Viva Video! 久保田成子

Viva Video! The Art and Life of Shigeko Kubota

ごあいさつ

新潟県立近代美術館、国立国際美術館、東京都現代美術館において、展覧会「Viva Video! 久保田成子展」を開催いたします。新潟に生まれ、ニューヨークを拠点に活躍した久保田成子（くぼたしげこ、1937–2015）の没後初となる本展は、日本では約30年ぶりの個展となります。

東京教育大学（現・筑波大学）で彫刻を学んだ久保田は、1960年代前半の東京でグループ音楽やハイレッド・センターといった同世代の前衛芸術家たちの仕事に触発され、さらなる可能性を切り開くべく1964年に渡米しました。ニューヨークでは、世界的に展開した芸術家集団であるフルクサスに参加するなど、表現の幅を広げました。1970年初頭には、ヴィデオという新しいメディアに出合い、アンソロジー・フィルム・アーカイヴズのヴィデオ・キュレーターを務めるなど、ニューヨークのヴィデオ・アート・シーンの中心的存在となります。そして1975年を皮切りに、ヴィデオの映像を立体的な構造物の中に取り込んだ「ヴィデオ彫刻」のシリーズを発表していきます。これらは久保田の代表作となり、その後、ドクメンタやヴェネチア・ビエンナーレといった数々の国際芸術祭に招待されるなど、このジャンルの先駆的な存在として国際的に評価されるようになりました。

ヴィデオ・アートという新しいジャンルが生まれたその黎明期から、世界を舞台に自らの芸術を展開する一人の女性作家として、久保田は何を考え、どのように表現を追求したのでしょうか。本展では、現代美術の父とも称されるマルセル・デュシャンを主題とした代表作「デュシャンピアナ」シリーズをはじめ、ヴィデオ彫刻、シングルチャンネル映像作品、それらのためのスケッチやアーカイブ資料などにより、久保田の仕事を展覧します。また、パートナーであるナムジュン・パイクら、同時代を生きたアーティストたちとの交流を通じて、久保田の芸術が生み出された背景を探っていくものです。

最後になりましたが、未知のウイルスによるパンデミックが世界的な猛威を振るうなか、本展の開催にあたって惜しみないご尽力を賜りました久保田成子ヴィデオ・アート財団の皆様、ご助成、ご協賛を賜りました機関、ならびに調査へのご協力、資料のご提供、さまざまなご助言などを頂きました関係各位に、心より御礼申し上げます。

主催者

Foreword

The Niigata Prefectural Museum of Modern Art, The National Museum of Art, Osaka, and Museum of Contemporary Art Tokyo are pleased to co-organize the exhibition *Viva Video!: The Art and Life of Shigeko Kubota*. This exhibition will be the first posthumous solo exhibition of Shigeko Kubota (1937–2015), who was born in Niigata and based in New York, and the first in Japan in approximately 30 years.

After studying sculpture at Tokyo University of Education (now University of Tsukuba), Kubota was inspired by the work of the avant-garde artists of her generation, such as Group Ongaku and the Hi-Red Center in Tokyo in the early 1960s. In 1964 she moved to the United States to explore further possibilities. In New York, she joined Fluxus, a worldwide group of artists, to expand her artistic horizon. In the early 1970s, she discovered the new medium of video and became a central figure in the New York video art scene, serving as Video Curator at Anthology Film Archives. Beginning in 1975, Kubota introduced a series of "video sculptures" that incorporated video images into three-dimensional structures. These became Kubota's signature works, and she was subsequently invited to participate in numerous international art festivals such as *documenta* and the *Venice Biennale*, gaining international recognition as a pioneer in this genre.

What was Kubota thinking and seeking as a woman artist, developing her art on the world stage at the dawn of media art? This exhibition explores Kubota's works through a series of video sculptures, single-channel video works, drawings related to these works, and archival materials, including her representative *Duchampiana* series which reinterprets the work of Marcel Duchamp—often referred to as the father of contemporary art. The exhibition will also explore the background behind the creation of Kubota's art through her interactions with her partner Nam June Paik and other artists who were active in the same milieu.

Finally, we would like to express our sincere gratitude to the Shigeko Kubota Video Art Foundation for their generous efforts in making this exhibition possible in the midst of an unforeseen pandemic, and to all those who gave us kind support, cooperation in the research, provision of materials, and advice.

Organizers

謝辞 Acknowledgements

本展覧会の開催にあたり、貴重な作品を貸与くださいました久保田成子ヴィデオ・アート財団、および美術館・画廊・所蔵家の皆様、ここにお名前を掲載することを差し控えられた皆様、多大なるご支援とご助言を賜りました関係者の皆様に心より御礼申し上げます。(順不同・敬称略)

We would like to express our deepest gratitude to the Shigeko Kubota Video Art Foundation as well as the museums, galleries, and collectors for kindly loaning us invaluable works, and to the many individuals and organizations who provided us with support and guidance to help realize this exhibition. (No particular order/honorifics omitted)

Shigeko Kubota Video Art Foundation
Norman Ballard
Jochen Saueracker
Reid Ballard
Lia Robinson
Kevin Harrison

久保田優子
中山孝子
法性桂子
法性玲子
長井順一

由本みどり

Mary Lucier
吉原悠博

Anthology Film Archives
Aspen Art Museum
DAAD
 - Deutscher Akademischer Austauschdienst
Electronic Arts Intermix (EAI)
Everson Museum of Art
Museum of Modern Art, New York
Whitney Museum of American Art
SCAI THE BATHHOUSE
慶應義塾大学アート・センター
東京国立近代美術館
富山県美術館
原美術館ARC
イメージフォーラム
ソニー株式会社

Karl McCool
Harry Ruhé
青野和子
赤瀬川尚子
阿部修也
蔵屋美香
柴田とし
坪内雅美
刀根康尚
西山輝夫
宮田有香
渡辺希利子

Carolee Schneemann Foundation
Fergus McCaffrey
Mother Gallery
HM Archive
ZEIT-FOTO SALON
鎌倉画廊
国立新美術館
東京文化財研究所
豊田市美術館
プロセスアート

Eric Andersen
Rachel Churner
Tom Haar
Larry Miller & Sara Seagull
Barbara Moore
Ian Roberts
Stephanie Tallering
内田芳孝
オノ・ヨーコ
橘川英規
菅谷幸
鈴木利佳
谷口英理
中谷芙二子
西﨑紀衣

Paul Garrin
Davidson Gigliotti
Robert Harris
Alison Knowles
Joan Logue
Barbara London
John Mhiripiri
Jeffrey Perkins
Liz Phillips
David Ross
Cecilia Sandoval
Trevor Shimizu
Gus Tsekenis
Lori Zippay
飯村昭子
飯村隆彦
石井宏枝
磯辺行久
奥岨玲子
神谷幸江
黒原繁夫
近藤学
斉藤陽子
佐々木奈美子
塩見允枝子
篠原有司男
篠原海苔こ
島敦彦
城之内美稲子
角田美奈子
宝田陽子
富山加津江
平沢剛
宮澤依子
山本圭吾
難波英夫

安齊重男
高晟埈

久保田成子ヴィデオ・アート財団からのメッセージ

久保田成子（1937–2015）の作品は大作であると同時に親密に語りかける魅力も持ち合わせています。彼女の作品はヴィデオと戦後現代美術の歴史において幅広く言及され、1970年代から90年代にかけて数多くの展覧会で発表されており、世界中の主要な美術館のコレクションに代表作が所蔵されています。しかし、彼女の活動範囲の広さと、現代美術に与えた影響はいまだ十分には知られていません。このたび、新潟県立近代美術館、国立国際美術館、東京都現代美術館との協働により、久保田の2015年の没後初の大型個展として、「Viva Video!　久保田成子」展を日本で開催し、彼女のユニークで影響力のある仕事を再び紹介できることは、久保田成子ヴィデオ・アート財団にとって名誉なことです。

久保田の長年の協働者である、ヨーヘン・ザウエラッカーの言葉を借りれば、久保田の作品は革新的で、「社会的かつ概念的な仕事」です。彼女の「ヴィデオ・ダイアリー」と「ヴィデオ彫刻」の試みのためには多くのドローイングが描かれ、協働者たちと会食しながらの議論があり、新しい技術の実験に溢れ、芸術と人生の境目を曖昧なものとしました。久保田のヴィデオ彫刻の構想と、アンソロジー・フィルム・アーカイヴズのキュレーターとして行なった企画の数々（1974年から82年）は、まだ生まれて間もなかったヴィデオという媒体を探究し、拡張することに大いに貢献しました。さまざまな形をとった彼女の彫刻作品を実際に鑑賞する経験は、偶然性、遊び、内省を促し、ヴィデオが遍在する今日の社会において強く共鳴するものです。

久保田ヴィデオ・アート財団は、2015年の久保田の逝去に際して遺贈を受けたノーマン・バラードによって設立されました。それは、ヴィデオの先駆者であった久保田と、夫であり協働者でもあったナムジュン・パイク（1932–2006）の夢でした。財団の使命は、久保田の遺産とヴィデオ・アートの広範な歴史を保存し、前進させることです。財団は、歴史研究に貢献し、現代芸術における実験を促し、そしてより多くの人々にヴィデオ・アートや新しいメディアに触れてもらう機会を設けるため、幅広い試みを実践しています。広域に及ぶ久保田のアーカイブの公開により、そしてヴィデオ・アート賞を創設することにより現代アーティストたちを支えることに徹して、財団は、ヴィデオ・アートの進化、ならびに、久保田と同時代の作家たちによって創始された思想や技術の発展に貢献することを目的としています。

「Viva Video!」の展覧会の原型は、新潟県立近代美術館のキュレーターである濱田真由美が2011年にニューヨークの久保田のロフトを訪れた際、久保田自身の同意を得て始まり、度重なる延期を乗り越え、財団および久保田の遺族、友人、協働者たちの協力を得て、このたび開催されることとなりました。

久保田の出身地である新潟を皮切りに、日本の代表的な美術館を巡回する、この重要な個展が、アーティストであり、キュレーターであり、批評家であり、協働者でもあった久保田成子という作家の成した多くの貢献についての、新たな問いかけと議論の契機となることを願っています。

久保田成子ヴィデオ・アート財団

ノーマン・L・バラード
遺言執行人／ディレクター

リード・N・バラード
コレクション・展示ディレクター

リア・ロビンソン
リサーチ兼プログラム・ディレクター

ヨーヘン・M・ザウエラッカー
アート・ディレクター／アーキヴィスト

ケヴィン・ハリソン
施設ディレクター

A Message from Shigeko Kubota Video Art Foundation

The work of Shigeko Kubota (1937–2015) is simultaneously monumental and intimate. Widely referenced in the histories of video and contemporary art, her work has been featured in numerous exhibitions from the 1970s to the 1990s, and examples are held in many major collections across the globe, yet the scope of her practice remains less well known. As the first major survey of the artist's oeuvre in Japan since her passing in 2015, The Shigeko Kubota Video Art Foundation is honored to collaborate with Niigata Prefectural Museum of Modern Art, National Museum of Modern Art, Osaka and Museum of Contemporary Art Tokyo to present a re-introduction to Kubota's unique and influential career with *Viva Video!: The Art and Life of Shigeko Kubota.*

In the words of longtime collaborator Jochen Saueracker, to describe Kubota's work is to describe an innovative "social and conceptual practice." Her ongoing experimentation with "video diary" and "video sculpture" often included extensive drawing, discussions with collaborators over drinks or meals, constant experimentation with new technologies, blurred distinctions between art and life. Kubota's inception of video sculpture and projects as Video Curator at Anthology Film Archives (1974–82), contributed significantly to the expansion of the video canon and exploration in this nascent media. A firsthand experience of the various iterations of her sculptural works invite indeterminacy, play and reflexivity that resonate perhaps even more strongly in society today where video is ubiquitous.

The Shigeko Kubota Video Art Foundation was established in 2015 by Norman L. Ballard at the bequest of the artist to realize the expressed vision of video pioneers Shigeko Kubota and her husband and collaborator Nam June Paik (1932–2006). Its mission is the preservation and advancement of Kubota's legacy and wider histories of video art. The Foundation is dedicated to supporting historical research, contemporary artistic experimentation, and broader public access to video art and new media through a wide range of initiatives. With its commitment to providing access to Kubota's extensive archive and support to contemporary artists through an Annual Video Art Prize, the Foundation aims to encourage the evolution of Video art, as well as the philosophies and techniques pioneered by Kubota and her contemporaries.

The concept for the exhibition *Viva Video!* was first initiated in cooperation with the artists herself, with a visit to Shigeko in New York by Mayumi Hamada, Curator, The Niigata Prefectural Museum of Modern Art in 2011, and was rescheduled in cooperation with the Foundation thanks to the support of many of the artist's family, colleagues and collaborators.

It is our hope that this important survey of Kubota's work, which began in the artist's hometown of Niigata and will tour to major institutions in Japan, will be a catalyst for renewed inquiry and discussions about Kubota's many significant contributions as an artist, curator, critic and collaborator.

Shigeko Kubota Video Art Foundation

Norman L. Ballard
Executor & Director

Reid N. Ballard
Director of Collections & Exhibitions

Lia Robinson
Director of Research & Programs

Jochen M. Saueracker
Art Director & Archivist

Kevin Harrison
Director of Infrastructure

目次

凡例

- 本カタログの図版ページは、「Viva Video! 久保田成子展」出品作を中心に、その他の主要な久保田成子作品および資料をおよそ年代順に掲載している。
- 特にキャプション記載のない展示写真は、新潟県立近代美術館における本展展示風景である。それ以外の写真については、判明した限りにおいて場所と年を記載したが、展示風景以外の作品画像はその限りではない。
- 使用画像の撮影者およびクレジットは、290頁に記載した。
- 図版ページ内のテキストは、作家自身による既発表のテキスト（明朝）と、書き下ろしの作品解説（ゴシック）とで構成している。

・作家によるテキスト
以下の文献より、再掲している。
［13頁］「しごとのデッサン　久保田成子：フルクサス・カップル」京都新聞、1999年5月29日。
［30、38-39頁］Shigeko Kubota, "Video Poems" *Arts Magazine*, vol. 49, no. 4 (Dec. 1974), p. 48.
［118-119頁］『第2回名古屋国際ビエンナーレARTEC '91』名古屋国際ビエンナーレ開催協議会編、1991年、38頁。
［129頁］*Et tous ils changent le monde/2ème Biennale d'art contemporain, Lyon* (Paris: Réunion des musèes nationaux, 1993), p. 179.
［133頁］"Work Sketches 1: Sexual Healing" from Shigeko Kubota, "Sexual Healing," *Shigeko Kubota: My Life With Nam June Paik* (New York: Maya Stendhal Gallery, 2007) pp. 67-68.
上記以外すべて、*Shigeko Kubota: Video Sculpture* (New York: American Museum of Moving Image, 1991)（以下「MMI」）。ただし、このうち一部のテキストは以下が初出。*Shigeko Kubota: Video Sculptures* (the Museum Folkwang Essen, the Berliner Künstlerprogramm des Deutschen Akademischen Austauschdienstes (DAAD), Berlin, the Kunsthaus Zürich, 1981)

・各作品解説
橋本梓［AH］、濱田真由美［MH］、西川美穂子［MN］、由本みどり［MY］が執筆を担当した。執筆にあたっては、MMIを中心とした既刊の個展カタログ等を参照している。
以下は、加筆修正の上、部分抜粋し再掲した。
［122、125、127、133、134、136頁］由本みどり「久保田成子展 ヴィデオで綴る人生の喜怒哀楽　My life with Nam June Paik at Maya Stendhal Gallery, New York, U. S. A. Sept. 6-Oct. 20. 2007」『イメージ&ジェンダー』Vol. 8、2008年3月24日、139-141頁。

Notes
- Plates of this catalog features the works included in the *Viva Video! : The Art and Life of Shigeko Kubota* exhibition as well as other major works and documents by the artist in a semi-chronological order.
- Installation views of the works without captions are those of the present exhibition at the Niigata Prefectural Museum of Modern Art. Captions of locations and years are provided for other installation views if known.
- Photographers and credit lines of the images are summarized on pp. 290.
- Texts in the plates consist of the artist's previously published writings (in a larger font)and new descriptions of the works (in a smaller font) in Japanese, while English texts and captions for images are located on pp. 238-256.

図版
Plates

1937-56

新潟時代

Niigata Years

毎日新聞

十七少女、みごと栄冠
久保田さん 二紀会展に入選

直江津高校普通科二年生同市八幡区久保田成子さん(一七)は九日から東京上野公園都美術館で開く第八回二紀会展に初入選した。これは二十号カンバスに"ひまわり"を画いた油絵で初出品が初入選しただけでなく、県下高校生で中央画展に名を出したのがこれがはじめてのことでベテラン級をあっといわせている。

成子さんは小学生当時から絵が好きだったが、高校へ入ってから図画教室担任の寺島展二教諭の指導を受け毎日スケッチやデッサンを十枚くらいもやるという大したエネルギーの持主で、去る六月から新大高田分校芸能科鳥取教授について本格的に油絵の勉強をはじめたのだが、よい素質に加えて不断の努力が急速な進歩を示しこんどの成果を上げたもので"入選ときいて胸がふるえてなにもいえません"とほおを紅潮させていた。手ほどきをやった寺島教諭は次のように語っている。

成子さんの絵は女子の作と思えぬ線の強さを持つ異色あるものです。個性からくる迫力の現れとみられ、構図も非常に大胆でこの先どこまで伸びるか楽しみです。

二紀会展に新入選の久保田成子さん

『毎日新聞』新潟版、1954年10月8日

1937年8月2日に新潟県西蒲原郡巻町（現・新潟市西蒲区巻町）で高校教師の久保田隆円（りゅうえん）と音楽教師の文枝の間に、4人姉妹の次女として生まれ、芸術的環境に育つ。南画系の画家であった祖父の影響を受け、幼い頃から絵が好きで、小学3年生で雑誌の絵画コンクールに入選。高校2年生の秋には、二紀展に初出品した油彩《向日葵》が入選、新聞にも大きく掲載された。（MH）

《向日葵》 1954年

1956-64

東京時代

Tokyo Years

叔母、邦千谷と　1956年

久保田は高校卒業後、美術の道に進むことを決意し、東京教育大学（現・筑波大学）の彫塑専攻に入学した。その当初から同郷の彫刻家・高橋清に師事し、彼が所属した新制作協会展に出展しており、出品作の写真からは人物をかたどった頭像が次第に抽象化していく様子がうかがえる。

大学を卒業し、中学校の美術教諭となった1960年、叔母の邦千谷（くにちや）が自身の舞踊研究所を開放すると、そこにはグループ音楽などの若い前衛芸術家たちが集うようになり、久保田もその輪の中に加わった。そして、1963年に初めて「第15回読売アンデパンダン展」に出品するが、それは細い金属棒を溶接した物体と既成の円筒形の物体を使った抽象的な作品で、新制作協会展の出品作からは作風が一変した。このように、久保田はこの頃から前衛美術への傾倒を加速させていく。（MH）

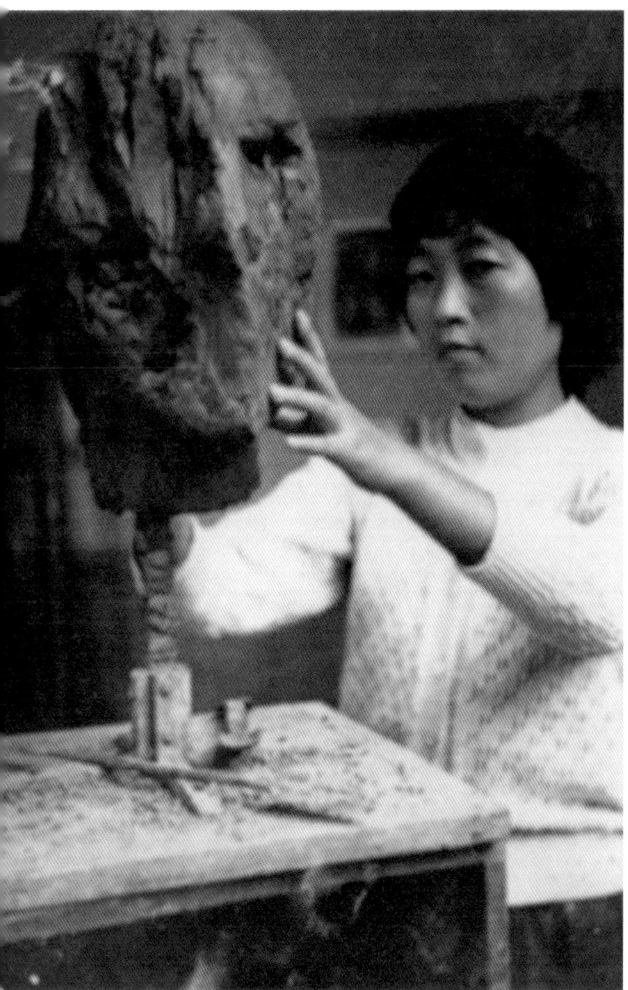

《死石T》を制作する久保田　1962年頃

制作中の久保田成子　1963年頃（上）
「第15回日本アンデパンダン展（読売アンデパンダン展）」（1963年）での展示（下）

1963

内科画廊

Solo Show at Naiqua Gallery

展覧会場に座る久保田

1963年12月1日から7日まで内科画廊で開催された初個展「1st. LOVE, 2nd. LOVE... 久保田成子彫刻個展」では、ラブレターに見立てた紙くずの山の上に読売アンデパンダンに出品したものと類似の立体物が設置され、来場者は山の上まで登って作品を見ることを余儀なくされた。久保田はこの展覧会の案内状と手紙を瀧口修造や中原佑介、東野芳明、三木多聞ら、当時活躍していた美術批評家たちに送って積極的にアピールし、その反応を期待したが、展評が出ることはなく大いに失望する。一方、この展覧会を見ていたナムジュン・パイクが好意的に評したことに勇気付けられた久保田は、この後、ニューヨークで活動することを決意した。

本展のタイトル「1st. Love, 2nd. Love...」は、展示された抽象彫刻の作品タイトルである。また案内状に印刷されている英語のテキストは、同時期に草月会館ホールで開催されたパフォーミング・フェスティバル「Sweet 16」のプログラムに掲載された久保田によると思われるテキストとも重複しており、両者の関連性がうかがえる。(MH)

御招待

1st.LOVE,2nd.LOVE... 久保田成子彫刻個展12月1日－7日Am11：00－Pm7：00内科画廊港区芝新橋2－12堤第2ビルTEL591－6795 Make a floor with waste paper which are all love letters to you, Spread a sheet of white cloth on the floor, Skin your lips by yourself, kiss a man who has mustach in audience.

案内状

出品作品《1st. love》《2nd. love》《3rd. love》 1963年

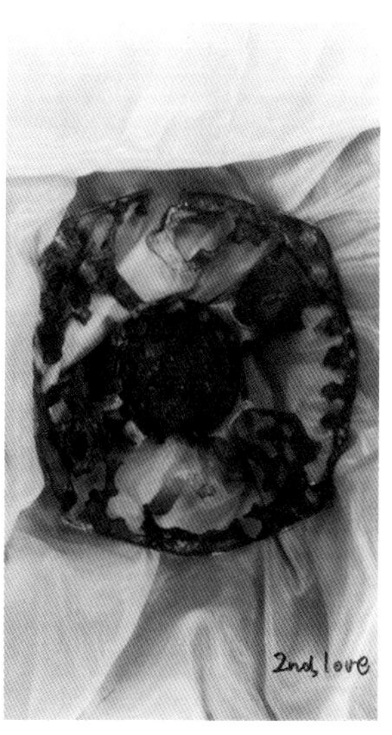

1963年、私は新橋の内科画廊で個展を開いた。医師がオーナーのこの画廊は、前衛的なアーティストのたまり場だった。私は、画廊の床から天井まで、ラブレターの切れ端を積み上げ、その上に白い布を敷き、メタルのパイプを配置した。会場を訪れた人は、紙くずの山をよじ登らなければならない。いわゆる参加型のパフォーマンス、環境芸術であった。自信をもって臨んだ個展だが、どの新聞にも美術雑誌にも批評は出なかった。当時24歳*の私は精神的にショックを受けた。日本では女性アーティストが認められるチャンスはないと思い、翌年、ニューヨークに渡った。

*実際には26歳

Sweet 16

Sweet 16

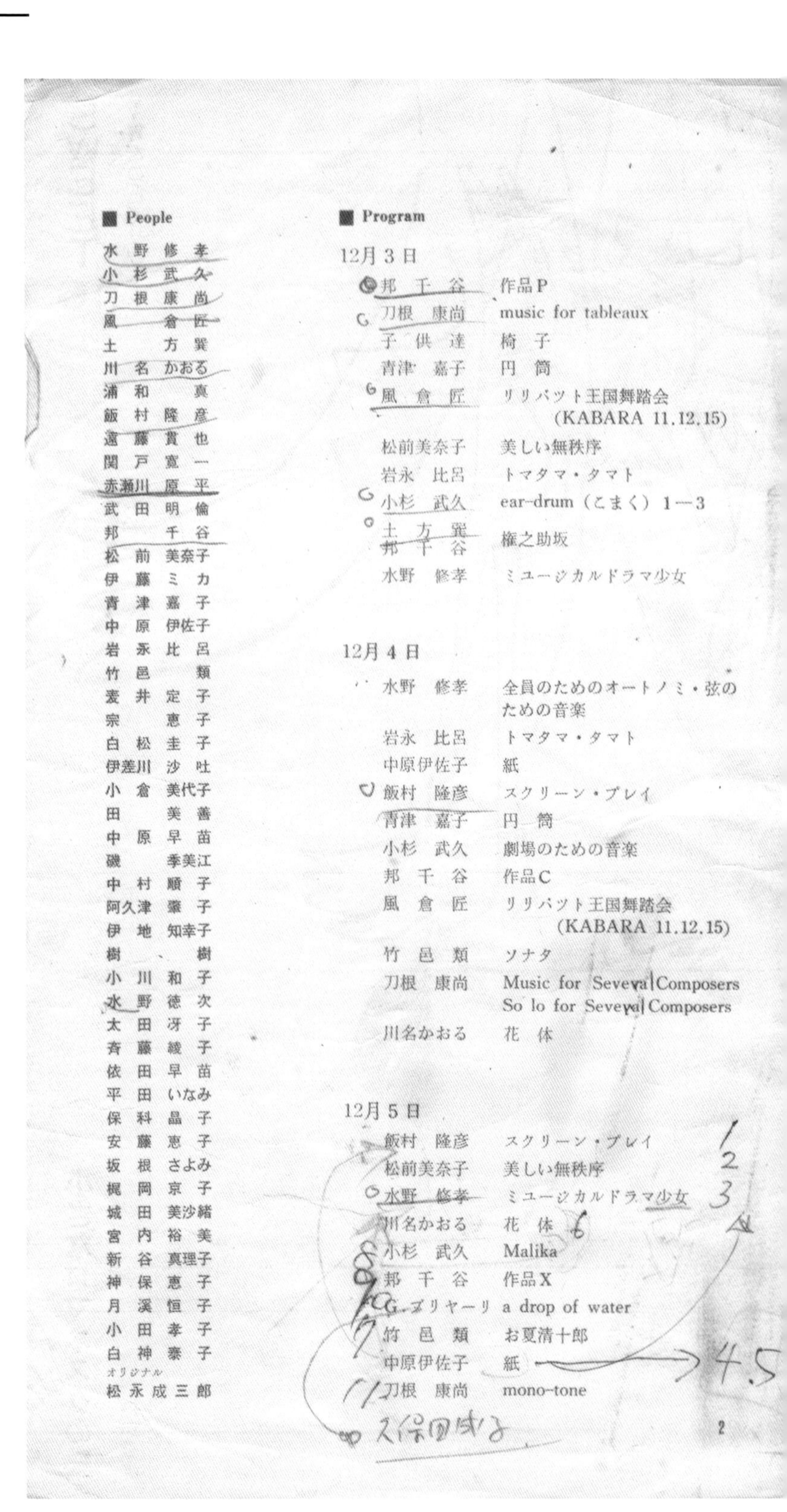

■ People

水野修孝
小杉武久
刀根康尚
風倉匠
土方巽
川名かおる
浦和真
飯村隆彦
遠藤貫也
関戸寛一
赤瀬川原平
武田明倫
邦千谷
松前美奈子
伊藤ミカ
青津嘉子
中原伊佐子
岩永比呂
竹邑類
麦井定子
宗恵子
白松圭子
伊差川沙吐
小倉美代子
田美善
中原早苗
磯季美江
中村順子
阿久津肇子
伊地知幸子
樹、樹
小川和子
水野徳次
太田冴子
斉藤綾子
依田早苗
平田いなみ
保科晶子
安藤恵子
坂根さよみ
梶岡京子
城田美沙緒
宮内裕美
新谷真理子
神保恵子
月渓恒子
小田孝子
白神泰子
オリジナル
松永成三郎

■ Program

12月3日

邦千谷	作品P
刀根康尚	music for tableaux
子供達	椅子
青津嘉子	円筒
風倉匠	リリパット王国舞踏会 (KABARA 11.12.15)
松前美奈子	美しい無秩序
岩永比呂	トマタマ・タマト
小杉武久	ear-drum(こまく) 1—3
土方巽 邦千谷	権之助坂
水野修孝	ミュージカルドラマ少女

12月4日

水野修孝	全員のためのオートノミ・弦のための音楽
岩永比呂	トマタマ・タマト
中原伊佐子	紙
飯村隆彦	スクリーン・プレイ
青津嘉子	円筒
小杉武久	劇場のための音楽
邦千谷	作品C
風倉匠	リリパット王国舞踏会 (KABARA 11.12.15)
竹邑類	ソナタ
刀根康尚	Music for Seveval Composers So lo for Seveval Composers
川名かおる	花体

12月5日

飯村隆彦	スクリーン・プレイ
松前美奈子	美しい無秩序
水野修孝	ミュージカルドラマ少女
川名かおる	花体
小杉武久	Malika
邦千谷	作品X
G.ブリヤーリ	a drop of water
竹邑類	お夏清十郎
中原伊佐子	紙
刀根康尚	mono-tone

2

プログラム 表紙(左)、P.2(右)

草月会館ホールで開催されたパフォーミング・フェスティバル「Sweet 16」は、同プログラムによると12月3日から3日間にわたって開催され、邦千谷をはじめ、グループ音楽の小杉武久、刀根康尚、水野修孝のほか、土方巽、風倉匠、飯村隆彦といった若手の前衛芸術家が多数出演していた。プログラムに名前はないが、久保田も本公演に参加し、「G.ブリヤーリ」という偽名でパフォーマンス作品を発表していたことが、友人の刀根康尚の証言とメモによって確認された。作品の詳細は不明のままだが、同プログラムに掲載された「マッキューナス様へ／G.ブリヤーリ」と題されたテキストが久保田の内科画廊の個展案内状に掲載されたテキストと重なるため、これが彼女のパフォーマンスのスコアであったのではないかと推測できる。(MH)

マッキューナス様へ／G.ブリヤーリ

My dear Mr. George Maciunas
Hello. . . . This is my christmas present to you.

Composition for K.
Skin your lips by yourself.
Kiss a man who has mustache in audience.

Blue love No.25.
Prick your pores of skin with a needle as far as far as your hand can touch.

Beehive No.1.
Make a floor with waste paper which are all love letters to you.
Spread a sheet of white cloth on the floor.

Beehive No.2.
Fill a room with waste paper which are all love letters to you.

1st Love.
Don't cast you shadow when a girl puts on the light in a small room.

Crying music No.9.
Let seven men stand in a line, starch (with a colored cloth,) a point of man's face which you find something wonderful. Moisten his head with a drop of hot water just as you water flowers.
Pull out a piece of hair from a part of his head which is gotten wet by the hat [hot] water.

Blue love No.1.
Shut your ears, Confess your 1st. love.

A drop of water.
Have dinner which is served only a white flower.
Put a drop of water from you[r] lips into long nylon pipe after dinner.
Shut the ends of the nylon pipe with two fingers.
Don't move until the white flower in your stomach becomes a drop of water.

Composition for only a man.
Put many women into a small room whose floor is covered with a sheet white cloth.
Keep them in the room for a month.
Make a wall by the sheet of white cloth after a month.
Print your shadow on the wall.
Erase other's shadows by that of your own.

Blue love No.8.
Send only a needle to your girl friend when you can't meet her. (or when you are too busy to meet her, or when you dislike to meet her.)

I do hope your asthma will get very well soon.
Good Bye.

G. Breyali

1964-65

渡米前後

Before and After Moving to the United States

ポートレート 1964年頃

久保田は1964年7月4日に渡米するが、その直前の6月に篠原有司男らが中心となって企画、開催されたグループ展「OFF MUSEUM」に《ミス・ユニバース》と題された作品を出品している。それは「久保田成子嬢がミス・ユニバースになる為の募金箱」と生きた白兎と時計によって構成され、観客は会場に貼られた指示書に記された時間に兎に餌をやったり散歩させたりすることを求められるという、一種のパフォーマンス作品であった。また、同年10月に内科画廊で開催された「刀根康尚個展」および、翌1965年9月に画廊クリスタルで開催されたグループ展「フルックス週間」では、どちらも女性用下着を壁に貼り付けた作品（タイトル不詳）を出品しており、表現の先鋭化が顕著となっている。
一方、東京時代に交流を深めたハイレッド・センターの資料をニューヨークに持参し、マチューナスと共に「ハイレッド・センター：イヴェント集」を制作。その活動を紹介するなど、東京とニューヨークの前衛の橋渡し役ともなった。(MH)

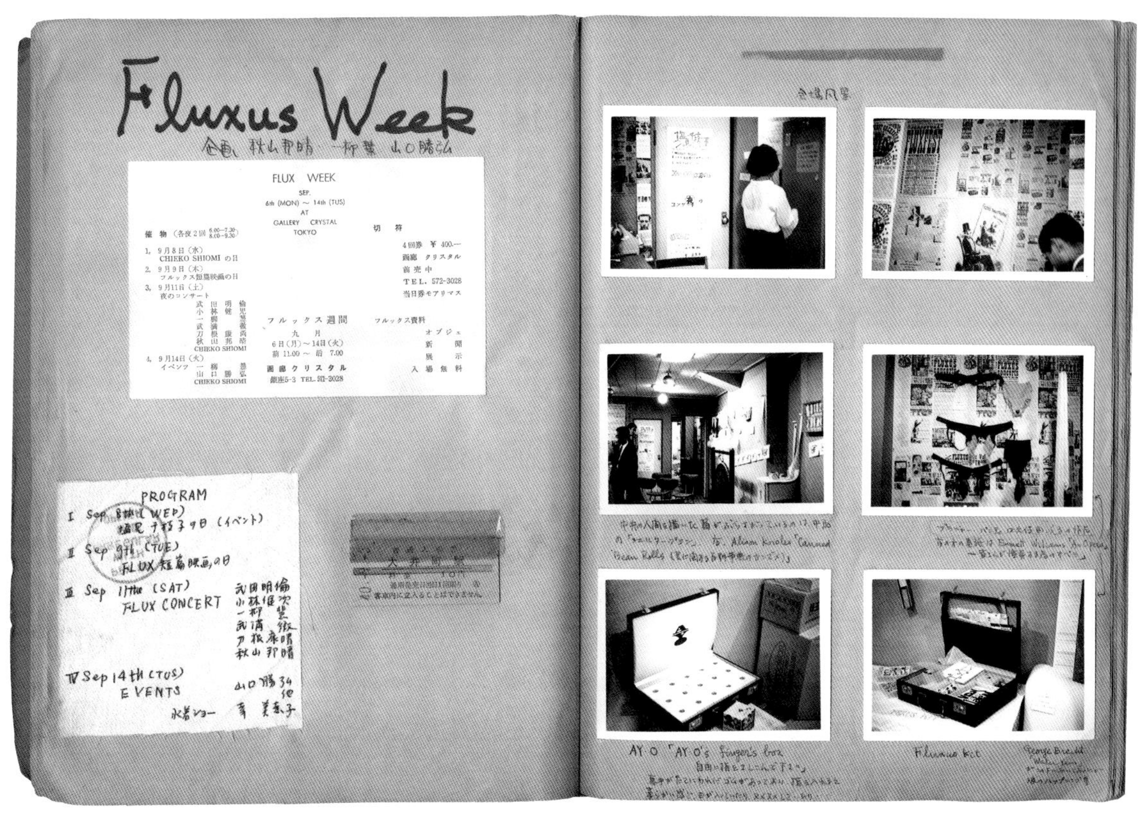

「ハイレッド・センター：イヴェント集」 1965年 編集：久保田成子 デザイン・製作：ジョージ・マチューナス（左上）
平田実《刀根康尚「インヴェスティゲイション・イヴェント」》より 「刀根康尚個展」（1964年）会場にて （刀根康尚の背後の壁に久保田成子の作品）（右上）
「フルックス週間」（1965年） 西山輝夫氏のスクラップ・ブックより 右ページ右中の写真 西山氏のメモ「ブラジャー、パンティーは久保田成子の作品」（下）

To. Miss. Shigeko
c/o
P.O Box 180
Mr. George
Maciunas.
New York

《フルクサス・スーツケース》1964年

1964-70s

フルクサス

Fluxus

我が親愛なるジョージ・マチューナス様

何度も手紙をくださって本当にありがとうございます。アーティストとして生きるために、東京がいいのか、ニューヨークがいいのか、私は毎日悩んでいます。しかしとうとう私は心を決めてニューヨークに行くことにしました。私がニューヨークへ行くということで、あなたを煩わせてしまって本当に申し訳なく思っています。私にとっては、アーティストとして生きるためにニューヨークへ行くことだけが希望なのですが、あなたにとってはとっても厄介なことでしかありませんね。でも私は、フルクサスというグループに接し、ニューヨークでひとりで生きることで、何かを見てみたいし、何かに触れてみたいのです。「今このタイミングで」ニューヨークへ行くことは、私にとって最大のハプニングです。[あなたという存在を、]私は生涯忘れることはないでしょう。

私は6月20日（土曜日）*夜10時半に、NW#6便（ノースウエスト航空）にてニューヨークの国際空港（ＪＦケネディ空港）に着く予定です。空港でお会いすることはできるでしょうか？　私のためにあなたの時間をお取りして申し訳ないのですが、あなたのご厚意に甘えて、空港でお会いできると信じたいのです。そのために、私は緑のコートとドレスを着ていきます。これで私はあなたと空港で会えると信じます。いや、これは不可能なことでしょうか……おお、どうすればいいのでしょう！　どうかよろしくお願いいたします。数日後にお会いしましょう。

さようなら、久保田成子より

*実際には7月4日

My dear Mr. George Maciunas

Thank you very much for your letter to me again and again.

In every day I was very worry which is better to be in Tokyo or to be in New York in order to live as an only artist.

But Now I made up my mind to go to New York. I'm very sorry to put you to a trouble by my act which is to go to New York.

It's my only hope to go to New York in order to live as a artist, but for you, it's no mean without the biggest trouble to you.

But I'd like to touch, to see and to feel something by touching a grop of Fluxus and living by myself in New York.

It's my biggest happening to go to New York "Now", I will not be able to forget to be you in a space of my eternal life.

I will arrive at International (J.F.Kennedy airport) in New York via NW#6 (Northwest orient airlines) at 10:30pm on 20th (saturday) June.

May I be able to meet you at airport?

I'm very sorry to eat your time for me but I'd like to blieve to meet you at airport, availing myself of your kindness.

So, as my mark, I will put on a dress and coat of green color.

1st my mark.

Now I do believe to be able to meet you at airport. but if it's impossible.....

oh. what shall I do!

Best regards to you
See you after few days.
Good-bye

Shigeko Kubota.

久保田成子からジョージ・マチューナスへの手紙　1964年

巻物状のマチューナスへの手紙で、アーティストとして生きる決心を表明し、そのためにニューヨークを選んだ久保田は、渡米を「最大のハプニング」と呼んだ。後に《フルクサス・スーツケース》と名づけたトランクに、作品を制作するための材料を入れ、事前に送った。1964年7月に塩見とニューヨークへ到着した久保田は、マチューナスらの歓迎を受けて彼の用意したソーホーのアパートで暮らし始める。近所には、先に渡米しフルクサスに参加していた靉嘔や斎藤陽子、ナムジュン・パイクもいた。マチューナス提案の「ディナー・コミューン」に参加して料理の腕を振るったり、メンバーのマルチプル制作を手伝う中、自身も《フルックス・ナプキン》や《フルックス・メディシン》を構想し、制作した。初期に限りLove-ko A*I*という、パイクにつけてもらったアーティスト・ネームを使った。(MY)

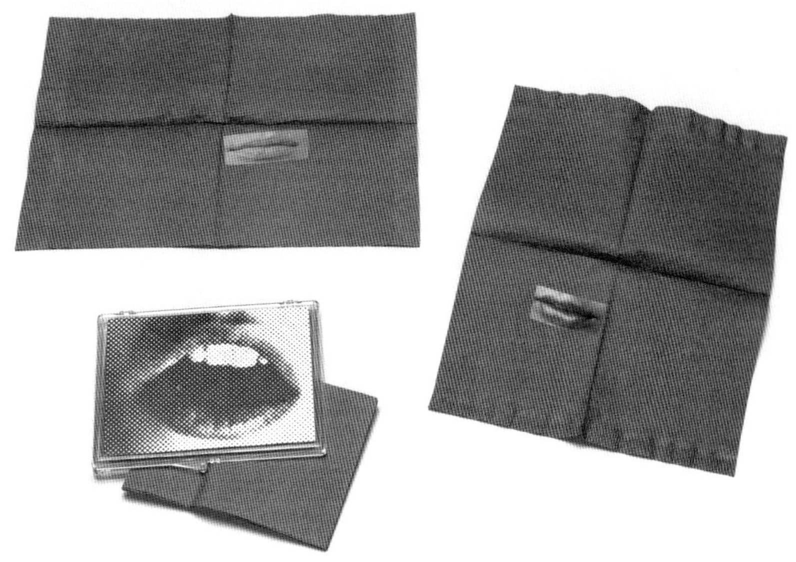

《フルクサスI》の中の封筒　1965年(上)
《フルックス・ナプキン》　1965年(中)
《フルックス・メディシン》　1966年(下)

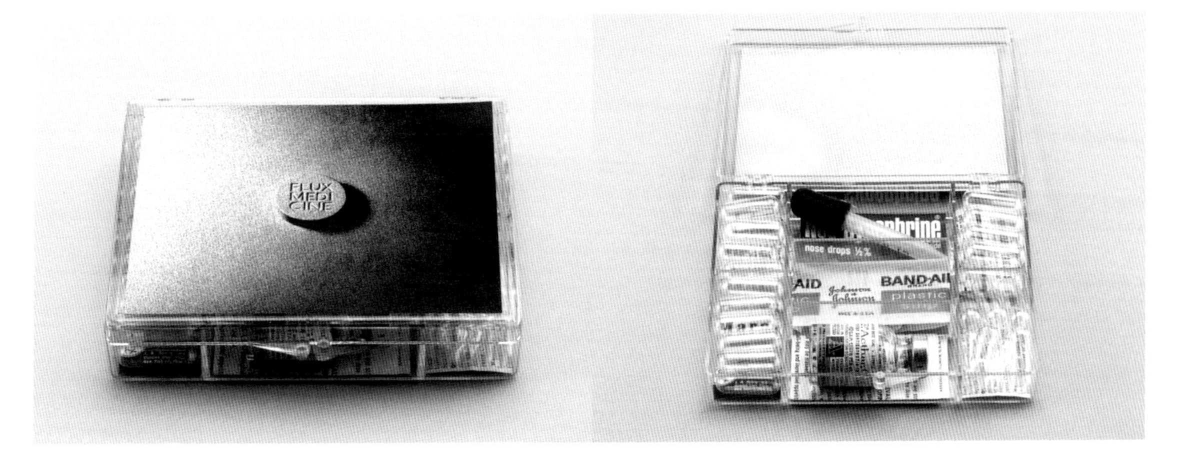

エリック・アンダーセン《OPUS45》に参加する久保田成子 1965年

TUNA FISH
COMPLIMENTS OF
Star-Kist Foods, Inc.
SHIGEKO KUBOTA
PERFORMS
THE IDENTICAL LUNCH

1964年から1965年にかけて複数回開催された、「永続的なフルックス・フェスト」で、エリック・アンダーセンのパフォーマンス《Opus45》、オノ・ヨーコ《ビート・ピース》などにも参加した。アリソン・ノールズの《アイデンティカル・ランチ》では、ノールズのインストラクションに従って、ツナ・サンドを食べている久保田の姿がプリントとして残る。1960年代後半にニューヨークを離れるメンバーが増えた中、久保田はマチューナスのそばを離れず、手伝いを続けたので、彼に「フルクサスの副議長」と呼ばれた。(MY)

アリソン・ノールズ《アイデンティカル・ランチをおこなう久保田成子》1969/1973年(上)
「フルックス・ゲーム」に参加する久保田成子とナムジュン・パイク　1973年(下)

1965

ヴァギナ・ペインティング

Vagina Painting

《ヴァギナ・ペインティング》1965年

フルクサスのイベント「永続的なフルックス・フェスト」において、久保田は《ヴァギナ・ペインティング》と称されたパフォーマンス作品を披露する。もともと1964年秋から毎週日曜に開かれる予定だった同イベントは幾度も延期され、最終的には久保田の番は1965年の夏に回ってきたようだが、日付の確証は得られていない。その名のとおり、女性器に装着した筆で描くというパフォーマンスだが、1964年11月にピーター・ムーアのスタジオで撮影された同作品の広報用らしき写真では、筆が留めてある下着を履いて描く久保田の姿が写っている。一方で、実際のパフォーマンスを見た靉嘔、塩見允枝子、エリック・アンダーセンといった仲間たちの証言によると、本番では実際に筆を女性器に挿入していたと推測される。
久保田はこのパフォーマンスについて、当時恋人であったパイクとマチューナスに依頼されてやったもので、自身のアイディアではないと晩年になって証言している。その真偽は確かめられないが、半年以上も前から入念に準備し、自身の作品として発表したことは紛れもない事実であり、久保田の芸術を語る上で欠かせない作品であることは間違いない。(MH)

「永続的なフルックス・フェスト」(フルクサス新聞No.5)より　1965年(上)
《ヴァギナ・ペインティング》ピーター・ムーアのスタジオでの写真　1964年(下)

1965-69

ソニック・アーツ・ユニオン

Sonic Arts Union

ヨーロッパ巡回中のソニック・アーツ・ユニオン、イタリア、アクィラにて、1969年
左から：ゴードン・ムンマ、バーバラ・ディリー、メアリー・ルシエ、アルヴィン・ルシエ、デイヴィッド・バーマン、久保田成子、ロバート・アシュリー、メアリー・アシュリー

久保田成子、S.N.バーマン（デイヴィッド・バーマンの父で劇作家Samuel Nathaniel Bearman）のニューヨークのアパートにて　1968年頃
＊本展展示のルシエによる《ポラロイド・イメージ・シリーズ：シゲコ》の元となった。

1965年、作曲家のデイヴィッド・バーマンに出会った久保田は、翌年、彼がロバート・アシュリー、アルヴィン・ルシエ、ゴードン・ムンマと共に結成した実験音楽集団、ソニック・アーツ・ユニオン（SAU）に参加する。1967年、バーマンと結婚し、SAUのヨーロッパ・ツアーに、メンバーの女性パートナーたち（メアリー・アシュリー、メアリー・ルシエ、バーバラ・ロイド）と同伴、時に声を出したり、光るセンサーを手につけて歩くなど、パフォーマーとしても参加した。1969年にも、北欧三か国、イギリス、ベルギー、イタリアなどをまわる、SAUの1か月間のツアーに部分的に参加している。（MY）

1967

スノーズ

Snows

1967年には、キャロリー・シュニーマンの《Snows》という、ヴェトナム戦争に対する怒りと悲しみを表現したパフォーマンス作品にも出演し、顔を白く塗られたり、足を引っ張られて吊り下げられるなど、負傷者や死者を象徴する役割を果たした。これらのパフォーマンスの体験が刺激になり、1972年に久保田はルシエと女性グループ「ホワイト ブラック レッド イエロー」を結成することになる。(MY)

記録映像《スノーズ》スチル(右上)
キャロリー・シュニーマン《スノーズ》にパフォーマーとして参加する久保田成子　1967年(他3点)

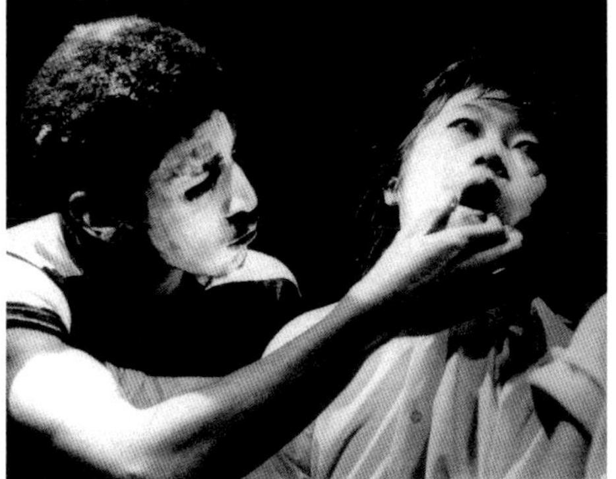

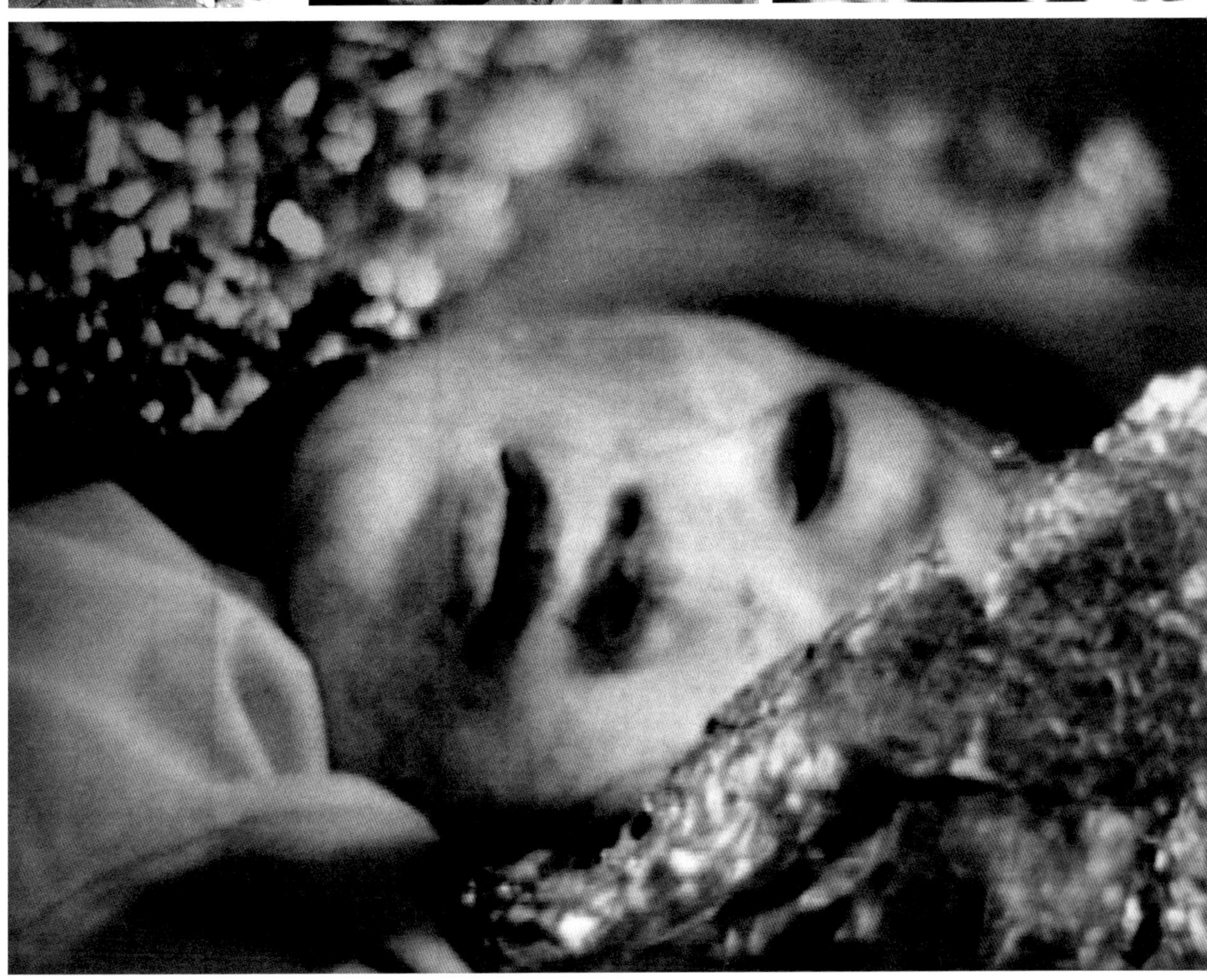

1970

マルセル・デュシャンとジョン・ケージ

Marcel Duchamp and John Cage

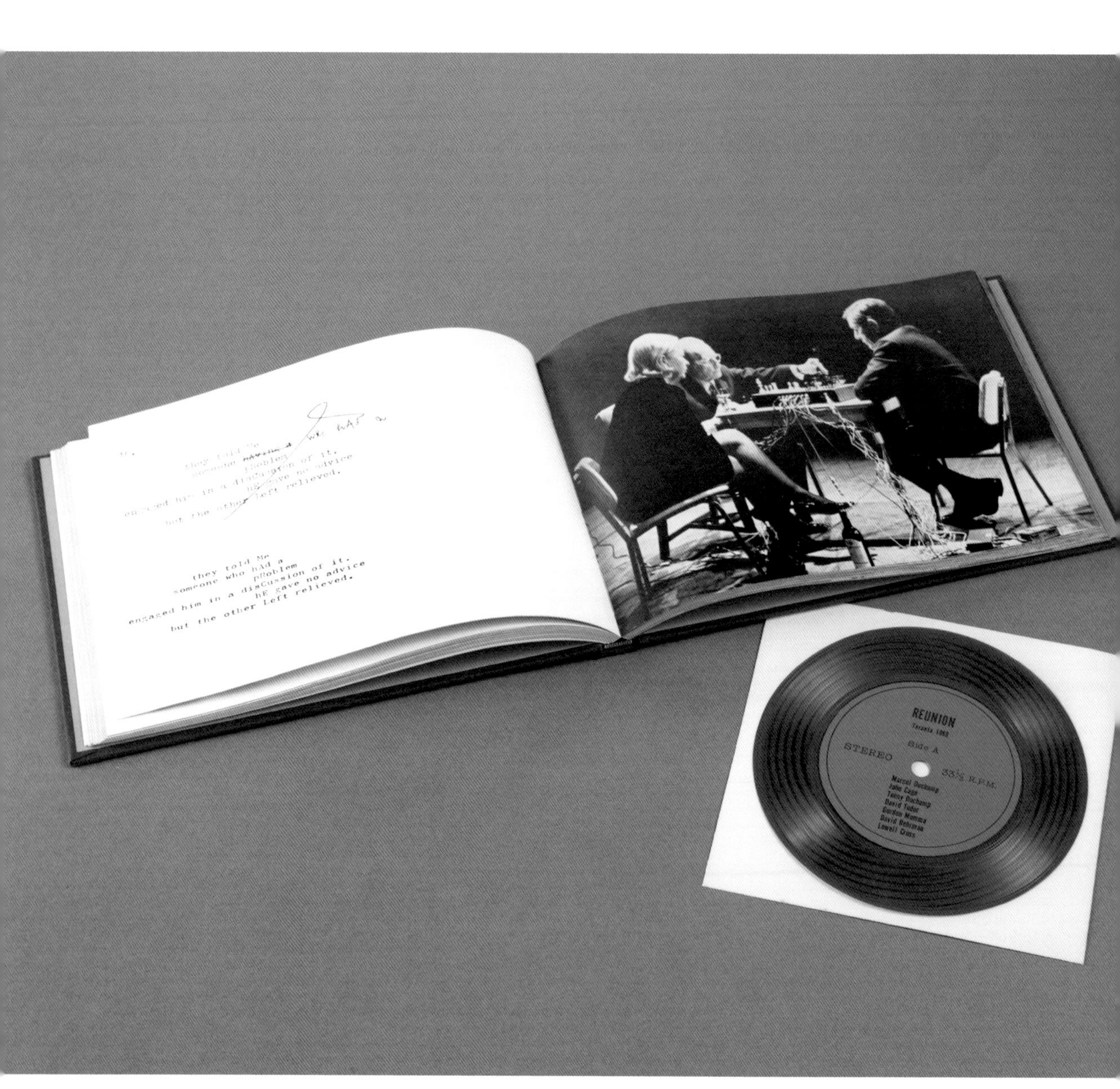

『マルセル・デュシャンとジョン・ケージ』 1970年

《マルセル・デュシャンとジョン・ケージ》写真　1968年

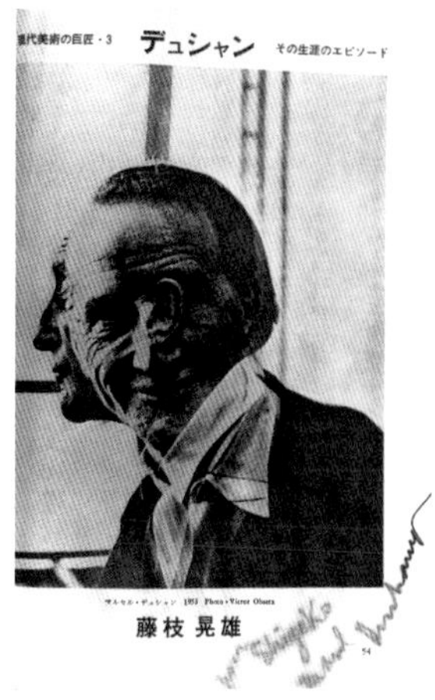

マルセル・デュシャンによるサインのある『美術手帖』1968年3月号

『マルセル・デュシャンとジョン・ケージ』は、2人の偉大なアーティストによるパフォーマンス／コンサート「リユニオン」の記録を久保田成子が編集した作品集。「リユニオン」は1968年3月5日にカナダのトロントでマルセル・デュシャンとジョン・ケージが行なったチェス対戦のイヴェントで、チェス盤には音響装置が仕掛けられており、会場内に設置されたスピーカーから流れる音が両者の駒の動きによって変化するというものだった。このパフォーマンスを企画したのはケージだが、演奏はディヴィッド・テュードア、ゴードン・ムンマ、デイヴィッド・バーマンの3人の気鋭の現代音楽家たちが担当していた。この模様を撮影した久保田の写真に、ジョン・ケージによるアクロスティック（言葉あそび）が添えられ、さらに同パフォーマンスの一部を録音したソノシートが付属した本書は、『美術手帖』の編集長であった宮澤壯佳が発行人となって日本で制作されたが、久保田が自費で出版し非売品としたため世の中に広く流通することはなかった。
久保田はのちに、この写真をもとにシングルチャンネル・ヴィデオ《マルセル・デュシャンとジョン・ケージ》（1972年）を制作し、さらにその映像をヴィデオ彫刻《ヴィデオ・チェス》へと展開していく。
（MH）

1972

ブロークン・ダイアリー：ヨーロッパを一日ハーフインチで

Broken Diary: Europe on 1/2 Inch a Day

《ブロークン・ダイアリー：ヨーロッパを一日ハーフインチで》 1972年（スチル）

ヴィデオ・ドアの背後で

私は旅するときはひとりで、ポータパックをヴェトナムの女性たちが赤ん坊を背負うみたいに背負って行く。

私はヴィデオが好き、重たいから。

ポータパックと私はヨーロッパ、ナヴァホ族の土地、日本を、男性の同伴者なしで旅してまわった。

ポータパックは私の肩、背骨、腰を引き裂く。

シベリア鉄道で働いているソ連の女性になったような気がする。

私は《ヨーロッパを一日ハーフインチで》というヴィデオを撮った。

私はアリゾナ州チンリーでナヴァホ族の家族とひと夏を過ごした。私は《あるアメリカの家族》というヴィデオを撮った。*

*この文章は1974年に書かれたものだが、最後の《あるアメリカの家族》が後に《ブロークン・ダイアリー：ヴィデオ・ガールズとナヴァホの空のためのヴィデオソング》と改題されたと思われる。

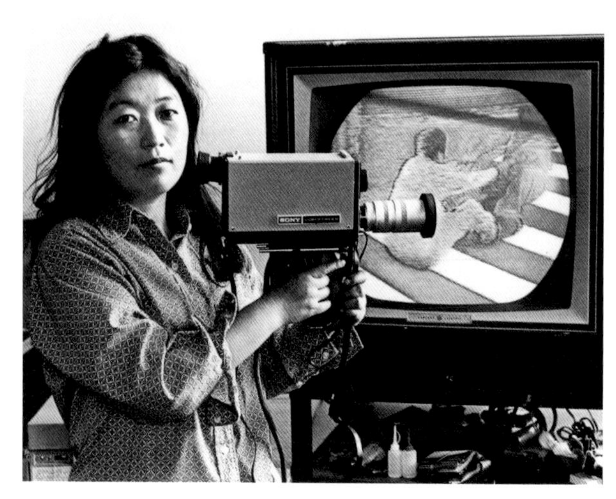

ポータパックを持つ久保田成子 1972年

1970年にデイヴィッド・バーマンと別れた久保田は、カリフォルニア芸術大学でヴィデオ・アートを教え始めたパイクと合流、ロサンジェルスでヴィデオ制作に着手した。1972年5月、新しいポータパックを手に、ヨーロッパを旅し、その録画からシングルチャネル・ヴィデオ、《ヨーロッパを一日ハーフインチで》を完成させた。それをニューヨークのザ・キッチンにおいて、初の「ライヴとヴィデオテープのコンサート」で発表した久保田は、ヴィデオ作家としての一歩を踏む。1968年のチェスのイヴェントで撮った写真を使って、ケージとデュシャンについてのヴィデオも作り、ケージの60歳のバースデイを祝うイヴェントなどで、それを上映した。1972年後半には既に、複数の回路のヴィデオを、積み重ねたブラウン管モニターで見せている。(MY)

SHIGEKO KUBOTA

LIVE & VIDEOTAPE CONCERT

JUNE 3O, 9:3O P.M
at THE KITCHEN
the mercer arts center
240 mercer st.

videotape 1,2

CAGE – TUDOR – DUCHAMP

half Inch

EUROPE on 5 ~~DOLLARS~~ A DAY

「久保田成子：ライヴとヴィデオテープのコンサート」ポスター　ザ・キッチン、1972年

1972-73

ホワイト ブラック レッド イエロー

White Black Red & Yellow

グループ「ホワイト ブラック レッド イエロー」
（左よりメアリー・ルシエ、シャーロット・ワレン、セシリア・サンドヴァル、久保田成子）

「ホワイト ブラック レッド イエロー」初公演ポスター 1972年 デザイン：久保田成子

1972年、久保田とルシエは、人種の異なる、「オリジナルの視覚的で音声も伴う劇場作品を発表することに徹する4人の女性」のグループ、「ホワイト ブラック レッド イエロー」を結成、ザ・キッチンで12月と翌年4月にライヴ・イヴェントを行なった。アジア人の久保田は「黄（イエロー）」、白人のルシエは「白（ホワイト）」、黒人のシャーロット・ワレンは「黒（ブラック）」、ナヴァホ族のセシリア・サンドヴァルは「赤（レッド）」を象徴し、グループ名の色の順番は不定であった。当時勃興したフェミニズムの第二波に呼応し、メンバーだけでなく、他の女性アーティストの作品も発表する「フェミニストの作品の交換所」のような役割を狙ったが、2度目のコンサートで解散する。最初のイヴェントで発表された、久保田の《リヴァーラン（川走）》は、30台もの12インチのモニターを、6個ずつ5列に重ね、一列ごとに異なる川を映すヴィデオの回路に繋ぐ予定だったが、実際にそこまで大掛かりであったかどうかの確証はなく、映像も見つかっていない。ここにある久保田の文章には、ジェイムズ・ジョイスの『フィネガンズ・ウェイク』への直接的言及があり、このヨーロッパとニューヨークで撮影した様々な川の様子を「走っていく時間の自伝」と呼んでいる。［同上グループの詳細については、184-86頁を参照。］（MY）

《リヴァーラン(川走)──ヴィデオ 水 詩》 1972年(スチル)

リヴァーラン(川走)──ヴィデオ水詩

水は動く映像をあらわす比喩だ。おのずと流れる自然の水、滝のように動く強制された水、それとも、池のようにきらきら輝く静かな水の溜まり──川走。

自然のエネルギーの異なる速度──走る水、水へと溶けていく誰かの生を映しながら、走る。血の川──洗い流され、永遠を通って何度も何度も戻ってくる。

1972年、私はハーフ〔インチ〕・オープンリール・ヴィデオ・ポータパックを持って旅行に出かけ、『一日5ドルでまわるヨーロッパ』ならぬ《ヨーロッパを一日ハーフインチで》と名づけたヴィデオ日記をつくった。このずっしり重いヴィデオ・ポータパックを肩から下げ、私はセーヌ川、ライン川、ハドソン川、アムステルダムの運河をボートで旅した。ヴェネツィアの運河では水上タクシーに乗った。

水はいつでも私の気持ちを落ち着かせ、人間は生の中で生き、生き残ることを思い出させてくれる。水がいろいろな面で私たちの生きる行為ととても密接であることは誰でも知っている。水のない砂漠では、私たちは喉が渇いて死んでしまうしかない。人間の身体の3分の2は水でできているし、赤ん坊は母親の子宮という水から生まれてくるし、等々。

川走は、長い私の人生から取り出した、個人的な時間のきれはしのようなもの。それは私の人生の感情面にかかわっている。それは走っていく時間の自伝なのだ、ジェイムズ・ジョイスの『フィネガンズ・ウェイク』のように。

少女だったころ、代々僧侶で、裏日本に寺を所有する父の実家を訪ねたものだった。水道が来ていなかったので、力持ちの若い衆がいつも、肩にかついだ天秤棒の両端に大きなバケツを吊るして、近くの山の泉から清水を汲んできていた。私はバケツを持って彼らのあとをついていったものだ。岩だらけの細道を泉まで歩き、滝からじかに手で汲んだ水を飲んだ──それはそれは冷たくておいしかった──官能的な体験だったことを今でも思い出せる。日本で氷柱(つらら)から滴るしずくを飲むのが私は大好きだ。

ほぼ同じころ、父の一番上の兄で僧侶だったおじが突然亡くなった。父は葬儀に参列しなければならなかった。葬儀から戻ってきた父に私は尋ねた。「おじさん、最後になんて言った?」 父は答えた。「砂糖が食べたいって言ったよ……」

おじの人生には甘さが足りなかったのだろうか? 戦時中に砂糖が不足していたから、食べたくてたまらなくなってしまったのだろうか? 何が真実なのか、よくわからなかった。私たちが今生きている傍らで、川走はいつも走っている。

> 川走(せんそう)、イブとアダム礼盃亭(らいはいてい)を過(す)ぎ、く寝(ね)る岸辺(きしべ)から輪(わ)ん曲(きょく)する湾(わん)へ、今(こん)も度(ど)失(う)せぬ巡(めぐ)り路(みち)を媚行(びこう)し、巡(めぐ)り戻(もど)るは栄地四囲委蛇(えいちしいいい)たるホウス城(じょう)とその周円(しゅうえん)。
>
> ジェイムズ・ジョイス『フィネガンズ・ウェイクI』〔柳瀬尚紀訳、19頁〕

1973

ブロークン・ダイアリー：ヴィデオ・ガールズとナヴァホの空のためのヴィデオソング

Broken Diary: Video Girls and Video Songs for Navajo Sky

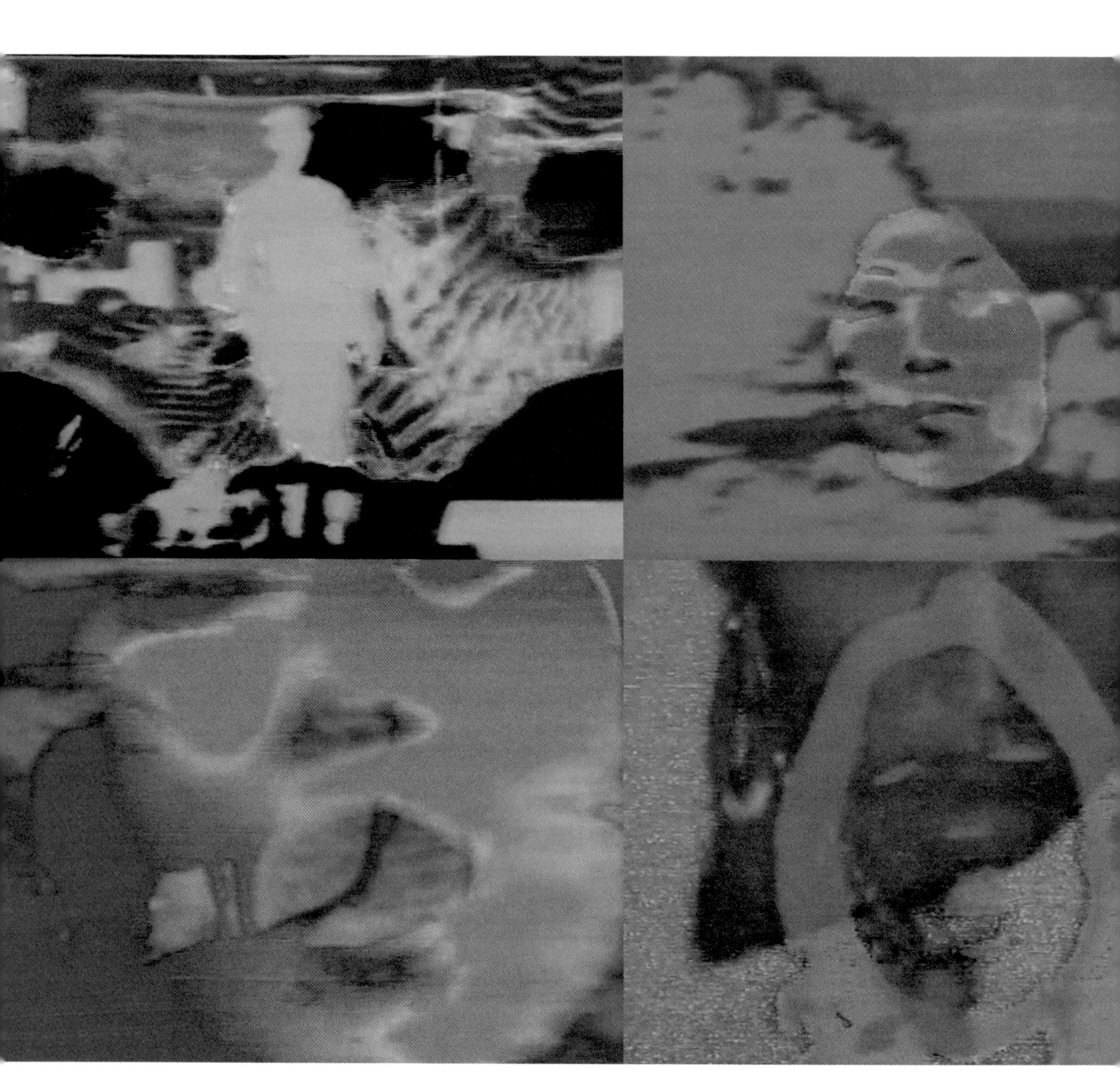

《ブロークン・ダイアリー：ヴィデオ・ガールズとナヴァホの空のためのヴィデオソング》（スチル）

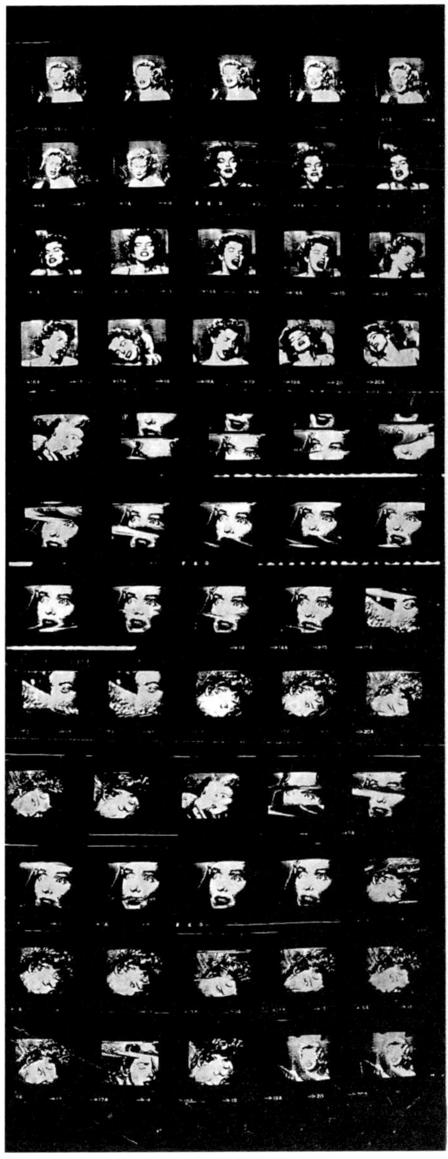

2nd Annual Video Arts Festival
may 1973

SHIGEKO
KUBOTA

A 36 - 24 - 36

MAY 28
8:30P.M
monday

AT
THE kitchen 475-9865
240 Mercer Street New York 10012
the mercer arts center

Photographed by mary Lucier

「第2回ヴィデオ・アーツ・フェスティヴァル　久保田成子:A36－24－36」ポスター　1973年

1973年５月、前年にザ・キッチンで始まったヴィデオ・アーツ・フェスティヴァルで、久保田は《A36－24－36》というマルチチャンネルの作品を見せた。メアリー・ルシエによれば、それはテレビに映ったマリリン・モンローの様々な姿をヴィデオに録ったもので、題名は、バストとヒップがほぼ同じサイズで腰がくびれているという、当時の女性の理想体型を指していたという。本作品は現存しないが、ルシエが撮った画面の記録写真を使い、当時のインスタレーションの状況を、本展用にプリントで再現してもらった。

翌月の６月、グループ「ホワイト ブラック レッド イエロー」のメンバー、セシリア・サンドヴァルに同行し、ルシエと久保田は、彼女の実家のある、チンリー（アリゾナ）のナヴァホ族の保留地を訪れた。少女の頃、父親の実家のお寺に水道がなく、若い衆がいつも肩に天秤棒とバケツをかついで、近くの山の泉から清水を汲んできたのを覚えていた久保田は、セシリアの家族も馬車を走らせて水汲みをしに行かなければならないことに共感する。久保田は、日本人とナヴァホ族は同一の祖先を持つと信じる彼らに特別な近親感を持つ。後に「ブロークン・ダイアリー」の一章となるシングルチャンネルのヴィデオ、《ヴィデオ・ガールズとナヴァホの空のためのヴィデオソング》は、彼らが井戸で水を汲んでいるシーンで始まって終わるが、抽象化された久保田の顔がその上に二重写しになるのが特徴的である。それは、あくまでも彼女という媒体を通して、見、聞き、感じたナヴァホ族の生活であることを強調するようだ。最後に「成子はナヴァホ語で、義理の妹か弟を意味する」と久保田が言う時、彼女の顔がナヴァホの女性の顔と重なる場面があるが、それも久保田の異文化を超えたアイデンティティの模索の表現であったのだろうか。
（MY）

1973-75

ブローークン・ダイアリー：私のお父さん

Broken Diary: My Father

JULY 14, 1974

MY FATHER DIED
THE DAY I BOUGHT
AN AIRPLANE
TICKET TO GO TO
SEE HIM.
I CALLED SHIRLEY
CLARKE. SHE ASK-
ED ME HOW I WAS.
I TOLD HER I WAS
CRYING. SHE SAID
"WHY DON'T YOU
MAKE A VIDEOTAPE
OF YOURSELF CRY-
ING".

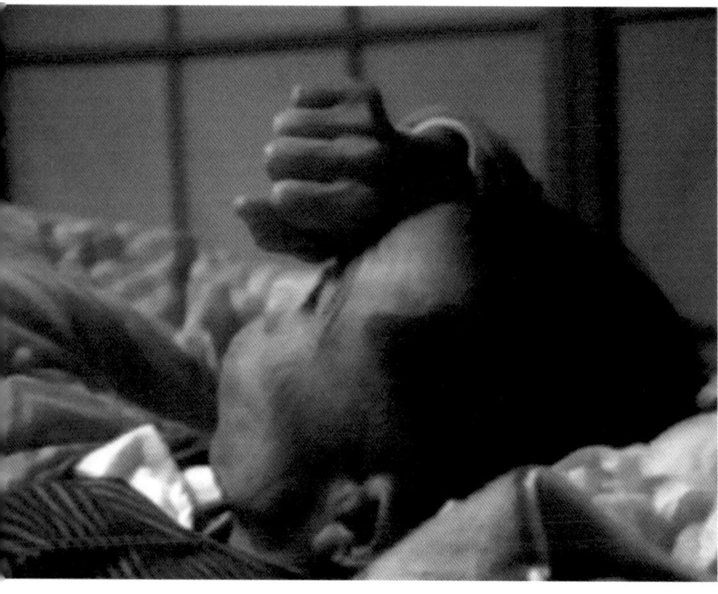

《ブローークン・ダイアリー：私のお父さん》（スチル）

1973年の年末に久々に帰省した久保田は、実家で病床の父を見舞う。大晦日に一緒に紅白歌合戦を観る様を記録したヴィデオは、翌年7月に父を亡くした時、《私のお父さん》というヴィデオ哀歌へと生まれ変わった。正月明けには、3夜に渡り、天井桟敷館でビデオひろばと協働して開かれた、「トーキョー・ニューヨーク・ビデオ・エキスプレス」で、ニューヨークから「手荷物便で持ってきた」アメリカ人作家のヴィデオテープを上映し、トークも行なったが、その時に見た日本のヴィデオ作家の作品について、1月末にニューヨーク近代美術館で行なわれた、「開かれた回路：テレビの未来」という国際会議でレポートをし、日米のヴィデオ・アートの交流に貢献した。同年、ジョージ・マチューナスが組織した、ソーホーのアーティストの共同住宅を購入し、パイクと移り住んだ久保田は、近所に移ったばかりのアンソロジー・フィルム・アーカイヴズで、ヴィデオ・キュレーターとして1982年まで勤めることになる。その頃、久保田の協力者となり、後にヴィデオ・キュレーターの仕事を後継するボブ（ロバート）・ハリスは、久保田の積極的でオープンな人柄が、新しい芸術分野であったヴィデオの人脈を繋げるのに適任であったと語っている。キュレーターとしての経験が効して、人とは違う「ヴィデオ彫刻」を編み出すこととなった。(MY)

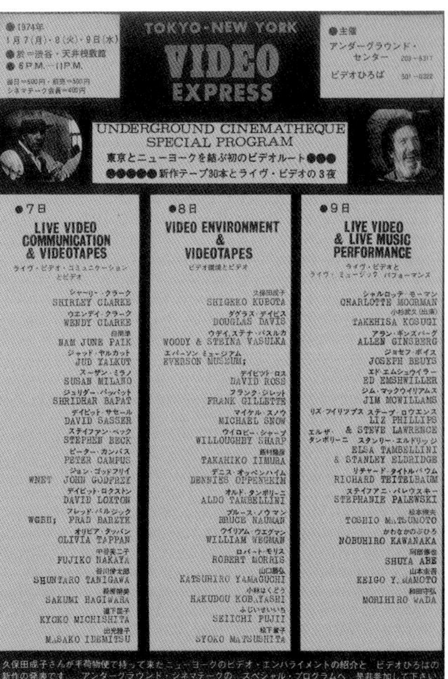

「トーキョー・ニューヨーク・ビデオ・エキスプレス」（1974年）会場にて（上）
「トーキョー・ニューヨーク・ビデオ・エキスプレス」チラシ　1974年（下）

1970-75

ヴィデオ・ポエム

Video Poem

ヴィデオ生活の背後で

男性は思う。「我思う、ゆえに我あり」。
女性である私は感じる。「我出血す、ゆえに我あり」。
近ごろ私は毎月ハーフインチ……３Ｍまたはソニー製……で１万フィートの長さの出血をする。
男性は毎晩私を撃つ＝撮る（シュート）……私は抵抗できない。
私は真っ昼間、露光過多で燃え上がるヴィデオまたはＴＶ撮像管で、男性を撃ち＝撮りかえす。

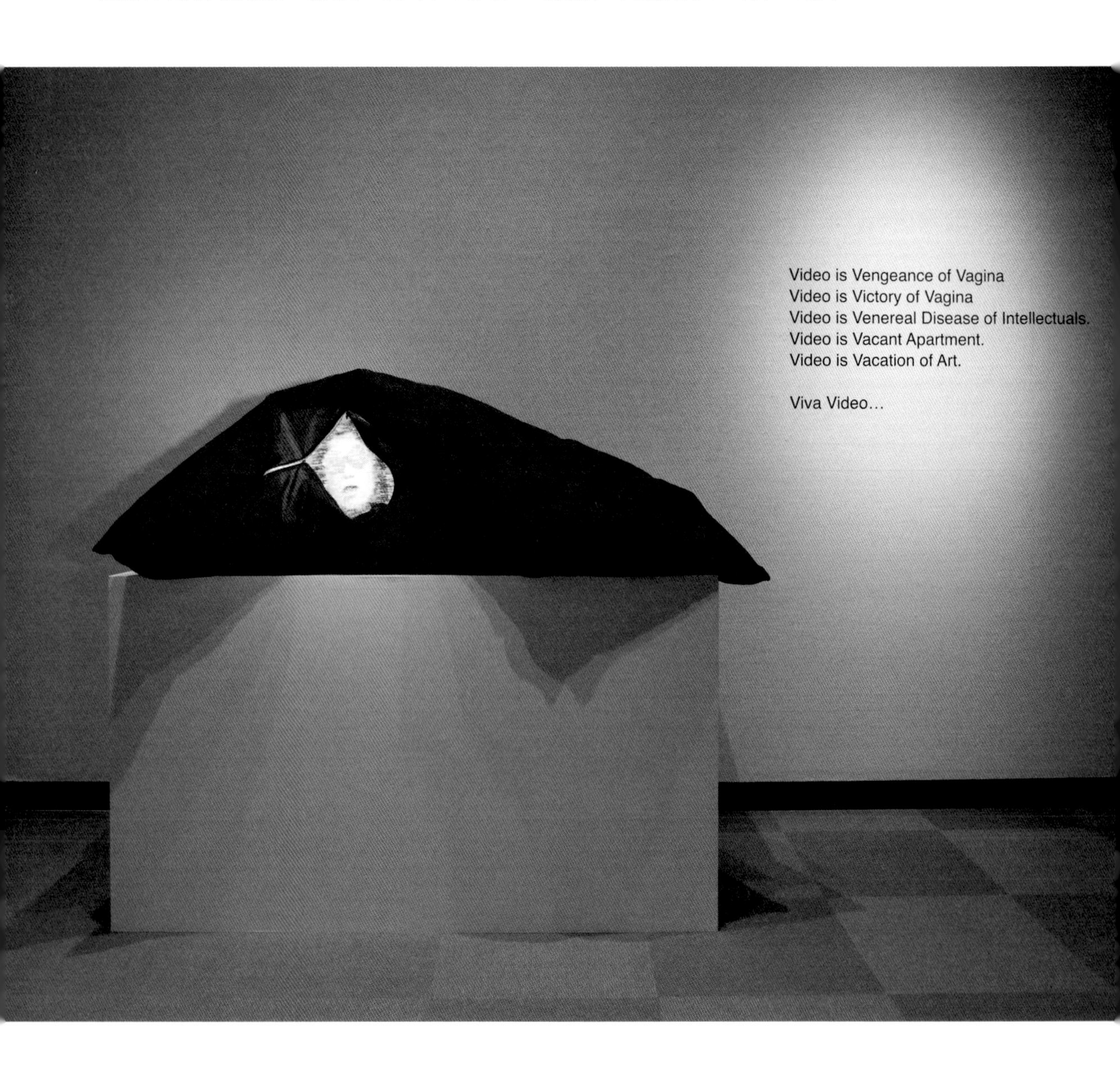

Video is Vengeance of Vagina
Video is Victory of Vagina
Video is Venereal Disease of Intellectuals.
Video is Vacant Apartment.
Video is Vacation of Art.
Viva Video...

Video is Vacation of Art.

久保田と《ヴィデオ・ポエム》 ザ・キッチン(1975年)での展示

ヴィデオは女性器(ヴァギナ)の復讐
ヴィデオは女性器(ヴァギナ)の勝利
ヴィデオは知識人たちの性病
ヴィデオは空室のアパート
ヴィデオはアートの休暇
ヴィデオ万歳……

布袋の一部が開いていて、そこから映像が見えている。袋の中にはテレビモニターと小型扇風機が設置されており、風によって柔らかく有機的な形に膨らむ。この袋はもともと、小杉武久のパフォーマンス作品《Anima2/Chamber Music》(1962年)のために久保田が縫ったものである。小杉の作品は、袋を室内に見立てその中に入り、窓やドアにあたる、大きさの異なる複数のジッパーから身体の一部を外側に出すというものだが、久保田はそこにテレビモニターを据え、無音で口をパクパクさせる自身の顔を覗かせた。このセルフ・ポートレートは、久保田がポーターパックを入手した最初期に撮影したものである。(MN)

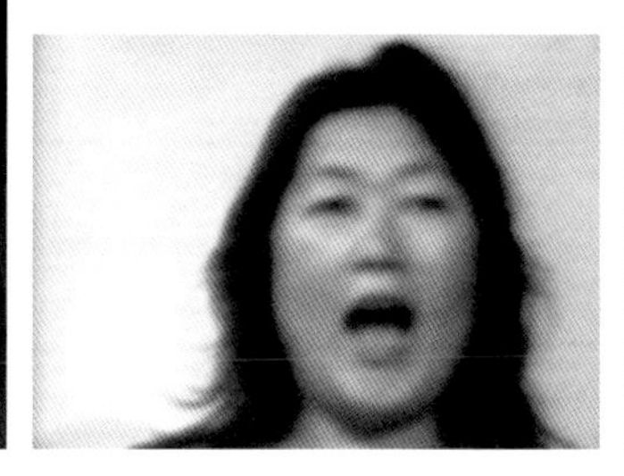
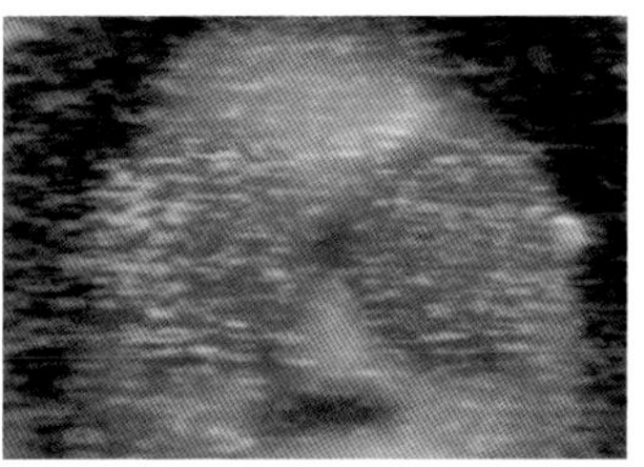

(スチル)

塩見允枝子
インタビュー

しおみ・みえこ：1938年生まれ、作曲家。

久保田成子さんと初めてお会いしたときのことはよく覚えていないんですけど、1963年ごろではないかと思います。「グループ音楽」の仲間、小杉武久さんを通じてのことでした。私がナムジュン・パイクに初めて紹介されたのもこの年の夏（「ニュー・ディレクション第二回演奏会」草月会館ホール）で、パイクとの出会いをきっかけに、私はフルクサスとのご縁ができ、翌年渡米することになりました。

当時私は、大学での勉強を一通り終えて故郷の岡山に戻っていたのですが、面白いコンサートなどがあると、時々上京していました。駒場にある、邦千谷さんの家の離れに住んでいた久保田さんのお部屋に泊めてもらったこともあります。内科画廊での久保田さんの初個展も見に行きました。トラック2台分の紙屑を集めてきて、その上に白い布がかけてあり、部屋の手前から奥に向かって少し高くなるように傾斜していました。その上に土管のようなものが置いてあったと思います*1。芳名帳のところにはいろんな色の鉛筆が置いてあったので、私が白で記名したら後で、「白で書くなんて独特なセンスの人だなと思ったら、貴女だったのね」って言われました。同じころ「Sweet 16」というイベントに私も久保田さんも参加したのだけど、久保田さんがそこで行なったパフォーマンスは残念ながら見ていません。

翌年6月の初めごろ、ニューヨークにいる秋山邦晴さんとジョージ・マチューナスから寄せ書きが届いて、渡米の決心をしました。その直後に同じようにニューヨークへ行こうかどうしようかと迷っていた久保田さんに会ったので、二人のほうが心丈夫だから一緒に行こう、ということになったんです。6月27日に開催されるフルクサスのコンサートに間に合うように行きたかったのですが、手続きに時間がかかって、結局到着は7月4日。マチューナスと秋山さんが空港へ迎えに来てくださり、キャナル・ストリートのロフトへ連れていってくれました。その後、隣のロフトに住んでいた靉嘔さん夫妻と斉藤陽子さんが、歓迎パーティをしてくださったのです。

久保田さんとはそれから2か月ほど一緒に暮らしました。マチューナスが紹介してくれたサリヴァン・ストリートのアパートは、2部屋あって良かったと思っていたら、翌日に管理人がやってきて、「君たちが契約した125ドルの部屋は、本当はここじゃないんだ」と言って、1つしかお部屋のない別のところへ移されてしまって……。そこで2週間ほど「ディナー・コミューン」をやりました。これはマチューナスの提案なのだけど、マチューナス、パイク、久保田さん、斉藤さんと私で、共同で食材を買って一緒に料理して食べるんです。共同体の夢を見ていたマチューナスらしい発想でしたが、私たちが日本食レストランでのアルバイトを見つけたので、このコミューンは解散になりました。このころは、マチューナスのロフトで、フルクサスのマルチプルを作る手伝いも久保田さんや斉藤さんと一緒にしていましたね。

ひと月あまり経ったころ、久保田さんは50cm角くらいの平面の板を4～5枚並べて、何か描き始めたのでいよいよ制作に取り組むんだなと思いました。彼女は突然、名前を「『Love-ko A*I*』に改名するわ！」などと言ったりして、驚かされたこともありますが、印象に残っているのは、彼女が強い覚悟を持ってアメリカに来たということです。今は下積みでいいけど、50歳になったころには華麗な生活を送っていたい、そのためにはちゃんと英語がしゃべれなきゃバカにされるからとニューヨーク大学の英語のコースにも通い始めました。私はちょうど1年間で帰国しましたが、その直前に彼女のパフォーマンス、《ヴァギナ・ペインティング》を見ました。

数年たって*2、彼女から突然電話をもらったのを覚えています。当時、私は結婚して箕面市に住んでいたのだけど、久保田さんは秋葉原にテレビを買いに来て、電話をかけてきてくれたんです。「パイクと一緒になったのよ」と報告してくれました。その後、私の「スペイシャル・ポエム No. 5」（1972年）にも参加してくれました。

その次に会ったのは1990年にヴェニスで、「Ubi Fluxus Ibi Motus 1962–1990」という展覧会に2人とも参加したんです。25年ぶりなので懐かしかったなあ……。初日に久保田さんから「あなた、なるべく自分の作品のところにいたほうがいいよ。いろんな人が訪ねてくるからね」って言われて、ああそういうものかと思って、2日目からはそうしていたら、たしかにいろんな人が来てくださいましたね。再会を喜んで、長年の積もる話をしたり、他の作家たちも交えて何度も食事をしました。私が先にヴェニスを発つときは水上タクシー乗り場まで、朝早いのに見送りにきてくれて、遠ざかっていく船と岸壁の上で2人とも大きく手を振って別れましたよ。あのシーンは忘れられませんね。ヴィデオ彫刻と音楽やパフォーマンスという仕事のジャンルは違っても、一種の戦友という思いを互いに抱いていましたから。

それから、1998年にパイクさんが京都賞を受賞なさったときは、京都までお祝いに駆け付けました。彼女がパイクさんの車椅子を押して、甲斐甲斐しく妻の役を演じていたのが印象的でした。最後に会ったのは、2004年に国立国際美術館の移転開館記念展「マルセル・デュシャンと20世紀美術」でのことです。ジョアン・ミロの作品の向かいのバルコニーのところで、2人でしばらくいろんな話をしました。「ニューヨークで生きていくのは大変なのよ」と、作家としての苦労や、長年にわたるパイクさんの看病のことなど、いろいろと話してくれたことを、つい最近のことのように思い出します。

2019年6月箕面市にて

インタビュアー：濱田真由美、橋本梓、西川美穂子、由本みどり

インタビュー編集：橋本梓

［註］

＊1――実際には鉄管。

＊2――おそらく1971年のことと思われる。

An interview with Mieko Shiomi

Composer. Born in 1938.

I don't remember exactly when, but the first time I met Shigeko was around 1963. I met her through Takehisa Kosugi, a friend from Group Ongaku. The summer of that year was also when I was first introduced to Nam June Paik (at the *New Direction 2nd Concert*, at Sogetsu Hall). Through my meeting Paik, I had the good luck to get to know Fluxus, and the following year, I went to the United States.

At that time I had finished my studies at university and returned to Okayama, my hometown, but I sometimes went to Tokyo when there were interesting concerts. I had stayed at Shigeko's place when she was living in a room built off of Chiya Kuni's house in Komaba. I also went to see Shigeko's first solo show at the Naiqua Gallery. She gathered two truckloads of paper scraps, and covered them with a white cloth, creating a slope that was slanted slightly upwards, from the front of the room towards the back. On top of that, something like clay pipes were placed ([metal pipes]). There were pencils of various colors for the guestbook, so I signed my name in white. She later told me, "I thought it was such a unique sensibility for someone to sign in white, and it turns out it was you." Around the same time, Shigeko and I both participated in an event titled, *Sweet 16*, but unfortunately I didn't get to see the performance Shigeko did there.

Around the beginning of June the following year, I got a message from Kuniharu Akiyama and George Maciunas in New York, and decided to go to the United States. Immediately after I made up my mind to go, I met Shigeko, who, like me, had been trying to decide whether to go to New York or not, so we decided to go together, since that would makes us feel more secure. We wanted to get there in time for the Fluxus concert scheduled for June 27th, but visa processing took too long, and we ended up arriving on July 4th. Maciunas and Akiyama picked us up at the airport and took us to their loft on Canal Street. Later Mr. and Mrs. Ay-O and Takako Saito, who were living in the loft next door, held a welcome party for us.

Shigeko and I lived together for about two months. Maciunas showed us an apartment on Sullivan St. We thought we were lucky to have two rooms, but the next day the building manager came and said, "Actually, this is not the $125 room you signed up for." We ended up being moved to another place with only one room . . . There we held a "dinner commune" for about two weeks. It was Maciunas who suggested it. Maciunas, Paik, Shigeko, Takako, and I bought the ingredients, cooked, and ate together. That was a typical Maciunas idea, as he was dreaming of having a commune at the time. However, this dinner commune fell apart, as we ended up finding part-time jobs at a Japanese restaurant. Around that time, Shigeko, Takako and I were also helping to make Fluxus multiples at

Maciunas's loft.

About a month passed, and Shigeko laid down four or five flat boards of about 50 x 50 centimeters and started drawing something, so I thought that she was finally going to work on production. I remember being surprised when she suddenly said, "I will change my name to 'Love-ko A*I*'!"

But what impressed me was that she went to the United States with such a strong determination. She started taking English courses at New York University, saying that it was fine, she was paying her dues now, but she wanted to live life splendidly by the time she turned fifty, so for that goal, she had to speak English properly so that people would not make fun of her. I returned to Japan after just one year, but just before that, I saw her performance *Vagina Painting.*

A few years later [probably in 1971], I suddenly got a call from her. At that time, I was married and was living in Minoo City, but Shigeko came to Akihabara to buy TVs and called me. Then she told me, "I married Nam June." Later, she also participated in my event, *Spatial Poem No. 5* (1972).

The next time I met her was at an exhibition called, *Ubi Fluxus Ibi Motus 1962–1990* in Venice in 1990, in which we both participated. That took me back, as it was my first time seeing her in twenty-five years! On the first day, Shigeko told me, "You should try to stay close to your work. Different people will come see you." I thought that sounded right, so from the second day on I did, and exactly as she said, many people came to say hi. We were delighted to see each other again and to catch up after so many years. We also went out to eat many times, with other artists too. When I was leaving Venice, Shigeko even came to the water taxi pier to see me off early in the morning, and we, one on the boat going away, the other staying on the quay, waved goodbye to each other and parted. I'll never forget that moment. Despite the fact that the genres of work we do—video sculpture vs. music and performance—are different, we both felt that we were comrades.

Also, at the time that Paik was awarded the Kyoto Prize in 1998, I went to Kyoto to congratulate him. It was impressive that Shigeko was pushing Paik's wheelchair and attending to him so carefully as his wife. The last time I met her was at the exhibition, *Mirrorical Returns: Marcel Duchamp and 20th Century Art*, commemorating the opening of the National Museum of Art, Osaka at a new location. We talked about a lot of things for a while, on the balcony across from Joan Miró's work. She said, "It's not easy living in New York," telling me different things such the hardships of living as an artist, and of her many years of caring for Paik. I still remember that time well, like something that just happened.

Interviewed in Minoh City, June, 2019
Interviewer: Mayumi Hamada, Azusa Hashimoto, Mihoko Nishikawa, Midori Yoshimoto
Editing: Azusa Hashimoto

Translation by Yuzo Sakuramoto

天衣無縫の人　久保田成子

メアリー・ルシエ

Mary Lucier：1944年生まれ、ニューヨーク在住、
ヴィデオ・アーティスト。

久保田成子に初めて会ったのは1965年、私が20歳になるかならないか、彼女が20代後半のときだった。しばらく前にニューヨークに来ていた彼女は作曲家デイヴィッド・バーマンと住んでいた。彼はのちに最初の夫になる。デイヴィッドと当時の私の夫アルヴィン・ルシエは友人であり仕事仲間だったので、私たち2人は最初はデイヴィッドの兄弟が93丁目に持っていたタウンハウスの3階、のちには本人がストーニー・ポイントに構えた家を訪ねていったものだ。ストーニー・ポイントの家にはジョン・ケージ、デイヴィッド・テュードア、シャーリ・ディーンズ（シャリ・ディアナシュ）、MCリチャーズなど、気の合うアーティストどうしが集まって一つの共同体を形成していた。

長年にわたって私はパワフルで複雑な女性アーティストたちと親しくなったが、成子もそのひとりだった。彼女には2つの顔があり、私は強く心を惹かれつつも、戸惑ってしまうことがあった。一方で成子は伝統的な日本女性だった——いつでも歓迎してくれ、陽気で、客が来ると喜んですばらしい寿司や天ぷらをふるまってくれた。他方で彼女は急進的なフェミニストであり、日本で女性アーティストとして自分が置かれている立場に不満を持っていて、少しでも不当な扱いを受けたと感じるとたちまち腹を立てた。彼女の癇癪は伝説だった。以前成子と付き合っていた作曲家の小杉武久はあるとき、親しみを込めて彼女のことを「台風」と呼んでいる。私は成子の両極端ぶりに恐れをなしていたが、同時に心のどこかで、激しやすく、アートにおいては野心的、何が何でも成功をつかもうと固く決意しているこの人物に深い親近感を覚えた。成子の気性とアートとは分かちがたく結びついており、彼女は途方もないエネルギーとバイタリティをもってすべてのプロジェクトに取り組んだ。私たちは親友となり、結局別々の人生を歩むことになったけれど、それまでのあいだには協働したりもした。

1960年代末から1970年代初めにかけてのアヴァンギャルドでは、アーティストが団結して「グループ」を結成するというのは、新音楽などの時間ベースのアートでは非常によく見られた。力を合わせ、自分自身や仲間の仕事を同じ旗印のもとで盛り上げていき、より広い層のオーディエンスに向けて公開しツアーしていく手段だったのだ。アルヴィン・ルシエ、ロバート・アシュリー、デイヴィッド・バーマン、ゴードン・ムンマといった作曲家たちは1966年、「ソニック・アーツ・ユニオン」を結成し、ヨーロッパや米国をまわる長期ツアーを企画した。これにはしばしば彼らの妻やパートナーたちが同行した。成子と私（にメアリー・アシュリーとバーバラ・ロイド）は1967年と69年、こうしたヨーロッパ・ツアーの最初の2回に参加し、全員で男性たちの作品の枠内で演奏（パフォーマンス）をしたほか、女性どうしで協働したり別々につくったりした独自の作品を披露することもあった。この経験に刺激され、フルクサスや「レインダンス」、「ヴィデオフリークス」といった同時期の他のいろいろな集団の影響もあって、私たちは独自のグループを結成することにした。多文化的でフェミニズム的な顔ぶれが揃ったから、注目を集められるだろうと私たちは考えた。

1970年には成子はバーマンと離婚し、ナムジュン・パイクと暮らしていた。エレクトロニック・アーティストはまだ稀だったが数は増えつつあり、彼らに対するナムジュンの影響力はすでに巨大だった。私はニューヨークに引っ越す前で、アルヴィンがウェスリアン大学の音楽学部で教えていたので、まだ〔同大のある〕コネティカット州ミドルタウンに住んでいた。とはいえ成子と私とは毎日のように手紙をやり取りし、独自のパフォーマンス・グループを結成すべくあれこれ策を練っていた。ナムジュンも成子も、自分とは違う文化出身の実践者たちを作品に取り込むところに特徴があり、私と成子のアンサンブルが人種的に多様なものになったのも、おそらくもともとは成子のアイデアだったと認めておこう。

私たちは友人2名に加わってもらった。私がウェスリアンで知りあったナヴァホ族の若い女性セシリア・サンドヴァル、そして私と成子共通の友人だったベルギー人作曲家ジャック・ベケルトを介して知りあったアフリカ系アメリカ人の詩人・教師シャーロット・ワレンだ。こうして「レッド ホワイト イエロー ブラック」（成子は「ホワイト ブラック レ

ッド イエロー」と表記していた）が誕生した。私たちの第1回マルチメディア・コンサートは1972年12月16日、まだマーサー通りにあった「ザ・キッチン」で開かれ、第2回と第3回は1年後の1973年4月20・21日に行われた。

こういった「コンサート」のひとつで成子は、モニターを複数台使ってヨーロッパを旅行したときに自分が撮影したいろいろな川や運河の映像を流した。セシリア・サンドヴァルと私は彼女が夢で見た結婚式を再演した（私はナレーター役）。米先住民がパフォーマンスをする白黒映像を背景に、セシリアは青の野球ユニフォームからセクシーな赤のドレスに着替え、オーディエンスとダンスを踊り、ナヴァホの言葉で語りかけた。シャーロットは著名なアフリカ系アメリカ人詩人の作品を朗読した。

こういったイベントは洗練された舞台というわけではなかったけれど、〔このころ〕即興的な作品に観客が集まるようになっていて、実験的で多様性に富み、絶えず変化する私たちの作品はとても好評だった。実を言えばこの種の精神風土（エートス）は当時、時間ベースのアートで大勢を占めていたようだった。1960年代のアート界でハプニングが行なわれていたおかげで、私たちがやっていたような音楽、ダンス、映画、演劇といった諸領域にまたがって存在するマルチメディア・パフォーマンスが可能になっていた。とはいえ最終的には成子も私もヴィデオ彫刻に活動の場を移した。ヴィデオ彫刻にはもっと規律や構造が必要で、寿命もパフォーマンスより長かった。

私たちはあいかわらず友だちだったが、グループとしてパフォーマンスを行なうことはなくなった。1974年、成子とナムジュンは〔アーティスト向けに低家賃で提供されていた〕「ウェストベス」のアパートメントからソーホー地区マーサー通り110番地の広大なロフトに引っ越し、芽ぐみつつあったヴィデオ・アート界にとってこのロフトは創造と出会いの一大中心となった。何年にもわたり、私は成子とナムジュンの仕事を写真に撮りつづけた。その中の一点に、恍惚とした姿態のマリリン・モンローをテレビから録画したクリップを含む成子のヴィデオ・インスタレーションがあった。インスタレーションには白黒のモニターが何台も使われて、それぞれが色付きのジェルで覆われていた。私は白黒映画をもとにした成子のヴィデオテープのスチル写真を撮り、うち何点かを選んで赤、白、青、黄色の特別な紙に印画した。成子のオリジナル作品のほうはもう存在しないから、私は今回の展覧会に向けて、色紙に印画しなおしたスチル写真の中から9点を選び、タテヨコ3点ずつグリッド状に並べた。このコラージュを私は《シゲコのヴィデオ・マリリン》と呼んでいる。

成子と並んで私も、よく同じ場で自分のインスタレーションを展示するようになった。あとで成子が当時ソーホー地区のウースター通りにあったアンソロジー・フィルム・アーカイヴズのヴィデオ・キュレーターになると、ヴィデオ・アーティストやキュレーター、友人たちが上映会に集い、しょっちゅう成子のロフトに移動して日本酒や寿司をごちそうに

ハロウィーン・パーティーでのメアリー・ルシエと久保田成子、1970年代半ば（メアリー・ルシエのポラロイド・カメラで撮影）
Mary Lucier and Shigeko Kubota at a Halloween Party, ca. mid 1970s (taken with Lucier's polaroid camera).

なった。このころソーホーのギャラリー街は最盛期で、土曜の午後「行くべき場所」といえば絶対に成子の家だった。ヴィデオ・アートが登場したてで映画界からもアート界からもはみ出していたこの時代、いつもどおり元気いっぱいで来る者拒まずといった態度で成子は私たちみんなを結びつけてくれた。

成子はリスクを冒すことの美学というものを理解していて、彼女の影響下でアンソロジーのヴィデオ・プログラムは、ヴィデオ・アートの将来に賭けるというばくちに出た。成子とアンソロジーのスタッフは、私の7チャンネル・インスタレーション《夜明けの過度露光》の公開を大いにサポートしてくれ、彼らの尽力の結果私は、予算や機材、スペース、信念が限られていたから、私一人ではとうてい不可能だったはずのアイデアを実現することができた。2年後、第10回パリ・ビエンナーレに招かれて現地で同じ作品を再制作することになった。成子とアンソロジー・フィルム・アーカイヴズには、こういう機会を与えてくれたことを感謝している。何年もあと、《夜明けの過度露光》はサンフランシスコ近代美術館に購入され同館コレクションに入った。

2020年12月22日

訳：近藤学

Shigeko Kubota: A Force of Nature

Mary Lucier

Video artist. Born in 1944.
Lives and works in New York.

When I first met Shigeko Kubota in 1965, I was barely 20 and she was then in her late 20s. Having recently arrived in New York, she was living with the composer David Behrman who would become her first husband. David and Alvin Lucier, to whom I was married at the time, were friends and colleagues, and we used to visit him regularly, first, on the third floor of his brother's town house on 93rd Street and later, in his house in Stony Point, where John Cage, David Tudor, Sari Dienes, MC Richards, and others shared a community of like-minded artists.

Shigeko was one of the powerful, complex women artists with whom I was friendly over the years. Her duality was fascinating though sometimes confusing. On the one hand, she seemed to be a traditional Japanese woman—accommodating, cheerful, and happy to cook for guests for whom she made fabulous sushi and tempura. On the other hand, she was a radical feminist, unhappy about her status as a woman artist in Japan and easily angered by the slightest perceived injustice. Her explosive nature was legendary. A previous boyfriend, the composer Takehisa Kosugi, once referred to her affectionately as "the typhoon." On one level, her extremes intimidated me but somewhere inside I felt a deep kinship with this volatile personality, ambitious in her art and determined to succeed. Her temperament and her art were inextricably bound together, and she brought tremendous energy and vitality to every project she undertook. We became close friends and, eventually, collaborators, before our lives drifted apart.

In the late 1960s and early 1970s Avant Garde, the idea of artists banding together to form a "group" was very prevalent in new music and the other time-based arts. It was a way for artists to join together to promote their own and their colleagues' work under a common rubric and to publish and tour that work to a broader audience. Composers Alvin Lucier, Robert Ashley, David Behrman, and Gordon Mumma formed the Sonic Arts Union in 1966, and organized extensive tours throughout Europe and the United States, frequently accompanied by their wives or partners. Shigeko and I (along with Mary Ashley and Barbara Lloyd) participated in the first two of those European tours in 1967 and 1969, during which we performed collectively in the men's works, occasionally presenting collaborative pieces and individual works of our own. This experience, along with the influence of other contemporary alliances such as Fluxus, Raindance, and the Videofreex, inspired us to form our own group, which we hoped would stand out due to its multicultural, feminist composition.

By 1970 Shigeko had divorced Behrman and was living with Nam June Paik, whose influence on the small but growing cadre of electronic artists was already huge. I had not yet moved to New York and was still living in Middletown, CT where Alvin was on the Wesleyan music faculty. But Shigeko and I were in almost constant contact by mail, scheming to form our own performing group. It was a signal characteristic of both Nam June's and Shigeko's work to incorporate practitioners from other cultures, and I will admit that it was probably Shigeko's idea in the beginning to form this diverse ethnic ensemble.

We enlisted two friends, Cecelia Sandoval, a young Navajo woman whom I had met at Wesleyan, and Charlotte Warren, an African-American poet and teacher whom we knew through our friendship with Belgian composer, Jacques Bekaert. And so was born "Red White Yellow and Black" (rendered by Shigeko as "White Black Red and Yellow"). Our first multi-media concert took place on December 16, 1972 at the original site of The Kitchen on Mercer Street, and the second and third, a year later on April 20 and 21, 1973.

In one of those "concerts" Shigeko presented multiple video monitor images of various rivers and canals she captured during her trip in Europe; Cecelia Sandoval and I reenacted a marriage dream of hers (with me narrating) against a background of black and white video images of Native American performers, while she changed costumes from a blue baseball uniform to a sexy red dress, dancing with the audience and speaking to them in Navajo; Charlotte read from the works of noted African American poets.

These events were not polished theater but there was a growing audience for improvisational work and the public was very appreciative of our experimental and diverse works-in-progress. In fact, this ethos seemed to dominate much time-based art of that era. Art world Happenings in the 1960s had paved the way for our kind of multi-media performances that existed across the fields of music, dance, film and theater. Eventually, however, both Shigeko and I moved on to video sculpture, which required more discipline and structure and had a longer lifespan.

We continued our friendship, but the group ceased to be as a performing entity. In 1974, Shigeko and Nam June moved from a Westbeth apartment to a sprawling SoHo loft at 110 Mercer Street, which became a hive of creative and social activity for the burgeoning video art world. Over the years I continued to photograph Shigeko's work, as well as Nam June's. One was Shigeko's video installation featuring clips of Marilyn Monroe in ecstatic postures that she had recorded from television. The installation used numerous black and white video monitors, each screen covered with a colored gel. I photographed offscreen still photos from her videotapes on black and white film and printed a select group of them on a special kind of colored paper in red, white, blue, and yellow. Since Shigeko's original work is no longer extant, I have chosen nine selected stills that I have reprinted in those colors and arranged in a 3 x 3 grid for the present exhibition. I am calling this collage *Shigeko's Video Marilyn.*

Along with Shigeko I was also beginning to show my own installations in many of the same venues. Eventually, when Shigeko became the video curator at Anthology Film Archives, then located on Wooster Street in SoHo, video artists, curators, and friends would gather for screenings, and often adjourn to her loft for sake and sushi. It was the heyday of SoHo galleries and [Shigeko's was] definitely "the place to be" on a Saturday afternoon. In her typically spirited and inclusive way, Shigeko helped to bring us all together at a time when video art was just emerging and did not fit comfortably in either the film or the art worlds.

Shigeko understood the aesthetic of risk, and under her influence the Anthology video program gambled on the future of video art. She and the staff were incredibly supportive in showing my seven-channel installation, *Dawn Burn*, in 1975, and as a result of their efforts I was able to realize an idea that otherwise I could not have pulled together by myself, given the limitations of budget, equipment, space, and faith. Two years later I was invited to recreate that work on location in the *10th Paris Biennale*, an opportunity for which I thank Shigeko and Anthology Film Archives. Years later, the work was acquired for the permanent collection of the San Francisco Museum of Modern Art.

December 22, 2020

私たちはみな、電子革命の一員だった

リズ・フィリップス

Liz Phillips：1951年生まれ、ニューヨーク市クイーンズ在住、マルチメディア・アーティスト。

1970年、ローズ美術館で開かれた「ヴィジョンとテレヴィジョン」展でナムジュン・パイクと知りあったとき、私はまだ19歳で、〔ヴァーモント州〕ベニントン・カレッジに籍を置きながらマサチューセッツ工科大学（MIT）先端視覚研究センターでインターンをしているところだった。ナムジュンを通じて久保田成子と知りあったのは、そのすぐあとのこと。私たちは親友になった。若いアーティストだった私の暮らしの中で、成子とナムジュンはとても大事な人たちだった。私の夫アール・ハワード、ナムジュン、成子、それに私は何晩も何日もともに過ごして、アートや音楽、テクノロジー、世界政治、いろいろな儀式、食べ物について語りあった。ナムジュンと成子が秘密で結婚式を挙げることに決めた際には、アールと私は市庁舎で証人を務め、チャイナタウンの456飯店で夕食を取ってから、上階にあった写真館で記念撮影をした。成子はよく、日本では自分を表現すること、ひとりの女性としてものをつくっていくことは本当に難しかったと言っていた。けれど彼女は日本のしきたりをいろいろと守り、ああ、またあれが食べたい、これが食べたいと懐かしんでいた。成子の料理は創造的で、ヴィデオでしていたのと同様に、台所でも自由に借用し合成した。成子とナムジュンが住んでいたマーサー通りのロフトにはアーティストやキュレーターたちが大勢集まり、食べ、飲み、アートについて議論した。あのころのニューヨーク・シティは、暮らすのにも仕事をするのにも最高の場所だった。

「ヴィジョンとテレヴィジョン」展カタログをいま見なおしてみると、略歴が載っている女性はシャーロット・モーマンだけであること、そして彼女は〔アーティストではなく〕演奏者（パフォーマー）という肩書で紹介されていたことに気づく。私が「レインダンス」に所属していたベリル・コローと知りあったのは〔ローズ美術館が附属する〕ブランダイス大学でのことだった。そのすぐあと、ナムジュンに頼まれて私はコネティカット州の〔オックスフォード市で共同生活を営みながら領域横断的な実験を行なっていた芸術集団〕パルサ・グループにメリーアン・アマチャーを迎えに行った。ナムジュンが〔マサチューセッツ州ケンブリッジ市〕ハーヴァード・スクエアで、ジョン・ケージの《サイレンス》をヴィデオ撮影するのに際して演奏してもらうためだった。また別の日、私たちはやはりナムジュンのヴィデオ用にウェスリアン大学でジョン・ケージの作品を演奏していた。私がメアリー・ルシエと知り合って、彼女が自室の居間のあちこちで撮影し、ひとコマひとコマ繋げた《私は部屋の中で座っている》のポラロイド写真を見たのはこのときだった。ナムジュンと成子は、私がつくっていたインタラクティブなインスタレーションや電子宴会を、「アヴァンギャルド・フェスティヴァル」などこの当時のグループ展に出品したらいいと勧めてくれた。私はさまざまなアート・グループや個人と知りあい、そのうちの何人か——久保田成子、メアリー・ルシエ、メリーアン・アマチャー、ベリル・コロー——は私にとって最も重要な女性アーティスト友だち・同僚になった。そのすぐあとには、彼女らと関連するアートをつくっていた他の女性たち——ルース・アンダーソン、アネア・ロックウッド、ローリー・スピーゲル、アリソン・ノールズ、ヘレーン・アイロン、スタイナ・ヴァスルカ、ジョーン・ローグ、ジョーン・ジョナス、メレディス・モンク、ハーマイン・フリード——とも知りあった。彼女たちの名前を挙げたのは、これ以前、女性アーティストが名指しで言及されることがあまりに少なかったからだ。私たちはインスタレーション、音楽、パフォーマンス、ニューメディアの創造と拡散に不可欠かつ活発な役割を果たした。

〔ブランダイス大やMITのある〕ボストン一帯で最初に成子と会ったときの思い出としては、一緒にハーヴァード・スクエアの〔セレクトショップ〕〈デザイン・リサーチ〉に行ったことなどがある。成子はマリメッコのドレスが大好きで、いつもこの店で買っていた。大きくてカラフルな柄を身にまとった彼女は本当にはなやかだった。マリメッコの布地は、成子のすばらしい笑い声、溢れ出る真心、アートや音楽、そして人生に彼女が注いだとてつもない熱情とよく響きあっていた。成子が着ていた明るい色を回想すると、しばしばヴィデオがくっきり生気に満ちた光線として天然木の彫刻から放出されア

ルミの水槽にぶつかって跳ね返る彼女の作品が思い浮かぶ。ヴィデオは明るく、合成されていて、その光は物理的な形態を貫く。

初めてニューヨーク・シティにナムジュンと成子を訪ねていったとき、私はまだ学生だった。2人はちょうど、元ベル研究所だった建物を公的助成を受けてアーティスト用住宅に改装した〈ウェストベス〉に引っ越したばかりだった。よく泊めてもらったり、ハドソン川を挟んだ対岸のニュージャージーにある私の実家から遊びに行ったりした。ナムジュンと成子はよく、あるとき私が思わず漏らしたセリフを引用したものだった。ある日の夕暮れ時、二人の家の窓から外を眺めていると、ナムジュンが「きれいだね」と言うので、私は「あんなのただのニュージャージーじゃない。向こうから見たほうがよっぽどきれいよ」と答えた。私は対岸からニューヨーク・シティを見て育っていたのだ。

この知りあって最初の夏、成子と私は2人で幾度か泊りがけの外出をしたり、何度も日帰り外出をしたりした。明け方にフラッシングやフルトン魚市場に行って、大きなマグロを買って帰った。ニュージャージー州のロングビーチ島に泊まって、私の弟ソール（当時11歳）が漁をし、成子は手に入れたばかりのポータパックで、ソールが獲った魚をおろしたり鳥たちが輪になって飛んでいたりするところを浜辺で撮影して大喜びだった。彼女は寿司をつくっ

久保田成子とリズ・フィリップス、久保田とパイクの110マーサー・ストリートのロフトにて、1974年
Shigeko Kubota and Liz Phillips in Kubota/Paik loft, 110 Mercer Street, New York City, 1974.

たが、この島始まって以来のことだったのではないかと思う。マグロなど当時は買う人もいなくて、漁師たちは缶詰用に1パウンド〔＝約450グラム〕69セントで売れれば儲けものだった。成子と知りあったおかげでソールは、マグロを主力商品にした世界的な漁業会社を築いてやろうと考えはじめた。

私たちはニューヨーク州北部のストーニー・ポイントに行った。泳いだり、きのこ狩りをしたり、すばらしい料理の腕前を持つアーティスト、サーリ・ディーンズやスタンとジョハンナのヴァンダービーク夫妻ほか、成子が作曲家デイヴィッド・バーマンと結婚していたときにお隣だった人たちを訪ねたりした。

私たちはみな、音楽、ヴィデオ、パフォーマンス、アートの領域で起きていた電子革命の一員だった。さまざまなツールや電子制御装置のおかげで、アートが作者やオーディエンスの手に戻ってきた。私たちは音声／映像シンセサイザー／オブジェクトを自作し、ファウンド・オブジェクトを使い、阿部修也やシュリダー・バパット、セルジュ・チェレプニンといったエンジニアたちと協働した。インスタレーション・アートと、転換や変容をテーマとするアートが、回路、モニター、スピーカーと絡みあい、パフォーマンスや彫刻、そして私にとって一番重要な成果として、インスタレーションを生み出した。当時の私たちは、作品が買われるとか売れるとかいうことはあまり考えなかった。作品を掘り下げ実現することが私たちにはできた。自分たちのアートからインスタレーションをつくり、観客がアクセスでき、私たちはフィードバックを得られるような、具合の良い空間に設営した。私たちは自由に議論を交わし、コラボレーションし、歌い、共同で研究し、時には共同で創作した。

成子はフルクサスのメンバーであることを誇りにしていて、私を〔この運動のリーダーである〕ジョージ・マチューナスに引きあわせようと、ウースター通りに建設中だったアンソロジー・フィルム・アーカイヴズに連れて行ってくれた。彼女はアンソロジー初のヴィデオ・アートのキュレーターになってほしいという依頼を受けていた。〔アンソロジーが体現していた〕実験映画がヴィデオ・アートの存在を認めたわけで、大いなる進歩だった！　私は成子がキュレーションした企画はほとんどすべてに足を運んだし、素晴らしいものが多かった。ジョーン・ジョナスのパフォーマンスを最初に見たのもここでだった。私の夫アール・ハワードが成子の機材を借り、彼女に励まされて《目隠し鬼》をつくったのもここでだった。アンソロジーから委嘱を受けて、ボブ〔＝ロバート〕・ハリス、アル・ロビンス、シュリダー・バパットの助力を得て制作されたコンセプチュアルな作品だ。この3名は成子を支える傑出したクルーで、私たちの親しい友だちそしてコラボレーターとなった。

成子の初期作品にはジョン・ケージとマルセル・デュシャンの仕事にオマージュを捧げたり参照したりしているものが多い。みんなそろってコラージュや電子加工に興味を持っていたから、成子、アール、ナムジュン、私はアプロプリエーション（流用）や電子加工、新テクノロジーをめぐって何時間でも語りあえた。ちょうどこのころ成子は特別な作品をたくさんつくった。父親の死去を扱った《私のお父さん》、《デュシャンピアナ：階段を降りる裸体》、《三つの山》などだ。

《メタ・マルセル：窓（雪）》で、窓枠の内側でノイズが雪に見立てられているのが私はとても好きで、初期のヴィデオ・アートにはあまり見られなかったような穏やかな性質や光を捉えていると感じた。《河》で成子は、いずれも流体が形態に変わるという特質をそなえている素材——水、ガラスを通したヴィデオ、金属、またこれらが示す歪みや反映すべて——から彫刻を創り出した。

訳：近藤学

We Were All Part of an Electronic Revolution

Liz Phillips

Murtimedia artist, born in 1951.
Lives and works in Queens, New York.

I was just 19 years old and on my first internship from Bennington College to MIT's Center for Advanced Visual Studies when I met Nam June Paik at the *Vision and Television* show at the Rose Art Museum in 1970. It was soon after this that I met Shigeko Kubota through Nam June. We became close friends. She and Nam June were very important people in my life as a young artist. My husband, Earl Howard, Nam June and Shigeko and I spent many evenings and days together talking about art, music, technology, world politics, rituals, and food. When Nam June and Shigeko decided to have a secret wedding, Earl and I were their witnesses at City Hall and then ate dinner at 456 Restaurant before photos in an upstairs Chinatown photography studio. Shigeko often said how difficult it had been in Japan to express herself and to create as a woman. Yet, she observed many Japanese customs and longed for foods from her past. She was a creative cook and freely borrowed and synthesized ingredients in the kitchen, as well as video. Many artists and curators gathered at their Mercer Street loft to eat, drink, and discuss art. New York City was a great place to live and work at that time.

Now, when I look back at the catalog from the Rose Art Museum, I realize that Charlotte Moorman is the only woman with a resume in the catalog, and she was a performer. It was at Brandeis that I first met Beryl Korot of Raindance, as well. Soon after, I was sent by Nam June to the Pulsa Group in Connecticut to pick up composer Maryanne Amacher to perform in conjunction with Nam June's videotaping of John Cage's *Silence* at Harvard Square. A different day we were performing a work of John Cage's at Wesleyan University for that film. I was then that I met Mary Lucier and saw her polaroids of *I am Sitting in a Room* sequenced frame by frame around her living room. Nam June and Shigeko encouraged me to present my interactive installations and electronic banquets in the Avant-garde Festivals and other group shows at that time. I met many art groups and individuals, including those who became my most significant women artist friends and colleagues: Shigeko Kubota, Mary Lucier, Maryanne Amacher and Beryl Korot. There were many other women making related art whom I met shortly after; Ruth Anderson, Annea Lockwood, Laurie Spiegel, Alison Knowles, Helene Aylon, Steina Vasulka, Joan Logue, Joan Jonas, Meredith Monk and Hermine Freed. I mention these women because there was so little mention of women artists before that time. We were so vital and active in installation, music, performance and new media creation and dissemination.

My first memories of Shigeko in Boston include going to Design Research in Harvard Square. Shigeko loved and always bought the Marimekko-designed clothes there. She looked so beautiful in those big colorful patterns. The fabrics resonated with her wonderful laugh, her bursts of honesty and her gigantic enthusiasm for art, music and life. The memory of wearing bright color leads me to Shigeko's work where video is often sharp and animated shafts of light emanating from natural wooden sculptures and bouncing off aluminum water containers. The video is bright and synthesized and its light pierces the physical forms.

I was still a student when I first visited Nam June and Shigeko in New York City. They had just moved to Westbeth, the subsidized artists' housing located in the former Bell Laboratory. I often stayed overnight with them or came in from my parent's house in New Jersey. Nam June and Shigeko often quoted me because one day when we looked out from their window at the sunset, Nam June said how beautiful it was. I said it was just New Jersey and it was all much more beautiful to see from the other side of the Hudson. I had grown up looking across the river at New York City.

That first summer Shigeko and I made some overnight trips together and many day trips. We went to Flushing and to the Fulton Fish market at dawn to carry home big tunas. We stayed on Long Beach Island in New Jersey where my brother (Saul was 11 years old at the time.) fished and Shigeko loved to shoot video with her new Portapak on the beach, of Saul fileting fish and of the birds that circled around. She made perhaps the first sushi on that Island when fisherman could only get 69 cents a pound for tuna to sell it to be canned. Through meeting Shigeko, Saul began to think of building his worldwide fishing business with tuna as a major item.

We went upstate to Stony Point. We went to swim, pick mushrooms and visit with the wonderful cook and artist Sari Dienes, and Stan and Johanna VanDerBeek and her other neighbors from her previous life and marriage to composer, David Behrman.

We were all part of an electronic revolution in music, video, performance and art, where tools and electronic controls returned to the hands of the art makers and audience. We made our own synthesizers and objects for sound and image, used found objects and worked with engineers including Shuya Abe, Shridhar Bapat and Serge Tcherepnin. Installation art and art about change and transformation mixed threads with circuits, monitors and loudspeakers to create performances, sculpture, and most important to me, installations. At that time, we did not think much about the work being bought and sold. We were able to explore and realize work. We made installations of our art in compatible spaces where the public had access and where we received feedback. We freely discussed, collaborated, sang, coresearched and sometimes co-created.

Shigeko was a proud member of Fluxus and took me to visit George Macuinas at Anthology Film Archives when it was being built on Wooster Street. She had been asked to be first video art curator there. That was enormous progress when experimental film acknowledged video art! I attended almost every show that Shigeko curated and many were wonderful. It was there that I first saw a Joan Jonas performance. It was there, with Shigeko's equipment and encouragement, that, my husband, Earl Howard created *Blind Man's Bluff*, a conceptual work, commissioned by Anthology, and produced with the help of Bob Harris, Al Robbins and Shridhar Bapat. They were the extraordinary crew of Shigeko and became our close friends and collaborators.

Shigeko's early video work often was in homage or reference to the work of John Cage and Marcel Duchamp. Because of all our mutual interest in collage and electronic processing Shigeko, Earl, Nam June and I could talk about appropriation, electronic processing and new technology for hours. It was during this time that Shigeko made her many special works; the work about her father's passing, *My Father*, *Duchampiana: Nude Descending a Staircase*, and *Three Mountains*.

In *Meta-Marcel: Window(Snow)* I loved the use of noise as snow within the window frames and felt it captured a peaceful quality and light that was not often embraced in early video art. In *River*, Shigeko created sculpture of common properties of fluid materials which became form; water, video through glass, metal and all their distortions and reflections.

久保田成子とリズ・フィリップス、久保田とパイクの110マーサー・ストリートのロフトにて、1974年
Shigeko Kubota and Liz Phillips in Kubota/Paik loft, 110 Mercer Street, New York City, 1974.

1972-75

デュシャンピアナ：マルセル・デュシャンの墓

Duchampiana: Marcel Duchamp's Grave

（スチル）

D'ailleurs, c'est toujours les autres qui meurent.
（それに、死ぬのはいつも他人）
マルセル・デュシャン

By the way, it is always others who die.
Marcel Duchamp

ヴィデオのないヴィデオ
死とのコミュニケーション
久保田成子

Video without Video
Communication with Death.
Shigeko Kubota

1972年、私はマルセル・デュシャンの墓に参った。私の青い本『マルセル・デュシャンとジョン・ケージ』を持っていって、とても風の強い日だった。パリからルーアンまで列車に乗って、それからタクシーで彼の墓地に向かった。女の人に「マルセル・デュシャンのお墓はどこですか？」と尋ねた。彼女は私を見て、「だれ、その人？」と言った。それから彼女は電話帳を開いた。私はとてもショックだった。たったひとりで、ポータパックの重みが肩に食い込む中、広い墓地を長いあいだ捜しまわったあげく、ようやく兄ジャック・ヴィロンの墓の隣にあるデュシャンの墓を見つけた。マルセルの皮肉な墓碑に私は驚いた……「D'ailleurs, c'est toujours les autres qui meurent.」

デュシャン本人は死に対してクールで感傷を排した態度をとっていたけれど、私はとても心を動かされた。代々僧侶である父の実家は裏日本に寺を所有していたので、葬儀を目にする機会は多かった。よく寺の部屋で宿題をしたが、そこには亡くなったばかりの人の遺骨がしまってあった。しょっちゅう幽霊と遊んだものだ……そんな子供時代の思い出がどっと頭の中にひらめいて、私は『マルセル・デュシャンとジョン・ケージ』を墓の上に置いた。東洋の家族が、ご先祖様の仏壇に煎餅を供えるみたいに。

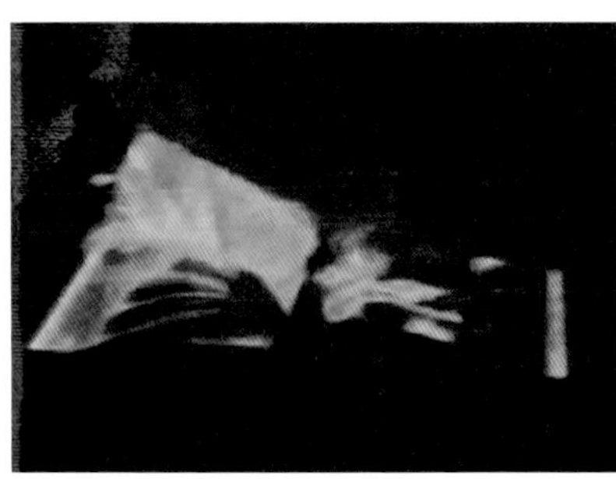
（スチル）

1975年のザ・キッチンにおける個展で発表された最初のヴィデオ彫刻の1つ。床から天井までテレビモニターを積み上げ、テレビの箱部分をベニヤ合板で覆い、モニター部分のみが覗く。床に置かれた鏡にモニターのイメージが映り込み、無限に増幅する。映像はデュシャンの墓を撮影したモノクロ映像を色加工したもので、縦に連なるモニターすべて（当初は9インチモニターが11台）に同一の映像が流れ、撮影時の風の音が重なる。1984年の展示で天井および対面にも鏡が追加されたほか、両脇の壁にプロジェクション投影を行なうなど、場所や時代によって展示方法が異なる。デュシャンとの掛け合いの言葉も、当初は鏡の続きとして対面に書かれたが、のちには横、あるいは両脇に付されるなど、バリエーションがある。(MN)

ザ・キッチンにおける個展（1984年）での展示

1968-75

デュシャンピアナ：ヴィデオ・チェス

Duchampiana: Video Chess

解決は存在しない、
なぜなら
問題がないのだから。
マルセル・デュシャン

There is no solution,
because
there is no problem.
Marcel Duchamp

問題は存在しない、
なぜなら
解決がないのだから。
久保田成子

There is no problem,
because
there is no solution.
Shigeko Kubota

私がマルセル・デュシャンと知り合ったのは、マース・カニンガム作『ウォーク・アラウンド・タイム』初演を見に、〔ニューヨーク州〕バッファローに行ったときのアメリカン航空の機上だった。ナイアガラの滝からの吹雪のせいで飛行機はバッファローの空港に着陸することができなかった。ロチェスター空港に着陸した私たちは、そこからバスでバッファローに向かった。そのあと1968年、トロントで私は、「リユニオン」コンサートでマルセルとジョン・ケージがチェスをしているところを写真に撮った。*

このときの写真を1972年から73年にかけ、ケン・ドミニクの助力を得てニューヨーク州ビンガムトンの実験TVセンターで、のちにはニューヨークのWNET-TVラボで、ヴィデオに変換し、露光調整、マット加工、着色を施した。

1975年、私はこのヴィデオテープを利用して彫刻をつくり、7年越しで本作を完成させた。ヴィデオ・モニターが1台、背を床と平行に置かれ、上を見あげている。透明な駒を並べた透明なチェス盤がTVモニターの上に据えてある。モニターはデュシャン氏とケージ氏のヴィデオテープを再生し、忘れられないこのコンサートのオリジナル・サウンドトラック、つまりジョン・ケージの曲を流す。チェス基盤（マトリクス）の交点にはどれも穴があいていてそこに光るセルが入っており、チェス勝負の進行に応じて変調する。響きの豊かな、相互変調するこのシステムを丹念に設計し操作したのは、電子音楽の達人（ヴィルトゥオーソ）たち——いずれも作曲家のデイヴィッド・テュードア、デイヴィッド・バーマン、ゴードン・ムンマ、ローウェル・クロス——だった。

TVはいつも夢と現実のあいだにある。チェスの対戦相手と《ヴィデオ・チェス》をプレイすると、この世界のかなたから偉大な名手ふたりがプレイするヴィデオテープが傍らで流れる。

ほかにもふたり、友人が手伝ってくれた。ジョージ・マチューナスとアル・ロビンスだ。ジョージは「ヒガン」（彼岸）に行ってしまった。

＊実際には「リユニオン」コンサートでの撮影の方が先である。詳細は濱田論文註31を参照。

daadギャラリー個展（1981年）オープニングにて　久保田とWieland Schmied（美術史家）

合板製の箱の中にモニターが上向きで設置され、その上に被せられたチェス盤が刻まれたガラス板には、透明のプラスチック製の駒が置かれている。モニターには、1968年にカナダのトロントで行なわれた『リユニオン』コンサートで久保田が撮影したデュシャンとケージの白黒写真に着色を施した映像が、コンサートのオリジナル・サウンドトラックと共に流れている（別のバージョンとして、着衣の久保田と裸のナムジュン・パイクがチェスで対戦している映像が存在するが、こちらは一度も展示されたことがない）。
作品近くの壁面には久保田が撮影した写真と共に、デュシャンと久保田によるテキスト（左頁）が添えられて展示されることもある。（MH）

1975-76

デュシャンピアナ：階段を降りる裸体

Duchampiana: Nude Descending a Staircase

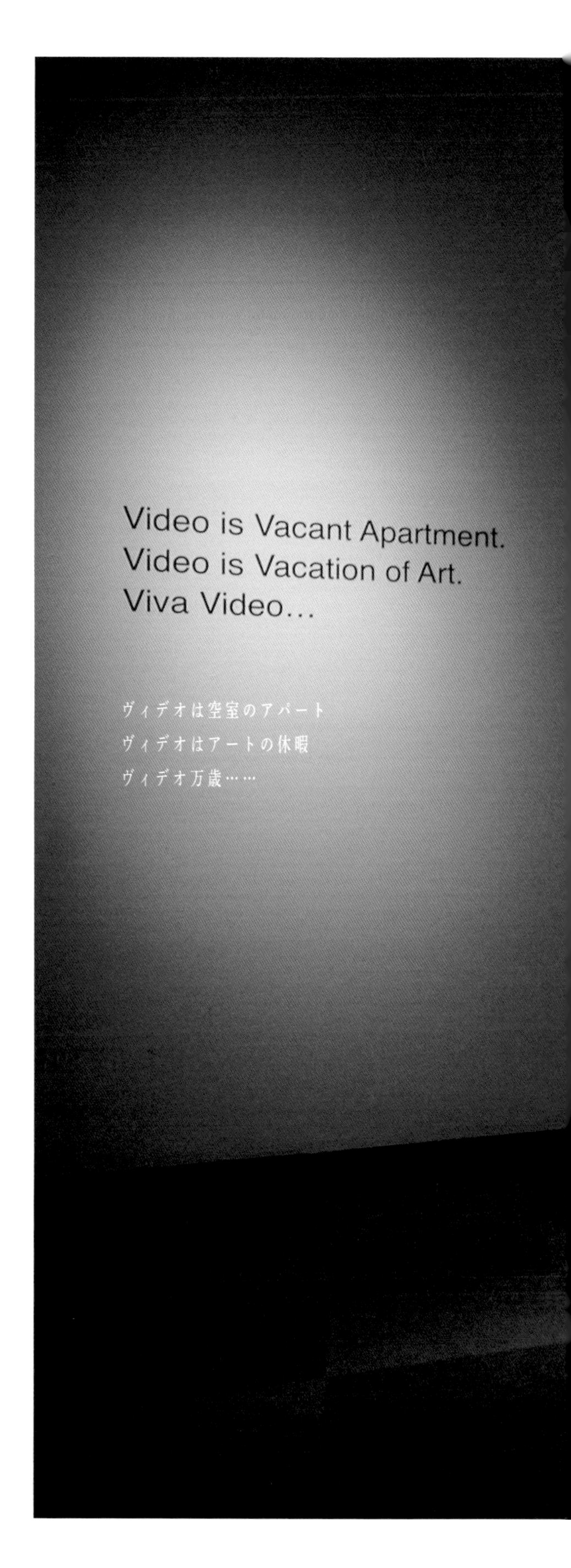

Video is Vacant Apartment.
Video is Vacation of Art.
Viva Video...
ヴィデオは空室のアパート
ヴィデオはアートの休暇
ヴィデオ万歳……

マルセル・デュシャンの油彩画、《階段を降りる裸体 No.2》（1912年）を引用した久保田の代表作のひとつ。4段の木製の階段に、ヌードの女性が階段を降りる映像が組み込まれている。制作当時所有していた4台のカラーテレビを使用し（オリジナルは13インチ3台と9インチ1台）、その画面の大きさに合わせて階段に穴が開けられている。映像の撮影は、アンソロジー・フィルム・アーカイヴズで行なわれ、スーパー8mmフィルムからヴィデオに変換され、カラー合成されている。本作は、1991年の段階で5つのエディションが確認されており、ヴィデオ作品としてニューヨーク近代美術館におけるコレクションとなったほか、世界各地に収蔵されている。1976年にアル・ロビンスが制作した最初の作品では後ろ側の角が斜めにカットされているが、本展出品の富山県美術館所蔵作（1983年制作）は直角のままであり、時代や場所に伴う機材や制作者の違いにより、バリエーションがある。（MN）

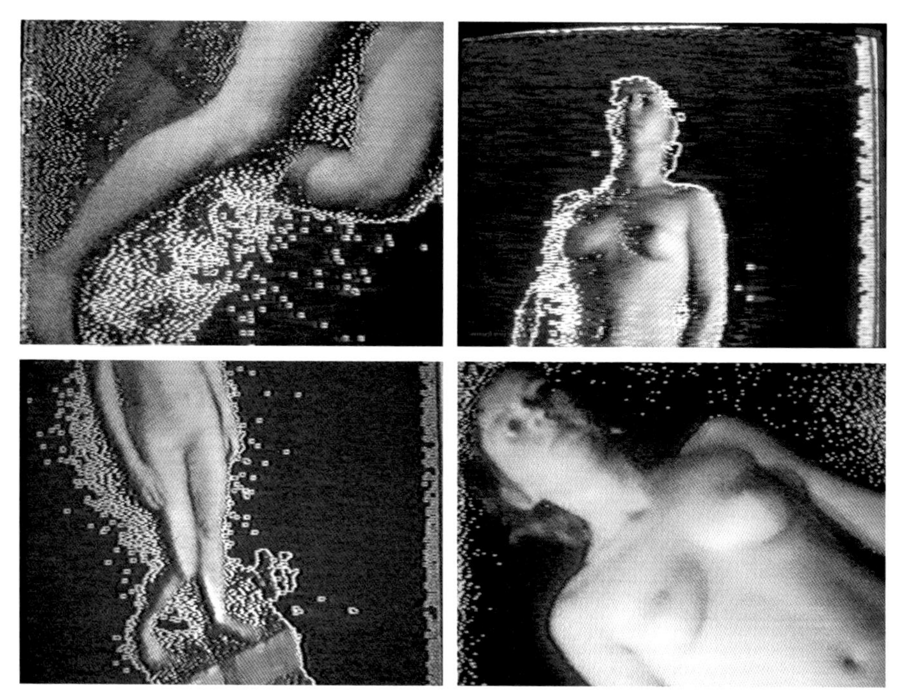
（スチル）

油彩による原作絵画では、デュシャンは「運動」する抽象的な裸体を描いている。ただし彼は疑似未来派ふうの時間表象に制約されていた……つまり複数の線で運動を描写するのである。四次元媒体であるヴィデオにそういった制約はない。私は本物の階段を、カラーモニターを4台使って組み立てた。きれいな裸の女性シーラ・マクラフリンが、ゆっくり／速く／飛ぶように、色や露光をさまざまに変えながら降りる。イメージはこの彫刻の内側で生きるかもしれない。私は視覚域とでもいうようなものを開発した。3分ごとにリピートするのだが、それでも見る人の注意をそらさないのである。ヴィデオ彫刻の中に時間構造を包装し梱包するには、特別に気を使ってよく考える必要がある。

ルネ・ブロック・ギャラリー個展（1976年）での展示

1976-77

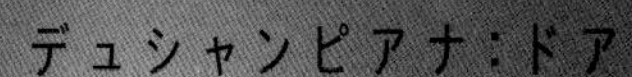

デュシャンピアナ：ドア

Duchampiana: Door

Door.
Door to open your mind.
Door to close your mind.

ドア。
あなたの精神を開くドア。
あなたの精神を閉じるドア。

90度の角度で接合された2つのドア枠にはドアが1つだけ取り付けられており、両方を同時に閉めることはできない。中に入ると小さな部屋になっている。テレビモニターの中ではマルセル・デュシャンが葉巻をくゆらせながら話をしており、間欠泉の水蒸気がそれに重ねられる。モニターの下をくぐるとまたモニターがあり（それらは背中合わせに設置されている）、まったく同じ映像が流れている。鑑賞者は入ったのと別のドアから出ることになる。ドアの外からは中のモニターは見えない。作品の要となるこのドアの構造は、マルセル・デュシャンのパリの家に実際にあったという作品《ドア：ラレー街11番地》（1927年）から着想を得ている。（AH）

1977年、私はニューヨークのルネ・ブロック・ギャラリーの内部に小さな部屋を組み立てた。部屋に入ってドアを閉じると、洞窟とかタイムトンネルの内部にいるような感じを受ける。ドアの枠はデュシャンの《ドア：ラレー街11番地》と同じ。２つの枠が直角を成すが、ドアは１枚しかなく、いつも同時に開いて／閉じている。中国には、タイムトンネルをテーマにした奇譚がかなりの数ある……ふと洞窟に足を踏み入れる、でなければ昼寝をしているとハンサムな案内人があらわれて洞窟の中へといざなう。しばらく歩いて宮殿にたどり着き、そこで君主と結婚して富を授かり、女王になる。突然夢から醒めると現実に逆戻りしているが、500年が過ぎ去っていて、友だちは１人もいなくなっているし、誰もあなたのことを覚えていない。時間や時間ワープをめぐる謎はよくフィクションに登場する。《デュシャンピアナ：ドア》を通って入っていくと、タイムトンネルに入り込む。デュシャン氏がそこで葉巻をくゆらせている。あの世に旅立つ前の最後のコンサートでしていたように。イエローストーン〔国立公園の間欠泉〕オールドフェイスフルの、永遠の中の１時間ごとに律儀に吹き出す水蒸気の映像がかぶさり、デュシャンはそこに溶け込んでいく。デュシャン本人がこう言うのが聞こえる。「アートは蜃気楼だ……アートは……蜃気楼だ……アートは蜃気楼だ」

ルネ・ブロック・ギャラリー個展（1977年）での展示

これはシゲコの「ヴィーコ・ヴィデオ」だ、と言った人がいた。私たちの因縁（カルマ）は永遠に再生されると考えたイタリアの哲学者ヴィーコ（1668-1744）にちなんだのだ。

> もうひとつ私に深い影響を与えたのは、成子がヴィデオにとっての死を発見したことだ。ヴィデオに撮影された死は単なる死ではない。現実の生は双方向的コミュニケーションと呼べるかもしれないのに対し、ヴィデオに撮影された死は一方向的コミュニケーションだ。「死後に生はある？」と聖書ふうに問いかけるかわりに、彼女は新しい問いを立てた。「死後にヴィデオはある？」と。生と可塑的な生があるように、死と可塑的な死があるだろう。あと何十年かして人工冬眠（低温学）が実現可能になったら、成子の革新はきわめてリアルで現代的な意味あいをもつだろう。
>
> ナムジュン・パイク　daadギャラリー久保田個展カタログ、1981年、31頁

1976-77, 1983

メタ・マルセル：窓

Meta-Marcel: Window

《メタ・マルセル：窓（雪）》 1976-77年

「デュシャンピアナ」シリーズの延長で、巨匠の呪縛からの脱却を意図して「メタ・マルセル」と名付けられている。窓の後ろにテレビを縦に置き、スノーノイズ（砂嵐）を雪に見立てた。制作当時、スノーノイズは、テープをかけずにオープンリールをテレビに繋げることによって作られた。後年の展示では、スノーノイズの画面を撮影したヴィデオ映像に置き換えられている。1983年には、窓に映す映像として、新たに「花」と「星」が制作された。録画された「雪」と「花」、「星」は個別に展示されることもあれば、「三つのテープ」（富山県美術館蔵）として1つの映像の中で順に見せることもある。（MN）

ヴィデオはきのうの窓。
ヴィデオはあすの窓。
心に雪が降るごとく、私のヴィデオに雪が降る。
私はデュシャン《なりたての未亡人（Fresh Widow）》の小型版を、合板を使ってつくった。その中では、古いRCAカラーテレビがガラス窓の背後に設置してある。TVはカラーの純度が不完全なので、雪はシュールな色合いに染まる。とてもとてもシンプルで明確で純粋な私の窓はきわめつきのヴィデオ彫刻、新たな一ジャンルの誕生を垣間見、把握するための手段だ。

ホイットニー美術館（2018年）での展示

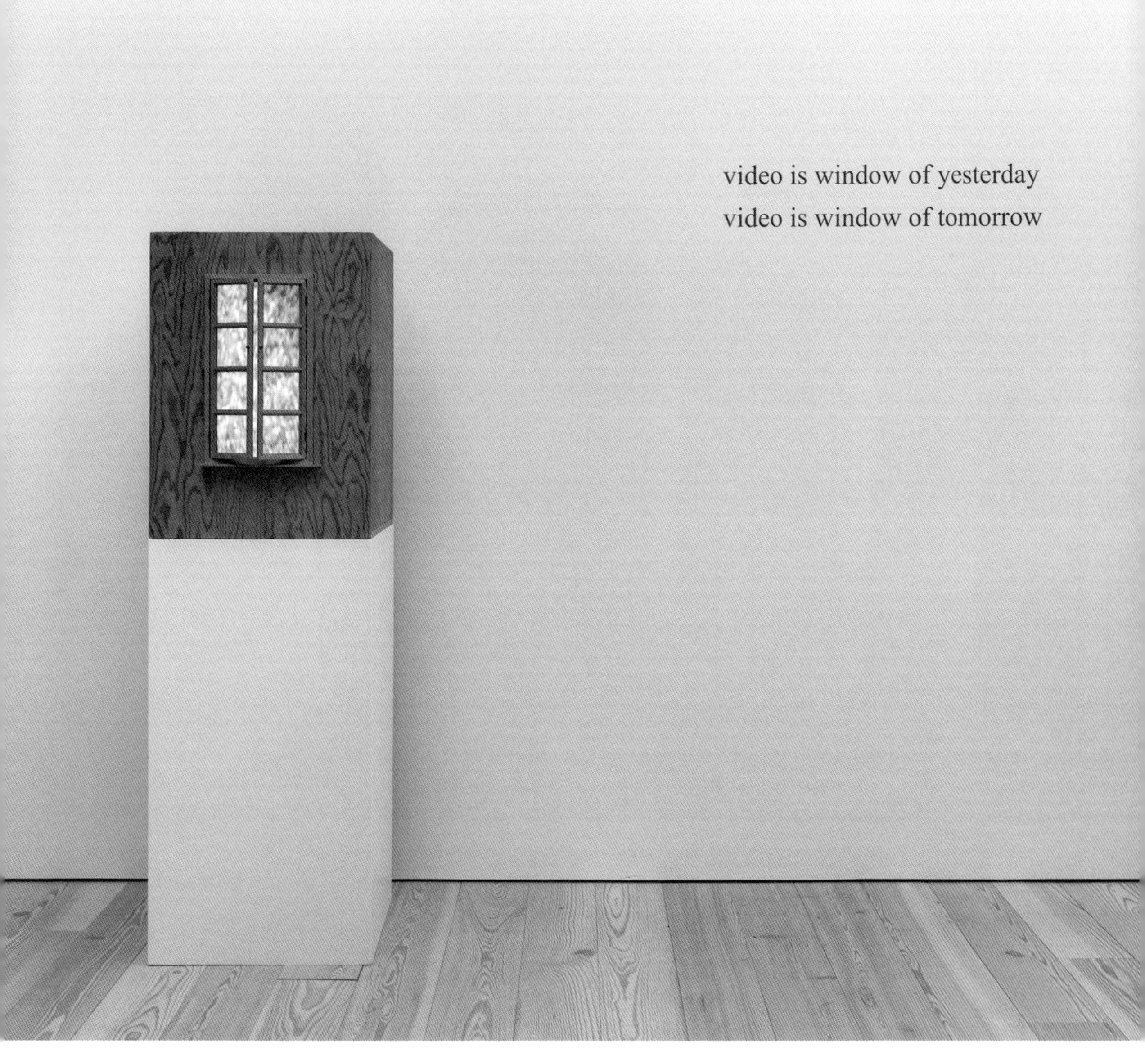
video is window of yesterday
video is window of tomorrow

《メタ・マルセル：窓（三つのテープ）》1983年

ミシガン湖畔で窓枠を持って立つ久保田(1981年頃)

新潟県立近代美術館（2021年）での展示

1977

構想スケッチ

Conceptual sketches

1977年10月の日記帳に残された構想スケッチ。ケネディ空港に《デュシャンの墓》を設置したいという、美術館での展示では飽き足らず、人々の往来する公共空間で作品を見せることへの関心がうかがえる。テレビモニターを床に敷き詰め部屋全体をチェス盤に見立てるインスタレーションや、部屋の窓を《メタ・マルセル：窓》の四季バージョンで作るなどのアイディアが見られる。(MN)

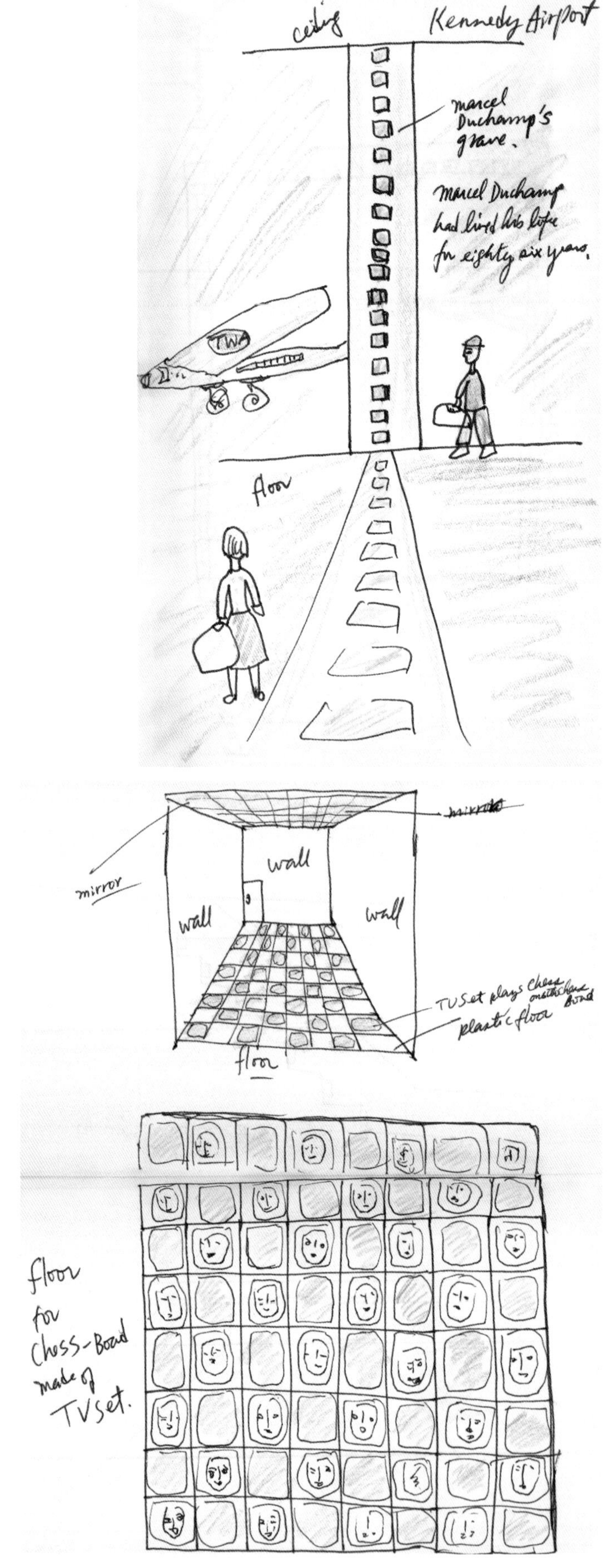

Video is window of yesterday.
Video is window of tomorrow.

1979

ベルリン時代のドローイング

Drawings in Berlin

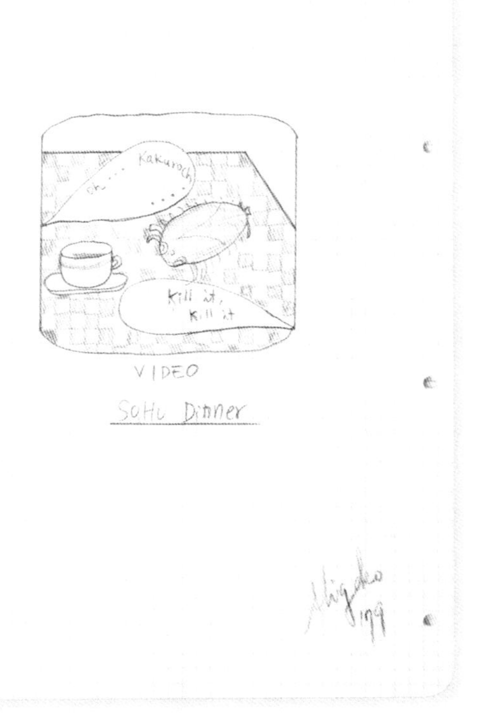

DAAD（ドイツ学術交流会）の奨学金を得てベルリンに滞在していた際に描いたスケッチ。1970年代前半から断続的にヴィデオ・ダイアリーを制作していたが、その1つとして1979年に《ベルリン・ダイアリー》を制作しており、これに関連する可能性がある。セリフの表現に吹き出しを使うなど、マンガのようタッチで何気ない生活の1コマを捉えている。また、久保田自身のメッセージとも読めるような、愛についてのイラストも印象的である。（AH）

NYC
Love is Air-MAIL
VIDEO
Berlin '79

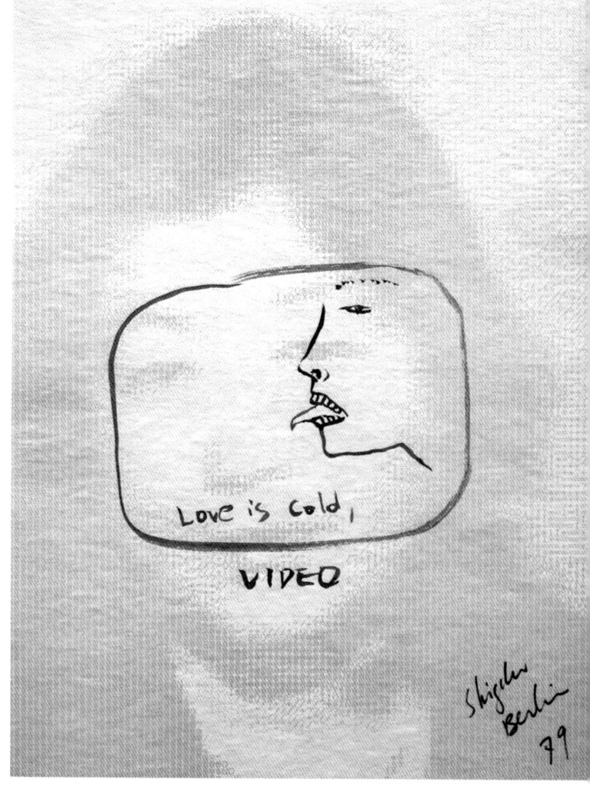
Love is cold,
VIDEO
Berlin 79

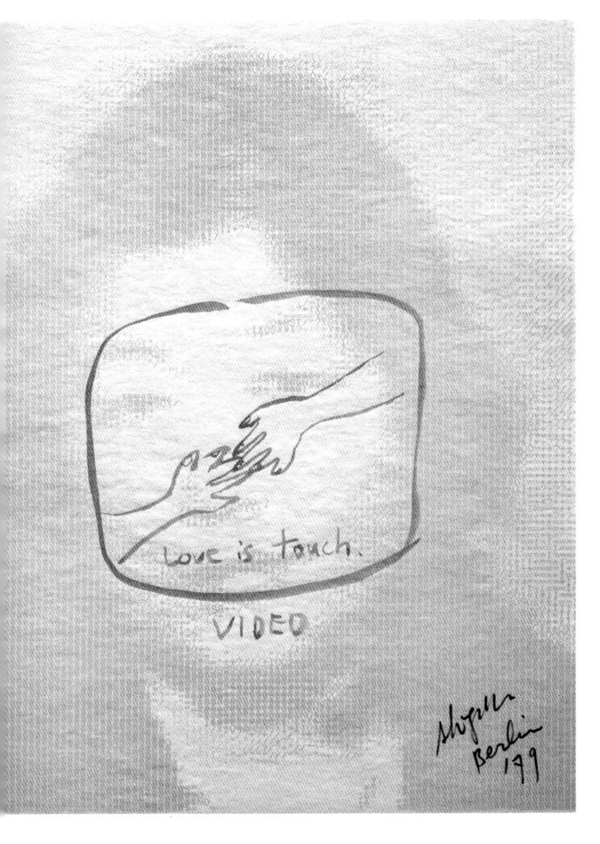
Love is touch.
VIDEO
Berlin
'79

Do you still Love me?
VIDEO
Berlin
'79

1976-79

三つの山

Three Mountains

3つの合板製の構造で構成され、うち2つは二等辺三角錐のような長細い形状で、一方の山には2つのモニターが、もう一方の山には3つのモニターが埋め込まれている。3つ目の、中央の山は正四角錐の上部を水平に切った形で、内部に2つのモニターを包含している。いずれのモニターも周囲に鏡が嵌め込まれ、モニターから映し出される4つの異なる映像——ヘリコプターから撮影したグランド・キャニオン、車窓からのエコー・クリフ、タオスの夕焼けの蜃気楼、ティートンの日没を複雑に反映している（映像に含まれる風や環境音がスピーカーから流れている）。

久保田が「ヴォルケーノ（火山）」と呼んでいた中央のピラピッド型が最初に作られ、1977年のルネ・ブロック・ギャラリーでの個展に単独で出品された（1978年のニューヨーク近代美術館の展覧会「Projects」にも出品予定であったが、最終的に出品されなかった）。「火山」の中は鏡で覆われ、映像と共に、覗き込んだ鑑賞者の姿も無限に増幅していく。

同作のドローイングからは、久保田が山を自画像的風景と考えていたことがわかる。また、関連するドローイングからは、山が2つから3つへと次第に展開していった様子がうかがえる。（MH）

《三つの山》をのぞく久保田（1977年頃）

私が創り出したいのは、アートと人生の融合、デュシャンピアナのモダニズムとレヴィ＝ストロースの未開状態（プリミティヴィズム）、クールな形式とホットなヴィデオ、そういった複雑な問題のすべてに取り組み、１万年以上前にベーリング海峡を越えた北方アジア人たちの部族的記憶を横断すること。そうして私はボーイング707に乗り、1964年７月４日、ニューヨークの光り輝くポップアートの世界に惹かれてやってきた。

ニューヨークの摩天楼群の高層鉄骨は、そのほとんどを偉大なモホーク族の末裔たちがつくったのだけれど、私が自分の古（いにしえ）のいとこと再会したのは乾いた砂漠の中、ぽつりぽつりと立つ砂岩の土柱に囲まれて、ナヴァホ族の人々と過ごしたときのことだった。ミッチェル＝サンドヴァル一家と私の交友が始まったのは、すぐれたアメリカ・インディアンのミュージシャンであるドゥーギー・ミッチェルと、1968年にウェスリアン大学で知り合ったのがきっかけだった。民族音楽学のティーチングフェローとして同大に在籍していたドゥーギーは元気いっぱいの、少しニヒリスティックな面のあるライフスタイルを持っていた。

私たちは日本語で、彼のブロークンなナヴァホ日本語で会話をしたものだった。25歳のとき、彼は謎の死を遂げた。彼の早逝を悼むことから、４人の女性アーティストから成るグループを結成し紹介することになった。人種は「白、黒、赤、黄」とさまざまで、メアリー・ルシエ、シャーロット・ワレン、セシリア・サンドヴァル（ドゥーギーのいとこ）、そして私という顔ぶれだった。1973年、メアリー・ルシエと私はセシリアの案内で、彼女の郷里であるアリゾナ州チンリーに行った。女家長制の彼らの家族のもとに滞在し、彼らの暮らしを生き、彼らの儀式や祭のいくつかを体験した。全体として、私は特段に暖かいもてなしを受けた。ある年取った男性は私に言った。「おお日本人、かわいそうにな、あんなに長いあいだ旅をして、たどり着いたのがあんなちっぽけな島だったとは。ずっとここアメリカにいたらよかったのに」。私は笑った。この老人は、アメリカ先住民たちが中国に移住して、紀元前４千年に中国文明を創設したと思っているのだ。また別の人は、シゲコという名はナヴァホ語で「私の義理の娘」という意味だと言った。ハローをあらわすナヴァホの単語は「ヤッテ、ヤッテ」と発音され、日本語では「私を愛して、私を愛して」の意味。

私はナヴァホの風景に魅了された。アリゾナの信じられないような色たち、高地の砂漠の空。とうとう出発の時が来たとき、私は必ず戻ってくると決心した。1976年、私はアメリカ西部を横断し、ワシントン、アイダホ、モンタナ、ワイオミングの山々で、ユタ、アリゾナ、ニューメキシコの砂漠や峡谷で、カラーヴィデオで風景を記録した。

古代の大彫刻的作品群――ストーンヘンジ、ピラミッド、ペルーのナスカ地上絵――には、その巨大なスケールや厳密に構成された形の中にもうひとつの宗教的で省察的な次元を宿しているものが多い。彫刻は自然を鏡のように映し出しつつ、つくり手の刻印を、意識を、内包しているのだ。

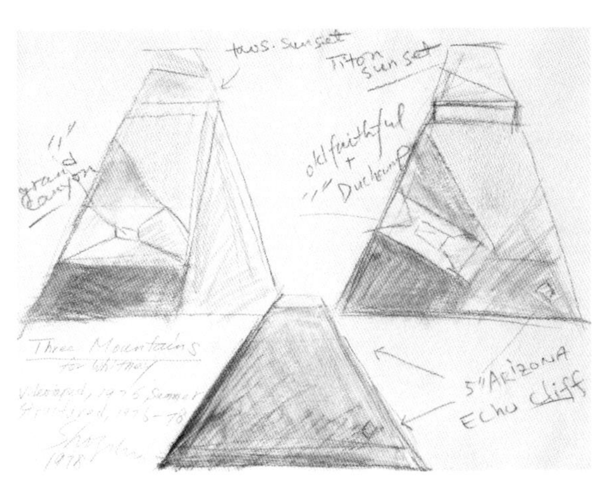

ドローイング　1978年

山――子宮
私の子宮は火山だ。
５インチ、11インチのイメージたちがその中で踊っている。
私の歴史を歌っている。

1964年、ハーバート・リードはこう書いた。「先史時代における発端から幾つもの時代を通じて、そして比較的最近まで、彫刻は堅固な形態の芸術、マッスを持った芸術と考えられてきた。その特質は空間に位置を占めること、つまり空間占有性に関係づけられてきた」〔ハーバード・リード『近代彫刻史』藤原えりみ訳、248頁〕。ヴィデオが彫刻のテリトリーに侵出することで、「もろい」とか「表層的だ」とか「一時的だ」とか「即時的だ」といった、ヴィデオに長くつきまとってきた偏見の数々は否定されることになるだろう。

私はなぜ山なんかつくっているのかと不思議がられている。

「なぜ山に登るのか？」「そこに山があるから」ではない。それは植民地主義／帝国主義的な考え方だ。そうではなくて、知覚し、見るためだ。

山々はほとんど理解不可能なまでのマッスとヴォリュームを持つセッティングの中で、知覚上複雑な視覚の嵐を提供してくれる。

……可能なかぎり速くクルマで走った、身体速度よりも速く、アリゾナの、エコー・クリフと呼ばれるハイウェイを、北の峡谷から南のグランドキャニオンまで、ナヴァホ族の居留地を通って走った、両手で自分のカメラを握りしめて、風はクルマの窓の外からマイクに強く吹きつけ……音は精神の速度より速くこだまする。インディアンの子どもたちが馬に乗っているような、雨乞いの踊りの儀式に向けて太鼓を叩いているような音がする。

「小千谷(おぢや)」、千の石のある小さな谷というのが、私の先祖の村の名だ。私は雪国で、日本の山村で生まれた。祖父は水墨画家だった。墨でひたすら山だけを描くことに生涯を費やした。学生時代、私は日本「アルプス」に登った。何週間も富士山の中腹で、冬の雪が降る中キャンプをした。山中に降る雪はヴィデオと彫刻に似ている。軽さ、速度、電子のはかない性質が、不動で無時間的なマッスと対照を成している。

私の山々は、裂けて膨張した時間と空間の中に存在する。私の消失点は逆転していて、あなたの脳のうしろにある。そして鏡とアングルのせいで歪められたそれは、多くの点で同時に消失する。遠近法の線はひたすら伸びつづけ、急角度で交差し、冷たく希薄な山の空気のように鋭い。時間は飛び去り、そしてじっと居座る。矛盾はない。

> バックミンスター・フラーは（…）つぎのように述べている。アジアを発ってヨーロッパに向かった者は風に逆らって進み、自然との戦いに適した機械と概念と西洋哲学を発展させたが、一方、アジアを発ってアメリカに向かった者は、帆を揚げ、風に乗って進み、自然の受容にふさわしい概念と東洋哲学を発展させた、と。この二つの傾向はアメリカで出会い、過去や伝統やそうしたものに縛られないひとつの動きを、空中に放出したのである。
>
> ジョン・ケージ『サイレンス』1958年〔柿沼敏江訳、131頁〕

1979-81

ヴィデオ・レリーフ

Video Relief

ヴィデオ・レリーフは私の自意識――鏡。
「鏡よ鏡、私はきれい？」
「鏡よ鏡、私はみにくい？」

私のヴィデオ鏡は二重鏡のようなものだ。レンズだけでなく旧式のTVスクリーンを磁気鏡のように使っている。レンズとスクリーンの中にはそれぞれ3インチの白黒TVがあって、私が西ベルリンの街路で子どもたちと喋るようすを流している。
TVスクリーンの表面上に、レンズ2枚の他、自分の姿が映っているのが見えるはず。
私の《ヴィデオ・レリーフ》のレンズを通して見つめる――鏡、私の過去と私の現在のような、二重のイメージ。
「成子、これは確かにあなた？　それとも、昔のあなた？」

現実と蜃気楼のあいだで――幻想、
ナルシシスティックな自己分析者。
私の《ヴィデオ・レリーフ》を見ていて飽きることは決してないはず、自分自身を見る、人生の中で、あなたにはいったいいくつ顔がある？

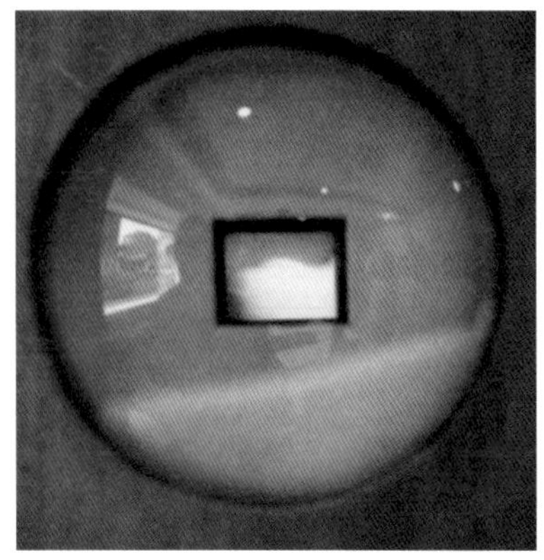

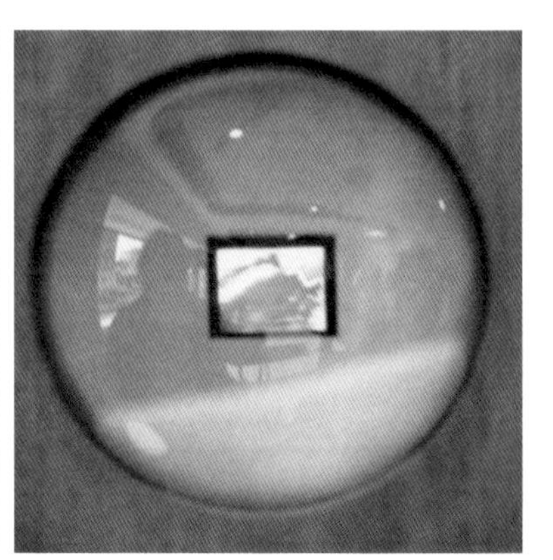

Daadギャラリー個展（1981年）での展示

ドイツに滞在している間に構想・制作された2つの作品《ヴィデオ・レリーフ》と《ベルリン・ダイアリー：先祖への感謝》に共通するのは、重層的なスクリーンの構造である。前者は合板にレンズまたはテレビモニターのスクリーン部分が埋め込まれ、その奥に3インチの小さなテレビモニターがセットされている。モニターにはシングルチャンネル作品《ベルリンのシゲコ》（1979-1980）が映し出され、久保田が街頭で子供たちにインタビューをする様子などが映し出される。レンズ部分には鑑賞者自体の顔が映り込むが、久保田にとってはそのことも重要な要素だったことが、彼女自身のテキストにより明らかである。MMIの個展カタログに記載された描写によれば、右と左に丸いレンズ、中央に四角いモニターが配された一組のインスタレーションのようだが、記録が見つかっておらず定かではない。また、この作品は後にヴィデオ彫刻《アダムとイヴ》の一部となった。（AH）

1981

ベルリン・ダイアリー：先祖への感謝

Berlin Diary: Thanks to My Ancestors

同じドイツ滞在中に制作した《ベルリン・ダイアリー》は、5インチのテレビモニターを通電させ、モニターの白い光が透過する桃色の水晶板が麻紐のようなもので取り付けられている。板には青い筆文字で文章が綴られており、漢詩のようにも見える久保田の独自の文章だ。「父母祖母姉妹涙」「友人飛行日本我心」「芸術生涯是中」などと読むことができる。この作品はドイツでは発表されず、初展示は1983年のニューヨークとなった。2021年、ニューヨーク近代美術館が収蔵。(AH)

「ナムジュン・パイクとの私の人生」展図録序文

ジョナス・メカス

Jonas Mekas：1922年リトアニア生まれ。2019年アメリカで没。
映像作家、詩人。

久保田成子、ナムジュン・パイク、ジョージ・マチューナス。

私の記憶のなかで切り離すことのできない３人の名前。

私自身の人生は、彼らの人生から離れられなくなるように運命づけられていた。

「ニューヨークの水道水を入れた瓶に小石を入れると、水道水が浄化されるのよ」と、成子は一度私に教えてくれた。その効果があり、以来ずっとそうしている。

彼女はいつもまわりにいた、けれどとても控えめに、ほとんど人目につかないように、一番後ろに立っていた。目立つのは、いつもナムジュン・パイクとジョージだった。２人にとって、彼女は母であり、姉であり、看護婦だった。ただし、彼女が、ヴィデオカメラを持って現われ、まわりで起こっていることすべてを記録したときを除いては。彼女がアーティスト、それも最高のアーティストだったのは、そのときだった。

1974年、私は、成子にアンソロジー・フィルム・アーカイヴズのヴィデオ・プログラムを運営するよう勧めた。ヴィデオ・プログラムは、それまでまったくなかった。彼女は、私からの誘いを快諾してくれた。アーカイヴズの移転を余儀なくされた1981年までの間、アンソロジーは、ヴィデオ・アートにとっての天国であり、世界一活気ある場所だった。彼女は、ものすごいエネルギーとインスピレーションの持ち主で、圧倒的に素晴らしかったし、いまでもそうだ。でも彼女はいつもとても謙虚だった。自分を隠し続けながら、いつでも人を助けていた。

いまこそ、アーティストとしての、ヴィデオ・アートを支えるうえで決定的に重要な、最高のアーティストとしての久保田成子を見るべきときだと思う。彼女のヴィデオ／エレクトロニクス彫刻は、これまで公の場で見る機会が少なかった。その今日性と、エネルギーと、われわれの全感覚と心への衝撃は、強烈だ。久保田成子が、彼女の生涯の友ナムジュン・パイクにどれほど貢献したか、本当に想像しがたいが、計り知れないほど大きかったにちがいない。

久保田成子を事実上日本からニューヨークに呼んだジョージ・マチューナスを彼女がどれほど支援してきたことか、言葉では到底言い表せないほどありがたいものだった。彼らの仕事でのパーフェクトな関係は、ジョージの生涯続いた。ジョージは、彼女のことをいつも褒め称えてばかりいた。尊い慈愛のようなものをお互い育んでいた。２人とも、とても特別で、本当に稀有なアーティストだった。

この展示会が実現したことをとても嬉しく思います。アートの世界に欠けていた何かが、いまこうしてここにある。それは、久保田成子である。

2007年８月 ニューヨーク

訳：桜本有三

Foreword for the exhibition catalog *Shigeko Kubota: My Life with Nam June Paik*

Jonas Mekas

Film maker, poet.
Born in Lithuania in 1922, died at New York, 2019.

Shigeko Kubota. Nam June Paik. George Maciunas.
Three names that are inseparable in my memory.

My own life, as it was destined, became inseparable from their lives.

"You should put pebbles in your New York tap water jar, they will purify New York tap water," Shigeko told me once, and I have been doing it since, and it works.

She was always there, but very humbly, almost invisible, standing in the very back. It was always Nam June Paik and George. She was a mother. she was a sister, and she was a nurse for both. Except when she came in with her video camera, recording it all. She was an artist then, one of the best there is.

In 1974 I invited Shigeko to run Anthology Film Archives video program. We had none till then. She gracefully accepted my invitation. Until 1981, when we had to relocate the Archives, Anthology was the heaven. and the most active video art place in the world. She was a mountain of energy and inspiration. She was amazing. And she still is. But always so humble. Always promoting others herself remaining invisible.

So it's time that we see Shigeko Kubota as an artist, a supreme artist in the art she was so crucial in assisting. Her video/electronic sculptures have been so rarely seen in public. Their modernity, their energy, their impact upon one's entire sensory and mental body are electrifying. I can only try to imagine, and it's not so easy to do, Shigeko Kubota's contribution to her life's friend, Nam June Paik. It must have been immense.

I cannot begin to tell you how much Shigeko Kubota had helped George Maciunas who had actually brought her to New York from Japan. They had a perfect working relationship that lasted to the end of George's life. George always had only the best words for her. A Zen love of a special kind. Both were very special, very very special.

I am so happy to see this exhibition become a reality. Something was missing in the art world but now it's here. Shigeko Kubota is her name.

August 2007 New York

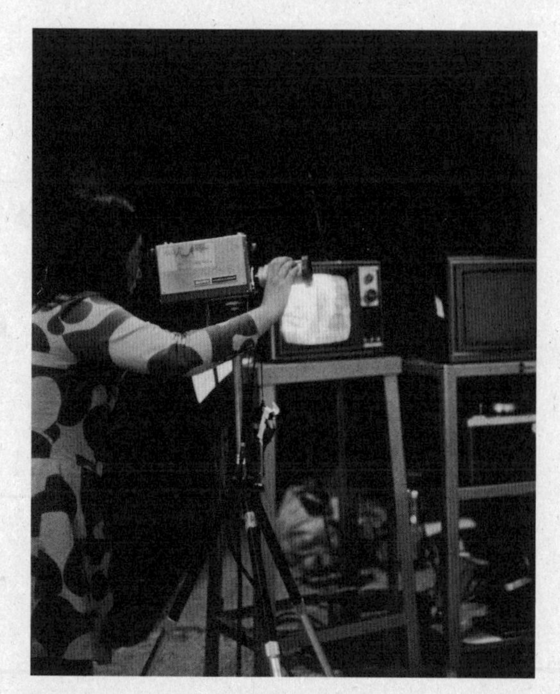

アンソロジー・フィルム・アーカイヴズで働く久保田成子、1974年頃。
Shigeko Kubota working at the Anthology Film Archives, ca. 1974.

成子と踊る

ロバート・ハリス

Robert Harris：教育者、映画詩人、旅人。マサチューセッツ在住。

1974年秋のある土曜日、スプリング通りとウースター通りの角で、私は久保田成子に初めて会った。ナムジュン・パイクと一緒に彼女はアンソロジー・フィルム・アーカイヴズに向かっているところだった。あちこち地面にヒビの入ったソーホー地区の歩道で、ヴィデオのモニターとデッキをガタガタいうカートに載せて運んでいた。奇遇なことにアーカイヴズは私の行き先でもあった。アーカイヴズはウースター通り80番地に再オープンしつつあるところで、私はスタン・ブラッケージの『光のテクスト』初上映のチケットを入手するつもりだったのだ。私は2人に手助けを申し出て、みんなで歩みを進めた。

その日の午後、成子は創立者・キュレーターとしてアンソロジーのヴィデオ・プログラムの活動の幕を切って落とし、それまで「アートとしての映画」のみを扱っていたこの場所にヴィデオを持ち込むことになる。偶然、好奇心、親和力から生まれた私たちの邂逅は、映画、ヴィデオ、労働、モニター、展覧会、美術館を混ざりあわせ、密接かつ永続的な友情をつくり出した。その日以降私は、生まれて間もなかったアンソロジーのヴィデオ・プログラムのすべての側面で成子を支援し、撮影や展覧会設営のほか、成子とナムジュン両方のアシスタントを務めることになった。

成子のキュレーションは彼女の性格を反映していた。大胆で創造的、気まぐれで意思が強く、民主的、衝動的、平等主義的で、自己矛盾している。まだ幼年期にあったヴィデオは粗削りかつ未熟な媒体で、限りないポテンシャルにいきいきと輝いていたが、映画純血主義者たちは、グレーでボケボケで自堕落で編集不可能なものとみなして、うさんくさげな、いささか見下すような視線を浴びせていた。あんなものは「家具」にすぎない、というわけだ[*1]。映画（セルロイド）の殿堂であるアンソロジーの中へと、私たちは撮像電子管（ヴィデオ）のエネルギーを忍び込ませた。

成子が打った最初の一手は、アルド・タンベリーニ、スタン・ヴァンダービーク、シャーリー・クラーク、ジャド・ヤルカット、エド・エムシュウィラーを招いて新作を上映するという大胆なものだった。いずれもすぐれた映画作家だが、このころにはヴィデオを使うようになっていた。彼らの作品がアンソロジーの中核をなす映画コレクションから排除されていたことは、人々の注意を引いていた。

先進的ヴィデオ作家たちの過去の経歴は、哲学者、映画作家、先見的エンジニア、コンピュータの開拓者、アクティヴィスト、ドキュメンタリー作家、コンセプチュアル・アーティスト、パフォーマンス・アーティスト、ダンサー、作曲家、詩人といったように多彩だった。成子はアンソロジーで上映されるヴィデオに、すべての領域のヴィデオ探求や実験が含まれるよう心がけ、特定のイデオロギーに肩入れすることはしなかった。まじめだが遊び心に満ちた、フルクサス精神にのっとった雰囲気が支配していた。私たちの上映プログラムにはヴィデオ・シンセサイザー作品、ヴィデオ・パフォーマンス、フェミニズム作品、ストリート・ヴィデオ／観察ヴィデオ、マルチチャンネル作品、ヴィデオ日記、すでに立場が確立しギャラリーもついている／大学で定職を得ているアーティスト、若手アーティスト、国際的アーティストが並んだ。アンソロジーのヴィデオ部門は、ヴィデオの可能性をぎりぎりまで追求しようとした。

成子がアンソロジーでキュレーションした代表的企画として、たとえば以下がある。

ホリス・フランプトンとデイヴィッド・ロスを迎えた「ヴィデオ・パネル」：ワインを飲みながら映画、ヴィデオ、アートについて討論。

ジョーン・ジョナスのパフォーマンス《黄昏》：ロビン・ウィンタース、アンディ・マン、ポーラ・ロンジェンダイクといったキラ星のような若手陣を迎え、モーターで動くアンソロジーのスクリーンを取り込んで、ふだんは動かないプロセニアムアーチを映画の付随的要素へとダイナミックに作り変える。

アール・ハワードの《目隠し鬼》：盲目の音楽家にしてホルン奏者が、ヴィデオの持つ知覚的可能性をめぐって挑発的、特異的、才気煥発な考察を繰り広げる。

アル・ロビンス：アンソロジーのヴィデオ部門は、まだまだ十分な評価がなされていないこの詩久保田成子と《三つの山》と友人たち（上から時計回り：ピーター・コルブ、アル・ロビンス、キャシー・ポリサー、シュリダー・バパット、ロバート・ハリス）、1979年。
Shigeko Kubota with her *Three Mountains*, with (clockwise from top) Peter Kolb, Al Robbins, Cathy Polisar, Shridar Bapat, and Robert Harris, 1979.

人／哲学者／電子キネティック・アーティストの仕事を公開した最初の会場だった。

ヴィデオフリークス：1か月間にわたりアンソロジーは、ウースター通りに面した窓で、同アーカイヴズが所蔵するこの先駆的ヴィデオ集団が制作したオープンリールテープのヴィデオ作品をすべて公開した。

フアン・ダウニーの《74年おめでとう、ペルー、マチュピチュ》：この多作なヴィデオ作家がアンソロジーで初上映したたくさんの作品の1点。

シャーリー・クラークのTPヴィデオスペース一座：クラークがチェルシー・ホテルで泊まっていたスイートルームを拠点とするこの先見的グループによる期間限定のワークショップ。空間、時間、インタラクティブ性の媒体として、ヴィデオを遊び心に満ちたやり方で活用。メンバーはウェンディ・クラーク、スーザン・ミラノ、ディーディー・ハレック、シュリダー・バパット、アンドリュー・グリアン。

私が成子のヴィデオ・アート制作に協力するようになる直前、彼女はシングルチャンネル作品《私のお父さん》を完成させていた。最初のヴィデオ彫刻《マルセル・デュシャンの墓》はまだ発展段階にあった。どちらの作品でも成子本人や押し殺した彼女自身の声、そしてカチカチとつまづくのが聞き取れるカメラが存在感を放っている。《私のお父さん》のカメラは小津安二郎ふうに静かで、新潟の実家でいまは亡き父親がテレビで新年の番組*2を見る姿を捉えた、燐光を放つスクリーン上の映像を成子がなでさする中、時間と空間、生と死を横断する。記憶と死をめぐる、究極の自己反省ヴィデオ／瞑想。

成子、シュリダー・バパット、アル・ロビンス、私は、落ちこぼれのイタズラ者一味だった。アルは木工にすぐれ、詩を書き、映画作家からヴィデオ作家に転向した哲学者だった。巨大で嵐のような存在感を放っていたアルは、「レインダンス」を設立したひとりであるポール・ライアンの言葉を借りれば、誠（まこと）、つまり「人間が自分の本心にしたがって真摯に振る舞うことを邪魔するようなものは、すべて打ち捨ててしまうほどの誠実さ」をそなえていた。アルが器用に組み立てた成子のオリジナル版「デュシャンピアナ」シリーズや《三つの山》彫刻は精巧、繊細、正確無比だ。《デュシャンピアナ：階段を降りる裸体》はその後「バージョン」がいくつも制作されているけれども、どれもアル独特の手つきや比率のセンスを欠いている。シュリダーは愛情深く献身的で感受性の強い心の持ち主で、つねに内なる悪魔のささやきに苛まれ、自分自身もかなり創造的だったが、その力を昇華させて、成子とナムジュン・パイクのインスタレーションや、他にも数え切れないほどの著名アーティストの仕事に、熟練の技術的手腕を提供した。

1976年夏、成子と私は、ロッキー山脈西部をあてどなく向こう見ずにさまようヴィデオ／映画制作の旅に乗り出した。私の愛する崇高な風景や山々を成子にも見てもらおうと私はクルマを借りてシアトルからアルバカーキまでドライブし、途中イエローストーン、グランド・ティートン、グランド・キャニオン、タオス、ブライス・キャニオン、ザイオン・キャニオン、ペインテッド・デザートなどの国立公園を通っていった。ニューヨークに戻った成子は《三つの山》をつくった。彼女がいくつも制作したすばらしいヴィデオ彫刻の中でも、私にとっては最良の一点だ。

訳：近藤学

［訳註］

*1――原著者の説明によれば、この表現は揶揄として、初期のヴィデオ・アートに関して繰り返し使われたものだという。TVやヴィデオは芸術や文化とは無縁であり、もっぱら家庭で大衆が楽しむ通俗的な物品とみなされたのである。

*2――正しくは年越しの番組。

Dancing with Shigeko

Robert Harris

Educator, film-poet, and traveler.
Lives and works in Massachusetts.

On a Saturday in the fall of 1974, at the corner of Spring and Wooster St., I first met Shigeko Kubota. With Nam June Paik, she was heading for Anthology Film Archives. They pushed a video monitor and deck on a wobbly cart over cracked Soho sidewalks. Serendipitously, the Archives was my destination as well. Anthology was reopening in its new 80 Wooster St. location, and I sought tickets to the premier of Stan Brakhage's *Text of Light*. I offered my assistance and we proceeded together.

Shigeko would, that afternoon, as founder and curator, inaugurate Anthology's Video Program, introducing video into an institution heretofore devoted exclusively to film-as-art. Our fortuitous meeting, born of chance, curiosity, and attraction; commingling film, video, labor, monitors, exhibitions, and museums, engendered a close and enduring friendship. From that day onward, I would assist Shigeko in all aspects of Anthology's nascent video program, and serve as cameraperson, exhibition installer, and assistant to both Shigeko and Nam June.

Shigeko's curation reflected her character; bold, creative, generous, whimsical, willful, democratic, impulsive, egalitarian, contradictory. Video, still in its infancy a raw and underdeveloped medium, luminous and vital with boundless potential, was eyed warily and with some condescension by the film purists who considered it gray, blurry, indulgent, and uneditable. "A piece of furniture." Into the celluloid cathedral of the Anthology, we insinuated a vidicon electron energy.

Shigeko's audacious first act was to invite and show new video work by Aldo Tambellini, Stan Vanderbeek, Shirley Clarke, Jud Yalkut, and Ed Emshwiller, prominent filmmakers now using video, whose films were conspicuously excluded from Anthology's Essential Film Collection.

The vanguard videomakers came from diverse backgrounds; philosophers, filmmakers, visionary engineers, computer pioneers, activists, documentarians, conceptual artists, performance artists, dancers, composers, and poets. Shigeko made video at Anthology inclusive and open to all areas of video exploration and experimentation without being aligned with any ideological camp. The tone was serious yet playful, in the Fluxus spirit. We showed image process synthesizer work; video performance, feminist work; street-video/observational video; multi-channel work, video diaries, established artists with gallery affiliations and/or academic credentials; young artists; international artists. Video at Anthology sought to explore the boundaries of what video could be.

Exemplary shows curated by Shigeko at the Anthology include:

"Video Panel" with Hollis Frampton/David Ross: A wine-fueled polemic on film, video, and art.

Joan Jonas's *Twilight* performance: featuring young luminaries Robin Winters, Andy Mann, and Paula Longendyke, incorporating Anthology's motorized screen edge in a dynamic para-cinematic repurposing of the static proscenium screen.

Earl Howard's *Blind Man's Bluff*: A controversial, singular and brilliant consideration of video's perceptual possibilities by the blind composer and horn player.

Al Robbins: Anthology Video was the first venue to show the work of the still underappreciated poet, philosopher, electronic kineticist.

Videofreex: Over the course of one month, Anthology screened, in the window facing onto Wooster St., the entire archive of reel to reel video tapes produced by the pioneering video collective.

Juan Downey's *Happy '74, Peru Machu Picchu*: The first of numerous premiers of the prolific videomaker.

Shirley Clarke's TP Videospace Troup: A live, evanescent workshop from the visionary group that, working from Clarke's Chelsea Hotel suite, playfully embraced video as a medium of space, time and interactivity. With Wendy Clarke, Susan Milano, DeeDee Halleck, Shridhar Bapat, and Andrew Gurian.

When I began to work with Shigeko on her video art, she had just completed the single channel piece *My Father*. Her first video sculpture, *Marcel Duchamp's Grave*, was in its formative stages. Both works are dirge-like eulogies. Both feature Shigeko's presence, her hushed voice, and the audible presence of the clicking, glitching camera. *My Father*, with its calm, Ozu-like camera, transverses through time and space, life and death, as Shigeko caresses the phosphorescent screen image of her now deceased father watching New Year's on TV at their home in Niigata. A quintessentially reflexive video/meditation on memory and death.

We were a misfit trickster team, Shigeko, Shridhar Bapat, Al Robbins and I. Al was a master woodworker, poet, filmmaker turned videomaker, and philosopher. An immense and tempestuous presence, Al, in the words of Raindance co-founder Paul Ryan, had *makoto*, "a kind of sincerity that discards anything that hinders a man from acting wholeheartedly on the impulses of his true feelings." Al's deft crafting of Shigeko's original *Duchampiana* series, and *Three Mountains* sculptures is exquisite, delicate and precise. Numerous "versions" of the staircase have been made; all lack

Al's touch and sense of proportion. Shridhar, a loving, dedicated, and sensitive soul, with his personal demons always near at hand, sublimated his own substantial creative abilities to provide expert technical prowess to Shigeko and Nam June's installations, as well as to the work of countless other prominent artists.

In the Summer of 1976 Shigeko and I embarked on a meandering, quixotic, vagabond, video/filmmaking tour of the Rocky Mountain west. To share my love of sublime landscape and mountains with Shigeko, I drove a rental car from Seattle to Albuquerque by way of Yellowstone, Grand Teton, Grand Canyon, Taos, Bryce Canyon, Zion Canyon, The Painted Desert. Returning to New York, Shigeko created her Three *Mountains*, in my mind, her finest of many wonderful video sculptures.

久保田のヴィデオ・ポートレイトと、私たち2人が知り合ったいきさつ

ジョーン・ローグ

Joan Logue：ヴィデオ・アーティスト。1942年生まれ。ニューヨーク在住。

私たちが知りあったのは1976年だった。久保田成子がカリフォルニア州のロングビーチ美術館に来て、「何やらまじめな仕事」という名義でアートの仕事をしていた友人2名（スーザン・マーティンとナンシー・ドルー）から、ヴェニスにあった私のスタジオに成子を連れていってもいいかとの問い合わせがあったのだ。到着した成子に私は、彼女を題材にした短いヴィデオ・ポートレイトを撮ってもいいかと聞いた。成子はちょっとためらった——できあがったポートレイトにもそれは見てとれる——が、いいわよと言った。あとになって私がニューヨークに引っ越してから、成子と私は友だちになった。

1977年、私はニューヨークに引っ越し、空港からタクシーに乗って、ソーホー地区クロスビー通りの新居に向かった。シャーリー・クラークの娘ウェンディがサブレット（又貸し）してくれたロフトだ。私はたちまち、これこそ私の街だという感覚を覚えた。ニューヨークでは女たちが活躍し、ヴィデオ・アートを作っている！　タクシーの運転手が「お客さん、仕事は？」と聞いたのを覚えている。「ヴィデオ・アーティストです、ヴィデオ・ポートレイトを撮ってるんです！」と私は答えた。運転手は眉ひとつ動かさず「そりゃいいね！」と言った。私はすっかり感心してしまった。タクシー運転手さえヴィデオ・アートのことを知っているのだ。まさに自分の街だと私は思った。ニューヨーク、ニューヨーク！

ニューヨークに着いてまだほんの数日しか経っていないころ、スプリング通りで久保田成子にばったり出くわした。彼女は私がニューヨークにいることに驚き、どうして電話くれなかったのと責めた。それから成子は、うちの下の階のロフトが空いてるんだけど、興味ない？と尋ねた。持ち主は日本人アーティスト靉嘔で、かわりに訊いておいてあげるからさ、と言う。それから夕食に招いてくれた。成子は先駆的女性ヴィデオ・アーティストのひとりだった。頭がよくて怖いものなしだった！　夕食の席で彼女は、ジョナス・メカスのアンソロジー・フィルム・アーカイヴズでヴィデオのキュレーターをしてるのよと話した。その後成子は自分が日曜の夜に企画し

ていた上映会に私を招いてくれ、彼女のおかげで私は、ニューヨーク・シティでヴィデオをやっている人たちと知りあえただけでなく、4階のロフトに引っ越すこともできて、ご近所さんになった！

訳：近藤学

Kubota's Video Portrait and How We Became Friends

Joan Logue

Joan Logue: Video artist.
Born in 1942 in Pennsylvania. Lives and works in New York.

We met in 1976. Shigeko Kubota came to the Long Beach Museum, and two friends who ran an art business, called Some Serious Business (Susan Martin and Nancy Drew), asked if they could bring Shigeko to my studio in Venice. When she arrived, I asked Shigeko if I could make a short video portrait of her. Shigeko was a bit hesitant—you can see it in the portrait—but she said yes. Later, after I moved to New York, Shigeko and I became friends.

In 1977 I moved to New York, took a cab from the airport to my new sublet in Soho on Crosby Street, a loft that Shirley Clark's daughter Wendy owned. I felt at home immediately: women were on the move in New York and working in video art! I remember a cab driver saying to me, what do you do? I replied, "I'm a video artist, I make video portraits!" The cabby didn't blink an eyelash and said "that's great!" I was amazed: even the cab drivers knew about video art it seemed. I knew I was home, New York New York!

I'd been in New York for only a few days when I ran into Shigeko Kubota on Spring Street. She was surprised to see me in New York and could not understand why I didn't call her! Shigeko then asked me if I was interested in renting a loft downstairs from her. It belonged to a Japanese Artist, Ay-O and she would ask him for me. Then she invited me to dinner. Shigeko was one of the first women pioneer video artists; she was smart, and fearless! At dinner, she told me she was the video curator at Jonas Mekas's Anthology Film Archives. Shigeko later invited me to her Sunday night video screenings and it was thanks to Shigeko I met the video community of New York City as well as moving into the fourth floor loft, making us neighbors!

1979-81

河

River

川があって水が走り、同じ水が走ることは決してなく、同じ人たちが同じ家に住んでいることは決してなく、四季のように、春、夏、秋、冬、時間に応じて、自然の中でと同じように、変わりつづけ……

目的のない方角へ、どこへ向かうのでもなく、ただただ流れ……私はどこへ行こうか……何の目的もなく終えるために……私は水流に乗って魚たちと泳いでいる、半分溺れながら、自分を探して……。

ニューヨークからベルリンへ飛び、飛行機の窓から下の風景を眺め、名もない川たちの描く線を見ていたら……自分の郷里の川のことを思った。信濃川、日本で一番長い川。

私は仏教徒の家系だ。仏教の中心にはいつでも川が、走る水があり、仏陀、石の仏陀はいつも雨に打たれている。一粒の雨がせせらぎになり、せせらぎが川になる。自然の中で水が演じる役割は、私たちの人生でヴィデオが果たす機能になぞらえることができる。川の物理的／時間的特性、そして情報伝達や省察といった「鏡」的な性質は、ヴィデオの中で再現されている。

産業化以前の時代、川は長い距離でへだてられたコミュニティとコミュニティをつなげ、情報を他のどんな手段よりも速く広めていた。今日、電子信号が私たちのメッセージを加速し、全地球規模で、そして宇宙へと私たちをつなげる。荷電電子が水滴のように私たちの受信画面を横切って流れ、以前のいつか（何年も前かもしれないし、100万分の数秒前かもしれない）、どこかから運ばれてきた情報が詰め込まれている……「上流」から来た情報が。

ある面では、ヴィデオと川は単線的な時間と空間をとおって進むが、別の面では、ヴィデオの閉回路フィードバックはそれ自体やまわりの環境を、円環的な、「渦巻状」の時間として反映するし、川はその表面の反映からイメージを投げ返してくる。泳ぐ身体は軽々と水に浮き、たやすくスピンし潜る。ヴィデオの現実の中に投じられると、無限のヴァリエーションが可能になり、重みのなさだけでなく、あらゆるかたち、形状、色、場所、速度、スケールをまったく自由に分解し、再構築し、変化させることができるようになる……液状の現実。

（スチル）

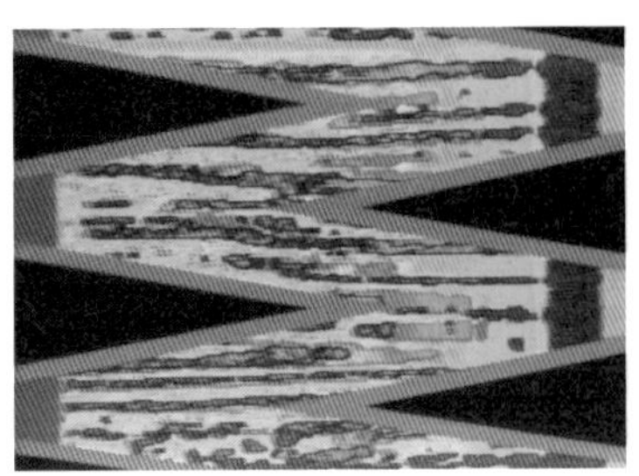

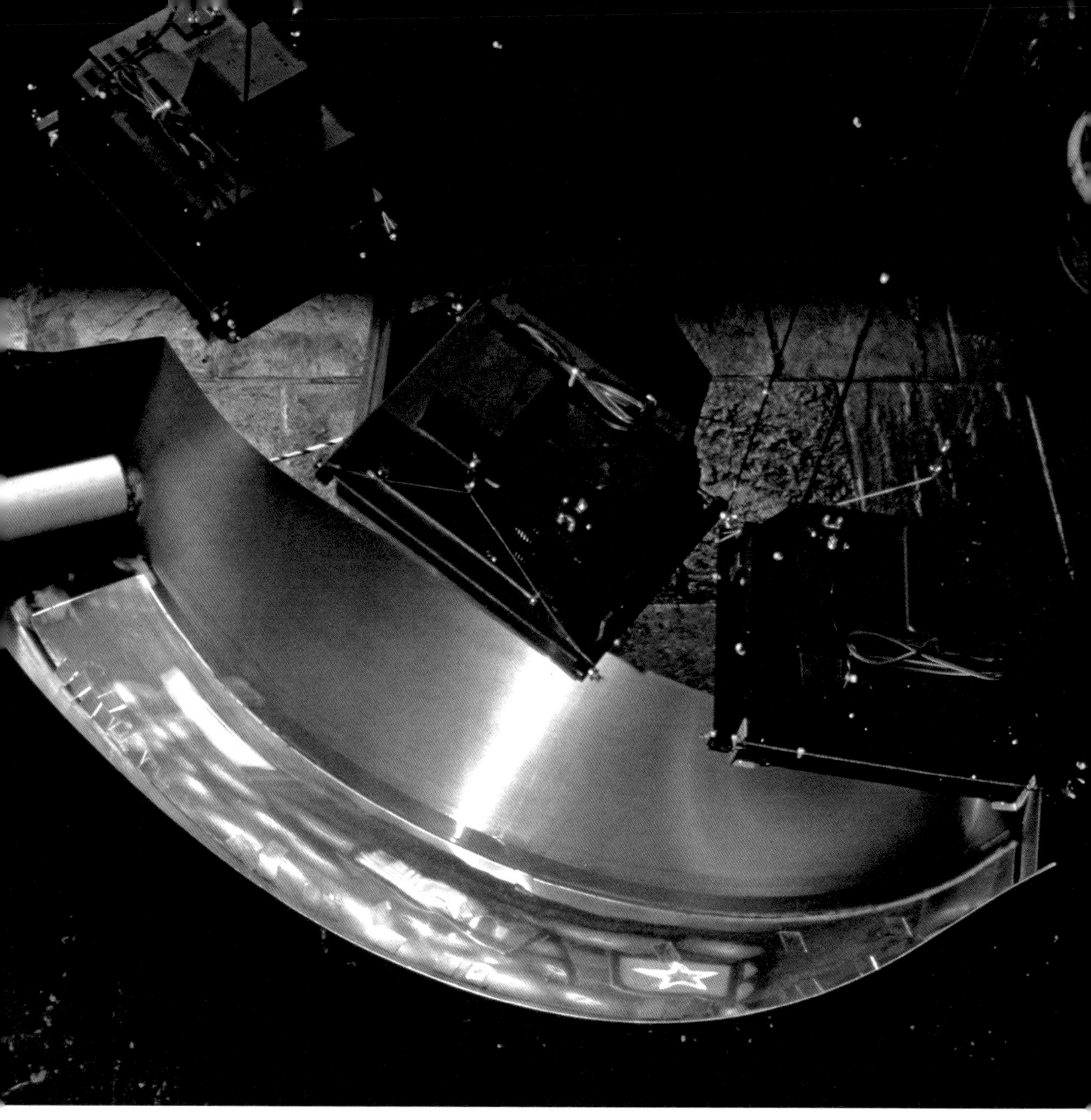

「ホイットニー・ビエンナーレ1983」での展示

折り紙の笹船を模したステンレス製の構造に水が張られ、川に見立てられている。回転する機械により、水は絶えず波を起こす。その上には3台のブラウン管テレビが吊り下げられており、その画面は覗き込まなければ直接見ることができないが、水の中を泳ぐ作家自身の姿を星やハート型のパターンと組み合わせた映像が水面に映し出される。本作は、作家にとって重要な自然をモチーフとし、ベルリン滞在中、金属という新しい素材を用いて制作された。1983年のホイットニー・ビエンナーレに出品され、その展示風景が美術雑誌『Art in America』の表紙を飾った。(MN)

daadギャラリー個展(1981年)のオープニングにて

1981

ヴィデオ俳句―ぶら下がり作品

Video Haiku – Hanging Piece

シカゴ現代美術館(1981年)での展示(上)
ファーガス・マカフリー・ギャラリー(2020年)での展示(右)

球体のテレビモニターが吊り下げられ、床に設置された丸く湾曲する鏡の上で振り子運動を続けている。テレビモニターはカメラで撮影しているモノクロ映像をライブで映し出しており、鑑賞者は床の鏡に映るモニターの映像を見ることになる。本作はシカゴの現代美術館で発表されたが、作品は窓際に設置されて、カメラは建物の外の様子を捉えていた。1983年の展示時では、天井にも丸い鏡が取り付けられた。(AH)

５、７、５
これが日本で一番短い詩である俳句の形式、俳句の音節数、俳句の精神。

詩人・芭蕉、その有名な俳句：

ふるいけや
１２３４５
かはづとびこむ
１２３４５６７
みづのをと
１２３４５

古池や
蛙飛びこむ
水の音

私のヴィデオ俳句は振り子、ぶら下がって、私の『生きる時間』の１分１分に合わせて揺れる、いち、に、さん……。

私はあと何年自分の人生を生きられるだろう！
私の〈生きる時間〉、私の〈物理的身体時間〉を知っているのは神様だけ、でも私の『精神の時間』と『アート時間』は永遠に生き残る……
ことを願っている。LOVE。

1983-90

デュシャンピアナ：自転車の車輪

Duchampiana: Bicycle Wheel

《デュシャンピアナ：自転車の車輪》 1983年（部分）

マルセル・デュシャンによる1913年の最初のレディメイド、《自転車の車輪》を引用し、スツールの上に自転車の車輪が乗っている。久保田の作品では、モーターの動力により、車輪が自動で回転する仕様になっている。車輪の中には小型モニターが取り付けてあり、風に揺れる花と風景の色加工された映像が流れる。1983年の制作時には、小型ブラウン管の重量が継続的な回転を難しくしていたが、1990年にはブラウン管に比べ軽量な液晶モニターを使用し、１つの車輪に１～３台の車輪を取り付けた「1、2、3」のバージョンが制作された。（MN）

《デュシャンピアナ：自転車の車輪　1、2、3》　1983-1990年

（スチル）

ドローイング　1977年

1980年代、アプロプリエーション（流用）は、ロバータ・スミスの表現を拝借するなら（『ニューヨーク・タイムズ』1989年12月27日）「あらゆるところで目にする戦略」となっている。

1976年、ルネ・ブロックと私は、ニューヨーク、ソーホーのルネ・ブロック・ギャラリーで私の個展を企画した。作品はすべてデュシャン関連にし、展覧会全体を「デュシャンピアナ：ヴィデオ彫刻」と題した。我知らず、私たちは重要なコンセプトを２つ、美術史に導入していた：

- アプロプリエーション。ヴィデオ・アートの領域だけでなくアート界そのもので1980年代に一世を風靡した。
- ヴィデオ彫刻。1970年代当時、ヴィデオ・アーティストたちは「ヴィデオ・インスタレーション」という用語を使っていたが、ルネ・ブロックは「インスタレーション」という言葉はドイツ語ではあまり響きが良くないとアドバイスしてくれた……トイレとかシャワーカーテンを「設置する」といった意味あいが強くなってしまうのだ。

アル・ロビンスに手伝ってもらって、私はこのヴィデオ彫刻を組み立てた。自己完結型の作品で、当時はヴィデオ機器をいいかげんに組み合わせるのがかなり流行っていたが、それには似ていなかった。私が造ったのは精巧に組み立てられた一点の芸術作品であって、ロダンやミケランジェロの伝統に連なる彫刻と呼ぶにふさわしいものだった。私は東京教育大学で伝統的な彫刻を専攻したのである。大教室で何時間も過ごし、組み立てや構造を学んだ。だからルネ・ブロックがデュシャンピアナ連作に与えたヴィデオ彫刻という解釈は、私にはとても素敵に思えた。彼は私が長いあいだ苦心して得ようとしていたものをたくみに言い当てていたのだ。

彫刻としての「デュシャンピアナ」第一弾は《マルセル・デュシャンの墓》。1972年、フランスのルーアンにあるデュシャンの墓を訪ねた直後に制作した。1975年、ザ・キッチンで初公開された。この作品のあと、《階段を降りる裸体》、《ヴィデオ・チェス》、《メタ・マルセル：窓》など、実にいろいろな作品が出てきて、《自転車の車輪》に行き着いた。これは1983年、ニューヨークのホワイト・コラム・ギャラリーで展示された。

デュシャンをほのめかしているのに加え、《自転車の車輪》は、田舎で過ごした私の子ども時代の懐かしい記憶を運んでいる。車輪は円の別名だ……始まりも終わりもなく、どんな秩序の感覚もなく、ひたすら動きつづける円。また、車輪は禅では肯定的な言葉で、煩悩にとらわれず、憂いのない澄明な人柄を示唆する。

グリーン・インスタレーション

Green Installation

（スチル）

2つの自立した構造物から構成され、一方の表面はフラットな斜面で、もう一方は階段状になっている。各パーツの表面にはそれぞれ5つのモニターが埋め込まれており、着色加工されたアリゾナの風景の映像が2チャンネルで同調しないで流れる。階段状の構造はモニターの周囲が鏡面になっているため、ヴィデオのイメージが反射し増幅する。（MH）

緑の公園、緑の遊び場、緑の野原、緑の葉、緑の森……。

マンハッタンで、緑の田舎から遠く離れて暮らしている私が緑色を見るにはどこを訪ねればいい？　セントラルパーク？

この《グリーン・インスタレーション》は私の頭の中の緑の風景、物理的な緑の脳。

緑を見に行くところがどこにもない？　緑はもうない？

子どものころ田舎で、野草の茂る緑の野原で遊びまわり、ちょうど日没前にはお腹がぺこぺこになったものだった。

マルセル・デュシャンは自分の仕事を緑のボックスに、緑のミニチュア・スーツケースに詰め込んだ〔『彼女の独身者たちによって裸にされた花嫁、さえも』（通称「グリーン・ボックス」）1934年〕。

この《グリーン・インスタレーション》は私の頭の中の遊び場、そこで私は夢を見て、私が眠っていたとき夢の中で、緑の水、緑色、無意識のうちに私の現実、日常に溶け込んでいく。

1984

ブロークン・ダイアリー：韓国への旅

Broken Diary: Trip to Korea

（スチル）

東京都美術館で「ナムジュン・パイク展 ヴィデオ・アートを中心に」展を成功させたナムジュン・パイクと久保田は、その足で共に韓国を訪れた。久保田にとっては夫の祖国を初めて訪れる旅となり、パイクにとっては、朝鮮戦争をきっかけに祖国を出て以来、実に34年ぶりの帰国となった。アーティストとして世界的に有名になったパイクをマスコミが出迎え、かつてパイクが住んでいた場所を訪れたり、祖先の墓参りや、伝統芸能を鑑賞する様子が撮影されている。撮影は同行した2人のアシスタントのポール・ギャリンと、久保田自身による。この際に目にした丸く土が盛り上がった墓をモチーフに、その後《韓国の墓》を発表している。(AH)

1985

ブロークン・ダイアリー：ソーホー・ソープ／雨の被害

Broken Diary: SoHo SoAp/Rain Damage

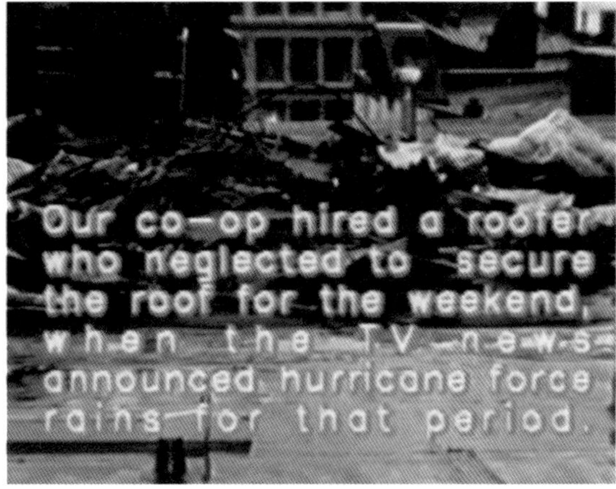

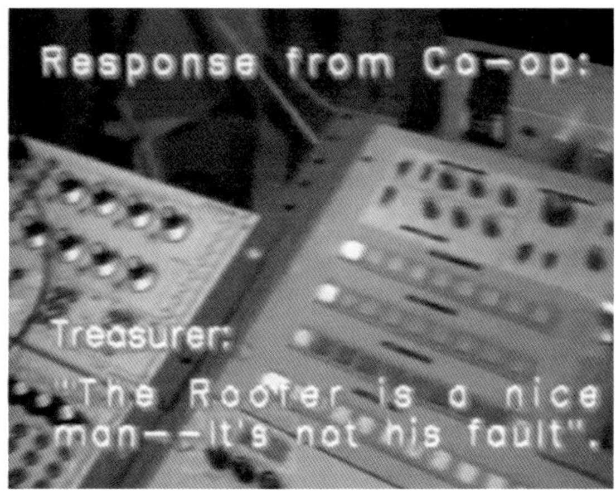

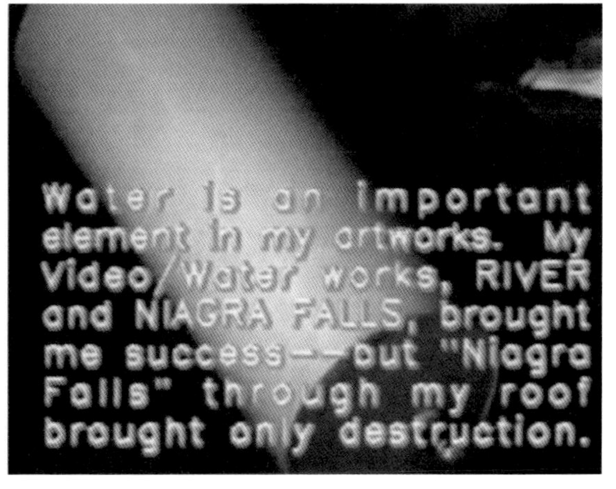

（スチル）

《ナイアガラの滝》をつくったすぐあと、
私のスタジオがナイアガラの滝になった、
屋根職人のミスで。
「芸術は自然を模倣し、
自然は芸術を模倣する」。

久保田はヴィデオによる日記的なシングルチャンネル作品を「ブロークン・ダイアリー」として、12章から成る一連のシリーズと1985年に位置付けた。その第一章は1970年の《One Day in California》で、これを含め《Video Curator Diary》（1974-1982）、《Berlin Diary》（1979-1980）《Shigeko in Chicago》（1982年）などは、現在公開されておらず近い将来の実現に向けて準備中である。完全なかたちで公開されたあかつきには、久保田がヴィデオ・アーティストであると共にヴィデオ・キュレーターであり、またひとりの女性としてもさまざまな苦難をくぐりぬけた人物であるということが浮き彫りになるであろう。いうまでもなく、こうした久保田の日記的な映像の仕事は、ジョナス・メカスに多大な影響を受けている。本作は「ブロークン・ダイアリー」シリーズの最終章に充てられる。パイクと共に暮らし、現在は久保田成子ヴィデオ・アート財団となっているロフトの屋根が大雨でひどい雨漏りを被った。機材やフィルムを損失した久保田とパイクの悲哀がコミカルに描かれる。「It rains in my heart/It rains on my video art（私の心に雨が降る／私のヴィデオ・アートに雨が降る）」というフレーズが印象的である。（AH）

1985-87

ナイアガラの滝

Niagara Falls

プラスチック製鏡の断片に覆われた、白い垂直な壁状の構造体に、大小10台のモニターが組み込まれている。色加工した4チャンネルのヴィデオはそれぞれ、ナイアガラの滝の春夏秋冬を表している。その上のシャワーから、滝のように水が滴り落ちる。水を受け止めるプールの底も鏡の断片で覆われ、四方八方に重ねられた反射素材により、映像が幾重にも増幅する。さらに、スピーカーから流れる夏のナイアガラの滝の音と、現実の水が落ちる音とが響き合う。1987年のドクメンタ8（カッセル）と東京での展示のために、モニターを14台に増やしたバージョンがそれぞれの地で制作されたが現存しない。(MN)

「JAPAN 87 ビデオ・テレビ・フェスティバル」（青山スパイラル）での展示（上）
ドローイング　1985年（下）

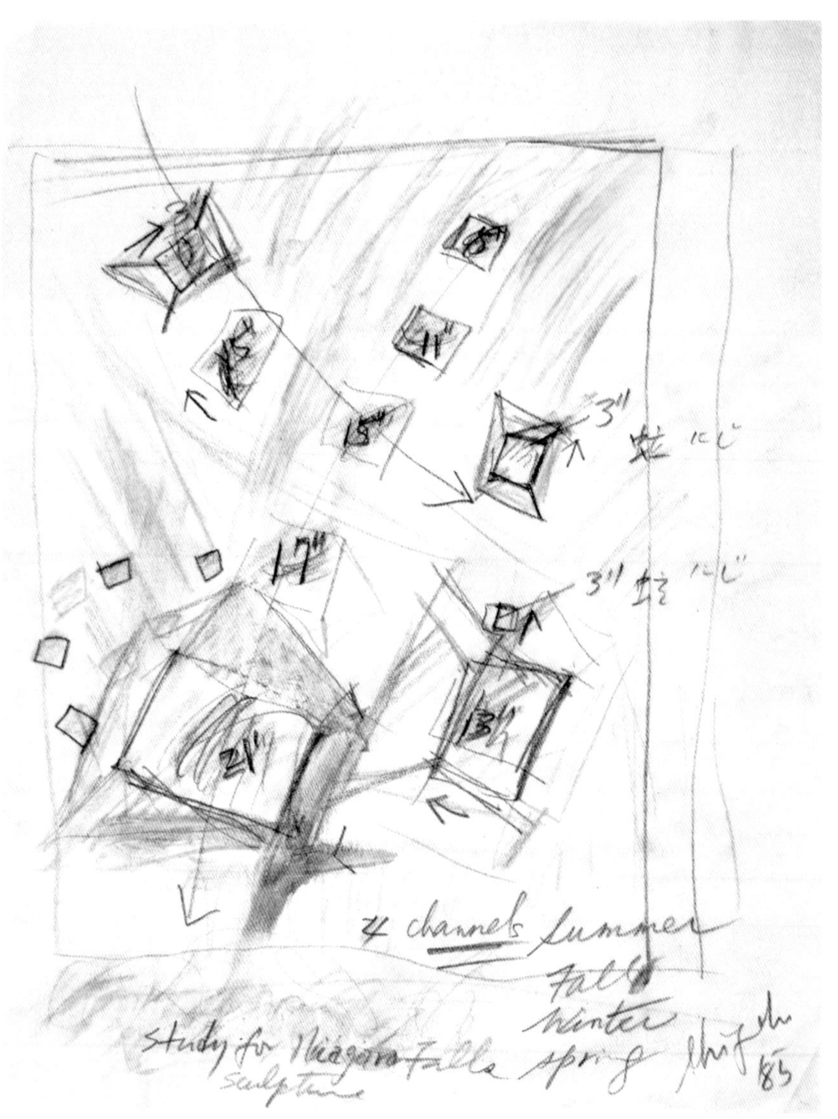

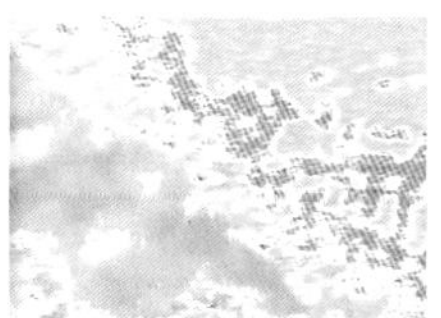

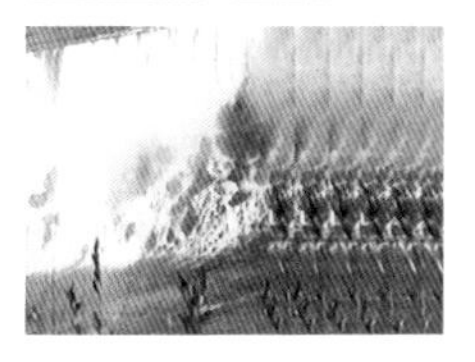

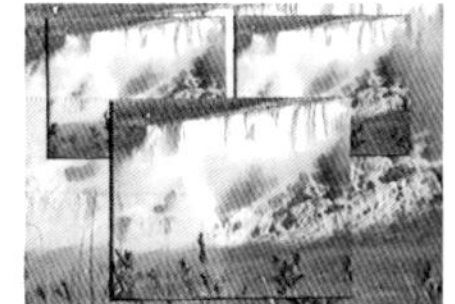

（スチル）

美しい自然は悪夢、おそれ、怖さ。ナイアガラの滝はとくに、壮大な自然の磁力のせいで、死に向かって身を投げ出し、自分の体を解き放って滝へとジャンプしようとする私の衝動にまっすぐ飛び込んでくる。

ナイアガラの滝には独特の美しさがあり、自我から解放された気分にしてくれる。カナダ側から滝を俯瞰すると、もっとずっと壮大だ。

真冬、空っぽのホテルに泊まり、真夜中に赤、青、緑の人工光で照らし出された滝を窓からじっと見つめた。私はこれを地獄の風景と考えた。

水が凍りついていたり、煙のように水蒸気がたなびいたりしているナイアガラの滝の眺めからは、狂乱状態の時間が凍りつく瞬間が思い浮かんだ。夏のナイアガラの滝のイメージは、溢れる水の渦巻や、地の底から鳴り響いてくる唸りだった。

三色レンズ・ヴィデオカメラで滝にズームインすると、滝のクロースアップは私をいっそう巻き込み、死の世界へと私を誘い、飲み込んだ。私は本当に怖かった。ヴィデオを撮るために私はポール・ギャリンとヴァーノン・ノーウッドに頼んでベルトで私の体を固定してもらい、カメラともども滝に落ちていってしまわないようにした。気がつけばこんなことを考えていた。もし自殺するならナイアガラの滝にしよう。そうすれば簡単に自然の中に消えていけるから。心の中では、自殺を懐かしく思う甘い郷愁と、そんなことをするなと自分に警告することで自殺を拒む気持ちとのあいだで葛藤があった。ナイアガラの滝は、美しい自然と物理的な死の存在が、同時にとても近く感じられる珍しい観光地だ。まるで観光とは地獄を見に行くことであるかのような気がした。観光客は、こんなふうな地獄めいたナイアガラの風景に興奮する。子どもも大人も大喜びで、金切り声で叫んでいる。カモメだけが、滝の奥深くに沈んだ自殺者たちの死体をエサにしているかのように、ゆっくり飛んでいた。

ナイアガラの滝が新婚旅行で有名なスポットなのは妙な話だ。きっと新婚旅行のあいだ、身体はナイアガラの滝と同じくらいぐらぐらするのだろうが、新婚旅行というのは入り口であって、死の世界に先立つ一歩であるような気もする。新婚旅行が男性と女性のあいだの生活の苦しみの始まりを意味するのだとしたら、人々は生きることに関して何かしら心を落ち着かせようとしてナイアガラを訪れるのかもしれない。

スタジオでジャクリーヌ・モニエにナイアガラの滝についてのヴィデオ彫刻を見せたら、マルセル・デュシャンの《与えられたとせよ：1．落水　2．照明ガス》（ニューヨーク、1946–66年）みたいだと言った。

デュシャンが自作の中で滝を創ったのは、自然の永遠性のシンボルに違いない。またはひょっとすると、男性の溢れる精液のシンボルなのかもしれない。

作品を完成させてからは一度もナイアガラに戻っていない。行きたい気がしない。実際のナイアガラも見たくない。一度見れば十分。それと同じで、また地獄の恐怖を見るのはいやだ。

1986

ロック・ヴィデオ　桜

Rock Video Cherry Blossoms

原美術館（1992年）での展示

フォームラバー製の岩に3つの水晶石が埋め込まれ、周囲には割れた鏡の破片が散りばめられている。同じ岩に埋め込まれた液晶カラーテレビのモニターからは、《桜》のシングルチャンネル・ヴィデオの映像が流れる。（MH）

子どものころ、父の実家の山寺を訪ねた。大きな石庭があり、そこで何度も何度も岩によじ登ったり飛び石にぴょんと載ったりするのが楽しかったものだ。

高校の修学旅行中、京都の龍安寺と銀閣寺に行く機会があった。旅行からは、こんなに崇高で芸術的な空間が自然と宗教のあいだで調和して存在しているんだ、という不思議な印象が残った。

現在ニューヨークを生活と仕事の場としてヴィデオ彫刻をつくっていて、岩にTVモニターを取り付けようと長いあいだ試みていたものの、TVが発する熱の扱いに困っていた。1986年に日本に帰国したとき、カシオが液晶カラーテレビ〔TV-〕2000を初めて生産し、「熱なし　ブラウン管なし」と宣伝していた。これは私の彫刻にベストの解決策だと私は考えた。熱という短所を持たずブラウン管を持たないTVが、鏡ガラスでできた液晶カラーTVがここにある。これを使えば、岩の中のTVが燃えるように熱くなるのも心配しなくていいだろうし、取り付けるのも楽だろうし、ファンも必要ないはずだと私は考えた。

（スチル）

《ロック・ヴィデオ　桜》は1986年、カリフォルニア州ヴェニスのピーゾ・エレクトリック・ギャラリーで、ディレクターのトム・ソロモンの招きで初公開された。サンフランシスコのニュー・ラングストン・アート・ギャラリーでも展示され、カタログにカラー図版が載った。評判は良く、3インチ液晶カラーTVという技術革新はオーディエンスをすっかり驚かせたので、サンフランシスコ・〔アート・〕インスティテュートの教員や学生、また多くのアーティストからかなりの称賛が寄せられた。

岩はきわめて固い本物の岩に見えたが、実はウレタンフォーム製の模造だった。岩を固くて重く見せるために私は鏡を1枚叩き割り、床いっぱいに破片を撒いて、岩に重量感を持たせた。

子どものころ、幼くして死ぬと「賽の河原」に行くという話を聞かされた。極楽か地獄のどちらかに行く前に小石を積み上げなければならず、どんなにがんばっても鬼が来て小石の塔を崩してしまうのだという。アルベール・カミュの『シジフォスの神話』でも似た話が語られていると聞いたことがある。

子どものころ、自分が死ぬだろうと思っていた年齢をもう過ぎてしまった。

私は桜のヴィデオテープを流すこのロック・ヴィデオ彫刻を、亡くなったシカゴ出身の友人たちに捧げた。

1987-88

枯山水

Dry Mountain, Dry Water

緑色のプラスチック製の鏡で覆われた、大きさや形も様々な7つの合板製の構造物から成る。床と壁に設置された4つのプロジェクターからは2種類の異なる桜の映像が投影され、立体物に映し出された映像が反射して壁に光を放つ。本作はのちに《アダムとイヴ》の一部となる。(MH)

生死（生と死）
事大（服従）
無常（生のはかなさ）
迅速（唐突さ）

京都、国宝・大仙院玄関に記された言葉

《河》と《ナイアガラの滝》の彫刻シリーズを、素材の面で対照的な水とヴィデオをコンセプトとして使いながら制作したあと、私は禅寺の枯山水を元にした彫刻石庭を組み立てることに決めた。

1987年の夏のこと、ヨーヘン・ザウエラッカーと私は猛暑の京都で石庭をいくつか訪ねた。ヨーヘンとともに、寺から寺へと、肩から重いカメラを下げて、汗だくになってまわっているうちに、ふと気づくと、唯一無二の個性を持つ石庭に向かい合っていた。

暑さのせいでヨーヒヘンは体重が激減し、どんどん痩せていく一方、私は体重が増えて中年太りした。このおかしな２人連れを目にした禅寺の僧が、ヨーヘンに、どこから来て何をしているのかと尋ねた。デュッセルドルフから来たとヨーヘンが答えると、僧はドイツ語で「すばらしい（ヴンダバール）カップル！」と言って私たちをからかった。ヨーヘンは恥ずかしがって真っ赤になった。この生臭坊主には本当にムッとした。

また、タクシーに乗ったら運転手が私たちを見て、皮肉な口調で言った。「どんな人でも死ぬ前に、何が何でもお寺にお参りしはんにゃなあ」。京の町の人の毒舌は本当にわずらわしかった。一言一句ヨーヘンに通訳はしなかった。きまりの悪い思いをさせたくなかったし、私たちがわざわざ京都まで来たのは観光のためではなくて、アートを追求し、石庭を研究するためだったのだから。

私は石庭を「枯れた」素材で構成した。緑色のプラスチック製の鏡をスパッと、刺身包丁でそいだかのように切ったかけらだ。

私の庭の岩は大きさや形がさまざまで、自然の中には見つからない。岩が自然に持っている外見を完全に超越している。またこれは、私の心の奥深くにつなぎとめられていた感情の岩だ。

禅寺の石庭には季節の花々も池も泉もない。かわりに砂利や小石、いろいろな形の岩が組み合わされ、これ以上ないほど小さく閉じた空間の中で、禅思想の発現として四季をあらわしている。こんなふうに概念上の出発点として最小限の素材を使うやり方に私はとても感動した。また、長細い巨岩は男根（ファロス）の象徴のようだったし、並んで横たわる丘のような小石は処女の乳房に似ていた。私にはとてもセクシーなものに見えた。

禅の石庭は西洋の庭園、とくに英国とフランスのデザインやスケールとは著しく対照的だ。禅の石庭はきちんとしていて、概念上の空間や、単純さと簡潔の域に達するまで切り詰められた空間を体現するようデザインされている。
禅僧たちが石庭をデザインしたのだろうか？　石庭は禁欲的な生活を送っている禅僧たちの幻想をあらわしているのだと私は思った。

1988-91 / 1989-91

ヴィデオ屏風／アダムとイヴ

Video Byobu / Adam and Eve

シカゴ出身の友人たちの思い出に捧げる
バーバラ・レイサム
リン・ブルーメンサル
２人ともあまりにも短い命だった、
桜の花のように。
桜は美しい
命が短くて
１週間くらいだから。
雨や雪が降ったり嵐が来たりすれば
桜はすぐに死んでしまう
若い乙女が死ぬのと同じくらい
悲劇的に美しいものが失われる。

1984年、東京の千鳥ヶ淵で桜をヴィデオに撮った。屏風とは伝統的な日本の衝立で、アコーディオンのように折りたたむ。屏風は折り紙、つまり和紙を折りたたんでまたたく間に作り上げる建築術のように、折られる。

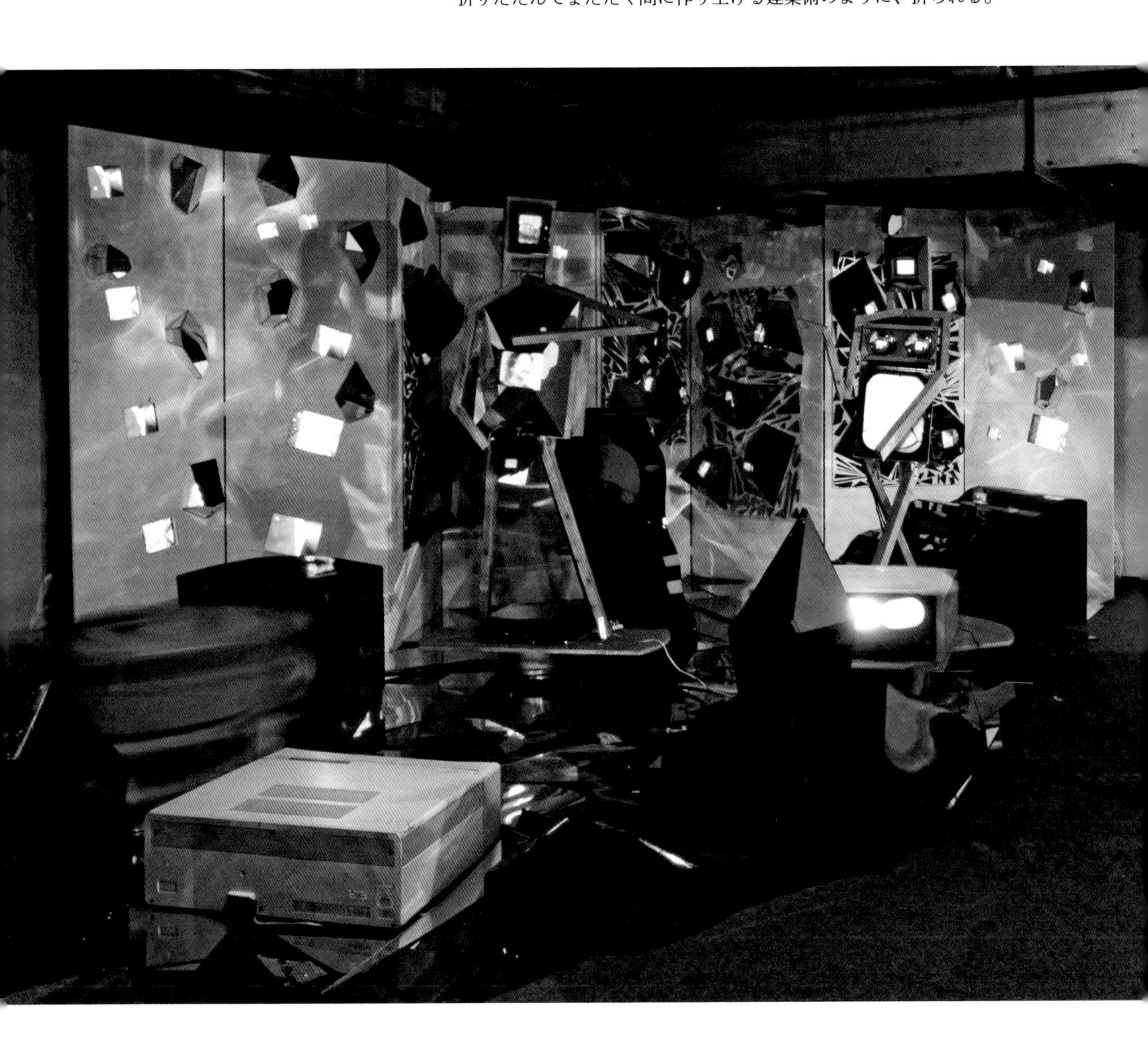

《ヴィデオ屏風》の最初のバージョンは、26個のモニターが埋め込まれたフォーマイカ（メラミン製素材）の平面構造で、その形はまるで日本の屏風を想起させる。モニターには2種類の桜の映像が映し出され、そのうちの1つにはコンピューター・ドローイングが施されている。同じ映像は作品の両脇の壁にも投影された。その後、白い合板製の構造物が赤、オレンジ、青、紫、緑、白の色とりどりのプラスチック製鏡面で覆われた2つめの屏風が制作されるが、内蔵された39個のモニターからは最初のバージョンと同じ2種類の桜の映像が流れる。最後に制作された3つめのバージョンは青のプラスチック製の鏡に覆われ、24個のモニターが内蔵された。そこに映るのは着色された空と夕日の空に鳥が飛ぶ2種類の映像で、同作はのちに《鳥》と改題された。
その後制作された《アダムとイヴ》では、中央に等身大サイズの2体の木製の人型彫刻がモーターで回転する台座の上に設置されている。各々には4つのモニター（その一部は《ヴィデオ・レリーフ》のモニターを再利用）が内蔵され、アダムのモニターにはアル・ロビンスの映像が、イヴのモニターには金閣寺の映像が流れる。彼らの前には《枯山水》が配置され、床と壁、さらに回転台に乗ったプロジェクターから2種類の桜の映像が投影される。背景には《ヴィデオ屏風II》が設置され、内蔵モニターと壁のプロジェクターには2種類の桜の映像が映し出される。このように、《アダムとイヴ》は複数の作品の組み合わせで構成され、また複数のプロジェクションにより周囲の空間全体を作品の一部として取り込んだ、環境型の作品である。（MH）

1987年2月8日、アル・ロビンスがサンフランシスコで心臓発作を起こして亡くなった。

私の家のクリスマスイヴ・パーティーで、青白い顔でアルは言った。「フロリダに行ってくるよ。ニューヨークの寒い冬から避難するんだ」。
「あらあら、あなたみたいなタフガイがフロリダに逃げるわけ？」と私は冗談を言った。
彼はフロリダに行ったものとばかり思っていた。窓や傷んだ天井がガタガタいってほとんど吹き飛ばされそうになっていた風の強い2月のある日、誰かが私のロフトを訪ねてきたのを私は感じ取った。祖国から遠く離れて暮らしているので、母かもしれないと思った。

次の日、友だちから電話がかかってきた。
「アルがサンフランシスコで死んだよ。」
「えっ、フロリダに行ったんじゃなかったの？」
友だちはこう続けた。「それがさ、アルはクリスマスイヴにカフェ・オーリンでサンフランシスコ出身の女の子と出会って、その子に飛行機のチケットを買ってもらったんだよ。彼女のアパートで死んだんだ」。
鉄の筋肉を持つアルが死んだ？

アルは建築家、詩人、ヴィデオ・アーティストで、私のヴィデオ彫刻をつくる大工でもあった。
1975年1月2日、アイラ・シュナイダーがザ・キッチンで開いた「ヴィデオ75、インスタレーション：20世紀最後の四半世紀の最初の数日」展で、私はアイラに、彼のインスタレーションの大工仕事をしたのは誰なのと尋ねた。
「アル・ロビンス」。
「誰、アル・ロビンスって？　どうやったら連絡とれる？」
「MoMA〔＝ニューヨーク近代美術館〕の彫刻庭園に行ってごらん。いつもあそこにいるから。ぼーっと座ってる」。
アルとつくった最初のヴィデオ彫刻は《マルセル・デュシャンの墓》だった。1975年6月にザ・キッチンで展示された。1976年の冬、アルと私は《階段を降りる裸体》と《メタ・マルセル：窓》をつくった。ルネ・ブロック・ギャラリーで初公開された。

アルはいつもふらりと立ち寄って、仕事をすると消えていった。1週間とか3か月、夏のあいだずっと姿を見せないこともあった。どこにいたのと聞くと、答えはいつも同じだった。「女の子のとこ。マディソン街を歩いてる青い目のブロンドの娘を追っかけるのが僕の趣味」。私は驚いた。アルは風呂に入っていなかったのはもちろん、もう10年も頭を洗ってなかった。ひどい臭いで、住所不定だった。女性のところに転がり込んで、追い出されるとグランドセントラル駅で寝たりさえしていた。ある意味でホームレスだったのだ。

シカゴで生まれたアル・ロビンスはバックミンスター・フラーに建築を学び、シカゴ大学を嫌ってハーヴァードに行き、退屈してドロップアウトした。マディソン街の建築事務所でしばらく働き、ペントハウスに住んだ。でもすぐに退屈し、浮浪者になった。
そして彼はいつも「僕はアインシュタイン」と言っていた。

（スチル）

父無し子だった。スキーヤーだった父親は家族を捨て、シカゴから逃げ出して山から山へと渡り歩いた。

アルと作業をしていて、この人は獰猛な動物だ、でなければときどき無邪気な赤ん坊だと思った。彼は私の仕事上の相棒だった。こんな人と関わり合いになってはいけないと何度も思った。それに、他に行き場がないときは、ただ私のところに来て仕事をしていた。まるで自分のことのように情熱を込めて作業をするので、私は言いたかった。「アル、どうしてそんなに一生懸命になって、こんなにきれいなものつくるの？」 彼はお金のためだけにやっていたのではなくて、心を込めていた。

アルはよく言っていた。「僕、あなた日本人だから好きだよ。日本に留学するチャンスもあったけど行かなかった。言葉も少し勉強したし。今になったら行っておけばよかった気がする。あなたといるとリラックスした気分になるよ」。そう言ってクラーク・ゲーブルみたいにウインクするのだ。

1924年、パリで、〔フランシス・〕ピカビアのバレエ『本日休演』中の『シネ・スケッチ』で、ルーカス・クラナッハの絵画を模して若きマルセル・デュシャンがアダムに扮し、ブロニア・ペルルミュテールという若い女性がイヴを演じた。これはアプロプリエーションのアプロプリエーションのアプロプリエーションのアプロプリエーションだった。若きデュシャンがアダムを演じている写真を見た私は、アルもアダムになれると思った。私にとっては当時も今も、あの大胆な体と荒削りな美しさとで、アルはアダムなのだ。

アルのガールフレンドは18歳の処女とポルノ女優だった。どちらもすごく純粋。２人はアルのモデルだった。

でも私のイヴは金閣寺だ。性別を超越した崇高な美を湛え、水晶のように沈黙し透明。京都の金閣寺は、精神に異常をきたした修行中の僧の放火で焼失した。でもふたたび立ち上がり、金で仕上げられた。これが私のイヴだ。頭を丸めた尼僧の純粋さ。

報せを聞いた私の最初の反応は「なんで無理やりベッドに引きずり込まなかったんだろ。しまったなあ、いつでもチャンスはあったのに。いつも一緒だったのに」だった。でも悲しいかな、彼の肉体は土に還ってしまった。こんなにすぐ逝ってしまうとは夢にも思わなかった。49歳だった。

《アダムとイヴ》と題したヴィデオ彫刻をつくることにした。これが私からアルへの手向け（たむけ）。私はアルに、こんなふうに永遠に生きてほしかった。

アルは私のアインシュタインだった。

1990

文化の門

The Gate for Culture

シチリアで毎年開催されていたアート・フェスティバルのタオルミーナ・アルテ内で、1987年から企画されたヴィデオ・アート部門、Rassegna Internazionale del video d' autoreに招待され、ヴィラ・コムナーレ公園に一時的に設置し、現在は残っていない。門のかたちに組み上げた構造体に32台（片側16台ずつ）のテレビモニターを設置した野外ヴィデオ・インスタレーションで、桜の映像が2種類用いられている。同年、久保田はヴェネチア・ビエンナーレ内の企画「Ubi Fluxus ibi motus 1990-1962」にも招待され、フルクサスのグループ・ショーではあったがヴィデオ彫刻を出品した。展覧会ではオノ・ヨーコ、塩見允枝子、アリソン・ノールズらの旧友たちと再会している。(AH)

タオルミーナにあるヴィラ・コムナーレの公園のヴィデオを見て私は、生涯でまだ目にしたことのない楽園だと思った。

公園のまわりには美しい青の大洋、緑の木々、花々がある。私は、岩だらけの風景の丘の中腹の平地に巧みに配された散歩道を自分が歩くところを想像し、ヴィデオ彫刻をこの風景の中、ヴィラの外に展示するんだと思ってとてもわくわくした。

雨が降る？　降ったっていいではないか？　濡れていようがいまいが、ヴィデオはヴィデオ・アートを通じて霊魂の乗り移りをコントロールするだろう。

とくに夜はきれいだろう。ヴィデオ光線とTVモニターのヴィデオスクリーンが無数の星々みたいに見えるから。暗い空のダイヤモンドのようにチカチカ光を発するのだ。私のヴィデオ門は、美しい自然公園への入り口であると同時に出口でもある。シチリアはギリシアやオリエントから来るさまざまな文化の入り口で、偉大な知識人や情報、着想、概念、哲学、財宝をヨーロッパに導入した。この門のところで私たちは姿勢を正し、自分自身に向き合うことになっている。門は神と仏陀の地への入り口をあらわすシンボルだ。

タオルミーナのヴィラ・コムナーレ公園に向けて私は門をひとつ造った。公園はまるで神の手で造られたかのような完璧な美しさだが、実は前〔＝19〕世紀、英国／インド人の〔原文ママ〕貴族の女性が建設したものだ。ヴィラは完璧な建築屋外劇場で、大洋に、タオルミーナの海に面し、エトナ山が見える。美しくエキゾチックな地中海の景観が、景色を描いた私の電子ヴィデオ・コンピューター・ドローイングと対照をなす。私は自然環境の中で両者を組み合わせ、変わりつづける光と時間の24時間を操作していくつもりだ。

自然の景観はそれはそれは完璧に見えることがある——絵ハガキなどの印刷媒体みたいに。ヴィデオに撮った自然の景観は自然の景観よりリアルに見える。いろいろなスケールのドラマや映画がたくさんタオルミーナで造られたに違いない。

この1990年の夏、このプロジェクトに参加できてとても嬉しい。1990年代というこの新たな10年間の幕開けにふさわしい良い夏になるだろう。

ヴェネツィアにて（1990年）　左より久保田成子、アリソン・ノールズ、塩見允枝子、オノ・ヨーコ、キャロリー・シュニーマン、サラ・シーガル（背後にビエンナーレのキュレーター、アキレ・ボニート・オリヴァ）

1991

自動車の車輪

Auto-Tire Wheel

自動車のタイヤの内側に、プラスチックの鏡と、小型の液晶モニター（5インチ、7インチ、12インチ）がはめこまれている。モニターには運転の様子のカラー映像が流れており、タイヤは回転している。3、5、7など奇数個で壁面に設置されることが多い。(AH)

夢は回り続ける輪
あなたは夢をみたくない
でも夢はいつもあなたの心を訪れる

私は、車のタイヤの中にTVセットを入れて、車のタイヤをグルグル、モーターでまわしてみたかった。車のタイヤの中のTVの映像は、ドライブのスピードによって、無色無形の映像をつくる。（ノイズ）

それは、ある暑い夏の日にスケッチブックに向っている時に浮かんだアイデアだった。(1977年）それは又、マンハッタンの街の中で、シフトの車に乗り、ライセンスをとった郊外のハイウェーを全スピードで、ドライブしたいナーという私の願望でもあった。

ベルリンからデュッセルドルフにドライブした時は、スピード制限のないドイツのハイウェー、当時はEast Germanyの畑の中をつっぱしった車のスピードが、私の体のスピードとなってさわやかな解放感を味わった。

1991年の春にやっと実現したこの作品には、ジョセフ・ボイスのとなえるSocial Sculpture、Air Pollutionからはじまり、この廃品となった（なるであろう）車のタイヤの中に、Industrial Artの美学とrecyclingのEcology の精神で、古いタイヤにも、もう一回、もう一つの人生を与えてやりたいと思った。このタイヤの機能美は、古タイヤでも美術館の壁にかかり、芸術作品として観衆に鑑賞してもらえるのだから、現代の美術である。それは、芸術が常に永遠性につながり、どんな溝泥（どぶ）の蓮花や平凡な日常の中の物体でも、美を発見できるのだ。

永遠にとっての芸術。

古びたタイヤは、風景を新たな荒地に変えてしまう。

その防止策の一つとして、古いタイヤを使って作品を創ることを考えた。

今はただの廃品でしかないものでも、何時かは財宝となり得るのである。

1991-92

スケート選手

Skater

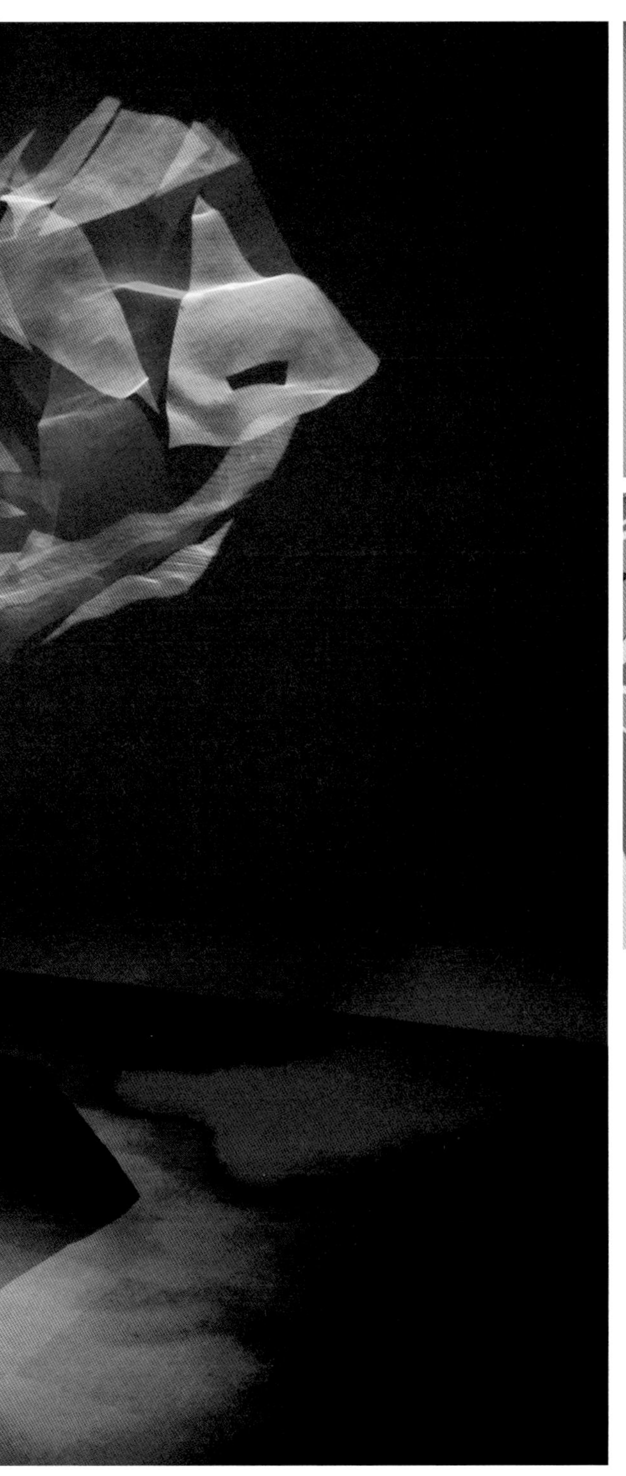

日本人のフィギュアスケート選手、伊藤みどりをモチーフにしている。回転する丸いリンクの上で、顔と胸にモニターを内蔵した木製の人形がリンクと反対方向に回っている。人形に向けて投影されるプロジェクションがリンクの上の鏡に反射し、周囲に色とりどりの光を投げかける。《アダムとイヴ》同様、木製の人型が回転するユーモラスな作品である。本作は伊藤がカルガリー五輪（1988年）でメダルを逃した後、銀メダルを獲ることになるアルベールヴィル五輪開催前の時期、彼女の出身地の名古屋での展覧会のために構想された。1994年、ニューヨークの公共空間で展示した後、1995年の光州ビエンナーレで展示されたことは判明しているが、その他の本作に関する記録は少なく、本展における展示は、本作の内容を明らかにする契機となった。(MN)

1991 / 1992

鳥Ⅰ／鳥Ⅱ

Bird I / Bird II

《鳥 II》 1992年

氷河のような形をした鏡の山の中に小型のモニターが無数にはめ込まれた、床に置かれたⅠと壁掛けのⅡの二点がある。ブロンクス動物園に鳥を撮影しに出かけた久保田は、冬で鳥がほとんど静止した状態だったので、それを「飛ばす」ために、ヴィデオのエンジニアと協働で、鳥の映像がプリズムのように左から右へ流れたり、上から下へ本のページをめくるように流れるような動画を制作したという。自然の鳥をヴィデオで解析し、人工の森に息づかせることで、久保田は自然と人工の対比を顕然とさせている。(MY)

《鳥 I》1991年

1993

ピッシング・マン／ジョギング・レディー

Pissing Man / Jogging Lady

《ピッシング・マン》 1993年

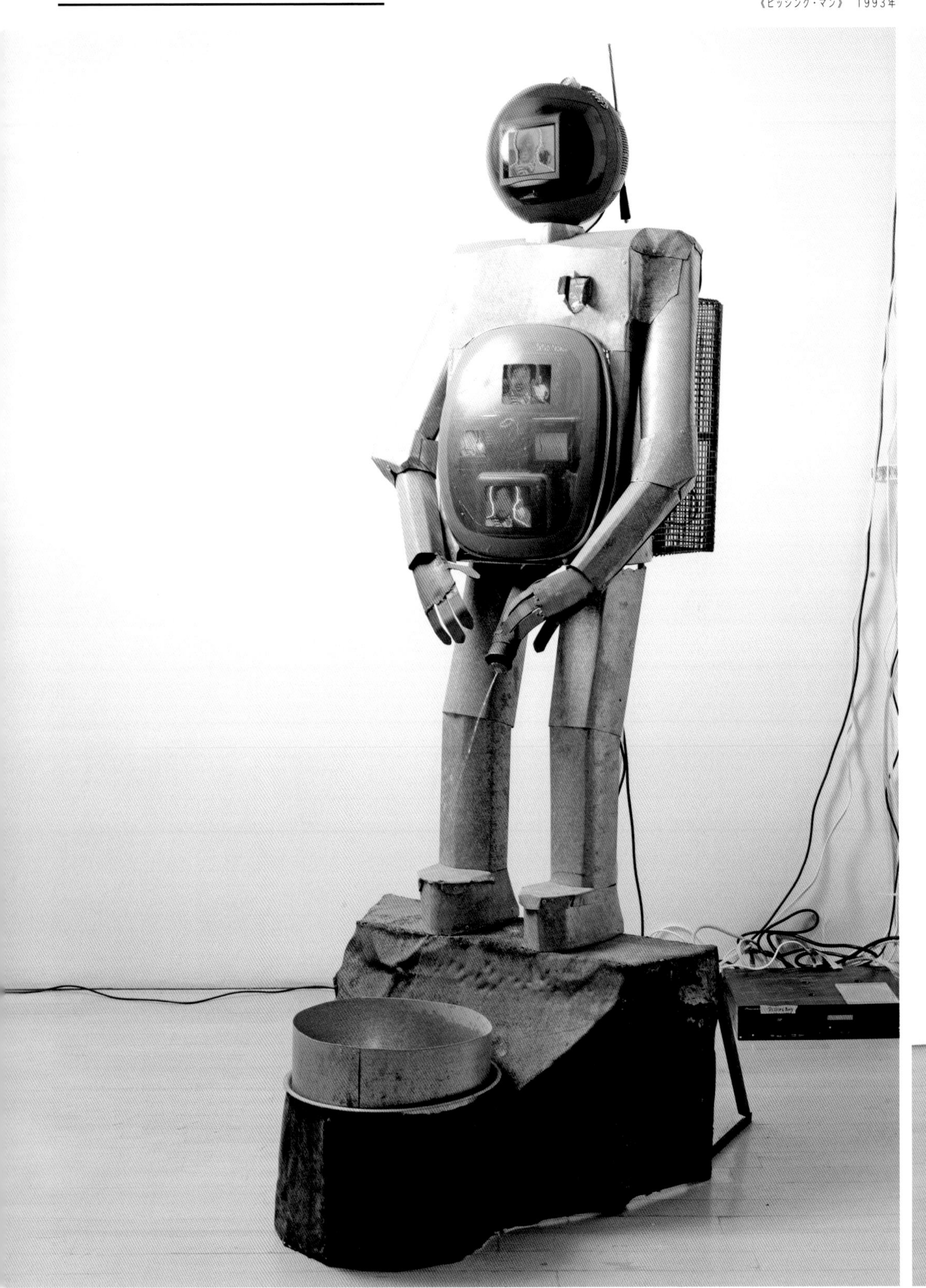

《ジョギング・レディー》 1993年

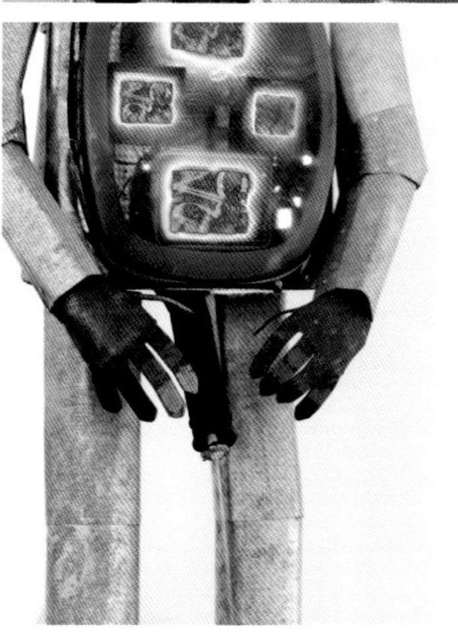

作家いわく、《ピッシング・マン》と《ジョギング・レディー》は、パイクと久保田の肖像であり、後者は、「いつもがんばって走り続けなければならない」という、久保田の抱く、女性一般のイメージの表象でもある。インスピレーションは、1991年5月13日発行の『ニューヨーカー』誌表紙に描かれた、ダンベルを持って、ウォークマンを聴きながらジョギングをする母の銅像で、久保田はその雑誌を大切に保管していた。(MY)

1993

韓国の墓

Korean Grave

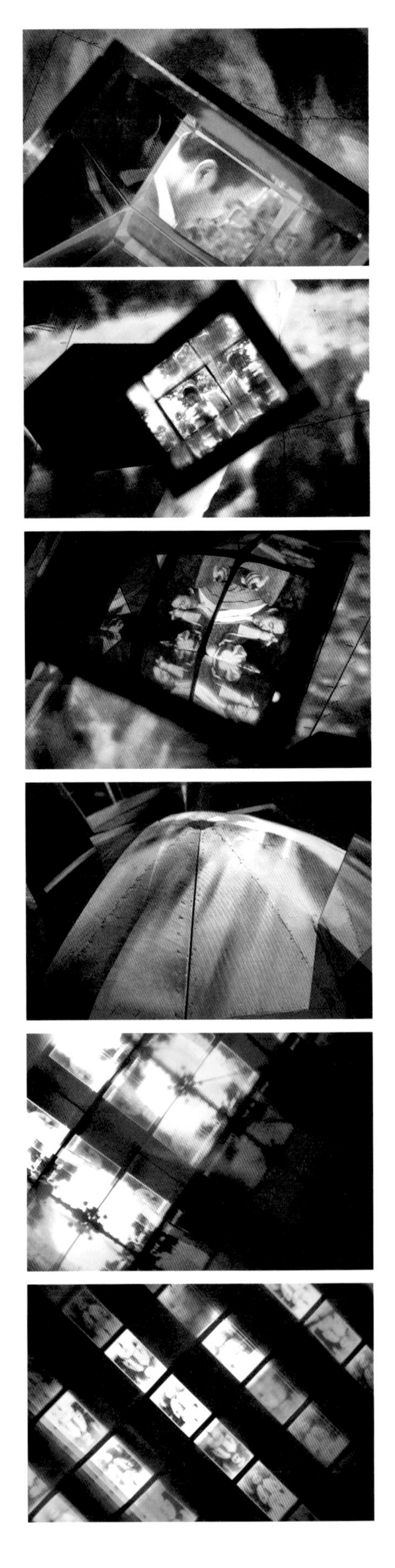

《韓国の墓》は、1984年に34年ぶりにパイクが韓国に帰国し、親戚に再会したり、家族の墓を参った時の様子を久保田が記録したシングルチャネル・ヴィデオ、《韓国への旅》が元になっている。韓国の墳墓の形を真似た半球体の彫刻が床に直接置かれ、その表面に不規則に開けられたいくつもの窓に、《韓国への旅》の映像が流れる。窓の一つ一つは、背の高い鏡の囲いで覆われているので、内側の映像が壁のあちこちに反射している。彫刻の表面にも、同じヴィデオがプロジェクターで投影されているので、木の物質性を感じさせない。この作品は1993年のものであるが、パイクの死を追悼する意味の強かった、久保田の2007年のマヤ・ステンダール画廊における個展の内容に最もふさわしく、墓の中のパイクの魂が、まるで、外の世界に向かって、メッセージを放っているような印象さえ与えた。ヴィデオはここでは、あの世とこの世を結ぶ臨界のようでもある。(MY)

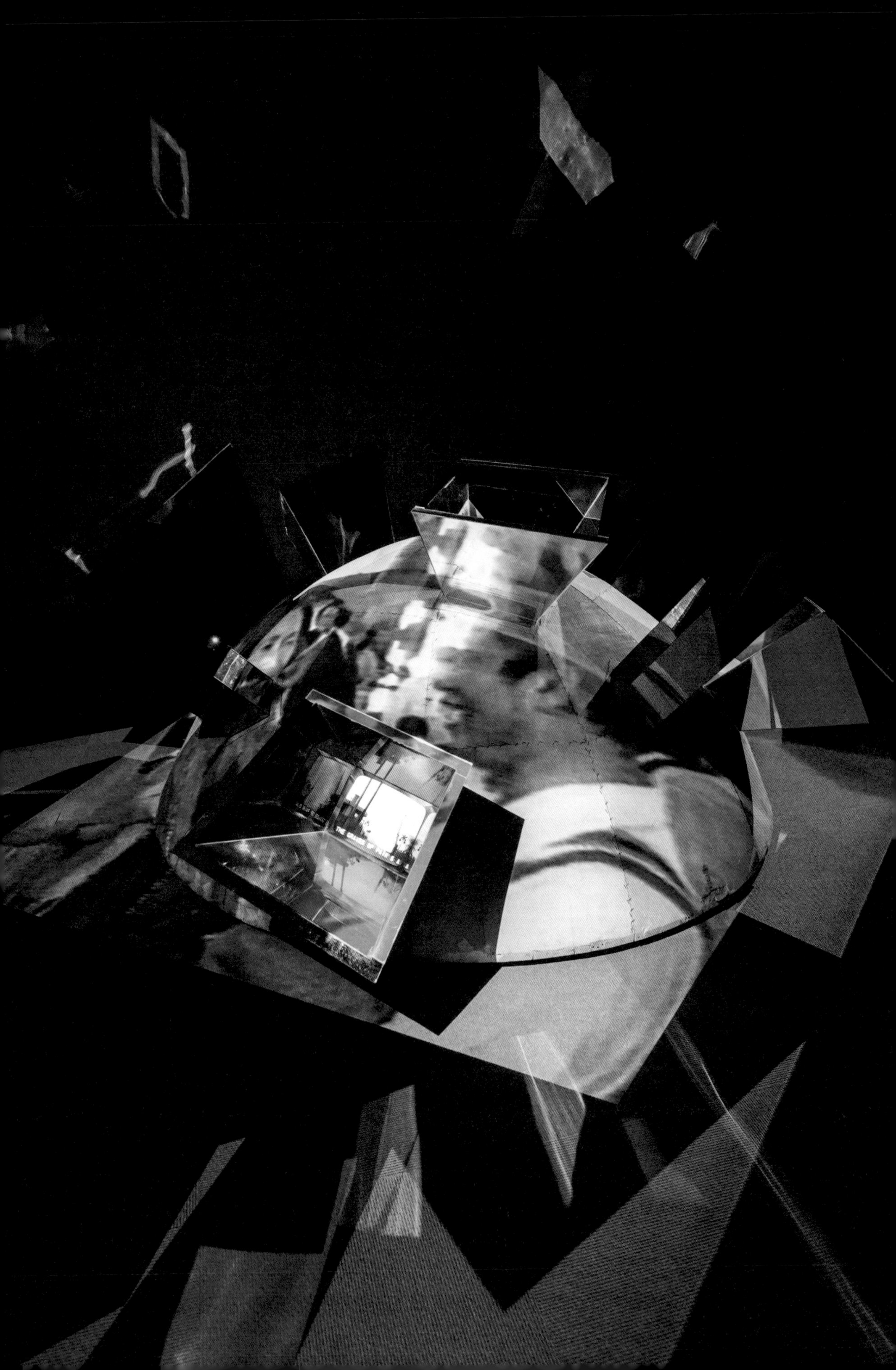

1993

風車（かざぐるま）／風の花（アネモネ）

Windmill

1993年のリヨン・ビエンナーレでは、「ヴィデオ・フィードバック　風車（かざぐるま）、風の花（アネモネ）」と題し、小型液晶モニターを中心に金属製の羽が回転する複数のレリーフ状の彫刻によるインスタレーションが行なわれた。（MN）

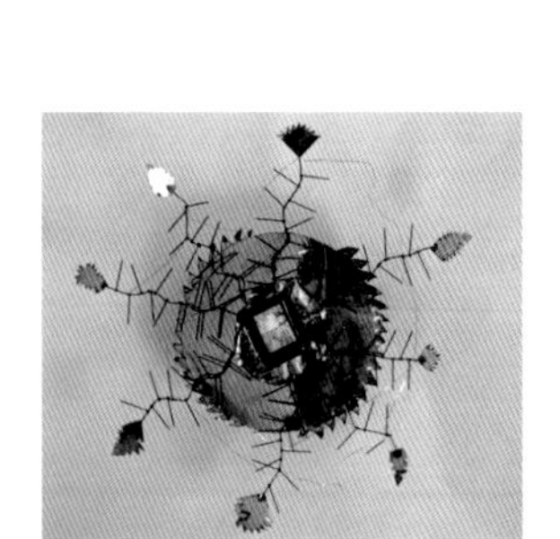

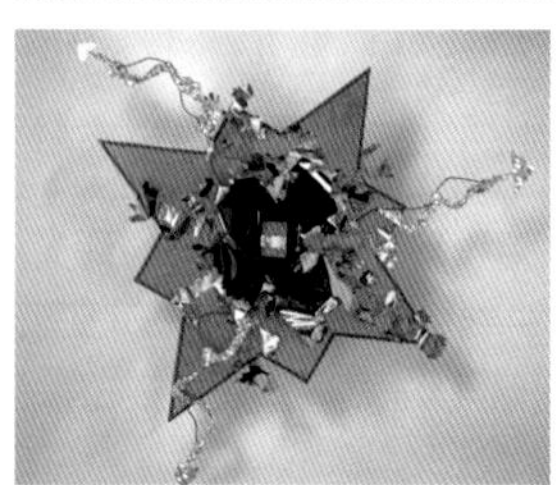

《風の花（アネモネ）》　1993年

《風車（かざぐるま）》　1993年

Video Poem; Windmill – Video Feed back

Wind from North
Wind from South
Wind from East
Wind from West
Wind from Ocean
Wind from Heaven

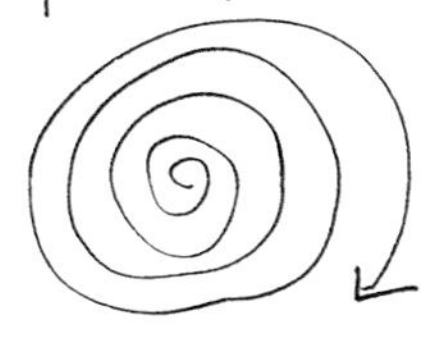

Wind from my heart, so soft wind, spring wind
wind from my head, so hard like Rock and stone,
Storm in my life,

Wind is hitting my face, hitting my body,
as faster as my mental speed,

please, pardon me,
what did I do wrong for you?

Wind, wind, wind, carrying my message,
for you, to whom I have ever, never met you yet
in my life.

P.S. This is my experience when I took a train from paris to Lyon – TVG.

リヨン・ビエンナーレ（1993年）カタログより

ヴィデオポエム、風車――ヴィデオ・フィードバック

北からの風
南からの風
東からの風
西らの風
海からの風
天国からの風

私の心から吹く風、それは優しい風、春風のよう
私の脳から吹く風、それは岩や石のように固い、
私の人生に吹き荒れる嵐のよう

風は私の顔に当たる、体に当たる
私の精神の速度と同じ速さで

すみませんが、
私は何かあなたに間違ったことをしたでしょうか？

風、風、風、メッセージを運ぶ
あなたへのメッセージ、まだこの人生で会ったことのないあなたへ

追伸　これは私がパリからリヨンへ向かう電車（TGV［本文ではTVG］）に乗っているときの経験

私が1976年にニューヨークのルネ・ブロック・ギャラリーでヴィデオによる作品《窓》を発表してから18年が経った。今年、1993年、リヨン・ビエンナーレで、私は《風―ヴィデオ［Wind-video］》を展示する。この18年のあいだに、《窓［Window］》は《風［Wind］》になった。つまり、《ow》が取り除かれて、より軽くなったのだ。

イヴ・クラインはセーヌの河岸で、袋に入った《セーヌの風》を売ったらしい。だがその時代、まだヴィデオは発明されていなかった。《風と共に去りぬ》は、20世紀前半を視聴覚的に描いたひとつの出来事だったわけだが、20世紀の後半、ヴィデオは人生と芸術の幸運な子供となった。来る世紀の幸運な子供*は何になるのだろうか？　21世紀、中国、旧ソ連、パキスタン、インドの20億もの人々が、大量消費の文化へと新たに突入していくだろう。

20世紀のあいだに大地を汚染したG7の国々は、こうした国の人々がこの先ずっと不幸で寒々とした生活を送ることを強いる道徳的権利などは持ち合わせていない。

こうした未来を前にして、新しいメディウムを風車として考えなければならない。

ヴェネツィアにて、1993年6月16日

＊この表現は、日本語で――筆者が強調するには――「風や雲を利用する子供」を意味し、それはつまり幸運のことである（日本語からフランス語への訳者註）。

1993

エデンの園

Garden of Eden

安齊重男《久保田成子、第45回ヴェネツィア・ビエンナーレ、ヴェネツィア、1993年6月》(上)
ヴェネツィア・ビエンナーレ(1993年)カタログより(下)

1996

ヴィデオ・イズ・ゴースト・オブ・ユアセルフ

Video is Ghost of Yourself

ランス・ファング・ギャラリー(1996年)での展示

《ヴィデオ・ツリー》、《ヴィデオ・フラワー I》、《風車》、《ヴィデオ・フラワー II》 1995年

1993年から96年にかけては、具象的な金属素材の彫刻が制作され、それらの組み合わせによるインスタレーションの発表が重なった。1993年のヴェネツィア・ビエンナーレの展示「エデンの園」のプランからは、実際の展示では作品数を絞ったと見られるものの、人型の彫刻を中心とした複数の作品を「物語的風景」として構成しようとしたことがうかがえる。1996年のホイットニー美術館での個展においても、《ジョギング・レディー》や《ピッシング・マン》の人型に加え、《鳥》や《韓国の墓》のようなプラスチック製鏡を多用した作品、回転する複数の《風車》、そして尖った金属片に小さなモニターが取り付けられた植物やコヨーテ、蛇などが床や壁いっぱいに設置され、それらを統合するように部屋全体にプロジェクションが投影された。観客は変化する色彩や反射にあふれる空間で、とげとげした金属彫刻のジャングルの中をかき分けるように進むことになる。同時期にランス・ファング・ギャラリーで開催された個展「ヴィデオ・イズ・ゴースト・オブ・ユアセルフ」でも同様に、プラスチック製鏡や金属素材の複数の作品が展示された。デジタルイメージの普及など映像イメージのあり方が変化した時代にあって、久保田の彫刻の中に使われる映像も液晶モニターによる小さなものになり、一方でそれらを組み合わせた環境的なインスタレーションによる新しい物語が紡がれるようになった。(MN)

1998

セクシュアル・ヒーリング

Sexual Healing

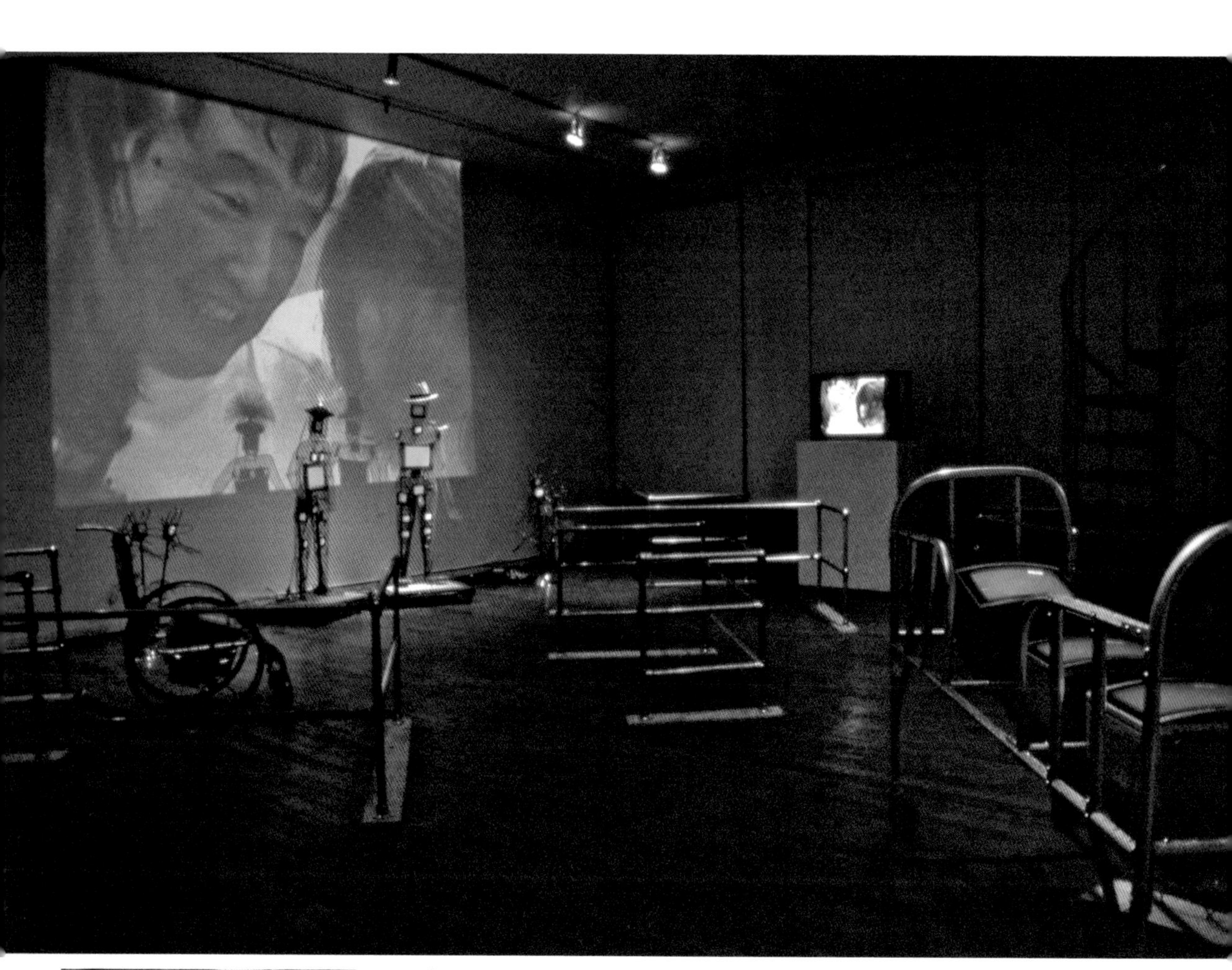

「セクシュアル・ヒーリング」展示風景

《セクシュアル・ヒーリング》1998年（スチル）

2000年のランス・ファング・ギャラリーでの「セクシュアル・ヒーリング」展は、同名のシングルチャンネル・ヴィデオを大きく映写した壁の前に、パイクと久保田自身を象徴したヴィデオ彫刻を置き、ベッドや車椅子に搭載されたモニターにも同じヴィデオを上映したインスタレーションであった。ヴィデオは、1996年に脳梗塞で半身麻痺となったパイクが、リハビリを行なう看護婦たちから、間接的に性的な刺激を受け、それが療養になっているということを、ユーモラスに描いた。同時期のヴィデオ、《4月は残酷極まる月》は、パイクが60年代初頭にドイツで行なったパフォーマンスや、ロボットを動かすなどの歴史的な映像を、自作の「韓国への旅」とマイアミで歩行のリハビリをする現在のパイクの映像などと組み合わせ、パイクへの長編オマージュとなった。2006年の《マイアミでの冬》は、パイクが13の時に作った曲をピアノで弾いた録音を背景に、ケアテイカーの撮った、公園のベンチに座る久保田とパイクの映像が流れる哀歌である。(MY)

「4月は残酷極まる月」と、かつてイギリスの詩人T. S.エリオットは言った。私の夫でヴィデオ・アーティストのナムジュン・パイクが 脳卒中で倒れたのも4月、3年前の復活祭の前夜だった。「僕はイースター・ベイビー。イエス様が復活したのだから、僕もきっとよくなるよ」と彼は言った。左半身が麻痺した身体で。

ナムジュンが入院した翌朝、健康的で若い女性セラピスト2人が、彼をベッドから連れ出しリハビリを始めた。大学を卒業したばかりのこの独身女性たちは、赤い口紅とタイツを身につけていた。彼女たちはナムジュンを赤ちゃんのように抱きしめ、その豊満な胸をぎゅっと押し付けた。

ナムジュンが初めてシャワーを浴びる練習をしたとき、彼女たちは興味深げに彼の裸を見て「肌も骨も、まるで40代のように若いですね」と褒めた。その時、彼は実際64歳だった。彼女たちは続けてこんなことも聞いた。「奥さんと正式に結婚しているの？」「子供はいるの？」もし子供がいないとしたら、不倫でもする気なのかしら？　私は戸惑った。

マーヴィン・ゲイの歌「セクシュアル・ヒーリング」よろしく、この病院では患者ひとりひとりに異性のセラピストを配してリハビリを行なっている。

彼女たちは私にこうも尋ねた。「あなたとパイクさんはヴィデオ・アーティストですよね？　カメラを持ってきたらどうですか？　彼の歩行療法をヴィデオに撮って、自分の姿を見られるようにしたらどうですか？」それまで私は、他の患者さんが怖がるのではないかと思って、病院にカメラを持ちこむことに抵抗があった。彼女たちの提案に勇気づけられ、私はリハビリをするナムジュンをヴィデオで撮影した。

「僕は見たくない」といって、ナムジュンはヴィデオを見ることを拒否した。たぶん彼は自分の身に起きた現実に向き合いたくなかったのだろう。

「セクシュアル・ヒーリング」のメロディに乗せて、私はナムジュンと彼のセラピストたちのためのヴィデオ作品をつくった。

2007

ナムジュン・パイクⅠ／ナムジュン・パイクⅡ

Nam June Paik I / Nam June Paik II

2006年に死去した長年の伴侶、パイクを弔い、彼の人生を湛えるため、久保田はパイクをかたどったヴィデオ彫刻2点を作った。１つは、鉄のパイプを使った抽象的な《ナムジュン・パイクⅠ》で、口、胸、両手、両足にあしらったモニターには、マイアミで療養しているパイクの姿が映っている。それでは飽き足らず、時代の反逆児パイクを描くには何がふさわしいかを考えた末、《ナムジュン・パイクⅡ》が生まれた。韓国からドイツ、日本、そしてアメリカと、地球を跨げたパイクは、文字どおり、半球体の上に載り、左手にバイオリン、右手に仏頭を手にしている。それらは、パイクの悪名高い、バイオリンを叩き壊すパフォーマンスと、後の《TV Buddha》という作品に言及している。目と口、体の内部がすべてヴィデオ・モニターになっており、そこには、パイクの人生のハイライトをモンタージュした《ナムジュン・パイクとの私の人生》が映る。(MY)

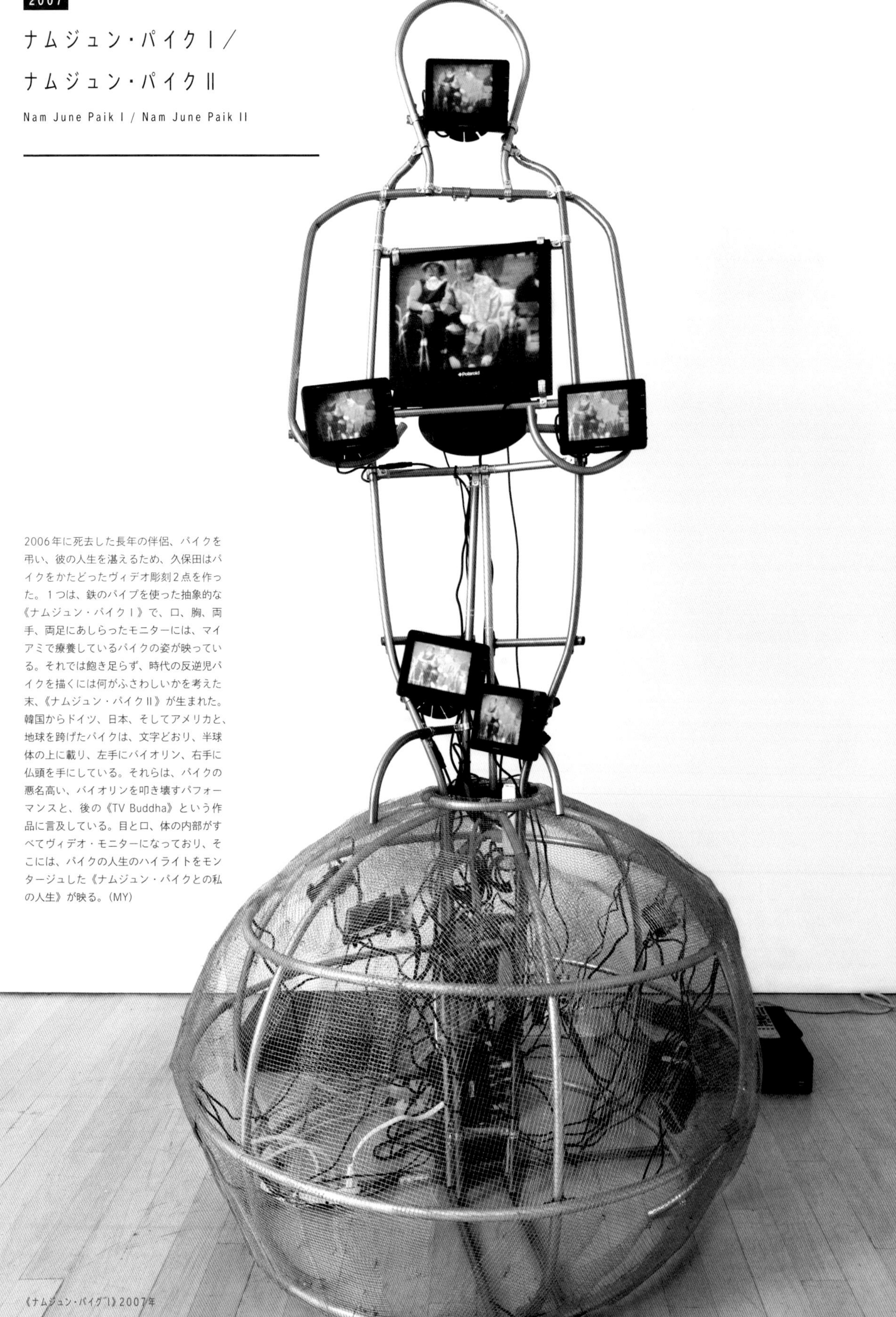

《ナムジュン・パイクⅠ》2007年

《ナムジュン・パイク II》2007年

2007

ナムジュン・パイクとの私の人生

My Life with Nam June Paik

ニューヨークで7年ぶりに、マヤ・ステンダール・ギャラリーで開かれた久保田の個展は、人生の半分以上を共に過ごし、喜怒哀楽を分かち合った、夫のパイクへの想い溢れるエレジーとなった。新作のパイクの彫刻2体に加えて、《鳥》の連作や《ジョギング・レディー》、《韓国の墓》などの1990年代の代表作が展示された。パイクは、久保田が「死」をヴィデオにした最初の作家だと語ったが、彼女の強みはたしかに、身内の死までも、芸術として昇華させることのできる、人生を冷静に見つめる目ではなかろうか。残念ながら、2010年以降、久保田自身も闘病し、制作活動の再開を見ず、この展覧会が最後の個展となった。(MY)

「ナムジュン・パイクとの私の人生」マヤ・ステンダール・ギャラリー（2007年）での展示

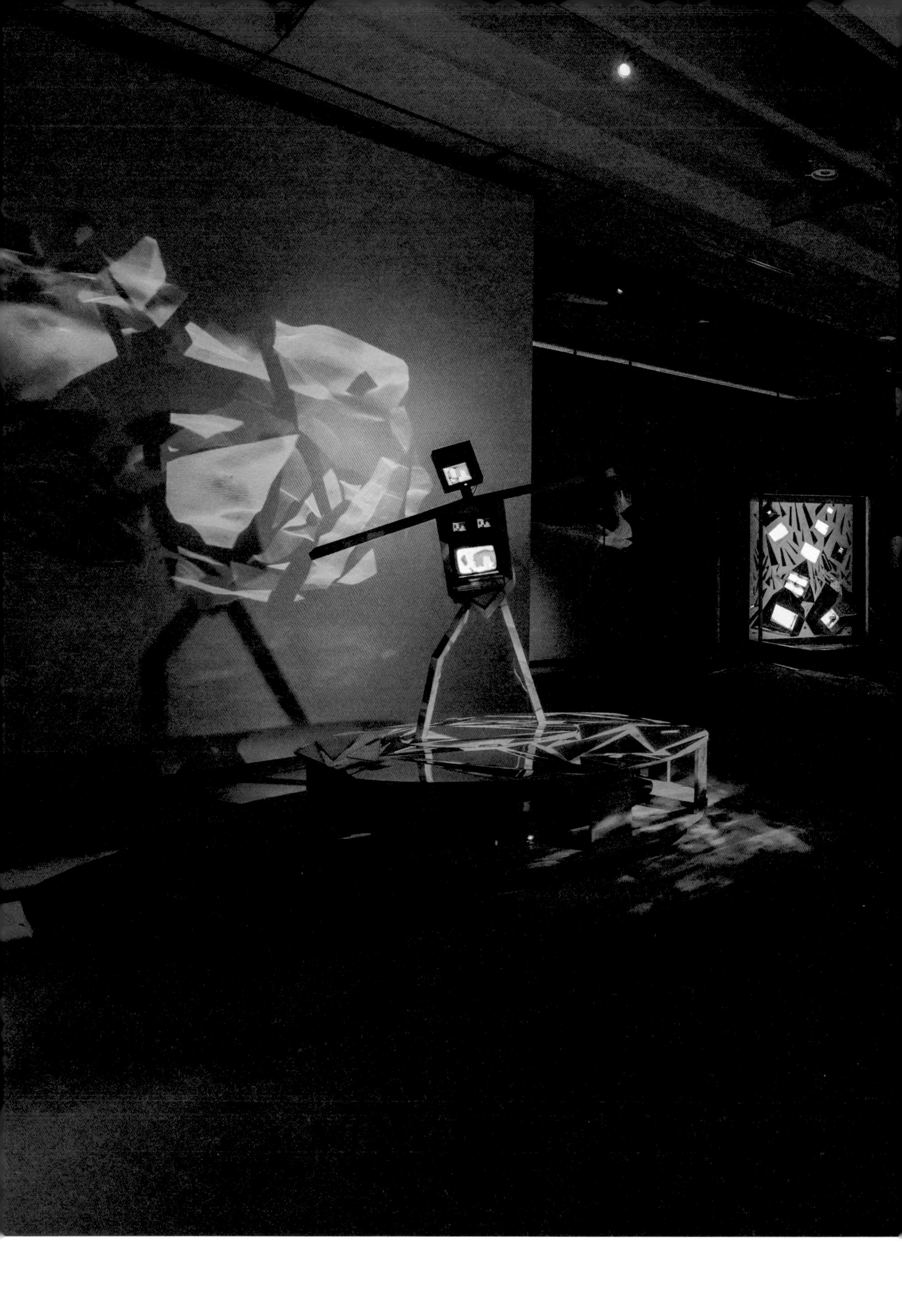

新潟県立近代美術館(2021年)での展示

唯一無二のヴィデオ・アーティスト

バーバラ・ロンドン

Barbara London：キュレーター、ライター。1946年生まれ。
ニューヨーク在住。

私が初めて久保田成子とナムジュン・パイクに会ったのは1973年、若いキュレーターだったころ。バスに飛び乗ると「こんにちは」とほがらかな声がして、私は2人の前の列に腰を下ろした。私たちが向かっていた先はシラキュース大学のシナプスTVスタジオ。学生だったビル・ヴィオラが、授業の一環で造った自作を熱心に見せていた。私を含めた30名ほどのヴィデオ通たちは、私と同じく若いキュレーターだったデイヴィッド・ロスがニューヨーク州芸術協議会の出資を得てシラキュース大付属エヴァーソン美術館で開催したカンファレンスに出席するために集まっていた。ヴィデオという、登場してまだ間もなかったこのアート形式をめぐって一同は白熱した議論を戦わせた。とくにヴィデオの生産、流通、展示がたがいにどのような関係にあるかが話題だった。参加者の顔ぶれは千差万別だったが、ヴィデオにのめり込んでいる点は共通していた。ヴィデオという媒体はまだ輪郭があやふやで、美術界の周縁でしかアートとして認知されていなかった。私たちはみな手さぐりで取り組んでいた。

このあとマンハッタンで成子とナムジュンは、2人を取り巻く多彩なアーティストや作曲家たちを惜しげもなく私に紹介してくれた。この人たちにかかれば、どんな思いつきも「天才的」、でなければ少なくとも「それ、ありでしょ！」ということになった。お互いに固く結ばれた、こうした仲間たちの騒々しい熱気が私の背を押してくれた。

付き合ううちに、「母権的」な性格の強い4人姉妹の家庭で育ったことが、成子の人格形成に影響を及ぼしているとわかってきた。舞踏家だったおばに触発された成子は、日本海沿いの雪山に囲まれた故郷を出て、彫刻を学ぼうと上京した。日本に深く根を張る、上下関係重視で愛国主義的な体制に逆らってあくまでひとりのアーティストとして生きた成子の勇気に、私はいまでも心を打たれる。

成子が1965年に行なったパフォーマンスはよく知られている。記録写真の彼女はヴァギナに絵筆を挿入して、足元に敷いた大きな紙に何か描いているところのように見える。いまではごくおとなしいものに（ひょっとすると人畜無害にさえ）感じられるかもしれないけれど、成子の行為がいかに大胆だったかは認識しておかなくてはいけない。同じころ世界の他の場所で、キャロリー・シュニーマンやヴァリー・エクスポートといった女性たちが力強い一歩を踏み出していたのと比べても、まったく遜色ない。家族や学校、教師、就職先などを基礎とする日本の社会秩序は、久保田のように独立心に富んだ女性たちに冷たかった。思ったことをズバズバ言う彼女は、外ではおしとやかに振る舞いうちでしか本音を出さないこの国の建前などおかまいなしだった。ニューヨークは彼女にぴったりだった。自分でいられる場所、アーティストとして伸びていける場所だったのだ。

友達思いで好奇心いっぱいの成子は面白い話が大好きで、すぐに腹を抱えて笑い転げた（とはいえ、前触れもなく心の奥底から怒りを爆発させることもたまにあり、そんなときは近寄らないのが得策だった）。パイクと暮らすマーサー通りの家で彼女はよく友人たちに夕食を振る舞った。ガタピシいうオンボロのオープン型エレベーターで建物の最上階にある2人の部屋に昇っていくのは命がけという感じがした。夫妻のスペースに足を踏み入れると、古いテレビや散らかった彫刻、ホコリをかぶった雑誌・カタログの山が行く手をはばんでいた。

私たちはキッチンに置かれた長いテーブルを囲み、初めはおとなしく何杯も緑茶を飲んだ。そのあと私たちが日本酒に切り替えるかたわらで、成子は包丁をふるって形の不ぞろいな刺身を切り分け、ご飯にお新香、味噌汁を添えて出してくれた。帽子をかぶったり友アレクサンダー・コールダーがデザインしたネックレスを着けたりした隣人のフランセス・ホイットニーが、よく裏口からぶらりと入ってきた。階下のロフトに住んでいるヨシ・ワダや嬰嘔が上がってきたり、場合によってはお隣のジョーン・ジョナス、近所の刀根康尚が姿を見せることもあった。ワイワイガヤガヤと会話は深夜までつづいた。

ある日、成子は《デュシャンピアナ：階段を降りる裸体》を見せてくれた。偶然マルセル・デュシャンに出会ったのがきっかけとなって生まれたヴィデオ彫刻だ。

興奮した口ぶりで彼女は、デュシャンと自分が乗っていた飛行機が、吹雪で〔ニューヨーク州〕ロチェスターに緊急着陸したのよ、と話してくれた。〔発想源となった〕デュシャンのコンセプチュアルな絵画に、成子の彫刻は第4の次元――時間――をつけ加える。彼女の手にかかると、人造の素材と自然の素材が二次元と三次元を優雅に調和させる。裸体が階段を歩いて降りるカラフルな抽象化されたイメージを映したモニター4台が蹴込に埋め込まれ、本彫刻の質素な合板に融合する。まぶたを閉じればいつでも、成子に頼まれてこの彫刻を制作した彼女の友人アル・ロビンスの姿が浮かんでくる。アルは熟練の職人であり、すごくいいアーティストだった。白人が髪をドレッドにすることなど思いもよらなかった当時から、もじゃもじゃのラスタヘアでキメていた。

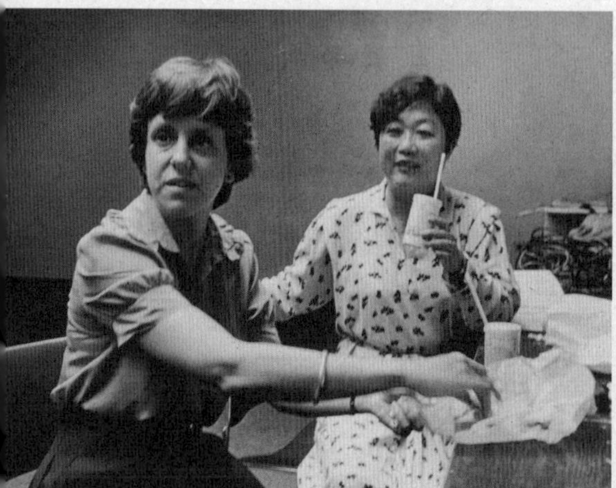

久保田成子とバーバラ・ロンドン、久保田成子「ヴィデオ彫刻―心理的風景から物理的風景へ」講演(ニューヨーク近代美術館)に際し、ロンドンのオフィスにて。1980年9月23日。
Shigeko Kubota and Barbara London in her office, on the occasion of Shigeko Kubota, "Video Sculpture: Mental Landscape into Physical Landscape," at MoMA on September 23, 1980.

私が資金集めをして《階段を降りる裸体》はニューヨーク近代美術館(MoMA)が購入した。同館コレクションに入った初めてのヴィデオ彫刻だった。成子はこれを誇らしく思い、スポーツクラブに入会するお金ができたと言ってとりわけ喜んでいた。

1970年代、アンソロジー・フィルム・アーカイヴズ(AFA)のヴィデオ部門キュレーターとして精力的に活動していた成子の姿はとくに強く印象に残っている。この当時AFAはウースター通り80番地の、フルクサスの煽動家ジョージ・マチューナスが特別に設計したスペースにあった。トイレに行こうと思ったら、とても踏面が狭く手すりのない階段を注意しいしい降りていかなければならなかった。

いつもアンテナを張り巡らせていた成子は、ニューヨーク内外の多彩なアーティストたちに呼びかけて毎週土曜の午後に彼らの新作を上映した。活発な質疑が交わされたあと、参加者のほとんどは近所の店に移動してビールを飲みながら議論を続けた。インターネットが登場する以前のこの時代、これこそが情報を共有するやり方だった。

パッとほほえむ成子、クックッと意味ありげに笑う成子、オシャレな服が大好きだった成子を私は一生忘れない。葬儀のとき、お気に入りのイッセイミヤケを着て、デザイナーものの大きな丸メガネをかけていたのは彼女らしかった。

12月に彼女の自宅でこぢんまりと開かれた追悼会では集まった人たちが、アーティストとして、キュレーターとして、そして友だちとして成子が重要な役割を演じたことを口々に証言した。現在、専任のスタッフが遺産管理にあたって彼女の名を冠した財団を設立しようとしているところだ。多産な生涯を通じてさまざまなことを成し遂げ、ヴィデオを周縁から本格的なアートの地位へと押し上げることに貢献した久保田成子の功績はもっと認められていい。

訳:近藤学

初出:『Millennium Film Journal』63号(Spring 2016)、85–86頁。

Media Maverick

Barbara London

Curator, writer. Born and lives in New York.
The first Video Curator at the Museum of Modern Art, New York.

As a young curator, I first met Shigeko Kubota and Nam June Paik in 1973. I heard a cheery hello when I hopped on a bus and grabbed a seat one row in front of them. We were en route to Syracuse University's Synapse TV studio, where an eager Bill Viola demonstrated his student work. Thirty or so of us video mavens were there to attend a New York State Council on the Arts funded conference at the Everson Museum organized by another young curator, David Ross. The group heatedly discussed particulars of the emerging art form, especially how its production, distribution, and exhibition go hand-in-hand. As disparate members of a fanatical community, we were all working seat-of-the-pants style with an amorphous medium that only the fringe deemed art.

Back in Manhattan, Shigeko and Nam June generously introduced me to their eclectic circle of artist and composer friends. They considered every idea brilliant, or at least plausible. Fiercely loyal, these rambunctious colleagues' enthusiasm encouraged me on.

I came to understand how Shigeko's strong "matriarchal" family of four sisters in Niigata shaped her. Emboldened by a choreographer aunt, she left her snowy mountainous home along the Sea of Japan to study sculpture in Tokyo. I am still struck by her courageous commitment as an artist contradicting Japan's deeply entrenched, hierarchical and chauvinist system.

The photo of her famous 1965 performance, in which she squats with paintbrush seemingly inserted in her vagina and draws on a large sheet of paper under her feet, might appear tame or even innocuous today. Yet we need to recognize the boldness of her action, equal to the strong steps taken in other parts of the world by her peers Carolee Schneemann and VALIE EXPORT. Japan—with its social order based on family, school and teacher (*sensei*), professional affiliation—did not support independent-minded women like Kubota. Outspoken, she broke the mold by not toeing the national line of presenting a polite face in public and a candid one in private. She was comfortable in New York, where she could be herself and develop as an artist.

Loyal and curious, Shigeko loved a funny story and readily exploded with a hearty belly laugh. (But you steered clear, when every once in a while a deep seated anger suddenly erupted.) She often invited friends for dinner in her and Paik's home on Mercer Street. Going up in the old rickety, open cage elevator to their loft on the building's top floor, you felt you were taking your life in your hands. Entering their space, you encountered a hodgepodge of old TV sets, sculpture in disarray, and dusty stacks of magazines and catalogs.

We would sit around their long kitchen table, at first formally drinking cup after cup of Japanese green tea. We would move on to sake, as Shigeko wielded her knife and cut large irregular slices of sashimi, accompanied by rice, oshinko, and miso soup. Their neighbor Frances Whitney would wander in through the back door, wearing a hat or necklace designed by friend Alexander Calder. Yoshi Wada and Ay-o would emerge from their lofts downstairs, maybe Joan Jonas from next door, and Yasunao Tone from around the corner. Boisterous conversations ran long into the night.

One day Shigeko showed me *Duchampiana: Nude Descending a Staircase*, her video sculpture that evolved out of a chance encounter with Marcel Duchamp.

She excitedly described how both had been grounded in Rochester during a blizzard to Duchamp's conceptual painting. In her hands manmade and natural materials elegantly harmonize two- and three-dimensions. She melded her electronic apparatus, including four monitors showing colorful abstracted image of a nude walking down a set of stairs, set in the risers within the humble plywood of the sculpture. In my mind's eye, I will always see her friend Al Robbins, who built the sculpture for her. Al was a master craftsman and terrific artist who sported a messy tangle of Rastafarian-style hair, long before Caucasian ever considered dreadlocks.

I raised the monies and MoMA acquired *Nude Descending a Staircase*, the first video installation to enter its collection. This made Shigeko proud and especially happy, because she now had enough money to join a health club.

I have strong memories of Shigeko as the energetic video curator at Anthology film Archives during the 1970s. These were the days of the 80 Wooster Street space, specially designed by Fluxus instigator George Maciunus. You proceeded with extreme caution, if you walked down the very narrow steps without railings to use the restrooms.

With her keen ear to the ground, Shigeko invited a broad spectrum of local and out-of-town artists to present new work on Saturday afternoons. After lively question-and-answer, most of us continued the conversation over a beer at a joint nearby. Pre-Internet, this was an essential form of information-sharing.

I will always remember Shigeko for her bright smile and meaningful chuckle, as well as her love of fashionable clothes. It was fitting that at her funeral she wore a favorite outfit designed by Issey Miyake and her large round designer glasses.

In December at a memorial in her home, a small group gathered to acknowledge the importance of her roles as artist, curator and friend. Now a dedicated team of executors of her estate is setting up a foundation in her name. Shigeko Kubota is most worthy of greater recognition for her many accomplishments and contributions to a field that she helped transition from fringe to full blown art during a productive lifetime.

First appearance: *Millenium Film Journal*, 63 (Spring, 2016), pp. 85–86.

久保田成子の破顔

島敦彦

しま・あつひこ：1956年生まれ。国立国際美術館館長。

ちょうど40年前の1981年、裸の女性が繰り返し階段を降りる映像に目を奪われた。映像は、現在のようなプロジェクションや液晶画面ではなく、階段状の木箱に組み込まれた4台のブラウン管時代のモニターTVに流れていた。

階段を降りる女性の動きは、時に急速に、時に緩慢に、時に顔だけがクローズアップされ、独特のリズムを刻む。カメラのアングルは上下斜めに激しく移り変わり、裸体はフォトグラムを思わせる妖しい光を纏う。約3分の短いループ映像だが、4台同時に映るので、増幅したイメージが観客を捉えて離さない。

久保田成子のヴィデオ彫刻《デュシャンピアナ：階段を降りる裸体》（以後、《階段》）との初めての出会いであった。展示場所は、かつて東京・池袋にあった西武美術館のロビー。開催中の「マルセル・デュシャン展」にちなんで、《メタ・マルセル　ウインドー》［タイトル表記は当時］（以後、《窓》）と共に賛助出品されていたのだ。その詳しい経緯は分からないが、デュシャン展の図録に「According to Marcel」と題した1ページが久保田成子に割かれているので、誰かからの提案があり、展覧会に関わった美術評論家の東野芳明らの了承があったのだろう。

それから2年後の1983年、久保田成子のヴィデオ彫刻を展示する機会が訪れる。富山県立近代美術館（現在の富山県美術館）で開かれた「第2回現代芸術祭－芸術と工学」展の出品作家に久保田成子が選ばれたのである。作家の選考は、彫刻家の伊藤隆道、九州芸術工科大学教授の松本俊夫、筑波大学教授の山口勝弘の3人の実行委員によって行われた。私は同館に学芸員として就職してまだ4年目であったが、理工学部出身という経歴であったことから、担当者となった。もっとも映像機器類の扱いには弱かった。ともあれ、ヴィデオ・アートはもとより、空気彫刻、キネティック、ライト、ホログラフィ、コンピュータ・グラフィックスなどアートとテクノロジーに関する総合的な展覧会を実現するべく奔走した。

久保田に早速、手紙と電話（FAXもメールもなかった）で連絡を取り合い、出品作は、デュシャン展と同様、《階段》と《窓》に決まった。階段状の木箱や窓枠を取り付ける展示台は、すべて富山の施工業者が作り、小型のモニターTVも調達した。税関から裸体を問題視する連絡が入った際は冷や汗をかいたが、西武美術館での展示歴を伝えて、ヴィデオテープは無事到着。掲載写真は、できたての《階段》の木箱を囲んで歓談する出品作家たちだ。

展覧会の終了後、富山県立近代美術館は《階段》を購入し、《窓》は寄贈という形で、いずれも同館のコレクションとなった。日本の公立美術館が、こうしたヴィデオ彫刻を所蔵する先鞭をつけることになった。ちなみにニューヨーク近代美術館は、バーバラ・ロンドン企画による「プロジェクツ」（1978年）で発表後の1981年に《階段》を所蔵している。

久保田は図録に寄せた文中、「抽象化された時間が、永遠にマルセル・デュシャンに捧げた作品が、瀧口修造先生の郷里で展示されるのも、非常にビデオ的な時間の体験と、その偶然性に感慨無量である」と記した。瀧口修造は、富山県出身の詩人・美術評論家で、デュシャンと深い親交があったことはよく知られている。

久保田は、富山県立近代美術館に作品が所蔵されたことを、過剰なほどに喜んでくれた。というのも、これは後になって気づいたことだが、久保田の夫で、ヴィデオ・アートの道を共に歩む同志でもあるナムジュン・パイクと絶えず比較されてきた久保田は「パートナーの芸術世界を真似ただけの二番煎じの作家であると後ろ指を指されるかも知れな」いという「強迫観念」に苦しんでいたからだ。こんな回想もある。「ナムジュンは、お金がいくらかかるか一切考えず数十台、数百台のテレビを買って作品を作る一方、生計を立てていかなくてはならない私は、多くて四、五台、しかも故障したテレビだけを使って作品を制作した」ことがしばしばであった*1。

ちなみに、久保田の作品が富山で紹介された翌1984年にはナムジュン・パイクの大規模な個展が東京都美術館で開催され、大変な注目を集めることになる。

久保田成子とは、その後、ニューヨークのスタジオで再会したし、脳梗塞で倒れたナムジュン・パイクがリハビリしていた頃、スタジオ近くのカフェでくつろいでいる場所に居合わせたこともある。フルクサスを特集した1990年のヴェネチア・ビエンナーレで偶然出くわしたこともあった。会うたびに「富山では本当にお世話になったわ。でもね、島さん、なぜかずっと展覧会貧乏よ！」と豪快に笑いとばしていた久保田の破顔を今でも忘れられない。

［註］
*1——久保田成子・南禎鎬著『私の愛、ナムジュン・パイク』高晟埈訳2013年、平凡社、151頁。

Shigeko Kubota's Big Smile

Atsuhiko Shima

Director of the National Museum of Art, Osaka.
Born in 1956.

Exactly forty years ago, in 1981, I was captivated by looping footage of a nude woman walking down stairs. Rather than being projected on a wall or an LCD screen as it would be today, the footage was shown on four CRT-era TV monitors encased in a wooden staircase construction.

The movement of the woman descending the stairs was sometimes rapid, sometimes slow.Occasionally only close-ups of her face were shown, and the footage played in time with its own peculiar rhythm. The camera shifted jerkily, pointing up or down, or diagonally across, to veil the nude body with mysterious, photogram-like lights. Although this short looping footage was only about three minutes long, as it was played simultaneously on four monitors, the multiplied visual images enchanted viewers.

「芸術と工学」展にて。1983年6月。
左：望月菊磨　中：幸村真佐男　右：久保田成子。
撮影：島敦彦
At the exhibition "Art and Technology," on June 1983.
Left: Kikuma Mochizuki Center: Masao Kohmura Right: Shigeko Kubota
Photo: Atsuhiko Shima

That was my first encounter with Shigeko Kubota's video sculpture *Duchampiana: Nude Descending a Staircase* (hereinafter *Staircase*). In conjunction with the *Exhibition of Marcel Duchamp*, it was exhibited in the lobby at the Seibu Museum of Art in Ikebukuro, Tokyo as an auxiliary work, alongside *Meta Marcel: Window* (hereinafter *Window*). I do not know the details of how this came to pass, however, since a page titled "According to Marcel," was devoted to Kubota in the exhibition catalog, it is likely that someone made a suggestion, and Yoshiaki Tono, an art critic involved in the exhibition, approved it.

Two years later, in 1983, there was another opportunity for Shigeko Kubota's video sculpture to be exhibited. Kubota was selected as one of the artists for the exhibition "The 2nd Contemporary Art Festival: Art and Technology" at the Museum of Modern Art, Toyama (now the Toyama Prefectural Museum of Art and Design). The artists were selected by three executive committee members—Takamichi Ito, a sculptor, Toshio Matsumoto, a professor at Kyushu Institute of Design, and Katsuhiro Yamaguchi, a professor at the University of Tsukuba. It was only four years since I had started working as a curator at the museum, however, as my academic background was science and engineering, I was tasked with organizing the exhibition. With that being said, I was not good at handling video equipment. In any event, I hustled to realize a comprehensive exhibition on art and technology, including air sculpture, kinetic art, light art, holography, and computer graphics, as well as video art.

I got in contact with Kubota right away—but still via letter and phone call, as there was neither fax nor email at the time. Similar to the Duchamp exhibition, we decided to exhibit *Staircase* and *Window*. The wooden staircase construction and the display pedestal for the window frame were all fabricated by a manufacturer in Toyama, and small-sized TV monitors were also procured. I broke out in a cold sweat when customs officials contacted us saying that they had a problem with the nude body. However, as we told them about the work's exhibition history at the Seibu Museum of Art, the videotape was allowed through and arrived safely. The photo shown here depicts the artists who participated in the show chatting around the freshly fabricated wooden construction for *Staircase*.

After the exhibition, both *Staircase*, which was purchased by the Museum of Modern Art, Toyama and *Window*, which was generously donated by the artist, became part of the museum's collection. The addition of these works into the Museum's collection paved the way for the inclusion of video sculptures in the collections of many public art museums in Japan. It might also be noted that the Museum of Modern Art in New York acquired the *Staircase* in 1981, after it was exhibited in *Projects* (1978), curated by Barbara London.

In her text for the catalog Kubota noted, "the fortuitous opportunity of having my work, a tribute to Marcel Duchamp, dealing with abstracted time—a temporal experience highly characteristic of video—exhibited in Mr. Shuzo Takiguchi's hometown makes me speechless with emotion." The poet and art critic Shuzo Takiguchi, well-known for his close friendship with Duchamp, was from Toyama prefecture.

Kubota was more than delighted that her work was acquired for the collection of the Museum of Modern Art, Toyama. As I later found out, Kubota, who was frequently compared with her husband and comrade Nam June Paik, with whom she pursued video art, had been suffering from an 'obsession' that people would criticize her as being an artist who was rehashing her partner's art. She also recalled, "Whereas Nam Jun would buy dozens or even hundreds of TVs to make his work without thinking of cost at all, I, who had to make a living, produced my work using only four or five TVs at the most, and what was worse, they were broken. "*1

Incidentally, in 1984, a year after Kubota's work was introduced at the Toyama, a large-scale solo exhibition of Nam June Paik's work was held at Tokyo Metropolitan Art Museum, and drew much attention.

I met Shigeko Kubota again at her studio in New York. I also happened to see her relaxing at a coffee shop by her studio, at the time when Nam June Paik was undergoing rehabilitation after collapsing from a stroke. I have also run into her at the Venice Biennale, which featured Fluxus artists in 1990. Every time we met, she would say, "Thanks for everything that you did for me in Toyama. But for some reason, Mr. Shima, don't ask me why, I have been going broke from having shows!" Then she would heartily laugh it off. Her big smile brings back fond memories. How I miss that smile.

Translation by Yuzo Sakuramoto

*1 —— Shigeko Kubota and Nam Jeong-ho, *My Love, Nam June Paik*, trans. by Seong-Jun Ko,(Tokyo: Heibonsha, 2013), p. 151.

光輝く存在

ローリ・ジッペイ

Lori Zippay：作家、キュレーター、コンサルタント。
元エレクトロニック・アーツ・インターミックス（EAI）の総合ディレクター

「芸術は生活を模倣する／生活は芸術を模倣する」は、成子の作品に頻出するテーマであって、私には彼女の芸術と生活はほぼ切り離せないように思えます。私はエレクトロニック・アーツ・インターミックス（EAI）で働き始めた1981年の夏に、成子とナムジュンに初めて出会いました。２人のアーティストは、1970年代初期のEAIの草創期からEAIと密接に関わっていました。彼らのシングルチャンネル作品はEAIにより、配給、保存、編集されており、仕事上でのわれわれの関係は、何十年も続く友人関係へと発展しました。

1970年から、成子は自分の日常生活を記録した、「ブロークン・ダイアリー」と総称される、類い稀な自伝的ヴィデオ作品を作り始めました。近年、私はこれらのヴィデオ日記を何時間もかけて鑑賞し、その率直性と親密性に魅了されてきました。また作品がもたらしてくれる、アーティストとして、また一個人としての彼女についての新たな発見にも魅了されてきました。これらの日記は、成子の大胆さ、元気のよさ、茶目っ気のあるユーモアを捉えると同時に、時に積極的で快活な彼女の裏側にある、稀にみる痛ましいほどの暗さを捉えています。カメラに写る彼女は、アーティスト、妻、キュレーター、フェミニスト、患者、看護人といった、プリズムのように分割された役割を同時に満たす上での矛盾と複雑性を湛えています。また、われわれが知り合う前の彼女の過去──例えば戦時中にお腹が減っていたことを低い声で語るとき──などの、個人史についての手がかりを与えてくれます。さらには、彼女を知る者たちはすぐに気付くであろう、女性としてのアイデンティティの力強い意識と強靭さも伝えてくれます。

EAIが1988年にブロードウェイ536番地に引っ越したとき、われわれの施設は成子とナムジュンの二次的なスタジオと化し、２人は頻繁にそこを訪れました。われわれは、19世紀のロンドンにあったような空気圧のチューブでマーサー・ストリートのスタジオとEAIを繋いでテープを送りあえたら、などと冗談を言ったものです。ナムジュンの死後は、成子がひとりでEAIのチェルシーの事務所に来て、当時技術監督であったトレヴァー・シミズとよく編集をしました。40年近く年下の彼を彼女は「ミスター・シミズ」と丁重に呼んでいました。歩くのが難しくてもイッセイ・ミヤケのドレスでお洒落をしていた彼女は、ソーホーに戻るためにタクシーを呼ぶ手助けを、いつも優しく、しかし堅く断るのでした。

2018年に成子のヴィデオ彫刻《河》が「Before Projection: Video Sculpture 1974–1995」展の一部として、スカルプチャー・センターに設置されたとき、私はとりわけ感動し、静かながらも強力な鑑賞体験だと感じました。1983年のホイットニー美術館での展示も見ていましたが、35年以上の時を経ても、この作品が並々ならぬものであることに感銘を受けました。流れる水をたたえる優雅な銀色の容器の上に、３台の重たいテレビモニターが、太いケーブルによって、絶妙な緊張感をもって逆さに宙吊りにされていました。その水に映るモニターのイメージは、成子に特徴的な電子プロセスを経て抽象化され、鮮やかな色をして、意識の流れのような視覚詩として作用するのです。鑑賞中にもうひとつはっと気付いたのは、若い女性である作家自身が泳いでいる姿でした。この泳ぐという動作によって、成子は自分の身体的な存在と個人的な物語とアイデンティティを、実際の水の流れのなかに、そして反射するヴィデオの川の流れのなかに持ち込んだのです。

成子は《河》についてこのように書きました。「泳ぐ身体は軽々と水に浮き、たやすくスピンし、潜る。ヴィデオの現実のなかに投じられると、無限のバリエーションが可能になり、重みのなさだけでなく、あらゆるかたち、形状、色、場所、速度、スケールをまったく自由に分解し、再構築し、変化させることができるようになる」。今になってようやくこの卓越したアーティストの貢献がより広く調査され、認められようとしています。成子は、ヴィデオのなかに「重みのなさと全くの自由」を見出すことで、人生から芸術を創り出し、芸術から人生を紡ぎ出した、光輝く存在でした。

訳：由本みどり

A Luminous Presence

Lori Zippay

Writer, curator, consultant, former Executive Director
of Electronic Arts Intermix (EAI).

"Art imitates life/Life imitates art" is a motif that recurs in Shigeko's works, and to me her art and her life were almost inseparable. I first met Shigeko and Nam June in the summer of 1981, when I started working at Electronic Arts Intermix (EAI), a nonprofit media art organization. Both artists were closely associated with EAI from its origins in the early 1970s—their single-channel video works were distributed and preserved by EAI, and often edited there—and our professional relationship grew into a friendship that spanned the decades.

Beginning in 1970, Shigeko created an extraordinary series of autobiographical video works—collectively titled *Broken Diary*—that chronicled her everyday life. I have spent hours with these video journals in recent years, fascinated by their candor and intimacy, and what they add to my experience of her as an artist and individual. The journals capture Shigeko's boldness, her spiritedness, her mischievous humor and, at times, a harrowing darkness rarely seen behind her outwardly bright demeanor. She appears on camera in all of her complexity and contradictions, inhabiting a prismatic series of roles—artist, wife, daughter, curator, feminist, patient, caregiver. Glimpses of a past that long predated our meeting—as when she speaks with a haunted voice about being hungry in wartime Japan—hint of a deeper personal history. The diaries also convey a forceful sense of female identity and strength that is immediately recognizable to those who knew her.

When EAI moved to a loft at 536 Broadway in 1988, our facilities became like an adjunct studio for Shigeko and Nam June, who made frequent and buoyant visits. We would joke about installing a pulley system across Broadway to shuttle tapes between their Mercer Street studio and EAI, or a network of pneumatic tubes, like those in nineteenth-century London. After Nam June's death Shigeko would come to EAI's offices in Chelsea alone to edit with our then-technical director Trevor Shimizu, whom she would invariably and respectfully address as "Mr. Shimizu," although he was some forty years her junior. Walking with difficulty but still dressed beautifully in Issey Miyake, she would always—graciously but firmly—refuse help in hailing a taxi back to SoHo.

In 2018, when Shigeko's video sculpture *River* (1979–1981) was installed at the Sculpture Center in New York as part of the exhibition *Before Projection: Video Sculpture 1974–1995*, I found it to be particularly moving, a quietly powerful revelation. I had seen the original installation at the Whitney Museum in 1983, but from a vantage of almost thirty-five years I was struck by its eloquence. Three bulky TV monitors, dangling from heavy cables, are suspended upside-down in exquisite tension over an elegant silver trough holding a flowing stream of water, upon which images from the monitors are reflected. The imagery mirrored in the water—Shigeko's signature electronic processing, shifting abstracted forms, vibrant colors—functions like a stream-of-consciousness visual poem. Upon this viewing I was struck by something else: images of the artist as a young woman, swimming. With this gesture, Shigeko brought her physical presence, her personal narrative and identity, into the literal flow and reflections of her video river.

Shigeko wrote of *River*: "The swimming body floats lightly upon the water, spins and dives with ease. Once cast into video's reality, infinite variations become possible, not only weightlessness but total freedom to dissolve, reconstruct, mutate. . . ." A remarkable artist whose contributions are only now being fully recognized and explored, Shigeko was a luminous presence who found in video the "weightlessness and total freedom" to create art from her life and life from her art.

論考・インタビュー

Texts

ヴィデオ―開かれた回路

久保田成子

初出:『芸術倶楽部』第9号、1974年6月30日発行、173-181頁。
言葉遣いは原文ママとしたが、明らかな誤植は訂正した。

ヴィデオ文化(カルチユア)のある大きい部分は、麻薬文化(ドラグ・カルチユア)やヒッピー文化(カルチユア)がそうであったように、反体制の哲学であり、共同体の文化である。

それは現代のリアリティを象徴し社会現象を反映する若者のエネルギーの融合である。

ヴィデオ芸術は、芸術が芸術自体をコミュニケートするメディア・コミュニケーションの一部分であり、芸術自体を日常化している。

ヴィデオ芸術は、あなたの生活の些細な部分、深く眠っている潜在意識を戦慄させ、マイナリティ・コンプレックスを表面化し、個々と個々への連帯感と問題意識を結ぶメディア・コミュニケーションである。

戦争やインフレーションになった時ほど、人間は、そのインフォメーションに飢餓する。それは、個々に迫る社会的危機感とインフォメーション・キャッチのルートの速度と浸透性を比例させ、あなたとメディア・コミュニケーションの関連は、あなたの生活にとって必然的なフィードバックとなる。

私は、常に芸術自体をコミュニケーションにし、コミュニケーション自体を芸術にするプロセスとコンセプトに興味を持っていた。それを実現させたのが、ヴィデオ芸術である。

ヴィデオ芸術は、“トゥー・ウェイズ・コミュニケーション”の芸術である。それは、上から与えられる芸術ではなく、横から横へ、地平線から地平線を結ぶグローヴァル・コミュニケーションであり、インフォメーションの社会学的な交換から、美学的に人間の存在感を確認し合うフィードバック系の芸術である。

恋人と恋人がベッド・インした時の感覚が、新鮮なスキンシップの体験であるように、ヴィデオ芸術を体験することは、あなたの人生観と空間的次元が拡大され、ニュー・ライフ・スタイルのメディア・コミュニケーションというメルヘンへ旅立つことである。その現代のメルヘンとは、犬も喰わぬウォーターゲートのスキャンダルであり、真昼下がりのソープ・オペラであり、そして私も含めたあなたのヴィデオ・ライフの体験である。

私の肉体は、ヴィデオ・ライフの体験と、インフォメーションのカクテルである。

私は何も好きこのんでソニーのヴィデオ・ポータパックを背中にかついでいるのではない。しかし、日本の古典的な女性が背中に赤ん坊を背負ったように、赤ん坊も生めない現代の女性は、何を背中に背負うことができるのか。

私は、ヴィデオ芸術というエレクトロニック・ハイウェイを突っ走っている無重力のオートモビールである。それはカルダーのモビールのようにゆっくりだったり、タージマハル旅行団[*1]の演奏のように、熱いトタン屋根を這い回る遊動の世界の密室であったりする。

ヴィデオ芸術は、ヴァジャイナのヴィクトリーであり、ヴェンジェンス（復讐）である。

ヴィデオ芸術は、その繁殖化と腐蝕化において、インテリの頭脳の反VD（反性病）である。

ヴィデオ芸術は、体制側の既成テレビのインフォメーションの独占からの解放である。
本当に重要でデリケートな現代の主題――政治、哲学、セックス、アヴァンギャルド活動などは、ヴィデオ芸術の本命であり、既成のテレビでは、けっして公平に公開されていない課題である。

VIDEO FREEXは、ウッドストックの村で無許可のテレビ海賊局を発信し[*2]、『ホール・アース・カタログ』のヴィデオ版のようなプログラムを制作している。数人のVIDEO FREEXのメンバーたちは畑を耕し、ヴィデオ・コミューンを作り、赤ん坊が生まれると、ちょうど彼らの畑の野菜の栽培をヴィデオで記録するように、その自然分娩をヴィデオで記録する。
ビンガムトンのエクスペリメンタル・テレビ・センターの連中が、ニューヨークのゲットーに潜伏して、スーパーマーケットの強盗略奪の現場をキャッチしたり、公道でヘロインを売買する子供たちをヴィデオ・テープにおさめたが、それはけっして、既成のテレビからあなたの家庭のリヴィング・ルームにとび込んでくるテレビ番組ではない。『ゲリラ・テレビジョン』の著者、かつて週刊誌『タイム』のメディア記者だったマイクル・シャンバーグは、マイアミの民主党大会へ行き、CBSのニュース・チーム自体を取材し、その報道性の真偽を正面から観客に訴えている。
これらは、ヴィデオ芸術におけるストリート・ゲリラの一環として行なわれた社会活動の一例である。
ヴィデオ芸術は、ニュー・ライフ・スタイルのレヴォリューションである。その日常性と観念の政治的なレヴォリューションが、メディア・コミュニケーションという媒体を通して芸術に再問するラディカルな行為である。
ヴィデオ・ポータパックとカメラは、一人でかつげて、一人でどこへでも危険を犯して潜伏でき、インフォメーションを多角度から採掘し、インフォメーションの地図を拡大し、観客にインフォメーションの選択のチャンスを与える。

非正統的なライフ・スタイルの革命的意義において、倒錯（パーヴァーション）していることは、反(サヴアージョン)乱することである。

第三の性の解放なしにセックスの解放がありえなかったように、メディアの改造なしに社会の改造はありえないのである。

そして、アーティストも、ストリート・ゲリラになるなんて、ずいぶんラディカルではないか！

現在、ヴィデオ芸術の人口が一番密集しているのはニューヨークであり、サンフランシスコである。そして、デュッセルドルフ、アムステルダム、パリへと点火している。

ヴィデオ芸術のハードウェアが高度に発達している場所は日本であるが、ヴィデオ芸術のソフトウェアが高度に発達している場所はニューヨークである。かつてポップ・アートが狂い咲きした土壌ニューヨークは、ポップ・アートの崩壊やアクション・ミュージックやストリート・ハプニングの細粉をカルチュアの肥料として、ヴィデオ芸術という種子を必然的に萌芽させた。

ハプニング、アース・アート、エレメンタル・アート、コンセプチュアル・アート、プロセス・アート、ボディ・アートは、自然や自我との相対的な概念を空間と観念の白紙の上に展開し、その記録性を必然とした消滅の芸術である。

飛行中に事故死したアース・アートの先駆者ロバート・スミッソンは、彼の作品が彼自身の事故死のように、アクシデントな芸術であることを知っていた。

観客も参加できない隔離された自然環境の中にアーティストが孤立した時、その疎外環境と疎外観念との接点は、インフォメーションを媒体としうるトゥール（道具）——写真、フィルム、ヴィデオ・テープレコーダー、立会人——なしに成立しない。コンセプチュアル・アートも、アヴァンギャルド・アートもメディアを排除しては存在しえなかった。

ヴィデオ芸術は、マイクル・スノウの延々と続くフィルムのコンセプトや、アンディ・ウォーホルの“リール・タイム”のフィルム、すなわち、現在の時限がだらだら続く、撮影しっぱなしの時限のコンセプトからその表現方法を影響されていることは確かだ。しかしそれは、ラ・モンテ・ヤングの永遠の旅への演奏——ドリーム・ミュージック（亀、その夢と旅）が、アンディ・ウォーホルの一連の初期のフィルム『エンパイア』『眠り』『食べる』『チェルシー・ガールズ』のリール・タイムのフィルムのコンセプトに影響を与えたように、ヴィデオ表現にフィードバックしてリサイクルしている。

リール・タイムの観念は、ニューヨークのロフトに住み、二十四時間が一日であるという観念を放棄した非日常性の中に棲息している現代のアーティストの呼吸のリズムである。

デュッセルドルフに住み、ヴィデオ・ギャラリーを唯一の表現方法としていたゲリー・シャムは、彼のフォルクスワーゲンのトラックの中をヴィデオ・スタジオとして、ヴェネチアの運河を渡り、不毛の大地へとコンセプチュアル・ヴィデオ・アートの表現の可能性を展開した。しかし、彼のエゴとコンセプチュアル・ヴィデオ・アートとの反比例化した進行度ゆえにか、若くして自殺してしまった。それは、彼の高度なエリート意識による行為と観念の挫折である。

現代の芸術は、額縁からはみ出し、ギャラリーや美術館に依存しない方向へ進行している。それは、かつてギャラリーや美術館が虚像にしたスターたちはソサイエティの伝説として生き、ポップ・アート以後、特定のスターを生めない、生んでいない芸術は、芸術自体をノー・サブジェクト、ノー・オブジェクトとして日常化している。

『コネクション』『クール・ワールド』『ジェイソンの肖像』などのフィルムを制作した女流フィルムメーカーだったシャーリー・クラークは、ある日、突然、フィルムを放棄し、ヴィデオにファック・インした。

彼女は、"ヴィデオは、わたしの新しいペニスだ"と宣言した。そして、その彼女の新しいペニスであるヴィデオの機能性、メカニズム、そしてその用途を、彼女流に研修し、マスターした。それは、けっしてフィルムの創作過程で、得ることのできなかったxの分野の芸術表現であった。

彼女の住むチェルシー・ホテルのペントハウスは、サイバネティックな玩具箱か、ジャンク・ボックスになった。三つの部屋と庭や空間は、カウンター、ウォーターゲートの方法で配線され、チェルシー・ホテルに住んでいる風来坊たちを電子的な線と点で結んだ。そしてニューヨークという風景――エンパイア・ステート・ビルディングやハドソン河を背景に、天然色の絵ハガキの毒々しい色のようにgroup psychotherapy（グループ精神治療）をくりひろげる。

これはHight Artにおきかえられた新しいHight Lifeとして、一つのヴィデオ環境を日常生活の中に提供している。それはアーティストばかりでなく、建築家、環境デザイナー、精神分析学者、社会主義者や医師が、ポスト＝インダストリーの時代の中に見出す未来の生活と芸術のヴィジョンを暗示している。

人間はたえず未来のヴィジョンに目を向ける創造的なカテゴリーに属する種属である。

一月二七～二九日、ニューヨークの現代美術館で開催された研究会議「オープン・サーキッツ――テレビジョンの将来」はその一例である*3。open circuits（開かれた回路）という言葉は、白南準の昔のマニフェスト（66年）からとられた。

第一日目は「テレビジョンの構造」という課題で、エクスペリメンタル・テレビジョンにおける世界的な傾向というパネル・ディスカッションで始まった。ドイツ、フランス、日本、そしてアメリカを中心に、各国におけるヴィデオ芸術のムーヴメントの現状報告。日本代表として、松本俊夫氏が日本のヴィデオ芸術に対する客観的な報告と、フィルムとヴィデオの相違や、その創作的な体験に関する深い洞察に充ちた論文を発表した。私は、たまたま一月七～九日、東京の天井桟敷でビデオひろばとアンダーグラウンド・センターの主催した「東京―ニューヨーク　ヴィデオ・エキスプレス」の報告をした。特にアメリカにおけるウーマン・ヴィデオと日本におけるウーマン・ヴィデオを中心にスピーチをした。ビデオひろばの主軸、中谷芙二子さんのヴィデオ活動とその作品、出光雅子〔編註・正しくは真子〕さんの『Work of Woman〔編註・おんなのさくひん〕』や、道下匡子さんの『Being woman in Japan,

Liberation within a Family』は、ウーマン・ヴィデオの分野においても、ヴィデオ芸術の総体的分野においても、優秀な作品である。
その第一日目の午後は、「ヴィデオ・シンセサイザーの起源」という題で、ヴィデオ・シンセサイザーを阿部修也氏とともにつくりあげた白南準と、サンフランシスコのKQED局で活躍しているスティーヴン・ベックの作品を中心に見ながら、パネル・ディスカッションに入った。
白南準と阿部修也氏が一九六三年以来、研究しているヴィデオ・シンセサイザーは、今までのテレビの映像のイメージのコンセプトをひっくりかえした。ジョン・ケージが沈黙の音楽を作曲したように、そしてマルセル・デュシャンが便器をアート・オブジェクトにしたように、そしてアンディ・ウォーホルが一ドル紙幣をシルクスクリーンに多量に刷ったように、白南準は、既成のテレビのイメージを破壊し、テレビというクールな媒体による芸術、ヴィデオ芸術を創造した。白南準は、テレビやヴィデオを油絵のように、そして粘土のように創造的媒体のトゥールとして、今まで誰も表現しなかったテレビ芸術、ヴィデオ芸術のジャンルを創造したのである。
「オープン・サーキッツ」の第二日目の課題は「テレビジョンの美学」で、朝の九時から『アート・マガジン』の編集長でミニマル美学の理論家であるグレゴリー・バトコックの「Not Good for the Family: the Sociology of the Set」という長文の論文で始まった。これは、マクルハーン以後の機知と英知が開花するメンタルテストのような論文であった。
その次に、ヌーボーとした風貌のホリス・フランプトンが、「The withering away of the State of the Art」という題で、淡々と演説する。ホリス・フランプトンは、マイクル・スノウやケン・ジェイコブズとともに構造映画の旗手であるが、最近はヴィデオにその触手を伸ばしている。
「映画は、芸術であるが、ヴィデオは神である」というジョナス・メカスの皮肉な格言をはさみながら、目をかたく閉じた時、瞼の裏に浮かぶ幻影を映画に表現しようと、二十年来格闘しているスタン・ブラッケージが、ヴィデオ・シンセサイザーの前で白南準と禅問答している仮想談を披瀝する。
第二日目の午後にエド・エムシュウィラーは講壇の裏に隠れ、自分のイメージをヴィデオで撮って、間接的に「Image Maker meets Video, or Psyche to Physics and Back」という題の奇妙なヴィデオ談義を行なった。
スタン・ヴァンダービークは、カリスマ性に充ちたスピード感で「Social Imagistics: the Artist and Television」という題で演説し、通信衛星で世界の隅々を照らし、壮大な宇宙大交響曲をテレ゠コミュニケーションで結ぼう、と宣言した。
その後、嬰児をかかえるように、丸いテレビ・モニターをかかえたシャーリー・クラークは、チェルシー・ホテルの浮浪人たちが泣いたり笑ったりするヴィデオ・テープをプレーして、観客にその表情を模倣させた。
ダグラス・デイヴィスは、「Time! Time! Time! the Context of Immediacy」という題で、通信衛星を通じて、ドイツのヨーゼフ・ボイスと交信する新しい芸術形態などについて話した。
夜のパネル「Video and Perception, the Place and Nature of the Viewer」では、帽子の型を四十分以上も変えてヴィデオで見せるジョン・バルデッサリ、エヴァソン美術館で植物、鉱物から光のスペクトルまで結ぶ大システム・アートを展開したフランク・ジレット、ヴィデオとの緊密な交流のもとに新しいダンス・フォームを開拓しつつあるジョン・ジョナス、ハプニングでおなじみのアラン・カプロー、若く精力的なヴィデオ・キューレーターのデイヴィッド・ロス、そしてコンセプチュアル・アーティストのリチャード・セラなどが、作家のヴィデオ的な意見を発表した。「オープン・サーキッツ」の最終日は、「The Politics and Philosophy of Television」という課題で開かれ、西ドイツのラディカルな詩人H・M・エンツェンスベルガーは、「Television and the Politics of Liberation」という論文を発表し、ケーブル・テレビ（＝CATV）、そしてポータパックのヴィデオ・テープも含めて、テレビとは、とかく体制側に利用されやすいと悲観的な見解を述べた。

その後、スイスの美術批評家ルネ・ベルガーは、「ヴィデオと神話の回復」という題で既存のマクロ・テレビ（たとえばNHK）と新しいテクノロジーであるメッゾ（中間）テレビ、ポータパックやカセットのようなミニ・テレビの三者が平行して、あるxへ到達するであろうという楽観的な見解を発表した。彼は、日本でリサーチした結果、日本でメッゾ・テレビやミニ・テレビが発達していない理由は、日本の社会が均質的な社会で、マイナリティがいないのに起因しているのではないか、と発言した。

日本でも翻訳された『未来の未来』の著者ジョン・マックヘールは、「The Future of Television: Some Theoretical Considerations」という講演をするはずだったが、これはくだらない会議であると宣言して、途中で家へ帰ってしまった。

夜の座談会は「ヴィデオと美術館」という題で開かれた。出席者のクリストファー・コックは、マサチューセッツの小さな町でアーティストが美術館を媒体として、回復期の精神病患者にヴィデオによる精神治療を行なっていることを報告している。アルゼンチンのホルヘ・グルースベルグは、チリ、ブラジル、アルゼンチンのような南米のファッシスト国でアーティストたちがいかに拷問され、傷つけられ、死んでいったかを切々と訴えた。シラキュウスのエヴァーソン美術館の館長であり、ヴィデオ芸術の発達に絶大な貢献をしたジム・ハリタスは、美術館とケーブル・テレビ局が融合して、各家庭に二十四時間、古今東西の美術の名作をカラーで送りとどけ、新しいアヴァンギャルドの芸術、ヴィデオ芸術を一家団欒のゴールデン・アワーの主軸にし、市民たちの同時参加を、電話とテレメトリーとテレビ電話を中心にして芸術化するロマンを展開した。

こうした「オープン・サーキッツ」の会議の総括として、ヴィデオ芸術において最も関心のある課題と方向を区分してみよう。

（1）エクスペリメンタル・アートとしてのエクスペリメンタル・テレビ。ネットワーク、特に教育テレビ局のWNET、WGBH、KQEDにおいてはヴィデオ・アーティスト、フィルムメーカー、ダンサー、音楽家による実験的な表現活動と作品を実際に放映している。一九六九年にボストンの教育テレビ局WGBHで制作された『Medium is Medium』は、もはやヴィデオ芸術における古典であり、現在、ニューヨークの教育テレビ局WNETでは、白南準の『Gloval Groove』、エド・エムシュウィラーのコンピューター・ヴィデオの作品『SCAPEMATE』、マイクル・シャンバーグの新作『TV, TV』を放映し、既成のテレビ番組に飽きた聴衆者に好評である。

（2）ヴィデオ芸術へのアプローチとして、カステリ・ギャラリーやソナベント・ギャラリーを代表とするコンセプチュアル・ヴィデオ芸術がある。たとえば、ウィリアム・ウェグマンのヴィデオ・テープは、二〜三分の作品の連続であるが、愛犬との日常些細な行為をシュールなウィットで知的に構成している。彼の愛犬が、アンディ・ウォーホルのフィルム『眠り』のように人間のベッドで毛布をかけて眠っていると、目覚時計のベルがけたたましく鳴る。愛犬は、彼自身のようにベッドからとび起きて走り出す。また、ヴィト・アコンチのコンセプチュアル・ヴィデオ・テープは、彼自身が床にひっくりかえっている時間が一時間も続く。また、彼自身が自分のセックスの体験を話し、どうしてもセックスができなかった体験から、第三の性へ転換する自己内部のプロセスをヴィデオ・カメラの前で告白する。

（3）ヴィデオ芸術の最もポピュラーな表現手段としてのdo it yourselfは、ヴィデオ・ドキュメンタリーである。ポータパックをかついでストリート・ゲリラとなり、ケーブル・テレビ、ゲリラ・テレビと、新しいラディカルなカウンター・カルチュアをグループで作る。

しかし、ヴィデオ芸術は、けっしてヴィデオ・テープ芸術だけではない。

（4）ヴィデオ芸術は、ヴィデオ環境、ヴィデオ・シアターをクリエートするライヴ・ヴィデオ・パフォーマンスを忘れることはできない。ヴィデオ・テープの上映が、電子音楽のテープ・コンサートであるとすれば、ライヴ・ヴィデオ・パフォーマンスはライヴ・ミュージックであり、チャンス・オペレーションが偶発し、観客の参加ハプニングも発生する。

「オープン・サーキッツ」では、ヴィデオ・テープはコマ切れのように短く上映された。むしろ、ヴィデオ・ディスカッションのほうに重点がおかれた。

ニューヨークでは、すでにヴィデオ・テープの氾濫で、過剰インフォメーションの中からわれわれが選択する段階に来ている。つまり、一方交通のコミュニケーションに観客は飽きてきている。

「東京―ニューヨーク　ヴィデオ・エキスプレス」の時、六時から十一時半まで、あのむさくるしい埃だらけの天井桟敷の冷たい床に座って、山もりのヴィデオ・テープを見ていた日本の観客に、私はたまげてしまった。まったくインフォメーションへの好奇心であり、飢えである。

メディアは、芸術を複雑化し、しかもそれをまき散らす。

メディアは、観念を物理的実体と同じレヴェルまでエスカレートさせる。

メディアは、公共的な、あるいは私有の経済構造に潜伏している力を拡散する。

メディアは、美術館やギャラリーに内在するようなハイ・エネルギー的露出に比べればロー・エネルギー的な露出だが、しかし、そのチャンネルはずっと広く、本性上、平等である。

［編註］

＊1――タージマハル旅行団（Taj Mahal Travelers）は1969年に小杉武久により結成された音楽集団で、伝統的な楽器を用いた即興演奏で知られる。小杉は久保田の東京時代のボーイフレンドだった。

＊2――Videofreexについては次を参照。https://www.vdb.org/content/videofreex-archive-preservation

＊3――同会議の発表者の名前、発表タイトルなどは次を参照。Douglas Davis, et al. *The new television a public/private art; essays, statements, and videotapes: based on "Open Circuits: An International Conference on the Future of Television"* (Cambridge, MA: MIT Press, 1978).

Video - Open Circuits

Shigeko Kubota

The first appearance: *Geijutsu Kurabu*, No. 9, 1974, Tokyo, pp. 173–187.

A large part of video culture is based on community and an anti-institutional philosophy, like the drug and hippy cultures were.

It is a fusion of youth energy, symbolizing contemporary reality and reflecting the social phenomenon.

Video art is part of media communication in which art communicates itself and turns into everyday life.

Video art electrifies minute aspects of your life and subconscious which are deeply asleep. It is media communication which connects the consciousness of individuals by revealing their insecurities.*1

Humans crave more information in times of wars and economic instability. This need accelerates the feeling of societal crises upon individuals and the speed and permeability of information follow suit. Media communication becomes a necessary feedback in your life.

I was always interested in the concept and process of art becoming communication and communication becoming art. Video art realizes this.

Video art is the art of "two-ways communication." It is not art which is given from the top, but global communication which connects one horizon to another, side to side. It is an art of feedback which confirms the presence of humans aesthetically through the sociological exchange of information.

As the feeling of lovers' intimacy in bed is the experience of fresh skinship, to experience video art is to expand on your life philosophy and special dimensions, and to depart for a fairy tale of media communication; your new lifestyle. The Watergate scandal is a contemporary fairy tale which even dogs wouldn't want to consume, while soap operas in the afternoon are your (and mine) experience of video life.

My body is a cocktail of video life experience and information. I don't necessarily prefer carrying this [SONY] Portapak on my back. As traditional Japanese women carried a baby on their back, what can a contemporary woman carry on her back when she can't even have a baby?

I am a levitating car which runs on an electronic highway called video art. It can be as slow as a [Alexander] Calder mobile, and as intimate a traveling space as a Taj Mahal Travelers' performance, moving about as on a hot tin-roof.*2

Video art is Victory of Vagina, and Vengeance of Vagina.

Video art is anti-Venereal Disease of Intellectuals in terms of its proliferation and corrosion.

Video art releases the media's monopolized information from institutions. Very delicate contemporary problems such as politics, philosophy, sex, and avant-garde movements are at the heart of video art, and they are never dealt with fairly in today's media.

VIDEO FREEX [Videofreex] is an illegal, pirate television station from the village of Woodstock which airs and produces programs which are like video versions of the *Whole Earth Catalog.**3 Several members of VIDEO FREEX cultivate the land, make a video commune, and document the natural births of their babies, just as they document the growth of the vegetables in their field.

People running the Experimental TV Center in Binghamton immersed themselves in the ghettos of New York and witnessed an armed robbery in a supermarket, and recorded kids who are selling heroin on the street. This content is far from the typical TV programs which invade your living room. The author of *Guerrilla Television*, Michael Shamberg, who used to be a journalist for *Time*, went to the Republican National Convention in Miami, (covered by the CBS news team), to directly ask the audience about the reliability of the reporting.

These are examples of social activities which are carried out as part of the street guerrilla tactics of video art.

Video art is a revolution of the new lifestyle. Its concept, and the political revolution of the ordinary, reframes art itself as a radical act, through the medium of media communication.

Portapaks enable one to carry a camera by oneself, take the risk of immersing yourself anywhere, collect information from various angles, expand the information landscape, and provide the audience a chance to select information.

In the revolutionary definition of the non-traditional lifestyle, to pervert is to subvert.

Sexual freedom was not possible without the freedom of the third sex. Similarly, the restructure of society is not possible without the restructure of media.

Isn't it quite radical for an artist to become a street guerrilla!

At present, the population of video art is most concentrated in New York City and San Francisco. It has spread to Dusseldorf, Amsterdam, and Paris.

While the hardware of video art was highly developed in Japan, the software of video art was highly developed in New York. As the land where Pop art crazily flourished, New York consequently germinated the seed of video art within the compost of the collapsed movements of Pop art, Action music, and Street Happenings.

Happenings, Earth art, Elemental art, Conceptual art, Process art, and Body art enfold the relationship between nature and self within concepts and on white sheets of space; ephemeral arts requiring documentation.

The pioneer of Earth art, Robert Smithson, who died in an airplane accident, knew that his work was accidental art, like his own accidental death.

When an artist isolates himself in a remote natural environment, where the audience cannot participate, the contact between the isolated environment and isolated concept is not possible without tools which use information as a medium—photography, film, a video recorder, and a witness. Conceptual art and avant-garde art could not exist without media.

Truly, video art derives its methods of expression from the temporal concept of continuous recording, where the present continues forever, such as in Michael Snow's films and Andy Warhol's "reel-time" films. But it is recycled in video expression as a feedback, as La Monte Young's performance for an endless journey—*Dream Music* (*The Tortoise: His Dream and Journeys*) influenced by the concept of early "reel-time" films by Warhol, such as *Empire*, *Sleep*, *Eat*, and *Chelsea Girls*.

The concept of "reel-time" is the breathing rhythm of contemporary artists who live in the extra-ordinary by forgetting the fact that a day consists of twenty-four hours, living in New York lofts.

Gerry Shum, who lived in Dusseldorf and had a video gallery as his only expressive outlet, turned his Volkswagen bus into a video studio, crossed Venetian canals, and brought the possibility of conceptual video art into the infertile land. But, perhaps because his ego and conceptual video art did not progress in parallel, he killed himself at a young age. It was an action taken due to his extreme elitist consciousness and failed concept.

Contemporary art stepped out of frames and is developing toward a direction not dependent on galleries and museums. Those stars whom galleries and museums made into virtual images continue to live as legends in society, while art, which hasn't produced a star since Pop art, becomes part of daily life by turning itself into no-subject and no-object.

Shirley Clark, the former woman film maker who produced such films as, *Connection*, *Cool World*, and *Portrait of Jason*, suddenly gave up on film and "fucked in" video.

She proclaimed that "video is my new penis." Then, in her own way, she learned and mastered the function, mechanism, and usage of video, which was her new penis. That was artistic expression in the "X"-field [unknown dimension], which she could never obtain in the filmmaking process.

The penthouse of the Chelsea Hotel where Shirley lives has turned into a cybernetic toy or junk box. Its three rooms and garden space are wired like a Watergate surveillance operation, which connects eccentric residents of the Chelsea Hotel through electric lines and dots. Group psychotherapy sessions unfolded against the backdrop of New York—the Empire State Building and Hudson River—in shocking, picture-postcard colors.

Video environments are offered in everyday life as a new "high life" instead of "high art." This suggests a vision for art and life in the future, to be sought in our post-industrial era not only by artists, but also by architects, environmental designers, psychoanalysts, socialists, and doctors.

Humans, as a species, belong to a creative category which constantly look toward a future vision.

The research conference, "Open Circuits—Future of Television," held at the Museum of Modern Art, New York, from January 27 to 29, was such an example. The term "open circuits" was borrowed from the old manifesto (1966) of Nam June Paik.

The first day, entitled, "Structure of Television," began with a panel discussion on global trends in experimental television. The current state of video art movements in Germany, France, Japan, and North America were reported. Representing Japan, Toshio Matsumoto gave an objective report on Japanese video art and presented a deeply insightful paper on the difference between film and video in his creative experience. I did a report on the "Tokyo—New York Video Express" organized by Video Hiroba and Underground Center at the Tenjō Sajiki Theater in Tokyo on January 7–9. I talked specifically about women's video in the United States and Japan. Video practice and the work of Fujiko Nakaya, the central figure of Video Hiroba, *Work of Woman* by Mako Idemitsu, and *Being Woman in Japan, Liberation Within a Family* by Kyoko Michishita are excellent works among women's video, and video art as a whole.

In the afternoon of the first day, a panel discussion entitled "Origins of Video Synthesizers," took place, primarily examining the works of Steven Beck from public television station, KQED in San Francisco and Nam June Paik, who created a video synthesizer with Shuya Abe.

The video synthesizer, which Nam June Paik and Shuya Abe have been developing since 1963, has subverted the pre-existing concept of images on television. As John Cage composed the music of silence, Marcel Duchamp turning a urinal into an art object, or Andy Warhol mass producing a dollar bill by silkscreen, Nam June Paik destroyed the existing image of television and founded video art with the cool medium of television. Paik created a genre of TV art or video art which no one had realized before by treating TV and video like oil painting and clay, as a creative "tool."

On the second day, the theme of "Open Circuits" was "Aesthetics of Television." It began at 9 a.m. with a long paper, "Not Good for the Family: The Sociology of the Set," by Gregory Battcock, the Minimalist theorist and the editor of *Art Magazine*. This was a mentally challenging examination of the flourishing of wisdom and knowledge since [Marshall] McLuhan.

Next, Hollis Frampton, with his enigmatic appearance, gave a matter-of-fact speech on "The Withering Away of the State of the Art." Along with Michael Snow and Ken Jacobs, Frampton was a leading figure in Structuralist films, but has recently touched on video as well.

Stan Brakhage presented a fictitious Zen-koan-like conversation with Paik in front of a video synthesizer, citing Jonas Mekas' satirical saying: "Film is art, but video is God." He has struggled over two decades to try and describe the impressions which appear on his retina when he shuts his eyes tight.

In the afternoon of the second day, Ed Emshwiller hid himself behind the stage, broadcasting his own image through video, while indirectly giving his strange lecture, "Image Maker meets Video, or, Psyche to Physics and Back."

Stan VanDerBeek gave a charismatic and lively speech, entitled, "Social Imagistics: the Artist and Television." He proclaimed his aim of using satellites from every corner of the world to broadcast and realize a big space symphony through telecommunication.

After that, Shirley Clark cradled a round TV monitor like a baby, played videotapes of vagrants at Chelsea Hotel crying and laughing, and asked the audience to imitate their facial expressions.

In his speech, entitled, "Time! Time! Time! The Context of Immediacy," Douglass Davis talked about a new form of art in which he can communicate with Joseph Beuys in Germany through a satellite.

The evening panel, "Video and Perception, the Place and Nature of the Viewer," consisted of presentations of John Baldessari's video of the continuously changing shape of a hat over 40 minutes, Frank Gillette, who developed a major art system which connects plants and minerals to the light spectrum at the Everson Museum, Joan Jonas who is exploring a new dance form based on intimate exchanges with video, Allan Kaprow, who is known for Happenings, the young and energetic curator, David Ross, and the conceptual artist, Richard Serra.

The last day of "Open Circuits" was titled "The Politics and Philosophy of Television." The radical poet from West Germany, H. M. Enzensberger, presented a paper, "Television and the Politics of Liberation," commenting pessimistically on the fact that television, including cable TV and videotapes made with [SONY] Portapak, have been taken advantage of by the institutions.

Later, in his talk, "Video and Restructuring of Myths," the Swiss art critic, René Berger, gave an optimistic vision in which the existing macro TV (such as NHK—Japanese public television station), the newer technologies of "mezzo (middle)" TV, and mini TV such as Portapak, will reach a certain "X" by developing in parallel. After conducting research in Japan, he concluded the reason why mezzo and mini TV haven't developed in Japan was because Japanese society is homogenous and doesn't have a significant minority.

Jon McHale, the author of *The Future of Future*, which has been translated into Japanese, was supposed to lecture on "Telefutures: Prospective Observations," but complained that it was uninteresting and left mid-conference.*4

The evening roundtable discussion was "Video and Museum." One of the participants, Christopher Cock, reported on the artists conducting psychotherapy using video to mental patients in recovery through a museum in a small village in Massachusetts. Jorge Glusberg from Argentine decried how artists were tortured, hurt, and killed in fascist countries in South America, such as Chile, Brazil, and Argentine. James Harithas, Director of the Everson Museum in Syracuse, New York, who made great contributions to the development of video art, presented a vision in which museums and cable television would merge and broadcast color images of art masterpieces from around the world to homes 24 hours a day. He also dreams of turning the new avant-garde art, video art, into a central pillar of prime-time family entertainment, and making the simultaneous participation of people through telephone, telemetry, and TV phone into art.

As a summary of the "Open Circuits" conference, let me isolate the most interesting issues and directions in video art.

1) Experimental television as an experimental art. Various networks, especially such public educational television stations, such as, WNET, WGBH, KQED, are actually broadcasting experimental artistic activities and works by video artists, filmmakers, dancers, and musicians. "[The] Medium is [the] Medium" produced by Boston's educational television, WGBH in 1969, has

become a classic in video art. At present, WNET, New York's educational television, is broadcasting Nam June Paik's *Global Groove*, Ed Elmshwiller's computer video, *SCRAPMATE*, Michael Shamberg's new work, *TV, TV*, and receiving good responses from an audience who are tired of the existing TV programs.

2) Conceptual video art represented by Castelli Gallery and Sonnabend Gallery exists as another approach to video art. For example, the videotape by Wiliam Wegman repeats a few-minutes segment depicting an ordinary action with his beloved dog, but in an intellectual composition filled with surrealistic wit. While his loving dog is sleeping with a blanket in a human bed, as in Andy Warhol's film, *Sleep*, an alarm clock rings loudly. The dog jumps up and starts running, like his surrogate. A conceptual videotape by Vito Acconci shows him lying on the floor for one hour. He confesses in front of a video camera his experience of sex and the internal process of him turning into the third sex from the difficulty of having a sex.

3) The most popular method of expression in video art, "do it yourself", is video documentary. Carrying a Portapak, an artist becomes a street guerrilla and becomes part of a group, producing a new, radical counter-culture through a cable TV and guerrilla TV.

But video art is never limited to videotapes.

4) In video art, one cannot forget about video environment and the live performances which create video theater. If the screening of a videotape becomes a concert of electronic tape music, a live video performance is a performance where chance operation and audience-participation Happenings can occur.

At the "Open Circuits," videotapes were screened in short excerpts. The focus was placed, rather, on video discussions.

In New York, videotapes have proliferated to the point where we have to make a selection from the excess information. The audience is growing tired of one-way communication.

At the time of *Tokyo—New York Video Express*, I was surprised by the Japanese audience who watched loads of videotapes while sitting on the dusty cold floor of the Tenjō Sajiki Theater from 6 p.m. to 11 p.m. It was due to their curiosity and thirst for information.

Media complicates art and distributes it everywhere.

Media elevates concepts to the level of physical substance.

Media disseminates the power inherent in public or private economic structure.

Media's exposure involves low energy compared to the high energy exposure of museums and galleries. But its channels are broad and essentially fair.

Translated by Midori Yoshimoto with editorial assistance by Gus Tsekenis

[Translator's Notes]

*1——Kubota used "minority complex" in Japanese here, but it seems to refer to inferiority complex or insecurities.

*2——The Taj Mahal Travelers were an experimental music group out of Tokyo, which performed improvisational drone music using Eastern and Western instruments, electronics, and vocal chants. The founder was the composer Takehisa Kosugi, Kubota's former boyfriend and a member of Fluxus.

*3——The *Whole Earth Catalog* was an American counterculture magazine and product catalog published by Stewart Brand several times a year between 1968 and 1972. See https://www.moma.org/interactives/exhibitions/2011/AccesstoTools/

*4——Although some of the presentation titles Kubota had were different, they have been replaced with the correct ones published as follows. Douglas Davis, et al. *The new television a public/private art; essays, statements, and videotapes; based on "Open Circuits: An International Conference on the Future of Television"* (Cambridge, MA: MIT Press, 1978).

久保田成子インタビュー

聞き手＝ジュディス・グリア

このインタビューは、1992年に原美術館で開催された個展「クボタ シゲコ ビデオ インスタレーション」に際して英語で行なわれ、未公開であった。本カタログ掲載のため、文字起こしと編集を行なった。編註は〔　〕内にまとめた。資料提供：公益財団法人アルカンシエール美術財団原美術館提供。文字起こし・編集・和訳：近藤学

―はじめに久保田さんの生い立ちについておうかがいします。大学は東京で？

K　美術系の、東京教育大っていうところの学生でした。いまの筑波大学。彫刻と構成と、美術史を勉強しました。

―お生まれは東京ですか？

K　いいえ、新潟生まれ、雪国の。

―きょう『雪国』読みました。

K　川端〔康成〕の有名なあれね。

―わたし〔ニューヨーク州〕バッファロー生まれなんです。バッファローにはいらしたことがありますよね？

K　ええ〔バッファローは〕知ってますよ。住んでたこともあるのよ。

―えっ、本当に？

K　半年間。

―そうなんですか。寒いですよね。

K　寒くて、冬は吹雪（笑）。でも寒いところは好きなのよ、雪国生まれだから。わたし冬はいつも運がいいのよ。シカゴにも教えに行ってた。シカゴ美術研究所。あそこも寒いでしょ。

―あそこは本当に寒いですね。

K　でも私の郷里はすごく寒くって。シベリアから風が日本海を渡ってくるから。でもなぜだかわからないけど、夏より冬のほうが調子がいいんですよ。

―夏は辛いですよね。

K　〔冬は〕脳が縮んで、凍りついて、鋭くなるのよね。

―私もそんな感じの脳です。

K　子供のころの冬のことはずっと覚えてる。いいわよね。幻想的よ、寒い冬は。半分凍ったイメージで。イリュージョンよね。

―ニューヨークの夏も辛いですね。

K　ええ、でもわたし、生まれたのは夏なのよ（笑）。でたらめでしょ。

―誕生日はいつですか？

K　８月２日。獅子座なのよ。

―いまこの夏の終わりに東京にいらっしゃるわけですけれども。

K　夏の終わりってなんだかおごそかよね。三島〔由紀夫〕の小説か何かみたいで。夏の終わりって季節の終わりでしょ。新しい季節の始まり。わたしも新しくスタートできる。だから夏の終わりに日本に戻ってきて、アーティストになりたいって思った自分の最初の野心を再スタートできるのはいいわね。

―前回東京に来られたのはいつですか？

K　２年前。

―東京にはよくいらっしゃいますか？

K　ううん。

―1986年に東京にいらしゃいました。それ以前には？

K　19歳でした、学生のとき。おばがいて。舞踊家で、邦正美（くにまさみ）に師事したの。邦さんというのは朝鮮の舞踊家で、東大に行った方。

―おばさまは邦正美の生徒だった、と。亡くなられましたか？

K　いえいえ、まだ踊ってますよ。

―まだ踊っていらっしゃる？

K　ええ、即興舞踊、創作舞踊。だからわたしが子どものころおばが東京にいたので、ときどき訪ねていって。わたしが高校生のとき、個人授業を受けに東京に来てたんです、彫刻の授業。

―そのころ東京で彫刻を習っていた先生はどなたですか？

K　高橋清（たかはしきよし）先生。

―有名な方ですか？

K　いいえ、わたしと同じ町の出だったから知られてたの。高校の先生の推薦で。高校の先生は寺島辰治（てらしまたつじ）先生。教育大（筑波）に行くのを進めてくださったのも寺島先生。

―どうして筑波を推薦なさったんですか？

K　先生も東京教育大のご出身だったから。

―個人的なつながりで。

K　そう。だから先生はいつも生徒に、わたしの行った学校に行くように推薦なさってたの。だからわたしも先生の歩んだ道をね。

―大学を卒業なさったのは何年ですか？

K　1960年だと思います。

―65年にジョン・ケージの音楽をお聴きになったんですね？

K　そう、63年。ジョン・ケージとデイヴィッド・テュードアが東京に来て〔正しくは1962年。1964年11月のコンサートは渡米後のため見ていない〕。

—ケージの音楽のテーマは？

K もっとチャンス・オペレーションとか自然な音楽をとか？ ダメだったわね。クラシックの指揮者が指揮してるような音楽が人気だったから。彼〔＝ケージ〕はだいたい自分の〔聞き取り不能〕は指揮してた。難解よ。こういう前衛音楽がニューヨークでは認められてるんだなあって思いましたね。だから、わたしニューヨークに行かなくちゃって。1964年、郷里を出て……。

—エモーショナルな面、個人的な面ではどういうお気持ちでしたか？

K 大学を卒業して、新橋の内科画廊で個展したんです。お医者さんが、心理学者〔原文ママ〕がオーナーだった。ハイレッド・センターも内科画廊で展覧会したのよ。高松〔次郎〕の「高」が「Hi」で、赤瀬川〔原平〕の「赤」が「Red」で、中西〔夏之〕の「中」が「Center」。とても前衛的でアナキストなパフォーマンス集団。いまではみんな有名なアーティストになって、赤瀬川さんは有名な作家で。芥川賞もらったのよ。わたしも機会があって1963年に〔内科画廊で〕個展したの。でも展覧会のあと、展評も何もぜんぜん出なくって。

—当時、ご自分のことをアナキストと思っていらっしゃいましたか？

K いいえ、ちょっと自分の道を模索してて、すごく進歩的な、前衛的なアーティストだったんです。それにわたし、当時はラディカルでね、全学連ってあるでしょ、政治的にアクティブだったの。そして内科画廊で個展やった。誰かひとりくらい展覧会評書いてくれる人いるだろうと思ったんだけど（笑）。でも何も出てこなかった。だからすごくがっかりしちゃって。それから読売新聞がやってたアンデパンダン展〔1963年〕にも出しました。すごく活発だったんだけど、やっぱり展評も何も出なくて。未来に希望がもてなかった。〔だから〕とにかく東京を、自分の国を出たんです。ニューヨークに行かなくちゃ、もっとチャンスがあるからって思って。〔日本は〕まるきり男社会だったし、あと、わたし芸大〔＝東京藝術大学〕を出たわけでもないから。わたしの出た大学は教員養成の学校で、美大じゃなかったのよね。〔だから〕自分にはちゃんとしたコネがないのかなって思った。だからニューヨークに行かないと、って。ニューヨークは新世界だし、誰でも運試しできる。ニューヨークではチャンスがもらえるってジョン・ケージの音楽を見たときに思いました。ジョン・ケージがちゃんとやれてるのなら、わたしだってやれるはずだ、って……。

—ニューヨークにいらしたときにはもう何人か……

K フルクサス・グループ。フルクサスとはコネがあったわね。

—それと、日本のアーティストも何人かいたんですよね。

K ええ、でもね、わたし芸大みたいなアートスクール行ってないでしょ。だからアート・グループともつきあいなかったのね。友だちだったのは、フルクサスのアーティストのジョージ・マチューナス。

—ええ。

K だからジョージ・マチューナスとか、ジョン・ケージみたいな音楽家とすぐに仲良くなったの。日本人で画家の友だちはいなかったわね。それよりもグループ音楽とか。小杉〔武久〕とか刀根〔康尚〕とかね。そういうのが日本人の友だちだったの。でもあの人たちは音楽家よね。いまでも友だちですよ。若くて実験的だった時代、辛くて楽しい時代を共有したのよ。画家より音楽家のほうが友だちとしてはいいわよ。

—どうしてですか？

K だって、音楽家って神様みたいだもの。悟ってて。音楽はやってて楽しいじゃない。アートはもっと苦しいのよ、オブジェクト作るとか、ペインティング作るとか。わたしは彫刻家〔だから〕とくにね。もっと体を使う仕事でしょ。でなきゃ、もっと深く考えるのよ、もっと体と心にかかわる空間。音楽もそうだけど、わたしたち〔アーティスト〕はかたちをつくらなきゃいけない。音楽は波なのよ。もっと心的なコミュニケーション。音楽家のほうが悟ってて、仏教徒っぽいのよね。ジョン・ケージとか。お坊さんみたい。音楽家の友だちのほうが遊んだり話したりするのは楽よ。ヴィデオ・アーティストとかアートの友だちだと、ときどき近すぎる感じするのよね。

—そうですよね。

K ええ、だからわたしあんまり友だちいないのよ。

＊＊＊

—ついこのあいだ、〔モーリス・〕ベジャール・バレエ団の男性第一舞踏手（プリモ・バレリーノ）のジョルジュ・ドンにインタビューしたんです。同じことを言っていました。「本当に、ダンサーとは友だちになれない。大好きだけど、親友は他の分野の人たちです」、と。「他の分野からは養分を、糧を得られますから」と言っていましたね。久保田さんも音楽から養分とか、知的な糧、エモーショナルな糧、精神的な糧を得ていらっしゃいますか？

K ええ、音楽って本当に抽象的よね、数学とか哲学みたい。

—そういう糧は、他にはどういうところから得ていらっしゃいますか？

K 自然だと思う。だから《三つの山》［本書78–81頁］とか《河》［本書84、93–95頁］とかいうようなわたしの作品は四季と関係があるんです。俳句みたいに。自然、それから、自分が毎日暮らしてる環境。スライド〔ショー〕みたいよね、変化する時間。

—お住まいは田舎ですか？

K いいえ、ニューヨークに住んでます。田舎は好きじゃないの。わたし田舎で生まれたのよ。新潟ってすごく田舎なの。山とか田んぼが見えて。だからニューヨークに住んでるんです。まあニューヨークも田舎だけどね。自分のロフトに閉じこもってたら、そこが田舎。どこも違わない。

—そうですか？

K ドア閉めるでしょ。

—ええ、でも緑がないですよね。

K 緑はないんですけどね。

──緑があったらなあ、と思われますか？

K　でも緑は自分でつくるわよ。わたしの作品、わたしのヴィデオでさ、緑とか庭のオブジェクトとか。《アダムとイヴ》［本書112-115頁］のためにつくったのよ。自分で緑つくるの。緑のロフト。自分で自分の緑をつくる。

──でしたら、作品に使うヴィデオテープと自然の事物のあいだには類似性があると感じていらっしゃいますか？

K　ヴィデオテープの緑は、自然の緑より自然なことがあるわよね。

──なぜでしょう？

K　だって、もっと透明だから。そこにあるみたいに見えたもの。

──じゃあ、透明性というのは久保田さんにとって非常に重要な質なんですね。

K　電子透明性とかね。シースルーってあるでしょ、どこか純粋なのよね、存在を透過して。わたしたち、いろいろな存在とかかわりがあるわけでしょ。

──存在というのはどういう意味ですか？

K　存在って光みたいなものよ。光、光源よね。ヴィデオは電子からくる光源。

──他に、久保田さんにとって重要な光源はどういうものですか？

K　日暮れとか。わたし、新潟の海に近い村で生まれたじゃない。海に日が沈むのを見ると素敵よ。変化しつづけて、消えてくのよ。海の向こうで太陽が２つに分かれるのよ。変化する光っていうか。

──わたし、ちょうどシチリアに行ってきたところなんです。本当にきれい！　海があって山があって、日暮れになる。日が沈んでいくんだけど、水面に着く前に消えてしまうんですね。わたしにとってはそれが本当に大事なんです。

K　そうそう、水面の反射があれをキャッチするのね。太陽は暮れちゃってもね。

──残るんですよね。

K　きれいよね、残るのね、そう。だから色なのよね、動く色。

──子ども時代とか育った場所とかが、久保田さんのアートの中にまた出てきているみたいですね。

K　人生を綴った風景みたいなね。心の中にあるのよね。自分のアートっていう領域の中に、自分の風景を創っていくわけでしょ。アートって自分の人生を綴った日記なのね。

──久保田さんにとって風景とはどういうものですか？

K　わたし山登りしてたんです。だから山登り好きなの。学生だった〔ころ〕、日本アルプス全制覇したのよ。それからアメリカに行って、ロッキー山脈に行って、ワイオミング〔州〕イエローストーン〔国立公園〕の〔グランド〕ティトンとか、大スケールの山に。

──お気に入りの山はどれですか？

K　富士山。

──あ、本当に？

K　富士山で冬にキャンプしたことあるのよ、クリスマスに、大学生のときに。登山部員だったの。

──富士山のどこがお好きですか？

K　バランスがいいと思うのよね（笑）。素敵な、おごそかな山。とってもきれい。〔セント・〕ヘレナ山が好きなのは、富士山に似てるから。〔セント・〕ヘレナ山は大噴火したのよ、シアトルの近くで。ずいぶんヴィデオに撮ったのよ、噴火前に。

──富士山に似てるんですか？

K　きれいな山ですよ。冬に登るときれいなんですよ。大雪崩も起きる。木はなくて。それがちょっと素敵なのよ。景色がすっかり見えて。風がすごく強くて、すごい雪崩で、それがアイスピックみたいなのよ、雪が。変化するスケールとボリュームの量みたい、彫刻みたいなの。風景みたいな。

＊＊＊

──〔話を戻しまして〕ニューヨークにいらして、フルクサスと関わられました。お仕事の媒体にヴィデオを選んだのはどうしてですか？

K　フルクサスのメンバーだったころ、ずいぶんストリート・ハプニングをしたんです。もっと攪乱的なね、イベントを。それでわたしたち、アート・オブジェクトには反対だったのね。

──どちらかというとゲームをプレイするみたいな。すごく反アート的ですね。

K　そりゃあ、フルクサスは反アートだったわよね。でも70年代に、ジョージ・マチューナスは不動産のほうに入れ込むようになって、ロフトとか、ソーホー風の。フルクサスのメンバーはみんな別々の方向に行ったのね。それから、わたしの彫刻家としてのバックグラウンドが表に出てきたんだけど、ただオブジェクトつくってもそんなに面白くないでしょ。オブジェクトって動かないから。映像とオブジェクトを組み合わせたいと思って。そしたらヴィデオとか新しい媒体が出てきて。だから、ヴィデオとオブジェクトっていう組み合わせは──ヴィデオ／彫刻の結婚よね。だから新しいものを発明する人間として仕事をしていったわけ。

──なぜ映画ではなくヴィデオだったんですか？

K　だってヴィデオのほうが瞬間的だから。玄米みたいなのよ、有機的で。映画はもっと化学的でしょ。もっと時間が要るのよね、処理するのに、見られるようになるまで待たなくちゃいけない。でもヴィデオはバックグラウンドで再生できるし、気に入らなければやりなおすこともできる。瞬間みたいなさ、速いのよ。簡単だし。自分でできるのよね。

──アート媒体としてのヴィデオに、最初どういう印象を受けましたか？　どういう方向に向かっていて、どういうことができそうだと思われましたか？

K　いろいろあったわよ。最初はドキュメンタリー・ヴィデオをやってみたかったし、それから一般放映用ヴィデオをやってみたかったし、いまはケーブル〔テレビ〕用ヴィデオをやってみたい。でもそういうのは物語性のあるヴィデオなのよね。でもわたしの場合、ニューヨークに住んでる日本人で、ブロークンな英語しゃべるから、一般放映用ヴィデオとしてはダメなのよね。試してみたことあるのよ。インディアンの居留地に行って、アメリカ・インディアンたちと暮らして、ドキュメンタリーつくったの。でもチャンネル13って、教育TV局ですけど、あそこはわたしのアメリカ・インディアンのヴィデオ流してくれなかった。だってアメリカ・インディアンたち自身がマイノリティだし、わたしもアメリカに住んでる外国人だからマイノリティでしょ。そういう二重のマイノリティだと、ドキュメンタリー・ヴィデオとか物語性のあるヴィデオとかのアーティストとしてやっていくには幸先が悪かったのね。ヴィデオ彫刻だったら英語、ブロークンな英語話す必要ない。〔話す〕必要なんかぜんぜんなくて、ただオブジェクトつくって、わたしのアート言語つくればいい。違う言語でしょ。ちょっとは話す必要あるけど、アート言語はデータである必要なくて、オブジェクトなのよね。

──すごくわかります。わたし、こちらに来て5年になるし、日本語も話すんですけど、英語でならできることができない感じがするんです。だからもうひとつ別の言葉が必要なんです。わたし、物書きなんですけど、かなり欲求不満がたまります。理解できますよ。久保田さんは日記をたくさん書いていらっしゃるんだなと気がついたんです。西洋美術史にたいへん感化されていらっしゃる。そして、自然や四季といった日本人に伝統的なテーマにもたいへん感化されている。それから俳句の力、はかなさ……たとえば桜が、あっという間に咲いて死んでしまうとか。そういう感覚、ありますよね。でも、そういった領域でお仕事をなさるときは隠していらっしゃる。ただ、〔作品の〕説明だけ読んでいると、個人的なステートメント(態度表明)はどこにあるの？　希望は？　愛は？　そういう気分がしてくるんです。そういうようなものは、久保田さんにとって、どこに出てきているんでしょうか？　それから、さらに探していって「ブロークン・ダイアリー」を見たら、久保田さんの個人的なステートメントはここから来るんだな、と思ったんです。そのことについてはどうお感じになりますか？

K　うーん、日記(ダイアリー)、文学は、日本人にとっては対話なんですよね。日記ってほんとうに親密なものだと思います。自分自身にとってはいいんだけど、他の人にとってはやりすぎかもしれない。親密すぎるのね。

──「ブロークン・ダイアリー」をつくっていらっしゃいます。どうして「ブロークン」なんですか？

K　だってわたしの英語はブロークンだし、エモーションはブロークンだから。完璧なものなんてないのよね。人生はすべてブロークンなのよ。

──イリュージョンにも関心がおありのようですね。ガラスが岩のように見えるというイリュージョンとか。でしたら、切れ目のない〔＝ブロークンではない〕日記のイリュージョンを創り出してみてもいいんじゃないでしょうか？

K　切れ目のない日記ねえ……でも、日記は好きだけど長いのはイヤって人もいるわよね。日記ってひとすじのヴィデオテープ、1本のヴィデオの流れみたいなものなのね。でもわたしはそのテープを越えて行きたいわけ。オブジェクト、もっと彫刻に近いもの。テープを越えた先っていうのは、すべての、情報と形の組み合わせとか。わたし、形のほうが興味あるの。

──テープよりもむしろ形。

K　そう。わたしは語り部じゃないし、日記って、ひとりの人間のストーリーとか経験とか、始まりのある物語みたいな何かってことになるわよね。でもわたしは始まりなんかいらないし、終わりもいらないの。それよりは真ん中の瞬間、ずっと続いていく時間じゃなくて。自分で自分をカットすることもあるのよ。

＊＊＊

──ええ。だからあんなにデュシャンにこだわっておられるのでしょうか？

K　デュシャンってループ、ループみたいな感じよね。でもわたしの《窓》［本書66–69頁］は「メタ・マルセル・デュシャン」なの。だからわたしはマルセル・デュシャンを越えて行かないといけない。

──ご自分を越えて行かなければいけない。

K　そう。

──デュシャンとともに、デュシャンを通じて？

K　通じて。

──では、デュシャンと彼の仕事は、久保田さんが越えていくための窓として機能しているわけですね。

K　そう。

──どうしてデュシャンなんでしょう？

K　それはわたし、彼に会ったから、1968年に、亡くなる3か月前に。飛行機の中で（笑）、バッファローに行く途中。偶然みたいに。

──でも、それ以前にもお会いになっていたんじゃ……

K　いいえ、マース・カニングハムのダンス公演〔《ウォーク・アラウンド・タイム》〕を見にバッファローに行く途中、飛行機の中で会ったの。〔この公演では〕デュシャンの大きなガラスの作品、フィラデルフィア美術館が持ってるあれ〔《彼女の独身者たちによって裸にされた花嫁、さえも》1915–23年〕を、ジャスパー・ジョーンズが舞台用に翻案したのね。それでわたし、偶然にあの方たち〔＝デュシャンと妻ティニー〕に会ったの。

──デュシャンに会うのはどういう感じでしたか？

K　飛行機の上で会ったわけよね。それが可笑(おか)しいところでさ。道で会ってたら、あんなに感動しなかったと思うわよ。飛行機にはあんまり人が座ってないでしょ。飛行機ってそんなに人が乗れないじゃない？

──彼は久保田さんの隣に座っていたんですか？

K　ううん、ファーストクラスにいた。わたしはツーリスト〔＝エコノミー〕クラス。

──では、ファーストクラスまでいらっしゃったんですか？

K　ううん、ティニー・デュシャンがトイレに行くのを見たの。それだから、あ、あの人知ってる、マルセルはファーストクラスにいるんだなって思ったの。トイレっていっつも後ろのほうの、飛行機の端にあるじゃない。ちょうどデュシャンの話を読んでたんです。『美術手帖』がマルセル・デュシャンの大特集を組んだところで〔305号、1968年12月号〕。だから、ひょっとすると自分のことが日本語で書いてあるのを見たら、彼は嬉しいかもしれないと思って。1968年には、まだ日本の印刷物って新鮮だったのよね。いまでも彼の写真持ってますよ。サインしてくれたのよ。わたし言ったの、「ほら、日本の雑誌に載っていらっしゃいますよ。ちょうどあなたの話を読んでたんですよ」って。それで、ナイアガラの滝のせいでバッファローで吹雪が強すぎて、着陸できなかったの。ロチェスターに着いたの。それから延々〔バスで〕行ったのよ、冬の野原を通って。

――バッファローまでデュシャンの隣に座って行かれましたか？

K　ええ、あんまり人はいなかった。彼のギャラリーの人と、ティニー・デュシャンと、ご本人と、わたし。4人。冬だった。だから冬が好きなのよね(笑)。こういうことがぜんぶ冬に起きたわけ。

――当時、デュシャンは何を教えてくれましたか？

K　うーん、とにかくフィーリングよね。「あ、この人がマルセル・デュシャンなんだ」って。フィーリングが伝わってくるのよ。媒体を通してじゃ伝わらないでしょ、印刷媒体とか、本当の、フィジカル（物理的・身体的）な、本当のフィーリングは。歴史を目の当たりにするわけよ。

――ひとつの歴史的瞬間。

K　歴史に触れる感じがするのよ。

――はい、はい。

K　安物のカメラ持ってたの。あとでその〔カニングハムの〕舞台の写真撮ったのね。でも現像しなかった。それである日、新聞を開いたら彼〔＝デュシャン〕が亡くなってたの。死ぬのは他人っていうあれよね。それで写真を現像したの。写真、まだくっきりしてた。それから写真本をつくったのよ。

――デュシャンのアートや作品で本当に惹きつけられた点は何ですか？

K　レディメイド。彼のコンセプト・アートよ。わたしたちのために、たくさん方向性を開いてくれたけど、わたしが知ってるのは、彼のレディメイドっていうコンセプト。

――なぜでしょう？

K　なぜって？　どんな物（オブジェクト）だって美しいし、どんな物だってアート・オブジェクトなの。わたしも既製品（レディメイド）使うわよ。TVも既製品でしょ。

――でも、レディメイドは周辺の空間に左右されますよね。

K　ええ、でも、レディメイドは「社会彫刻」っていうような、政治的な感覚の延長なのよ。

――どういうところが？　どの点がそうだと思われますか？

K　なんでもアートになりうる。もっと政治的な、ステートメント（意見表明）的なオブジェクト、「社会彫刻」みたいな。みんないろいろなもの使うでしょ。わたし、自動車のタイヤの作品つくったのよ。タイヤの中にTVを〔入れた〕。それをわたしはアートとして展示したいわけ〔《自動車の車輪》本書118-119頁〕。美術館でも展示したい。映像も。タイヤは捨てられちゃう、ジャンクよね。でも、ジャンクもアートになる。ジャンクにもう一度命を吹き込めるのよ。既製品（レディメイド）はジャンクでしょ。10セント均一の店で買える。でも彼〔＝デュシャン〕は既製品をアートの作品にしたのよ。

――でも、美術館で既製品を目にするのは、当時は驚きだったわけですけど、いまはそれほどでもないですよね。

K　そうね。

――だとすると、久保田さんにとってレディメイドはどういう点でいまでも新鮮なんでしょうか？

K　スーパーマーケット的なコンセプトってあるじゃない？　技能訓練は、それはそれで大事。でも、もっと簡単なアートへのアプローチ〔がある〕。幼稚園とか、子どもとか……

――では、誰でもアートをつくれると。

K　それはそうよ。彼〔＝デュシャン〕は、特別じゃないアートへの扉を開いてくれたのよ。自分自身でできるアート。〈自分でやってみよう（DIY）〉的な態度ね。

＊＊＊

――そういうこともあって久保田さんはヴィデオに惹かれたんでしょうか？

K　ヴィデオは既製品。「社会彫刻」でもある。TVはどんどん安くなってるから、いま。カラーTVはむかしはずいぶん高かったのよ。お金持ちだけのもの。

――ヴィデオカメラも本当に安くなりつつありますね。

K　そうなのよ。ポラロイドみたいになったわよね。誰でもアーティストに、フォトグラファーになれる。フォトグラファーってどういう人？　プロのフォトグラファー？〔でも〕アマチュアのフォトグラファーなんていないのよ。〔もうプロ／アマの〕境界線なんてない。ヴィデオアーティストみたいなものよ、いま。8ミリヴィデオなら、カメラを手にとったらそれでもう日記のできあがりでしょ。それが自分のアートなのよ。

――それについてはどうお感じになりますか？

K　すばらしいわよね。

――ヴィデオカメラが入手しやすくなったというこの状況は、人々が久保田さんのアートを見るときの見方にどういうふうに影響するのでしょうか？何かお考えはありますか？

K　子どもはわたしのアートが好きなんだと思うのよね。それはすごく嬉しい。ミュージアム・オブ・ムーヴィング・イメージで展覧会したとき……〔ニューヨーク市クイーンズ地区の〕アストリアにあって、移民の町みたいなところなの。ポーランドとか、プエルトリコとか、もっと貧乏な子たちが学校の見学でそこのミュージアムに来るの。そしたらその子たちが気に入ってくれて。マンハッタンも移民よ。でもマンハッタンはすごく〔物価が〕高い。でもクイーンズとかブルックリンだったら、子どもたちも気に入ってくれるかもしれない。参加型のアートを。子どもたちが「あっ、自分が映ってる」って言うのよ。ライブカメラ〔《ヴィデオ俳句――ぶら下がり作品》本書96-97頁〕があるの。子どもは自分がTVに映ってるのを見たり参加したりするのが好きなのよ。「あれは自分だ」とか「TVアナウンサーだけじゃなくて、自分も」みたいな、インタラクティブな参加。参加型の作品は、子どもたちにとってもオーディエンスにとってもすごくいいのよ。巻き込まれて、アートの一部になるから。傍観するだけじゃなくて。

――ただ、久保田さんのお仕事について評を読んだのですけど、久保田さんがご自身のアートの中で実験したり使ったりされたヴィデオのエフェクトは、MTVや巨大ショッピングモールでも見られると……

K そうなのよ。わたしたちからアイデアを盗むから。MTVはもっとお金があるでしょ（笑）。

――それについてはどうお感じになりますか？

K そう、ピーター・キャンパスみたいなアートのほうがすごいのよ。ボストンのTV局WGBHでクロマキー作品とかすばらしい実験的作品をつくった方ですけどね。でもMTVの人たちはもっとお金がある。製作の規模もずっと大きい。ずっとハイテクな設備があるから、もっとうまくできるのよ。でもアイデアとかコンセプトの面では、ピーター・キャンパスみたいなヴィデオアーティストに影響受けてるのよ。それは社会的な影響だと思う。別にいいんだと思うの、彼ら〔＝MTV〕が奪っていったって。わたしたちのほうでも何かしら奪い返せるからね。でもそういうのは社会現象というか、ヴィデオアートの一部よ。

――久保田さんは本当にたくさんのものをアプロプリエーションされましたが、今度は他の人が久保田さんの仕事をアプロプリエーションしています。

K そうよ。それは違う方向性だわね。でも社会はいつもそういうふうに起こってきたのよ。とくにMTVみたいな若い世代はデスクトップとかでしょ。暗さとか明るさとか音楽とかダンスとかプロジェクションしたイメージとか、そういうのがすごく性に合ってるのよ。

――久保田さんがヴィデオで行なった実験が取られ、ポピュラーカルチャーの中で、ショッピングモール、ヴィデオ、スーパーマーケット、TVなどあらゆるところで使われるようになっています。久保田さんは人々が自分のまわりの環境を見るときの仕方に、環境の中に何を見て取るかに、本当に大きな効果を与えました。

K 前よりよく見えるようになるんならいいんですけどね。

――〔自分のアートが〕人々の見え方をよくする助けになると思われますか？　久保田さんのイメージや、なさってきたことは、ポピュラーカルチャーに入っていくと、また別の内容になるとお考えですか？

K でもライフスタイルが変わったわよね。誰にでも居間があって、ヴィデオプロジェクターがあって、ヴィデオニュースを、TVニュースを見てるでしょ、TV画面でだけじゃなくて。映画とかヴィデオプロジェクターとか、もっと大きな画面を使えて、壁には版画があって。壁に動画があるわけよね。それが高級ライフスタイルの一部で、若い人もそういうの好きでしょ。素敵よね。それで幸せなら素敵じゃない。むかしはアイスボックス買って喜んでたでしょ。いまは居間にヴィデオプロジェクターがあるから嬉しいのよ。生活改善、生活の豊かさよ。自分たちの空間とか、生活体験を楽しんでるのよ。だったらいい生活よね。

＊＊＊

――久保田さんの作品が子どもたちに人気があるとおっしゃったときに、自分の姿を見られるからだというお話がありました。ヴィデオでインタラクティブをたくさん使われています。

K そんなに使わないけど、鏡とライブカメラで使うことはあるわよ。隠しライブカメラ。あと、わたしが展覧会をしたとき、あのミュージアム〔・オブ・ムーヴィング・イメージ〕のまわりは子どもがいっぱいいるから、生活保護を受けてる子たちを楽しませる一番安上がりな方法は美術館に連れてくことだから（笑）。美術館では普通さわれないでしょ、ダメなのよね。ただ突っ立って眺めるしかない。

――久保田さんの展示では何でもさわれるわけですね。ここ〔＝原美術館〕でも展示物に触れられる。

K そうよ。だから、そういうフィジカルな接触とかアートへの招待とか、若い世代は好きなのよ。

――すばらしいですね。

K 環境の一部になりたいのよ、アートの一部に。インタラクティブなヴィデオがあったらアート作品だと思うのかもね。子どもがいなくて、参加もなくて、人がいなかったら、退屈、ただ来て、ふつうの見方、ちょっとめずらしい情景。

――カメラはご自分で操作されますか？

K ときどき。

――それはいつですか？

K 最初にカメラを使ったときはそうしてたわよ。

――写真で。

K ポートレイト。

――ヴィデオ・ポートレイトですか？

K そう。自分。

――ヴィデオ・ポートレイトをされていたのはいつですか？

K まあ、スタジオのこともあったし、自分の居間のこともあったわね。いまはあんまりしませんけど、前はしてましたね。あれはちょっと中毒みたいなものよ。最初にカメラ、新しいカメラを手に入れたときは。自分をヴィデオに撮るのが好きなのよ。ヴィデオは中毒性があるわよ、ナルシスティックだから。自分が楽しくて、自分自身を何度も何度も何度も何度も見るの。ヴィデオっていつも、もっともっと、なのよね。

――ただ、現代のフェミニスト・ヴィデオではたくさんの女性が自分自身を何度も何度も何度も撮っていますよね。それはどう思われますか？

K いいと思う。ご本人たちは満足してるし。

――あれはナルシスティックではない？

K ナルシスティックだけど、本人だけのものだからさ。でもケーブルTVではだめよ、たぶん。あんなの全部見る時間ある人なんかいないじゃない。みんな忙しいのよ。

──ええ、でもそこら中で目にします。

K だからわたしヴィデオ彫刻つくるのよ。まわりを一周したら〔見〕終わるでしょ。腰を下ろす必要ない。前にアンソロジー・フィルム・アーカイヴズでヴィデオのキュレーターしてたんだけど、同じプログラム何度も何度も何度も見ると飽きちゃうの。シングルチャンネル・ヴィデオ、アーティスト・ヴィデオよね。でもそのうち、自分でもあの人たちがつくってるような作品つくりたくなってきた。ヴィデオ彫刻のことよ。わたし、オーディエンスを拘束しないのよ。オーディエンスは楽しんで、立ち去ればいい。とどまる必要ないわよ。忙しいんだし。だからわたし、ヴィデオ・インスタレーションとかヴィデオ彫刻を公共の場所、広場みたいなところにつくってみたいのよ。人が歩いて通ってるような、空港とかショッピングセンターに。

──最近つくられた作品に、タオルミーナの《文化の門》〔本書116–117頁〕があります。

K はいはい、シチリアにね。あれはきれいだったわね。

──タオルミーナにはきれいなギリシアの劇場があって……

K そうなのよ！

──眺めが……

K 海に面した眺めね。

──久保田さんの《文化の門》は見る場所を形成し、創り出す。その仕方が、あの劇場を思い出させました。ただ、さきほどヴィデオの役割と文化の話をなさいましたよね。《ヴィデオ・ゲート》〔《文化の門》を指す〕を見ていると、久保田さんにとってアートはすごくもったいぶった精神的なものなのではなくて、久保田さんのアートは、その人が自分で探しに行けるゲートを創り出せるんだなという気がしてくるんです。どうお感じになりますか？

K あと、それはフレームよね。窓のフレームみたいな、眺めを枠付けるフレーム、考えを枠付けるフレーム、風景を枠付けるフレーム、自分が歩く公園を枠付けるフレーム。フレームがあって、そこを通過していくのね。きれいな公園が見えて、視角（アングル）が〔見え方の〕決め手なのね。タオルミーナ庭園はとくに。地中海だけど山も〔ある〕。

──フレームはなぜ重要なんでしょうか？

K 自分がフレームをつくるところにはいつもフレームがあるっていう感じがする。世界をどういうふうに見るか〔に関係がある〕と思う。それを自分でつくるわけ。好きなところに自分で触れて、目がそれをストップする。それがフレーム。通過してる、いつも何かが見えてるんだけど、時々ストップして何かをまなざす。

──日本文化の中では、フレームはどういうふうに機能しているのでしょうか？

K わからないけど、脳経由じゃない？

──どういうふうにですか？

K 自分の心にとっての風景に脳が反応する仕方、環境を生きる仕方。フレームって、どこに自分が生きてるか、その位置を決めるようなものだったのよ。だから、自分のバックグラウンドよね。その眺めに関心を持ったのなら、それがフレームなのよ。

──おっしゃることはわたしにとって興味深いです。掛け軸などを見ると……

K ああ、掛け軸、あれはフレームよね（笑）。

──掛け軸はフレームである。でも硬いフレームではありません。

K そう、柔らかいのよ。丸いフレームでもある。輪郭があって……

──あと、西洋のわたしからすると、研究者や書き手にとって、枠組み（フレーム）を持っているというのは本当に大事なことです。でもここ〔＝日本〕ではそれほど大事ではないみたいですね。だから思ったんですが、久保田さんがフレームに興味を持ったのは米国にいらしたときですか？

K 映画館からだわね。あと、とくに自分でカメラを操作するとき。自分が動くところでは目がカメラになって、ここでストップすると、それがフレーム。自分の身体的なリズム、自分の心身のリズムがカメラをコントロールするわけ。カメラは手の一部で、手は目とフィーリングの一部。フィーリングはいつも脳の一部。だからカメラも自分の体の一部なのよ。ただ、心理的なもの、意識がすべてコントロールしてる。

──意識が何もかもコントロールしていると。

K そう、それがフレーム。

──すると、久保田さんが創られるものはすべて意識的に創られていて、完全に計画してあるわけですね。

K でなければ無意識。でもそれがわたしのフレームになったわけ。フレームを延長したものが時間。時間は運動。フレームを切り取る、フレームを分析することも運動、運動の始まりに戻ること。

＊＊＊

──いま取りかかっていらっしゃるのはどういう作品ですか？

K 風景をつくったあとで、身体をつくってるところ。《アダムとイヴ》のあと、スケート選手と知り合いになったの。〔伊藤〕みどりちゃん。名古屋〔にある画廊〕が招いてくれて、新作をつくらなくちゃいけなくって。そしてある日『ニューヨークタイムズ』を開いたんです。みどりちゃんは名古屋生まれだったのね。でもこの作品は、残念だけど、名古屋では展覧会しないの。「社会彫刻」っていうのよ。もっと具象的で。体の像をやってるの。次は顔か体型、石膏製で。石膏とブロンズ。内側に液晶TV使うのよ。小さい小さい液晶TV。熱もブラウン管もないから、小さいTVを石膏とかブロンズの中に入れられるのよ。いまではTVは本当に小さくなって、液晶TVは……。いまは具象をやってるの。学生時代、石膏とブロンズを使ってたときみたいに。

──一周して元のところに戻ってきたという感覚がありますか？

K うん、いま完全に一周したわね、学生に戻って（笑）。いろんな素材を使ってたころに、木とか合板とか金属とか、川、水、音符を使って、いま

〔また〕石膏とブロンズ、それから液晶TV、具象の身体を、人体をつくってるのね。

——いま具象作品がトレンドだから久保田さんも具象に惹かれるのだと思われますか？

K それよりは、「これがひとりの女性の感じていることだ」とか、もっとエモーショナルなことが言えるようになりたいのね。ストーリー〔が必要だ〕って言うんなら、怒りとかエモーションとか何かについてストーリー書いてやるわよ（笑）。

——何か人間的なこと。

K 人間的。そう、そうね。わたしの作品、前はとても冷たかったから。だから作品の中にもっとエモーションを入れたかったの。それはもっと具象をってことね。ステートメントとメッセージがあるようにしておきたかったの。前はとても抽象的なメッセージ〔だったから〕。でもいまはもっと口頭よ。わたし、よくしゃべるでしょ、エモーショナル。

——エモーショナルな言葉を？

K そう。

——これもまた別の新しい言語ですね。

K そう。去年の夏から試してみてるの。まったく新しいツールを借りてきて、石膏とブロンズをつくってるの。スタジオにあるのよ。

——話すための新しいツールですか？

K そう、新しい彫刻ツール。

——どういうものなんですか？

K 新しいツールよ、石膏つくるための。もっと伝統的な彫刻。

——それの写真はお持ちですか？

K ううん、写真はまだ撮ってない。そのうち撮らないといけないわね。

＊＊＊

——〔原美術館での〕展覧会の作品を選んだのは久保田さんでいらっしゃいますか？

K あら、原［俊夫、原美術館館長（当時）］さんよ。

——ご一緒に？　それとも原さんが選ばれたんでしょうか？

K 原さんがわたしの《河》の作品を見て気に入ってくださったの。ホイットニー〔美術館〕で、1983年のバイアニュアルのとき。《河》はベルリンで、1979年から81年に、ベルリンのDAAD〔ドイツ学芸交流会〕でレジデンスしてたときに。

——教えていらしたんですか？

K いえ、そうじゃなくて、ドイツ政府が招いてくれたのよ。アーティストをベルリンに招いてるのよ。ただベルリンに住んでアートつくってたの。それがレジデンスだったのよ。それで《河》つくったの。金属と水と波の機械を使ったのはあのときが初めてで。ドイツでプール行ったのよね。10分ごとに大きな波がプールに起きるの。海みたいって思ったけどプールなの。いいアイデアだと思って。大きな波の機械をつくりたかったんだけど、小型版をつくったの。

——ご自分でつくられたんですか？

K モーターで。それから動くモーターとか回転機械を使うようになったの。原さんはそれをとっても気に入ってくださって。日本人でありながらホイットニー・アメリカ美術館のビエンナーレに出るのって大変なのよ。

——女性でありながら出るのも大変ですよね。

K そりゃあ女性であるのは大変よ。でもね、いまは女性であるのはそんなに悪くないのよ。米在住の外国人アーティストで、アメリカ人アーティストじゃないほうが大変なのよ。

——なるほど、そうですよね。

K ホイットニー・アメリカ美術館っていうところは、アメリカ人アーティストによるアメリカ美術しかコレクションしないから。わたしはニューヨークに長く住んでるから、ホイットニー美術館はわたしが日系アメリカ人なんだと思ったのね（笑）。でもわたしまだ日本のパスポート持ってるのよ。

——ご自身のことをアメリカ系日本人と考えてらっしゃいますか？

K どうだろう、考えたことないわ。そうであってもいいわよね。そしたらホイットニー美術館が《河》を買いたがったかもしれない。結局わたしがまだ日本人なんだって知って、「シゲコ、あなたまだ日本人なの？　アメリカ系日本人なのかと思った」って言うの。「どういうこと？」って聞いたら、「ごめんなさい。あなたの作品は好きなんだけど、買えません」って。わたし「ええっ？」って言ったの。不公平だと思ったわ。

——人種差別ですよね。

K うーん、人種差別かどうかはわからないけど、わたし米国で税金払ってるのよ。まるで戦時中よ。でもわたし、自分の国を出てきたのよね。ちょっと迷子みたいなものよね。「どこに行けばいいの」って。ここ〔＝日本〕では私が帰ってくると、ニューヨークに長居しすぎですよって言われる。それで米国に行ったら、「まだ日本人なんだね」って。

——そういうお気持ちをどれか作品に込めたことはおありですか？

K まだない。だからもっと具象やろうと思ったの。自分の怒りとかエモーションとかを入れたポートレイトを、ときどき。わたしの言語はそこにあるの。わたしがアートを好きなのは、国際的な言語だからなのよ。戦時中みたいな状況に直面しなきゃならないなんて知らなかった。いま、みんなすごく国家主義的になってるじゃない。

——ホイットニーはまだ久保田さんの作品はひとつも……

K ないのよ、買えないのよ、わたしはアメリカ人じゃないから。アメリカ美術館っていう名前でしょ。アートは国際的な言語なのよ。だからわたしアートやってるのよ。でも大変よ。違う国に住んでたら、自分の国ではないけど、自分の世界で作業してるのよね。境界線を引くのが好きな人たちみたいに……。

——久保田さんの仕事を理解するということに関して、アメリカ人と日本人のあいだに境界線があると思いますか？

K アメリカ人にはずいぶん助けてもらったと思うわよ。アメリカ人のほうがわたしの仕事をわかってくれる。

──助けてくれたんですか？

K　そう、そう。それもあってホイットニーに文句言えないの。アメリカ人はわたしの仕事、とっても気に入ってくれたのよ。あと、ドクメンタに2回出たわ〔ドクメンタ6（1977年)、ドクメンタ8（1987年)〕。

──じゃあ、ドイツ人ですね。ヨーロッパの人たちは久保田さんのお仕事が好きだ、と。

K　そう、ヨーロッパの人たちも。でもわたし、全米芸術基金とか、ニューヨーク芸術協議会とかからもずいぶんと助成金もらったのよ。それがわたしの仕事を支えてくれて続けられた。けっこうな額なのよ。

──今回が日本では初の大きな展覧会ですか？

K　そうです。

──どんなお気持ちですか？

K　すばらしいわよ（笑)。みなさん喜んでくださってるし。

──ええ、わたしたちもワクワクしています。ご旅行をヴィデオで撮られているとか？

K　ううん、撮ってない。撮ったほうがいいんだろうけど、どうなのかしらね。日本は……（笑)。

──おふたりで韓国を再訪されたときにナムジュン・パイクのヴィデオを撮っていらっしゃるので、うかがったんです。

K　そうなんだけどねえ……。

──カメラに映るのが恥ずかしくていらっしゃる。ご自分でもなぜなのかおわかりにならないのでしょうか？

K　わたしは自分の目を信じてるから。

＊＊＊

──『ニューヨーカー』誌のインタビューでは、ヴィデオ・アートは重いとおっしゃいましたね。

K　そうよ。カメラが重いもの。

──カメラが重いんですか。

K　でもいまではカメラも軽くなってるわよね。重労働ではない。でもわたしたちはいまでも重いカメラが好きなのよね。ソニーは小型のカメラをつくってる。片手に載せられるのよ。でも重いカメラには、何ていうか、重みがあるのよね。

〔録音が一時中断〕

K　わたしがシカゴ〔美術〕研究所でヴィデオを教えてたら、マッチョな学生がいっぱいいたのよ、筋肉モリモリの。

──男性のほうが女性より多かったですか？

K　半々ね。シカゴってすごく中西部なのよ。すごく極端なの。「重いヴィデオがいい？　それとも小さいのがいい？」って言ったの。そしたら全員が「重いほう」って。

──みんな重いのがいいんですね。

K　〔機材が〕重いから、映画作家はいつも健康なのよ、スポーツマンみたいに。体をカメラの一部みたいに、踊るみたいに使う。いまではソニーがあんなに小さいカメラつくってるから重労働じゃない。カセットテープみたいにポケットに入れるっていうのが近いかもね。

──小型のヴィデオを使う人は軽量級アーティストなんでしょうか？

K　うーん、小型ヴィデオはいいんだけどね。ヴィデオ・アートも変わりましたよ。

──どういうふうに変わりつつあるのでしょうか？

K　重いカメラはドキュメンタリーっていう感じのほうが強いと思うのね。もっとフィジカルっていうか、もっとデモンストレーションっぽいっていうか、もっとエモーショナルなものよね。軽いほうはもっと優雅。カメラの重さやサイズは、コンセプトやヴィデオの動きを変えると思う。重いカメラは、これから何かするぞっていう気分がするわよね。息をひそめて。軽いほうは本当に簡単で。

──小型カメラに切り替えるという飛躍は難しかったですか？

K　ううん、わたし小型カメラ好きよ。ずっと簡単で。アシスタントがいなくていいのよ。自分ひとりでできる。でも重いほう好きよ、古典的なほう。

──アートに重みが出ますよね。

K　水中銃みたいよね（笑)。

＊＊＊

──60年代のアートは反アートだったというお話をなさいました。70年代のアートはアート、反アート、ヴィデオという3部構成の進化なんだと。80年代はどうでしょう？

K　80年代と90年代は、インタラクティブ・アートっていう感じのほうが強いと思うわね。もっとインタラクティブ・アートとか参加型アート。それに、アートはもっとポピュラーになったわね。誰でもできるみたいに。アートはもう大真面目なものじゃない。それは前よりいいと思うわよ。

＊＊＊

──久保田さんにはアート面で父親がたくさんいます。デュシャンや、久保田さんのヴィデオにも登場される実のお父様。アート面での母親についてはいかがでしょう？　実のお母様は？

K　わたしの実の母はとっても芸術的なの。上野音楽学校出たの。いまでいう東京藝術大学、上野公園の。きれいな音楽演奏するのよ。だからわたしみたいな娘ができたのよ（笑)。とても伝統的で。ショパンとモーツァルト演奏してた。ピアニストなのよ。上野〔音楽学校〕を出て。〔当時は〕簡単じゃなかったのよ。〔いま〕80歳くらいですけど。

──いつ卒業なさったんですか？　お若いころですよね。

K　もちろん。でも、新潟からだと簡単じゃないのよ。家庭教師がいたのよね。

──他にアート面での母親は？

K　アート的な部分だと、わたしのおばが舞踏家だった話したでしょ。わたしのうちは女家族なんです。兄弟いないの。だからおじはいなくて、どっちかっていうとおばが……。

──では、身近な方たちが久保田さんのアート面の母親でいらっしゃるわけですね。父親のほうはむしろ……

K　散らばってる。

──他にはどういうアート面での父親がいらっしゃいますか？

K　ううん、それで全部。もう十分。

—アルはどうですか？

K アル・ロビンス？　ええ、好きですよ。でも父親じゃなかったわね（笑）。わたしの男の子、赤ちゃんみたいなさ。

—久保田さんの赤ちゃんだったんですか？

K 厄介者の子ども。

—ああ、なるほど。不良ですね。お子さんはいらっしゃいますか？

K いいえ。だからわたしアーティストなのよ。何かしなくちゃいけないじゃない。でもアーティストってみんな子どもよ、これ本当（笑）。

—そんなことおっしゃらないで。

K 子どもはいいわよ。

—わたし、結婚したばかりなんです。

K あら、いいわね。子どもはいいけど、アートをつくると楽しいわよ。子どもも楽しいけど、違う楽しさよね。〔アートは〕もっと満足感〔がある〕。アートは自分でコントロールできる。子どもは別人格でしょ。子どもはいつ卒業していくかわからないじゃない。アート・オブジェクトはいつもいっしょに〔いてくれる〕。

—でも、作品を売却されたときはどうですか？　作品が久保田さんのもとを去っていくときは？

K そりゃ悲しいわよ。

—お子さんを亡くされたような気持ちがしますか？

K そうそう。残念だけど、わたしそんなには作品売れてないの（笑）。ニューヨーク近代美術館に1点売った。《階段を降りる裸体》。〔あの場所で〕自分の作品を見るのはいいものよ。前はうちの居間に置いてた。いまは美術館。わたしあれ好きなの。《階段を降りる裸体》をうちのロフトに置いてたときは、棚みたいだった。オシャレな棚なんて持ってないから。段の上に本とか日常のものを置いてたの。いまでは美術館に行って、自分のアート見るわけ。

—重要な美術館にご自分の作品が受け入れられるのはどんなお気持ちですか？　受け入れられるのが遅すぎたと思われますか？

K ええ。どうしていま、自分の国に招かれるんだろうって思うのよね。遅いって気がするか？　遅すぎはしないけど、ねえ。

—すごく時間がかかりましたよね。

K そうよ、わたしの仕事と同じ。

—これ〔＝今回の展覧会〕は日本のヴィデオ・アートに効果を及ぼすと思われますか？　久保田さんがどんどん受け入れられていって、作品がメインストリームに入っていく、そういうことがいま起きてるわけですが、そのおかげで、受け入れられようとがんばっている他のヴィデオ・アーティストにとって状況が楽になると思われますか？

K ヴィデオ・アーティストだけじゃなくて、一般的アーティストにとっても。

—なぜでしょう？

K だってわたし、自分は単なるヴィデオ・アーティストじゃなくて、一般的アーティストだと思ってるから。

—ヴィデオ・アーティストという肩書はお好きでないんですね。

K まあ、ヴィデオをやってるけど、いつもポストモダン・アートの展覧会に招かれるのよ。ヴィデオ・アートじゃなくて。ヴィデオ・アートの歴史の展覧会に招かれることもあるけど、〔たいていは〕ポストモダン・アートの展覧会よ。ヴィデオ・アーテイストはわたしひとりのこともあるのよ。いいわよね。

—ポストモダン・アートの創始者のひとりであるという自負がおありですか？

K いいえ、そうは思わない。わたしの仕事はヴィデオ・アートを超えてるから。

＊＊＊

—新しいカタログでは久保田さんの歩みが語られていますが、1976年にアプロプリエーションを使われたとか？

K 大昔にね。ええ、いま流行ってるわよね。みんなやってる。

—アプロプリエーションはポストモダニズムの最重要テーマのひとつです。

K ええ、そうなのよ。だからわたし招かれるのよ。ヴィデオのおかげでわたしもそれができたのよね。新しい媒体を使ってたらもっと良かったはずよ。じっさいとてもうまくやってきてる。過去を通じた、新鮮な新しい創造。新しい媒体だったから良かったのよね。

—新しい媒体はどこへ向かっていると思われますか？　どういう方向性で？　他よりも重要な方向性は何でしょうか？

K 見当もつかない。インタラクティブ・ヴィデオってみんな言うけど、オーディエンスが行きたいと思う方向なんじゃないかしら。

—周囲の他のアートもたくさんご覧になりますか？

K いいえ、わたしソーホーに住んでるの。ギャラリー〔街〕の真ん中。

—お気に入りのアーティストはいますか？

K ええ、ジャスパー・ジョーンズ。色が華麗よね。ヴィデオでも色を何層も重ねるのよ。彼の筆、何層も重ねた色……

—ご自分のヴィデオでジョーンズの重ね塗り効果を使われたことはありますか？

K まあ、あんまりやりませんけどね。でも彼の何層もの色を、グレーだって、念頭に置いてたのよ。何層ものグレー。とっても透明。何層もあるんだなって感じられる。彼の筆。華麗だと思う。ヴィデオにもあれがもっとあるといいわよね。感動的っていうか。

—それに取り組んでいらっしゃるんですか？

K そうしたいわね。でもやるの難しいの。

—いろいろなさりたいことがあるみたいですね。

K そうだと思う（笑）。

—他に取り組んでみたいことは何でしょう？

K もっとオブジェクトつくりたいわね。石膏とかブロンズとかいろいろ。

—久保田さんの彫刻はヴィデオに対して単純すぎると批判する人もいます。

K だってTVは箱だから。TVの形のせいでヴィデオ彫刻がちょっと制限されたのよね。でもTVのサイズは前より多様になった。一度なんてJVCが丸いTVやったのよ。わたし使ったけど。バスケットボールみたいにまん丸。《ヴィデオ俳句──ぶら下がり作品》がいい見本。

──へー、まだつくってますか？

K　ううん。生産中止になっちゃった、残念だけど。熱が入りすぎるからだと思う。四角い箱なら熱が入らないようにするのがもっと簡単なのよ。でもいまは液晶TVで。熱もブラウン管もない。だからTVはサイズと形が変わったのよね。もっと面白い形がつくれる。でも箱も悪くないと思うわよ。コンセプチュアルだから。正方形のかたち。

──そうですね、もっとひどい形だった可能性もあるわけですから（両名笑）。この新しい自由にワクワクしていらっしゃいますか？

K　ええ。

＊＊＊

──瞑想はなさいますか？　禅を実践なさっていますか？

K　お医者さんにはもっと瞑想しなさいって言われるし、ヨガはしてる。でもいまお医者さんの言うこと聞いてないの。

──ご自分のアートについて考えているときは瞑想なさっているような感じがしますか？

K　そりゃあもう。あれは純然たる瞑想と満足感よ。創造的な時間よね。ドローイングをやってる〔あいだ〕考えるの。いい瞑想になるし、わたしドローイング好きなのよ。手作業ね。夜のあいだはあれ、瞑想よ。

──１日に何時間くらいなさいますか？

K　もっとやらなくちゃいけないんだけどね。わたし怠け者なのよ。ナムジュンは違った。たくさん働いてた。わたしよりも。わたし、あまり自分を追い詰めたくないのよね。いつも自分を追い詰めてたのよ。だから自分で抑えてる。楽しんでアートをつくれるように、リラックスしたいわね。もっと優雅にね、こんなふうにガーッとじゃなく（笑）。

──そのほうが人間的ですよね。

K　そうなのよ、だからわたしあんまり働きたくないの（笑）。

──作品をつくられるとき、ヴィデオ編集室で過ごされることのほうが多くていらっしゃいますか？　それとも彫刻にかける時間のほうが長いでしょうか？

K　彫刻と、考えることと、ドローイングと。ヴィデオ編集はわたしそんなに好きじゃないわね。ひとりで編集するか、エンジニアと編集するんです。編集室に行くとすぐに胃が痛くなっちゃう、緊張するから。怖いし。機械がジジジって音してね。それに、夜の９時から３時までずっと編集してるから。

──自前の編集室は……

K　ブロードウェイ。うちにも編集室はあるけど、本当にプロフェッショナルにやるの。すごくお金が高いし、編集時間も。

──ではそこを９時から３時まで使われて。

K　そうそうそう。そういうものだから。割引してくれるのよ。それから大真面目でやるから緊張しちゃう。

──恐ろしいですよね、ヴィデオ編集……。

K　ヴィデオの人たちって中毒なのよね。編集者はすごく頭がシャキッとして鋭いのよ。アーティストとは違う。エンジニアなのよね、違う脳なのよ。

＊＊＊

──いまでもご自分はフェミニストだと思われますか？

K　そういうふうにみんな言うのよね。わたしフェミニストかもしれないけど、自分がフェミニストだと思ったことないの。でも昔やってたセルフ・ヴィデオ〔＝《ヴィデオ・ポエム》〕はちょっと……。可笑しいわよね。あれはフェミニズムの時代の前にやったんだから。

──では、久保田さんはいつも他に先駆けているわけですね。

K　そうなの。いつも他の人より先なの。時代が来るときにはいつもわかる。でも〔ヴィデオ・〕ポエムを書いたときは、自分がフェミニストだなんて思わなかったのよ。

＊＊＊

──これまでのところ、ご自分が美術史に対してなさったいちばん重要な貢献は何だと思われますか？

K　ヴィデオ彫刻。オブジェクトと映像。

──ヴィデオ彫刻とヴィデオ・インスタレーションの違いとは何でしょう？

K　ヴィデオ・インスタレーションのほうが簡単なのよ。建築のスケールの一部みたいなもので。ヴィデオ彫刻はもっとオブジェクト・アート、アート作品なのよ。ヴィデオ・インスタレーションはもっとスケールが大きくて、美の一部。アートの絵とか空間の一部。

──反アートでいらしたのが、アート支持にまわられたみたいですね。

K　そうよ。どうなんだろう。それがわたしのバックグラウンドなのよね……。また、大学で受けた教育に戻っていっているところだから。４年間大学で教育受けて……だから……。

訳：近藤学

Interview with Shigeko Kubota

by Judith Greer

Conducted on the occasion of the solo exhibition *Kubota Shigeko Video Installation*, this interview remained unpublished. The text was transcribed from the original recording provided by the Foundation Arc-en-Ciel, Hara Museum, and edited by Gaku Kondō for the present catalog. Square brackets indicate the editor's notes.

—Okay, let's start with chronological information. You studied in Tokyo.

K I was (a) student at an art school, Tokyo University of Education. Tsukuba University, now they are called. I studied sculpture, structure, construction, and art history.

—Were you born in Tokyo?

K No, I was born in Niigata, the snow country.

—I read that today, *Snow Country*.

K Yeah, the famous *Snow Country* by [Yasunari] Kawabata.

—I was born in Buffalo. You've been to Buffalo, right?

K Yeah, I know [Buffalo]. I used to live in Buffalo, too.

—Oh, really?

K For six months.

—Oh, it's cold there.

K Cold and blizzard [*laughs*] in winter, but I love a cold place because I was born in the snow country. Winter always brings me good luck. I used to go to Chicago to teach, too. Chicago Art Institute. That's cold, too.

—That's really cold.

K But my hometown is very cold because of the wind from Siberia over the Sea of Japan. But somehow during winter I do better than during summer.

—Summer is hard.

K [In Winter] the brain shrinks, [gets] frozen and kind of sharper, you know.

—I have a brain like that, too.

K I always remember my winter experience when I was a kid. Nice. It's a kind of fantasy, cold winter. Half-frozen image. The Illusion.

—Summer in New York is hard, too.

K Yeah, but I was born in summer. [*laughs*] Crazy.

—When is your birthday?

K August 2. I'm a Leo.

—So now you are in Tokyo at the end of summer.

K At the end of summer is like noble. It's like in a story by [Yukio] Mishima or something. The end of summer is the end of a season, the beginning of a new season. I can make a fresh start. So it's nice to come back to Japan at the end of summer to start again my first ambition to be an artist.

—When is the last time you came to Tokyo?

K Two years ago.

—Do you come often to Tokyo?

K No.

—You were in Tokyo in 1986. Were you in Tokyo before that?

K I was nineteen. Yeah, when I was a student. I had my aunt. She was a dancer and studied with Masami Kuni as her teacher. He's a Korean dancer and studied at the University of Tokyo.

—Your aunt was a student of Masami Kuni's. And she died?

K No, no. She still dances.

—She still dances?

K Yeah, improvisation dance and creative dance. So I had my aunt. She was in Tokyo when I was a kid and I used to visit her once in a while. And when I was a high school kid, I used to come to Tokyo to take private lessons, my sculpture class.

—Who was your teacher in Tokyo then? Of sculpture?

K Kiyoshi Takahashi.

—Is he famous?

K No, he was known because he was from my hometown. My high school teacher recommended him, and my high school teacher was Tatsuji Terashima. He also encouraged me to study at the University of Education (Tsukuba).

—Why did they recommend Tsukuba?

K Because my teacher graduated from the Tokyo University of Education.

—Personal connections.

K Yeah. So the teacher always recommended students to go to my college. So I just followed in his steps.

—What year did you graduate from college?

K I think 1960.

—In '65 you heard John Cage's music?

K Yeah, '63 [*sic.* October 1962]. John Cage and David Tudor came to Tokyo.

—What was it about Cage's music?

K About more chance operation and natural music? No luck. They loved music conducted by a classical conductor. And he conducted his [*inaudible*] most of the time. Difficult. I thought this kind of avant-garde music was approved in New York. So I thought I should go to New York. In 1964, I left hometown and. . . .

—How did you feel emotionally or personally about it?

K After I graduated from university, I had a show at the Naiqua Gallery in Shinbashi. It was owned by a doctor, psychologist [*sic*]. Hi-Red Center is a group who got also an exhibition at the Naiqua Gallery. Hi is Takamatsu, Red is Akasegawa, Center is Nakanishi, three artists [who] organized Hi-Red Center. It was a very avant-garde, anarchist performance group. Now they are famous artists, and Akasegawa is a famous writer. Won the Akutagawa prize, too. I had the opportunity and I had my one-man show in 1963. But after my show, no review, nothing.

—Did you consider yourself an anarchist in those [days]?

K No, I was kind of, you know, finding the way, and very advanced, avant-garde artist. At that time, I was very radical, too, you know, Zengakuren [All-Japan League of Student Self-Government], politically active. Then, I had a one-man show at the Naiqua Gallery. I thought at least in the city [someone would] write a review or something. [*laughs*] But nothing came out. So I was very disappointed. Then I participated in the *Indépendant* [exhibition, organized by the] Yomiuri newspaper. They were active, but [again] no review, nothing. I didn't see my future.

—This was in '63?

K 1964. [So] I just left Tokyo, my own country. I said [to myself], I should go to New York [for] more chance. [In Japan, it wouldn't work because] it was all male-oriented, and maybe, I didn't graduate from Geidai [Tokyo University of the Arts], too. My university is a teacher's university, not an artist's university. Maybe I didn't have the right connections, I thought. So maybe I should go to New York. New York is a new world, anybody can try. You get a chance there, I thought, when I saw [*sic*] John Cage's music. If John Cage can be good, I should be good, too.

—When you got to New York, there were already some. . . .

K The Fluxus group. I had a connection with Fluxus.

—Also, there were some young Japanese artists there.

K Yeah, but you know, I didn't go to art school like Geidai. So I didn't go to art groups. My friend was the Fluxus artist George Maciunas.

—Yeah.

K So I was right away with George Maciunas or music[ians] like John Cage. I didn't have a particular Japanese friend who is a painter. More like Group Ongaku. [Takehisa] Kosugi or [Yasunao] Tone. They were my Japanese friends. But they are musicians. They are still my friends. We share our young and experimental time, hard life and joyful life. Musician friends are better than painters.

—Why?

K Because musicians are like gods, they're so nice. Enlightened. Music makes people happy. But art is more like a struggle, making an object, making a painting. Especially [because] I'm a sculptor, more physical work. Or you think more deeply, more physical and mental space. Music, too, but we have to make a shape. Music is a wave, more like a psychic kind of communication. Musicians are more enlightened, kind of like a Buddhist, like John Cage. Like a monk. Musician friends are easier to have fun and talk [with]. You know, sometimes a video artist or art friend feels too close [to] each other.

—Well, that's true.

K Yeah, so I don't have so many friends.

* * *

—I just interviewed the primo ballerino for [Maurice] Béjart's group. His name is Jorge Donn. Jorge Donn said the same, "I can't have friends who are dancers, really. I love them, but my close friends are in other fields." He said, "Because I can get a nurturing, nourishment from other fields." So, do you take nurturing and intellectual, emotional and spiritual food from music?

K Yeah, I think music is so abstract, like mathematics or philosophy.

—Where else do you take that nourishment from?

K I think nature. That's why my works, like *Three Mountains* or the *River* piece, are relating to four seasons, like Japanese haiku, nature, and environment where you live every day. Kind of slide [show] to you, changing time.

—Do you live in the country?

K No, I live in New York. I don't like the country. I was born in the country. Niigata is so much country. You see mountains and rice fields. That's why I live in New York. Well, New York is the country, too. Once you stay inside of your loft, it's the country. What's the difference?

—Yeah?

K You close the door.

—Yeah, but there is no green.

K No green, I know.

—Do you miss the green?

K But I make the green. You see my work, in my video, the color green or objects of garden, I made them for *Adam and Eve*? I made the green myself. Green lofts. I make my green myself.

—So, do you feel like there is a similarity between the video tape that you work with and natural things?

K I think the video tape green is more natural than

the natural green sometimes.

—Why?

K Oh, because more transparent. I saw it like it's there.

—So transparence is a very important quality for you.

K Like electronic transparency. You've got see-through, kind of purity there, through being. Because we deal with lots of being.

—What do you mean, being?

K Being is like a light, you know, light, light sources. Video is a light source from electron.

—What are other important light sources for you?

K Like sunset. I was born in a village near the ocean in Niigata. Nice to see the sun set in ocean. Always changing and disappearing, too. The sun is separating beyond the ocean. Kind of changing light.

—I was just in Sicily. It's beautiful! You have the sea, and there are mountains. And then it's the sunset. And the sun comes down, but it disappears before it touches the water. This is really important to me.

K Yeah, and the reflection of the water catches it. Even when the sun is gone.

—It remains.

K It's beautiful, it remains, yeah. So, that's color, moving color.

—It seems like that your childhood and where you grew up, it comes out again in your art.

K Like sort of biographical landscape which you have, in your mind. You are going to create your landscape in the field of your art. Art is your autobiographical diary.

—What's a landscape for you?

K I was a mountain climber, so I like mountain climbing. [When] I was a student, I climbed all the Japanese Alps. Then, I went to America, I went to Rocky Mountains, and [Grand] Teton, Wyoming, Yellowstone, big scale mountains.

—What's your favorite mountain?

K Mount Fuji.

—Ah, really?

K I camped there in winter, Christmas, when I was a university student. I was a member of the mountain climbing club.

—What do you like about Mt. Fuji?

K I think it's well-balanced. [*laughs*] A nice, noble mountain. Very beautiful. And then I like Mount [St.] Helen[s] because it looks like Mount Fuji. Mount [St.] Helen[s] had a big blow-up, near Seattle. I video-taped it a lot, too, before the blow-up.

—That looks like Mt. Fuji?

K It's a beautiful mountain. When you climb up, in winter time, it's beautiful. Big avalanche comes, too. No tree. That's nice, in a way. You can see all the view. Winds, very strong, and incredible avalanche, that's like ice pick, snow. It's like a changing quantity of scale and volume, like sculptures. Like landscape.

* * *

—[Getting back to New York,] you went to New York. You got involved with Fluxus. What made you choose video as a medium for work?

K When I was a member of Fluxus, I did lots of street happenings, more disruptive ones, events, and we were against art object.

—It's more like playing, game, very anti-art.

K Oh, Fluxus was anti-art. But [in the] late seventies, George Maciunas was getting more involved in real estates, like in lofts, SoHo-style. All the Fluxus artists went in different directions. Then, my background as a sculptor came out, but just making an object is not that interesting. Because an object doesn't move. I wanted to combine moving image and object together. Then new media like video came out. So combination of video and object—that's marriage of video/sculpture. So I was going to work [as] an inventor.

—Why video and not film?

K Oh, because video is more instant [aneous]. It's like brown rice, organic, you know. And film is more chemical. You need more time, to process, and you have to wait to see it. But video plays background, or if you don't like it you can try again, too. Like instance [*sic.* instant], you know, quick. And easy, too: you can do it yourself.

—What were your first impressions about video as a medium for art? Where did you think it could go, what did you think it could do then?

K There were many ways. First you would like a documentary video and also broadcast video and now the cable [TV] video. But, that's narrative video. But my case, being a Japanese living in New York, speaking my broken English, wouldn't qualify as a broadcast video. I tried, you know. I used to go to an Indian reservation and live with American Indians and made a documentary. But Channel 13, the educational TV station, didn't play my American Indian tape because American Indian themselves were minority, and myself, being a foreigner living in America, is minority, too. So that double minority didn't make it a good start for a documentary video artist or a narrative video artist. With video sculpture, I don't need to speak English, broken English. I don't need [to speak] at all, just make object and make my art language. It's a different language, you know, you don't need to speak little now, but art language doesn't need to be data, it's object.

—God, I can relate. I've been here five years and I speak Japanese, but I don't feel like I can do what I can do in English. So I need another language. I'm a writer, but the frustration that I feel is pretty intense. I can understand [what you mean]. I noticed you write a lot of diaries. You seem very affected by western art history. Also, very affected by traditional themes in Japanese like nature and the four seasons. And the power of haiku, the ephemerality and . . . like the cherry blossoms, how quickly they bloom and they die. You know that feeling. But then, it seems like when you work in those areas, you are hiding. Sometimes, just looking at the description, I feel, where is the personal statement? Where is hope? And, where is love? Where does that come out for you? And then, looking more, I saw the *Broken Diaries*, and I thought, this is where your personal statement comes from. How do you feel about that?

K Well, a diary, literature, is a dialog for Japanese. I think diaries are so intimate. It's all right for yourself, but for some people may be too much. Too intimate.

—I noticed you make *Broken Diaries*. Why "broken"?

K Oh, because my English is broken and also, emotion is broken. Nothing is perfect. Everything in life is broken.

—Also, you seem interested in illusions, like the illusion of glass looking like a rock. So, why not make an illusion of a seamless diary?

K Seamless diary . . . but some people like a diary but not long. Diaries are like one strip or stream of video tape. But, I would like to go beyond the strip. Object, more sculpture. Beyond the strip means more like combination of all, information and shape. I'm more interested in shape.

—And shape rather than strip.

K Yeah. Because I'm no storyteller, and, diary would be one person's story or experience, something more like a narrative with a beginning. But I don't want to have any start, any end. More like a middle moment, not a continuous time. I cut myself sometimes.

* * *

—Yes. Is this one of the reasons why you are so involved with Duchamp?

K Duchamp's like loop, loop, yeah. But my *Window* is "meta Marcel Duchamp." So I have to go beyond Marcel Duchamp.

—You have to go beyond yourself.

K Yeah.

—With, through Duchamp?

K Through.

—So Duchamp and his work acts as a window for you to go beyond.

K Yeah.

—Why Duchamp?

K Because I met him in 1968, three months before he died, in an airplane (*laughs*), on my way to Buffalo. Like coincidence.

—But, did you meet him before . . .

K No, I just met him on an airplane on my way to Buffalo to attend Merce Cunningham's dance concert.*1 Duchamp [was going to Buffalo because his] big glass piece, which the Philadelphia Museum has,*2 [was adapted] for the stage, by Jasper Johns. Then by chance I met them [i.e., Duchamp and his wife Teeny].

—What was it like to meet Duchamp?

K Well, I met him in an airplane. That was the funny thing. If I had met him on a street, I wouldn't have been so moved. [On an] airplane, not many people are in the seats. How many people airplane can carry?

—Was he sitting next to you?

K No, he was [in] first class, I was in tourist class.

—So, you went to first class?

K No, I saw Teeny Duchamp who went to the toilet. That's why I thought, oh, I know her, then Marcel must be in the first class. The toilet is always behind, at the end of the airplane. I was [just] reading about Duchamp, because *Bijutsu Techō* had a big special issue on Marcel Duchamp. So I thought, oh, he might be happy to see himself written in Japanese. In 1968, Japanese print was still fresh at that time. I still have a picture of him, on which he gave me his signature. I said, "Here you are in a Japanese magazine. I was just reading about you." Then because the blizzard in Buffalo was so strong because of the Niagara Falls, we couldn't land. We landed in Rochester. Then a long [bus] trip through the winter field.

—Did you sit by him on the way to Buffalo?

K Yeah, not many people were there. His gallery person, and Teeny Duchamp and himself, and me. Four. It was winter. That's why I like winter. [*laughs*] It all happened in winter.

—What did he teach you at that time?

K Well, just a feeling. "Oh, this is the man, Marcel Duchamp." You get your feeling. You can't get a feeling through the media, like printed media, not the real feeling, the physical, real one. You see the history there.

K A moment of history.

—You feel like you touch history.

K Yeah, yeah.

K I had a cheap camera. I took a photograph of that stage later. But I didn't develop the photograph. Then one day I opened a newspaper, and he [Duchamp] was dead. That was like someone who dies. Then I developed the photograph. The photo was still clear. Then I made a photo-book. [see pp. 28–29]

—What is it about his art or his work that really attracts you?

K Ready-made. His concept art. He opened many directions for us, but one I know [is] his concept of the ready-made.

—Why?

K Why? Any object is beautiful, any object is an art object and a ready-made object. I myself use ready-mades. A TV is a ready-made, too.

—But ready-made depends on the space that the object is around.

K Yeah, but ready-made continues the political sense like social sculpture.

—How? Where do you see it?

K Anything could be art, more political, statement-like object, like social sculpture. People use lots of things. I made an auto tire piece. I [put] a TV inside of an auto tire, which I want to show as art [*Auto-tire Whleel*, cat. pp. 118–119]. And I show it at museums, too. Moving image, too. Auto tire is thrown away, it's a junk. Well, junk will be art, too. [You can] give a junk a life again. Ready-made is a junk. You can buy it at a ten-cent store. But he [Duchamp] made ready-made as art piece.

—But, it was surprising then to see ready-mades in a museum. It's not so surprising now, though.

K No.

—So, what is it about ready-made that is still fresh for you?

K I think you know that supermarket kind of concept? Technical training, that's important, too. But [there's] an easier approach for art, like kindergarten, children. . . .

—So, anybody can make art.

K Oh, sure. He [Duchamp] opened the door for art that is not special. You can do it yourself. Do-it-yourself kind of attitude.

* * *

—Is that another reason why you were drawn to video?

K Video is a ready-made. And social sculpture, because TV is now getting cheaper and cheaper. Color TV used to be very expensive, only for rich people.

—Also, video cameras are becoming really cheap.

K I know. It became like a Polaroid. Anybody can be an artist, a photographer. Who is a photographer, a professional photographer? [But there is] no amateur photographer, no border line [any more], no. Like a video artist, too, now. Because [with] Video8 you grab the camera, then you have your diary. That's your art.

—How do you feel about that?

K Wonderful.

—How does this situation, the change in the availability of video cameras, how does that affect how people see your art? Do you have any idea?

K I think kids liked my art. That pleases me lot. And when I had a show at the Museum of Moving Image. . . . It's in Astoria, which is like an immigrant town. Polish kids, Puerto Rican and more poor kids came to the museum on a school tour. Then they liked it. Manhattan is also immigrant. But Manhattan is very expensive. But in Queens or Brooklyn, maybe kids like it, participation art. Kids say "Oh, that me?" They have a live camera [*Video Haiku—Hanging Piece*, cat. pp. 96–97]. They like to see themselves on TV and participate. "That's me," or, "Not only TV announcer on screen, me too" kind of participation, interactive kind of participation. A participation piece is very good for children and for audience, because they are involved, part of the art, not just observe.

—But one review about your work that I read was that the techniques and the video effects that you experimented with and used in your art now can be seen on MTV, and in the big shopping malls. . . .

K I know. Because they stole the idea from us. MTV, they have more money. [*laughs*]

—How do you feel about that?

K I know, not only art like Peter Campus' is greater, the video artist who did lots of chroma key work and wonderful experimental work at WGBH in Boston. But MTV people have more money. And they have much bigger scale of production. They do better because they have more high-tech facilities. But [in terms of] ideas and concepts they got influenced by video artists like Peter Campus. I think it's a social influence. I think it's all right, they can take it. We can take back something. But that's like a social phenomenon, part of video art.

—You have appropriated so much, but now people appropriate your work.

K Yeah. That's like a different direction. But always society has happened so. Especially the young generation like MTV, more like a desktop. It fits them very well, darkness and brightness and music and dance and projected image.

—Your experiments in video have been taken and used in popular culture, everywhere, shopping malls, videos, supermarkets, TV. You had a really big effect on the way people look at their environment, what they see in their environment.

K I hope they can see better.

—You think that help them see better? Do you think your images and the content of what you have done changes when it moves into popular culture?

K But the living style has changed. Anybody has a living room, a video projector, watch video news, TV news, not just [on a] TV screen. They get to use a bigger screen like film and a video projector, and a print on the wall. Moving image on the wall. [That's] part of your high living style, and young people like it, too. It's nice. If they're happy, then it's nice. In old times people were happy they got an ice box. Now they are happy they've got a video projector in their living room. Life improvement, life richness. And they enjoy their space, their life experience. Then, it's a good life.

* * *

—One thing that you mentioned about children liking your work is that they can see themselves. You use a lot of interactive in your video.

K I don't use it so much, but I use it with mirror and live cameras sometimes. Hidden live camera. Then, when I had a show, because this museum is surrounded by lots of children, because the cheapest way to entertain welfare kids is to take them to a museum. That's for teachers. [*laughs*] But they have good time. In video art they can participate, they can touch, too. Because [usually] in an art museum, you cannot touch, you cannot do. You just have to stand and watch.

—So they can touch everything in your exhibit. Also, we can touch your exhibits here [at the Hara Museum].

K Yeah. So, you know, that kind of physical activity and invitation to the art, I think the young generation likes it.

—That's wonderful.

K They want to be part of the environment, part of the art, too. Maybe they think it an art piece if it [is] interactive video. If [there's] no kids, no participation, people, boring, just come and there, normal watching.

—Do you operate your own camera?

K Sometimes.

—When?

K I used to do when I used a camera first.

—With photographs.

K Portrait.

—Video portrait?

K Yeah. Myself.

—When were you doing video portraits?

K Well, sometimes studio, sometimes my living room. I don't do it now so often, but I used to do. That's like addicted, when you have your first camera, your new camera. You like to videotape yourself. Video is addictive, because it's narcissistic. You enjoy yourself, and you like to see yourself again and again and again and again. In a video it is always more, more, more, you know.

—But feminist video these days includes a lot of women taking pictures of themselves again and again and again. What do you think?

K I think it's all right. They're happy.

—It's not narcissistic?

K It's narcissistic, but it's just for themselves. But not on a cable TV, maybe. You know, who has time to watch all that? People are busy.

—Yeah, but I see it everywhere.

K That's why I make video sculptures. You just walk around and [you are] gone. You don't need to sit. I used to be a video curator at the Anthology Film Archive, and I got bored to watch the same program again and again and again, a single-channel tape, an artist tape, you know. Until I wanted to make a piece like they were making, I mean video sculpture. I don't hold the audience. The audience can enjoy and go. You don't need to stay. You are busy. That's why I would like to make my video installation or video sculpture for the public space like a plaza, [where] people [are] walking through, like [in] an airport or a shopping center.

—A recent work that you've made *The Gate for Culture* [cat. pp. 116–117] in Taormina.

K Oh, yeah, in Sicily. That was beautiful.

—In Taormina there's that beautiful Greek theater.

K I know!

—And the view. . . .

K View facing the ocean.

—Your *Gate for Culture* reminded me of that in the way it shapes, creates the viewing place. And yet you just talked to me about the role of video and the culture. This "Video Gate" makes me feel like for you maybe, art isn't this spiritual thing that is so important, but your video can create a gate for the person to go and find it themselves. How do you feel?.

K And also, that was by frame. Like frame for your window, frame for your view, frame for your mind, frame for your landscape, frame for your park you walk in. You have a frame, you passing through. And you see a beautiful park determined by angle. Garden of Taormina especially. Mediterranean and [it has] also mountains.

—Why are frames important?

K I feel, where you make a frame, you have always a frame. I think [it is related to] how you view your world. You make it. You touch [it] yourself where you like, and your eyes stop it. That [is the] frame. You are passing through and you always see something, but you sometimes stop and you gaze [at] something.

—How do frames operate in Japanese culture?

K I don't know, but through your brain, no?

—How?

K How your brain [is] reacting to your landscape for your mind and you're living the environment. Your frame was like locating where you live. So, that's your background. You've got interest in that view, then that's frame.

—What you are saying is interesting for me because, if you see a scroll, *kakejiku*. . . .

K Oh, *kakejiku*, that's a frame. [*laughs*]

—*Kakejiku* is a frame, but it's not a hard frame.

K I know, it's a soft one. Round one, too. You've got a contour. . . .

—And also, for me in the West, it's really an important idea for a scholar or a writer to have a frame. But it doesn't seem so important here. So I'm wondering, did you get interested in frames when you were in the States?

K I think from film theater, and also especially when

you work your camera. Your eyes are camera where you move and you stop here and that's frame. Your physical rhythm, your body and mental rhythm control the camera. Your camera is a part of your hand, and [your] hand is part of your eyes and feeling. Feeling [is] constantly part of your brain. So camera is part of your body, too, but all is controlled by the psychological, the consciousness.

—The consciousness is controlling everything.

K Yeah, I think that's [the] frame.

—So everything you create is created consciously and planned out.

K Or unconsciousness. But it became my frame. Continuation of frame is time. Time is a movement. And cutting a frame, and analyzing a frame is a movement again, going back to the beginning of the movement.

* * *

—What are you working on now?

K After I made a landscape, I'm making a body. After *Adam and Eve* [cat. pp. 112–115] I met a skater, a Japanese skater, [Itō] Midori-chan. I was invited by Nagoya, and I had to make a new piece for Nagoya. Then, one day I opened the *New York Times*. Midori-chan was born in Nagoya. But this piece, unfortunately I'm not showing in Nagoya. I'm showing it now in New York. It's called *Social Sculpture*. More figurative. I'm working on body figures. Next is more like face, or type of the body, made with clay. Clay and bronze. I am going to use a liquid-crystal TV inside. A small, small liquid-crystal TV. Because [it has] no heat, no tube, I can put a small TV inside the clay, or inside the bronze. TV set used to be hot and couldn't be put inside. Now TV became so small, and now liquid-crystal TV. . . . Now I'm working figurative, like when I was a student, I used clay and bronze.

—So do you feel like you've gone the whole circle?

K Yeah, whole circle now, I think, going back to a student [*laughs*], when I was using materials, because I used wood, plywood, and metal, river, water, and notes, and now, [back] to clay and bronze, and liquid-crystal TV, and making figurative bodies, of human bodies.

—Do you think you are being pulled toward figurative work because that's the trend now?

K I wanted to be more like, I can say "This is like a woman's feeling there," or, something more emotional. You say story, but I will write a story about anger or emotion or something. [*laughs*]

—Something human.

K Human. Yeah, yeah. Because my work was very cold before. So I wanted to have more emotion in the piece, which is more figure. I wanted to keep some statement and message. Before [it was] very abstract message. But now more oral. I talk a lot, emotional.

—Emotional words?

K Yeah.

—This is another new language.

K Yeah. Which I've been trying since last summer. I borrowed my whole new tool to make clay and bronze. I have it in my studio.

—A new speaking tool?

K Yeah, a new, sculpture tool.

—What does it look like?

K Like a new tool, a new tool to make clay. More traditional sculptures.

—Do you have a picture?

K No, I haven't made a picture yet. Sometime I have to do it.

* * *

—Did you choose the work for the show?

K Oh, Mr. Hara [Toshio Hara, the director of Hara Museum at the time].

—Together? Or he chose?

K Well he liked my River piece, when he saw it at *The Whitney Biennial* [in] 1983. The *River* piece, I made it in Berlin, 1979 to 1981, when I was a DAAD Berlin.

—Were you teaching.?

K No, no. I was invited by the German government. They invite artists to Berlin. I was just living in Berlin and making art. That was my residency. And I made the *River* piece. [It was the] first time I used metal and water and wave machines. I went to a swimming pool in Germany. Every ten minutes, the big wave came in the swimming pool. I thought it's like the ocean, but it's a swimming pool. Good idea, I thought. And kids are excited and challenging [for] big waves. I thought, I want to make a big wave machine, but I made a small wave machine.

—You made your own?

K With motor. Since then, I started using a moving motor, or a rotating machine. And Mr. Hara liked it very much. Being a Japanese artist is hard, to be in the Biannual at the Whitney Museum of American Art.

—It's hard to be a woman in that.

K Oh, [it's] hard to be a woman, but, now being woman is not so bad. To be a foreign artist living in America, not an American artist is harder.

—Hmm, I think so.

K Because the Whitney Museum of American Art, they only collect American art by American artists. I have been in New York for a long time, and the Whitney Museum thinks I'm an American Japanese. [*chuckles*] And I still keep my Japanese passport.

—Do you consider yourself American Japanese or not?

K I don't know. I never thought of it. I could be. Then the Whitney Museum wanted to buy my *River* piece. They finally learned I'm still Japanese [and asked], "Shigeko, Are you still Japanese? I thought you were an American Japanese." I said, "What do you mean?" "I'm sorry, we like your piece, but we cannot buy it." I said, "What?" I thought it's not fair.

—It's racist.

K Oh, I don't know it's racist or not, but, you know, I paid tax in America. War.

K But I left my country. I'm like a lost child in a way. Where can I go? Here I come back and people say, oh, you have been in New York too long. Now I'm going to America, then they say, "You're still Japanese."

—Have you ever put that feeling into any of your art?

K Not yet. That's why I thought I'm going to make more figurative, portraits with my anger or my emotion sometimes. My language, it's there. I thought, I like art because [it's an] international language. I didn't know I had to face a war-like situation. People have become very nationalistic now.

—The Whitney still hasn't bought any of your. . . .

K No, I [don't] think they can because I'm [not] an American. They are called Museum of American Art. Art is an international language. That's why I'm working art. But it's hard, you know. When you live in a different country, it's not your country, but you are working in your own world. Like some people who like to have a border line between. . . .

—Do you think there is a border line between Americans and Japanese in terms of understanding your work?

K I think Americans helped me lot. Americans understand my work better.

—They helped you a lot?

K Yeah, yeah. This is another reason I cannot complain about the Whitney. Americans like lots of my work. And also, I was in Documenta twice.

—So, Germans, Europeans like your work.

K Yeah, Europeans, too. But also, I got lots of grant from American National Endowment for Art or, New York State Council of Art. That supported my own work to keep going on. It's not cheap, you know.

—Is this your first big show in Japan?

K Yes.

—How do you feel about that?

K Wonderful. [*chuckles*] And they are happy.

—Yeah, we're excited, too. Are you making a video tape of your trip now?

K No, no. I should, but I don't know, Japan. . . . [*laughs*]

—It's a question because you made a tape of Nam June Paik when you re-visited Korea. This is a kind of special re-visit for you, too.

K I know, but. . . .

—You are shy for the camera. You don't know why?

K I believe in my eyes.

* * *

—In the interview with the *New Yorker*, you called video art heavy.

K Oh, yeah, because camera is heavy.

—It's the camera that's heavy.

K But now camera is getting light. It's not challenging. But we still like heavy camera. Sony is making a small camera. You can put it on a hand. But heavy camera has something like, you know, weight.

[*Gap in the tape*]

K When I was teaching video at Chicago Institute there are a lot of macho students, you know, big muscle.

—More men than women?

K Oh, fifty-fifty. Chicago is very Midwest. You go very far. And I said, "Do you like a heavy video or a small one?" And they all said, "The heavy one."

—They all like heavy.

K Because [of the] weight [of the equipment], filmmakers are always in good shape, like a sportsman. They use body like part of your cam, like dancing. Now Sony makes such a small camera it's not challenging. Maybe it's more like [you] put [it] in a pocket like a cassette tape.

—People who use small videos are light-weight artists?

K Well, small video is all right. Video art got changed.

—How is it changing?

K I think a heavy camera is more like documentary, more physical or more like demonstration, something more emotional. Light one is more elegant. I think the weight and size of the camera change the concept and video's movement. Heavy camera is like you feel you are going to do something. You hold your breath. Light one's so easy.

—Did you find it hard to make the jump to using a small camera?

K No, I like small cameras, much easier. You don't need to have an assistant. You can do it yourself. But, I like the heavy one, classic.

—It lends weight to your art.

K Yeah, like a sea gun. [*laughs*]

* * *

—You talked about art in the sixties being anti-art, and art in the seventies being the tripartite evolution: art, anti-art, and video. What were the eighties?

K The eighties and nineties, I think it's more like interactive art. More interactive art and participation art. And art became more popular, like anybody can do. Art is no [longer] serious. I think that's better.

* * *

—You have a lot of artistic fathers. Duchamp, your own father you put into your video. What about your artistic mother? What about your real mother?

K My real mother is very artistic. She graduated from the Ueno Music School, Ueno Ongaku Gakko. Now Tokyo University of Art [and] Music in the Ueno

Park. She plays beautiful music. That's why she has a daughter like me. [*chuckles*] She's very traditional. She played Chopin and Mozart. She's a pianist, she graduated from Ueno. That [was] not easy [back then]. She's like eighty something [now].

—When did she graduate? When she was young?

K Of course. But from Niigata it's not easy. She had a private teacher in piano.

—Now, other artistic mothers?

K Artistic part, my aunt was a dancer, I told you. My family is like *onna* [female] family, no brothers, so no uncle, more like aunt and. . . .

—So people who are close to you are more like your artistic mothers. Then, your fathers are more. . . .

K Spread out.

—What other artistic fathers do you have?

K No, that's it. I have enough.

—What about Al?

K Al Robbins? Yeah, I like him. But he was not my father. [*laughs*] He was my boy, baby or something.

—He was like your baby?

K Trouble kid.

—Ah, yeah. Delinquent. Do you have any children?

K No. That's why I'm an artist. You have to do something. But artists are like kids, I tell you. [*laughs*]

—Don't tell me that.

K Kids are nice.

—I just got married.

K Oh, It's nice. Kids are nice, but you make art and it is enjoyable. Kids are enjoyable, too, but it's a different enjoyment. [Art brings] more satisfaction. Art, you can control it yourself. A kid is another personality. Kids graduate from you any time. Your art object always [stays] with you.

—Well, what about when you sell your work? When your work leaves you?

K Oh, I feel sorry.

—Do you feel like you lost your kid?

K Oh, yeah. Unfortunately, I haven't sold so many. [*chuckles*] One I sold to Museum Modern Art in New York, *Nude Descending A Staircase*. It's nice to see my piece [there]. I used to have it in my living room. Now [it's] in a museum. I like it. When I had my *Nude Descending a Staircase* at my loft, it was like shelves. I didn't have a fancy shelves. I put my books and everyday kind of object on its steps. Now you go to the museum, and you see your art.

—How do you feel about having your work being accepted by important museums? Do you think it was accepted too late?

K Yes. I think, why am I invited now by my own country? I feel too late? Not too late, but, you know.

—It took a lot of time

K Yeah. Like my job.

—Do you think this one'll have an effect on video art in Japan? The more you are accepted, and your work enters the mainstream, which is happening now, do you think it will make it easier for other video artists who work to be more accepted?

K I think not only for video artists, but general artists, too.

—Why?

K Because I don't think I'm just a video artist, more like a general artist.

—You don't like the title video artist.

K Well, I work on video, but I'm always invited to post-modern art shows, not video shows. Sometimes, of course, I am invited by a history of video art show, but [it's mostly] post-modern art show. Sometimes I'm the only video artist. It's nice.

—Do you take credit for being one of the originators of the post-modern art?

K No, I don't think so. Because my work is beyond video art

* * *

—Your new catalogue talks about your development, your use of appropriation in 1976?

K A long time ago. Yeah, now it's fashionable. Everybody is doing [it].

—Appropriation is one of the most important themes in post-modernism.

K Yeah, I know. That's why I'm invited. Because of video I was able to do it, too. Using new media, it could have been better. And it has done very well. Fresh new creation through past. Because of new media, it was nice.

—Where do you see new media going now? And in what directions? What are more important directions?

K I have no idea. Interactive video, people say, but, I think where the audience would like to go.

—Do you look at other art around you very much?

K No. I live in SoHo, in the middle of the gallery [district, so I don't have to go out (?)].

—Do you have a favorite artist?

K Yeah, Jasper Johns. His color is gorgeous. We make many layers of color in video. His brush, touch of many layers of color. . . .

—Do you ever use his layering effects in your videos?

K Well, I don't do it so often. But I had in my mind his many layers of color, even gray. Many layers of grays. Very transparent. There are many layers, I can feel. His brush. I think that's gorgeous. We would like to have it in video more. Kind of touching.

—Are you working on that?

K I'd like to. But, it's hard to do.

—Sounds like you have a lot of things you want to work on.

K I think so. [*chuckles*]

—What else do you want to work on?

K I'd like to make more objects. Clay and bronze and more.

—Some people have criticized your sculpture as being too simple for your video.

K Because TV is a box. Its shape kind of limited video sculpture. But TV size became more varied. Once JVC had a round TV, too, I used [it], like a basketball, round and round. *Video Haiku*,[is a] good model. . . . [cat. pp. 96–97]

—Oh, do they still make that?

K No. They discontinued, unfortunately, I think because too much heat was involved. Square box is easier to keep heat off. But now, with liquid-crystal TV, no heat, no tube. So made it easier. So TV size and shape have changed. We can make more interesting shape[s]. But I think box is not bad because it's conceptual. Shape of the cube.

—Yeah. It could have been worse. [Both laugh] Are you excited about this new freedom?

K Yeah.

* * *

—Do you meditate? Do you practice Zen?

K My doctor says I should meditate more and I do yoga. But now I'm not listening to him.

—Do you feel like you are meditating when you are thinking about your art?

K Oh, yeah. That's a pure meditation and satisfaction. You know, creative time. I think [while I'm] drawing. It's a good meditation and I like drawing, hand work, you know. During nights, it's meditation.

—How many hours a day do you spend?

K I should do more often. I'm lazy. Nam June wasn't. He worked hard, he worked harder than I. I don't want to push myself to the edge, you know. I always went to the edge, you know. So I control myself. I would like to relax in a way to enjoy myself and making art. You know, more elegant way, not hard like this. [*laughs*]

—It's more human way.

K I know, so I don't want to work hard. [*laughs*]

* * *

—When you are making a work, do you spend more time in the video editing room? Or do you spend more time on the sculptures?

K Sculpture and thinking and drawing. Video editing, I don't like it so much. I edit with myself or with my engineer. As soon as I go to the editing room, I get stomach ache, because I get nervous. I also get scared. The machine makes zzzz noise, you know. And because we go on editing like 9 o'clock at night to 3 o'clock.

—Do you have an. . . .

K Broadway. We have an editing room at my home, but we do it really professional way. And money is very expensive, and editing time.

—So you use it from 9 to 3.

K Yes, yes, yes, because that's how it's done. You can get discount. Then we get so serious I get nervous.

—It's terrible, video editing. . . .

K Video people are addicted and always, editors are very sharp and keen. Not like an artist. They are engineers, different brain.

—Do you call yourself a feminist, still?

K You know, people say it. I might be a feminist, but I never thought I'm a feminist. But my old self-video is like. . . . It's funny. Because I made it before the feminist time.

—So you're always early.

K I know. I'm always early. I know always [when the] time comes. But when I wrote a [video] poem [cat. pp. 38–39], I never thought I that was a feminist.

* * *

—What do you think your most important contribution to art history so far?

K Video sculpture. Object and moving image.

—What's the difference between video sculpture and video installation?

K Video installation is easier, in a way like part of architectural scale. But video sculpture is more [of an]object art, art piece. Because video installation is bigger [in] scale, like part of beauty. Part of the art picture, space.

—It sounds like you've gone from anti-art to pro-art.

K Yeah. I don't know. It's my background. . . . Because I'm going back again to my university [training]. I had training there for 4 years. . . so. . . .

[NOTES]

*1——*Walkaround Time*, premiered on March 10, 1968, at Buffalo State College, State University of New York.

*2——*The Bride Stripped Bare By Her Bachelors, Even*, 1915–1923, also known as *The Large Glass*.

ヴィデオは人生の窓 ― 久保田成子の芸術と人生

濱田真由美

はじめに

新潟県に生まれ、ニューヨークを拠点に活動したヴィデオ・アーティスト、久保田成子。彼女の作品を語る際に必ず使われる「ヴィデオ彫刻」*1とは、ヴィデオと立体的な構造物あるいはインスタレーションを組み合わせた表現で、ヴィデオ・アートの一形式として1970年代半ばより展開した。それと並行するように、久保田の活躍は1970年代半ばから90年代半ばまでの20年間に最も際立っていた。「ドクメンタVI」(1977年)への出品をはじめ、彼女の作品は欧米各地で繰り返し紹介されたが、その多くはヴィデオ彫刻を紹介するもので、それ以前の創作活動をまとめて紹介するのは本展覧会が初の試みとなる。

他方で、久保田成子という作家についてのもうひとつのイメージは、《ヴァギナ・ペインティング》(1965年)［本書24頁］と題する過激なパフォーマンスを写した1枚の写真によって形成されてきた。それは観客であった同じフルクサスのメンバーたちからも不評を買ったといわれているが、のちにフェミニズムのコンテクストなどから注目され、現在も新たな視点から再評価が進んでいる。

ヴィデオ彫刻とヴァギナ・ペインティング。この2つの異質な作品を生み出した久保田成子の作家像に迫るため、本稿では、初期を中心に彼女の人生と作品の変遷を辿っていく。それによって、原点である彫刻、初期に強い影響を受けたパフォーマンス、生涯のメディアとして選んだヴィデオと手法を変えながらも、空間芸術と時間芸術の融合を目指してヴィデオ彫刻を展開し、さらに空間や鑑賞者をも包含した表現へと向かったことを検証する。そして、そのテーマは常に自らの人生や体験に由来するものであった点も確認したい*2。

1. 出自

1937年8月2日に新潟県西蒲原郡巻町(現・新潟市西蒲区巻町)で久保田隆円（りゅうえん）と文枝の次女として生まれた成子は、父が旧制中学校(のちの県立高等学校)の教師であったため幼少期から転校を繰り返し、新潟県内各地で過ごした(図1)。新潟市にある新潟第一師範学校男子部附属小学校に入学するが、小学2年生の頃には戦況の悪化で父の実家である新潟県中頸城郡美守村（ひだもりむら）(現・上越市三和区)の西勝寺に一時疎開し、終戦まで同地で過ごした。4年生から再び巻町の小学校に通ったのち、中学から高校までの6年間は上越地方の直江津で過ごすこととなる。こうした自然豊かな田舎での生活やお寺で過ごした幼少期の体験が、彼女の作品の中に自然や死といったテーマへの関心をもたらしていると、後年の回想でしばしば述べている*3。

そのような田舎の自然とともに育った久保田が美術の道を志したのは、彼女の特殊な家庭環境による*4。母方の久保田家は小千谷の出身で、成子の曽祖父である久保田右作の時代には詩人・西脇順三郎の実家である西脇家と並ぶ地元の二大名主

図1 生後間もない久保田　1937年
fig. 1 Kubota soon after birth, 1937.

として栄えていた。右作の息子、彌太郎は京都で南画を勉強しており、成子自身はこの祖父に最も影響を受けたという。彌太郎の長女である母、文枝は東京音楽学校を卒業して教師をしていた、当時としては先進的な女性であった。彌太郎の三女で叔母にあたる久保田芳枝は前衛舞踊家として知られた人物で、成子に大きな影響を与えることになる。また、文枝の母で成子の祖母にあたる久保田トシは、元柏崎市長で中村彝（つね）のパトロンでもあった洲崎義郎の実姉にあたる。このような久保田家の芸術的環境に生まれ育った成子ら4姉妹は、幼少期から音楽や美術に親しみ、自然と芸術の道へと進んだ。特に、子供の頃から絵を描くのが好きだったという成子は、小学3年生で雑誌の絵画コンクールに入選するなど、早くから才能を示していた。美術の道を進むことを望んだ娘のために、父は校長を務めていた直江津高校の美術教員に佐渡出身で東京教育大学（現・筑波大学）を出た彫刻家・寺島辰治を東京から招聘し、さらに新潟大学高田分校芸能科の教授から特別レッスンを受けられるよう尽力した。「毎日スケッチやデッサンを十枚くらいやる」*5という久保田は、高校2年生の秋に二紀展に初出品した油彩《向日葵》が入選、新聞にも大きく掲載された［本書8頁］。そのインタビューで寺島教諭は次のように語っている。「成子さんの絵は女子の作と思えぬ線の強さを持つ異色あるものです。個性からくる迫力の現れとみられ、構図も非常に大胆でこの先どこまで伸びるか楽しみです」。その後、彫塑専攻出身だった寺島の影響と女流彫刻家が少なかったという理由から、久保田は彫刻の道を目指すこととなったが*6、高校時代のこうしたエピソードと作風からは、彼女の生来の豪快さや上昇志向がうかがえる。また、音楽や舞踊の実践者が身内にいたことによって、美術以外の芸術活動に対する親近感や感受性が早くから育まれていたことが理解される。

2．東京へ──「ほんとの彫刻家に成りたい」

東京教育大学の彫塑専攻に入学した久保田成子は、大学の保守的な教員養成課程の授業に飽き足らず、高校時代から師事していた新潟出身の彫刻家・高橋清のアトリエで制作していた。高橋は終戦後に彫刻家を志して東京美術学校に入学、第21回新制作展（1957年）で新作家賞、大阪市長賞を受賞した新進気鋭の作家であった。久保田は高橋と同じ新制作協会展に第22回展（1958年）から3回出品している。いずれも頭像であるが、第22回展の出品作が《首A》（図2）と題された女性の頭像だったのに対し、第25、26回展の出品作は同じ頭像でも抽象化が進み、タイトルも《死石》となっている（図3）［本書11頁左］。実は後者2回の出品に先立つ1959年、久保田は故郷で開催された「第十四回新潟県美術展覧会（県展）」に出品し、奨励賞を受

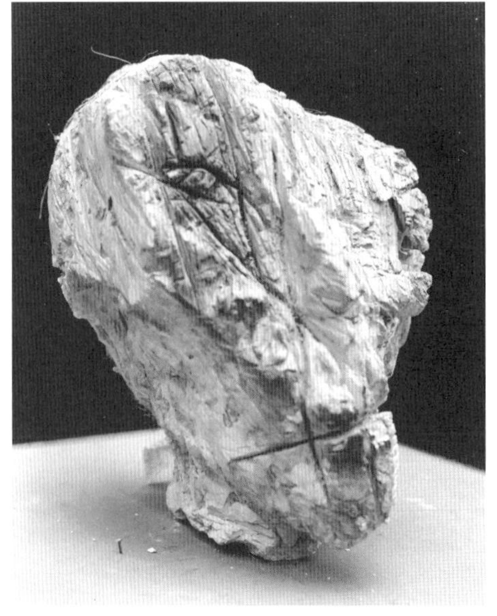

図2 《首A》1958年
fig. 2 *Kubi (Head) A*, 1958.
図3 《死石5》1961年
fig. 3 *Shiseki (Death Stone) 5*, 1961.

賞しており、その際の出品作のタイトルがまさしく《死石》であった[*7]。作品図版が残っていないため断定はできないが、翌々年の第25回新制作展に出品された「死石」シリーズの最初の作品であったと推察される。具象的な《首A》と比べ、《死石》は単純化された荒削りな彫像であり、人間の頭像というよりも民間信仰の神像や儀式用マスクのような、アニミズム的な力を感じさせる造形となっている[*8]。奇しくもその転換期の直前にあたる1958年に、師であった高橋が古代美術の研究のためメキシコへと渡ってしまうが、久保田はその後も引き続き彫刻家として自己のスタイルを模索し続けた(図4)。

図4 大学卒業後の久保田 1960年8月頃
fig. 4 Kubota after graduating from university, C. Aug. 1960.

大学卒業後も彫刻制作を続けていた久保田に、他方で大きな芸術的影響を与えていたのが叔母で前衛舞踊家の邦千谷（本名・久保田芳枝）の存在であった。舞踊家・邦正美に師事した千谷は、1947年に舞踊教室を開設し各地で公演を行なった後、1957年目黒区駒場に「邦千谷舞踊研究所」を設立。ジャンルを超えた芸術活動を展開するために、1960年には若い芸術家たちの活動の場として研究所を開放した。そこには大野一雄や土方巽といったダンサーのほか、グループ音楽のメンバーらが集まり、ジャンルを超えた前衛芸術家たちの交流の場となっていた[*9]。ちょうどこの頃、同敷地内に居候していた久保田はこれらの前衛作家と接し、その作品やパフォーマンスを目にする機会を得たのだった。そこで親交を持ったグループ音楽の塩見允枝子とはのちに共に渡米し、フルクサスに合流することとなる。

早くからアカデミックな美術に反感を抱いていた久保田は、新しい芸術を目指すエネルギッシュな作家たちとの交流から、次第に前衛美術のコミュニティに深く入り込んでいった。1963年には、過激化が最高潮に達していた第15回読売アンデパンダン展に参加し、それまでとはまったく異なる作風の抽象彫刻《We can make it》(図5)と《Suddenly》(図6)を出品、その年の12月には内科画廊での個展を実現する。「1st. LOVE, 2nd. LOVE... 久保田成子彫刻個展」は1963年12月1日から7日まで開催され、作家自ら評論家たちに案内状を送っている[*10]。内科画廊での個展とあって訪れた評論家も少なからずいたようだが[*11]、その展評が出ることはなく、久保田は大いに落胆した。この「彫刻個展」で展示した作品は、同年初頭に読売アンデパンダン展に出品した鉄を溶接した抽象彫刻を再構

図5《We can make it》1963年
fig. 5 *We can make it*, 1963.
図6《Suddenly》1963年
fig. 6 *Suddenly*, 1963.

成したものとみられるが、注目すべきはその展示方法にあった［本書12頁］。彫刻本体は「ラブレター」に見立てた紙くずを部屋いっぱいに詰め込みシーツで覆った山の上に置かれていたため、観客は彫刻を見るためにその山を這い上がっていかなくてはならなかった。それは展示空間全体を使ったインスタレーション作品ともいえるもので、観客が登るという行為も含めて成立する一種のハプニングであり、また、人が登り降りすることによって山の高さや空間の見え方が日々変化していくというインスタレーション作品でもあった*12。「彫刻個展」とあえて名付けながらも、伝統的な彫刻展とはかけ離れたこの作品展からは、久保田が次第に彫刻の枠に囚われない創造性へと進んでいく様子がはっきりと見て取れる。

さらに、同展会期中に草月会館ホールで開催された「Sweet 16」（12月3–5日）と題するパフォーミング・フェスティバルにも参加しており、そこで久保田はG.ブリヤーリという偽名でパフォーマンスを行なっていたことが確認された*13。パフォーマンスの詳細は不明だが、「マッキューナス様へ／G.ブリヤーリ」と題されたテキストがプログラムに掲載され［本書15頁］、パフォーマンスのスコアとみられるこのテキストの一部が内科画廊の個展案内状［本書13頁上］に印刷された英文と一致することから、久保田の作品であることは疑いない。小野洋子を介してフルクサスの活動を知り、関心を抱いていた久保田は、ほぼ同時期にフルクサスの代表ジョージ・マチューナスに「永続的なフルックス・フェスト」のためのイベント・スコアを送っており、その内容が先のプログラムに掲載された文章とも大きく重なることが確認できる*14。

このように、1963年頃から急速に前衛美術に傾倒し、ハイレッド・センター（HRC）による《シェルター計画》や小野洋子の《モーニング・ピース》など同時代を象徴するイベントにも参加していた久保田は、この後、自らの表現においてもさらに変化をみせる。例えば、篠原有司男らが参加したアナーキーなグループ展「OFF MUSEUM」（椿近代画廊、1964年6月17–22日）では、《ミス・ユニバース》と題した生きたうさぎを使った観客参加型の作品を発表*15。また、「刀根康尚個展」（内科画廊、1964年10月12–17日）と「フルックス週間」（画廊クリスタル、1965年9月6–14日）［いずれも本書17頁］では同様の下着を使った作品を出品していたことが本展のための調査で確認されたが、そこにはもはや彫刻家としての面影はなく、パフォーマンスやイベントという新しい表現を模索する前衛芸術家としての姿がうかがえる。

その背景として、久保田が東京で美術家としてのスタートを切った1950年代末は草月アートセンターが設立され、その招聘によって60年代初頭には世界の最前衛のアーティストが多数来日していたことが挙げられる。その中には「小野洋子作品発表会」（1962年）やジョン・ケージおよびデイヴィッド・テュードアの演奏会（1962年）などがあったが、彼女に最も影響を与えたのが1964年5月29日に開催された「白南準作品発表会」であった。この時の衝撃について、彼女は自身の著書で詳しく語っているが、かねてから惹かれていたナムジュン・パイクの公演を実見し、直接話を聞いたことで、彼が参加していたフルクサスへの関心と渡米への欲求は一気に高まっていった*16。このように東京時代の後半から急速に増したパフォーマンス・アートへの関わりは、渡米後の久保田の活動の素地を準備することとなる。

3．渡米——自己の表現を探し求めて

1964年7月4日に塩見と共にニューヨークへ到着した久保田は、マチューナスの歓迎を受けて彼の用意したアパートで暮らし始める。そこには、先に渡米しフルクサスに参加していた日本人芸術家の靉嘔や斉藤陽子（たかこ）のほか、敬愛するパイクもいた。マチューナスは共同体としてのフルクサスの組織化を目指しており、久保田と塩見は直後から彼らの「ディナー・コミューン」（食費を節約するための当番制の食事会）に参加することとなる。また、マチューナスはメンバーの作品をマルチプルとして「フルクサス・ショップ」で販売しており、久保田はその手伝いをしながら、自身も《フルックス・ナプキン》、《フルックス・メディシン》［いずれも本書21頁］を制作しているが、こうしたマルチプル作品をさらに展開させることはなかった。

他方、エリック・アンダーセンのパフォーマンス《OPUS45》［本書22頁］やオノ・ヨーコの《ビート・ピース》（1965年）*17といった、フルクサス

のパフォーマンスにも参加していた。そうした中で、「永続的なフルックス・フェスト」の一演目として久保田自身もパフォーマンス作品を発表することとなるが、それがマチューナスの数枚の写真によって知られる《ヴァギナ・ペインティング》である。これは明らかに60年代初頭にパイクが行なっていた《頭のための禅》を想起させるものだったが、観客たちの反応は否定的であったという*18。晩年の久保田はこのパフォーマンスについて、パイクの発案で頼まれてやむをえずやったものだったと述懐しているが*19、本展の調査で、前年秋にピーター・ムーアのスタジオで広報用と思しき写真を撮影していたことが判明した［本書25頁］。写真には刷毛のようなブラシが取り付けられた下着とそれを身につけて描く久保田の姿がはっきりと写っており、実際に本番を見た観客の感想とは異なっている。事前準備と本番で手法を大きく変更した意図や誰のアイディアであったかということは、久保田とパイクが不在の今となっては知る由(よし)もない。しかしながら、彼女が本作を入念に準備し発表したこと、また同時期にパフォーマンスにたびたび参加していたことを踏まえると、フルクサスの一員として独自のパフォーマンス作品を残したいという意志を持って臨んでいたであろうと推測できる。

その後もキャロリー・シュニーマンの《スノーズ》(1967年)［本書27頁］や電子音楽のパフォーマンス・グループ「ソニック・アーツ・ユニオン」のツアーにパフォーマーとして参加してはいるが、形として残らないパフォーマンス・アートの儚さと自らの目指す表現とのズレを感じ始めていた*20。結果として、《ヴァギナ・ペインティング》が久保田の唯一のパフォーマンス作品として知られているが*21、その要素は続く初期ヴィデオ作品の中にも引き継がれていく*22。

4. ヴィデオとの出会い

1960年代半ばからヴィデオ作品を制作していたパイクと共同生活を始めた久保田は、1970年頃には自身もヴィデオを使った作品に着手している。最初のシングルチャンネル・ヴィデオ作品として発表された《ブロークン・ダイアリー：ヨーロッパを一日ハーフインチで》(1972年)［本書30頁］は、ソニーのハンディカメラ「ポータパック」を担いで一人でヨーロッパを旅しながら撮影した映像によるもので、同一とみられる映像から異なる編集や形式でも作品発表するなど、ここから久保田成子のヴィデオ・アーティストとしての歩みが始まる。

女性が一人でも扱うことができ、また、スタートを同じくする男性と対等に戦うことができる小型ヴィデオの発明によって、多くの女性のヴィデオ作家がこの頃に誕生した。久保田も女性グループの展覧会にたびたび参加しているが、彼女が同世代の女性アーティストと積極的に協働するのはこの時期だけであり、中でも「ホワイト ブラック レッド イエロー」と名付けられた異なる人種の4人の女性アーティストによるグループ展は、のちに同じく国際的に活躍するメアリー・ルシエと協働した初期ヴィデオ・アートの活動としても注目される*23。

久保田は自らのヴィデオ作品を制作する一方で、彼女のオープンな性格とパイクとの共同生活によって、他のヴィデオ・アーティストの作品を目にしたり、彼らと交流する機会に多く恵まれた。その経験からアンソロジー・フィルム・アーカイヴズのヴィデオ・キュレーターに採用され、1974年から82年まで多くの作家を紹介することとなる*24。また、同年には東京で開催された「トーキョー・ニューヨーク・ビデオ・エキスプレス」［本書37頁］でニューヨークのヴィデオ作品を紹介し、逆にそれをニューヨーク近代美術館で開催されたヴィデオについてのシンポジウム「Open Circuits」で報告するなど、日本とアメリカのヴィデオ・アートを媒介する役割も果たしている*25。

このように、ヴィデオという新しいメディアとの出会いは、久保田の活動や表現の幅を大きく広げていった。その一方で、ヴィデオ作品として鑑賞されるということは、モニターに映し出される映像の内容で評価されるということでもある。しかし、久保田は当初からマルチ・チャンネルでモニターを複数台使って、時には立体物のように積み重ねて発表していたことがわかっている*26。複数のモニターを使った展示は当時から珍しいことではなかったようだが、久保田にとってそれは造形的要素の強調であり、その後のヴィデオ彫刻へと繋がる重要な意味をもっていたと言える。

5．ヴィデオ彫刻の誕生

ヴィデオを撮り始めた当初、久保田は自分の顔などナルシスティックで、ダイアリーのような映像を撮っていたと語っているが*27、その最初期の映像が《カリフォルニアでの一日》（のちに《セルフ・ポートレート》と名付けられる）であり、久保田の最初のヴィデオ彫刻作品《ヴィデオ・ポエム》（1975年）［本書38-39頁］に使われている*28。パイクをはじめとするヴィデオ・アーティストの多くが映像そのものを重視して造形性に無頓着であったことに久保田は失望しており、また映像作品が鑑賞者の時間を占有し、最初から最後まで画面を見続けなければならないことにも不満を感じていた*29。そこで誕生したのが、四角いブラウン管を袋で隠し、送風機で袋を膨らませながらジッパーの隙間から映像をのぞかせるという《ヴィデオ・ポエム》であった。袋で半ば隠れたモニターに映し出される映像ははっきりと見ることができないため、そこに物語性を見出すことは意図されていない*30。そして、同作が立体作品として成立するヴィデオ・アート、いわゆるヴィデオ彫刻の最初の試みであったといえる。ヴィデオ彫刻は、久保田の作家としての原点である彫刻と、新しく切り開いたヴィデオ・アートを結びつける格好の表現方法であり、そこから作品を急展開することとなる。

「デュシャンピアナ」シリーズ

久保田成子の代表作として知られる「デュシャンピアナ」は、1975年から1990年までの15年にわたって生み出された連作で、マルセル・デュシャンとその作品にインスピレーションを受けて作られた、いわばアプロプリエーションの先駆けともいえる作品群である。彼女がデュシャンと出会ったのは1968年のことで*31、その数か月後のデュシャンの死をきっかけに、まずは自身が撮影した写真をもとにした作品集『マルセル・デュシャンとジョン・ケージ』（1970年）［本書28頁］を自費出版し、続いてその写真を編集したシングルチャンネル・ヴィデオ作品《マルセル・デュシャンとジョン・ケージ》（1972年）を制作する。さらに、1972年のヨーロッパ旅行の際に撮影したデュシャンの墓の映像を使って作られたのがヴィデオ彫刻《マルセル・デュシャンの墓》［本書54-55頁］であり、これが最初に発表された「デュシャンピアナ」シリーズとなった。その後、《ヴィデオ・チェス》［本書56-59頁］、《階段を降りる裸体》［本書60-62頁］、《ドア》［本書63-65頁］、《メタ・マルセル：窓》［本書66-69頁］（以下、《窓》）がわずか2年の間に発表され、《自転車の車輪》［本書98-100頁］が数年後に登場する。「デュシャンピアナ」として発表されているのはこれら6作品であるが、1990年に発表された《アダムとイヴ》［本書112-115頁］のアダムは、フランシス・ピカビアのバレエ『本日休演』で（クラナッハの絵画に倣って）デュシャンが扮した裸のアダムを引用するなど、その影響は後年まで続いた。

そのうち、《ヴィデオ・チェス》、《マルセル・デュシャンの墓》、《階段を降りる裸体》、《ドア》は立体部分のみではなく映像でもデュシャンに言及した表現であったのに対し、《窓》と《自転車の車輪》では作品の造形面でデュシャンを引用しながらも、映像は久保田独自の自然の表現へと移行している。特に《窓》の最初のバージョンである「雪」においては、テレビのノイズという機械的な特性を生かしながら、そこに自然現象である雪のイメージを重ねるという久保田特有の感性を発揮し、ヴィデオ彫刻に新たな美学を取り入れた傑作となった*32。

ルネ・ブロック・ギャラリーで開催された1976年、77年の2度の個展は、「デュシャンピアナ」をテーマに構成されたが、その成功によって久保田は一躍ヴィデオ彫刻の作家として知られるようになる*33。かくして、デュシャンという明快なテーマと確固とした造形表現は、久保田成子を美術史上に位置づけることに貢献した。

自然をテーマとした作品へ

《窓》で自然のモチーフを表現に取り入れた久保田は、同時期にアメリカ南西部の風景を撮影した映像を用いて《三つの山》［本書78-81頁］を1979年に発表するが、それは自然をメインテーマに制作した最初のヴィデオ彫刻となった。それ以降、《河》［本書84、93-95頁］、《グリーン・インスタレーション》［本書101頁］、《ナイアガラの滝》［本書104-107頁］、《ロック・ヴィデオ　桜》［本書108-109頁］、《枯山水》

［本書110–111頁］と、自然や風景をテーマにした作品を次々と生み出すことになる。大学時代に山岳部に所属し、また、幼い頃から慣れ親しんだ身近な対象でもあった山というテーマに取り組む中で*34、久保田は多くのドローイングを残している。そこには、「自分の型をどのように残すか」、「ヴィデオ彫刻は人生を映し出す」、「自伝的風景」（図7）といった言葉が書き込まれており、「デュシャンピアナ」シリーズで一つのスタイルを築いた久保田が、独自の表現を模索し、自らの芸術観をこの作品で表現しようとしていたことがうかがえる。

《三つの山》と《グリーン・インスタレーション》ではアリゾナの映像が使われており、前者では立体の内部に、後者では表面の半分に鏡が貼られ、砂漠の太陽のようにギラギラと光を反射して輝いている。《河》では、水を湛えた水槽の形状がカーブした川のラインを暗示しながら、水面に映し出された映像には作家の泳ぐ姿が見える。そこに施されたカラーシンセサイザーによる星やハートの形はポップで都会的な印象を与えるが、同作のためのドローイングからは、それらが夜の川に映り込んだ月や星の光にインスピレーションを受けたものであったことがわかり、風景的特質を強調する要素となっている。また《ナイアガラの滝》では、実際に同地を訪れてクローズアップで撮影した滝の迫力ある映像をもとに、4チャンネルで滝の四季を描き出しており、その激しい映像と上部に取り付けられたシャワーから降り注ぐ水の飛沫やスピーカーから流れる滝の音が重なり合い、抽象的で破壊力のある滝のイメージを現出している。いずれも自然そのものを対象としながら、久保田はそれらを映像によって抽象化されたイメージへと変換させ、独自の感性で作品化している。本格的に美術に取り組み始めた高校時代から彼女にとって最も身近なモチーフであった自然が、ヴィデオによって新たな表現として展開されていく*35。

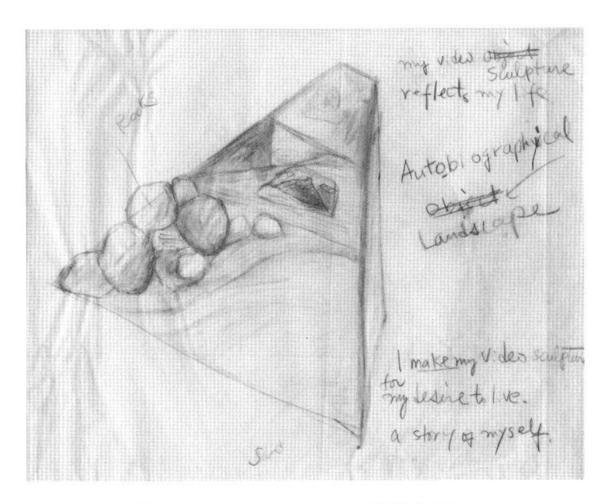

図7 ドローイング［Autobiographical Landspace］制作年不詳
久保田成子ヴィデオ・アート財団蔵
fig. 7 Drawing [Autobiographical Landspace], year unknown.
Collection of Shigeko Kubota Video Art Foundation

6．拡張する表現

久保田の作品で1980年頃から頻繁に使用されるのが、水や鏡といった反射する素材と、作品に動きを導入するための仕掛けとしてのモーターである。モチーフとしての水は初期のヴィデオ作品《リヴァーラン（川走）―ヴィデオ 水 詩》［本書33頁］にも登場するが、それはあくまでも映像による水の描写であった。他方、《河》と《ナイアガラの滝》では実際の水を使用し、水底には鏡の破片が散りばめられ、底からも光が反射する仕組みとなっている。《三つの山》《グリーン・インスタレーション》《枯山水》といった内部あるいは表面に鏡面素材が使われている作品では、映像の光を反射するのみならず、鑑賞者や周囲の環境をも反映し、空間を作品の一部として取り込むことに成功している*36。《ヴィデオ俳句―ぶら下がり作品》［本書96–97頁］では、床に置かれた楕円形の鏡面に天井から吊るされたモニターの映像が映り込んでいるが、その映像は天井近くに設置されたカメラによってリアルタイムで撮影された鑑賞者の姿である。これによって観者は作品の一部ともなり、みる／みられるの関係は曖昧となる。

久保田の作品をよりダイナミックな空間表現としているもうひとつの重要な素材がモーターであり、これが80年代以降の作品に欠かせない「動き」の要素を付与している。最初にモーターが採用されたのは《河》であり、作品内の水の表面に動きをつけるために取り付けられた。水面が動くことで、そこに映り込んだ映像の光がさまざまに反射し、変化することを意図したためである。その後、《ヴィデオ俳句》や《ナイアガラの滝》でもモーターが使用されるが、さらに顕著な効果は《自転車の車輪1、2、3》にみられる*37。1980

年代後半に流通し始める小型液晶ディスプレイによって実現した同作では、モニターから映し出される映像の動きに加え、それを設置している車輪自体が動くという二重の運動効果によって、作品はより重層的な時間表現を獲得している。

モーターの使用はその後さらに進化し、《アダムとイヴ》と《スケート選手》[本書120–121頁]では作品の台座部分にモーターが仕込まれ、彫刻本体が回転するに至る。また、80年代半ばから彫刻自体にプロジェクターの映像をかぶせて投映する手法を取り入れ始めるが、次第にそれは周囲の空間にも広がり、プロジェクター自体を回転させるなど、展示空間全体が動きを伴うものとなっていった。そこでは観者が作品の一部を成すが、これはまさに久保田が最初の個展で試みたインスタレーションの発展と見做すことができる。

おわりに

1991年にアメリカン・ミュージアム・オブ・ザ・ムーヴィング・イメージから始まった国際巡回展でそれまでの集大成となる個展を開催した久保田成子は、彫刻家を目指していた1960年頃以来、約30年ぶりに再び人物をテーマに制作を始めた。《アダムとイヴ》に始まり、《スケート選手》、《ジョギング・レディー》[本書125頁]、《ピッシング・マン》[本書124頁]へと続く一連の人型彫刻は、類型化されているようでありながら、実際には久保田の個人的な記憶や人生と結びついた、特定の人格を持った人物像である。そして、晩年に制作する《パイクⅠ》と《パイクⅡ》[本書134–135頁]は最愛の夫のポートレートであり、一連の人物彫刻の帰結とも言える。これらの人物像と自然をモチーフにしたヴィデオ彫刻をひとつの展示空間で一体的に見せるようになったのが、1993年のヴェネチア・ビエンナーレの「エデンの園：ヴィデオ・ドリームの光景」[本書130頁]や1996年のランス・ファング・ギャラリーとホイットニー美術館での個展[本書131頁]においてであった。そこでは、1991年の《アダムとイヴ》の展示で実現された複数作品の組み合わせによるエンバイロメンタルな表現が、彼女の展示スタイルとして繰り返されていることがうかがえる。

その後、1996年にパイクが脳梗塞によって半身不随となると、その介護とグッゲンハイムでの彼の個展実現のために全精力を注いだため、自身の作品制作は中断せざるをえなくなる。その一方で、久保田の作品のテーマはパイクその人となり、2000年に開催した個展「セクシュアル・ヒーリング」(ランス・ファング・ギャラリー)や2007年の個展「ナムジュン・パイクとの私の人生」(マヤ・ステンダール・ギャラリー)では、パイクをモチーフにした一連の映像やヴィデオ彫刻を発表した。中でも「セクシュアル・ヒーリング」では、パイクのリハビリの様子をユーモラスに表現した映像作品を中心に、その周囲にベッドや車椅子といった介護を象徴するオブジェとモニターが設置され、空間全体がひとつのインスタレーションとして体感される展示となっており、彼女が目指した表現スタイルが最後まで貫かれている。

久保田が行き着いた空間全体を作品化するという表現は、1963年の内科画廊での試みから始まっていた＊38。その展示を認め、励ましてくれたパイクと共に歩んだ人生であったことからも、内科画廊での個展は、久保田成子の芸術と人生におけるスタート地点だったと言える。そして、ヴィデオこそが二人を繋ぎ、彼女の人生を世界に向かって開いた窓であった。

本展では残念ながら久保田成子を「回顧」するには至らなかったが、30年ぶりに展示される作品や発見された資料を通して、彼女の芸術活動があらためて評価される契機となることを願っている。

(はまだ・まゆみ＝新潟県立近代美術館主任学芸員)

久保田成子に関する調査にあたり、準備段階でご協力くださった故・久保田成子氏と美術館の同僚であった故・高晟埈氏、そして多大なる助成を頂きました公益財団法人ポーラ美術振興財団および公益財団法人鹿島美術財団、美術館連絡協議会に深く感謝申し上げます。

[註]

＊1――こと久保田に関しては、画商のルネ・ブロックが1976年に彼女の作品をドイツで紹介するにあたって「デュシャンピアナ：ヴィデオ彫刻」と題したことに由来する(本書100頁《自転車の車輪》のテキストより)。詳細は橋本論文を参照。

＊2――「私は彫刻家だから、記憶からもっと何かを作りたかった。(中略)ヴィデオのパートは私の人生の記憶から立ち昇る蜃気楼なのです」("On Art and Artists: Shigeko Kubota," *Profile*, vol. 3, No. 6, November 1983, p. 15)。

*3——例えば、山をテーマにした作品《三つの山》の制作動機として、母の実家のある中越地方の小千谷を自らのルーツとして挙げている（本書81頁《三つの山》のテキストより）。

*4——久保田家の歴史については以下を参照。中山孝子「久保田芳枝（邦千谷）と家族のこと」、邦千谷舞踊研究所編集委員会（編）『凛として、花として　舞踊の前衛、邦千谷の世界』アトリエサード、2008年、6、14–15頁。

*5——「十七歳少女、みごと栄冠　久保田さん二紀会展に入選」『毎日新聞』新潟版、1954年10月8日、8面。

*6——久保田成子・南禎鎬著、高晟埈訳『私の愛、ナムジュン・パイク』平凡社、2013年、47頁。

*7——「第十四回『県展』出品目録」（主催：新潟日報社、新潟県教育委員会、新潟・長岡・高田三市教育委員会）、1959年5月26日–6月7日、小林百貨店、新潟市。

*8——実妹の中山孝子氏へのインタビューによると、成子はこの頃、奈良や京都で見た仏像に感銘を受け、熱心に頭像を制作していたとのことである（2019年2月3日のインタビュー）。手塚美和子による「日本美術オーラル・ヒストリー・アーカイヴ　久保田成子インタヴュー」（2009年10月11日、http://www.oralarthistory.org/archives/kubota_shigeko/interview_01.php）にも奈良や京都の仏像について語っている部分がある。

*9——邦千谷の活動については以下に詳しい。邦千谷舞踊研究所編集委員会（編）、前掲書、2008年。

*10——慶應義塾大学アート・センターに瀧口修造宛、東京文化財研究所のアーカイブに三木多聞宛の手紙が残されている。

*11——残された記録写真には東野芳明が写っており、また中原佑介も訪れていたことが判明している（宮田有香の質問に対する回答、1999年7月30日消印書簡）。

*12——「環境芸術、反美術館アート、反エスタブリッシュの表現で、新しいアートの形態を表現したかった。（中略）観客が参加し、パーテスペーション（ママ）するハプニング——これは、ジョンケージの偶然性とチャンスオペレーションに強く影響されていたからである。時のアヴンギャルド（ママ）も、ハイレットセンター（ママ）や土方巽や、草月ホールでのコンサートにとても刺激された」（宮田、同上書簡）。実際に展示を見た塩見允枝子や刀根康尚、実妹の中山孝子らの各証言において山の高さの描写が異なっていることから、展示を見た時期によって実際の高さやその印象がかなり違っていたことがわかる。

*13——同公演のプログラムに久保田成子の名前は見当たらないが、当日参加していた友人の刀根康尚のメモによりそれが久保田の作品であったことが判明した（本書14–15頁参照）。

*14——小野と久保田の交流およびマチューナスへの手紙については以下に詳しい。Midori Yoshimoto, “Self-Exploration in Multimedia: The Experiments of Shigeko Kubota,” *Into Performance: Japanese Women Artists in New York* (New Brunswick, New Jersey and London, Rutgers University Press), 2005, pp. 171–172.

*15——篠原有司男『前衛の道』、美術出版社、1968年、132頁。「OFF MUSEUM ’64 6/17–22 椿近代画廊」『美術ジャーナル』46号、頁無し。

*16——久保田、前掲書、2013年、33–40頁。

*17——ジョン・ヘンドリックス「オノ・ヨーコとフルクサス」『YES オノ・ヨーコ』展カタログ、朝日新聞社、2003年、43頁。

*18——久保田、前掲書、2013年、98–100頁。このパフォーマンスを見ていた塩見も、見ていて痛々しかったという感想を述べている（塩見允枝子へのインタビュー、2019年7月1日）。一方で、同じくパフォーマンスを目撃したエリック・アンダーセンは「成子のパフォーマンスは過去に彼女が行なったもののなかで最高でした。信じられないほど詩的で驚異的。筆は確かに彼女のヴァギナから出ていましたが、それが衝撃的だったとは全く思いません。とても感動的で、官能的で、繊細でした。私たちは皆、非常に感銘を受けました」（西川美穂子宛メール、2020年8月2日付）と述べており、一概にネガティブな反応だったとは断定できない。

*19——手塚、前掲インタビュー、2013年。久保田はこの事実をパイクによって口止めされていたため晩年まで明かさなかったとしている。

*20——「でも、あんなのはその、戯れみたいなもんで。自分を彫刻家と思ってたから。ちょっとこの人たちと違うなって思ってた。（中略）なんとなく一瞬で消えるっていうのはね、儚いわね。あまりにも儚すぎると思って」（手塚、前掲インタビュー、2013年）。同様の失望感は1983年時点でも語られている。*Profile*, op. cit., p. 15.

*21——ジャン・デュピュイ企画のグループ展に出品した作品もタイトルからパフォーマンスとみられるが、詳細は不明である。Jean Dupuy (ed.), *Collective Consciousness: Art Performances in the Seventies*, Performing Arts Journal Publications, New York, 1980, pp. 109, 121, 189.

*22——最初のヴィデオ・ライヴ・パフォーマンスや《川走——ヴィデオ・水・詩》（1972年）などの作品にもパフォーマンスの要素が見られる。久保田の初期ヴィデオ作品および活動の詳細は、本書の由本論文を参照。

*23——Melinda Barlow, “Red, White, Yellow, and Black: Women, Multiculturalism, and Video History,” *Quarterly Review of Film and Video*, 17(4), 2000, pp. 297–316. この時期の久保田の活動については、本書の由本論文を参照。

*24——“Video Programming,” *Bulletin for Film and Video Information, Anthology Film Archives*, Vol.1, No.3, June 1974.

*25——Shigeko Kubota, “Women’s Video in the U.S. and Japan,” Douglas Davis and Allison Simmons (eds.), *Essay, Statements and Videotapes Based on “Open Circuits: An International Conference on the Future of Television” organized by Fred Barzyk, Douglas Davis, Gerald O’grady, and Willard Van Dyke For the Museum of Modern Art, New York City*, MIT Press, Cambridge, Massachusetts, and London, England, pp. 96–101. これに先立つ1969年から71年にかけて、久保田は在ニューヨークのリポーターとして『美術手帖』に不定期で記事を執筆している。そのテーマは、アートからエコロジー、セックス、ドラッグ・カルチャーと幅広い内容に及んでいるが、それはまさに同時代のアメリカ文化のアクチュアリティを日本に伝えるという役割を担っていたと言える。このことも含めて考えた時、制作者としての立場だけでなく、他の作家や作品、また国を超えて文化を紹介する「媒介者」としての久保田成子の姿が浮かび上がってくる。

*26——1972年9月30日の Experimental Television Center Binghamtonのポスターに3チャンネルのヴィデオ・パフォーマンスと掲載されている。また、「第9回ニューヨーク・アヴァンギャルド・フェスティヴァル」の写真でもスタッキングされたモニターの前に立つ久保田の姿が映し出され、「第2回ヴィデオ・アーツ・フェスティヴァル」には複数のモニターに色とりどりのセロファンを貼ってマリリン・モンローの映像を映した作品《A36-24-36》を出品している（本書35頁参照）。

*27——手塚、前掲インタビュー、2013年。

*28——Moira Roth, “The Voice of Shigeko Kubota: ‘A Fusion of Art and Life, Asia and America . . . ’” in exh.cat., *Shigeko Kubota Video Sculpture, American Museum of the Moving Image*, NY, 1991, p. 81.

*29——Shigeko Kubota and Jonathan Price, [Interview] Feb. 17, 1976.（アンソロジー・フィルム・アーカイヴズの資料より）

*30——「ビデオ・インスタレーションていうのは、ビデオのもつ時間がもっと抽象的になると思ったのよ。」（「久保田成

子インタヴュー　ビデオ／アート／人生を語る」『月刊イメージフォーラム』1984年11月号)。

＊31——久保田がマルセル・デュシャンと初めて会ったのは、彼とジョン・ケージのチェス・コンサート「リユニオン」においてであり、その様子を撮影する機会に恵まれた。詳細は以下を参照。久保田成子「晩年のデュシャンとチェス・ゲーム」『美術手帖』第319号、1969年11月、80–89頁。なお、その後のインタビューや記述においてはデュシャンとの再会と撮影のタイミングが逆になった、誤った記録が繰り返されているが、久保田が撮影した「リユニオン」は1968年3月5日にトロントで開催され、一方、マース・カニングハムの「ウォークアラウンド・タイム」はバッファローで開催されたのが1968年3月10日であることから、1969年の最初の記事が正しい。

＊32——1979年に描かれた《窓》のためのドローイング（本書73頁）では、四季の景色が見えるような映像を使った4つの《窓》（春夏秋冬）の構想を残しているし、久保田が《窓》の枠を手に持って川辺でポーズする写真（本書69ページ右）は、窓が自然に向かって開かれていることを暗示しているようでもある。

＊33——1977年のルネ・ブロック・ギャラリーでの2度目の個展「久保田成子によるメタ・マルセル」では3点の作品が発表されるが、そのうちの1点であった《山》はのちに《三つの山》へと発展する作品であるため、本展では「デュシャンピアナ」シリーズとはみなしていない。

＊34——久保田は山というテーマについて、デュシャンピアナと並んでひとつのシリーズと考えていたようだ。“Shigeko Kubota—Mountain Series,” *Shigeko Kubota—Video Sculptures*, in exh. cat., Museum Folkwang Essen, daadgalerie, Berlin, Kunsthaus Zürich, 1981, pp. 34–37.

＊35——原美術館でのインタビュー、1992年（本書163–164頁）。

＊36——鏡を使った最初の作品は《マルセル・デュシャンの墓》（1975年）であるが、1975年の最初の展示では床にのみ鏡面が設置され、その後、1984年の再展示で天井と向かい側の壁にも設置され、より環境的な作品へと進化している。同作の展開については、本書の西川論文を参照。

＊37——1983年に制作された《デュシャンピアナ：自転車の車輪》の最初のバージョンにもモーターが仕込まれたが、この時はまだモニターが大きく重量があったため、回転し続けることができなかった。

＊38——久保田は後年、内科画廊での展示について「環境芸術であった」と述べている（久保田成子「しごとのデッサン」『京都新聞』1999年5月29日）。それ自体は回顧的な発言であり、久保田がどのような意味でその語を使ったのかは定かではない。しかし、彼女が1960年代にアラン・カプローの講義を実際に受け、彼のハプニングやエンバイロメンツという発想に影響を受けていたことは事実である（*Profile*, op. cit., p. 3.)。また、久保田と山口勝弘は長年親交があり、たびたび同じグループ展に出品していた事実も考え合わせると、今後あらためて環境芸術の文脈から久保田の作品を捉え直す必要があるだろう。

Video Is the Window of Her Life: The Art and Life of Shigeko Kubota

Mayumi Hamada

Foreword

The video artist Shigeko Kubota was born in Niigata Prefecture, and was based in New York throughout her career. "Video sculpture,"*1 the term we always use when describing her work, refers to a combination of video with three-dimensional objects or installations, and developed as a video art format from the mid-1970s onward. It was around this time that Kubota rose to prominence, and the two decades from the mid-1970s through the mid-1990s were the peak of her career. Her works were shown many times in various parts of Europe and the United States, including at *documenta VI* (1977), but most of them were video sculptures. The current exhibition represents the first comprehensive endeavor to present art she created prior to this period.

Meanwhile, another image of Shigeko Kubota as an artist was formed by a photograph of a radical performance entitled *Vagina Painting* (1965) [cat. p. 24]. It is said to have been unpopular with the audience, who were fellow members of the Fluxus group, but it later drew attention in other contexts such as that of feminism, and continues to be re-evaluated from new perspectives.

Video sculptures and *Vagina Painting*: to gain a clearer picture of Shigeko Kubota, the artist who created these two very different types of works, this essay traces the arc of her life and work with a focus on her early days. This is intended to shed light on her development of video sculpture, in a manner that pursued fusion of spatial and temporal art and sought to incorporate the space and the viewer into the work, while her approach evolved, from its origins in sculpture, through performance which played a strong role early in her career, to video which remained her medium of choice for the remainder of her life.*2

1. Origins

Shigeko Kubota was born on August 2, 1937 in Makimachi, Nishikambara-gun, Niigata (present-day Makimachi, Nishikan-ku, Niigata), the second daughter of Ryuen and Fumie Kubota [fig. 1. p. 183.]. Her father was a junior high school (after prefectural high school) teacher, and from early childhood she transferred schools many times and lived in various areas of Niigata Prefecture. She enrolled at Niigata Fuzoku Elementary School in Niigata City, but by the time she was in second grade the tide of the war in the Pacific was turning against Japan, and she was temporarily evacuated to her father's parents' home at Saijo-ji Temple in Hidamori-mura, Nakakubiki-gun, Niigata (present Sanwa-ku, Joetsu), where she remained until the end of the war. After attending elementary school in Maki-machi from the fourth grade, she spent the six years of junior high school and high school in the city of Naoetsu in the Joetsu region. In recollections in her later years, she frequently spoke of her childhood in rustic rural surroundings and of living at a temple, and how this awakened the interest in themes of nature and death that characterized her later work.*3

As she grew up in these rural surroundings, Kubota's artistic aspirations were stirred by her unique home and family environment.*4 The Kubota name was that of the maternal side of her family, who were from the city of Ojiya and prospered as one of two local daimyo (noble households) alongside the Nishiwaki family, into which the famous poet Junzaburo Nishiwaki was born, during the time of Shigeko's great-grandfather Usaku Kubota. Usaku's son Yataro studied *nanga* (Southern School or literati painting) in Kyoto, and Shigeko cited her grandfather as her greatest influence. Yataro's eldest daughter, Shigeko's mother Fumie, graduated from the Tokyo College of Music and worked as a teacher, making her quite a progressive woman for her time. Yataro's third daughter and Shigeko's aunt Yoshie Kubota was known as an avant-garde dancer and was also a significant influence on Shigeko. Also, Fumie's mother and Shigeko's grandmother, Toshi Kubota, was the sister of Giro Sunosaki, a former mayor of Kashiwazaki and a patron of the painter Tsune Nakamura. Born and raised in the artistic environment of the Kubota family, Shigeko and her three sisters were well versed in music and art from an early age and naturally gravitated toward the arts. Shigeko in particular was fond of drawing from childhood onward and showed talent early on, winning a prize in art contest sponsored by the publisher in her third year of elementary school. Her father was the principal of Naoetsu High School, and for the sake of his aspiring artist daughter, he invited the sculptor Tatsuji Terashima, who was from Sado in Niigata and graduated from Tokyo University of Education (present-day University of Tsukuba), to be an art teacher at the school. He also went to great lengths to enable her to take special lessons from a professor in the arts department of Niigata University's Takada branch. Kubota recalled that she "produced around ten sketches and drawings a day,"*5 and in her second year of high school her first submission to the Niki-kai art association's exhibition, an oil painting entitled *Sunflowers*, was accepted [cat. p. 8]. In an interview related to screening of works for this exhibition, her teacher Mr. Terashima said: "Shigeko's painting is unique, with a strength of line one would not think was that of a girl. It seems to manifest the power she derives from her originality, and the composition is very bold as well. I look forward to seeing how she will grow in the future." Due to the influence of Terajima, originally a sculptor, and the fact that there were so few female sculptors, Kubota elected to pursue sculpture herself.*6 Anecdotes like this one, and the artistic style of her high school years, show her innate dynamism and ambition, and it is also evident that the presence of people around her practicing music and dance fostered familiarity and sensitivity to creative activities other than the visual arts from her early years.

2. Moving to Tokyo: "I Want to Be a Real Sculptor"

Having enrolled at the Tokyo University of Education (present-day University of Tsukuba) as a sculpture major, Kubota was frustrated with the university's conservative teacher-training classes, and began working at the studio of sculptor Kiyoshi Takahashi, a fellow native of Niigata who she had been studying under since high school. Mr. Takahashi entered the Tokyo School of Fine Arts after World War II with the goal of becoming a sculptor, and was an up-and-coming artist who won a prize for new artists and also the Osaka Mayor's Award at the 21st Shinseisaku Exhibition (1957). Kubota showed work in the Shinseisaku Exhibition, like Takahashi, three times beginning with the 22nd exhibition (1958). Each time the subject was a head, but while the work featured in the 22nd exhibition was an image of a woman's head entitled *Kubi (Head) A* [fig. 2. p. 184, top], those in the 25th and 26th exhibitions were increasingly abstract heads given the title *Shiseki (Death Stone)* [fig. 3. p. 184, bottom] [cat. p.11, left]. In fact, in 1959, prior to the latter two works, Kubota participated in the 14th Niigata Prefectural Art Exhibition ("Kenten" for short) in her home prefecture and won an honorable mention, also for a work titled *Shiseki*.*7 There are no existent images of the work and it cannot be said for certain, but we can infer that this was the first work in the *Shiseki* series featured in the 25th Shinseisaku Exhibition two years later. Compared with the figurative *Kubi A*, in *Shiseki* we see a rough, simplified sculpture with animistic power, more like a deity from folk religion or a ceremonial mask than a human head.*8 As it happened, shortly before this turning point, in 1958, Kubota's teacher Mr. Takahashi went to Mexico to study its ancient art, but Kubota continued to explore her style as a sculptor. [fig. 4. p. 185, left]

Kubota continued producing sculpture after graduating from university, while also undergoing a different kind of artistic influence from her aunt, the avant-garde dancer Chiya Kuni (born Yoshie Kubota). Chiya studied under the dancer Masami Kuni, opened a dance school in 1947, and performed in various locations. In 1957 she established the Chiya Kuni Dance Institute in Komaba, Meguro-ku, Tokyo, and in 1960 she opened up the institute to young people as a place to pursue creative activities across multiple disciplines. In addition to dancers such as Kazuo Ohno and Tatsumi Hijikata, creators who gathered there included the members of Group Ongaku, and it became a nexus of interaction among avant-garde artists of various genres.*9 Kubota, who was living on the premises around this time, had the opportunity to meet these avant-garde artists and see their works and performances. She later traveled to the United States with Group Ongaku member Mieko Shiomi, with whom she had developed a close relationship at the institute, and joined the Fluxus group.

Kubota, who had been resistant to academic art studies from early on, gradually became part of the avant-garde art community by engaging with energetic artists seeking to create something completely new. In 1963 she participated in the 15th edition of the *Yomiuri Independent Exhibition*, which was then at its height of outrageous experimentation, and presented two abstract sculptures in completely different styles, *We can make it* [fig. 5. p. 185, top-right] and *Suddenly* [fig. 6. p. 185, bottom-right]. In December of the same year she had her first solo exhibition at Naiqua Gallery, *1st. LOVE, 2nd. LOVE...Shigeko Kubota Solo Sculpture Exhibition*, held from December 1–7, 1963, and the artist herself sent invitations to critics.*10 It seems that a fair number of critics visited this exhibition,*11 but no reviews of it were published, and Kubota was deeply disappointed. The works at this "solo sculpture exhibition" seem to have been reconstructions of the abstract welded iron sculptures she showed at the Yomiuri Independent Exhibition earlier the same year, but what was noteworthy was the manner in which they were presented. [cat. p. 12] The room was filled with scraps of paper intended to resemble "love letters," and the sculptures placed atop mounds covered with sheets, so that viewers had to crawl up these mounds to see the sculptures. It could be called an installation, making use of the entire exhibition space, and a happening, in that it incorporated the act of visitors' climbing and the height of the mounds and the appearance of the space changed from day to day as people climbed up and down.*[12] While she deliberately labeled it a "solo sculpture exhibition," it was far removed from traditional sculpture and clearly showed Kubota progressing toward creative endeavors unconfined by the conventional framework of sculpture.

While this exhibition was on view Kubota took part in a performance festival called *Sweet 16* (December 3–5) at Sogetsu Kaikan Hall, performing under the pseudonym "G. Breyali."*[13] The content of her performance is unknown, but a text entitled "To Mr. Maciunas/G. Breyali" appeared in the festival program [cat. p. 15], and as a part of this text, which appears to be a score for the performance, matches the English printed on the invitation to her solo show at Naiqua Gallery [cat. p. 13, top], it is unquestionably Kubota's work. Kubota had learned of the activities of the Fluxus group through Yoko Ono and taken an interest, and around the same time she sent an event score for "Perpetual Fluxfest" to George Maciunas, the organizer of Fluxus, the content of which has also been verified as largely the same as that of the text printed in the above-mentioned festival program.*[14]

As the above examples indicate, around 1963 Kubota rapidly turned toward avant-garde art, participating in some iconic events of the period such as Hi-Red Center's *Shelter Plan* and Yoko Ono's *Morning Piece*, and her own work evolved. For example, at the anarchic group exhibition *OFF MUSEUM* (Tsubaki-Kindai Gallery, June 17–22, 1964) in which Ushio Shinohara and others took part, she presented *Miss Universe*, an audience-participation piece incorporating a live rabbit.*[15] During research for the current exhibition it was confirmed that she showed the same work incorporating underwear at Yasunao Tone's exhibition at Naiqua Gallery (October 12–17, 1964) [cat. p. 17, top right] and at Flux Week (Gallery Crystal, September 6–14, 1965) [cat. p. 17, bottom], and showed a definite shift away from sculpture, reshaping herself as an avant-garde artist exploring new modes of expression such as performances and events.

Underlying this evolution was the establishment in the late 1950s, when Kubota was beginning as an artist in Tokyo, of the Sogetsu Art Center, which invited many of the world's most experimental avant-garde artists to Japan in the early 1960s. Events included a presentation of works by Yoko Ono (1962) and a concert by John Cage and David Tudor (1962), but it was a presentation of work by Nam June Paik on May 29, 1964 that had the most profound impact on Kubota. She discussed the impact of this event in detail in her own book, but after seeing the performance by Nam June Paik, to whom she had long been drawn, and hearing him speak in person, her ambition to move to the United States and her interest in Fluxus (of which Paik was a member) grew dramatically.*[16] The rapid increase in Kubota's involvement performance art in the later part of her Tokyo days set the stage for her subsequent activities after moving to the US.

3. Moving to the US: Exploring Original Modes of Expression

Arriving in New York City along with Mieko Shiomi on July 4, 1964, Kubota was welcomed by Maciunas and took up residence in an apartment he had prepared. Fellow Japanese artists Ay-O and Takako Saito, who had already moved to the US and joined Fluxus, were in the city, as was Paik whom she so greatly admired. Maciunas aimed to organize Fluxus as a community, including arranging "dinner communes" (dinner parties with rotating hosts aimed at saving members money), in which Kubota and Shiomi began participating shortly afterwards. Maciunas also sold members' works as multiples at the Fluxus Shop, and Kubota helped out at the shop and produced the pieces *Flux Napkins* [cat. p. 21, middle] and *Flux Medicine* [cat. p. 21, bottom], but she did not develop these multiples further.

She also took part in Fluxus performances such as Eric Andersen's *Opus 45* [cat. p. 22] and Yoko Ono's *Beat Piece* (1965).*[17] Kubota herself began performing, presenting her first piece in the Perpetual Fluxfest event, *Vagina Painting*, known through several photographs taken by Maciunas. It was clearly related to Paik's early 1960s work *Zen for Head*, but evidently the audience reaction was negative.*[18] In later years Kubota recollected that the performance had been Paik's idea, and that he asked her to do it and she reluctantly complied,*[19] but during research for this exhibition, what appear to be publicity photographs of the piece at Peter Moore's studio in the fall of the previous year were discovered [cat. p. 25, bottom]. The photographs clearly show the mechanism for the piece, underwear with something like a housepainter's brush attached to it, and Kubota painting while wearing it in a manner quite different from what the audience at the actual performance recalled. Now that Kubota and Paik are both deceased there is no way to determine whose idea it was or the reasons for changing the approach between the preparatory stages and the actual event. However, given that she thoroughly prepared for and presented this work, and was frequently participating in others' performances around the same time, we can infer that at least she had the aspiration to stage her own original performance piece as a member of Fluxus, and this motivated her to go through with it.

She later participated as a performer in Carolee Schneemann's *Snows* (1967) [cat. p. 27] and a tour by the electronic music performance group Sonic Arts Union, but she was starting to sense a gap between the transitory medium of performance art, which did not endure in tangible form, and what she wanted to accomplish.*20 As a result, *Vagina Painting* came to be known as Kubota's only performance piece,*21 but elements of it were carried on in her subsequent early video works.*22

4. Encountering Video

Kubota began living with Paik, who had been producing video works since the mid-1960s, and started working with video herself around 1970. *Broken Diary: Europe on 1/2 Inch a Day* (1972) [cat. p. 30, top], presented as her first single-channel video work, was made while traveling alone in Europe with a hand-held Sony Portapak camera. This was the start of Kubota's career as a video artist, and was marked by signature approaches such as presenting what appears to be the same source material in a variety of different edits and formats.

Many female video artists emerged around this time thanks in part to the invention of compact video equipment that could be handled by a woman alone, and enabled women to compete with men on an equal footing. Kubota frequently participated in group exhibitions of women artists, but this was the only period in which she actively collaborated with female artists of the same generation, most notably in *White Black Red and Yellow*, a group show featuring four female artists of different races that is also noteworthy as an early video art project in collaboration with Mary Lucier, who went on to international prominence.*23

While Kubota was producing her own video pieces, thanks to her outgoing personality and the fact that she lived with Paik, she also had many opportunities to view works by other video artists and interact with them. Through these experiences she was hired as a video curator at Anthology Film Archives in 1974, and from then until 1982 introduced works by numerous artists.*24 She acted as a conduit between the Japanese and American video art scenes, introducing works from New York for *Tokyo-New York Video Express* [cat. p. 37, bottom] held in Tokyo and then reporting on this event at a videotaped symposium, "Open Circuits," held at MoMA.*25

Encountering the new medium of video greatly expanded the range of Kubota's activities and creative practice. On the other hand, having one of her works viewed as a video piece meant its being judged primarily by the content of a video playing on a screen. However, Kubota is known to have used multiple monitors for multi-channel works early on, sometimes stacking them in the manner of sculptural objects.*26 From this time onward use of multiple monitors was not an uncommon practice in general, but for Kubota there was a particular emphasis on the sculptural element, and this is significant in that it connects to her subsequent video sculpture.

5. The Birth of Video Sculpture

Kubota remarked that when she first started shooting video she was somewhat narcissistic, taking diary-like footage that often featured her own face,*27 and the earliest work that fits this description is *One Day in California* (later retitled *Self-Portrait*), which was incorporated into Kubota's first video sculpture *Video Poem* (1975) [cat. pp. 38-39].*28 She was disappointed that many video artists, including Paik, emphasized videos themselves and were indifferent to formal aspects of the works, and dissatisfied with the way video art made demands on viewers' time and compelled them to keep watching a screen from beginning to end.*29 In response she produced *Video Poem*, in which a square cathode-ray tube monitor is shrouded by a sack and the sack inflated with a blower, the images on the screen only visible through the gap of an open zipper. These images cannot be clearly made out, as they are largely concealed by the sack, and the intent is not to convey a narrative.*30 This work can be described as her first so-called video sculpture, i.e. video art that takes the form of a three-dimensional work. Video sculpture was an optimal way for Kubota to connect sculpture, her foundation as an artist, and the newly pioneered medium of video art, and having arrived at this mode her work rapidly developed.

The Duchampiana Series

Duchampiana, one of Shigeko Kubota's best-known series of works, was produced over 15 years from 1975 to 1990. Inspired by Marcel Duchamp and his work, it can be regarded as a pioneering example of appropriation. She met Duchamp in 1968,*31 and he died a few months later, inspiring her first of all to publish the book *Marcel Duchamp and John Cage* (1970) [cat. p. 28], a collection of works based on photographs she had taken herself, at her own expense, then to compile and edit these photographs into a single-channel video piece also titled *Marcel Duchamp and John Cage* (1972). She subsequently produced the video sculpture *Marcel Duchamp's Grave* [cat. p. 54–55] using footage of Duchamp's grave shot during a trip to Europe, which was the first work exhibited as part of the Duchampiana series. Thereafter, in the short span of two years she exhibited *Video Chess* [cat. pp. 56–59], *Nude Descending a Staircase* [cat. pp. 60–62], *Door* [cat. pp. 63–65], and *Meta-Marcel: Window* [cat. pp. 66–69] (referred to below as *Window*), followed by *Bicycle Wheel* [cat. pp. 98–100] several years later. These six works constitute the series shown with the title *Duchampiana*, but his influence continued into her later years as reflected in *Adam and Eve* [cat. pp. 112–115], released in 1990, which quotes from Duchamp's appearance as the naked Adam in Francis Picabia's ballet *Relâche* (based on a painting by Lucas Cranach).

Of these works, *Video Chess*, *Marcel Duchamp's Grave*, *Nude Descending a Staircase*, and *Door* referenced Duchamp in their video as well as in their three-dimensional elements, while *Window* and *Bicycle Wheel* appropriated Duchamp in terms of the work's visual elements while the videos had shifted to Kubota's distinctive portrayals of nature. The first version of *Window*, entitled *Snow*, was a particularly masterful example of a new video-sculpture aesthetic that showcased Kubota's unique sensibility in its juxtaposition of the natural phenomenon of snow with the technical side effect of static known by the same name.*[32]

Kubota's two solo exhibitions in 1976 and 1977 at the René Block Gallery, organized around the theme of *Duchampiana*, were successes that rocketed Kubota to prominence as a video sculpture artist.*[33] It is clear that this series, with its well-defined theme of Duchamp and solid sculptural qualities, contributed to the establishment of Shigeko Kubota's position in the history of art.

Toward Works on the Theme of Nature

Having incorporated natural motifs into *Window*, Kubota produced *Three Mountains* [cat. pp. 78–81] around the same time, in 1979, using images of the American southwest landscape in her first video sculpture primarily focused on nature. She subsequently produced a series of works with themes of nature and landscape: *River* [cat. pp. 84, 93–95], *Green Installation* [cat. p. 101], *Niagara Falls* [cat. pp. 104–107], *Rock Video: Cherry Blossom* [cat. pp. 108–109], *Dry Mountain, Dry Water* [cat. pp. 110–111]. Kubota belonged to the mountaineering club in university, and before that had spent her childhood surrounded by mountains, making this a theme close to her heart,*[34] on which she produced a large number of drawings. Inscribed on these are phrases such as "how to leave a pattern of the self," "video sculpture portrays life," and *Autobiographical Landscape* [fig. 7. p. 189], and it is evident that Kubota, having developed a distinctive style in the *Duchampiana* series, was further exploring unique modes of expression and seeking to convey her own views of art in these works.

Images of Arizona appear in *Three Mountains* and *Green Installation*, and both works feature mirrors, affixed to the interior of a 3D object in the former and to half of the surface in the latter, reflecting brilliant light reminiscent of the sun in the desert. In *River*, the form of a water-filled tank hints at the curving line of a river, and a moving image of the artist swimming is projected on the water's surface. Star and heart shapes generated with a color synthesizer create an urban, Pop-like impression, but drawings for the work indicate that it was inspired by the light of the moon and stars reflected in a river at night, and they become elements that emphasize the landscape. *Niagara Falls* presents the waterfall in the four seasons of the year, in a four-channel juxtaposition of powerful footage of the falls shot in close-up during actual visits to the area, and physical splashes of water from a shower attached at the top of the piece combine with the sound of a waterfall emerging from speakers, producing an image of the waterfall that is both abstract and full of destructive power. All of these works depict nature itself, but it is nature rendered abstract and transformed into art with a highly personal sensibility through the medium of video. Through this medium, nature, a most familiar of subjects for Kubota since her high school days when she turned to art in earnest, developed into a new field for personal expression.*[35]

6. Expansion of Expression

From around 1980 onward, Kubota made frequent use of reflective materials such as water and mirrors, and of motors as a mechanism to introduce movement into the works. Water as a motif also appeared in the early video piece *Riverrun–Video Water Poem* [cat. p. 33], but this was only water captured as a moving image, while *River* and *Niagara Falls* utilized actual water, with mirror fragments scattered at the bottom of the water reflecting light from below. Works such as *Three Mountains*, *Green Installation*, *Dry Mountain, Dry Water*, in which mirror material is applied inside or on the surface of an object, reflect not only the light of the moving image but also the viewer and the surrounding environment, and succeed in incorporating the space around them into the work.*[36] In *Video Haiku—Hanging Piece* [cat. pp. 96–97], the moving image on a monitor hung from the ceiling is reflected in an oval mirrored surface on the floor, but that image is of the viewer filmed in real time by a camera installed near the ceiling. This makes the viewer part of the work, and renders ambiguous the relationship between the acts of to see and to be seen.

Motors were another important mechanism that made Kubota's work more dynamic in terms of spatial expression and added the element of movement that was indispensable in her work from the 1980s onwards. A motor was first used in *River*, where it was installed to generate movement on the surface of the water so as to change the light of the moving image reflected on it in various ways. She went on to use motors in *Video Haiku* and *Niagara Falls*, and to even more pronounced effect in *Bicycle Wheel One, Two, and Three*.*37 That work, which utilizes small LCD displays that became available in the late 1980s, achieves more multi-layered temporal expression through the dual motion effects of the moving image on the monitor and the movement of the wheel on which it is installed.

Her use of motors evolved further thereafter, and in *Adam and Eve* and *Skater* [cat. pp. 120–121] motors are installed in the pedestal of the work, causing the body of the sculpture to rotate. In the mid-1980s she began superimposing multiple moving images on the sculptures themselves using projectors, and this approach gradually spread to the surrounding environment, creating movement throughout the entire space, for example by rotating the projector. This turned the viewer into part of the work, and can be seen as an extension, many years later, of the installation Kubota created for her first solo exhibition.

In Closing

In 1991 Shigeko Kubota had an international traveling exhibition, beginning at the American Museum of the Moving Image, that represented a culmination of her solo shows thus far, and afterwards she refocused on people as subjects for the first time in around 30 years, since around 1960 when she was an aspiring sculptor. A series of humanoid sculptures, starting with *Adam and Eve* and continuing with *Skater, Jogging Lady* [cat. p. 125], and *Pissing Man* [cat. p. 124], portray individuals that seem typified but are actually human beings with distinct personalities linked to Kubota's personal memory and life. Her late works *Nam June Paik I* [cat. p. 134]and *Nam June Paik II* [cat. p. 135] are portraits of her beloved husband, and can be seen as the conclusion of a long series of sculptures featuring the human figure. At the 1993 Venice Biennale, where she presented *Garden of Eden: Video Dream Landscape* [cat. p. 130], and in solo exhibitions [cat. p.131] at the Lance Fung Gallery and Whitney Museum of American Art in 1996, these depictions of the human figure and video sculptures with nature as a motif came to be shown together in the same venue. Environments combining multiple works, as in *Adam and Eve* (1991), can be seen as a style that consistently characterized her presentation. After Paik was paralyzed due to a stroke in 1996, Kubota devoted herself to caring for him and ensuring the success of his solo exhibition at the Guggenheim, and production of her own work fell by the wayside. When it resumed the subject of her work became Paik himself, who was the subject of a series of videos and video sculptures shown in the solo exhibitions *Sexual Healing* (Lance Fung Gallery, 2000) and *My Life with Nam June Paik* (Maya Stendhal Gallery, 2007). *Sexual Healing* was an exhibition centered on a video that dealt humorously with Paik's rehabilitation, surrounded by monitors and objects symbolizing long-term care such as beds and wheelchairs, and the entire space could be experienced as a single installation, maintaining a style she pursued to the end.

Kubota's endeavors to create works that utilized entire spaces went back to her first solo show in 1963 at the Naiqua Gallery.*38 That exhibition was a starting point in terms of both art and life, as Paik viewed and appreciated it, encouraged her and went on to become her partner in life. Video was a window that connected the two of them and opened her life to the world.

This exhibition unfortunately falls short of a "retrospective" of the work of Shigeko Kubota, but I sincerely hope that the exhibition of these works, some of them for the first time in 30 years, and the newly discovered materials will be an occasion for reappraisal and recognition of her work.

(Curator, The Niigata Prefectural Museum of Modern Art)

Translation by Christopher Stephens

Finally, I am deeply grateful for assistance in research on Shigeko Kubota from the late Kubota herself and from my museum colleague the late Ko Seong-Jun, both of whom cooperated during the preparatory stages, as well as for the generous support of the Pola Art Foundation, the Kajima Foundation for the Arts, and the Japan Association of Art Museums.

[Notes]

*1——This term originated with the gallerist René Block's presentation of her work in Germany in 1976 under the title *Duchampiana: Video Sculpture* (from the text on *Bicycle Wheel* on p.100 of this book)。 For details, refer to the essay by Hashimoto.

*2——"Because I am a sculptor, I wanted to work more from memory . . . The video part is a mirage that arises from memories of my life." ("On Art and Artists: Shigeko Kubota," *Profile*, vol. 3, no.6, November 1983, p. 15.)

*3——For example, Kubota cited her roots in her mother's hometown of Ojiya, in the Chuetsu region, as an inspiration for her mountain-themed work *Three Mountains* (from the text on Three Mountains on p. 81 of this book).

*4——For a history of the Kubota family, cf. Takako Nakayama,

"Yoshie Kubota (Chiya Kuni) and Her Family," Chiya Kuni Dance Institute Editorial Committee (ed.), *Dignified, Like a Flower: the Avant-Garde Dance World of Chiya Kuni*, Atelier Third, 2008, pp. 14–15.

*5——"High Honor for 17-Year-Old Girl: Ms. Kubota's Work Accepted for Niki-kai Exhibition," *Mainichi Shimbun* Niigata edition, October 8, 1954, p. 8.

*6——Shigeko Kubota and Nam Jeong-ho, *My Love, Nam June Paik*, translated by Ko Seon-Jun, Heibonsha, 2013, p. 47.

*7——*14th Niigata Art Exhibition (Kenten) Catalog* (organized by the Niigata Nippo, the Niigata Prefectural Board of Education and the Boards of Education of Niigata City, Nagaoka City and Takada City), Kobayashi Department Store, Niigata City, May 26-June 7,1959.

*8——According to an interview with her younger sister Takako Nakayama, Shigeko was impressed with Buddhist statues she saw in Nara and Kyoto around this time, and was enthusiastic about sculpting heads (interview on February 3, 2019). There are also mentions of Buddhist statues in Nara and Kyoto in Miwako Tezuka's *Oral History Archives of Japanese Art, Kubota Shigeko Interview* (October 11, 2009) http://www.oralarthistory.org/archives/kubota_shigeko/interview_01.php).

*9——For details on the activities of Chiya Kuni, cf.: Op. cit., Chiya Kuni Dance Institute Editorial Committee (ed.), 2008.

*10——There are letters existent today addressed to Shuzo Takiguchi at the Keio University Art Center, and to Tamon Miki in the archive of the Independent Administrative Institution National Institutes for Cultural Heritage Tokyo National Research Institute for Cultural Properties.

*11——Yoshiaki Tono appears in existing documentary photographs, and it is known that Yusuke Nakahara visited as well. (Response to inquiry from Yuuka Miyata, letter postmarked July 30, 1999).

*12——"I wanted to make art in new formats, like environmental art, anti-museum art, anti-establishment expression . . . audience participation, participatory happenings—because I was strongly influenced by John Cage's work with randomness and chance operations. The avant-garde at the time was also very inspired by Hi-Red Center, Hijikata Tatsumi, concerts at Sogetsu Hall." (Miyata letter, ibid.) Statements from Mieko Shiomi, Yasunao Tone, and her younger sister Takako Nakayama, all of whom saw the exhibition in person, differ in their descriptions of the mountain's height, it is evident that the actual height and the impression it made differed considerably depending on when the exhibition was viewed.

*13——Kubota's name does not appear in the performance program, but notes written by her friend Yasunao Tone, who participated in the event, indicate that it was Kubota's work. See also this catalog pp. 14–15.

*14——For details on interaction between Ono and Kubota and the letter to Maciunas, cf. Midori Yoshimoto, "Self-Exploration in Multimedia: The Experiments of Shigeko Kubota," *Into Performance: Japanese Women Artists in New York* (New Brunswick, New Jersey and London, Rutgers University Press), 2005, pp. 171–172.

*15——Ushio Shinohara, *Avant-Garde Road*, Bijutsu Shuppan-sha, 1968, p. 132. "*OFF MUSEUM* '64 6/17–22 Tsubaki-Kindai Gallery," *Bijutsu Journal* no. 46, page number unknown.

*16——Kubota, op. cit., 2013, pp. 33–40.

*17——Jon Hendricks, "Yoko Ono and Fluxus," *YES Yoko Ono* exhibition catalogue, Asahi Shimbun-sha, 2003, p. 43.

*18——Kubota, op. cit., 2013, pp. 98–100. Shiomi, who viewed the performance, also commented that it was painful to watch (interview with Mieko Shiomi, July 1, 2019). On the other hand, Eric Andersen, who also saw it, described it as "the greatest performance Shigeko ever did. It was astonishing and incredibly poetic. The brush was emerging from her vagina, but I didn't think there was anything shocking about it. It was deeply moving, sensual and delicate. All of us were extremely impressed." (E-mail to Mihoko Nishikawa dated August 2, 2020). Thus the audience reaction cannot be called uniformly negative.

*19——Tezuka, op. cit. interview, 2013. Kubota claimed that she did not reveal this fact until late in life because Paik had discouraged her from doing so.

*20——"To me, that kind of thing seemed like playing around. I thought of myself as a sculptor. I felt I was a little different from these people . . . a performance is ephemeral, it's over in an instant. It was just too ephemeral, I thought." (Tezuka, op. cit. interview, 2013). She also spoke of a similar sense of dismay in 1983 (*Profile*, op. cit., p. 15.)

*21——A work in a group exhibition organized by Jean Dupuy was evidently a performance, judging by the title, but the details are unknown. *Collective Consciousness: Art Performances in the Seventies*, Jean Dupuy (ed.), Performing Arts Journal Publications, New York, 1980, pp. 109, 121, 189.

*22——There are elements of performance in her first video performance, *Riverrun* (1972). For more information on Kubota's early video works and activities, see the Yoshimoto essay in this book.

*23——Melinda Barlow, "Red, White, Yellow, and Black: Women, Multiculturalism, and Video History," *Quarterly Review of Film and Video*, 17(4), 2000, pp. 297–316. For more information on Kubota's early video works and activities, see the Yoshimoto essay in this book.

*24——"Video Programming," *Bulletin for Film and Video Information*, Anthology Film Archives, Vol. 1, No. 3, June 1974.

*25——Shigeko Kubota, "Women's Video in the U.S. and Japan," Douglas Davis and Allison Simmons (eds.), *Essay, Statements and Videotapes Based on "Open Circuits: An International Conference on the Future of Television" Organized by Fred Barzyk, Douglas Davis, Gerald O'Grady, and Willard Van Dyke for the Museum of Modern Art, New York City*, MIT Press, Cambridge, Massachusetts, and London, England, pp. 96–101. Prior to this, from 1969 to 1971, Kubota contributed articles irregularly to *Bijutsu Techo* magazine as a New York-based reporter. The these covered a wide range of topics, from art to ecology, sex, and drug culture, and played a role in conveying the realities of American culture of the day to readers in Japan. In this respect, too, a picture emerges of Kubota as not only a creator but also as an intermediary who brought other artists and their works to people's attention and bridged the divide between countries and cultures.

*26——A poster for the Experimental Television Center Binghamton from September 30, 1972 mentions a three-channel video performance, and a photo from the *9th Annual Avant-Garde Festival* of New York shows Kubota standing in front of a stack of monitors. Also, the work *A36 - 24 - 36*, in which moving images of Marilyn Monroe appear on multiple monitors with multicolored cellophane affixed, was exhibited at the 2nd Video Arts Festival (cat. p. 35).

*27——Tezuka, op. cit. interview, 2013.

*28——Moira Roth, "The Voice of Shigeko Kubota: 'A Fusion of Art and Life, Asia and America . . .'", in exh. cat., *Shigeko Kubota Video Sculpture*, American Museum of the Moving Image, NY, 1991, p. 81.

*29——Shigeko Kubota and Jonathan Price, Feb. 17, 1976 (the

document from Anthology Video Arhchive).

*30——"I thought the medium of video installation would render the element of time in video more abstract." ("Kubota Shigeko Interview: Talking about Video, Art, and Life," *Monthly Image Forum*, November 1984).

*31——Kubota first met Marcel Duchamp at John Cage's chess concert Reunion, which she was able to film. For details, cf. Kubota Shigeko, "Chess Game with Duchamp in His Final Years," *Bijutsu Techo* no. 319, November 1969, pp. 80–89. It should be noted that in subsequent interviews and descriptions, the chronology of her second meeting with Duchamp and shooting of footage is repeatedly incorrectly reversed, but Kubota's *Reunion* took place in March 5, 1968 in Toronto while Merce Cunningham's *Walkaround Time* was staged in March 10, 1968 in Buffalo, thus the initial 1969 article is correct.

*32——In a drawing for *Window* [cat. p. 73] made in 1979, Kubota maintained the concept of four windows representing spring, summer, autumn and winter using images of scenery of the four seasons. In the video piece *Window*, the image of her holding the window frame in her hand and posing (cat. p. 69, right) by the waterside also seems to imply the natural opening of windows.

*33——Three works were presented at *Meta-Marcel by Shigeko Kubota*, her second solo exhibition at René Block Gallery in 1977. One of these was *Mountain*, which later evolved into *Three Mountains*, which for the purposes of this exhibition is not considered part of the Duchampiana series.

*34——Kubota apparently intended to make a mountain-themed series on the scale of her *Duchampiana* series. "Shigeko Kubota - Mountain Series," *Shigeko Kubota—Video Sculptures*, in exh. cat., Museum Folkwang Essen, daadgalerie, Berlin, Kunsthaus Zürich, 1981, pp. 34–37.

*35——Interview at the Hara Museum, 1992 [cat. p. 174].

*36——Her first work employing mirrors was *Marcel Duchamp's Grave* (1975), but when it was first shown in 1975 a mirrored surface was installed only on the floor, but when it was shown once more in 1984 it was also mounted on the wall opposite the ceiling, giving the work a more environmental character. For details on the development of this work, see Nishikawa's essay in this book.

*37——The first version of *Duchampiana: Bicycle Wheel*, produced in 1983, was also equipped with a motor, but at this time the monitor was still too large and heavy for it to rotate continuously.

*38——Kubota later described her exhibition at the Naiqua Gallery as "environmental art" ("Kubota Shigeko's 'Working Drawings,'" *Kyoto Shimbun*, May 29, 1990). This remark was in the context of a recollection, and what exactly she meant by this phrase is unclear. However, it is known that she attended a lecture by Allan Kaprow in the 1960s and was influenced by his ideas on happenings and environments (*Profile*, op. cit., p. 3.) Also, in light of Kubota's longtime friendship with Katsuhiro Yamaguchi and the fact that they often exhibited together in group shows, there is a need to reconsider Kubota's work in the context of environmental art in the future.

「我ヴィデオする、ゆえに我あり」

久保田成子のヴィデオ人生の始まり

由本みどり

「結局、ホンモノが大量生産される映画が演劇をつぶし、レコードがナマのコンサートをこえて、音楽を大産業にした歴史が、美術でも繰り返されるのではなかろうか？　比較的造形力の可塑性に乏しい写真でさえ、すでに芸術に成長したが、写真のように簡単に再生産され、しかも油絵よりも何倍も造形力のあるTVアートが、本格化されれば、将来、美術文化に大きな変革が起きるだろう *[1]

1969年5月にハワード・ワイズ・ギャラリーで開かれた画期的な展覧会「創造的媒体としてのTV」展の評を書くなかで、久保田成子は上記のように、予言的に締めくくった。当時久保田は、日本の代表的美術雑誌である『美術手帖』に、ニューヨークのアートシーンについての記事を書き始めたばかりであったが、テレビを用いた美術が広い美術界にパラダイム変換をもたらす予感を強く抱いていた。もっとも、彼女自身が、来（きた）る変革において大きな役割を果たすことになることは知る由（よし）もなかったのだが。

久保田はこの展評を「ヴィデオ・アート」の語さえない頃に書いた。「２部屋を鈎状につなげたこのうす暗く幽閉された会場には、10人のTVアーティストによる25個のTVセットが、ちょうど秋葉原のTV屋の店先のように立体的に配置されていた」*[2]。フランク・ジレットとアイラ・シュナイダーの《ワイプ・サイクル》やナムジュン・パイクの《参加型テレビⅠ－Ⅱ》などの、最も早いヴィデオ・インスタレーション作品の例をあげながら、久保田は、観者の生の、または録画された姿がモニターに映るクローズト・サーキット（閉回路）の参加型テレビ作品の重要性を指摘した。彼女はこう強調している。「創造的媒体としてのTV」展で浮かびあがったのは、大衆がじかに参加して、今まで一方通行であったTV文化を体制側から奪い返して、本当の『電子性』にふさわしい二方交通、多重コミュニケーションにつくりなおそうとする動きである」*[3]。

同展に刺激を受け、久保田は自分でヴィデオを撮り始める。60年代半ばまでにアートを作ることをいったんあきらめた彼女だが、1970年までにはヴィデオという媒体を通して「画像、音、アクションを取り戻し」、融合させたい気持ちに駆り立てられた*[4]。作曲家デイヴィッド・バーマンと別れた久保田は、アラン・カプローによってカリフォルニア芸術大学に初のヴィデオ・アートの教授として招聘されたナムジュン・パイクと合流すべく、ロサンゼルスへと飛んだ。パイクはヴィデオ・シンセサイザーを協働して作った、電機技師の阿部修也を日本から呼んでいた。実験のるつぼで、久保田はまず自分自身をヴィデオで録画したが、それは後に彫刻作品《ヴィデオ・ポエム》に使われることになった。だが、カリフォルニアの雰囲気があまりにもリラックスしていると感じた彼女は、パイクが翌年の契約を更新しないよう説得し、1971年暮れにニューヨークに戻った*[5]。1972年春、アメリカに夫を訪ねた阿部夫人に頼んで、久保田は新しいSONYポータパックを入手した*[6]。同年5月、久保田はヨーロッパを旅し、ルーアン（デュシャンの墓を参るため）、ニース（フルクサスの友人、斉藤陽子を訪ねて）、ブリュッセル、アムステルダム、ブレーメン（ジョン・ケージに会いに）、ヴェネツィアで観たものを撮影してきた。ニューヨークに戻るなり、それらの録画映像を使って、後に「ブロークン・ダイアリー」の第２章となる、初期のシングルチャンネル・ヴィデオ作品《ヨーロッパを一日ハーフインチで》を制作した。

6月30日のザ・キッチンにおける、初の「ライヴとヴィデオテープのコンサート」をきっかけに、久保田はヴィデオ作家として飛躍していった［本書31頁］*7。当初のヴィデオの映写には、ライブ・コンサートのような即興性があり、夜遅く行なわれた。久保田によれば、観客が多すぎて、一晩に2度の映写をしなければならなかったという*8。《ヨーロッパを一日ハーフインチで》の他に、1968年のチェスのイベントで撮った写真を使って作った、ケージとデュシャンについてのヴィデオも上映した。

同年秋、ニューヨーク北部のシラキュースのエヴァーソン美術館内の実験テレビ・センターと、マンハッタンのサウスストリート・シーポートに停留していた船、アレクサンダー・ハミルトン号で開かれた、「第9回ニューヨーク・アヴァンギャルド・フェスティヴァル」において、久保田は3チャンネル（3回路）のヴィデオ・インスタレーションを発表し、ケージの60歳の誕生日を祝った。「ジョン・ケージのためのヴィデオ・バースデイパーティ」と題されたアヴァンギャルド・フェスティヴァルでの発表では、もう1つモニターが設置してあり、それにはクローズト・サーキットで生の観者の姿が映されていたようだ*9(図1)。ヴィデオ・アーティストとしてデビューしてわずか数か月のうちに、久保田は複数の回路のヴィデオに取り組み、1969年の「創造的媒体としてのTV」展で、彼女が重要な要素として報告した、ライブ・フィードのカメラとモニターを使って、観者を巻き込もうとした。1シーズンに5回も発表の機会を得た久保田は、生まれたばかりのヴィデオ・アート・シーンで、自分の名を成していった。

久保田のヴィデオ・アーティストとしての台頭は、アメリカにおけるフェミニズム運動の第二波の勃興と同時期であったが、それは単なる偶然ではない*10。キュレーターのメアリー・ジェーン・ジェイコブズが述べているように、「これらの新しいジャンル（ヴィデオ、パフォーマンス、写真、インスタレーション・アートなど）を通して、彼女らは、西洋男性優勢の絵画界では不可能であった、自分たちの場所を獲得したのだ」*11。絵画よりもさらに男性優勢であった分野は、久保田も日本で学んだ彫刻であった。久保田は戦略的に考え、エリート主義な東京の前衛界を去り、環境的芸術やパフォーマンスについての興味を探究することのできる、より開かれたニューヨークのアートコミュニティを選んだ。ヴィデオに出合った時、彼女は自分の即興的で行動的な性格にそれが向いていることを直感的に悟った。プロセスが「非常に化学的な」映画に比べ、久保田はヴィデオを「玄米みたいに有機的で、のりみたいに東洋的、日本製だ」と、最初のポータブルなヴィデオ・レコーダーがソニーによって開発されたことにユーモラスに言及した*12。さらに、久保田は、最も本能的な言い方で、ヴィデオとその創造過程を女性の身体とその機能に喩えて、こう宣言した。「ヴィデオはヴァギナの勝利」、「私は毎月半インチ……3Mまたはソニー製……で1万フィートの長さの出血をする」*13。このような隠喩は、（しばしば男性の「天才」に帰されがちな）芸術的創造と生殖とを直接的に結びつけた久保田のパフォーマンス、《ヴァギナ・ペインティング》を思わせる*14。彼女のフェミニスト的宣言は、久保田と同時期に映画からヴィデオに転向した、シャーリー・クラークの「ヴィデオは私の男根である」というような挑発

図1　「第9回アヴァンギャルド・フェスティヴァル」で自作の前に立つ久保田成子
Fig. 1. Shigeko Kubota in front of her work at *the 9th Annual Avant Garde Festival*, 1972.

的発言に部分的に影響を受けているかもしれない*[15]。

ヴィデオ・アートの初期には多くの女性作家がいたが、彼女らは男性作家と同等の機会や支持を得られたわけではなかった。ザ・キッチン創始者のスタイナ・ヴァスルカは、彼女らのニーズを察知し、ヴィデオ・アーティストのスーザン・ミラノに持ちかけて、女性ヴィデオ・フェスティヴァルの開催を実現した。同フェスティバルは、1972年から76年までほぼ毎年、女性ヴィデオ作家に発表の機会を与えた*[16]。久保田はニューヨーク市で開かれた4回のフェスティヴァルのすべてに参加し、ひときわ注目を浴びた*[17]。このフェスティバルで久保田が最初に見せたのは、《ジョア：不貞の袋小路》で、評によれば、それは、スクリーンを2分割にし、一方では女装男性を含む、風変わりな性的ダンス劇団を見せ、もう一方では、乳房の部分だけ穴をあけた、網目のレオタードを着た女性やその他の映像を見せた、下俗なストリップを様式的にパロディ化したうえに「性行為を様式化」した作品であったということだ*[18]。残念ながら、本作品はいまだ見つからず、紛失の恐れがあるが、乳房を露にした女性のダンサーは《ヨーロッパを一日ハーフインチで》にも登場するので、内容的に重複した可能性が高い。2分割のスクリーンは、アンディ・ウォーホルのダブル・スクリーン方式の《チェルシー・ガールズ》(1966年)からインスピレーションを得た可能性もあり、注目に値する*[19]。性について評するような実験的な作品を他の女性作家のいる場で公開できたことは、久保田にとって、貴重な肯定的な経験となったに違いない。少し後で、アンソロジー・フィルム・アーカイヴズのヴィデオ・キュレーターになった時、久保田はミラノを招待し、過去の女性フィルム・フェスティヴァルで見せた作品を再公開し、仲間の女性アーティストたちの発表の機会を増やすことに協力した*[20]。

ホワイト ブラック レッド イエロー：ヴィデオ、ダンス、ストーリー、イメージ劇

> グループのメンバーと他の女性芸術家による、オリジナルの視覚的で音声も伴う劇場作品を発表することに徹する4人の女性。生と録画されたヴィデオ、大小複数の映写画像、そして生のパフォーマンスを駆使して、私たちはフェミニズムの資料を考察し、その芸術品を創造しようと試みる*[21]。

1972年夏、久保田とメアリー・ルシエは、多人種の女性アーティスト集団のアイディアを一緒に構想した。2人は、60年代後半に前衛音楽のパフォーマンス・グループ、ソニック・アーツ・ユニオンに共に参加した親友であったが、その経験が彼女ら自身のグループのアイディアへと結びついた［本書32頁］。アリゾナのナヴァホ族の友人を久保田に紹介したのもルシエだった。ブレッシングウェイと呼ばれるナヴァホ民謡の優れた歌い手として、ルシエの夫の教えていたウェズレイアン大学に招聘されていたダグラス（ドゥーギー)・ミッチェルを最初に紹介し、ルシエは次に、彼のいとこであるセシリア・サンドヴァルをこのように紹介した。「ナヴァホの友達で私たちのグループ、レッド ホワイト イエロー ブラックに入りたいっていう子がいるんだけど」*[22]。返事で久保田はこう提案した。「この10月にキッチンで、環境的なコンサートを皆で一緒にやれるかしら……。メアリー、私たちは一緒に仕事をするリユニオンが必要よ。それこそ本当のウーマン・リブ」*[23]。9月に久保田はもうひとりのメンバーとして、シャーロット・ワレンを勧誘する手紙を書いた。「数年前に、あなたがブラックゲート・シアターでジャックとデイヴィッドと一緒に美しいパフォーマンスをしたのを覚えてる。知ってると思うけど、今年は女性の年よ。私たちはとても面白い女性のグループを作れると信じてる。グループを白黄黒赤とでも呼んで、メアリーが私たちのきれいに微笑んだ肖像写真を撮ってくれる」*[24]。ルシエによれば、グループの名前の色の順番は不定だったが、彼女はアメリカの国旗にならって、レッド ホワイト イエロー ブラックを最も頻繁に用いた*[25]。彼女の撮った個々の肖像写真は「きれい」でも「微笑んで」もなく、どちらかというと犯行者の写真を思わせる横向きの無愛想なもので、彼女らの「内にある反抗心」を示唆していた*[26]。久保田は肖像写真を横に並べ、それぞれのメンバーの人種を指す色の語を斜めにあしらって、衝撃的なデザインを作った［本書32頁］。久保田とルシエは、グループが「フェミニストの作品の交換所のような場、

もしくは前衛におけるフェミニストの焦点として役立てる」よう願っていた*27。

彼女らの野心は、1972年12月の初コンサートで、3点のマルチメディア作品の同時発表として実現された*28。録音と生の要素を組み合わせ、ワレンは、アメリカ中の都市部で立ち上がる黒人たちを称える詩や、アンジェラ・デイヴィスの逮捕を批判する詩を含むさまざまな詩からなる《黒人たちの声》を発表した。《目くらましの日記：ボストンの絞殺犯は女性だった》で、ルシエは、性別と人種にまつわるステレオタイプを赤、黒、白、黄色でアクセントをつけた、約80名の女性犯罪者の写真を映写しながら、女性の犯罪性について男性著者が書いたさまざまな記事からの抜粋を読んだ。この2作が明らかに政治的なのに対して、久保田のインスタレーション《川走―ヴィデオ 水 詩》は、「人の人生、生存」についての「ヴィデオの水の詩」を隠喩的に発表したものだった。30もの12インチのモニターを、6個ずつ5列に重ねるよう構想されたこの作品は、5つの川と運河（セーヌ川、ライン川、ハドソン川、ヴェネツィアとアムステルダムの運河）を1列ごとに異なるヴィデオの回路に繋げて見せた*29。自伝的な要素もあるが、人の人生がさまざまな段階や場所を通過する旅路という普遍的なテーマを表現したのかもしれない。彼女らの最初の発表会にかなりの前評判があったのにもかかわらず、実際何も評が出なかったことでアーティストたちは落胆したが、絶望したわけではなかった。翌年4月のザ・キッチンでの2回目の発表の後、グループは解散したが、彼女らの友情が、久保田にとって目の覚めるような経験を導くこととなった*30。

1973年6月、ルシエと久保田は、チンリー（アリゾナ）のナヴァホ族の保留地に、サンドヴァルの家族を訪ねた。サンドヴァルのいとこ、ドゥーギー・ミッチェルが12月に急死したので、ミッチェル・サンドヴァル家への慰問の意図もあった。彼らの温かいもてなしに感動した久保田は、このナヴァホ族の家族に特別な近親感を持つ。呪術医としても知られるこの家族の長老、フランク・ミッチェルは日本人とナヴァホ族は同一の祖先を持つと信じていた。久保田は、成子という名がナヴァホ語で「義理の妹」の意味であることを知る。久保田の「ブロークン・ダイアリー」の一章である《ヴィデオ・ガールズとナヴァホの空のためのヴィデオソング》は、久保田の異文化の垣根を越えた、トランスカルチュラル的体験を鮮やかに要約している［本書35頁］。サングラスをして、極端なコントラストによって抽象化された久保田の顔が、初めと終わりの部分で画面に浮かび、これが彼女の見て感じたことであることを強調するかのように、「これは私のヴィデオ・ダイアリーです」と宣言する。羊を殺し、皮をはぎ、肉を切り分けるところを記録した、真ん中の白黒の部分を除いて、ナヴァホの音楽がヴィデオを通して聴こえる(図2)。ナヴァホの人々、生き方と風景に強く魅了された久保田は、1976年に同地に戻り、アリゾナとその近隣の風景を録画し、それをもとに、代表作となる《三つの山》［本書78–81頁］を制作した。3つの三角形を基本とした、ベニヤ板と鏡でできた構造体は、アメリカ西部の起伏のある地形だけでなく、若い頃日本で登った山々や、ギザのピラミッドなどの古代の遺跡からもアイディアを得ている。同時に、それらは自叙伝的でもあり、彼女が山好きであることと、山と自分を重ねていることに繋がっている。ナヴァホの人々とその土地と関わることで、久保田は彼女のルーツを見つけると共に、自分がいかに山と水と緊密に繋がっているかということを悟る。久保田は、ナヴァホ族と日本人の間の文化的相似性に気付いたことで、自分が日本人かアメリカ人かという、二項対立のアイデンティティの問いかけを乗り越えることができた。そのようなトランスカルチュラルな意識が、久保田の強みのひとつとなり、しばしば人種的に二極化した社会で生き抜くすべとなった。

図2 《ヴィデオ・ガールズとナヴァホの空のためのヴィデオソング》からのスチル、1973年
Fig. 2. Still from *Video Girls and Video Songs for Navajo Sky*, 1973.

フェミニスト的でトランスカルチュラル的な意識が、久保田の初期のヴィデオ活動のひとつの重要な側面を特徴付けることとなる。1974年の秋、久保田は、ウースター・ストリート80番地で再オープンした、アンソロジー・フィルム・アーカイヴズで、ヴィデオ・キュレーターとして新しい仕事を始めた。同年前半に、久保田とパイクは、アンソロジーから数ブロックの、マーサー・ストリート110番地に、ジョージ・マチューナスを通して、アーティストの共同住宅を購入し、移り住む。また、マチューナスは久保田を、アンソロジーの創設者である、リトアニアの同胞のジョナス・メカスに推薦した。久保田の協力者で、ヴィデオ・キュレーターの後継者となるボブ・ハリスは、誰に対しても分け隔てがなく、心の広い久保田が、アーカイヴズで新しいヴィデオ・プログラムを立ち上げるのに適任であったことを証言している。毎週土曜の午後、久保田はヴィデオ・アーティストを何人か招待して、自分たちの作品を見せた後、観客と対話のできる機会を設けた。また、彼女は「ゲスト・キュレーターによる上映会」も導入し、そこでは、「ザグレブ、バルセロナ、エルサルバドル、ニカラグア、イギリス、カナダからの作品や、アフリカ系アメリカ人、アジア人、フェミニスト、ラテン・アメリカ系、ネイティブ・アメリカ系の感受性を反映した作品」などが公開された*31。前述の、スーザン・ミラノによって選ばれた、女性によるヴィデオ作品の数々もこのシリーズの一部だった。ニューヨーク近代美術館でヴィデオのキュレーションを始めてすぐのバーバラ・ロンドンも、ヴィデオ・アートについての情報が少ない当時、これらの上映会の多くに足を運び、新しいアーティストや傾向を発見したという*32。さらに久保田は、「ヴィデオ・オープン上映会」も始め、ロンドンなどのヴィデオのキュレーターたちを招待して、アーティストが持ってきたヴィデオテープを観てもらい、直接アーティストと作品について話してもらった。「モバイル・ヴィデオ・コミュニケーション」というタイトルの下に書かれた「アーティストが居ます」という予告は、このヴィデオという若い媒体の即発性と直接性を表現すると共に、久保田がはぐくもうとしていたコミュニティの雰囲気を湛えていた*33。彼女の率直で積極的な性格が、駆け出しのアーティストがキュレーターや他のアーティストと知り合うきっかけ作りと、新しいヴィデオのコミュニティを築くことに役立ったのだ。

ヴィデオがまだ揺籃期の頃、久保田はアーティストとして、書き手として、キュレーターとして、多大な貢献をした。我々は今ようやく、久保田のヴィデオ活動の初期のいくつかの側面を詳細に垣間見れたが、これから彼女の芸術的活動のさまざまな段階と経歴がより明確になることで、この複雑なアーティストのさらに包括的な全体像がわかり、評価されることを望んでいる。

（よしもと・みどり＝ニュージャージー・シティー大学准教授／ギャラリーディレクター）

訳：筆者

ここで本論のためのインタビューに応じてくださった、久保田成子の元ご旧友の皆様（敬称略：メアリー・ルシエー、エリザベス・フィリップス、セシリア・サンドヴァル、ジョアン・ローグ、ボブ・ハリス、デイヴィッド・ジグリオッティ、アン・サージェント・ウースター、スーザン・ミラノ、バーバラ・ロンドン、刀根康尚）に心からの感謝を表します。
本展調査のための初期のリサーチはMetropolitan Institute for Far Eastern StudiesとThe Shigeko Kubota Video Art Foundationからの助成を受けました。

［註］

＊1――久保田成子、「創造的媒体としてのTV」、『美術手帖』317号（1969年9月）、175頁。

＊2――同上、168頁。

＊3――同上、174頁。

＊4――Shigeko Kubota, Interview by Jonathan Price, February 17, 1976, transcript, 1, Anthology Film Archives, New York.

＊5――タイミングが良く、パイクはすぐにテレビ局WNETに雇われ、パイク・阿部シンセサイザーを使って、番組を革新した。久保田成子、『私の愛、ナムジュン・パイク』（平凡社、2013年）、125–128頁。

＊6――西川美穂子、阿部修也氏とのインタビュー聞き取り文、2020年8月14日。この中で阿部は、久保田が自画像のヴィデオを作る時にカメラを時々持って手伝ったと語っている。

＊7――1971年春、ヴィデオ・アーティスト、スタイナとウッディ・ヴァスルカ夫妻により、ザ・キッチンは、マーサー通り240番地の元ブロードウェイ・セントラル・ホテルの台所に、マルチメディアの劇場として設立された。http://www.vasulka.org/Kitchen/KRT.htmlを参照。

＊8――久保田成子からメアリー・ルシエ宛葉書、1972年7月頃。Courtesy Mary Lucier.

＊9――同秋に2つの他の発表で、1つのモニターを使って、観者の姿を生で見せていることから推測される。Experimental Television Center Binghamton at Everson Museum, Syracuse, NY, “Shigeko Kubota: Video Tapes,” program, September 30, 1972.

＊10――久保田の複雑なフェミニズムとの関係については、次を参照されたい。Helena Shaskevich, “‘With my portapak on my back': Identity and Belonging in Shigeko Kubota's *Broken Diary*," in *Transnational Belonging and Female Agency in the Arts* (London: Bloomsbury Press, 2021, forthcoming).

*11——Mary Jane Jacobs, "Introduction," in *Shigeko Kubota: Video Sculpture* (New York: American Museum of Moving Image and University of Washington Press, 1991), pp. 6–7.

*12——Shigeko Kubota, quoted in Jeanine Mellinger and D. I. Bean, "On Art and Artists: Shigeko Kubota," *Profile*, no. 3 (1983), p. 2.

*13——本書38頁。Shigeko Kubota, "Behind the Video Life," from "Video Birthday Party for John Cage," in Dan Cameron, "The Grammar of the Video Image." *Arts Magazine*, 49, 4 (Dec. 1974), p. 48, reprinted in Toni Stooss, et al., *Shigeko Kubota: Video Sculptures* (Berlin: daadgalerie, Essen: Museum Folkwang, Zurich: Kunsthaus Zürich, 1981), p. 42. 元MoMAのキュレーターであるバーバラ・ロンドンは、1974年1月に同館で催された「開かれた回路：テレビの未来についての国際会議」で、久保田がこの文章を声高々に読み、低い声で笑って着席したと書いている。Barbara London, *Video Art: The First Fifty Years* (Phaidon Press, 2020), p. 35.

*14——《ヴァギナ・ペインティング》についての詳細は、本書25頁と、拙著*Into Performance: Japanese Women Artists in New York* (New Brunswick, NJ: Rutgers University Press, 2005), pp. 178–183を参照のこと。

*15——久保田成子、「ヴィデオ—開かれた回路」、『芸術倶楽部』(1975年)、175–77頁。本書の154–160頁に再掲載。クラークは久保田がキュレーターとしてアンソロジー・フィルム・アーカイヴズでヴィデオを紹介した最初のアーティストの一人。

*16——Susan Milano, "Introduction," in *Women's Video Festival NYC 1976* (New York: Women's Interart Center, 1976), unpaginated.

*17——例えば、久保田と作品のカラー写真が掲載されたものに次のような記事がある。Unidentified author, "Tattler: New York," *VIVA: The International Magazine for Women* (June 1976), page unknown. Courtesy Susan Milano.

*18——Maryse Holder, "Counter Culture: Women's Video Festival," *Off Our Backs*, 3:2 (October 1972), p. 18.

*19——久保田はウォーホルに強い関心を抱いていた。下の書評で、彼による長い映画の中に《チェルシー・ガールズ》も挙げている。久保田成子、「アンディー・ウォーホルの小説《a》」、『美術手帖』312号 (1969年5月)、133頁。

*20——Anthology Film Archives, "Mobile Video Communication," Program, November 1975, Courtesy Susan Milano. 11月22、23、29、30日に計26名の女性アーティストの作品が上映された。

*21——Mary Lucier, typed note, November 15, 1972. Courtesy Mary Lucier.

*22——Mary Lucier, a carbon copy of a typed letter to Shigeko Kubota, August 28, 1972. Courtesy Mary Lucier.

*23——久保田成子からメアリー・ルシエ宛の書簡、1972年8月30日付。Courtesy Mary Lucier. リユニオンは単に再会を意味しただけでなく、久保田が1968年に写真を撮った、ケージとデュシャンのチェスイベントのタイトルに言及していた。

*24——久保田成子とメアリー・ルシエ、シャーロット・ワレン宛の手紙の草稿、1972年9月11日付。メアリー・ルシエの提供協力。ワレンは夫がベルギーの医学部に留学中、そこで作曲家のジャック・ベカールと知り合った。ニューヨークに戻った1968年に、彼は当時久保田の夫であったデイヴィッド・バーマンと共同企画した《今》というパフォーマンスにワレンに参加して欲しいと依頼した。このいきさつについて、さらにグループのメンバーの背景の詳細については次を参照。Melinda Barlow, "Red, White, Yellow, and Black: Women, Multiculturalism, and Video History," *Quarterly Review of Film and Video*, 17:4 (2000), p. 307.

*25——筆者のメアリー・ルシエとのインタビュー、コチェクトン、ニューヨークにて、2019年6月17日。

*26——Barlow, "Red, White, Yellow, and Black," p. 299.

*27——Mary Lucier to Shigeko Kubota, a typed letter copy, dated November 10, 1972. Courtesy Mary Lucier. この手紙の中で、ルシエは彼女たちが演じる作品を募る、他の女性アーティストの名前を挙げている。リストにはメアリー・アシュリー、ポーリーン・オリヴェロス、アリソン・ノールズ、バーバラ・ロイド、シャーロット・モーマン、ジル・ジョンストン、ヨーコ・オノ、キャロリー・シュニーマンの名があった。

*28——White Black Red & Yellow, Program Notes (December 16, 1972), The Kitchen Archives. https://www.eai.org/supporting-documents/224/a.8654.34. サンドヴァルの遠距離電話を通しての読み聞かせは、技術的困難のため実現しなかった。Emily Watlington, "Red, White, Yellow, Black: A Multiracial Feminist Video Collective, 1972–73," *Another Gaze* (Dec. 23, 2019), https://www.anothergaze.com/red-white-yellow-black-multiracial-feminist-video-collective-1972-73/.

*29——1991年の『ヴィデオ彫刻』展カタログ (The American Museum of Moving Image, pp. 21–22) は、この作品に30台のモニターが用いられたと述べ、それを示すような写真を掲載したが (似た写真は1982年のDAADでの個展カタログにも掲載、pp. 22–23)、実際に30台もモニターが使われたかどうかは確証がなく、写真はヴィデオの静止画像を繋ぎ合わせたものである可能性が高い。本書33頁上に一部掲載。

*30——第2回の公演で、久保田は、《ヴィデオ占い》を発表したが、それは、前年のケージとチュードアのコンサート、《鳥かご》の映像を2つのモニターで見せ、3つめのモニターで、読書したり食事をしたりといった久保田の日常生活を見せ、4つめのモニターで、久保田が観客の手相占いをしているところを生放送で流すという作品だった。Barlow, p. 309.

*31——Bob Harris, "Video at Anthology," in David E. James, ed., *Free the Cinema* (Princeton: Princeton University Press, 1992), p. 288.

*32——London, *Video Art*, p. 32.

*33——Anthology Film Archives, "Mobile Video Communication," Program, November 1975.

"I video, therefore I am":
Shigeko Kubota's Early Video Life
Midori Yoshimoto

After all, doesn't history repeat itself in art, too? The history in which mass-production of the real by films destroyed theater. The history in which (vinyl) records turned music into a major industry beyond live music? Even photography, which lacks relative plasticity and flexibility, has grown into an art form. TV art can easily be reproduced like a photograph and has so much more plasticity than oil paintings. There will be a major revolution in art in the future if TV art gets into full swing. —— Shigeko Kubota*1

Shigeko Kubota prophetically concluded the above upon reviewing the groundbreaking exhibition, "TV as a Creative Medium," at the Howard Wise Gallery in May 1969. Although she had just begun to write about the New York art scene for the leading Japanese art magazine *Bijutsu Techō* (Art Notebook), Kubota had a strong premonition that TV art would cause a paradigm shift in the wider art world. Little did she know that she would play a major role in that upcoming revolution.

Kubota wrote this review before the field of "video art" was established: "In a darkened, enclosed space, two connected rooms house a chain of twenty-five television sets, by ten TV artists, laid out in a three-dimensional fashion like a TV store front in Akihabara."*2 Describing the earliest examples of video installation art, such as *Wipe Cycle* by Frank Gillette and Ira Schneider, or *Participation TV I–II* by Nam June Paik, Kubota pointed out the importance of closed-circuit, participatory TV art, whereby live and recorded images of the viewer appeared on the monitors. She asserted: "What has become clear through *TV as a Creative Medium*, is a movement to take the institution of TV culture, which had been one-way communication, and reimagine it as a two-way, multi-layered communication, appropriate for the true 'electricity' of audience involvement."*3

Profoundly inspired by this exhibition, Kubota started shooting her own video. Even though she had given up art making by the mid-1960s, by 1970 she felt an urge to "bring back the image, sound, and action," all of which could come together through the medium of video.*4 After separating from composer David Behrman, Kubota flew to Los Angeles to join Nam June Paik, who had just been invited by Allan Kaprow to teach at Cal Arts as its first video faculty. Paik had brought electronic engineer Shuya Abe, whom he collaborated with in Japan to build a video synthesizer. In this crucible of experimentation, Kubota tried video recording herself—which would become the basis for her later sculpture, *Video Poem* [see p. 38]. Feeling, however, that the California atmosphere was too "laid back", she urged Paik not to renew the contract the following year and the couple returned to New York in late 1971.*5 In the spring of 1972, Kubota acquired a new Portapak by asking Mrs. Abe to procure it from Japan while visiting her husband.*6 She traveled throughout Europe in May that year, capturing her visits to Rouen (to visit Duchamp's grave), Paris, Nice (to see her Fluxus colleague, Takako Saito), Brussels, Amsterdam, Bremen (to see John Cage), and Venice. Upon returning to New York, she turned some of the footage into *Europe on ½ inch a day*, one of her earliest single-channel videos, which later became the second chapter of her *Broken Diary* series.

Beginning with her first "Live and Videotape Concert" at the Kitchen on June 30, Kubota's video career took off.*7 [see p. 31] Early video screenings had the spontaneity of a live concert, and were held late at night. According to Kubota, too many people came, and she had to offer a second screening that same night.*8 *In addition to Europe on ½ inch a day*, she played tapes about John Cage, David Tudor, and Duchamp, which utilized still photographs she had taken at their chess event in Toronto in 1968. On a couple of occasions that fall, Kubota celebrated Cage's 60th birthday by presenting a three-channel video installation at the Experimental Television Center at Everson Museum in Syracuse, and at the ninth annual New York Avant Garde Festival—which took place inside the Alexander Hamilton Boat docked at the South Street Seaport. The latter presentation, entitled *Video Birthday Party for John Cage II*, had an additional monitor setup which may have live-fed the image of the audience through a closed circuit.*9 [fig. 1: p. 202] Just a few months after her debut as a video artist, Kubota was experimenting with multiple-channel videos and involving the audience through the use of live-feed cameras and monitors, a significant feature of the 1969 *TV as a Creative Medium* exhibition on which she had reported. With more than five showings in one fall, Kubota was quickly making her name known in the nascent video art scene.

Kubota's emergence as a video artist coincided with the rise of a second-wave feminist movement in America, which was more than mere coincidence.*10 Curator, Mary Jane Jacobs stated that "Through these new genres (of video, performance, photography, and installation art) they (women) could proclaim a place for themselves in the art world that could not be achieved through the Western, male-dominated field of painting."*11 Even more male-dominated than painting was the field of sculpture, which Kubota studied while in Japan. It was Kubota's strategic thinking that prompted her to leave the elitist, avant-garde circles of Tokyo for the more open art community of New York, where she could explore her earlier interests in environments and performance art. When Kubota discovered video, she instinctively knew that this medium suited her spontaneous and active personality. Compared to film, whose process Kubota considered "very chemical," she saw video as "organic, like brown rice . . . very oriental like seaweed, made in Japan," wittily referencing the fact that the first truly portable video recorder was produced by SONY.*12 Furthermore, Kubota associated video and its creative process to the female body and its functions in the most visceral manner imaginable, proclaiming: "Video is Victory of Vagina," "I bleed in half-inch . . . 3M or SONY . . . ten thousand feet long every month."*13 Such associations harken back to her *Vagina Painting* performances, in which she draws direct connections between artistic creation (often attributed to male genius) and procreation.*14 Her feminist manifesto may have been partly inspired by statements such as "Video is my dick," by Shirley Clarke (1919–97), former film maker who turned to video at around the same time as Kubota. *15

In the early days of video art, there were many women creators, but they were not receiving the same opportunities or support as men. Recognizing the need, founder of the Kitchen, Steina Vasulka, suggested to video artist Susan Milano to organize the Women's Video Festival, which became an almost annual showcase between 1972 and 1976.*16 Kubota participated in all four of the festivals held in New York City, and benefited from the publicity received.*17 The first work she showed for the occasion was *Joa: The Impasse of Infidelity*, which, according to a review, was a stylish parody of raunchy strip as well as "stylizations of love making," featuring "split-screen effects of the two sets of images; one was of an extraordinary sex-dance-theater troupe which included transvestites, and among others a woman wearing a transparent net leotard with cut-outs for breasts."*18 Unfortunately, this work has not yet been found and may well be lost, but a female dancer with exposed breasts also appeared in *Europe on ½ inch a day* and there may be some overlap. The split-screen format is noteworthy, as it may be indicative of a possible inspiration from Andy Warhol's double-screen film, *Chelsea Girls* (1966).*19 To be able to show such edgy work commenting on sexuality in the company of other women artists must have been a valuable experience of affirmation for Kubota. Later when she became the video curator at Anthology Film Archives, Kubota invited Milano to showcase selections from past festivals, to help increase visibility of fellow artists.*20

White Black Red and Yellow: Video, Dance, Story, Image Theater

> Four women dedicated to the presentation of original visual and vocal theater work by members of the group as well as by other women artists. Using live and pre-recorded video, multiple projection both giant and miniature, and aspects of live performance we attempt to examine documents and produce artifacts of feminism.*21

During the summer of 1972, Kubota came up with an idea for a multiracial women's artist collective. Developed in close collaboration with Mary Lucier, whom she had been close friends with since the mid-1960s through their mutual involvement in the Sonic Arts Union. Their experience of being part of an avant-garde music performance group inspired them to form a group of their own. [see p. 32] In one of her letters, Lucier introduces Cecilia Sandoval, whom Lucier had just visited in Arizona: "I have a Navajo friend interested in being in our group: Red, White, Yellow, and Black?"*22 In her reply, Kubota suggested, "Maybe we all have an environmental concert together this October at the Kitchen . . . Mary, we need Reunion to work together. It will be a really women's lib. . . ."*23 In September Kubota drafted a letter to invite another member, Charlotte Warren, in which she wrote: "We remember you had a beautiful performance with Jacque and David at the Black Gate Theater several years ago. . . . As you know, this year is a women's year. We believe we make a very interesting women's group together. Maybe we call our group White, Yellow, Black, and Red, and the beautiful smiling portrait pictures witch Mary is going to take."*24 According to Lucier, the order of the colors in the group name varied, but she often used "Red, White, Yellow, and Black," to parody that of the American flag.*[25] The individual portraits taken were neither "beautiful" nor "smiling," but rather were neutral profiles reminiscent of criminal mug shots, and suggested the "possibility of the outlaw within." *[26] Kubota laid out the portraits in a high impact, line-up design [see p. 32]. They envisioned that the group "can serve as a kind of clearing house for feminist pieces and perhaps act as a feminist focal point in the avant-garde."*[27]

Their ambitions were realized at their first concert in December 1972, with a simultaneous presentation of three multimedia pieces.*[28] Combining pre-recorded and live elements, Warren presented *Black Voices*, consisting of various poems—including a piece celebrating the rise of black American from inner cities across the nation, and another critiquing the arrest of Angela Davis. For her *Red Herring Journal: The Boston Strangler Was a Woman*, Lucier read excerpts from various publications on female criminality written by male authors, while projecting slides of approximately eighty female criminals which she accented in red, black, white, and yellow, to highlight the gender and racial stereotypes which stigmatized those women. While these two works were decisively political, Kubota's installation, *Riverrun*, was metaphorically presented as a "video water poem" about "living and survival of the human being." Conceived for thirty twelve-inch monitors stacked in five rows of six, it showed five different rivers and canals (Seine, Rhine, Hudson, Venice and Amsterdam Canals) with each row being connected to a different video channel. While it was partly autobiographical, it could also represent the universal theme of life's journey through various stages and locales. Although there was preliminary excitement over their first show, it failed to garner any reviews, leaving the artists disappointed, but not daunted. Nonetheless, Lucier cheered up Kubota by writing that she "had absolute confidence in" Kubota because her work was "very strong and [her] presentation was always successful."*[29] After their second show at the Kitchen in April, the group disbanded, but their friendship led to an eye-opening experience for Kubota.*[30]

In June 1973, Lucier and Kubota visited Sandoval's family on the Navajo reservation in Chinle, Arizona. Since Sandoval's cousin, Doogie Mitchell, whom Lucier and Kubota knew as a visiting Blessingway singer at Wesleyan University, had suddenly died in December, this visit was also to console the Mitchell-Sandoval family. Kubota felt an extraordinary kinship with this Navajo family. The elder of the family, a medicine man, believed that the Japanese and the Navajo shared ancestry. Kubota was also told that the name Shigeko meant "my sister-in-law" in the Navajo language.

Video Girls and Video Songs for Navajo Sky, another chapter in Kubota's *Broken Diary* series, vividly encapsulates her transcultural experiences. Kubota's face, wearing sunglasses and abstracted through extreme contrasts, floats over the beginning and end, announcing "this is my video diary," and emphasizing the fact this is what she saw and felt. Navajo songs are heard throughout the video, except during the middle of the film, which is shot in black and white and documents the disturbing killing, skinning, and butchering of a sheep. [fig. 2: p. 204]"Video girls" may also express Kubota's comradery with Lucier who introduced her to the indigenous culture and Kubota introduced Lucier to video making.

The people, lifestyle, and landscapes of the Navajo enchanted her so much that she returned in 1976 to film the landscapes in Arizona and surrounding regions to develop into her seminal video sculpture, *Three Mountains* [see pp. 78–81]. Three triangular structures made of plywood and mirrors were not only inspired by rocky terrains of American West, but also by mountains she climbed in Japan and ancient monuments such as the Pyramids. Simultaneously, they were autobiographical, pointing to her love of mountains and self-identification with them. Through her interaction with the Navajo people and their land, Kubota discovered her roots, her close relationship to mountains and water. Cultural affinities she found between the Navajo and the Japanese helped her to move beyond the binary question of her identify of being Japanese or American. Such transcultural awareness became Kubota's strength and a means to survive the often racially politicized society.

Both feminist and transcultural conscience defined another important aspect of Kubota's early video career. In fall 1974, Kubota began her new job as the Video Curator at the Anthology Film Archives upon its reopening at 80 Wooster Street. Earlier that year, Kubota and Paik had bought a coop through George Maciunas at 110 Mercer Street, which was a few blocks away from the Archives. Maciunas also recommended Kubota to his fellow Lithuanian filmmaker and the founder of the Archives, Jonas Mekas. Her collaborator and later successor, Bob Harris attests that Kubota was perfectly suited for launching the new video program at the Archives because of her egalitarian openness. Every Saturday afternoon, a few videomakers would present their works and have a dialogue with the audience. She also incorporated "guest-curated screenings" which included "works from Zagreb, Barcelona, El Salvador, Nicaragua, Great Britain, and Canada, as well as works reflecting African American, Asian, feminist, Latin-American and Native American sensibilities."*[31] Aforementioned presentations of women's video select by

Susan Milano were part of this series. Barbara London, who had just begun curating video at MoMA, attended many of these screenings to discover new artists and trends when media coverage of video art was scarce.*32 Kubota also started "Video Open Screening" where video curators like London were invited to review tapes and discuss them directly with the artists. The announcement "artists will be present" written directly below the title of the program, "Mobile Video Communication," expressed the spontaneity and immediacy of this young medium and its community Kubota wanted to nurture.*33 Her candid and proactive personality helped emerging artists to connect with one another and with curators, building the community from ground up.

In video's infancy, Kubota made a great contribution as an artist, writer, and curator. Although these details provide just glimpses into some facets of Kubota's early video life, more facts about varied phases of her career will hopefully become uncovered soon to paint a fuller portrait of this complex artist.

(Associate Professor of Art History/Gallery Director, New Jersey City University, U.S.A.)

The author deeply appreciates former friends of Shigeko Kubota for offering interviews: Mary Lucier, Elizabeth Phillips, Cecilia Sandoval, Joan Rogue, Bob Harris, David Gigliotti, Susan Milano, Barbara London, and Yasunao Tone. The early research trip in preparation for this exhibition was generously funded by the Metropolitan Center for Far Eastern Studies and the Shigeko Kubota Video Art Foundation.

[Notes]

*1——Shigeko Kubota, "TV as a Creative Medium," *Bijutsu Techo*, no. 317 (September 1969), pp. 168–175. Translated by the author.

*2——Ibid., p. 168.

*3——Ibid., p. 174.

*4——Shigeko Kubota, Interview by Jonathan Price, February 17, 1976, transcript, 1, Anthology Film Archives, New York.

*5——The timing was just right because Paik was soon hired by WNET to spice up its programs using the Paik-Abe synthesizer. Shigeko Kubota, *Watashi no ai, Nam June Paik/My Love, Nam June Paik* (Tokyo: Heibonsha, 2013), pp. 125–128.

*6——Mihoko Nishikawa, Transcript of her interview with Shuya Abe, August 14, 2020. Abe also told Nishikawa that he held the camera sometime for Kubota to make her self-portrait video.

*7——Just the year before in spring 1971, the Kitchen was founded as a multimedia theater by video artists Steina and Woody Vasulka in the kitchen of the Mercer Arts Center, in the former Broadway Central Hotel at 240 Mercer Street. See http://www.vasulka.org/Kitchen/KRT.html

*8——Shigeko Kubota, postcard to Mary Lucier, ca. July 1972. Courtesy Mary Lucier.

*9——This is my deduction based on the fact that she used one of the monitors for showing the live-feed mage of the audience in two other presentations that fall. See Experimental Television Center Binghamton at Everson Museum, Syracuse, NY, "Shigeko Kubota: Video Tapes," program, September 30, 1972.

*10——For a detailed discussion of Kubota's complex relationship to feminism, see Helena Shaskevich, "With my portapak on my back: Identity and Belonging in Shigeko Kubota's *Broken Diary*," in *Transnational Belonging and Female Agency in the Arts* (London: Bloomsbury Press, 2021, forthcoming).

*11——Mary Jane Jacobs, "Introduction," in *Shigeko Kubota: Video Sculpture* (New York: American Museum of Moving Image and University of Washington Press, 1991), pp. 6–7.

*12——Shigeko Kubota, quoted in Jeanine Mellinger and D.I. Bean, "On Art and Artists: Shigeko Kubota," *Profile*, no. 3 (1983), p. 2.

*13——See p. 247. Shigeko Kubota, "Behind the Video Life," from "Video Birthday Party for John Cage," 1974, *Arts Magazine*, 49, 4 (Dec. 1974), p. 48, reprinted in Toni Stooss, et al., *Shigeko Kubota: Video Sculpture* (Berlin: daadgalerie, Essen: Museum Folkwang, Zürich: Kunsthaus Zurich, 1981), p. 42. The former MoMA curator Barbara London recalls Kubota standing up and reading this statement aloud, concluding it with a "hearty belly laugh" and sitting down at "Open Circuits: An International Conference on the Future of Television," held at MoMA in January 1974. Barbara London, *Video Art: The First Fifty Years* (Phaidon Press, 2020), p. 35.

*14——For a detailed discussion of *Vagina Painting*, see Midori Yoshimoto, *Into Performance: Japanese Women Artists in New York* (New Brunswick, NJ: Rutgers University Press, 2005), pp. 178–183, and p. 25 of this book.

*15——Shigeko Kubota, "Video—Open Circuit," *Geijutsu Kurabu* (1975), pp. 175–77. Clarke was among the first artists whose videos Kubota introduced as the curator at Anthology Film Archives.

*16——Susan Milano, "Introduction," in *Women's Video Festival NYC 1976* (New York: Women's Interart Center, 1976), unpaginated.

*17——The publicity includes: Unidentified author, "Tattler: New York," *VIVA: The International Magazine for Women* (June 1976), page unknown. Courtesy Susan Milano.

*18——Maryse Holder, "Counter Culture: Women's Video Festival," *Off Our Backs*, 3:2 (October 1972), p. 18.

*19——Kubota was very interested in Warhol in general. In her review of his novel, *a*, she mentions *Chelsea Girls* among other long films. Shigeko Kubota, "A Novel by Andy Warhol." *Bijutsu Techō*, no. 312 (May 1969), p. 133.

*20——Anthology Film Archives, "Mobile Video Communication," Program, November 1975, Courtesy Susan Milano. The total of 26 women's videos were screened on Nov. 22, 23, 29, 30.

*21——Mary Lucier, typed note, November 15, 1972. Courtesy Mary Lucier.

*22——Mary Lucier, a carbon copy of a typed letter to Shigeko Kubota, August 28, 1972. Courtesy Mary Lucier.

*23——Shigeko Kubota, a letter to Mary Lucier, August 30, 1972. Courtesy Mary Lucier.

*24——Shigeko Kubota with Mary Lucier, a copy of a draft letter to Charlotte Warren, September 11, 1972. Courtesy Mary Lucier. Warren had met composer Jacques Bekaert in Belgium while her husband was studying in a medical school there. When she returned to New York in 1968, she was asked to participate in the performance of *Now* which was developed in collaboration with composer David Behrman, Kubota's then husband. Melinda Barlow, "Red, White, Yellow, and Black: Women, Multiculturalism, and Video History," *Quarterly Review of Film and Video*, 17:4 (2000), p. 307. Barlow's article contextualizes the group with each member's background and offers insightful analyses.

*25——Mary Lucier, Interview with the author, Cochecton, New York, June 17, 2019.

*26——Barlow, "Red, White, Yellow, and Black," p. 299.

*27——Mary Lucier to Shigeko Kubota, a typed letter copy, dated November 10, 1972. Courtesy Mary Lucier. In it, Lucier listed the names of other women artists they are considering of inviting to contribute a piece for them to perform. The list read: Mary Ashley, Pauline Oliveros, Alison Knowles, Barbara Lloyd, Charlotte Mooreman, Jill Johnston, Yoko Ono, and Carolee Schneemann.

*28——Sandoval's storytelling over a long-distance telephone call did not happen due to the technical difficulty. Emily Watlington, "Red, White, Yellow, Black: A Multiracial Feminist Video Collective, 1972–73," *Another Gaze* (Dec. 23, 2019), https://www.anothergaze.com/red-white-yellow-black-multiracial-feminist-video-collective-1972-73/.

*29——Although the use of thirty twelve-inch monitors was mentioned in Kubota's 1991 *Video Sculpture* catalog (The American Museum of Moving Image, pp. 21–22) and an image including thirty monitors was reproduced there as well as in the 1982 DAAD catalog (pp.22–23), this vision may not have been fully realized and the image was most likely made of still images from the videos. As such, installation photographs of this work have not been found.

*30——Kubota presented *Video Fortune-telling*, which included two monitors showing Cage and Tudor's concert, *Birdcage* from the previous year, the third showing Kubota's daily life such as reading a book or eating, and the last showing the live-feed image of Kubota reading palms of an audience member. Barlow, p. 309.

*31——Bob Harris, "Video at Anthology," in David E. James, ed., *Free the Cinema* (Princeton: Princeton University Press, 1992), p. 288.

*32——London, *Video Art*, p.32.

*33——Anthology Film Archives, "Mobile Video Communication," Program, November 1975.

久保田成子のヴィデオ彫刻

過去からのメッセージを受け継ぐために

西川美穂子

はじめに

「ヴィデオ彫刻（Video Sculpture）」は久保田成子の作品を語る上で欠かせない要素であり、作家本人が用いると同時に、彼女の作品の評価に使われてきた語でもある。この言葉から一般に想起されるのは、ヴィデオ・モニターと立体構造物が合わさった自律した彫刻としての形態であろう。しかし、久保田作品におけるヴィデオ彫刻は、じつに環境的である。電気製品としてのテレビモニターの箱部分を覆い隠し、スクリーンのみを切り離してオブジェクトに取り込んだのが、久保田のヴィデオ彫刻の特徴である。強い光を放つ色や動きなど、ヴィデオ映像の持つ抽象的な美しさを彫刻的オブジェクトに取り入れることにより、空間的に体験させる装置を作り出した。映像を取り入れた彫刻的な形や素材は、彼女の作品概念を示す重要なものであると同時に、表れる形は、実質的物質性には依拠しない。久保田は展示ごとに空間や条件、その時々の自身の関心に合わせ、作品の形態や展示方法を変化させている。それは、マルセル・デュシャンに代表されるアプロプリエーション（引用）や、フルクサス的複製（マルティプル）の考え方など現代美術における重要な概念に基づくものであり、ヴィデオという電子的メディアの持つ脆弱性や流動性に対応したものでもあった。本稿は、久保田がどのようにヴィデオを作品に取り入れたのか、その背景や意図を紐解くことで、メディア・アートの可能性を探るものである。

1. インスタレーションとしてのヴィデオ彫刻

1972年にザ・キッチンで最初のヴィデオ・コンサートを行なって以来、アンソロジー・フィルム・アーカイヴズでのヴィデオ・キュレーターとしての活動や女性作家たちとの交流など、当時、アートシーンのなかで急速に興隆しつつあったヴィデオの文脈において、久保田の名前を見ることができる*1。1970年代前半は、シングルチャンネルのスクリーニングのほか、複数のモニターを用いるなど、実験的な試みを行なっているものの、彫刻家出身の自負を持つ久保田は、一過性のライブ・パフォーマンスをより普遍的な形に残すことに関心を持っていた。アンソロジーでのヴィデオ・キュレーターの経験は同時代のヴィデオとその可能性について触れる重要な経験だったが、ただスクリーンを見るという経験では飽き足らなかったと後に述べている*2。そんな折、ザ・キッチンにおける個展開催の機会を得た久保田は、モニターを床から天井まで積み上げ、床に鏡を置いて、映像イメージを反射させた《デュシャンピアナ：マルセル・デュシャンの墓》［本書54–55頁］（以下《墓》）*3を制作した。当時まだインスタレーションを手掛ける作家が少ないなか、自分自身の独自の表現として、規模の大きなヴィデオ・インスタレーションを意識的に発表したという*4。当時流行していたヴィデオ機器を適当に組み合わせたようなものではなく、構成や構造について熟考して制作された、自律した彫刻作品として*5、本作はその後の久保田の美術作家としてのキャリアの転換点となった。

当時、ヴィデオの展示方法が多様化し始めるなかで、「ヴィデオ・インスタレーション」の語が用いられるようになり、久保田自身もたびたびその語を自身の作品に対して使用しているものの、彼女が「ヴィデオ彫刻」の語を好んだのは、美術作品としての性質を強調したかったためである*6。その意義は、作品としての自律性を持つことにより、鑑賞に際し、空間との身体的関係が生まれることにある。以下、作家の言葉に意図がよく表されている。
「ビデオ彫刻になると、作品に空間や時間という要素が入ってくる。それに美術館とか公共のスペースにどう展示するかという建築的要素も入って、表現が三次元に拡大されてくるわね。観客を一定の時間で縛らないから、作品の前でちょっと立ち止まったり、腕を組んでじっと見ていたり、観客と作家との対話ができる。シングルテープは文学的ストーリーの意味を理解するにはいいけれど、文学性を乗り越えてより視覚的な表現を目指そうとするときに、ビデオ彫刻という表現形式が出てきた。ビデオ彫刻は宇宙的で抽象的な世界だから、そういう謎の世界に観客を引き摺り込むのが面白いのね」*7。

2．彫刻に取り込まれたヴィデオ映像

久保田のヴィデオ彫刻で重要なのは、テレビの機械部分を覆い隠し、画面を切り離してコラージュした点である*8。これにより、ヴィデオというメディアに物理的な形を与え、空間における彫刻的な対峙を可能にした。《墓》についてのジョン・ハンハートの次の評がその点をよく指摘している。「久保田は画面以外のすべてを隠し、11台のモニターでイメージを反復させ、それらを垂直に配置することで、映像が織りなす色彩やカメラの動き、パターンを溶け合わせ、テレビモニターの見慣れたイメージから私たちを引き離した。それにより、ヴィデオを、映像や画面の抽象化をもたらす彫刻、あるいはコラージュとして経験させることになるのである」*9。

久保田は美術作品の伝統に則りつつ、そこにヴィデオという新しいメディアが持つ今日性がもたらす、五感に訴える効果にいちはやく気づき、作品に取り入れたのである。彼女にとってヴィデオ映像は、美術作品を構成する上での魅力的な素材であった。「1960年代にソニーがポータパックを開発した時、それは革命的なことだった。映画は科学的なものだけど、ヴィデオはもっと有機的なもの。私にとってポータパックは新しい絵筆みたいだった。フルクサスのDIY精神とも同じだったわ」*10と彼女は言う。ヴィデオ映像は光を発するメディアで、絵具顔料に比べて鮮やかな輝きを持っており、コントラスト（明度や輝度の差）をあげることも可能である*11。彼女は鮮やかな色彩と激しいコントラストを好んだと言われる*12。さらにヴィデオを使えば、電気信号の編集により、像を重ねたり、ゆがみや引き延ばしを行なったりすることもできる。ヴィデオは、イメージの抽象化が効果的に行なえるメディアなのである。

また、物語性を排した映像はユニバーサルな言語であり、空間のなかに置くことで、鑑賞者との対話が生まれうる。ヴィデオは話さなくても良いから、英語話者ではないマイノリティとして適していたし*13、「ヴィデオ彫刻として視覚的な強度を得ることで、言葉を必要としない自律した作品とすることを選択した」*14と作家自身が語っている。

ヴィデオは、繰り返しによる反復を容易にするという特性も持っている。久保田はマルセル・デュシャンからのアプロプリエーションばかりでなく、しばしば自身の過去の作品を素材としたバリエーションも制作した。ヴィデオは複製可能で同じ素材を繰り返し利用でき、撮影から時を経て作品化することも可能である*15。久保田はヴィデオの時間を取り込むことにより過去を反復させ、線的時間を変形させた*16。繰り返しにより、終わりは始まりとなり、循環するのである。作家は次のように述べている。
「時間がない時間はビデオの時間だと思う」*17。
「ビデオは死の世界と生の世界とのコミュニケーションでもあるし、永続性に結びつくイメージがあると思うよ。消えないもの」*18。

3．映像を取り囲む素材とフォルム

ヴィデオ映像を取り込む彫刻的外形はもちろん、ただ機械部分を覆い隠すためだけに作られたものではない。その素材やフォルムの選択には、彫刻的かつコンセプチュアルな意図が込められている。

まず素材の選択について見てみると、電気的なヴィデオ信号と有機的な自然物との融合が一つの動機になっていることを指摘できる。初期作品の多くで用いられているベニヤ合板構造*19では、自然のままの木目の見える松材が用いられ*20、電気的な映像が柔らかな木材のなかに取り込まれている。のちの《河》［本書84、93-95頁］や《ナイアガラの滝》［本書104-107頁］ではさらに、実際の水が使わ

れている点もユニークである。「テクノロジーはハードだけど、材質は木やプラスチック・ミラー（中略）水のように柔らかい」*21ものを意識的に選んだと言うとおり、異なる素材が生む違和感と、それらが融合することによる、誰も見たことのないような新しい造形が、久保田のヴィデオ彫刻を特徴づけている。

モチーフの選択においても、「山」や「河」といった自然を象徴する概念が多く見られる。彼女のスケッチブックには、アリゾナやモンタナで見た山が繰り返し描かれているが*22、そこにはしばしば、「ゆく河の流れは絶えずして、しかももとの水にあらず」という『方丈記』の一説や、父や故郷への郷愁を表す文章が共に記されている。久保田にとっての「山」や「河」は、自身の人生を投影する自伝的なモチーフでもあった［本書189頁図7参照］。

久保田は鏡も好んで用いたが、鏡によってもたらされる反射や繰り返しも、久保田作品の重要な要素だった。鏡はデュシャンへのオマージュであると同時に彼の精神の投影であり、宇宙的な広がりを持たせたかったという*23。最初期のヴィデオ彫刻である《墓》において、複数モニターと鏡を用い、ループし続ける円環をつくりだしたように、《デュシャンピアナ：自転車の車輪》［本書98–100頁］、《自動車の車輪》［本書118–119頁］、《スケート選手》［本書120–121頁］ではモーター動力を用い、実際の動的な回転を作品に取り入れ、円環を形として表現した*24。

物質的な素材に加え、とくに初期においては、壁に書かれた文字による言葉が作品に付随している点も久保田のヴィデオ彫刻の特徴である。オブジェクトに接する身体感覚、映像を目で追う視覚、書かれた言葉を読む言語的思考というように、複数の知覚に働きかける体験を生み出している。デュシャンピアナ・シリーズ以後は、壁の文字に代わり、オーバープロジェクションを行なったり、複数の作品をインスタレーションとして組み合わせて見せたりすることで、その多層的な鑑賞体験はより拡張していく。

4. 概念としてのモチーフ──表われとしての彫刻

ヴィデオ彫刻のフォルムに選ばれるモチーフは、概念的なものであり、その形は、制作当時の機材の形や作家が所有していた数によって規定されている場合もある。《デュシャンピアナ：階段を降りる裸体》［本書60–62頁］（以下《階段》）について、なぜ4段で制作したのかという質問に対し久保田は、「テレビがうちに四つしかなかったの（笑）」「それも大きいのが三つで小さいのが一つ。みんなはそれがバランスがいいって言うんだけど、それしかなかったのよ。もし二〇〇あったら、天への階段みたいになってるかもね（笑）」*25と答えている。

米国に活動拠点があるなか、日本で展示するにあたり、当初は「私の『階段』はSONY Trinitron 15インチのTVset、ただし高さは13.5インチ。そうでないと私のデザインした階段に入らない」と指定しながらも、その後、同じ規格の古い製品が日本では手に入らないことが判明した際には、「階段の寸法がTVの寸法に合わせて変えるより仕方ないです。階段のなかにTVが入らなければなりませんので、階段の寸法が少し高くなるでしょう」「そちらの大工さんのセンスにまかせて、良くバランスを私の図面から計算して下さい」*26と指示している。このことからも、モニターと階段構造を組み合わせるというコンセプトをもとに、素材となる機材等の物理的な条件に合わせ、柔軟に対応していたことがうかがえる。

階段は、のちの《グリーン・インスタレーション》［本書101頁］などでも用いられているように、久保田が好んだモチーフである。先に引用したインタビューで、もしモニターが200あったら天まで続く階段をつくっていたかもしれないと冗談めかして語っているように、そのコンセプトは、数や形を変えて展開する可能性も秘めていた。公共空間でのインスタレーションを構想したと見られる日記に残されたスケッチのひとつには、床から天井に続くような背の高い階段が描かれているし（図1）、2008年の豊田市美術館での展示では、同館の階段の上から下まで、8段の大きな階段を重ねるようなインスタレーションを行なっている（図2）。階段の昇り降りは、アップダウンを繰り返す人生を象徴するものでもあった*27。まるで実際に昇り降りできるかのような階段を物理的に出現させた上、そのなかにヌードの女性が繰り返し階段を降り続ける映像が挿入された《階段》は、実空間と

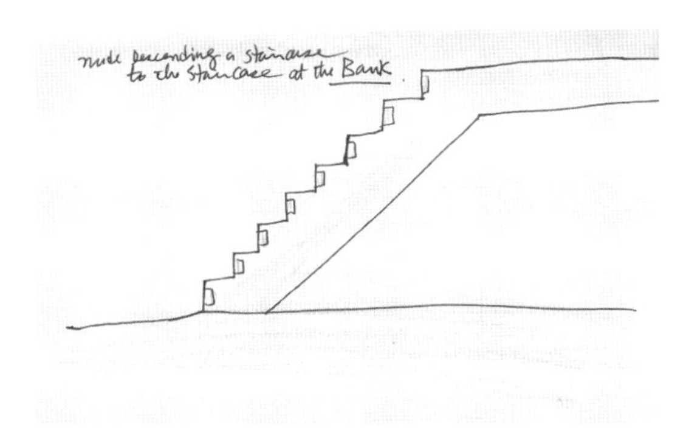

図1 「銀行の階段での《階段を降りる裸体》」構想スケッチ（1977年10月の日記帳より）
fig. 1. Concept sketch for installation of *Nude Descending a Staircase* on stairway of bank (from Kubota's diary, October 1977).
図2 《デュシャンピアナ：階段を降りる裸体》「不協和音ー日本のアーティスト6人」（豊田市美術館、2008年）のための再制作
fig. 2. Reproduction of *Duchampiana: Nude Descending Stairs* for *Dissonances: Six Japanese Artists* (Toyota Municipal Museum of Art, 2008)

電子的空間、あるいは撮影された時間と鑑賞される時間など、異なる時空が重ね合わされ、終わりがない時間を現前させている。

《メタ・マルセル：窓》［本書66–69頁］（以下《窓》）でも同様に、その表れについて、使用する機材等の素材の物理的条件がひとつの要件となっていたことを指摘できる。本作はデュシャンの《なりたての未亡人（Fresh Widow）》（1920年）を模し、格子状で両開きのフランス窓の形を取っているが、その大きさは原作より小さく、当時所有していたテレビモニターの大きさがそのまま作品サイズに反映したと考えられる。デュシャンの窓枠が緑なのに対し、久保田のそれは塗装なしの木目のままであり、何より原作では窓枠だけが独立しているが、久保田作品では窓枠の周囲が木の箱状になっている。木の箱形は、画面部分のみを見せるために、テレビモニターの機材部分を覆う機能を果たしている。それが白い展示台に乗っているスタイルは、美術館における彫刻の展示方法を採用しつつ、人の目線の高さに窓を置く目的などが考えられるが、加えてこの台は、再生機を隠す役割も持っていた。本作は、カラーテレビにオープンリールの再生機をつなぎ、砂嵐（スノーノイズ）を作るという作品である*[28]。テープをかけないオープンリールから信号が送られることで、それを受けたカラーテレビの画面は砂嵐になる。電子機器が作り出すドットのことを久保田は「ヴィデオスノー」と呼び、通常横に平行して走っている走査線を、テレビを縦に置くことで90°回転させ、窓の外に降る雪に見立てた*[29]。本作は後に、実際の砂嵐を毎回作成するのではなく、それを録画した映像が用いられるようになり、「花」と「星」という別のバージョンもつくられる*[30]。いずれにしても映像再生機が必要になるため、展示台が機材を隠す機能を果たすことには変わりない*[31]。このように本作の形状が当時の機材の大きさや形に依拠していると見られる一方、久保田にとっての「窓」は、過去や未来をつなぐ開かれた窓という概念的なものであるとも言える*[32]。日記に描かれた構想スケッチでは、実際に制作された「雪」「花」「星」以外にも、窓の奥に広がる四季を描くことを考えていたことがうかがえるし、壁に直接穿たれた窓の様子も描かれている(図3)。また、展示台なしで個展会場の入口の壁に直接窓を埋め込んだり、道路に面したガラス窓に向けた展示(図4)も行なっており、《窓》が箱型の形状にのみ限定されるものではなかったことが確認できる。

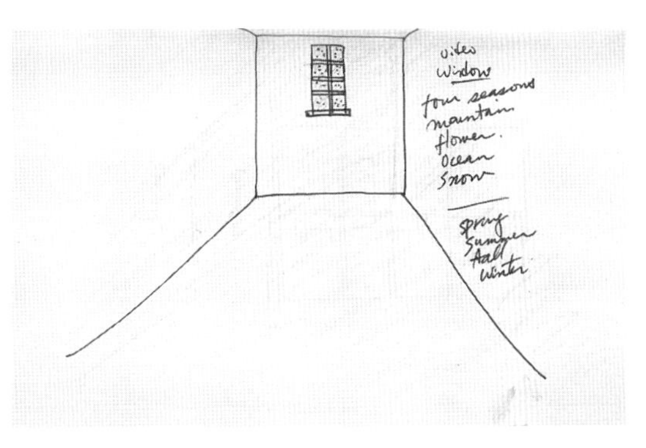

図3　四季による「窓」の構想スケッチ（1977年10月の日記帳より）
fig. 3. Concept sketch for *Window* in four seasons (from Kubota's diary, October 1977).

図4 「Ten-day Video "Snow"」(グレイ・アートギャラリー、ニューヨーク大学、1983年)展示風景
fig. 4. Installation view of *Ten-day Video "Show"* (Grey Art Gallery, New York University, 1983)

5. テクノロジーの変化への応答

ヴィデオ作品にまつわる課題として、機材やメディアの技術的な進化への対応がある。久保田は変化に柔軟に対応しながら、新しい機材の誕生を喜び、自身の作品の発展につなげていった作家である。撮影機材が軽量化したり、編集機材に新しい機能が加われば、映像のパターンが増え、表現の幅が広がる。また、初期の再生機がテープの架け替えを手動で行なわなければならなかったのに比べ、ループ機能ができ、自動的に再生できるようになれば展示運用における作業工程が減じるなど、技術の進化は展示の利便性を高めるものでもあった*33。久保田がヴィデオ彫刻に使用するモニターは、初期はブラウン管テレビだが、1980年代後半に液晶テレビが普及するようになると、小型で軽量なうえ、熱を持たない液晶のモニターになり、《ロック・ヴィデオ　桜》(1986年)[本書108-109頁]などの作品が誕生した*34。《自転車の車輪》の場合でも、1983年に制作した当時は小型ブラウン管が重過ぎて、車輪を継続的に動かし続けることができなかったが、1990年には軽量な液晶テレビを使用し、最大3台のモニターを車輪のなかに組み込んだバージョンを実際に回転させて展示できるようになった*35。

メディア・アート特有の問題としては、過去の記録・再生媒体は時代と共に陳腐化してしまい、常に別の新しい媒体への変換を必要とする点もあげられる。久保田の作品においても、複数の媒体の変遷を見ることができる。富山県美術館では、1983年に同館(当時の富山県立近代美術館)で開催された展覧会「第2回現代芸術祭—芸術と工学」をきっかけに、1984年に《階段》、1985年に《窓》を収蔵しているが、現在では複数の映像媒体が保管されている。もっとも古い媒体としてユーマチックがあり、収蔵時のものと考えられる。さらにベータカムが存在し、1989年に開催された「第4回現代芸術祭—映像の今日」の際に複製、あるいは作家から送付されたものではないかと推測される。1991年、1992年のラベル表記のあるレーザーディスクもあり、両作品が出品された「彫刻の遠心力—この十年の展開」(国立国際美術館)の開催が1992年であることから、同展の素材として作家が制作したものと考えられる*36。このように、収蔵後も展覧会出品等をきっかけに、作家が新たな映像媒体を送付している場合もある*37。

6. マルティプルとしてのヴィデオ彫刻

久保田は現代美術の作家として、展示場所や企画内容に合わせ、その都度制作を行なった。既存作品を出品する場合でも、初期にはスライドの映写で行なっていた壁テキストを、後年の多くの展示で切り文字貼り付けに変更するなど、環境や予算等、物理的条件にも柔軟に対応していたことがうかがえる*38。先述したとおり、久保田のヴィデオ彫刻は、コンセプチュアルな成り立ちを持っているからこそ、最初のコンセプトおよび形を元に、場所ごとに制作することが可能なのである。とくに《階段》や《窓》は彫刻的な独立した形状で、サイトスペシフィックなインスタレーションに比べ、輸送に適していた。さらに、直線的な箱型とモニターの組み合わせであることから、設計図を元に現地制作がしやすい作品だったと言える。久保田の代表作として最初に思い浮かべられる両作品は、このように美術館や展覧会という制度になじみやすい形を持っていたことも、展示頻度を高めたひとつの要因と考えられよう。そのように展示に適した形状は、保存のうえでも扱いやすいということであり、それにより、展示制作後にそのまま収蔵されることとなり、両作品は世界各地にエディションを残す結果となった*39。

世界各地のアーカイブに自身の作品を残し、広めるという考え方は、ジョージ・マチューナスをはじめとしたフルクサスの作家たちに共通するものでもある。彼らは、作家のコンセプトを凝縮したオブジェクトやテキストを廉価なマルティプルとして販売することにより、世界中に頒布させようとした。一方で久保田は、スクリーニングや放映の形で消費されるシングルチャンネル・ヴィデオとは異なり、オブジェクトとしての形を持つことが、美術作品の価格をコントロールする上でも役立つことを認識していた。物質的な形を持つことで保存され、のちの展示を可能にする美術作品としての形式を意識的に選択していたのである*40。

7. バリエーションとしての作品 ――メディア・アートの未来

これまで見てきたように、コンセプチュアルな形を表すための物理的なオブジェクトは重要であるが、唯一無二のものというわけではなく、バリエーションとして再生可能なものである。本展開催にあたり、作家没後に行なわれる初めての回顧展として、ヴィデオ彫刻をどのように再現するかという点が大きな課題となった。久保田のヴィデオ彫刻のほとんどは、展示のたびに機材を用意し、組み立てる必要がある。作家の遺産を引き継ぎ、作品を保存している久保田成子ヴィデオ・アート財団は、作品の所蔵者という以上に、出品にあたっての作品修復、展示指導という点においても、本展のために大きな貢献を果たしている。メディア・アートの再生についてのひとつの実践として、その仕事は、今後も美術界に引き継がれるべき遺産である。

本展における機材は、現在において用意することができ、会期中の安定的な運用が可能なことから、多くの作品で液晶モニターとメディアプレイヤーが採用されている*41。前述したとおり、久保田のヴィデオ彫刻では、機材部分を隠し、映像部分のみを見せる構造が多いため、ブラウン管から液晶モニターへの変更による大きな美的変化は起きない。ただし、ブラウン管テレビの周囲にある枠が、ベニヤによる構造体との間に隙間を作っていたものが、液晶モニターにはないため、《墓》では、3Dプリンターで再現した枠を用い、液晶モニターを一部ブラウン管に似せた形にする工夫をしている。

彫刻外形部分についても、一部が失われていたり、損傷が大きかったりして、残っている部材のみで再現することは難しかった。財団は、作品コンセプトとそのフォルムや質感を作家の意図したとおりに再現するため、オリジナルの部材を損傷などを含めてそのまま使うのではなく、できるかぎりの修復や置き換えを行なうことを選択した。その結果、木目を活かしたベニヤ構造ではアル・ロビンスが制作した当時のフォルムと質感が再現され、プラスチック製鏡を使用した作品では欠けや汚れのない新しい素材に置き換えられ曇りのないリフレクションが再現された。

サイトスペシフィックなインスタレーションを行なう場合はとくに、久保田は展示のたびにオーバープロジェクションの有無や映像の内容を変えることもあった*42。作家が行なった過去の展示のうち、どの時点の何の要素を採用すべきか、難しい判断を求められる場合がある。本展における、財団と私たち展覧会企画者との一致した考え方は、資料や記録を元に、歴史的にさかのぼることを基本としながらも、展示としての魅力を損なうような原理主義的になり過ぎることは避けるというものだった。作品の本質に近づくため、作品ごとに状態や条件を鑑み、素材や展示方法を選択している。今後さらに機材の技術革新が起こり、作品調査が進むなかで新しい発見があれば、再解釈による変更がされていくであろう。本展は、メディア・アート特有の課題に溢れ、各要素において多くの調査と議論、判断、作業が必要とされる展覧会で、その過程は財団との長い旅路のようであった。ここで判明した事柄や現時点での判断は、未来の展示や研究に引き継がれていくことだろう。未来においても再生可能な久保田のヴィデオ彫刻はまさに、終わりのない時間を内包し、私たちに語りかける、作家からのポジティブなメッセージなのである。

（にしかわ・みほこ＝東京都現代美術館学芸員）

［註］

＊1――1970年代のニューヨークのヴィデオ・アート・シーンにおける久保田の活動は、本書の由本論考に詳しい。

＊2――“In Conversation, Shigeko Kubota with Phong Bui,” *The Brooklyn Rail*, September 2007（https://brooklynrail.org/2007/09/art/kubota）アンソロジーの創始者であるメカスからの影響と、その後の展開について、作家自身が以下のように述べている。「ジョージ（・マチューナス）を通して、ジョナス・メカスを知って、大きな影響を受けたのは、映像とヴィデオの関係について理解できたということ。だからパフォーマンス・シーンが下火になった時、私はやり方を変えたの」

＊3――1975年のザ・キッチンでの発表時には、本作に加え、その後も《ヴィデオ・ポエム》と称されるセルフポートレートの作品［本書38–39頁］との2点による展示全体を「ヴィデオ・ポエム」と称していた。本作に《チェス》［本書56–59頁］と《階段》が加わった翌年のルネ・ブロック・ギャラリーでの展示が「デュシャンピアナ」の名を冠していることから、1976年以降、シリーズ名として「デュシャンピアナ」を作品タイトルに付すようになったと推測される。

＊4――Jeanine Mellinger and D. L. Bean, “Shigeko Kubota,” Interview in *Profile* (Video Data Bank) 3, 6 (Nov. 1983), entire volume. pp. 3–4. 本作以前にも多くのシングルチャンネル・ヴィデオを発表する機会はあったが、それは自身の作家としての経歴とは考えておらず、ヴィデオをより複雑に拡張したヴィデオ・インスタレーションあるいはヴィデオ彫刻を目指したとも語っている。

＊5――*Shigeko Kubota: Video Sculpture* (New York: American Museum of Moving Image［MMI］, 1991), p. 48.（本書100頁）。

＊6――*Ibid.* 1976年のルネ・ブロック・ギャラリーでの個展「デュシャンピアナ：ヴィデオ彫刻」において、ブロックの指摘により「インスタレーション」の語を避け、「ヴィデオ彫刻」としたこと、そしてその考え方が自分の考えと合致したとも述べている。「彫刻」という語によって、久保田作品の今日的な意味でのインスタレーション性についての解釈が減じている可能性も考えられる。しかし、久保田はスクリーニングや放送を主体としたヴィデオの利用とは一線を画した美術作品としての自律性を目指したのであり、彼女にとって彫刻的であることと、その規模を拡張させたインスタレーションとは相反するものではなく、不可分な形式だったと言えよう。

＊7――松下電器産業株式会社ビデオ事業部、ビデオムービー事業部「特集　HOW TO MAKE A VIDEO インタビュー久保田成子」『VIDEO CULTURE』No. 19、1992年5月1日、2–3頁、3頁。

＊8――ザ・キッチンにて《墓》と共に展示したヴィデオ彫刻の萌芽とも言えるセルフポートレートの映像を使用した《ヴィデオ・ポエム》でも、TVモニターを袋で覆い、画面だけを覗かせる構造を作っている。小杉武久が《Anima2/Chamber Music》で袋から体の一部を出してパフォーマンスしたのに対し、久保田はそこに映像を挿入した。

＊9――拙訳。John Hanhardt, “Video / Television Space,” *Video Art: An Anthology* (New York and London: Harcourt Brace Jovanovich, 1976), pp. 223–224. ハンハートの本テキスト所収の同書は、1970年代半ばのヴィデオ・アート・シーンの様相を反映したものである。ヴィデオを文化的コミュニケーションとして活用しようとした集団、レインダンスによって1975から76年にかけて編纂された本書では、久保田と親交のあったヴィデオ作家のメアリー・ルシエも編集に携わっている。久保田は70名のヴィデオ・アート作家のうちのひとりとして、発表されたばかりのザ・キッチンでの個展「ヴィデオ・ポエム」の展示写真（ルシエによる撮影）と「ヴィデオ・ポエム」の詩が紹介されている。さらに本書には、アンソロジー・フィルム・アーカイヴズにおける久保田によるキュレーション・プログラムの全リストも掲載されている。

＊10――拙訳。“In Conversation, Phong Bui,” *op.cit.*.

＊11――ジュディス・グリアによるインタビュー、1992年頃、本書164頁。電子的な光が持つ透明性の重要性についても語っている。また、色へのこだわりについては、「マルセル・デュシャン展」（1981年、高輪美術館、西武美術館）への作家からの指示書でも、「必ずソニーのトリニトロン（を使用すること）　色が美しい」（カッコ内は筆者補足）と述べていることからもうかがえる。以下すべて、「マルセル・デュシャン展」（1981年、高輪美術館、西武美術館）における作家からの指示書等資料は、富山県美術館への調査に基づく。

＊12――技術者の阿部修也は、久保田が通常の画像では飽き足らず、コントラストを上げていたと証言する。西武美術館での展示の際、《階段》の映像のコントラストを上げるため、久保田に頼まれ、増幅器を付けたこともあったという。筆者より阿部修也へのインタビュー、2018年12月7日。

＊13――ジュディス・グリーアによるインタビュー、1992年頃、原美術館（本書165頁参照）

＊14――Mellinger and Bean, *op.cit.*, p.13, p.15. 一方で、日記としてのヴィデオの機能も多いに利用し、1970年代から80年代にかけて《ブロークン・ダイアリー》のシリーズを制作した。そのうち、公開しているのは、本展で出品している5作品を中心とした一部である。シングルチャンネル・ヴィデオは日記的、個人的なものであり、多くの人に見せるものとは異なる性質のものであるとも述べている。

＊15――1968年に撮影した写真を元に私家版『マルセル・デュシャンとジョン・ケージ』（1970年）を制作した後、1972年の欧州への旅ではケージのコンサートやデュシャンの墓をポータパックで撮影。両巨匠との出会いという私的経験に基づく日記的なモノクロヴィデオはその後、1975年の《墓》においてカラーライズされ、複数のモニターと鏡による反射で増幅したインスタレーションに展開される。1976年のルネ・ブロック・ギャラリーで《墓》を含むヴィデオ彫刻は「デュシャンピアナ」の名を冠すようになるが、翌年の同ギャラリーではデュシャンからの超克を意識して「メタ・マルセル」にその名を変える。しかしその後、山や河といった自然をモチーフにした独自の作品を制作した後、83年には再び、《自転車の車輪》や雪以外の《窓》など、デュシャンピアナ・シリーズを再開するなど、年代をまたいで繰り返し、自身のシリーズを継続させている。このように、久保田は素材やモチーフを含め、様々な形でアプロプリエーションを繰り返した。本カタログ所収のリズ・フィリップスによるテキストからも、彼らが当時の現代美術の動向のなかで意識的にアプロプリエーションを行なったことがうかがえる。本書50頁。

＊16――ナムジュン・パイクはこのことについて、久保田が発見したのがヴィデオの死、つまり可塑的な死であることを指摘している。*Shigeko Kubota Video Scultpures* (daadgalerie, 1981), p. 31（本書65頁）。

＊17――インタビュー「総特集　映像の現在　久保田成子インタビュー　ビデオ／アート／人生／を語る」『月刊イメージフォーラム』第50号、1984年11月号、48頁。引用箇所は、クライマックスのないのがヴィデオの時間であり、そのあり方がフルクサスと共通しているという趣旨のなかで発言されている。

＊18――インタビュー「一つのオデッセイが終わった　NYで大規模なビデオ・スカルプチャー個展を開く　インタビュー　久保田成子　聞き手：富山加津江」『月刊イメージフォーラム』第139号、1991年10月号、24頁。

＊19――初期作品の多くは、久保田がその高い技術を認めていたアル・ロビンスが、ベニヤ合板による構造体を制作した。ロビンスが木材を用いた構造物の制作に長けていたことも、初期作品にベニヤ合板を用いたものが多かった要因になって

いる。

＊20——日本で合板構造を制作する際の指示書では、「Plywood（松）、ニスはぬらないで下さい。自然色」と素材を指定し、さらに木目を横向きにするようにと図と共に示している。「マルセル・デュシャン展」における作家からの指示書。

＊21——インタビュー「一つのオデッセイが終わった　NYで大規模なビデオ・スカルプチャー個展を開く　インタビュー久保田成子　聞き手：富山加津江」『月刊イメージフォーラム』第139号、1991年10月号、15–29頁、22頁。《三つの山》についての言及。

＊22——アリゾナやモンタナで見た独特な山の形は、日本では見られないアメリカ的な風景として、作家の記憶に強く刻まれていたという。Mellinger and Bean, *op.cit.*, p.10.《三つの山》が直線のみで構成されているのに対し、直後にベルリンで制作した《河》以降、《枯山水》等の作品では、アジア的な自然観を反映した曲線が使用されている。

＊23——*Ibid.*, pp. 3–4.

＊24——《河》や《自転車の車輪》には当初、ペダルが付いていて、観客が踏むことにより回転するインタラクティブな作品と構想されていた。作品がすでに包含する回転の要素に観客による能動的な偶然性も加わり、何重にも動きが付加されるのである。*Ibid.*, p. 7.

＊25——前掲インタビュー「一つのオデッセイが終わった」、22頁。

＊26——「マルセル・デュシャン展」（1981年、高輪美術館、西武美術館）における作家からの指示書。

＊27——Mellinger and Bean, *op.cit.*, p.13. ここでも最初の個展でラブレターの山のインスタレーションに観客をよじ登らせたことが思い出される。

＊28——ポール・ギャリンおよび阿部修也からの聞き取りによる。彼らによると、カラーテレビがつくるスノーノイズは、単純なモノクロではなく、赤や緑といった色彩を含む複雑さを持つため見飽きなかったという。本展に関連して行なわれた両氏への調査については以下に詳しい。濱田真由美「久保田成子ヴィデオ・アート財団における作品調査」『新潟県立近代美術館紀要第17号』2019年3月、52–58頁。

＊29——制作時を知る阿部は、久保田の代表作として本作を高く評価しており、ニューヨークの放送局WNBCが2001年1月1日、21世紀を迎えた朝の最初の放送時に久保田の《雪》を流したとパイクから聞いたと語る。筆者による阿部修也への電話インタビュー、2020年8月14日。

＊30——《窓》の新しいバージョンがつくられたことで、複数の窓を並列または点在させて展示することが可能になり、さらに、一つの窓に「雪」、「花」、「星」の三つの自然をループで一緒に見せることもできるようになった。

＊31——現在の展示では、メディアプレイヤーを再生機として用いているが、小さいため、それを隠すために下の展示台を利用する必要性はない。また、ブラウン管テレビに比べ各段に薄い液晶モニターを使う場合、木の箱のなかは大きな空洞になっている。

＊32——本作に付される作品テキストは、「ヴィデオはきのうの窓。ヴィデオはあすの窓。」であり、ヴィデオを過去と未来をつなぐ窓とみなしているとみなすことができる。

＊33——1991年から92年にかけ、アメリカン・ミュージアム・オブ・ムーヴィング・イメージおよび原美術館他で開催した個展では、ヴィデオ・ディスク（レーザーディスクを指すと考えられる）48台を使ったとしており、それまでテープで再生していた作品をディスクに変換したことがわかる。これに対し久保田は、テープの巻き戻しの時間（リワインド・タイム）やクリーニングの必要がないことを喜ぶ発言をしている。前掲インタビュー「一つのオデッセイが終わった」、27頁。

なお、ポール・ギャリンによると、レーザーディスクへの切り替えは、1985年頃から行なわれたという。ポール・ギャリンへの本展調査のためのインタビュー、ニューヨーク、2018年11月20日。

＊34——MMI, *op.cit.*, p. 59.（本書109頁）。

＊35——前掲インタビュー「一つのオデッセイが終わった」、24頁。

本作の制作に関わったポール・ギャリンに対する聞き取りでも、1983年当時も回転させることはできたが、展示のために回転を継続させることは難しかったということが確認できた。前掲インタビュー。

＊36——その他、展示用に日本で複製されたVHS（《窓》のみ）およびDVDが存在する。なお、《窓》のレーザーディスクのラベルには「SNOW」のみが表記され、DVDも「雪」のみで、「３つのテープ」ではない「雪」のみのバージョンが存在するが、その経緯は不明である。富山県美術館所蔵作品の媒体変遷については、富山県美術館提供の資料を参照した。当時、展覧会を担当した島敦彦氏への聞き取りでも、収蔵後に数回、作家からデータが送られてきた可能性が確認できた。島敦彦への本展調査のためのインタビュー、金沢21世紀美術館、2019年6月6日。また、原美術館に収蔵されている《デュシャンピアナ：自転車の車輪1, 2, 3》についても、ベータカム、レーザーディスクとDVDが存在している。再生機器がないなどの理由で、現段階での確認はできていないが、これら国内収蔵作品で残されている複数の媒体には異なるラベルが貼られているものもあり、映像の内容そのものに、なんらかの違いがある可能性も残されている。

＊37——一般に、美術館における映像作品の収蔵保存において、媒体の変換についての考え方とルールを作家と共有することは、現在においても大きな課題である。

＊38——「マルセル・デュシャン展」（1981年、高輪美術館、西武美術館）における作家からの指示書。「部屋は暗いのですか？　あかるいのですか？　スライドか壁に字を書く必要があるのです。壁に字を書いた方が経済的でしょう」と述べており、暗室や機材を用意しなければならないスライド投影よりも、経済的で効率的な切り文字に変更した理由がわかる。

＊39——《階段》がニューヨーク近代美術館に収蔵された最初のヴィデオ作品となったことはもちろんのこと、国内初の久保田作品の収蔵となった富山県美術館をはじめ、イタリア、アルゼンチン等、世界の異なる地域に収蔵されている。前掲インタビュー「一つのオデッセイが終わった」、22頁。

＊40——Mellinger and Bean, *op.cit.*, p.7.

＊41——《河》のように、機材が彫刻的外形の一部を担う部分については、制作当時に使用されていたものに類似したブラウン管を用いている。

＊42——《墓》の1975年の展示では、鏡が床のみで、その続きには壁テキストがあったが、1984年の展示では天井にも鏡が付され、さらにモニターの左右にプロジェクションがされ、横側の壁にテキストが書かれた。再現にあたっては、それらの要素について、いつの何を採用するか、複数の可能性が残されている。

The Video Sculpture of Shigeko Kubota:
Transmissions from the Past

Mihoko Nishikawa

Foreword

"Video sculpture" is an indispensable element of any discussion of Shigeko Kubota's work, and a term consistently used by the artist herself, as well as in evaluations of her work. The term generally suggests free-standing sculpture that combines one or more video monitors with a three-dimensional structure, but Kubota's video sculpture is markedly environmental in nature. It is characterized by covering of the casings of TV monitors, concealing their presence as electrical appliances and incorporating only their screens into the objects. By incorporating the abstract beauty of moving images, their luminous colors and dynamic movements, into sculptural objects, she created mechanisms that enable viewers to experience works spatially. Sculptural forms and materials incorporating moving images are important means of presenting her works' concepts, while at the same time these presentations are not dependent on physical materiality. With each exhibition, Kubota altered formats and display methods according to the venue, conditions, and her own concerns. This flexibility was rooted in basic contemporary art concepts, such as appropriation as exemplified by Marcel Duchamp and multiples as practiced by the Fluxus group, and was also a response to the fragility and fluidity of the electronic medium of video. This essay considers various possibilities in media art by exploring the underpinnings and intent of Kubota's incorporation of video into her works.

1. Video Sculpture as Installation

After staging her first video concert at The Kitchen in 1972, Kubota emerged as a presence in the burgeoning video art scene, working as Video Curator at Anthology Film Archives and interacting with other female artists.*[1] In the early 1970s, Kubota viewed herself as a sculptor and was concerned with giving one-time-only performances more lasting and universal form, while at the same time experimenting with single-channel screenings and use of multiple monitors. Her experience as Video Curator at Anthology Film Archives provided important opportunities to engage with contemporary video and its potential, but she later remarked on the repetitive nature of the work, which involved showing the same videos over and over again.*[2] Around this time she was offered the chance to have a solo show at The Kitchen, and produced *Duchampiana: Marcel Duchamp's Grave**[3] [cat. pp. 54–55] (referred to below as *Grave*), which featured monitors stacked from floor to ceiling and a mirror on the floor to reflect the screens' moving images. At the time there were still few artists working with installation, but the artist stated that she deliberately presented this large-scale video installation as a mode of expression distinctly her own.*[4] Rather than a somewhat random-looking array of video equipment in the style that was popular at the time, Kubota created a free-standing sculpture with a carefully considered composition and structure,*[5] and the work marked a turning point in her career as an artist.

At this time, approaches to exhibiting video were beginning to diversify and the term "video installation" was coming into use, and although Kubota herself often applied this term to her work, she said that she preferred "video sculpture" because she wanted to emphasize the pieces' character as autonomous works of art.*[6] This was significant in that making the works autonomous and self-contained gave them physical relationships to spaces when viewed. The following quote aptly expresses the artist's intent:

"With video sculpture, space and time become elements of the work. Architectural factors also come into play, such as how to install the work in a museum or public space, and expression is expanded in three dimensions. Viewers are not detained for a certain length of time while they watch a video, meaning they can just pause for a moment in front of the work, or fold their arms and gaze at it for a good while, and a dialogue between the viewer and the artist can emerge. Single-channel video is well suited to conveying the meaning of a literary narrative, but I arrived at the video sculpture format when attempting to transcend the literary and achieve a more visual mode of expression. The world of video sculpture is cosmic and abstract, and pulling the viewer into such a mysterious world is a fascinating process."*7

2. Video Images Incorporated into Sculpture

A crucial point regarding Kubota's video sculptures is that mechanical parts of TV sets are obscured, and only the screens are isolated as collage-like elements.*8 This gave physical substance to the medium of video, and facilitated encounters between viewer and artwork in space, in the manner of sculpture. John G. Hanhardt focuses on this point in his commentary on *Grave*: "Kubota has distanced us from the familiar connotations of the television set by masking everything except the screen, repeating the image in each of the eleven monitors, and placing them vertically in such a way that the images dissolve into a matrix of weaving colors, camera movements, and recognizable patterns. In a sense one is experiencing the video as a sculpture/collage whose effectiveness is achieved through an abstraction of image and of video screen."*9

While adhering to traditions surrounding works of fine art, Kubota was quick to perceive the new medium of video's appeal to multiple senses, and to incorporate it into her work. For her, video imagery was a fascinating material with which to compose works of art, and she recollected: "In the 1960s Sony invented the Portapack, which was revolutionary; like what you'd just said, film was chemical, but video was more organic. To me Portapack was like a new paintbrush. It was certainly in the same spirit as Fluxus, 'do it yourself.'"*10 Video is a medium that emits light from within, glows more brightly than the pigment of paint, and can easily have its contrast heightened,*11 and it has been noted that Kubota preferred to work with vivid colors and stark contrasts.*12 Also, working with video meant having the ability to modulate electrical signals so as to overlay, distort, or stretch images. The medium of video offered efficient means of rendering images abstract.

Furthermore, moving pictures without narrative content constitute a universal language, while positioning works as objects in spaces generated dialogue with the viewer. As a minority and nonnative English speaker, video was an ideal medium, as she was not required to speak,*13 and the artist remarked that " I chose to make autonomous works, which did not require language, by strengthening their presence as video sculptures."*14

Another property of video is ease of repetition and duplication. Kubota not only appropriated from Marcel Duchamp, but also often produced variations based on her own past works. Video can be copied, the same material can be used repeatedly, and footage can be used to create art regardless of the time elapsed since it was shot.*15 In assimilating 'video time' into the works, she put parts of the past on repeating loops and transformed the linear flow of time.*16 With repetition, the end becomes the beginning and time becomes cyclical. The artist stated:

"To me, 'video time' is time without time."*17

"Video is a form of communication between the world of the dead and the world of the living, and it produces images that connect to the eternal, that will never disappear."*18

3. Materials and Forms Surrounding Moving Images

The materials and forms employed in Kubota's works created sculptural frameworks surrounding the video images, but were not made simply to cover the mechanical parts of equipment. Her selection of materials and forms had both a sculptural and a conceptual intent.

Turning first to selection of materials, one notable motivating factor was the fusion of the electrical (video signal) and the organic (natural materials). Many of the plywood structures*19 used in early works are of pine featuring conspicuous wood grain,*20 the organic wood enfolding the electrical video image. The later works *River* [cat. pp. 84, 93–95] and *Niagara Falls* [cat. pp. 104–107] take this juxtaposition even further and are unique in their use of actual water. Kubota stated that she consciously selected "materials such as wood or plastic mirrors which are soft like water, while the technology is hard,"*21 and her video sculpture is characterized by both dissonance, resulting from the use of contrasting materials, and new and unprecedented forms arising from their fusion.

Her selection of subject matter, as well, is marked by many motifs from nature such as mountains and rivers. In her sketchbook she repeatedly drew mountains she had seen in Arizona and Montana,*22 frequently accompanied by text such as "The flow of the water is ceaseless and its water is never the same," a quotation from the Japanese classic *Hojoki* ("The Ten-Foot-Square Hut"), or nostalgic recollections of her father and her hometown. For Kubota, mountains and rivers were also autobiographical motifs onto which she projected her own life [see Fig. 7 on p. 189].

Kubota also made frequent use of mirrors, and their effects of reflection and repetition were important elements of her work. She described the mirror as both an homage to Duchamp and a projection of his spirit, and spoke of wanting to imbue it with cosmic expansiveness.*23 As in her very early video sculpture *Grave*, which used multiple monitors and mirrors to create a continually looping circle, in *Duchampiana: Bicycle Wheel* [cat. pp. 98–100], *Auto-*

Tire Wheel [cat. pp. 118–119], and *Skater* [cat. pp. 120–121] she employed motor power to incorporate actual dynamic rotation into the work, and gave physical form to circles.*24

In addition to the physicality of the materials, Kubota's video sculptures, especially from the early years, are also characterized by text on walls accompanying the works. This generates experiences that work on multiple perceptual levels: the physical sensation of touching an object, the visual sensation of following images, the linguistic thought-process of reading written text. From the *Duchampiana* series onward, in place of text on the wall, Kubota further expanded the multi-layered viewing experience through over-projection (multiple overlapping projections), or presentation of installations combining multiple works.

4. Motif as Concept / Sculpture as Manifestation

The forms Kubota selected for her video sculptures were conceptual, in terms of motif, and were in some cases defined by the forms of equipment available at the time of production and the number of pieces of equipment owned by the artist. When asked about *Duchampiana: Nude Descending a Staircase* (referred to below as *Staircase*) [cat. pp. 60–62], Kubota responded, "I had only four TVs in the house [laughs] . . . There were three large units and one small one. People tell me they're well-balanced, but actually those were all I had. If there were 200 of them, it might be like a staircase to heaven [laughs]."*25

Kubota was based in the United States, but when exhibiting in Japan, she initially stipulated that "*Staircase* uses 15-inch Sony Trinitron TV sets, the height of which is 13.5 inches. Otherwise, they will not fit in the stairs I designed." However, when it became clear that older products meeting these specifications were not available in Japan, she instructed that "the size of the staircase must be changed to match the TVs. The TVs need to fit inside the staircase, so each stair step must be made a bit higher . . . please leave the practicalities to the carpenter, and calculate the balance as best you can based on my drawings."*26 These instructions indicate that in working with the basic concept of incorporating monitors into a staircase structure, Kubota responded flexibly to physical conditions imposed by equipment and other materials.

The staircase was a favorite motif of Kubota's, also appearing in later works such as *Green Installation* [cat. p. 101]. As suggested by her joking in the interview quoted above that if she had 200 monitors she might have created a staircase reaching the heavens, the concept had the potential for expansion with different numbers of steps and different forms. A sketch in her diary, which seems to be a concept for an installation in a public space, depicts a tall staircase leading from floor to ceiling [fig. 1. p. 215, top-left], and her 2008 exhibition at the Toyota Municipal Museum of Art featured an installation in which eight large staircases are connected, extending from top to bottom of a stairway in the museum [fig. 2. p. 215, bottom-left]. Ascending and descending of a staircase was also symbolic of a life of recurring ups and downs.*27 In addition to the staircase as a physical spaces that the viewer feels they could actually ascend and descend, a looping video of a nude woman descending a staircase is embedded in the steps of the staircase. Different times and spaces—real space and electronic space, time captured on video and time spent viewing the video—are superimposed, manifesting a time continuum with no beginning or end.

Similarly, in *Meta-Marcel: Window* [cat. pp. 66–69] (referred to below as *Window*), it is notable that physical qualities of materials, such as types of equipment to be used, were among the conditions specified. This work takes the form of a latticed double-door French window, modeled on Duchamp's *Fresh Widow* (1920), but it is smaller than the original, and this probably resulted from the size of TV monitor available to Kubota at the time. While the Duchamp window frame is green, Kubota's wood is unpainted and shows its grain, and above all, in the original the window-frame stands on its own but in Kubota's it is enveloped by a wooden box. This wooden box functions to conceal the mechanical parts of the TV monitor so only the screen can be seen. Its placement on a white pedestal may be intended to put the window at eye level while adhering to a conventional method of displaying sculpture in a museum, but the pedestal also plays the role of hiding an open-reel video player, which is connected to a color TV to produce static.*28 When an open-reel player with no videotape inserted sends a signal, the screen of the color TV receiving it shows static. Kubota referred to these moving dots produced by electronic devices as "video snow," and here the parallel scanning lines that run horizontally on a TV screen are made vertical by rotating the TV set 90 degrees, evoking snow falling outside the window.*29 In later works the artist used prerecorded footage rather than producing static in real time each time the work was exhibited, and produced other versions termed "flowers" and "stars."*30 Whichever approach was used, a video player was required, so the pedestal continued serving to conceal this piece of equipment.*31 As the above examples show, the forms sculptures took evidently depended on sizes and shapes of equipment available at the time, but for Kubota the window also represented a conceptual "open window" connecting the past and the future.*32 In a concept sketch in her diary, we see that in addition to the actually realized "snow," "flowers," and "stars," she was considering rendering the four seasons unfolding outside the window, and she made drawings in which the window is embedded in a wall [fig. 3, p. 215, right]. In one exhibition she embedded a window directly in the wall of at the gallery entrance, without a pedestal, and in another the window was displayed facing the glass windows looking out on the street [fig. 4, p. 216]. It is clear that *Window* was not limited to the format of enclosure in a box.

5. Responses to Changing Technology

One issue in video art is how to deal with the technological advancement of equipment and media. Kubota was an artist who responded flexibly to change, celebrated the emergence of new technology, and connected it to the development of her own work. When camera equipment became lighter, or new functions were added to editing equipment, she was able to produce videos with more diverse patterns and broaden her range of expression. The evolution of technology smoothed the process of exhibiting: while early playback devices required manually replacing videotape, newer models had a loop function, and with automatic repeating playback, managing an exhibition was less labor-intensive.*33 Kubota initially used cathode ray tube TVs for her video sculptures, but as LCD became more prevalent in the late 1980s she began using smaller, lighter, heat-free LCD monitors and created works such as *Rock Video: Cherry Blossom* (1986) [cat. pp. 108–109].*34 In the case of *Bicycle Wheel*, when she initially made it in 1983 the small cathode ray tube TV was too heavy for the wheel to keep moving continuously, but in 1990 she replaced it with lightweight LCD, enabling a version in which the wheel could spin with up to three monitors mounted.*35

Another issue peculiar to media art is that as times change, past recording and playback media become obsolete, and content needs to be transferred to new media. Over the course of Kubota's career, there were multiple transitions from one medium to another. After the *2nd Contemporary Art Festival: Art and Technology* at the Toyama Prefectural Museum of Art and Design (then known as the Museum of Modern Art, Toyama) in 1983, *Staircase* entered the museum's possession in 1984, followed by *Window* in 1985, and today its collection contains work by the artist in multiple media. The oldest of these media is U-matic, which was evidently used in the original work. Another work uses the Betacam format, and is thought to have been duplicated in 1989 for the *4th Contemporary Art Festival: Image of Today*, or to have been sent to the museum by the artist. There are laser discs labeled with the dates 1991 and 1992, apparently produced by the artist as materials for the exhibition *Centrifugal Sculpture: An Aspect of Japanese Sculpture in the Last Decade* (The National Museum of Art, Osaka) in 1992, as both works were exhibited there.*36 These are some examples of the artist sending work in new formats to venues, even if these works were already in their collections, on occasions such as exhibitions.*37

6. Video Sculptures as Multiples

As a thoroughly contemporary artist, Kubota was willing to produce modified iterations of her work each time it was shown depending on the venue and exhibition content. Even when showing works in their existing form, she was clearly flexible in making changes, such as presenting wall texts that originally took the form of slide projections as cutout lettering affixed to the wall, based on physical conditions such as environment and budget.*38 As discussed earlier, because Kubota's video sculptures are conceptually structured, they can be recreated at each new venue based on the initial concept and format. *Staircase* and *Window* in particular are in free-standing sculptural formats, making them more suitable for transportation than site-specific installations. And because they are simply assembled from linear boxes and monitors, these works must have been relatively easy to reproduce on site based on design drawings. These two works, easily identifiable as representative of Kubota's oeuvre, are in formats highly compatible with museums and exhibitions on a systemic level, and this seems to be a factor contributing to the frequency with which they are exhibited. These easy-to-exhibit formats mean the works are also easy to preserve, resulting in their being added to venues' collections after exhibitions, and in iterations of both works exist throughout the world today.*39

The idea of widely distributing one's work in archives around the world is one she shared with George Maciunas and other Fluxus artists. They sought to spread objects and texts encapsulating artists' concepts worldwide by selling them as inexpensive multiples. At the same time, Kubota recognized that giving an artwork the form of a physical object, unlike a single-channel video consumed through screening or projection, also helped to control the price of the work. She consciously selected the format of a work of fine art, which would be preserved in material form and could be exhibited at a later date.*40

7. Works as Iterations: The Future of Media Art

As we have seen, physical objects—used to represent conceptual forms—are important but not unique, and can be reproduced as iterations. Specific means of recreating video sculpture were a crucial concern in organizing this exhibition, the first survey since the death of the artist. The majority of Kubota's video sculptures require procurement of equipment and assembly each time they are exhibited. The Shigeko Kubota Video Art Foundation, which carries on the artist's legacy and preserves her works, contributed greatly to this exhibition not only as the owner of works but also in terms of their restoration and provision of practical guidance for installing the exhibition. As a regenerative practice in media art, this work represents heritage that should be handed down to the art world of the future.

In terms of equipment, many works exhibited in this exhibition employ LCD monitors and digital media players, as these can be prepared and stably operated throughout the exhibition period under current circumstances.*41 As described above, Kubota's video sculpture is often structured so as to conceal mechanical parts and reveal only screens showing video, so the update from cathode ray tubes to LCD monitors does not result in major aesthetic changes. However, as LCD monitors do not necessitate a gap between monitor and bezel like that resulting from the use of cathode ray tube TVs, *Grave* features a bezel reproduced with a 3D printer, and in some ways the LCD monitor has been made to resemble its cathode ray tube predecessor.

Reproducing outer sculptural forms using only surviving materials was difficult, as parts of these structures had been lost or severely damaged. To reproduce the works' concepts, form, and texture as the artist intended, the Foundation chose to repair or replace the original materials to the greatest possible extent, rather than presenting them in their existing, damaged forms. As a result, plywood structures emphasizing wood grain reproduce the forms and textures they had when first fabricated by Al Robbins, and in works incorporating plastic mirrors, these mirrors are replaced with new material that is not chipped or dirtied, restoring their unclouded reflections.

Kubota sometimes chose to use or not use over-projection, or altered the contents of videos, for each exhibition, especially when producing site-specific installations.*42 In some cases, difficult decisions needed to be made as to which elements of the artist's past exhibitions from which times should be adopted. The Foundation and those of us organizing this exhibition were able to agree on an approach that involved tracing the historical record based on materials and documents, while avoiding excessive didacticism that would undermine the appeal of the exhibition. Materials and exhibition methods were selected in consideration of the status and conditions of each work in order to draw closer to the work's essence. In the future, if further technological innovations occur and new discoveries are made while the work is being surveyed, reinterpretations will result in further changes. This exhibition involved numerous issues peculiar to media art, each element requiring a large amount of research, discussion, judgment, and labor, and the process was a long quest undertaken in close cooperation with the Foundation. It is our hope that the resulting findings, and our judgments at this point in time, will contribute to future exhibitions and research. As works with documented plans to be restored and reinstalled in the future, Kubota's video sculptures encapsulate the vast endlessness of time, and convey the endlessly positive message the artist was dedicated to delivering.

(Curator, Museum of Contemporary Art Tokyo)

Translation by Christopher Stephens

[Notes]

*1——For an in-depth discussion of Kubota's activities in the 1970s New York video art scene, see the essay by Yoshimoto in this catalogue.

*2——"In Conversation, Shigeko Kubota with Phong Bui," *The Brooklyn Rail*, September 2007 (https://brooklynrail.org/2007/09/art/kubota). The artist described the influence of Mekas, the founder of Anthology Film Archives, and subsequent developments as follows: "Through George I met Jonas Mekas, who had a great deal of influence on me and, because I recognized the connection between image and video, and since the whole performance scene became less active, I began to change my process as a result."

*3——In addition to *Grave*, her exhibition at The Kitchen in 1975 featured a self-portrait work [cat. pp. 38–39.] and the two pieces together were titled *Video Poem*, while the self-portrait went on to be called *Video Poem* thereafter. It can be inferred that the series name *Duchampiana* was added to the title *Grave* after her exhibition at René Block Gallery the following year (1976), when it was shown alongside *Chess* [cat. pp. 56–59] and *Staircase*.

*4——Jeanine Mellinger and D.L. Bean, "Shigeko Kubota," Interview in *Profile* (Video Data Bank) 3, 6 (Nov. 1983), entire volume. pp. 3, 4. She noted that prior to this work she had opportunities to present many single-channel videos, but did not consider this an important part of her artistic career, seeking instead to pursue video installation or video sculpture that extended the medium of video in a more complex manner.

*5——*Shigeko Kubota: Video Sculpture* (New York: American Museum of Moving Image [MMI], 1991), p. 48. (See p. 248 of this catalogue.)

*6——*Ibid.* Kubota has noted that for her solo exhibition *Duchampiana: Video Sculpture* at René Block Gallery in 1976, she avoided the word "installation" and instead used "video sculpture" at Block's suggestion, the gallerist's thinking being in line with her own ideas. It is possible that the use of the word "sculpture" has diminished perceptions of her work in terms of installation in the contemporary sense. However, Kubota aimed to create works with autonomy as art objects which differentiated them from the conventional use of video primarily for screening and broadcasting, and the "sculptural" nature of these works according to Kubota's definition does not preclude their being "installation" when expanded in scale, rather these are two inseparable aspects of her format.

*7——Matsushita Electric Industrial Co., Ltd. Video Equipment Division and Video Movie Division, "Special Feature: How to Make a Video, Interview with Shigeko Kubota," *Video Culture*, No. 19, May 1, 1992, p. 3.

*8——Even as early as *Video Poem* [cat. pp. 38–39], which incorporates a video self-portrait and was exhibited together with *Grave*, the two marking the origins of Kubota's video sculpture practice, the TV monitor was covered with a bag to create a structure in which only the screen could be seen. While Takehisa Kosugi's *Anima2/Chamber Music* was performed in a bag with parts of the performer's body emerging, Kubota here replaced the human body with video footage.

*9——John Hanhardt, "Video/Television Space," *Video Art: An Anthology* (New York and London: Harcourt Brace Jovanovich, 1976), pp. 223–24. This book containing Hanhardt's text reflects the state of the video art scene in the mid-1970s. Compiled in 1975 to 1976 by the Raindance Foundation, a group that sought to use video for cultural communication, and among its editors was Mary Lucier, a video artist who had close ties with Kubota. As one of 70 video artists featured in the book, Kubota is represented by an installation view (photographed by Lucier) of her recent solo exhibition *Video Poem* at The Kitchen, along with the text of the poem *Video Poem*. The book also includes a complete list of programs curated by Kubota at Anthology Film Archives.

*10——"In Conversation, Phong Bui," op. cit.

*11——Interview by Judith Greer, p. 175 of this catalogue. Kubota also spoke about the importance of electronic light's transparency. Meanwhile, the artist's strong focus on color can be seen in her instructions for installation of the exhibition *Marcel Duchamp* (1981, Takanawa Art Museum, Seibu Museum of Art), which states that "Absolutely Sony Trinitron TVs [must be used]. Their color is beautiful" (text in brackets added by author). Below, all of the materials cited with regard to the 1981 *Marcel Duchamp* exhibition, such as instructions from the artist, are based on a survey at the Toyama Prefectural Museum of Art and Design.

*12——The engineer Shuya Abe has stated that Kubota was not satisfied with standard picture quality and sought higher contrast. For her exhibition at the Seibu Museum of Art, Kubota asked him to add an amplifier to boost the contrast of the footage in Staircase. Interview with Shuya Abe by the author, December 7, 2018.

*13——See interview by Greer, pp. 175–176 of this catalogue.

*14——Mellinger and Bean, *op. cit.*, p. 13, p. 15. At the same time, Kubota frequently used video in the manner of a diary, and produced the *Broken Diary* series in the 1970s and 1980s. Some entries have been made available for public release, including the five shown in this exhibition. The artist noted that her single-channel videos, diaristic and personal, were qualitatively different from what she presented for wider audiences.

*15——After producing a private printing of *Marcel Duchamp and John Cage* (1970) based on photographs taken in 1968, she shot footage of a Cage concert and Duchamp's grave on a trip to Europe in 1972. A diaristic black-and-white video based on her personal experiences encountering the two masters was subsequently colorized for *Grave* in 1975, and expanded into an installation amplified by multiple monitors and mirror reflections. At the René Block Gallery in 1976, the series title *Duchampiana* was applied to her video sculptures including *Grave*, but at the same gallery the following year, this title was changed to *Meta-Marcel* in light of her attempt to transcend Duchamp's influence. However, after creating original works with motifs from nature such as mountains and rivers, in 1983 she resumed the *Duchampiana* series, including *Bicycle Wheel* and the *Window* works other than those featuring snow, so in effect the series continued over multiple decades as part of Kubota's own practice. This is an example of how Kubota repeatedly used appropriation in various ways, including with regard to materials and motifs. The text by Liz Phillips in this catalogue makes it clear that she consciously worked with appropriation in the context of current contemporary art trends. See p. 52 of this catalogue.

*16——With regard to this, Nam June Paik stated that what Kubota had revealed was the death of video, albeit death with plasticity. *Shigeko Kubota Video Scultpures* (daadgalerie, 1987), p. 31. See p. 244 of this catalogue.

*17——Interview, "Comprehensive Special Feature: Video Today – Shigeko Kubota on Video/Art/Life," *Gekkan* [Monthly] *Image Forum* No. 50, November 1984, p. 48. This quotation is part of a passage describing "video time" as lacking a climax, and in that sense having commonalities with Fluxus.

*18——Interview, "An Odyssey Completed: Major New York Exhibition of Video Sculpture—Shigeko Kubota interviewed by Katsue Tomiyama," *Gekkan* [Monthly] *Image Forum* No. 139, October 1991, p. 24.

*19——Many of Kubota's early works were fabricated with plywood by Al Robbins, who was trusted by Kubota for the quality of his workmanship. Robbins's woodworking skills contributed to the fact that many of her early works employed plywood.

*20——In her instructions for making plywood structures in Japan, she specified: "Please use plywood (pine) and do not apply varnish. Natural color," with an illustration showing that the wood grain should run horizontally. From the artist's instructions for the exhibition *Marcel Duchamp* (1981).

*21——Interview, "An Odyssey Completed: Major New York Exhibition of Video Sculpture—Shigeko Kubota interviewed by Katsue Tomiyama," *Gekkan* [Monthly] *Image Forum* No. 139, October 1991, p. 22. The comment is with regard to *Three Mountains*.

*22——The artist said that as American scenery unlike any in Japan, the distinctive shapes of mountains she saw in Arizona and Montana were strongly engraved in her memory. Mellinger and Bean, *op. cit.*, p. 10. While *Three Mountains* consists of only straight lines, her subsequent works feature curving lines that reflect an Asian view of nature, beginning with *River*, which she made in Berlin immediately following *Three Mountains*, and continuing with others such as *Rock Garden*.

*23——*Ibid.*, pp. 3–4.

*24——Initially, *River* and *Bicycle Wheel* were interactive works with pedals that caused them to rotate when viewers operated them. The active, chance participation of viewers added to the rotational elements already present in the work, adding many multiple layers of movement. *Ibid.*, p. 7.

*25——*Op. cit.* interview, "An Odyssey Completed," p. 22.

＊26——Instructions from the artist for the exhibition *Marcel Duchamp* (1981).

＊27——Mellinger and Bean, *op. cit.*, p. 13. This recalls Kubota's first solo exhibition, featuring an installation in which the audience climbed a mountain of love letters.

＊28——From interviews with Paul Garrin and Shuya Abe. According to them, snow (static) on a color television is not simply black-and-white, but has a complex palette including red, green and other colors, so the viewer never tires of watching. Details of the surveys they conducted in connection with this exhibition can be found in: Mayumi Hamada, "Survey of Works by the Shigeko Kubota Video Art Foundation," *Bulletin of the Niigata Prefectural Museum of Modern Art* No. 17, March 2019, pp. 52–58.

＊29——Abe, who had been conscious of this work since it was produced, praised it as Kubota's masterpiece, and he heard from Paik that the New York broadcaster WNBC showed Kubota's *Snow* as its first broadcast on the morning of January 1, 2001, when the 21st century began. Telephone interview with Shuya Abe by the author, August 14, 2020.

＊30——With the new version of *Window*, it was possible to display multiple windows in a row or scattered around, and in addition, one window could show three aspects of nature—snow, flowers, and stars—ogether on a loop.

＊31——The current exhibition uses a media player for playback, but because of its small size there is no need to use the pedestal to conceal it. Also, when using LCD monitors that are thinner than cathode ray tube TVs, the inside of the wooden box becomes a large empty space.

＊32——The text accompanying this work reads, "Video is a window on yesterday. Video is a window on tomorrow." Video can be regarded as a window that connects the past and the future.

＊33——In her solo exhibitions at the American Museum of the Moving Image, Hara Museum of Contemporary Art and elsewhere in 1991 and 1992, 48 "video discs" (thought to be Laser Discs) were used, and discs were clearly adopted for works that previously employed tape for playback. Kubota was pleased that there was no need to spend time rewinding or cleaning videotape (see the above-mentioned interview "An Odyssey Completed," p. 27). According to Garrin, the switch to LaserDisc began around 1985. Interview with Paul Garrin for survey connected with this exhibition, New York, November 20, 2018.

＊34 ——MMI, *op. cit.*, p. 59. (See p. 250 of this catalogue.)

＊35——*Op. cit.* interview, "An Odyssey Completed," p. 24. An interview with Paul Garrin, who was involved in production of this work, confirmed that it was possible to rotate it in 1983, but it was difficult to make this rotation to continue throughout the exhibition. *Op. cit.* interview.

＊36——VHS (only of *Window*) and DVDs reproduced in Japan for exhibition purposes also exist. The label on the LaserDisc for *Window* reads only "SNOW" and the DVD only "snow," and there is a version with only "snow" rather than the usual three tapes, but the circumstances of its usage are unknown. For details on the evolution of media in works at the Toyama Prefectural Museum of Art and Design, reference was made to materials provided by the Toyama Prefectural Museum of Art and Design. An interview with Atsuhiko Shima, the person in charge of that exhibition, confirmed that the artist may have sent data several times after the work was acquired for the collection. Interview with Atsuhiko Shima for the survey of this exhibition, 21st Century Museum of Contemporary Art, Kanazawa, June 6, 2019. Also, there are Betacam, LaserDisc, and DVD versions for *Duchampiana: Bicycle Wheel One, Two, Three* in Hara Museum ARC. Although it has not been confirmed at this stage due to lack of playback equipment and other factors, some media in Japanese collections have differing labels attached, and it is possible that the contents of the videos themselves may differ.

＊37——Generally speaking, sharing approaches and rules regarding conversion of media with artists remains a major issue with regard to the storage and preservation of video works at museums.

＊38——From instructions from the artist for the exhibition *Marcel Duchamp* (1981): "Is the room dark? Is it bright? Either slides need to be projected, or text should be written on the wall. Writing on the wall would be more economical." The reason for transitioning from slide projection to more economical and efficient cutout lettering is evident.

＊39——Not only was *Staircase* the first video work acquired by The Museum of Modern Art, New York, but it was also the first of Kubota's works acquired for a Japanese collection, at the Toyama Prefectural Museum of Art and Design, and is in collections throughout the world including in Italy and Argentina. *Op. cit.* interview, "An Odyssey Completed," p. 22.

＊40——Mellinger and Bean, *op. cit.*, p. 7.

＊41——In cases where the equipment forms a part of the outer sculptural form, such as *River*, a cathode ray tube similar to that used at the time of production is used.

＊42——When *Grave* was exhibited in 1975, the mirror was only on the floor, followed by a wall text, but in the 1984 exhibition a mirror was also mounted on the ceiling, and there were projections to the left and right of the monitor, with text on the wall to the side. In reproducing the work, there are multiple possibilities as to which elements to adopt from what point in time.

久保田成子のサーキュレーション

橋本梓

0

久保田成子は1964年に日本からニューヨークへ移り、フルクサスへの参加、ヴィデオを用いたパフォーマンスの発表などを経て、1975年にヴィデオを使った立体作品を初めて発表した。その2年後には早くも大規模な国際展で発表の機会を得、とりわけ80年代から90年代半ばにかけて、欧米を中心としたアートシーンで存在感を示し続けた。本稿は、そうした久保田の受容に関して、以下の二段階で考察する。すなわち、まず1970年代半ばから久保田が国際的な評価を得るに至る道筋を確認し、次に彼女の作品の構造をより概念的に検討した上で、1990年代から今日までの受容を概略する。

1

1960年代から1970年代を通して、ヴィデオを用いた実験的な表現は、とりわけドイツやアメリカ、日本、その他機材を入手可能な国々で同時多発的にさまざまな展開を見せた。そうしたなか、ヴィデオを使って立体表現に取り組んだ久保田は、自らの仕事に沿う言葉として「ヴィデオ・インスタレーション」ではなく「ヴィデオ彫刻」という語を掲げた。

この名付けには、当時ギャラリストでありキュレーターで、1980年代以後はヨーロッパを中心に多数の展覧会のキュレーションを手がけることとなる、ドイツ出身のルネ・ブロックが関係している。ブロックは1960年代にドイツでそのキャリアをスタートさせたが、フルクサス関連の作家や、ヨーゼフ・ボイス、ナムジュン・パイクなどと協働し、ベルリンやニューヨークで先鋭的な仕事を手掛けていた。1974年から77年の間にソーホーでギャラリーを運営していたブロックと久保田が出会ったのは、後に久保田の夫となるナムジュン・パイクを通じてのことだった。

1976年、ルネ・ブロック・ギャラリーでの久保田の初個展のDMには「SHIGEKO KUBOTA: 3 VIDEO INSTALLATIONS」と記されている。《マルセル・デュシャンの墓》[本書54–55頁]、《ヴィデオ・ポエム》[本書38–39頁]はこの前年にThe Kitchenでの初個展で発表されており、ここに新作《階段を降りる裸体》[本書60–62頁](以後《階段》)を加え、「デュシャンピアナ」シリーズとして発表した。その際にギャラリーの出したプレスリリースや、新聞等に出た批評には「video sculpture」という語はまだ見当たらず、唯一Arts Magazineだけが「彼女の三つの作品はヴィデオ=彫刻みたいなもの(Her three pieces are a kind of video-sculpture)」と評している*[1]。久保田は後年、ブロックが1976年に個展を企画した時に展覧会を「デュシャンピアナ:ヴィデオ彫刻」と題したと述懐しているが、正確にはそれがヴィデオ彫刻の名を得たのは、ブロックがドイツでこの後の翻訳を検討したことがきっかけだった*[2]。1976年、ブロックのキュレーションによりベルリンで開催された展覧会「New York-Downtown Manhattan: SoHo-Berlin Festival」(Academie der Kunste, Berlin)に、久保田の《階段》も出品された。先と同じ久保田の述懐によれば、英語のvideo installationをドイツ語に翻訳する際、ドイツ語のInstallationが主に配管工事などを意味するため、語の印象が良くないという理由で、ブロックは久保田の作品を「ヴィデオ彫刻」と名付けたというが、それがこの展覧会ではないかと推測される*[3]。翌1977年にニューヨークのルネ・ブロック・ギャラリーで開催された久保田の個展のDMには「Meta-Marcel by Shigeko Kubota/3 Video Sculptures」と記されている。久保田はこの名称を気に入ったようで、以下のように記している。「アル・ロビンスに手伝ってもらって、私はこのヴィデオ彫刻を組み立てた。自己完結型の作品で、当時はヴィデオ機器をいいかげんに組み合わせるのがかなり流行っていたが、それには似ていなかった。私が造ったのは精巧に組み立てられた一点の芸術作品であって、ロダンやミケランジェロの伝統に連なる彫刻と呼ぶにふさわしいものだった」*4。

フルクサスでは領域横断的な実践に飛び込み、1970年代前半にはヴィデオ・パフォーマンスも試み、1974年からはアンソロジー・フィルム・アーカイヴズでヴィデオ・キュレーターとして毎週末同時代を生きるヴィデオ・アーティストの企画に取り組み、絵画や彫刻といった近代的なメディウム論を超越した新しい表現をたっぷりと浴びた久保田が、彫刻というクラシックなジャンルに自らの置き所を設定したのは興味深い*5。東京教育大学（のちの筑波大学）で彫刻を学び、内科画廊で彫刻の仕事を組み込んだ新しい体験型の作品を発表したにもかかわらず、批評家たちの手応えを得られなかった悔しい経験が久保田の作家としての出発点にはある。「女流彫刻家」として名を成したいと切望していた久保田*6は、「ヴィデオ彫刻」という新たな表現の担い手として、彫刻というジャンルのマチズモを、ヴィデオをもって解体できると考えたのではないか。こう考えた時、やはりあの《ヴィデオ・ポエム》を想起せずにはおれない。曰く「ヴィデオはヴァギナの復讐／ヴィデオはヴァギナの勝利」と*7。

ただし久保田は、木材を削り粘土をこねるような古典的な意味での彫刻の仕事への関心は薄かった。自ら設計はするが、実際に素材と格闘するのはアシスタントの仕事であった*8。このことから、久保田が「彫刻」に執着したのは彫塑の作業ではなく、空間を占める物体としてヴィデオに形を与えることであったと言える。代表作の多くを手伝ったアシスタントのアル・ロビンスを久保田が評価したのも、木材を使った作品の仕上げの美しさによってであった。とりわけ1970年代に手掛けた「デュシャンピアナ」シリーズや《三つの山》〔本書78–81頁〕では、テレビモニターはその縁部分がすべて木材で覆われて見えず、画面だけが露出している。このため作品の見え掛かりはすっきりしていて、ヴィデオ映像を見せつつも「彫刻」としての造形性を保つことに成功している。久保田は晩年に著した『私の愛、ナムジュン・パイク』の中で、パイクに以下のように提案したと言う。「ビデオを使ってオブジェを作ってみなさいよ。そうすれば美術館にも収集されるし」*9。いつ頃の発言だったのか著書の中では明らかにならないが、久保田の彫刻指向にこうした意図があったのは事実だろう。

ヴィデオという点で新しく、しかし彫刻というクラシックな「ヴィデオ彫刻」を提示したということに加えて重要なのが、久保田がそこにマルセル・デュシャンをかけ合わせたということである。ネオ・ダダやフルクサス、ポップ・アートに直結していたアメリカでのデュシャンの受容は、死後（1968年）に遺作が公開されたことで大きく変化し、芸術の成立基盤を問うのにますます不可欠な存在となっていた*10。造形的な部分でのアプロプリエーションや、ヴィデオの素材として本人の姿を用いるなど、いくつかのアプローチを（時には複合して）デュシャンを召喚したことで、ヴィデオを用いた彫刻というメディウム論とは別の批評性が明らかとなり、作品が受容される文脈を広げたと言える。その意味でやはり《階段》は久保田の出世作と言えるだろう。ヴィデオ・アートを専門とするキュレーターのバーバラ・ロンドンによってニューヨーク近代美術館初のヴィデオ・インスタレーションとして1981年にコレクションに加わった本作は、デュシャンの《階段を降りる裸体》（1912年）をモチーフとし、階段状の彫刻の中に埋め込まれたヴィデオ画面に、階段を降りる裸の女性が映し出されるというストレートな表現ながら、キュビスム以後の芸術の諸問題を内包する。本作の収蔵は1981年だが、1978年には同美術館の「Projects」にて展示を行なっており、その前年の1977年には、Manfred Schneckenburgerのキュレーションにより、ドクメンタ史上初めてフィルムやヴィデオを用いた表現が大規模に紹介された歴史的な舞台で、ビル・ヴィオラ、ナムジュン・パイク、ブルース・ナウマンらのヴィデオ・インスタレーションと共に展覧される機会を得ている*11。

その後、久保田は自然をテーマにしたより普遍的なモチーフへと仕事を展開させた。実際に流れる水や回転の仕掛けなどを取り入れ、よりスケールの大きな作品に挑戦していく。夫のパイクがドイツと縁が深かったことや、また1979年には自らもDAADのフェローシップを得たことから、ベルリンやデュッセルドルフにはたびたび滞在するだけでなく作品発表の機会も増えた。1981年からはドイツとスイスでまとまった規模の個展を開催し、アメリカより先にドイツ語圏で英語とのバイリンガル・カタログを出版した*12。

1980年代には、その始まりから約20年あまりのヴィデオ・アートを振り返るグループ展が多々企画されたが、「The Luminous Image」(Stedelijk Museum、アムステルダム、1984年)、「Video: A Retrospective, Long Beach Museum of Art 1974–1984」(Long Beach Museum、カリフォルニア、1984年)、「Video Skulptur: retrospectiv und aktuell 1963–1989」(Kölnischer Kunstverein、ケルン、1989)など、今日ヴィデオ・アートの歴史を語るに欠かせない展覧会に作品を出品し、「ヴィデオ彫刻」を確実に歴史に刻んでいる。

こうした舞台への後押しをしたのは、1971年にEverson Museum of Art in Syracuseで初めてヴィデオ・アート・シリーズを立ち上げたDavid A. Rossや、1974年からWhitney Museum of American Artのフィルム&ヴィデオ・キュレーターとなったJohn G. Hanhardt、前述のバーバラ・ロンドンなど、1970年代前半から親交のあったヴィデオ・アートを専門とするキュレーターたちであった。とりわけハンハートは、1979年に久保田と飯村隆彦の2人展を手掛けた後、キュレーターのひとりを務めた1983年のホイットニー・バイアニュアルにはドイツで制作した大作《河》[本書84、93–95頁]を出品し、『Art in America』の表紙となりインパクトを与えるものであった*13。久保田が生前に美術館で開催した最後の個展も、ホイットニー美術館でのハンハートのキュレーションによるものである*14。この頃、すなわち1990年代、映像を用いた表現は一般化し、プロジェクターで見せる作品や、より複合的なヴィデオ・インスタレーションといった作品発表も珍しいものではなくなった。久保田はこの展覧会で小さな液晶モニターを採用して彫刻に埋め込み、さらに彫刻の表面にプロジェクターで映像を投影したり、また複数の作品を組み合わせて展示することで、空間全体を作品化するような試みを行なっている。

2

こうして久保田が最初にヴィデオに触れてから20年以上がたち、現代美術にまつわる状況は大きく変化した。ビエンナーレなどの大規模な国際展が多数開催され、とりわけ1990年代前半には久保田はそうした展覧会に頻繁に招待された。1991年にはアメリカン・ミュージアム・オブ・ムーヴィング・イメージでまとまった規模の個展を開催し、ヴィデオ彫刻の代表作が一堂に介した。本展は日本およびヨーロッパに巡回、その評価を決定づけたと言ってもよいだろう*15。しかし久保田のキャリアには1996年でブレーキがかかる。同年、夫のパイクが病に倒れ、彼を献身的に支える人生を選択したからだ。以後、作品発表の機会は激減し、2006年にパイクが他界した後には自身も病を得、最後に新作を発表したのは2007年だった。晩年の仕事については紙幅の関係で本稿では対象としないが、1990年代以後の久保田の受容について、その作品の構造を踏まえて記しておきたい。代表的な作例を中心に据える理由は、現在に至るまで、グループ展で展示される作品の多くが《階段》《車輪》など1980年代以前の代表作だからである*16。

久保田の作品に埋め込まれた数分から数十分のヴィデオ素材の多くは、「始め」と「終わり」があるような直線的な提示を意図しておらず、「終わり」まで再生されたら自動的に「始め」に戻りまた繰り返す、循環構造となる*17。筆者がわざわざ声高に言うまでもないが、無論これは久保田の作品に限ったことではなく、多くのヴィデオ・インスタレーションに通じる構造である。しかし久保田の作品に特徴的なのは、このループ再生に加えて、ヴィデオを内包する彫刻自体の形式にも、循環してもとに戻る構造を意識的に取り入れているという点である。

典型的な作例として《自転車の車輪》[本書98–100頁]を挙げよう。久保田は1977年の時点で回転する車輪を大きく描いたドローイングを何枚も描いており、この主題が彼女にとって長らく重要なものであったことがわかる。当時久保田は、マルセル・デュシャンの作品を流用したシリーズ「デュシャンピアナ」を手がけており、デュシャンの《自転車の車輪》(1913/64年)のヴィデオを用いた流用というのがこの作品の基本的なコンセプトである。が、ここで注目したいのは作品の運動だ。スポーク部分に液晶テレビが取り付けられた自転車の車輪は、モーターによってゆっくりと回転し続ける。鑑賞者は、自転車を回転させるモーターの音を聞きながら、回転する車輪に取り付けられた液晶モニターを目で追うことになる。小さなモニターに映し出されるのは、ハイコントラストに加工された人工的な自然の風景である。植物が揺れる映像が回転していくのをただ見つめる体験は、奇妙に観想的だ。

《自転車の車輪》のみならず、久保田の彫刻作品には円環構造や回転運動、さらに踏み込んで言えば、無限に続く反復構造が特徴的である。1975年に発表したヴィデオ・インスタレーション《マルセル・デュシャンの墓》は、天井と床に鏡を配することで、壁に積み上げられたテレビ・モニターが無限にループするような構造を理想とした（実際は展示空間の制限上、モニターに向かった鑑賞者の背後にまで鏡を設置することは難しかった）。以後、鏡は久保田の気に入りの手段であり、テレビモニターを増幅させる道具として《三つの山》、《ヴィデオ俳句―ぶらさがり作品》［本書96–97頁］、《河》、《ナイアガラの滝》［本書104–107頁］などに効果的に用いられている。

鏡と同時に水も重要な役割を果たす。《河》ではぶら下げられたテレビ・モニターがいわばプロジェクターのように水面に映像を映し、水面がモニターの役割を果たす。モーターが作り出す水の動きが、水音と共に映像を揺らす作品である。《ナイアガラの滝》では滝のように落水し続けるシャワーの水がやはりテレビ・モニターの発光を受けて光り、また水槽部分に溜まった水が立ち上がる彫刻の姿を揺れながら映している。いずれも、水は止むことなく流れ、水槽から吸い上げられてはまた滝となって落水し、映像を反復するという循環を続けている。

《自動車の車輪》［本書118–119頁］はタイヤの中央にモニターを嵌め込んで回転をする作品で、風車の羽を模した作品その名も《風車（かざぐるま）》［本書128–129頁］も同様に、モニターを嵌め込んだ壁付けの羽根が回転する構造である。《アダムとイヴ》［本書112–115頁］、《スケート選手》［本書120–121頁］は、人物彫刻自体がステージの上でダンスを踊るかのように回転を続ける。《ヴィデオ俳句―ぶらさがり作品》は、回ることこそないものの、吊り下げられた丸いモニターは終わることのない振り子運動を行なう。多くの作品にはループする映像が複数埋め込まれ、彫刻といういわば堅牢な表現に、終わりなき運動を内包させている。

このように、久保田の作品には「回る」構造、回転運動、反復運動、それがもたらす独特の感覚がある。動物が動いているものに目を奪われるがごとく、鑑賞者は半ば自動的にモニターの光を追い、動きを追い、終わることなく水の流れる音を聞き続ける。それらは初めに戻ってまた繰り返し、終わらない時間の只中にいるような、思考停止して感覚が文字どおり宙づりにされたような、観想的でもあり、瞑想的でもあるような感覚だ。

これを確認したうえで、久保田自身が記した《自転車の車輪》についての記述の一部に注目したい。「…デュシャンをほのめかしているのに加え、《自転車の車輪》は、田舎で過ごした私の子ども時代の懐かしい記憶を運んでいる。輪は円の別名だ……始まりも終わりもなく、どんな秩序の感覚もなく、ひたすら動き続ける円。また、輪は禅では肯定的な言葉で、煩悩に捉われず、憂いのない透明な人柄を示唆する」*[18]。久保田は自転車の車輪を回転し続ける円と読み替え、それを禅の哲学に接続して、作品解釈に自ら仏教の思想を導入している*[19]。

父方の実家が仏寺であり、少女時代まで仏教にまつわる文化に親しんだことは、久保田が自らの身の上話をする際に必ず言及する事柄である。他の作品に添えたテキストのなかでも、たとえば誰かの死、既に他界した人について仏教に絡めて語っているし、先に触れた「河」も仏教において重要な要素であると記している*[20]。久保田の生い立ち背景を抜きにして《自転車の車輪》に向かい合った時、ただちに仏教や禅を導き出すのはやや唐突な印象があったとしても、作家自身がこのように私たちの耳元で囁くことで、作品はどこか東洋的な色彩を帯びて見えてきたとしても不思議ではない。渡米以後、久保田が新作を発表する舞台は常にアメリカやドイツであったことを思い出しておきたい。そうした前提において、ヴィデオを用いた彫刻やインスタレーションという（とりわけ1970–80年代）当時新しい芸術に、東洋の文脈を重ねることでより強調されるどこか瞑想的な様相は、久保田の作品の大きな魅力であったことは間違いないと言えるだろう。先に触れたデュシャンをモチーフとした一連の作品の後、久保田は時折作品タイトルに「俳句」「枯山水」「桜」といった言葉も織り交ぜた。

1993年のヴェネチア・ビエンナーレに久保田が招聘されたのはまさに、「Passagio dal Oriente（東方への道）」と題されたヴェネチア・パヴィリオンであった。展示記録写真を見るかぎり展示は混沌とし、与えられたスペースに代表作と新作を詰め込んだかのような印象である［本書130頁上］。欧米のキュレーターたちがそれ以外の地域の作家を国際展で積極的に紹介し始めた1990年代にあって、作家としてのキャリアは日本国外のほうがとうに長くなった久保田が、ヴィデオ・アートの文脈を離れて、マルチカルチュラリズムの文脈でグループ展に配されたのは興味深い。この展示を企画したアキレ・ボニート・オリヴァは、1980年代から90年代にイタリアのみならず世界的に活躍した重要なキュレーターのひとりであることは言うまでもないが、翌1994年にムディマ財団が発行した久保田のカタログに寄せた文章では、西洋の物質社会と東洋の精神性を二元的に語り、それを解決する存在として久保田を称揚している。さらに1995年には、ヴェネチア・ビエンナーレと同時にパラッツォで開催された「Asiana」にも久保田は招聘された。これは、韓国・中国・日本のキュレーターが協働し、東アジア出身の作家を紹介する展覧会であった。1996年の光州ビエンナーレではパイクが企画を担当した主に東アジア圏のヴィデオ・アートを紹介した「INFO ART」に参加もしている。また振り返ってみればバーバラ・ロンドンも、1981年にドイツで発行された久保田の個展カタログに寄せた文章でこのように述べていた。「久保田成子は西洋化した世界における物理的な諸現実に対して東洋哲学的にアプローチしている（Shigeko Kubota has an Eastern philosophical approach to the physical realities of a Westernized world）」*21。

3

以上を踏まえるなら、久保田はヴィデオ・アートの担い手であると同時に、あるいはそれ以前に、日本という母国を離れて欧米のアートワールドに身を置いたひとりの女性であったということがあらためて印象付けられる。ヴィデオ・アーティストとして久保田よりもさらにグローバルに活躍した夫パイクへの敬愛、そして時には嫉妬や悔しさを糧に、自らの作品世界を確立しようともがいてきた。これまでのアートとフェミニズムの議論において頻繁に召喚されてきた《ヴァギナ・ペインティング》［本書24–25頁］のセンセーショナルな記録写真はあまりに有名である。ただし、渡米翌年、フルクサスに身を投じる中で行なったこのパフォーマンスは、ジョージ・マチューナスやパイクに依頼されて実行したにすぎないという久保田自身による晩年の発言もあり、その真偽が定かでないことは強調しておこう*22。1960年代から1990年代まで、現代美術のフロンティアにい続けた女性作家女性作家として検証された展覧会に「The First Generation Women and Video, 1970–75」（Independent Curators Incorporated, New Yorkによる巡回展、1993–95年）、「前衛の女性1950–1975」（栃木県立美術館、2005年）などがあるが、近年はアーカイブ資料の調査や周辺作家へのヒアリングなどが進み、1970年代前半に久保田が行なった女性作家たちとの協働についての研究も発表されている*24。

ヴィデオという新たな手段を「ヴィデオ彫刻」として我が物にし、歴史を踏まえつつ新規性を取り混ぜ、さらには自らのアイデンティティと重ね合わせて作品を提示してみせた久保田成子。渡米前を含めた久保田の仕事を本展の規模で展覧するのは日本初であり、中には20年以上の時を経て息を吹き返す作品もある。再生機もモニターも更新されたヴィデオ彫刻を、私たちは今日の環境でどのように受け止め、またいかなる歴史の中へと送り返すことが可能なのか。本稿で概観した作家・作品受容が大いに更新されることを期待している。

（はしもと・あずさ＝国立国際美術館主任研究員）

［註］

*1——Nancy Grove, “Shigeko Kubota at René Block,” *Arts Magazine*, 50, 8 (Apr. 1976), p. 18.

*2——*Shigeko Kubota: Video Sculpture* (New York: American Museum of Moving Image, 1991), p. 46. このカタログに掲載さ

れた久保田のテキストは、本カタログにも掲載されている。日本語訳は近藤学による。

＊3——Ibid.

＊4——Ibid.

＊5——ただし、シングルチャンネル・ヴィデオ作品は断続的に発表を続けた。久保田にとってシングルチャンネル作品は、より日記的、文学的な実践として、ヴィデオ彫刻とはまた別のフェーズにあるものだった。継続的に制作したシリーズ「ブロークン・ダイアリー」のうち、所在不明となっていた《Berlin Diary》（1970–80年）、《Video Curator Diary》（1974–82年）、《Shigeko in Chicago》（1981年）が発見された。2021年1月時点では公開されておらず、公開が待たれる。

＊6——久保田成子オーラル・ヒストリー、手塚美和子によるインタヴュー、2009年10月11日、日本美術オーラル・ヒストリー・アーカイヴ、URL（http://www.oralarthistory.org/archives/kubota_shigeko/interview_01.php）

＊7——《ヴィデオ・ポエム》は、1974年にニューヨーク近代美術館で開催されたヴィデオ・アート関連のシンポジウムで久保田が読み上げたこともあった（Shigeko Kubota, "Women's Video in the U.S. and Japan," In Douglas Davis and Allison Simmons, eds. *The New Television: A Public/Private Art* (Cambridge, Mass.: The MIT Press, 1977), pp. 97.）。久保田とフェミニズムについては本稿にて後述。また、久保田の作品を彫刻の文脈で評価した企画として「彫刻の遠心力　この十年の展開」（1992年、国立国際美術館）がある。

＊8——アル・ロビンスの追悼として《アダムとイヴ》を制作し、その思い出を以下に綴っている。Op cit., *Shigeko Kubota: Video Sculpture*, pp. 66–68. 木材の加工に長けたアシスタント、アル・ロビンスの没後、ヴィデオ彫刻のいわば彫刻部分は大きく変わった。1990年代以後は金属を用いた造形が多用される。これも久保田自身ではなくアシスタントによるものだった。

＊9——久保田成子・南禎鎬、高晟埈訳『私の愛、ナムジュン・パイク』平凡社、2013年、148頁。

＊10——戦後アメリカのマルセル・デュシャン受容については以下を参照。平芳幸浩『マルセル・デュシャンとアメリカ　戦後アメリカ美術の進展とデュシャン受容の変遷』ナカニシヤ出版、2016年。

＊11——同キュレーターはドクメンタ8にも久保田を招待し、代表作《ナイアガラ》とシングルチャンネル・ヴィデオ作品《ブロークン・ダイアリー：ソーホー・ソープ／雨の被害》の出品を果たした。

＊12——展覧会情報は以下。*Shigeko Kubota Video Sculptures*, daadgalerie, Berlin, 1981, Museum Folkwang, Essen, 1982, Kunsthaus Zürich, 1982. カタログはShigeko Kubota Video Sculptures (Berlin: daadgalerie; Essen: Museum Folkwang; Kunsthaus Zürich, 1981).

＊13——*Art in America*, 1984 February, cover.

＊14——Shigeko Kubota (Whitney Museum of American Art, June 29–August 25, 1996)

＊15——*Shigeko Kubota Video Sculpture* (American Museum of Moving Image, 1991). 詳細は本書の年表を参照。

＊16——《デュシャンピアナ：自転車の車輪》の最初の制作は1983年。まだ小型の液晶モニターが発売されておらず、テレビモニターが重いため、車輪を回転させるのが難しかった。

＊17——ただし1970年代は自動再生が叶わず、都度手動で巻き戻し再生が必要だった。

＊18——*Shigeko Kubota: Video Sculpture* (New York: American Museum of Moving Image, 1991), p. 49.

＊19——紙幅の関係で深く立ち入らないが、久保田は1981年に初めて個展のカタログを発行した時から、掲載された主要な作品図版にテキストを添えている。これについては、別の考察の機会が必要となるだろう。

＊20——*Shigeko Kubota: Video Sculpture* (New York: American Museum of Moving Image, 1991), p. 21.

＊21——日本語は拙訳。*Shigeko Kubota Video Sculptures* (Berlin: daadgalerie; Essen: Museum Folkwang; Kunsthaus Zürich, 1981) p. 11.

＊22——前出オーラル・ヒストリー「『やれ』って言われたの。私やりたくなかったの、ほんとは」。前出『私の愛、ナムジュン・パイク』、97–100頁。

＊23——本書の年譜を参照。

＊24——本書、由本みどり氏の論考の他、以下も参照されたい。Melinda Barlow, "Red, White, Yellow, and Black: Women, Multiculturalism, and Video History," *Quarterly Review of Film and Video*, 17, 4 (2000), pp. 297–312.

Shigeko Kubota and the Cyclical

Azusa Hashimoto

0.

In 1964, Shigeko Kubota moved from Japan to New York City, where she became involved with the Fluxus group and presented works including performances incorporating video. She exhibited her first three-dimensional work utilizing video in 1975. Two years later she participated in a major international exhibition, and she remained a significant presence on the Western art scene especially from the 1980s until the mid-1990s. This essay will discuss the reception of Kubota's work in two stages: first tracing her career up until the mid-1970s when she gained international acclaim, and then examining the structure of her work on a more conceptual basis before outlining its reception from the 1990s until the present day.

1.

Throughout the 1960s and 1970s, experimental art involving video concurrently developed along various paths, particularly in Germany, the United States, Japan and other countries where video equipment was available. In this context, Kubota, who produced three-dimensional works using video, adopted "video sculpture" rather than "video installation" as an appropriate term for her work. This term is connected to the German-born René Block, then a gallerist and curator, who since the 1980s has organized numerous exhibitions primarily in Europe. Block began his career in Germany in the 1960s and went on to work with the Fluxus artists, Joseph Beuys, Nam June Paik and others to present avant-garde art in Berlin and New York. Block, who ran a gallery in New York's SoHo district between 1974 and 1977, came to know Kubota through her husband Nam June Paik.

A mailed announcement of Kubota's first solo exhibition at René Block Gallery, in 1976, reads "Shigeko Kubota: 3 Video Installations." Two of these, *Marcel Duchamp's Grave* [cat. pp. 54–55] and *Video Poem* [cat. pp. 38–39], had been presented in her first solo show at The Kitchen the year before, and to these was added the new work *Nude Descending a Staircase* (referred to below as *Staircase*), [cat. pp. 60–62] with the series collectively titled *Duchampiana*. The term "video sculpture" was not yet used in gallery press releases and reviews in the press at this time, with the exception of *Arts Magazine*, which noted that "Her three pieces are a kind of video-sculpture."*[1] Kubota later recalled that when Block organized her solo exhibition in 1976 he gave it the title *Duchampiana: Video Sculpture*, but strictly speaking, the term "video sculpture" subsequently came into use as a result of Block's consideration of how the title should be translated into German.*[2] Kubota's *Staircase* was also shown in the 1976 exhibition *New York-Downtown Manhattan: SoHo-Berlin Festival* (Academie der Kunste, Berlin), curated by Block. According to Kubota's recollections cited above, when translating the English term "video installation" into German, Block wanted to avoid using the word "Installation," which in German primarily refers to plumbing work and thus has negative connotations, and thus described Kubota's art as "video sculpture." We can infer that this was connected with the abovementioned Berlin exhibition.*[3] The following year, in 1977, a mailed announcement of Kubota's solo exhibition at René Block Gallery in New York read "Meta-Marcel by Shigeko Kubota/3 Video Sculptures." Kubota evidently liked the term, and later wrote: "I assembled this video sculpture with the help of Al Robbins. It's a self-contained piece, and it wasn't like the works many people were producing at the time that incorporated video equipment in sloppy ways. It was an elaborately constructed work of art, worthy of being called 'sculpture' in the tradition of Rodin and Michelangelo."*[4]

As an artist with ties to Fluxus, she embraced an interdisciplinary practice, staging video performances in the early 1970s, and from 1974 onward working weekends as video curator at Anthology Film Archives, where she was involved in planning works by video artists who were her contemporaries, and developed the Video Program. It is interesting that being thus immersed in new modes of expression that transcended traditional ideas of art mediums such as painting and sculpture, Kubota chose to position her practice in the classic genre of sculpture.*5 Despite having studied sculpture at the Tokyo University of Education (predecessor of the University of Tsukuba) and presenting new experiential pieces incorporating sculpture at Naiqua Gallery, the response from critics was indifferent, and this was the starting point of Kubota's career as an artist. It seems that she was determined to make her name as a "female sculptor"*6 and believed she could employ video to undermine the machismo of the sculpture medium. Thinking along these lines, one cannot help but be reminded of a line from her *Video Poem*: "Video is Vengeance and Victory of Vagina."*7

That being said, Kubota had little interest in sculptural processes in the classical sense, such as carving wood or shaping clay. While she executed designs by herself, physically grappling with the materials was the job of her assistants.*8 This indicates that Kubota's fixation on "sculpture" related not to the work of sculpting per se, but to giving physical form to her video pieces as objects that occupy space. Because of the beautiful finish of his woodwork, Kubota thought very highly of Al Robbins, the assistant who helped produce many of her best-known works. Especially in works from the 1970s—the *Duchampiana* series and *Three Mountains* [cat. pp. 78–81] —wood conceals the edges of TV monitors, exposing only the screen. This gives the works a crisp, clean look, and they successfully maintain the formal clarity of sculpture while also employing video. In *My Love, Nam June Paik*, which she wrote late in life, Kubota states that she suggested to Paik: "Why don't you try using video, but incorporating it into objects? Then you can have your work acquired by museums."*9 The book does not specify when this was said, but it is certainly true that the same intent underlay Kubota's own orientation toward sculpture.

In addition to her "video sculpture," new in terms of video but classical in terms of sculpture, it is important to note Kubota's incorporation of Marcel Duchamp. Duchamp's reception in the United States, which was directly linked to Neo-Dada, Fluxus, and Pop Art, changed drastically with the posthumous exhibition of work following his death in 1968, and he became increasingly essential to questioning of the basic foundations of art.*10 Her invocation of Duchamp through several approaches (sometimes combined), such as appropriation of figurative elements and use of his images in her videos, clarified critical aspects separate from the mediumistic exploration of sculpture utilizing video, and evidently broadened the scope of her work's reception. The Museum of Modern Art, New York's first video installation acquisition in 1981, handled by Barbara London, a curator specializing in video art, was Kubota's work appropriating the motif of Duchamp's *Nude Descending a Staircase* (1912). Video screens embedded in the sculpture, which takes the form of stairs, straightforwardly present a female nude descending a staircase, while also conveying implications for various issues relating to modern art since Cubism. The work was acquired in 1981, but it had been shown as part of MoMA's *Projects* series in 1978, and the year before it was part of the historic first large-scale showcasing of film and video art at Documenta (1977), curated by Manfred Schneckenburger, exhibited along with video installations by Bill Viola, Nam June Paik, Bruce Nauman and others.*11

Kubota subsequently expanded her practice to deal with more universal motifs, focusing on themes from nature. She incorporated actual flowing water and rotating mechanisms, and began working at a larger scale. Due to her husband Paik's close ties to Germany and her own DAAD fellowship in 1979, she not only spent much time in Berlin and Düsseldorf, but also began exhibiting more frequently in the region. Starting in 1981, she had large-scale solo exhibitions in Germany and Switzerland, and a bilingual (German and English) exhibition catalogue was published in these German-speaking countries before anything comparable appeared in the US.*12

In the 1980s there were many group shows that looked back on the development of video art in the 20-plus years since its emergence. Kubota's work was included in several exhibitions indispensable to discussions of the history of video art, including *The Luminous Image* (Stedelijk Museum Amsterdam, 1984), *Video: A Retrospective: Long Beach Museum of Art, 1974–1984* (Long Beach Museum of Art, California, 1984), and *Video Skulptur: retrospectiv und aktuell 1963–1989* (Kolnischer Kunstverein, Cologne, 1989), ensuring that her "video sculpture" made an indelible mark on this history.

This was thanks in large part to curators specializing in video art with whom Kubota had ties since the early 1970s, such as David A. Ross, who she became friendly with around the time he launched the first video art series at the Everson Museum of Art in Syracuse in 1971, and John G. Hanhardt, who became a film and video curator at the Whitney Museum of American Art in 1974, as well as the above-mentioned Barbara London. Notably, Hanhardt curated a two-person exhibition of Kubota and Iimura Takahiko in 1979, and subsequently included her large-scale work *River* [cat. pp. 84, 93–95], produced in Germany, in the 1983 Whitney Biennial, where he was on the curatorial team. This was featured on the cover of *Art in America* and made a significant impact.*13 Hanhardt also curated Kubota's last solo museum show during her lifetime.*14 Around this time, in the 1990s, video art had become commonplace, and showing films with projectors or staging more complex video installations was not at all unusual. In this exhibition, Kubota embedded small LCD monitors in sculptures, and also projected films on the sculptures' surfaces, or combined multiple pieces, with the effect of transforming the entire space into a single work.

2.

More than 20 years after since Kubota began working with video, the contemporary art scene had changed dramatically. Biennials and other large-scale international exhibitions had proliferated, and Kubota was frequently invited to participate in them, especially in the early 1990s. In 1991 she had a solo exhibition of substantial size at American Museum of Moving Image, and presented all her best-known works of video sculpture at once. The exhibition traveled to Japan and Europe, and can be said to have cemented her reputation.*15 However, Kubota's career was brought to a halt in 1996 when her husband Paik fell ill and she chose to dedicate herself selflessly to being his primary caregiver. Opportunities to exhibit drastically dwindled, and after Paik's death in 2006 she too fell ill, showing new work for the last time in 2007. This essay will not discuss her late works due to space constraints, but instead let us examine how Kubota has been recognized since the 1990s, after touching on the structure of some of her works. Here the examples given are primarily her best-known pieces, because in recent years and to this day, most of the works shown in group exhibitions are well-known ones from the 1980s and earlier, such as *Staircase* and *Bicycle Wheel.**16

Many of the videos embedded in Kubota's sculptures, ranging in length from several minutes to tens of minutes, are not intended to be shown linearly with a "beginning" and an "end" but rather cyclically, automatically starting again when they reach the end.*17 There is no need to underscore the fact that this description is obviously not limited to Kubota, and indeed applies to the majority of video installations. However, what characterizes Kubota's work is that in addition to looping playback, the sculptures containing the videos are also deliberately given cyclically structured forms, circulating back to their beginnings.

A classic example is *Bicycle Wheel* [cat. pp. 98–100]. By 1977, Kubota had already produced numerous drawings featuring large rotating wheels, indicating that the subject had long been important to her. At that time Kubota was working on the series *Duchampiana*, an homage that appropriated the work of Marcel Duchamp, and the basic concept of this work was also appropriation, recreating his *Bicycle Wheel* (1913/1964) with video introduced. However, let us turn our attention to the movement of the work. A bicycle wheel with an LCD TV attached to its spokes slowly and continuously rotates, powered by a motor. The viewer's eyes follow the LCD display attached to the rotating wheel while listening to the sound of the motor that rotates the wheel. On the small monitor is footage of artificial-looking natural scenery, processed to heighten the contrast. The experience of simply gazing at the spinning video of swaying plants is strangely contemplative.

Other sculptural works besides *Bicycle Wheel* are also characterized by circular forms, rotational movement, and, on a somewhat deeper level, infinitely repeating structures. Her video installation *Marcel Duchamp's Grave*, first exhibited in 1975, was under ideal circumstances to be structured so that mirrors on the ceiling and floor would reflect TV monitors stacked against the opposite wall from floor to ceiling, thus forming an infinite loop (in practice, the limitations of the venue meant that it was not feasible to place mirrors behind the viewer as he or she faced the monitors.) From then on, mirrors were among Kubota's preferred devices, and were put to dramatic use as a means of amplifying TV monitors in *Three Mountains*, *Video Haiku – Hanging Piece* [cat. pp. 96–97], *River*, *Niagara Falls* [cat. pp. 104–107] and other works.

In addition to mirrors, water plays an important role. In *River*, suspended TV monitors act like projectors, sending video to a receiving surface, the rippling water, that plays the role of a screen. A motor agitates the water, creating rippling water sounds and causing the projected image to vibrate. In *Niagara Falls*, water from a shower continuously falls like a waterfall, glowing with reflected light emitted by a TV screen as in *River*. The water falls into and accumulates in a tank, where it vibrates the entire sculpture. In both cases water flows without stopping, and the water in the tank is sucked up and falls like a waterfall once again, while reflecting and repeating the video in an overall cycle.

Auto-Tire Wheel [cat. pp. 118–119] is a piece in which a monitor is embedded in the center of the tire and endlessly rotates, while the wall-mounted *Windmill* [cat. pp. 128–129] has a similar structure, except with fan-like blades on the wheel. *Adam and Eve* [cat. pp. 112–115] and *Skater* [cat. pp. 120–121] create an effect like a human sculpture dancing on stage, as a figure continuously turns in circles. *Video Haiku* does not involve rotation, but a suspended circular monitor swings back and forth endlessly like a pendulum, which the viewer gazes at as if hypnotized. Many works incorporate multiple looped videos, introducing never-ending movement into the generally solid and stable medium of sculpture.

As these examples illustrate, Kubota's work is characterized by rotating structures, rotational movement, repetitive motion, and the unique sensations these produce. The viewer semi-automatically follows the light from the screens, follows the movement, and hears the ceaseless sound of flowing water, like an animal fascinated by a moving object. Like being in the midst of a never-ending time loop, the effect is both contemplative and meditative, as if thought had ceased and the senses were literally suspended.

In light of the above, note the following quote from a text that Kubota wrote about *Bicycle Wheel*: " . . . In addition to evoking Duchamp, this *Bicycle Wheel* also carries nostalgic memories of my childhood in the countryside. A wheel is a circle by another name . . . A circle that has no beginning or end, no sense of order, only ceaseless motion. In Zen, the circle has positive implications, suggesting a transparent personality unburdened by distress."*[18] Kubota reinterprets the bicycle wheel as an endlessly spinning circle, connects it to Zen philosophy, and introduces Buddhist concepts into the interpretation of the work.*[19]

When speaking about herself, Kubota never failed to mention the fact that she was born into a Buddhist temple family, on her father's side, and throughout childhood was steeped in the culture of Buddhism. In texts accompanying other works, she wrote at times of a person's death, or of someone who has already gone, in Buddhist terms, and wrote that the theme of the river mentioned earlier is also an important one in Buddhism.*[20] While it may be a bit of a stretch to say that *Bicycle Wheel* immediately evokes Buddhism or Zen unless the viewer is aware of Kubota's upbringing and background, the artist herself frequently hinted at these implications, and it is not surprising that the works should take on a somehow East Asian atmosphere. We should keep in mind that after moving to the US, Kubota always exhibited new works first in that country or in Germany. Under these circumstances, it is certain that a significant part of her art's appeal was its somehow meditative aspect, emphasized by its East Asian contextualization of the then-novel media of video sculpture and video installation (especially during the 1970s and 1980s). Following the series of works with Duchampian themes discussed above, Kubota from time to time included words such as "haiku," "rock garden," and "cherry blossoms" in her titles.

When Kubota was invited to show at the Venice Biennale in 1993, it was in the Venetian Pavilion show entitled *Passagio dal Oriente* (Passage to the Orient). Judging by photographs documenting the exhibition, it was a chaotic one, and it appears that she packed her allotted space with both well-known past works and new pieces [cat. p. 130, top]. It is interesting that in the 1990s, when Western curators had begun proactively featuring work by non-Western artists in international exhibitions, Kubota—who had been active far longer in the West than in Japan—was included in a group show in the context of multiculturalism rather than that of video art. Achille Bonito Oliva, who organized this exhibition, is widely known as an important curator active not only in Italy but also worldwide in the 1980s and 1990s, and in 1993, the year after the Biennale, he contributed a text to a catalogue of Kubota's work published by the Fondazione Mudima in which he praised her as an artist who dealt with the duality of Western materialist society and Eastern spirituality in a way that reconciled and resolved their conflicts. In 1995, Kubota was invited to show work in *Asiana*, held at a Venetian palazzo concurrently with the Venice Biennale. This was an exhibition featuring artists from East Asia, produced in collaboration with curators from South Korea, China, and Japan. At the 1996 Gwangju Biennale she participated in *INFO ART*, primarily organized by Paik, which showcased video art primarily from East Asia. And looking back further in the past, Barbara London noted in a statement for Kubota's solo exhibition catalogue published in Germany in 1981: "Shigeko Kubota has an Eastern philosophical approach to the physical realities of a Westernized world."*[21]

3.

Based on all of the above, we are left with an image of Kubota both as a pioneering practitioner of video art, and as a woman who left her home country of Japan and made a place for herself in the Western art world. She strove and sometimes struggled to establish her own independent practice, and derived energy and frustration from working alongside her longtime collaborator and husband Paik, who achieved even greater success as a globally renowned video artist. The sensational photographs of *Vagina Painting* [cat. pp. 24–25], which have frequently come up in previous discussions of art and feminism, are certainly well known. However, it should be emphasized that the true story behind them is uncertain, in that Kubota herself said this performance, staged the year after her arrival in the US when she was involved with Fluxus, was done at the urging of George Maciunas and Paik.*[22] There have been exhibitions focusing on female artists at the forefront of contemporary art from the 1960s through the 1990s, including *The First Generation Women and Video, 1970–75* (traveling exhibition organized by Independent Curators Incorporated, New York, 1993–1995) and *Japanese Women Artists in Avant-Garde Movements 1950–1975* (Tochigi Prefectural Museum of Fine Arts, 2005), but in recent years there has also been progress in the study of archival materials and interviews with related artists, and research on Kubota's collaborations with female artists in the early 1970s has also been presented.*24

Shigeko Kubota made the new medium of video her own through the development of "video sculpture," introduced brash novelty while referencing history, and incorporated her own identity into the presentation of her art. The current exhibition of Kubota's work is the largest ever held in Japan, including when she lived here prior to departure for the US, and some pieces are being reactivated for the first time in more than 20 years. How do viewers engage with video sculpture in today's environment, with playback equipment and monitors having greatly advanced, and how do we place the works back into what historical context? I hope that recognition of the artist and her work, of which this essay has given an overview, will be greatly advanced by this exhibition.

(Curator, the National Museum of Art, Osaka)

Translation by Christopher Stephens

[Notes]

*1——Nancy Grove, "Shigeko Kubota at René Block," *Arts Magazine*, 50, 8 (Apr. 1976), p. 18.

*2——*Shigeko Kubota: Video Sculpture* (New York: American Museum of the Moving Image, 1991), p. 46. Kubota's text in the exhibition's catalogue is reprinted in the current catalogue, with Japanese translation by Gaku Kondo.

*3——Ibid.

*4——Ibid.

*5——However, she continued showing single-channel video pieces intermittently. For Kubota, the single-channel format was more of a diaristic and literary approach, and played a different role than that of her video sculpture. From her series *Broken Diary*, produced on an ongoing basis, *Berlin Diary*, *Video Curator Diary*, and *Shigeko in Chicago*—the whereabouts of which were unknown—have been discovered. As of January 2021 they have never been shown publicly, but there are high expectations for their screening.

*6——Shigeko Kubota oral history, interview by Miwako Tezuka, October 11, 2009, Oral History Archives of Japanese Art (http://www.oralarthistory.org/archives/kubota_shigeko/interview_01.php)

*7——One presentation of *Video Poem* was a recitation by Kubota during a video art symposium at MoMA in 1974 (Shigeko Kubota, "Women's Video in the US and Japan," in Douglas Davis and Allison Simmons, eds. *The New Television: A Public/Private Art* [Cambridge, Mass.: The MIT Press, 1977], p. 97.) Kubota's relation to feminism will be discussed later in this essay. Meanwhile, an example of an exhibition that interpreted Kubota's work in the context of sculpture is *The Centrifugal Force of Sculpture* (1992, The National Museum of Art, Osaka).

*8——Kubota produced *Adam and Eve* in memory of Al Robbins, and related memories of him in: op cit., *Shigeko Kubota: Video Sculpture*, pp. 66–68. The sculptural aspects of her video sculpture changed drastically after the death of Robbins, her assistant who was such a skilled woodworker. From the 1990s onward, she often utilized metal, which was also handled by an assistant, not by Kubota herself.

*9——Shigeko Kubota and Nam Jeong-ho, *My Love, Nam June Paik*, translated by Ko Seong-Jun, Heibonsha, 2013, p. 148.

*10——Regarding the reception of Marcel Duchamp in the postwar US, cf. Yukihiro Hirayoshi, *Marcel Duchamp and the United States: The Development of Post-WWII American Art and the Trajectory of Duchamp's Reception*, Nakanishiya Shuppan, 2016.

*11——The same curator also invited Kubota to exhibit her well-known work *Niagara Falls* and the single-channel video piece *Broken Diary: SoHo SoAp / Rain Damage*, both of which were featured in Documenta 8.

*12——Exhibition details are as follows. *Shigeko Kubota Video Sculptures*, daadgalerie (Berlin, 1982), Museum Folkwang (Essen, 1982), Kunsthaus Zürich, 1982). The catalogue is *Shigeko Kubota Video Sculptures* (Berlin: daadgalerie; Essen: Museum Folkwang; Kunsthaus Zürich, 1981).

*13——*Art in America*, 1984 February, cover.

*14——*Shigeko Kubota* (Whitney Museum of American Art, 1996).

*15——*Shigeko Kubota Video Sculpture* (American Museum of the Moving Image, 1991). The exhibition traveled, with changes to title and content, to the Hara Museum and the Stedelijk Museum Amsterdam (both 1992), Ford Astistico, Eisfabrik, Wiesser Raum, and Kusthalle in Kiel, Kiel (all Germany, 1993). The Stedelijk Museum Amsterdam exhibition was titled *Shigeko Kubota 1975–1992*.

*16——*Duchampiana: Bicycle Wheel* was first fabricated in 1983. As small LCD monitors were not yet on the market, and the TV monitor was heavy, it was difficult to make the wheel rotate.

*17——However, in the 1970s automatic playback was not yet possible, and it was necessary to rewind manually each time.

*18——*Shigeko Kubota: Video Sculpture* (New York: American Museum of the Moving Image, 1991), p. 49.

*19——It is not discussed in depth here due to space limitations, but Kubota wrote texts to accompany her major works exhibited from the time of first solo exhibition catalogue's publication in 1981. This requires further study on another occasion.

*20——*Shigeko Kubota: Video Sculpture* (New York: American Museum of the Moving Image, 1991), p. 21.

*21——*Shigeko Kubota Video Sculptures* (Berlin: daadgalerie; Essen: Museum Folkwang; Kunsthaus Zürich, 1981), p. 11.

*22——Op. cit. oral history. "They urged me, 'Do it.' It was something I didn't want to do, actually." Op. cit. *My Love, Nam June Paik*, pp. 97–100.

*23——Cf. chronology in this catalogue.

*24——In addition to the essay by Midori Yoshimoto in this catalogue, cf. Melinda Barlow, "Red, White, Yellow, and Black: Women, Multiculturalism, and Video History," *Quarterly Review of Film and Video*, 17, 4 (2000), pp. 297–312.

English Translations of Plates

pp. 8–9

1937-56
Niigata Years

Shigeko Kubota was born on August 2, 1937; the second daughter among four sisters, between junior high school teacher, Ryuen Kubota and music teacher, Fumie Kubota in Maki-machi, Nishi-kambara-gun (currently Maki-machi, Nishian Ward, Niigata City). She grew up in an artistic environment, and due to the influence of her grandfather, who was a Nanga-style painter, Shigeko took to painting at a young age. When she was a third grader, her painting was selected for an art competition of a magazine. In the fall of her high school sophomore year, her oil painting, *Sunflower*, entered the juried exhibition Nika-ten for the first time, and was featured in a local newspaper. (MH)

Captions:
Mainichi Shimbun, Niigata edition, October 8, 1954.
Sunflower, oil on canvas, 1954.

pp. 10–11

1956-64
Tokyo Years

After graduating from high school, Kubota decided to pursue the path of becoming an artist and entered Tokyo University of Education (currently Tsukuba University)—majoring in sculpture. She apprenticed to sculptor Kiyoshi Takahashi, also from Niigata, and submitted her works to the annual exhibitions of the Shinseisaku Society, of which Takahashi was a member. The photographs of her submitted works show the transition in which her sculptural heads gradually became more abstracted.

After graduating from university, she became a middle school art teacher in 1960 and her aunt, Chiya Kuni, opened her dance studio to artists. Soon young avant-garde artists, including members of Group Ongaku, started to gather there and Kubota befriended them. In 1963, she entered her works in *the 15th Yomiuri Independent Exhibition* for the first time. These abstract pieces utilized pre-existing cylinders and welded thin metal poles, marking a notable turn from her earlier sculptures shown at *Shinseisaku* exhibitions. Kubota quickly gravitated toward the avant-garde around this time. (MH)

Captions (from left):
Kubota with her aunt, Chiya Kuni, 1956.
Kubota sculpting *Shiseki (Death Stone) T*, c. 1962.
Top: Kubota welding her sculpture, c. 1963.
Bottom: Installation view of Kubota's work at the 15th Yomiuri Independent Exhibition, 1963.

pp. 12–13

1963
Solo Show at Naiqua Gallery

At her solo show, *1st. LOVE, 2nd. LOVE..., Shigeko Kubota Sculpture Exhibition*, held at the Naiqua Gallery from December 1 to 7, 1963, paper scraps, considered to be love

Notes

- The following texts consist of the artist's previously published writings (in bold, san serif) and new descriptions of the works (not in bold, serif). The first page numbers point to the pages where the corresponding Japanese texts and images are printed in this catalog.
- The descriptions of the works were written by Azusa Hashimoto (AH), Mayumi Hamada (MH), Mihoko Nishikawa (MN), and Midori Yoshimoto (MY) by referencing the catalog of *Shigeko Kubota: Video Sculpture* (New York: American Museum of Moving Image, 1991) (hereinafter MMI cat.). The descriptions on the following pages, however, were drawn from, expanded on the following review.

[p. 122, 125, 127, 133, 134, 136] Midori Yoshimoto, "Emotions of Life Expressed through Video: My Life with Nam June Paik at Stendhal Gallery, New York, U.S.A. Sept. 6-Oct. 20, 2007," *Image & Gender*, vol. 8 (March 2008), pp. 139-141.

letters, were piled up with sculptures resembling those shown at the Yomiuri Independent Exhibition placed above, forcing visitors to climb up. Kubota sent a letter and invitation to the show to active curators at the time, such as Shuzo Takiguchi, Yusuke Nakahara, Yoshiaki Tono, and Tamon Miki, expecting their responses, but was deeply disappointed to find no review. Encouraged by positive comments from Nam June Paik, who saw the exhibition, she decided to live and work in New York. "1st. love," "2nd. love" of the title individually referenced the abstract sculptures which were displayed. Furthermore, the English text printed on the invitation corresponded to the text which was supposedly written by Kubota and included in the program of a performing festival, *Sweet 16*. (MH)

In 1963, I held my solo exhibition at Naiqua Gallery in Shimbashi (Tokyo). Owned by a doctor [of internal medicine], this gallery was a magnet of avant-garde artists. I filled the gallery space from the floor to the ceiling with scraps of love letters, covered them with a white cloth, and placed metal pipes on top of those. Visitors had to climb a mountain of paper scraps. It was like a participatory performance and a piece of Environment art. Although I was confident, I received no review from newspapers and magazines. At the age of twenty-four,* I received a psychological shock. Thinking that women artists had no chance, I moved to New York in the following year.

*She was actually twenty-six at the time.

Excerpted from "Dessin of Works Shigeko Kubota: Fluxus Couple", *Kyoto Shimbun*, May 29, 1999.

Captions:
Kubota seated at her solo exhibit at Naiqua Gallery, 1963.
Top: An invitation.
Bottom: *1st. love, 2nd. love, 3rd. love*, sculptures shown, 1963.

---

pp. 14–15

1963
Sweet 16

The performance festival, *Sweet 16*, was held at the Sogetsu Kaikan Hall for three days from December 3, 1963. Young avant-garde artists, including Takehisa Kosugi, Yasunao Tone, Shuko Mizuno of Group Ongaku, Tatsumi Hijikata, Kazakura Sho, Takahiko Iimura—who frequented Chiya Kuni Dance Institute participated in it. While Kubota's name is missing from the program, she participated and presented a performance under the pseudo name of G. Breyali, according to notes and confirmation from her friend, Tone. Although details are unknown about the work, the text, "To Mr. Maciunas/G. Breyali" printed in this program overlapped in content with the text included in the invitation to Kubota's solo exhibition at Naiqua Gallery and can be considered her performance score. (MH)

My dear Mr. George Maciunas
Hello. . . . This is my Christmas present to you.

Composition for K.
Skin your lips by yourself.
Kiss a man who has mustache in audience.

Blue love No. 25.
Prick your pores of skin with a needle as far as far as your hand can touch.

Beehive No. 1.
Make a floor with waste paper which are all love letters to you.
Spread a sheet of white cloth on the floor.

Beehive No. 2.
Fill a room with waste paper which are all love letters to you.

1st Love.
Don't cast you shadow when a girl puts on the light in a small room.

Crying music No. 9.
Let seven men stand in a line, starch (with a colored cloth,) a point of man's face which you find something wonderful.
Moisten his head with a drop of hot water just as you water flowers.
Pull out a piece of hair from a part of his head which is gotten wet by the hat [hot] water.

Blue love No. 1.
Shut your ears, Confess your 1st. love.

A drop of water.
Have dinner which is served only a white flower.
Put a drop of water from you[r] lips into long nylon pipe after dinner.
Shut the ends of the nylon pipe with two fingers.
Don't move until the white flower in your stomach becomes a drop of water.

Composition for only a man.
Put many women into a small room whose floor is covered with a sheet white cloth.
Keep them in the room for a month.
Make a wall by the sheet of white cloth after a month.
Print your shadow on the wall.
Erase other's shadows by that of your own.

Blue love No. 8.
Send only a needle to your girl friend when you can't meet her. (or when you are too busy to meet her, or when you dislike to meet her.)

I do hope your asthma will get very well soon.

Good Bye.

G. Breyali

Instruction from the brochure of *Sweet 16*

Caption:
The brochure of *Sweet 16*.

pp. 16–17

1964-65
Before and After Moving to the United States

In June 1964, before her move to the United States in July, Kubota submitted a work entitled, Miss Universe, to the group show *Off Museum*, organized by artists represented by Ushio Shinohara. The work consisted of a "donation box for Ms. Shigeko Kubota to become Ms. Universe," a live white rabbit, and a clock. It was a sort of performance piece in which the viewer was asked to feed food to the rabbit or take it for a walk at times designated by an instruction posted in the gallery. In addition, Kubota submitted a work consisting of women's underwear, which suggests her concern with women's bodies, both to the Yasunao Tone solo exhibition in October of the same year and to the Flux Week exhibition at Gallery Crystal in September 1965. Kubota brought documents on Hi-Red Center, whose members she was friendly with in Tokyo, and produced Hi-Red Center Events with George Maciunas. By introducing their work in New York, she served as a bridge between vanguard communities in Tokyo and New York. (MH)

Captions:
p. 16: Self-Portrait, ca. 1964.
p.17 top left: *Hi-Red Center "Bundle of Events,"* Edited by Shigeko Kubota, Designed and produced by George Maciunas.
p.17 top right: Kubota's work behind Yasunao Tone, at his solo exhibition at Naiqua Gallery, October 12, 1964.
P.17 bottom: Photographs and notes about "Flux Week", Gallery Crystal, September 1965, from Teruo Nishiyama's scrapbook. The middle-right photo shows a bra and panty which were part of Kubota's work according to Teruo Nishiyama.

pp. 20–21

1964-70s
Fluxus

Kubota expressed her determination to live as an artist in New York in her scroll letter to Maciunas and called going to the United States "the biggest Happening." She sent art materials for her work in advance in a trunk which she named "Fluxus Suitcase" (see pp. 18–19). After arriving in New York with Shiomi in July 1964, Kubota received a welcome from Maciunas and others and began living in an apartment he had prepared for them in SoHo. Ay-O, Takako Saito, and Nam June Paik, who had come to New York earlier, lived nearby. While participating in the "dinner commune" proposed by Maciunas to take turns cooking, Kubota helped the production of Flux multiples by members and conceived and made Flux *Napkins* and *Flux Medicine*. Only in the beginning, Kubota used a pseudo name of Love-ko AI which was given by Paik. (MY)

Captions:
Left: Shigeko Kubota, Letter to George Maciunas, 1964.
Top right: An envelope inside *Fluxus I*, ca. 1965.
Middle right: *Flux Napkins*, ca. 1965.
Bottom right: *Flux Medicine*, ca. 1966.

pp. 22–23

At the *Perpetual Flux Fest* which was held a number of times from 1964 to 1965, Kubota participated in Eric Andersen's *Opus 45* and Yoko Ono's *Beat Piece* as a performer. One of the prints Alison Knowles made for *The Identical Lunch* documents Kubota eating a tuna sandwich according to Knowles' instruction. Although many members left New York in the late 1960s, Kubota stayed near Maciunas and continued helping him, for which he was grateful and called her "Fluxus Vice Chairman." (MY)

Captions:
Kubota Performing in Eric Andersen's *Opus 45*, 1965.
Top right: Alison Knowles, *Shigeko Kubota Performs The Identical Lunch*, 1969/1973.
Bottom right: Kubota and Paik participating in "Flux Games," 1973.

pp. 24–25

1965
Vagina Painting

Kubota presented a performance, entitled, *Vagina Painting* as part of *the Perpetual Flux Fest*. Although the Fest was supposed to be held every Sunday from the fall of 1964, it was postponed many times. Kubota's turn eventually came in the summer of 1965, but there are some confusing accounts on the exact date. While the title made one think of a performance to paint with a brush inserted in her vagina, the contact sheet of the photographs possibly taken for publicity at Peter Moore's studio in November 1964 shows a panty with a brush attached and the artist painting with this equipment. According to the statements of Ay-O, Shiomi, and Andersen, who watched the actual performance, Kubota might have inserted a brush into her vulva. In her late years, Kubota stated that she did this performance at the request of Paik and Maciunas, and it was not her idea. It is impossible to know the truth now, but the fact is that she prepared for the performance more than a half year in advance and presented it as her work. This piece cannot be overlooked when discussing Kubota's art. (MH)

Captions:
Shigeko Kubota, *Vagina Painting*, 1965 at New Cinemateque, New York.
Top right: "Perpetual Flux Fest" in *Flux Newspaper* No. 5, 1965.
Bottom right: Shigeko Kubota, *Vagina Painting*, contact sheet of the photos taken at Peter Moore's Studio, November 1964.

p. 26

1965-69
Sonic Arts Union

p. 27

1967
Snows

Kubota met composer David Behrman in 1965. In the following year, she began participating in performances by the Sonic Arts Union (SAU), which Behrman co-founded with Robert Ashley, Alvin Lucier, and Gordon Mumma. In 1967, Kubota married Behrman and accompanied SAU's tour in Europe along with the female partners of other members (Mary Ashley, Mary Lucier, Barbara Lloyd), occasionally performing in pieces through voice or walking with sensors on her hands. She also joined SAU's 1969 tour in Northern Europe, England, Belgium, and Italy for some time.

In addition, Kubota performed the role of a Vietnamese woman, injured or dead, in Carolee Schneemann's multimedia work, *Snows* (1967). With her face painted in white and hung upside down by her ankles, the piece expressed sorrow toward and anger against the Vietnam War. These performance experiences stimulated Kubota and led her to form the women's collective, White Black Red & Yellow with Lucier in 1972. (MY)

Captions:
Shigeko Kubota at the apartment of S. N. Behrman (David Behrman's father and playwright), ca. 1968.
*This became the base image for Mary Lucier's *Polaroid Series: Shigeko* included in the present exhibition.
Right (all 4 images): Shigeko Kubota performing in Carolee Schneemann's *Snows*, 1967.
*Top right is a still from the documentary film of Carolee Schneemann's *Snows*.

---

pp. 28–29
1970
Marcel Duchamp and John Cage

Marcel Duchamp and John Cage is Kubota's book which documents the performance and concert, *Reunion* by these two great artists. *Reunion* was a chess match between Duchamp and Cage held in Toronto, Canada, on March 5, 1968. The chess board was equipped with an acoustic system which would pick up the movements of chess pieces and alter the sound broadcasted from speakers in the space. Although this idea came from Cage, the realization became possible by three contemporary composers, David Tudor, Gordon Mumma, and David Behrman. The book is comprised of Kubota's photographs of this event, Cage's acrostic poem, and a sound sheet which has become a part of the recording of the event. Because it was published by the then chief editor of *Bijutsu Techo*, Takeyoshi Miyazawa in Japan, and was funded by Kubota and not intended for sale, it was not widely distributed.

Later, Kubota turned these photographs into a single-channel video, *Marcel Duchamp and John Cage* (1972), and incorporated the video into another video sculpture, *Video Chess*. (MH)

Captions:
Marcel Duchamp and John Cage, 1970.
Middle: *Marcel Duchamp and John Cage*, photograph, 1968.
Top right: A page in *Bijutsu Techo* (March 1968) with Marcel Duchamp's autograph.

---

pp. 30–31
1972
Broken Diary: Europe on 1/2 inch a Day

Separated from David Behrman in 1970, Kubota joined Paik, who started teaching video art at the California Institute of Arts, and began her video art. In May 1972, she traveled through Europe with a new Portapack in her hand. She created a single-channel video, *Europe on 1/2 inch a Day* from her recordings of the trip. She presented it at her first *Live and Videotape Concert* at the Kitchen in New York and took her first step in becoming a video artist. She also made a video using her photos of the 1968 chess event by Cage and Duchamp and played it at the 60th birthday party event for Cage. She had already shown multiple-channel video on stacked CRT monitors by the late 1970s. (MY)

Behind the Video Door

I travel alone with my portapack on my back, as Vietnamese women do with their babies.
I like video, because it is heavy.
Portapack and I traveled over Europe, Navajo land, and Japan without male accompany.
Portapack tears down my shoulder, backbone, and waist.
I feel like a Soviet woman, working on the Siberian Railway.
I made a videotape called *Europe on 1/2 Inch a Day*.
I had one summer with a Navajo family in Chinle, Arizona. I made a videotape called *An American Family*.*

**An American Family* mentioned above seems to have evolved into *Video Girls and Video Songs for Navajo Sky* later.

Excerpted from Shigeko Kubota, "Video Poem." *Arts Magazine*, vol. 49, no.4 (Dec. 1974), p.48.

Captions:
Shigeko Kubota with a Portapak, 1972.
Poster for *Shigeko Kubota, Live and Video Concert*, 1972.

---

pp. 32
1972-73
White Black Red & Yellow

In 1972, Kubota and Lucier formed White Black Red & Yellow, a group of "[F]our women dedicated to the presentation of original visual and vocal theater work," and held a live event at the Kitchen in December 1972 and April 1973. Kubota was "yellow" as an Asian, Lucier was "white" as a Caucasian, Charlotte Warren was "black" as an African American, and Cecilia Sandoval was "red" as a Navajo, though the order of colors in the name was unfixed. Corresponding to a rising second wave of the feminist movement, the group aimed to "serve as a kind of clearing house for feminist pieces," but it dissolved after the second event. Although Kubota's *Riverrun* was intended to consist of thirty twelve-inch monitors, with five rows of six, and each row connected to a different channel of video showing a different river, there was no visual documentation found. Kubota's text here directly refers to *Finnegan's Wake* by James Joyce. She called diverse riverscapes in Europe and New York an "autobiography of running time." For more about this collective, see pp. 208–210. (MY)

Riverrun—Video Water Poem

Water is a metaphor for moving images; natural water spontaneously flowing, forced water moving like waterfalls or the calm pool of water shimmering like a pond—Riverrun.

A different speed of the natural energy—running water, reflecting the life of someone melting into the water, running.

River of blood—washed away, coming back again and again through eternity.

In 1972 I traveled with a half-open-reel video portapack in order to make my video diary *Europe on 1/2 Inch a Day* instead of *Europe on Five Dollars o Day*. Carrying this heavy video portapack on my shoulder, I took a boat trip on the Seine, the Rhine, the Hudson, and the Amsterdam Canal; for the Venice Canal I boarded a water-taxi.

Water always calms me down, reminding me of living and survival of the human being in life. We all know that water, in many ways, is very close to our living; in the desert without water, we have only to die of thirst. Two-thirds of a human body is made out of water, and a baby is born from the water of the mother's womb, etc.

Riverrun is like a strip of personal time from my long life. It is about my emotional life. It is an autobiography of running time like "riverrun" of James Joyce.

When I was a little girl, I used to visit my father's family of monk s lineage who owned a monastery in the hinterlands of Japan. Since they didn't have plumbing, strong young fellows always fetched fresh water from the mountain spring nearby, carrying on their shoulders a pole with two big buckets on each end. I used to follow them with buckets, walking along the rocky narrow paths to the spring and drink a handful of water directly from the waterfalls—so cold, so delicious—I still remember it as a sensuous experience. I loved to drink drops of water from the glacier in Japan.

Around this time, my uncle, who was a monk and my father's oldest brother, died suddenly. My father had to attend his funeral. When my father returned from the funeral, I asked him "what were his last words?" My father answered, "He said he wanted to taste sugar . . ."

Was his life not sweet enough? Did running short of sugar during the war force him to crave sugar? I was not sure of the truth. Riverrun is always running as we are living now.

riverrun, past Eve and Adam's, from swerve of shore to bend of boy, brings us by a commodius [sic] vicus of recirculation back to Howth Castle and Environs.

James Joyce, Finnegans Wake

Excerpted from MMI cat., pp. 21-23

Captions:
Top left: Portrait of White Black Red & Yellow (from left: Mary Lucier, Charlotte Warren, Cecilia Sandoval, and Shigeko Kubota), 1973.
Bottom left: Poster for the first concert of White Black Red & Yellow, 1972. Design by Shigeko Kubota.
Right: Still images from *Riverrun—Video Water Poem*, 1972.

---

pp. 34–35
1973
Broken Diary: Video Girls and Video Songs for Navajo Sky

In May 1973, Kubota showed a multiple-channel video, *A36 – 24 – 36* at *the Second Video Arts Festival*, which began the year before at the Kitchen. According to her friend, Mary Lucier, it consisted of recordings of various appearances of Marilyn Monroe on a television, and the title probably referred to an ideal "hourglass" female body shape—having the same sized bust and hip size with a smaller waist. Although this work is no longer extant, Lucier reconstructed a partial view of the installation as prints for the present exhibition, using her photographs of Kubota's screens.

Next month, Lucier and Kubota accompanied Cecilia Sandoval of White Black Red & Yellow to her family home in the Navajo reservation in Chinle, Arizona. Remembering that the temple of her father's family did not have running water, requiring a young apprentice to fetch fresh water from a spring in the mountain nearby, Kubota sympathized with Cecilia's family, who had to drive a horse carriage to get water from a distant well. Kubota found a special affinity with this Navajo family who believed that they had shared ancestry with the Japanese. Her single-channel video, *Video Girls and Video Songs for Navajo Sky*, a chapter of the *Broken Diary* series, begins and ends with a scene of drawing water from a well. Kubota's abstracted face is superimposed over those scenes to striking effect. It seems to emphasize the fact that the video presents a Navajo lifestyle as seen, heard, and felt through her agency. When Kubota says "Shigeko means a sibling-in-law in Navajo," her face overlaps with that of a Navajo woman. Was it part of Kubota's transcultural exploration of her identity? (MY)

Captions:
Stills from *Video Girls and Video Songs for Navajo Sky*.
Poster for the *Second Annual Video Arts Festival, Shigeko Kubota: A36 – 24 – 36*, 1973.

---

pp. 36–37
1973-75
Broken Diary: My Father

Kubota visited her father at his sick bed when she returned to Japan, following years of absence, at the end of 1973. Her video recording of her father and herself watching the singing competition program in New Year's Eve turned into a video elegy, *My Father*, after he passed away in July of the following year. In early January, Kubota presented and talked about many videotapes of American artists which she "brought in a carry-on luggage" from New York at the *Tokyo New York Video Express*, co-organized with Video Hiroba at Tenjo Sajiki Hall in Tokyo over three nights. She also reported on the works of Japanese video artists at the international conference, "Open Circuits: The Future of Television," held at the Museum of Modern Art, New York in late January, contributing to a bridging of the video art scenes of Japan and the United States.

In 1974, Kubota and Paik purchased one of the first co-op lofts which George Maciunas organized in SoHo and moved in there. Kubota began working as a Video Curator at the Anthology Film Archives, which had just moved nearby, and continued until 1982. Robert Harris, who became Kubota's assistant around then and inherited her video curatorial work later, pointed out that Kubota's active and open character was well suited for connecting people in the nascent field of video art. Her experience as a curator led Kubota to conceive of "video sculpture"; a field distinct from other video art. (MY)

Captions:
Stills from single-channel video, *My Father*, 1974.
Top right: Kubota presenting videotapes at *Tokyo New York Video Express*, 1974.
Bottom right: Flyer for *Tokyo New York Video Express*, 1974.

---

pp. 38–39
1970-1975
Video Poem

The middle of a cloth bag is open and a video peaks through that hole. A television monitor and a small fan are hidden inside it and the wind from the fan makes its soft and organic form. This bag was originally sewn by Kubota for Takehisa Kosugi's *Anima 2/Chamber Music* (1962). Whereas Kosugi entered the bag, which he considered a chamber, and revealed a part of his body through variously sized zippers functioning as windows and doors, Kubota placed a monitor there instead which broadcasts her silently screaming face through the opening. Kubota took this self-portrait in video initially around 1970 when she gained access to a Portapak. (MN)

Behind the Video Life

Man thinks "I think, therefore I am."
I, a woman, feel, "I bleed, therefore I am."
Recently I bleed in half-inch . . . 3M or SONY . . . ten thousand feet long every month.
Man shoots me every night . . . I can't resist.
I shoot him back at broad daylight with vidicon or tivicon flaming in over-exposure.
Video is Vengeance of Vagina
Video is Victory of Vagina
Video is Venereal Disease of Intellectuals
Video is Vacant Apartment
Video is Vacation of Art
Viva Video. . .

Excerpted from Shigeko Kubota, "Video Poem." *Arts Magazine*, vol. 49, no.4 (Dec. 1974), p.48.

Captions:
Left: The installation view at the Niigata Prefectural Museum of Modern Art, 2021.
Right: Kubota and *Video Poem* at the Kitchen, 1975.
Bottom: Stills from *Video Poem*.

---

p. 40, p. 53

A view of Kubota's studio on Mercer Street, ca. 1976.

---

pp. 54–55
1972-75
Duchampiana: Marcel Duchamp's Grave

This work, one of the first video sculptures produced by Kubota, was included in her solo show at the Kitchen in 1975. Television monitors were stacked within a plywood structure, revealing the screens within. The images from the monitors were reflected from mirrors placed on the floor and multiplied. The video was a colorized version of the black and white recording of Kubota's visit to Duchamp's grave, shown on all the monitors (11 nine-inch monitors in the beginning) and accompanied by the sound of wind. At her 1984 solo show in the Kitchen, mirrors were added to the ceiling and on the opposite side with the same video being projected onto adjacent walls. Depending on the site and time, the exhibition method differs. The location of the wall text varied as well; being placed on the opposite wall at first, and later separated onto two side walls, for example. (MN)

D'ailleurs, c'est toujours les autres qui meurent.
(By the way, it is always others who die.)
Marcel Duchamp

Video without Video
Communication with Death.
Shigeko Kubota

In 1972 I visited Marcel Duchamp's grave. I took my blue book, *Marcel Duchamp and John Cage*, with me. It was a very windy day. I took a train from Paris to Rouen, then took a cab to his cemetery. I asked a woman, "Where is Marcel Duchamp's grave?" She looked at me and said, "Who is he?" Then, she opened the telephone book. I was very shocked. Alone, after a long search in the vast cemetery, the weight of my portapack crushing on my shoulder, I finally found Duchamp's grave next to that of Jacques Villon, his brother. Marcel's ironic epitaph surprised me . . . "D'ailleurs, c'est toujours les autres qui meurent."

Despite the cool unsentimentality of Duchamp's own attitude toward death, I was very moved. My father's family, of monk's lineage, owns a monastery in the hinterlands of Japan, so I used to see a lot of funerals. I often did homework inside a temple room where fresh bones were stored. How I played with ghosts . . . all these childhood memories flashed back into my head, I put my Duchamp and Cage book on his grave, as in the oriental family custom of putting rice cookies on the dead ancestor's altar.

Excerpted from MMI cat. p. 24.

Captions:
Left (all 3): Stills from *Marcel Duchamp's Grave*.
Right: *Shigeko Kubota: Marcel Duchamp's Grave (Revived)* at the Kitchen, 1984.

---

pp. 56–59
1968-75
Duchampiana: Video Chess

The monitor is placed upwards inside a plywood box. A sheet of glass on top, engraved with a chessboard pattern, holds transparent plastic chess pieces. The monitor played a colorized video made from black and white photographs Kubota took of Duchamp and Cage at the *Reunion* concert held in Toronto, Canada, in 1968. The soundtrack consists of a recording from the concert. (A different version, namely a video of clothed Kubota playing chess with a naked Paik exists, but it has been never shown.) The wall nearby holds Kubota's photographs from the *Reunion* and the texts by Duchamp and Kubota. (MH)

There is no solution,
because
there is no problem.
Marcel Duchamp

There is no problem,
because
there is no solution.
Shigeko Kubota

I met Marcel Duchamp on an American Airlines flight to Buffalo for the opening of *Walk Around Time* by Merce Cunningham. It was a cold winter in 1968. The airplane couldn't land at the airport in Buffalo because there was a blizzard from Niagara Falls. We landed at the airport in Rochester, then took a bus to Buffalo. In Toronto, later in 1968, I photographed Marcel and John Cage playing chess at the *Reunion* concert.

In 1972–73 these pictures were transferred, keyed, matted, and colorized at the Experimental TV Center in Binghamton, New York, with the assistance of Ken Dominik, and later at WNET-TV Lab in New York.

In 1975 I made a sculptural entity utilizing this videotape, concluding the piece after seven years. A video monitor looks up, its back parallel to the floor. A transparent chessboard with transparent chess pieces sits above the TV monitor. The monitor plays the videotape of Mr. Duchamp and Mr. Cage, and emits the original soundtrack of this unforgettable concert, a composition by John Cage. Every cross-point of the chess matrix has a hole and light cell, which is modulated by the proceeding of a chess game. This rich-sounding, intermodulated system was painstakingly designed and operated by virtuoso electronic musicians-composers David Tudor, David Behrman, Gordon Mumma, and Lowell Cross.

TV is always somewhere between dream and reality. When you and your chess partner play *Video Chess*, you are accompanied by the videotape of the two great masters playing from the other side of this world.

Two other friends helped me, George Maciunas and Al Robbins. George has gone to "Higan" (the other side).

Excerpted from MMI cat. p. 16.

p. 56 and 58: The installation view at the Niigata Prefectural Museum of Modern Art, 2021.
p. 57: Kubota and Wieland Schmied (art historian) during the opening of her exhibition, *Shigeko Kubota Video Sculptures* at daadgalerie, Berlin, 1981.

---

pp. 60–62
1975-76
Duchampiana: Nude Descending a Staircase

One of Kubota's representative works appropriates Duchamp's oil painting, *Nude Descending a Staircase, No. 2* (1912). Monitors inside the four wooden steps show a video of a nude woman descending a staircase. The first one utilized the four pre-existing color televisions (three 13-inch and one 9-inch); the holes in the steps corresponding to the sizes of those monitors. The recording was originally done in Super 8mm film at the Anthology Film Archives, transferred to video, and color synthesized. There were five iterations noted in 1991. The 1976 iteration made by Al Robbins became the first video sculpture acquired by the Museum of Modern Art, New York in 1981, and the rest are in collections worldwide. While the first one has a rear corner cut off, the 1983 iteration in the Toyama Museum of Art and Design (shown in the present exhibition) has a square corner. (MN)

Video is Vacant Apartment.
Video is Vacation of Art.
Viva Video . . .

In the original oil painting, Duchamp showed an abstract nude in "motion." But he was restricted to a quasi-futuristic representation of time . . . that is, multilineal motion depiction. The four-dimensional medium of video knows no such restriction. I constructed a real staircase, made of four color monitors; a lovely nude woman, Sheila McLaughlin, descends slowly/rapidly/flying in many colors and exposures, The image might live within the sculpture. I developed a sort of visual range that repeats itself every three minutes, yet still keeps the attention of the viewer, Packaging and parceling of the temporal structure in video sculpture require special care and consideration.

Excerpted from MMI cat. p. 28.

Captions:
The installation view of the 1983 iteration from the collection of the Toyama Museum of Art and design at the Niigata Prefectural Museum of Modern Art, 2021.

---

p. 62

Top: Stills from *Duchampiana: Nude Descending a Staircase*
Bottom: Installation view at René Block Gallery, New York, 1976.

---

pp. 63–65
1976-77
Duchampiana: Door

A single hinged door is attached to two frame joints at a 90-degree angle with the result being that both sides cannot be closed simultaneously. Inside the small room, a monitor set up above the viewer's head plays a video of Marcel Duchamp talking while smoking a cigar. Its image is superimposed with a video of vapor from a geyser. When the viewer goes under this monitor, they find a monitor on the other side (installed back to back), playing the same video. The viewer goes out from the opposite side of the door. The monitors cannot be seen from outside. The door structure is based on Marcel Duchamp's work, *Door, 11 rue Larrey* (1927), which was installed inside his apartment in Paris. (AH)

Door.
Door to open your mind.
Door to close your mind.

In 1977 I constructed a small room inside the René Block Gallery in New York. When one goes into the room and shuts the door, it gives the feeling of being inside a cave or a time tunnel. The door's frame is like that of Duchamp's *Doors: 11, rue Larrey*; with two frames at ninety-degree angles for one door, which is always opening/closing at the same time. In China there are quite a few mystery stories with the theme of time tunnels . . . you stumble into a cave; or, taking a nap, you meet a handsome guide who leads you inside the cave. Walking a distance, you arrive at a palace where you marry the prince, get rich, and become a queen. Suddenly, you awake from the dream, you are back in reality, but 500 years have passed, you don't see any of your friends, no one remembers you. Mysteries of time, time-warps, occur frequently in fiction. When you enter by my *Duchampiana: Door,* you enter a time tunnel. Mr. Duchamp is there smoking a cigar, as in his last concert before departing to the other world. He blends into the superimposed view of steam from Yellowstone's Old Faithful, dutifully blowing off every hour of eternity. Duchamp himself can be heard, "Art is mirage . . . Art is . . . mirage . . . Art is mirage."

Someone called this my "Vico-Video," after Vico, the Italian philosopher (1668-1744) who believed in the eternal recycling of our karma.

Another thing that has influenced me profoundly is that Shigeko discovered death for video. Videotaped death is not a simple death. Whereas you can term the real life a two-way communication, videotaped death is a one-way communication. Instead of asking the biblical question, "Is there life after death?," she formulated a new question, "Is there video after death?" As there ore life und plastic life, so there will be a death and plastic death. Her innovations will become extremely real and pertinent when artificial hibernation (cryogenics) becomes practical in a few decades.

The text by Nam June Paik
in *Shigeko Kubota Video Sculpture*,
(daadgalerie, 1981), p. 31

Excerpted from MMI cat. p. 30.

Captions:
p. 63 and p. 64: Installation view at the Niigata Prefectural Museum of Modern Art, 2021.
p. 65: Installation view at René Block Gallery, New York, 1977.

---

p. 66–69
1976-77, 1983
Meta-Marcel: Window

This series, entitled Meta-Marcel, is an extension of the "Duchampiana" series. Kubota intended to break free from the spell of the master (Duchamp) and overcoming his influence. Kubota placed a television on its side, presenting its noise as snow. In the beginning, the noise was made by connecting an open reel to a television. In later years, it was replaced by a video recording of the noise on a screen. In 1983, new videos of "Flowers" and "Stars" were created. "Snow," "Flowers," and "Stars" can be shown individually, while a videotape with all three variations (in the collection of the Toyama Museum of Art and Design) can be shown on one window. (MN)

Video is the window of yesterday.
Video is the window of tomorrow.
It snows in my video window as it snows in my mind.

I made a small version of Duchamp's *Fresh Widow*, using plywood. Inside, an old RCA color TV is set behind the glass window. A character generator produces a snow pattern. The TV set has imperfect purity of color, so the snow becomes surreally tinted. So simple, clear, pure, my window is the quintessential video sculpture, a means to glimpse and grasp the birth of a new genre.

Excerpted from MMI cat. p. 33.

Captions:
p. 66: *Meta-Marcel: Window (Snow)*, location and date unknown.
p. 67: Installation view at the *Programmed: Rules, Codes and Choreographies in Art, 1965–2018* at the Whitney Museum, 2018.
pp. 68–69 (first three): Installation views at the Niigata Prefectural Museum of Art, 2021.
p. 69: Shigeko Kubota holding a frame, Chicago, ca. 1981.

---

pp. 70–71

Installation view at the Niigata Prefectural Museum of Modern Art, 2021

---

pp. 72–73
1977
Conceptual sketches

These conceptual sketches in Kubota's diary date from October 1977. Dissatisfied with exhibiting in museums, she expressed interest in displaying her works in public spaces to people passing by. The most notable sketch depicts the placement of *Duchamp's Grave* at the J. F. Kennedy airport. Others included the installation of monitors on the floor, turning an entire room into a chess board, and embedding a window on a wall which would play the four season's version of *Meta-Marcel: Window.* (MN)

---

pp. 74–77
1979
Drawings in Berlin

Kubota drew these during her residency at DAAD (Deutscher Akademischer Austauschdienst; German Academic Exchange Service). These may relate to a single-channel video, *Berlin Diary,* created in 1979 as part of a series of video diaries. The work began in the early 1970s, though the series was combined and renamed *Broken Diary* in 1985. Utilizing speech balloons, she managed to capture a fleeting moment of everyday life in comic book style. (AH)

---

pp. 78–81
1976-79
Three Mountains

It consists of three plywood structures, two of which are elongated, equilateral triangular forms, containing 2 or 3 monitors, and the last one being a quadrangular pyramid, with the top cut off, containing two monitors. All monitors are inset with mirrors around them which reflect a four-channel video of the Grand Canyon as seen from helicopter, the Echo Cliffs as seen from a car window, a mirage over a sunset in Taos, and a sunset scene in the Grand Tetons. The speaker plays the sound of wind and other environmental noises.

The pyramid in the center, which the artist referred to as a "volcano," was created first and shown at the René Block Gallery in a 1977 solo show. (Although it was supposed to be included in the "Projects" exhibition at the Museum of Modern Art, New York in 1978, in the end—it was not.) The interior of the "volcano" was lined with mirrors, which infinitely reflected a moving image from the monitors to the viewer. Related drawings suggest that Kubota considered these mountains an "autobiographical landscape," while also showing how the two-mountain composition grew into three. (MH)

I want to create a fusion of art and life, Asia and America, Duchampiana modernism and Levi-Straussian savagism, cool form and hot video, dealing with all of those complex problems, spanning the tribal memory of the Nomadic Asians who crossed over the Bering Strait over 10,000 years ago. Then, I came, flying in a Boeing 707, on July 4th in 1964, drawn to the glittering Pop Art world of New York

Although the descendants of the great Mohawk Nation did much of the high steel work on New York's skyscrapers, my reunion with my ancient cousin came in a dry desert amidst lonely sandstone spires, with the Navajo people. My friendship with the Mitchell-Sandovar family started with Doggie Mitchell, an outstanding American Indian musician, at Wesleyan University in 1968. Doggie, there as a teaching fellow in ethno-musicology, had an ebullient, partially nihilistic lifestyle.

We used to converse in Japanese, his broken Navajo-Japanese. He met a mysterious death at the age of twenty-five. The mourning of his untimely departure led to the formation and presentation of a multiracial group of four women artists, "White, Black, Red and Yellow," including Mary Lucier, Charlotte Warren, Cecilia Sandovar (Doggie's cousin), and myself. In 1973 Mary Lucier and I followed Cecilia to her hometown in Chinle, Arizona. We stayed with their matriarchal family lived their lives, experienced some of their rites and festivals. Generally speaking, I was treated with exceptional warmth. An elder man told me, "Oh, poor Japanese, you traveled so long to such a small island, you should have stayed here in America." I laughed. This old man thinks that the Native Americans immigrated to China and founded Chinese civilization in 4000 B.C. Another person told me that my name, Shigeko, means "my daughter-in-law" in the Navajo language. The Navajo word for hello, pronounced "Ya-tu-hey, ya-tu-hey" means "Love me, love me" in Japanese.

The landscape of the Navajo enchanted me: the incredible colors of Arizona, the skies of the high desert. When I finally had to leave, I resolved to return. In 1976 I traveled throughout western America, recording the landscape in color video in the mountains of Washington, Idaho, Montana, Wyoming, and the deserts and canyons of Utah, Arizona, and New Mexico.

Many great ancient sculptural works—Stonehenge, the Pyramids, Peru's Nazca Lines—bear within their grand scale and precisely composed form another, religious and reflexive, dimension. Sculpture mirrors nature while containing the imprint, the consciousness, of its maker.

Mountain—womb
My womb is a volcano.
Five-inch and eleven-inch images are dancing inside of it.
They sing of my history.

Herbert Read wrote in 1964 that, "From its inception in pre-historic times down through the ages, and until comparatively recently sculpture was conceived as an art of solid form, of mass, and its virtues were related to spatial occupancy." Video's incursion into sculptural territory will negate the long-held prejudices concerning video that suggest that video is "fragile," "superficial," "temporal," and "instant."

People wonder why I am making mountains.

"Why do I climb the mountain?" Not, "Because it is there," a colonialist/imperialist notion, but to perceive, to see.

The mountains provide a visual storm of perceptual complexity in a setting of almost incomprehensible mass and volume.

. . . drove as fast as possible, faster than body speed, drove on the highway in Arizona called the Echo Cliff, from the north canyon to the south Grand Canyon through Navajo reservation, grabbed my camera with both hands, the wind was hitting the microphone out of the window of the car . . . the sound echoes faster than mental speed, it sounds like the Indian kids are riding the horse, drumming for the raindance ceremony.

"O ji Ya," a small valley of a thousand rocks is the name of my ancestor's village. I was born in the snow country, in a mountain village in Japan. My grandfather was a sumi-e painter. He spent his entire life painting only mountains. As a student, I climbed in the Japanese "alps." I camped for weeks on the slope of Mt. Fuji during the winter snows. Snow in the mountains is like video and sculpture. Lightness, speed, the ephemeral quality of the electron set against an unmoving, timeless mass.

My mountains exist in fractured and distended time and space. My vanishing point is reversed, located behind your brain. Then, distorted by mirrors and angles, it vanishes in many points at once. Lines of perspective stretch on and on, crossing at steep angles, sharp like cold, thin mountain air. Time flies and sits still, no contradiction.

Buckminster Fuller . . . explains that men leaving Asia to go to Europe went against the wind and developed machines, ideas and occidental philosophies in accord with a struggle against nature: that, on the other hand, men leaving Asia to go to America went with the wind, put up a soil, and developed ideas and oriental philosophies in accord with an acceptance of nature, These two tendencies met in America, producing a movement into the air, not bound to the past, traditions, or whatever.

John Cage, *Silence*, 1958

Excerpted from MMI cat. pp. 35–36.

Captions:
Top: Installation view at the Whitney Museum of American Art, 1979.
Bottom: Kubota looking inside the "volcano" of *Three Mountains*, ca. 1979.
Right: [Three Mountains for the Whitney], drawing, 1978.
pp. 80–81: Installation views at the Niigata Prefectural Museum of Modern Art.

---

p. 82
1979-81
Video Relief

The commonality between these two works is the layered screens. *Video Relief* consisted of three plywood panels, two with round lenses and one with a television screen covered with calligraphy. Behind each panel was a three-inch monitor which played a single-channel video, *Shigeko in Berlin*. The video included a scene of Kubota interviewing children on a street. Her text here makes it clear that a viewer's face became reflected on the lens or screen. According to the MMI catalog, it seemed to have been an installation of two lenses on the sides with a rectangular screen in the middle, but there is no clear record remaining. The work was later absorbed into the video sculpture, *Adam and Eve*. (AH)

Video Relief is my self-consciousness—mirror.
"Mirror, mirror, am I beautiful?"
"Mirror, mirror, am I ugly?"

My video mirror is like double mirrors, using lenses as well as an old-fashioned TV screen like a magnetic mirror. Inside each of the lenses and the screen is a three-inch, black-and-white TV playing a videotape of myself talking to children in the streets of West Berlin.

You will see your own reflection on the surface of the TV screen as well as the two lenses.

Looking through my *Video Relief* lenses—mirror, double images like my past and my present.

"Are you sure that this is you, Shigeko? Or is this you who used to be?"

Between reality and mirage—fantasy, a narcissistic self-analyst.

You will never get bored, watching my *Video Relief*, you see yourself, how many faces do you have in your life?

Excerpted from MMI cat. pp. 38–39.

Caption:
All 3: Partial views of Video Relief at Kubota's exhibition at daadgalerie, Berlin, 1981.

---

p. 83
1981
Berlin Diary: Thanks to My Ancestors

A pink crystal board is attached to a five-inch monitor with twine, and then backlit with white light.

Kubota wrote a Chinese-style poem in blue ink on the board, which reads, in part, "father, mother, grandmother, sisters, (in) tear," "a friend, flight, Japan, my heart," and "in art and life." This work was never shown in Germany and only shown at White Columns in New York in 1983. In 2021, The Museum of Modern Art, New York acquired this work for its collection. (AH)

---

pp. 84, 93–95
1979-81
River

A stainless steel basin resembling an origami boat is filled with water, as a metaphor for a river. A motorized roller creates a constant wave in the water. Three CRT monitors are hung above it. By looking down, the viewer can see a single-channel video mixing the motifs of a star and heart with the artist swimming, reflected on the surface of the water. Kubota created this work about nature, which is significant to her, using the new material of metal, during her residency in Berlin. It was shown at the *1983 Whitney Biennial* and a photograph from the exhibition was later featured on the cover of *Art in America*. (MN)

There is river running water, all the time, never the same water running, never be the same people at the same house living, it's changing like four seasons, spring, summer, fall, and winter, function of Time, like in Nature. . . .

Floating on and on to the endless direction and nowhere . . . where shall I go . . . to end for no end . . . I'm swimming on the current with fishes, half being drowned, looking for myself. . . .

When I flew to Berlin from New York, looking upon the landscape from the window of the airplane, seeing the lines of nameless rivers . . . I thought of my hometown river: the Shinano River, the longest river in Japan.

I'm of a religious Buddhist family. At the center of Buddhism is always river, running water, Buddha, the stone Buddha is always washed by rain. A drop of rain becomes a brook, a brook becomes a river. The role of water in nature is comparable to the function of video in our life. A river is replicated in video in its physical/temporal properties and in its information-carrying and reflective, "mirror" qualities.

In preindustrial times, rivers connected communities separated by great distances, spreading information faster than any other means. Today the electronic signals speed our messages and connect us globally and into space. Charged electrons flow across our receiver screens like drops of water, laden with information carried from some previous time (be it years or microseconds) and space . . . from "upstream."

In one of their aspects, video and rivers progress through linear time and space, in another, video's closed circuit feedback reflects itself and its environment in cyclical, "whirlpool" time, and rivers throw back images from their surface reflections.

The swimming body floats lightly upon the water, spins and dives with ease. Once cast into video's reality, infinite variation becomes possible, not only weightlessness, but total freedom to dissolve, reconstruct, mutate all forms, shape, color, location, speed, scale . . . liquid reality.

Excerpted from MMI cat. pp. 40–41.

Captions:
Left: Stills from *River*.
Top right: Installation view at the *Whitney Biennial 1983*.
Bottom right: Kubota with *River* at her exhibition at daadgalerie, Berlin, 1981.

---

pp. 96–97
1981
Video Haiku - Hanging Piece

A circular monitor is suspended over a curved, round mirror on the floor, and moves back and forth by motor. The monitor shows a live black and white image of a viewer looking into the mirror, captured by a camera installed on the wall. When the work was premiered at the Museum of Contemporary Art, Chicago, it was placed near a window with the camera directed outside of the building. In 1983, a round mirror was added to the ceiling. (AH)

5, 7, 5
This is the form of Haiku, the number of syllables of Haiku, a spirit of Haiku, the shortest poem in Japan.

Poet, Bashoo, his famous Haiku:

FU RU I KE YA
1 2 3 4 5
KA WA ZU TO BI KO MU
1 2 3 4 5 6 7

MI ZU NO O TO
1 2 3 4 5

An old pond,
a frog jumps in,
the sound of water

My Video Haiku is a pendulum, hanging, swinging the time of a minute to a minute of my Living Time, one, two, three. . . .

How many more years can I live in my life!
Only God knows my Living Time, my Physical-Body Time, but my Mental Time and Art-Time will survive forever . . .
I hope, LOVE.

Excerpted from MMI cat. p. 44.

Captions:
Left: Installation view at Museum of Contemporary Art, Chicago, 1981.
Middle: Installation view at Fergus McCaffrey Gallery, New York, 2020.
Right: Installation view at the Niigata Prefectural Museum of Modern Art, 2021.

---

pp. 98–100
1983-1990
Duchampiana: Bicycle Wheel

Referencing Marcel Duchamp's first readymade, *Bicycle Wheel* (1913), a bicycle wheel is placed on top of a stool. In Kubota's work, the wheel turns automatically by motor. A small monitor attached to the wheel plays a colorized video of a flower blowing in the wind against a landscape. In 1983, the weight of the CRT monitor made a continuous rotation difficult. In 1990, lighter LCD monitors were attached to each wheel to create the version One, Two, and Three; one of the triptychs became part of the collection of the Hara Museum ARC. (MN)

In the 1980s appropriation has become the "ubiquitous strategy," if I may borrow the expression from Roberta Smith (*The New York Times*, Dec. 27, 1989).

Back in 1976, René Block and I organized my one-person exhibition at the René Block Gallery in SoHo, New York. We decided to make every piece Marcel Duchamp-related and title the whole exhibition "Duchampiana: Video Sculpture." Without knowing, we introduced two important concepts into art history:
1. Appropriation, which became à la mode in the 1980s, not only within the field of video art, but also in the art world itself.
2. Video Sculpture, At that time during the 1970s, video artists used the term "Video Installation," but René Block advised me that the word "installation" did not sound good in German . . . relating more to the toilet-installation or shower curtain.

With the help of Al Robbins, I constructed this video sculpture, a self-contained piece, not similar to the loose combinations of video hardware that were quite popular then. I made a well-crafted artwork which could naturally be called a sculpture as in the tradition of Rodin or Michelangelo.

I majored in traditional art sculpture at the Tokyo University of Education. I spent many hours in the lecture hall, studying construction and structure. Therefore, René Block's interpretation of video sculpture in the *Duchampiana* series sounded very sweet to me. He was in tune with what I had long been striving for.

My first "Duchampiana" as sculpture was *Marcel Duchamp's Grave*, done just after I had visited Duchamp's grave in Rouen, France, in 1972. It was premiered at The Kitchen in 1975. After this piece, the whole series of works developed, including *Nude Descending a Staircase*, *Video Chess*, and *Meta-Marcel: Window*, leading me to the *Bicycle Wheel*, which was shown at the White Columns gallery in New York in 1983.

Besides the Duchamp allusion, the *Bicycle Wheel* conveys fond memories of my childhood in the countryside.

Wheel is one name of the circle . . . endlessly moving with no beginning, no ending and without any sense of order. Wheel is also a positive word in Zen Buddhism, suggesting a trouble-free, transparent personality without an ego trap.

Excerpted from MMI cat. pp. 46–49.

Captions:
Left: *Duchampiana: Bicycle Wheel*, 1983.
Right: *Duchampiana: Bicycle Wheel, One, Two, Three*, 1983–1990.
p. 100 left (both): Stills from *Duchampiana: Bicycle Wheel*, 1983.
p. 100 right: [3-Speed Bicycle], drawing, 1977.

---

p. 101
1983
Green Installation

It is comprised of two freestanding structures: one has a flat slope and the other has steps. Each side contains five monitors each, which play a two-channel, color-synthesized video of an Arizona landscape which are asynchronous. The monitors on the stairs are surrounded by mirrors which reflect the moving image. (MH)

Green park, green playground, green field, green leaf, green forest. . . .

Living in Manhattan, far away from a green country, where shall I visit to see green color? Central Park?

This Green Installation is my mental green landscape, a physical green brain.

Nowhere to go to see green? No green anymore?

When I was a kid, I used to play around in the countryside, a green field with wild weeds, until I got hungry just before the sunset.

Marcel Duchamp packed his work inside a green box, a miniature green suitcase.

This Green Installation is my mental playground where I had a dream, in my dream when I was sleeping, a green water color green, melting into my reality—everyday life unconsciously.

Caption:
Green Installation and its still.

---

p. 102
1984
Broken Diary: Trip to Korea

After the success of the opening *Nam June Paik: Mostly Video* exhibition at the Tokyo Metropolitan Museum of Art, Kubota and Paik visited South Korea together. For Kubota, it was her first time to visit her husband's country. Paik returned home after 34 years of absence, having left at the onset of the Korean War. The media welcomed Paik as a world-famous artist. Kubota met Paik's family and friends and visited the place where he used to live. Video recording was done by Paul Garrin, who assisted both Kubota and Paik, and Kubota herself. She made the video sculpture, *Korean Grave*, by replicating the round form of a tomb mound. (AH)

Caption:
Stills from *Broken Diary: Trip to Korea*.

---

pp. 103
1985
Broken Diary: SoHo SoAp/Rain Damage

Kubota titled her single-channel videos *Broken Diary*; consisting of twelve chapters, including *Trip to Korea* in 1985. The first chapter, *One Day in California* (1970). *Video Curator Diary* (1974–82), *Video Diary* (1979–80), and *Shigeko in Chicago* (1982), have recently been discovered by her foundation and are being prepared for an upcoming premier. When all the chapters are shown, it will become apparent that Kubota overcame many obstacles as a video artist, video curator, and being a woman as well. Needless to say, these works by Kubota were partly influenced by Jonas Mekas. *SoHo SoAp/Rain Damage* became the last chapter of *Broken Diary*. It depicts the horrible leak which developed in her SoHo loft (purchased through George Maciunas) due to a storm, which was exacerbated by faulty repair in the building. Not only did it affect their life, but it also damaged tapes and equipment. Her statement in the video, "It rains in my heart. It rains in my video art" poetically encapsulates this tragicomedy. Like *River* and *Niagara Falls*, water was always an important motif for Kubota. (AH)

Just after I made *Niagara Falls*,
my studio became Niagara Falls,
because of roofer's mistake.
"Art imitates Nature,
Nature imitates Art."

Excerpted from MMI cat. p. 53.

Caption:
Still from *Broken Diary: SoHo SoAp/Rain Damage*, 1985.

---

pp. 104–107
1985-87
Niagara Falls

Ten monitors of varying sizes are embedded onto a white, wall-like structure, covered with plastic mirror pieces. A 4-channel, color-synthesized video shows four seasons of the Niagara Falls separately. The shower installed at the top drips water constantly, while the resulting pool covers a bottom with mirror shards below. The reflective materials installed ubiquitously multiply the moving images. The sound of the Falls in the summer and the sound of the real dripping water echo each other. In 1987, two other versions were made with fourteen monitors in Kassel (documenta 8) and Tokyo (Spiral Gallery), but they are no longer extant. (MN)

Beauty of nature is nightmare, fear, and terror. Niagara Falls particularly, because of its magnetic force of magnificent nature, plunges into my impulse to thrust myself to death, releasing my body and jumping into the falls.

Niagara Falls has a particular kind of beauty that makes you feel liberates from your self. Commanding the falls from the Canadian side, the falls look much more magnificent.

I stayed in an empty hotel in the middle of winter and from the window I stares at the falls illuminated by the artificial colors of red, blue, and green at midnight. I thought of this as a landscape in hell.

Such a view of Niagara Falls as frozen water and steam drifting like smoke suggested the frozen moment of frenzied time. The images of Niagara Falls in the summer were the whirlpool of overflowing water and its howling sound from the bottom of the earth.

With the three-color lens video camera zoomed into the falls, the close-up view of the falls got me more involved, inviting me and swallowing me into the world of death. I was so frightened. In order to shoot the video, I asked Pau Garrin and Vernon Norwood to hold my body with a belt so that I would not fall into the falls with the camera. I found myself thinking, if I commit suicide, I would choose Niagara Falls so that I would be able to easily disappear into nature. In my mind there was conflict between a sweet nostalgia for suicide and a refusal of it by warning myself not to do so. Niagara Falls is one of the few sightseeing places where you feel so close to natural beauty and to presence of physical death at the same time.

I felt as if sightseeing meant going to see hell. Tourists are excited about such a hellish landscape of the falls. Children as well as adults are having fun, screaming and shouting. Only seagulls were flying slowly as if they were feeding on the corpses of the suicides deeply sunk under the falls.

It is strange that Niagara Falls is a famous spot for honeymoons. Perhaps your body is as shaky as Niagara Falls during a honeymoon, but I also feel a honeymoon is the entrance, a step before the world of death, If a honeymoon implies the beginning of hardship between man and woman in life, people may visit the falls to make some kind of reassurance about living.

When I showed Jacqueline Monnier my video sculpture of Niagara Falls at the studio, she said it was like Marcel Duchamp's *Etants Donnés: 1 ° La Chute d'eau 2 ° Le Gaz d'éclairage* (Given: 1. The Waterfall, 2. The Illuminating Gas) (New York, 1946–66)

Duchamp's creation of the falls in his works must be a symbol of the eternity of nature, or perhaps it might be a symbol of man's overflowing semen.

I have never been back to the falls since I completed the work. I don't feel like going back there. I don't want to see the actual falls, either. Once you see it, that is enough, just as I don't want to see the horror of hell again.

Excerpted from MMI cat. p. 55, p. 58.

Captions:
Top: Installation view at Spiral Hall, Tokyo, 1987.
Right: Stills.
Bottom: *Niagara Falls*, drawing, 1985.
pp. 105, 107: Installation view at the Niigata Prefectural Museum of Modern Art, 2021.

---

pp. 108–109
1986
Rock Video Cherry Blossoms

A piece of foam rubber which looks like a boulder is embedded with three crystal rocks and surrounded by broken shards of mirror on the floor. A small LCD monitor on top of it plays a single-channel video of cherry blossoms. (MH)

As a child, I visited the house of my father's parents, a temple in the mountains, where there was a big rock garden. There, I used to enjoy climbing the rocks and hopping onto the stepping stones over and over again.

During a school trip in my high school days I had a chance to see the gardens of Ryoan-ji and Ginkaku-ji in Kyoto. The trip left me with a strange impression that such sublime and artistic spaces existed in harmony between nature and religion.

Currently living and working in New York, producing video sculptures, I had tried for a long time to install a TV monitor into rock, but had trouble dealing with the heat coining out from the TV.

I went back to Japan in 1986 when Casio produced a liquid crystal color television 2000 for the first time, advertising: "NO HEAT NO PICTURE TUBE." I thought this was the best solution for my sculpture. Here was a TV without the disadvantage of heat, without a picture tube, a crystal color TV made of mirror glass. With this, I thought, I wouldn't have to worry about the heat burning the TV in the rock, it would be easy to install, and it wouldn't need fans.

Rock Video Cherry Blossoms was premiered in 1986 at Piezo Electric Gallery in Venice, California, at the invitation of Tom Solomon, the director. It was also shown at the New Langston Art Gallery in San Francisco, and it was reproduced in color for the catalogue. It was well-received and the innovation of the three-inch liquid-color TV was such a surprise to the audience that it drew considerable praise from instructors and students at the Sari Francisco Institute, as well as from many artists.

The rock looked like an extremely solid, authentic rock, but was actually an imitation made of foam rubber. In order to make it look solid and heavy, I smashed a mirror and filled the floor with the broken pieces, thus giving the rock a sense of weight.

In my childhood I was told the story of going to the "Shore of Dice" when dying young; it says that before going to either heaven or hell, you have to pile pebbles one on top of the other, and no matter how hard you try this, the demon comes and smashes the tower of pebbles. I have heard that a similar story is told in the *Myth of Sisyphus* by Albert Camus.

I have already passed the age at which, as a child, I thought I would die.

I made this rock video sculpture showing the videotape of cherry blossoms which I dedicated to my deceased friends from Chicago.

Excerpted from MMI cat. pp. 59–60.

Captions:
Left: Installation view at Hara Museum, 1992.
Right: Stills from *Rock Video Cherry Blossoms*.

pp. 110–111
1987-88
Dry Mountain, Dry Water

It consists of seven differently sized and formed plywood structures, covered in green mylar. Five projectors installed on the floor and walls show a two-channel video of cherry blossoms. Projected images get reflected on the surfaces of the sculptures and shed lights onto the walls. This work later became part of *Adam and Eve*. (MH)

Life and death
submission
evanescence of life
suddenness

Inscribed on the entrance of the temple of Daisenin in Kyoto, a national treasure

After I produced a series of sculptures, *River* and *Niagara Falls*, using as their concept water and video which are contrasting in their materials, I decided to construct a sculptural rock garden based upon the dry landscape of Zen Buddhism.

It was in the summer of 1987 that Jochen Saueracker and I visited the rock gardens in scorching Kyoto.

Going from visiting one temple to another with Jochen, carrying heavy cameras on our shoulders and perspiring, I found myself confronted by rock gardens that were uniquely individual in character.

Because of the heat, Jochen lost a lot of weight and became thinner and thinner, while I, on the other hand, gained more weight and acquired middle-age flab. One of the Zen monks caught sight of this strange couple and asked Jochen where we were from and what we did. He answered that we were from Düsseldorf, and the monk teased us by saying in German "Wunderbar couple!" Jochen was embarrassed and turned red. This secular monk really got on my nerves.

Also, when we took a taxi, the driver looked at us and ironically said: "Everyone makes a visit to temples for worship at any cost before he dies, you know." Venomous tongues of Kyoto townsmen were really annoying. I didn't bother to translate every word for Jochen because I didn't want to make him feel bad, and also because we came the distance to Kyoto, not for sightseeing, but for the pursuit of art and the study of the rock gardens.

I composed my rock garden with "dry" materials, pieces of green plastic mirror cut at sharp angles as if they were sliced with a sashimi knife.

Each of the rocks for my garden varies in size and shape, and cannot be found in nature. They completely transcend the natural appearance of rocks. Also, these were rocks of my emotion which had been deeply anchored in my mind.

In the rock gardens of Zen temples there are no seasonal flowers, no pond, no fountain water. Instead, gravel, pebbles, and various shapes of rocks are composed to represent the four seasons in an ultimately confined space as a manifestation of Zen philosophy. Such a minimum use of materials as its conceptual starting point moved me a lot. Also, a big elongated stone seemed to be like a phallic symbol, while small mountlike pebbles lying next to each other were like the breasts of a virgin. They looked very sexy to me.

Zen rock gardens contrast sharply with Western gardens, especially those of British and French design, and in their scale. Many of the Zen rock gardens are neat and are designed to represent a conceptual space as well as a space reduced to the point of simplicity and economy.

Did Zen monks design the rock gardens? I thought that the rock gardens were the representation of the fantasies of Zen monks living ascetic lives.

Excerpted from MMI cat. pp. 62–64.

pp. 112–115
1988-91/1989-91
Video Byobu/Adam and Eve

The first version was made of Formica boards embedded with 26 monitors. Its structure was reminiscent of a traditional Japanese folding screen. The monitors show a two-channel video of cherry blossoms. One of them includes superimposed computer drawings. These videos were also projected on the sides of the screen. The second version, which was made of white plywood boards covered with red, orange, blue, purple, green, and white plastic mirrors, contained 39 monitors playing the same two-channel video as the earlier iteration. The third was covered with blue and white plastic mirrors and included 24 monitors. They showed a two-channel video of birds flying through a colorized sky and sunset. The work evolved into *Birds*. The work *Video Byobu II* was incorporated into *Adam and Eve*.

Two equal-sized wooden figurative sculptures stand on top of a rotating, motorized stage. Each figure contains four monitors, some of which were recycled from *Video Relief*. Monitors on Adam played a video of Al Robbins, while Eve's played that of the Golden Pavilion. *Dry Mountains, Dry Water* was placed in front of them. In addition to the projectors on the floor and walls, there was another projector on a rotating disc which played a two-channel video of cherry blossoms. Behind the figures was *Video Byobu II*, whose monitors also played a two-channel video of cherry blossoms. Consisting of several different works and incorporating the surrounding space through multiple projections, *Adam and Eve* was an environmental piece. (MH)

Dedicated to the memory of
my friends from Chicago,
Barbara Latham
and
Lyn Blumenthal
their lives were so short
like cherry blossoms
Cherry blossoms are very beautiful
because their lives are short,
about one week.
If it rains, snows or storms,
cherry blossoms will die immediately
a loss of beauty as tragic

as the death of a young virgin girl.

I videotaped cherry blossoms at Chidorigafuchi in Tokyo in 1984. *Byobu* is a traditional Japanese folding screen like an accordion. *Byobu* is folded like origami, the instant architectural art of folded rice paper.

Excerpted from MMI cat. p. 64.

*

It was on February 8, 1987, that Al Robbins died of a heart attack in San Francisco.

At my Christmas Eve party, Al, with a paper-white face, said: "I'm going to Florida to get out of New York's cold winter."

"Oh! A tough guy like you has to run away to Florida?" I joked.

I was sure he had gone to Florida. One windy February day when my windows and dilapidated roof rattled, almost blew off, I sensed that someone visited my loft. Living far from my homeland, it could have been my mother, I thought.

Next day I got a call from a friend.

"Al died in San Francisco."

"Oh, hasn't he gone to Florida?"

He continued: "Well, Al met a girl from San Francisco at Café Orlin on Christmas Eve and she bought him an airline ticket. He died in her apartment."

Iron-muscled Al is dead?

Al was an architect, a poet, a video artist, and the carpenter who built my video sculpture.

January 2, 1975, at Ira Schneider's "Video 75, Installation: First Days Of The Last Quarter Of the Twentieth Century" at The Kitchen, I asked Ira who did the carpentry on his installation.

"Al Robbins."

"Who is Al Robbins and how can I reach him?"

"Go to MoMA's Sculpture Garden, He is always there, just sitting."

The first video sculpture I did with Al was *Marcel Duchamp's Grave*. It was exhibited at The Kitchen in June 1975. In the winter of 1976, Al and I made *Nude Descending a Staircase* and *Meta-Marcel: Window*. They premiered at the René Block Gallery.

Al always casually stopped by and worked and disappeared. He sometimes did not show up for a week, three months, the entire summer at a time, When I asked him where he was, his answer was always "at a girl's. My hobby is to chase blue-eyed blondes walking down on Madison Avenue." I was surprised. Al had not washed his hair for ten years, let alone taken a bath. He stank like hell, He never had a permanent pad, He would crash at a woman's place, and when kicked out, he would even sleep at Grand Central Station; he was homeless in a way.

Al Robbins, born in Chicago, studied architecture with Buckminster Fuller, hated the University of Chicago, went to Harvard, got bored and dropped out. Worked at an architectural office on Madison Avenue for a while, living in a penthouse. But soon got bored, became a hobo.
And he always said "I am Einstein."

Fatherless, his father, a skier, had abandoned his family and run away from Chicago to mountain after mountain.

Working with Al, I found him a fierce animal, or sometimes an innocent baby. I thought, many times, that I should not get involved with such a man. He was my business partner. Besides, he just came and worked for me when he did not have any other place to go. As he worked passionately as if it were his own, I wanted to say "Al, why do you work so hard and make such beautiful things?" He did not do it just for money, he put his spirit into it.

Al used to say, "I like you because you are Japanese. I had an opportunity to go study in Japan but I didn't go. I studied the language a little, Now I feel I should have gone. I feel relaxed when I'm with you," and winked like Clark Gable.

In 1924, in Paris, young Marcel Duchamp performed as Adam with a young woman, Brogna Perlmutter, playing Eve in Picabia's Ciné Sketch, in the ballet *Relâche*, which was done after Lucas Cranach's painting. This was an appropriation of an appropriation of an appropriation of an appropriation. When I saw the picture of young Duchamp playing Adam, I thought AL could be Adam, too. Al was Adam then, and still for me with that intrepid body and wild beauty.

Al's girlfriends were an eighteen-year-old virgin and a porno actress. Both very pure. They were Al's models.

But my Eve is the Temple of the Golden Pavilion, which stands in sublime beauty that transcends the gender, like crystal, silent and transparent. The Temple of the Golden Pavilion in Kyoto was destroyed by arson, by a demented acolyte priest. But it rose again, finished in gold. That's my Eve. The purity of a nun who has shaved her head.

The first reaction I had when I heard the news was "why hadn't I forced him into bed with me. Damn, I always had an opportunity with him. We were always together."

But, alas now his flesh went back to the earth. I never, ever dreamed that he would go so fast. He was forty-nine.

I decided to make a video sculpture called *Adam and Eve*. This is my tribute to Al.

This is how I wanted Al to live forever.

Al was my Einstein.

Excerpted from MMI cat. pp. 62-64.

Captions:
p. 112: Installation view at Kamakura Gallery, 1998.
p. 114: *Adam and Eve*.
Right: Stills from *Adam and Eve*.

---

pp. 116–117
1990
The Gate of Culture

This work was commissioned by Rassegna internazionale del video d'autore, the video section begun in 1987, as part of the *Taormina Arte*, the annual art festival in Sicily, and installed temporarily in the park of the Villa Comunale. For this outdoor installation, 32 monitors (16 on each side) were attached to the gate-shaped metal structure and played a two-channel video of cherry blossoms. In the same year, Kubota was also invited to the exhibition within the Venice Biennial, *Ubi Fluxus Ibi Motus 1990–1962*, and showed video sculptures. There she reunited with her old Fluxus friends, such as Yoko Ono, Mieko Shiomi, and Alison Knowles. (AH)

When I saw a videotape of the Villa Comunale's Park in Taormina, I thought that it was a heaven which I had not yet seen in my lifetime.

Around the park, there is a beautiful blue ocean, green trees, and flowers. I imagined myself walking through the well-designed paths in the hilly plateau of rocky landscape, and I became very excited about exhibiting my video sculpture within this landscape, outside of the villa.

Does it rain? Even if it rains, what does it matter? Whether it is dry or wet the video will control a transmigration of souls through Video Art.

It will be beautiful, especially at night, because video beams and video screens of TV sets and monitors look like countless stars; blinking lights like diamonds in the dark sky. My video gate is an entrance as well as an exit into the beautiful natural park. Sicily used to be an entrance for cultures from Greece and the Orient, introducing great intellectuals, information, ideas, concepts, philosophies, and treasures to Europe. When we Japanese visit temples or shrines, there is always a gate. At this gate, we are supposed to straighten our attitude and face ourselves. The gate is a symbol of entrance to the land of God and Buddha.

I have made a gate for the park of the Villa Comunale in Taormina of perfect beauty as if it were made by God, although it was actually built last century by an Anglo-Indian princess. The villa is a perfect architectural outdoor theater facing the ocean, the sea of Taormina, with a view of Mt. Etna. Beautiful and exotic Mediterranean scenery stands in contrast to my electronic video computer drawing of scenery. I am going to combine them together in the natural environment, manipulating twenty-four hours of changing light and time.

Sometimes natural scenery looks so perfect—like a postcard or like some other printed media. Videotaped natural scenery looks more real than natural scenery. Many dramas and movies of various scales must have been made in Taormina.

I am very happy to participate in this project this summer of 1990. It is going to be a good summer to open this new decade of the 1990s.

Excerpted from MMI cat. pp. 67–68.

Captions:
Left: Installation in the Villa Communare, as part of *Taormina Arte*, 1990.
Right: Women of Fluxus (from left: Shigeko Kubota, Alison Knowles, Mieko Shiomi, Yoko Ono, Carolee Schneemann, Sara Seagull) and the curator Achille Bonito Oliva at Venice Biennale, 1990.

---

pp. 118–119
1991
Auto-Tire Wheel

Plastic mirrors and small monitors (5, 7, or 12 inches) are inserted in the middle of tires. Monitors play a video of a driving scene while tires turn by motors. Uneven number of tires, such as, 3, 5, and 7 are shown together on a wall. (AH)

Dream is a wheel turning around,
You don't want to have a dream,
But dream always visits your mind.

Excerpted from MMI cat. p. 71.

I wanted to install a television set into a car tire and have it spin by using a motor. By accelerating this tire to driving speed, the images on the TV-set would then become neutral images in color and form.

This idea occurred to me on a hot summer day in 1977 as I was facing a sketchbook. At that time I had just gotten my driver's license by using a stickshift which I slowly drove through the city of Manhattan. It made me have a strong desire to drive full-speed on a suburban high-way.

Before the unification, I drove through a field in East Germany on my way from Berlin to Dusseldorf on the autobahn, a German expressway with no speed limit. It was so refreshing that I enjoyed an incredible sense of freedom feeling the high speed with my body.

In the spring of 1991, I finally materialized this piece. The concept of this piece was originally based upon the idea of social sculpture advocated by Joseph Beuys and also upon my concern to the problem of air pollution. Combining the aesthetics of Industrial Art with the spirit of ecology through recycling, I wanted to give a new life to the old tires which would have otherwise a mere waste. The functional beauty of these old tires mounted against a museum wall can be appreciated as a work of art representing modern times.

As far as art implies eternity, its beauty can be found in a lotus flower even if it is in the mud or in simple things in everyday life.

Art is for the millennia.
Old tires transform a landscape into a new wasteland.
Creating Art form old tires is one way to prevent waste.
Today's waste can become tomorrow's riches.

Excerpted from the catalog of *The 2nd International Biennale in Nagoya-ARTEC '91*, p. 38.

---

pp. 120–121
1991-92
Skater

Inspired by the Japanese figure skater, Midori Ito, a wooden figure embedded with monitors in its face and chest turns in the opposite direction from a rotating, round rink. A projector directed toward the figure casts moving images onto the mirrors on the rink, while colorful lights move around the space. Like *Adam and Eve*, this work is unique in that a wooden figure turns around. Kubota made this work after Ito missed a medal at the 1988 Calgary Olympics, and before the 1992 Olympics where she won a silver medal, initially for an exhibition in Nagoya where Ito was from. After it was shown in a public space in New York in 1992, it was also displayed at the 1995 Kwangju Biennial, but here is no sufficient information to prove subsequent showings. The present exhibition became an opportunity to learn more about this piece. (MN)

Caption:
Installation views at the Niigata Prefectural Museum of Modern Art, 2021.

---

pp. 122–123
1991/1992
Birds I, II

There are two iterations of *Birds I* on the floor and *Birds II* on the wall. Both are shaped like glacier mountains, covered with mirrors, and equipped with numerous small monitors. When Kubota went to record video for the project at the Bronx Zoo, the birds were rather static because it was winter. In order to help them "fly," she collaborated with a video engineer and made a video in which an image of a bird transitioned from left to right, as in a prism, or from top to bottom as in a book. By synthesizing birds through video and having them live in an artificial forest, Kubota made apparent the juxtaposition of nature and artifice. (MY)*

Captions:
Right: Birds I, shown at Maya Stendhal Gallery, 2007.
Left: Birds II, shown at Maya Stendhal Gallery, 2007.

---

pp. 124–125
1993
Pissing Man/Jogging Lady

Pissing Man and *Jogging Lady* represented Paik and Kubota according to the artist. The latter was also a commentary on the general perception of women who always felt the need to run. Its inspiration came from the illustration of a jogging mother, shown listening to music on a Walkman and carrying weights, on the cover of *The New Yorker* magazine (May 13, 1991) which was kept by the artist. (MY)*

Captions:
Pissing Man, shown at Maya Stendhal Gallery, 2007.
Left: *Jogging Lady*, shown at Maya Stendhal Gallery, 2007.

---

pp. 126–127
1993
Korean Grave

Korean Grave was based on the single-channel video, *Trip to Korea* (1984), in which Kubota documented Paik's visit to South Korea after thirty-four years to reunite with his relatives and pay their respects at his family tomb. Placed directly on the floor, the semi-spherical sculpture resembles a traditional Korean tomb and contains a few dozen window frames on its surface, where the same video is being looped. Each window is encased by tall walls which are covered with mirrors, reflecting an internal video image onto the adjacent walls. As the same video is also projected onto the whole sculpture, the materiality of the wood seems to disappear. Even though this work was from 1993, it seemed appropriate for Kubota's 2007 exhibition at Maya Stendhal Gallery which memorializes Paik's death and gave an impression of Paik's soul as being inside the tomb, sending messages to the outer world. Video served as a threshold or conduit which connected this world to the next. (MY)*

Caption:
Installation views at the Niigata Prefectural Museum of Modern Art, 2021.

---

pp. 128–129
1993
Windmill/Windflower

At the 1993 Lyon Biennial, Kubota showed an installation titled, *Video Feedback, Wnidmill, and Windflower*, which consisted of a handful of relief sculptures whose metal wings rotate around a small LCD monitor in the center. (MN)

Video Poem; Windmill—Video Feedback

Wind from North
Wind from South
Wind from East
Wind from West
Wind from Ocean
Wind from Heaven

Wind from my heart, so soft wind, spring wind
Wind from my head, so had like Rock and Stone,
Storm in my life.

Wind is hitting my face, hitting my body,
as faster as my mental speed,

please, pardon me,
what did I do wrong for you?

Wind, Wind , Wind, Carrying my message,
for you, to whom I have ever, never met you yet
in my life.

P. S. This is my experience when I took a train from Paris to Lyon—TGV.

Excerpted from the illustration for the catalog of 2ème Biennale d'art contemporain, Lyon, p. 179.

Dix-huit ans se sont passés depuis que j'ai organisé une manifestation-vidéo "Window," en 1976, à New York à la galerie René Block. Cette année, en 1993, á la Biennale de Lyon, j'expose "Wind-video." Pendant ces dix-huit années, "Window" est devenu "Wind," c'est-à dire qu'en supprimant "ow" elle est devenue plus légère.

Il paraît qu'Yves Klein a vendu du "vent de la Seine," sur les quais de la Seine, dans un sac. Mais à cette époque la video n'était pas encore inventée." Autant en emporte le vent" etait l'evenement audiovisual qui a represente la première motié de ce siècle et la vidéo est devenue, pendant la seconde, l'enfant fortuné de la vie de l'art.

Que sera l'enfant fortuné* du debut du prochain siècle? Au XXI siècle, la nouvelle humanite des deux milliards d'habitants de la Chine, de l'ex-URSS, du Pakistan et de l'Inde va entrer dans la culture de consummation de masse.

Les nations du G-7 qui ont pollué la terre entire au cours du XX siècle n'ont pas le droit moral d'exiger des nouveaux peuples de ces nations une vie de misère et de froid pour l'éternité.

Devant cet avenir, il faut penser aux nouveaux médias comme à des roues de moulin à vent.

Venise, le 16 juin 1993

*Cette expression, en japonais—et l'auteur le souligne—signifie "l'enfant qui profite du vent et des nuages"—et qui a donc de la chance. (Note des traducteurs)

Excerpted from the artist's statement for the catalog of *2ème Biennale d'art contemporain, Lyon*, p. 179.

Captions:
Left: *Windflower*, 1993.
Right: *Windmill*, 1993.

---

p. 130
1993
Garden of Eden

p. 131
1996
Video is a Ghost of Yourself

Kubota created figurative metal sculptures from about 1993 to 1996 and presented several installations combining those sculptures. Her plan for the "Garden of Eden" at the 1993 Venice Biennial suggests a narrative landscape using many of these anthropomorphic sculptures, though she later reduced the number of works in the end. At her 1996 solo exhibition at the Whitney Museum, she filled the floor and walls of the space with figurative sculptures such as *Jogging Lady*, and *Pissing Man*, alongside pieces covered with plastic mirrors, such as *Birds* and *Korean Grave*, the rotating *Windmill* piece, as well as plants, a coyote, and a snake made of pointy metal pieces with small monitors. She even added projected moving images around the room to integrate these disparate elements. The viewers needed to grope their way through a jungle of metal plants in the colorful, reflection-filled space. Her solo exhibition, *Video is a Ghost of Yourself*, at the Lance Fung Gallery held in the same year also displayed works made of metal or plastic mirrors. Around the time when the nature of images was transitioning to digital, the monitors used in Kubota's sculptures changed to small LCDs. New narratives were being told through environmental installations combining these sculptures. (MN)

Captions:
p.130 top: Shigeo Anzaï, *Shigeko Kubota, The 45th Venice Biennale, Venice, June 1993.*, 1993.
p. 130 bottom: Kubota, preparatory sketch of *Garden of Eden* at the 1993 Venice Biennial, 1993.
p. 131 top: Installation view of *Video is a Ghost of Yourself* at Lance Fung Gallery, 1996.
p. 131 bottom: *Videotree*, *Videoflower I*, *Windmill*, and *Videoflower II*, 1995.

---

pp. 132–133
1998
Sexual Healing

Kubota's *Sexual Healing* exhibition at Lance Fung Gallery in 2000 was an installation, consisting of a large-scale projection of the eponymous video on the wall, a paired figurative video sculptures representing Paik and Kubota, and monitors inside a bed and wheelchair playing the same video. The video humorously depicted the fact that Paik was receiving indirect sexual stimulation from the nurses helping his rehabilitation, which Kubota insinuates contributed to his healing process. Another single-channel video made around the same time, *April Is The Cruelest Month*, was a long homage to Paik, combining historic footage of Paik's performance in Germany in the early 1960s, her video excerpts from Trip to Korea, and the recent video of Paik in walking rehabilitation in Miami. *Winter in Miami* (2006) became an elegy for Paik, using a piano composition he composed at age thirteen as background music, and an image of Kubota and Paik sitting on a bench, taken by his caretaker. (MY)*

"April is the cruelest month," once wrote British poet T. S. Eliot. It was also in April, when my husband and video artist, Nam June Paik, due to stroke, collapsed the night before Easter three years ago. "I'm an Easter baby. Since Jesus resurrected, I will get better for sure," he said, with the left side of his body paralyzed.

The following morning after Nam June was hospitalized, two healthy and young female therapists took him out of the bed to start his rehabilitation. These single women, who just graduated from college, were wearing red lipstick and tights. They held Nam June like a baby, pressing him hard against their voluptuous breasts.

When Nam June practiced taking a shower for the first time, these girls curiously looked at his naked body and complimented by saying "Your skin and bones looks as young as if you were in your forties." At that time he was actually sixty-four years old. They went on asking things like, "Are you officially married with your wife?" or, "Do you have children?" If didn't have children, were they interested in having an affair? I was puzzled.

Like the song "Sexual Healing" by Marvin Gaye, this hospital conducts rehabilitation by assigning each patient with therapists of the opposite sex.

They also asked me, "You and Mr. Paik are video artists, right? Why don't you bring your camera? Why don't you videotape his walking therapy so he can watch himself?" Until then, I was reluctant to take the camera to the hospital, thinking maybe the other patients would feel

intimidated. Encouraged by their suggestion, I shot the video of Nam June engaged in exercise.

"I don't want to see it," Nam June said, and refused to watch the video. Perhaps he did not want to confront the reality of what had happened to him.

To the melody of "Sexual Healing," I made a video work for healing, for Nam June and his therapists.

Excerpted from Kubota, 'Work Sketches 1: Sexual Healing,' "Sexual Healing" from the catalog of *Shigeko Kubota: My Life With Nam June Paik* (Maya Stendhal Gallery, 2007).

Captions:
Top: *Shigeko Kubota: Sexual Healing* exhibition at Lance Fung Gallery, 2000.
Bottom: Still from single-channel video, *Sexual Healing*, 1998.

---

pp. 134–135
2007
Nam June Paik I/Nam June Paik II

In order to mourn her long-term partner, Paik's death, and also celebrate his life, Kubota created two video sculptures modeled after him. The first one, entitled *Nam June Paik I*, was rather abstract, and was constructed of metal pipes. The monitors embedded in his mouth, chest, arms, and legs looped video of Paik engaged in physical rehabilitation in Miami. After considering how best to represent Paik's rebellious and untamed spirit, Kubota came up with *Nam June Paik II*. To express him as a globe trotter who traveled from South Korea to Germany, Japan, and the United States, Paik is literally placed on top of a half sphere, holding a violin in his left hand and a Buddha head in his right. The sculpture references Paik's notorious performance of shattering a violin and his later *TV Buddha*. His eyes, mouth, and internal body were embedded with video monitors. These monitors played the video collage, *My Life with Nam June Paik*, which presented highlights of Paik's life. (MY)*

Captions:
Left: *Nam June Paik I*, shown at Maya Stendhal Gallery, 2007.
Right: *Nam June Paik II*, shown at Maya Stendhal Gallery, 2007.

---

pp. 136–137
2007
Shigeko Kubota: My Life with Nam June Paik

Kubota's solo show at the Maya Stendhal Gallery in New York after seven years was an emotional elegy to her husband, Nam June Paik, with whom she spent more than the half of her life and shared an intense bond with. In addition to the new sculptures representing Paik, representative works from the 1990s such as the two *Birds* sculptures, *Jogging Lady*, and *Korean Grave* were exhibited. Paik mentioned that Kubota was the first artist who created video about death. Indeed, her strength lies in a calm perspective on life, through which she could elevate her partner's death into art. Unfortunately, Kubota struggled with her own with illnesses, and after 2010 she could not return to work. This became her last exhibition. (MY)*

Caption:
Both pages: Installation views at Maya Stendhal Gallery, 2007.

資料篇

References

久保田成子
年譜

凡例

［全体について］
- 本年表は、個展、グループ展、そのほか作家にとって重要と思われる出来事を時系列で整理したものである。
- 作成にあたっては図録、パンフレット、雑誌等の刊行物の他、自筆の日記等の資料、また下記のインタビューも参照した。

  久保田成子オーラル・ヒストリー、手塚美和子によるインタヴュー、2009年10月11日、日本美術オーラル・ヒストリー・アーカイヴ（URL: www.oralarthistory.org/archives/kubota_shigeko/interview_01.php）

［展覧会について］
- 日本国内およびアメリカで開催されたものを中心に、ヨーロッパやアジア地域での活動も調査したが、特に日本とアメリカ以外での活動については網羅できていない可能性がある。
- 展覧会情報は、［会期］（不明の場合省略）展覧会名（不明の場合は〔展覧会名不明〕）、会場名（表記は開催当時）、都道府県名（海外の場合は都市名。会場名に都道府県名・都市名が入っている美術館については省略）の順で記載した。ただし、繰り返し開催される国際展（ヴェネチア・ビエンナーレほか）は会場名、都市名を省略した。会場が複数ある場合および巡回展の場合には、主要なものを選び、都市名及び国名のあとに「ほか」としてその他の会場・開催地を省略した。ただし個展は例外とし、巡回先も記した。
- 個展は太字とし、また特に展覧会名の付されていない場合は［個展］と記した。
- 久保田自身が過去に記したCVおよび、下記の展覧会カタログに出品歴等で記載のある展覧会については、一次資料を調査できていない場合でも、参考のために記載した。その場合、展覧会タイトルは〔不明〕と記す。

  Shigeko Kubota: Video Sculpture (New York: American Museum of Moving Image, 1991).

  Shigeko Kubota (New York: Whitney Museum of American Art, 1996).

［出品作品について］
- 出品作品のタイトルについては、久保田が基本的に英語でタイトルを付していることに鑑み、英語のみ記載する。図録や作品リストで明らかとなっている場合は◎の後に記載し、不明の場合は［タイトル不明］または［出品作不明］または［カタログに記載なし］と記す。掲載順不同。作品名は/で繋いだ。制作年は省いた。ヴィデオ彫刻およびシングルチャンネル作品以外（ドローイングなど）の出品については［　］で点数のみ記す。シングルチャンネル・ヴィデオ作品と同名の作品が存在する場合、シングルチャンネルには（SC）と付す。

1937
- ［8月2日］新潟県西蒲原郡巻町赤鰯（現・新潟市西蒲区巻町）で久保田隆円と文枝の4人姉妹の次女として誕生。

1944
- ［4月］新潟第一師範学校男子部附属新潟小学校に入学。

1945
- 戦況悪化に伴い一時、父の実家のある高田市の美守村（現・上越市三和区）に疎開。

1947
- ［4月］西蒲原郡巻町の小学校に転入。

1950
- ［3月］西蒲原郡巻町の小学校を卒業。

1953
- ［4月］直江津町立直江津中学校を卒業。
- ［4月］新潟県立直江津高等学校に入学。久保田の父は同校の初代校長を務めており、久保田のために東京から美術教師として寺島辰治を招致。
- ［夏］家出をして、親戚宅である浄善寺（上越市）に数ヶ月間下宿。

1954
- ［10月9日–10月26日］「第8回二紀展」（東京都美術館）に《向日葵》が入選。

1956
- ［3月］新潟県立直江津高等学校を卒業。
- ［4月］東京教育大学（現・筑波大学）教育学部芸術学科彫塑専攻に入学。大学時代に学生運動（全学連）に参加。

1958
- ［9月22日–10月10日］「第22回新制作協会展」（東京都美術館）に《首A》が入選。

1959
- ［5月26日–6月7日］「第14回新潟県美術展覧会」（小林百貨店、新潟市）にて《死石》が奨励賞受賞。

1960
- ［3月］東京教育大学を卒業。
- ［4月］美術教諭として品川区立荏原第二中学校に着任。品川教員組合婦人部副部長を務める（正確な期間は不明）。
- ［4月以降］叔母の邦千谷の舞踊研究所に下宿し、そこでグループ音楽（塩見允枝子、小杉武久、刀根康尚ほか）と知り合う。

1961

- [9月22日–10月10日]「第25回新制作協会展(東京都美術館)」に《死石5》《死石34》が入選。

1962

- [9月22日–10月10日]「第26回新制作協会展(東京都美術館)」に《死石T》が入選。

1963

- [3月2日–3月16日]第15回読売アンデパンダン展(東京都美術館)で《We can make it》《Suddenly》を出品。
- [12月1日–12月7日]**初個展「1st. LOVE, 2nd. LOVE… 久保田成子彫刻個展」(内科画廊、東京)を開催**
  ◎1st. love/2nd. love/3rd. love
- [12月3日–12月5日]「Sweet 16」(草月会館ホール、東京)に参加。G.ブリヤーリの名でパフォーマンス《a drop of water》を行う。

1964

- [1月26日–1月27日]東京の帝国ホテルで行われたハイレッド・センター《シェルター計画》に参加。
- [3月(?)]荏原第二中学校を退職。
- [5月24日 か 31日]小野洋子のイヴェント《モーニング・ピース》に参加し、作品を購入。
- [5月29日]草月会館ホールで開催された「白南準作品発表会」を観覧、ナムジュン・パイクに会い、内科画廊での個展を賞賛される。
- [6月17日–22日]篠原有司男が中心となって企画した「OFF MUSEUM」(椿近代画廊、東京)に参加。
  ◎ミス・ユニバース
- [7月4日]作家活動を行うため渡米する。塩見允枝子(千枝子)と同便でニューヨーク着。ジョージ・マチューナスが部屋などを世話し、フルクサスに参加し始める。
- [10月12日–10月17日]「刀根康尚　個展」内科画廊(東京)
  ◎[タイトル不明、黒い下着を壁に展示]
- [11月4日]翌年1月に行う予定のイヴェント《ヴァギナ・ペインティング》広報用(?)の写真をPeter Mooreのスタジオにて撮影。このイヴェントは延期となった。

1965

- [6月27日前後か 7月4日前後]「永続的なフルックス・フェスティヴァル」(New Cinematheque、ニューヨーク)にてパフォーマンス《ヴァギナ・ペインティング》を行う。
- New York Universityに在籍(学生ビザ取得のため、1966年まで)。
- [9月6日–9月14日]「フルックス週間」(画廊クリスタル、東京)に出品(?)。
  ◎[タイトル不明、「刀根康尚個展(1964年)」の出品作に類似]
- [9月8日]「3rd Annual New York Avant Garde Festival」(Judson Hall、ニューヨーク)で行われたDick Higginsのパフォーマンス《Long Constellation(No.10) Graphis No.131》にパフォーマーとして参加。
- [9月25日]「THE 83RD FLUXUS CONCERT: FLUXORCHESTRA」(Carnegie Recital Hall、ニューヨーク)にバイオリンで参加。

1966

- New School for Social Research に在籍(学生ビザ取得のため、1967年まで)。
- [9月9日]「4th Annual New York Avant Garde Festival」(セントラル・パーク、ニューヨーク)に参加。
  ◎peeping into the balla

1967

- [1月21日、22日、27日–29日、2月3日–5日]キャロリー・シュニーマンのパフォーマンス作品《SNOWS》(Martinique Theater、ニューヨーク)にヴェトナム人役として出演。
- Brooklyn Museum Art School に在籍(学生ビザ取得のため、1968年まで)。
- デイヴィッド・バーマンがメンバーだったソニック・アーツ・ユニオンの活動にパフォーマーとしてたびたび参加。4月にはイタリアとベルギーでのコンサート・ツアーに同伴した。バーマンと結婚し、ニューヨーク市の中心から約60km離れたストーニー・ポイントに転居。

1968

- [3月5日]ジョン・ケージとマルセル・デュシャンによるチェス・コンサート《リユニオン》(Ryerson Theatre、トロント)の写真を公式に撮影。バーマンはゴードン・ムンマらとこのコンサートの電子音楽を手がけた。
- [3月9日]マース・カニングハム《ウォーク・アラウンド・タイム》を見に行くために搭乗したバッファロー行きの飛行機でマルセル・デュシャン夫妻に偶然出会う。
- この頃、日本語教室で日本語を教えて生計を立てていた。

1969

- [4月–5月]ソニック・アーツ・ユニオンのヨーロッパツアー(スウェーデン、イタリア、ベルギー)に参加。
- [5月]この頃から約2年間、不定期で雑誌『美術手帖』に執筆。ニューヨークやアメリカの美術動向などについてレポートする。

1970

- 書籍『Marcel Duchamp and John Cage』(私家版)を出版。
- [11月]バーマンと別れ、パイクを追ってロサンゼルスへ転居。

1971

- カリフォルニア芸術大学でアラン・カプローの授業などを聴講。正式な学生ではなかった。ヴィデオ機材に触れ、《セルフ・ポートレイト》を制作。
- [6月1日]パイクとニューヨークに戻る。
- [11月19日]「8th Annual New York Avant Garde Festival」(69th Regiment Armory、ニューヨーク)
  ◎[出品作不明]

1972

- [3月]阿部修也の妻の渡米を機に、自分用のポータパックを入手。
- [5月1日–]ヨーロッパ旅行し、方々でヴィデオ撮影する(フランクフルト、ブレーメン、アムステルダム、パリ、ルーアン、ニース、ヴェネツィアなど)。
- ウエストベス(アーティストの共同アパート、ニューヨーク)に入居。
- [6月30日]**初のヴィデオライヴ発表となる「Live and Videotape Concert」(ザ・キッチン、ニューヨーク)を開催。**
  ◎Cage-Tudor-Duchamp/Europe on half inch a Day
- [9月5日]**「Video Birthday Party (60th) of John Cage by Shigeko Kubota」(ザ・キッチン、ニューヨーク)**
  ◎John Cage in Bremen, New York, San Francisco and Toronto
- [9月16日、23日、30日]「Women's Video Festival」(ザ・キッチン、ニューヨーク)に参加。
  ◎Joa: Impasse of the Infidelity
- [9月30日]**「Daily Performance: Shigeko Kubota Video Tapes」(Experimental Television Center Binghamton at Everson Museum、シラキュース、ニューヨーク)**
  ◎Three Channels Video Performance (Marcel Duchamp-John Cage Chess match/Europe on a Tape a Day with slight time variations.) (sic.)
- [10月3日-10月29日]「Videotapes」(de Saisset Art Gallery, University of Santa Clara、カリフォルニア)
  ◎[出品作不明]
- [10月28日-30日]「9th Annual New York Avant Garde Festival」(South Street Seaport、Alexander Hamilton Boat)
  ◎Video Birthday Party for John Cage II
- [11月21日]「An Evening of Video Exhibition」(Wesleyan University, Middletown、コネチカット)に参加。
  ◎Video Birthday Party for John Cage, No.3/Europe on 1/2 inch a day/Impasse of Infidelity/Marcel Duchamp and John Cage
- [12月16日]女性グループ「ホワイト ブラック レッド イエロー」として初公演(ザ・キッチン、ニューヨーク)。
  ◎Riverrun–Video Water Poem
- 「First Annual New York Video Festival」(ザ・キッチン、ニューヨーク)
  ◎[出品作不明]

1973

- School of the Art Institute Chicago(イリノイ)でヴィデオ・アーティスト・イン・レジデンスに参加(1981年、1982年、1984年も同様)。
  ◎[出品作不明]
- **[個展](Wabash Transit Gallery、School of the Art Institute of Chicago)**
  ◎[出品作不明]
- [4月17日-5月18日]「Circuit: A Video International」(Everson Museum of Art、シラキュース、ニューヨーク、ほかアメリカ巡回)
  ◎Europe on 1/2 inch a day
- [4月20日、21日]女性グループ「ホワイト ブラック レッド イエロー」の第2回(最後の)公演(ザ・キッチン、ニューヨーク)。
  ◎Video Fortunetelling
- [5月4-14日]「About 405 East 13th Street (#1)」(405 East 13 Street、ニューヨーク)
  ◎Water Event
- [5月28日]「Second Annual Video Arts Festival: Shigeko Kubota」(ザ・キッチン、ニューヨーク)
  ◎A36-24-36
- [6月]アリゾナ州チンリーのナヴァホ族居住地に滞在し《ヴィデオ・ガールズとナヴァホの空のためのヴィデオ・ソング》の撮影を行う。
- [9月28日、10月12日、10月14日]「Second Annual Women's Video Festival」(ザ・キッチン、ニューヨーク)
  ◎Video Girls and Video Songs for Navajo Sky(以降Navajo Sky)
- [12月9日]「10th Annual New York Avant Garde Festival」(Grand Central Station、ニューヨーク)に参加。
  ◎[出品作不明]
- [12月31日]帰郷し、病を得た父を撮影。

1974

- [1月7日-9日]「トーキョー・ニューヨーク・ビデオ・エキスプレス」(天井桟敷館、東京)をビデオひろば、アンダーグラウンド・センターと共同企画。
  ◎[出品作不明]
- [1月23日-25日]シンポジウム「Open Circuits: The Future of Television」(ニューヨーク近代美術館)にゲスト参加。
- [2月13日]「Video Celebration for John Cage」(Harvard University、ケンブリッジ)
  ◎[出品作不明]
- [2月18日]「Women in Film and Video」(ニューヨーク州立バッファロー大学)
  ◎Navajo Sky
- [4月18, 19, 20, 21日]「About 405 East 13th Street (#2)」(405 East 13 Street、ニューヨーク)
  ◎[出品作不明]
- [5月30日-6月16日]「ART NOW 74: A Celebration of the American Arts」(John F. Kennedy Center for the Performing Arts、ワシントンD.C.)
  ◎Navajo Sky
- [6月15日-6月30日]「第11回日本国際美術展」(京都市美術館)
  ◎作品(work)
- マーサー・ストリート(ソーホー地区)にあるロフトをジョージ・マチューナスから購入し転居。
- [7月7日]父死去。《私のお父さん》を制作。
- [7月-8月]「Project 1974」(Kölnischer Kunsteverein、ケルン)
  ◎[出品作不明]
- [11月]アンソロジー・フィルム・アーカイヴズでビデオ・キュレーターを勤める(82年まで)。
- [11月16日]「11th Annual Avant Garde Festival of New York」(Shea Stadium、ニューヨーク)
  ◎Video Wind, Video Stripe
- [11月30日]「Soup and Tart」(ザ・キッチン、ニューヨーク)
  ◎[出品作不明]

1975

- 流産を経験。《Hospital Diary》をヴィデオで撮影。
- Creative Artists Public Service Program Grantを得る。
- National Endowment for the Arts Fellowshipを得る(1978年、1980年も同様)。
- [4月10日-4月26日]「Women's Video Festival」(Women's Interart Center、ニューヨーク)
  ◎Marcel Duchamp and John Cage
- [5月30日-6月7日]**ヴィデオ彫刻の初個展「Video Poem by Shigeko Kubota」(ザ・キッチン、ニューヨーク)を開催。**
  ◎Duchamp's Grave(以降Grave)/Self-portrait(後にVideo Poem)
- [6月]「Projected Video」(ホイットニー美術館、ニューヨーク)
  ◎Chess (tape)
- [9月17日-11月2日]「Video Art」(Institute of Contemporary Art, University of Pennsylvania、フィラデルフィア)
  ◎Europe on 1/2 inch a day
- [9月27日]「12th Annual Avant Garde Festival of New York」

(Gateway National Recreation Area、ニューヨーク)
◎[出品作不明]
- [11月1日-1976年1月31日]「Projects: Video VI」(ニューヨーク近代美術館)
◎Navajo Sky
- [11月25日-12月19日]「Shigeko Kubota: Two Pieces」(Everson Museum of Art, Syracuse、ニューヨーク)
◎[出品作不明]
- 「Two Installations」(and/or Gallery、シアトル、ワシントン)
◎Grave/Video Poem
- 「Southland Video Anthology」(Long Beach Museum of Art、カリフォルニア)
◎[A Day at the California Institute of the Arts(with Shuya Abe)]

1976

- [1月24日-2月17日]「Shigeko Kubota: 3 Video Installations. Duchampiana」(René Block Gallery、ニューヨーク)。デュシャンピアナ・シリーズを発表。
◎Nude Descending A Staircase(以降Staircase)/Video Chess/Grave
- [4月1日-4月3日]「Living Video Environment Video Installations by Shigeko Kubota at her studio」(アンソロジー・フィルム・アーカイヴズによるThe Moving Image New York Cityの一部として)
◎Staircase/Grave
- [4月19日-6月20日]「Projects: Video III」(ニューヨーク近代美術館)
◎My Father
- [6月9日-6月26日]「Rooms」(MoMA PS1、ニューヨーク)
◎[出品作不明]
- [6月10日-6月27日]「Women's Video Festival NYC」(Women's Interart Center、ニューヨーク)
◎My Father/Grave
- 「New York-Downtown Manhattan: SoHo-Berlin Festival」(Academie der Kunste、ベルリン)
◎Grave
- [7月23日-8月1日][個展](and/or Gallery、シアトル、ワシントン)
◎Staircase
- [8月]ロバート・ハリスとロッキー山脈の西部へ撮影旅行に出かける。撮影素材は後に《三つの山》に用いられた。

1977

- 「インディ」賞(Association of Independent Video and Filmmakers、ニューヨーク)
- [1月22日-2月26日]「Meta-Marcel by Shigeko Kubota 3 Video Sculptures: Window, Door, Mountain」(René Block Gallery、ニューヨーク)
◎Meta Marcel: Window(以降Window)/Door/Mountain
- [3月21日]ナムジュン・パイクと結婚。同年、子宮ガンのため入院・手術を行う。
- [6月19日]「13th Annual Avant Garde Festival of New York」(The World Trade Center、ニューヨーク)
◎[出品作不明]
- [6月24日-10月2日]「documenta 6」(カッセル、ドイツ)
◎Staircase
- [9月18日-10月16日]「Duchampiana: 3 Video Sculptures Shigeko Kubota」(Long Beach Museum of Art、カリフォルニア)
◎Staircase/Grave/Window
- 「Duchampiana」(Museo de Arte Carrillo Gil, Mexico City)
◎Staircase

1978

- School of Visual Arts(ニューヨーク)およびKunst Akademie(デュッセルドルフ)でヴィデオ・アートを教える。
- [1月21日-2月3日]「Shigeo Kubota 4 Video Sculptures: Duchampiana」(Japan House Gallery、ニューヨーク)
◎Grave/Window/Chess/Video Poem
- [2月6日-2月19日]「PAN-CONCEPTUALS '78 ヴィデオによる作品を中心に」(田村画廊、東京)
◎[出品作不明]
- [3月16日-5月2日]「Projects: Shigeko Kubota」(ニューヨーク近代美術館)
◎Staircase
- [5月20日]「14th Annual Avant Garde Festival of New York and the 2nd Annual Cambridge River Festival」(Cambridge、マサチューセッツ)
◎[出品作不明]
- [7月14日-7月18日]「Shigeko Kubota: Video Poem」(Galerie René Block、西ベルリン)
◎Video Poem
- [10月5日-10月29日][個展](Art Gallery of Ontario、トロント)
◎Video Poem/Staircase/My Father
- [11月10日-12月31日]「Shigeko Kubota: Nude Descending a Staircase」(Everson Museum of Art, Syracuse、ニューヨーク)
◎Staircase
- [12月3日-1979年1月21日]「Couples」(Institute for Art & Urban Resources, P.S.1, Long Island City、ニューヨーク)
◎Window (Snow)

1979

- ロックフェラー財団の奨学金を得る。
- DAAD(ドイツ学術交流会)の奨学金を得てベルリンに滞在。
- [5月22日-6月3日]「Shigeko Kubota, Taka Iimura, New Video」(Whitney Museum of American Art、ニューヨーク)
◎Three Mountains
- [9月28日-10月21日]「Three Mountains & Snow」(Aspen Center for the Visual Arts、コロラド)
◎Three Mountains/Window (Snow)
- [10月28日-12月16日]Videoweeks Essen '79(Museum Folkwang、エッセン)
◎[出品作不明]

1980

- New York State Council on the Arts Fellowshipを得る(1982年、1984年も同様)。
- [1月20日-3月2日]「Fur Augen und Ohren: von der Spieluhr zum akustischen Environment」(Akademie der Kunste、ベルリン)
◎Three Mountains
- [5月9日-11日]「Video-Informative Series 2」(Institut Alemany de Barcelona)
◎Staircase
- [6月18日-8月24日]「Encounter par les yeux: objets et environments sonores」(パリ市立近代美術館)
◎Video Chess/Window

- ［9月23日］講演「Video Sculpture: Mental Landscape into Physical Landscape」『Video Viewpoints』（ニューヨーク近代美術館）

1981

- ヴィデオ・アーティスト・イン・レジデンス（ブラウン大学、プロヴィデンス、ロード・アイランド）
- ニューヨーク近代美術館が《デュシャンピアナ：階段を降りる裸体》をヴィデオ・インスタレーションとして初めて収蔵。
- ［6月26日–8月23日］「Options 9」（Museum of Contemporary Art、シカゴ）
  ◎Grave/Staircase/Chess/Window/Video Haiku - Hanging Piece（以降Video Haiku）
- ［8月1日–9月6日、9月11日–28日］「マルセル・デュシャン展」（高輪美術館、長野、ほか）に特別出品
  ◎Window/Staircase
- ［9月30–10月17日］**［個展］（Atholl McBean Gallery、San Francisco Art institute Annual Exhibition）**
  ◎Staircase/Window
- ［12月12日–1982年1月24日］**初の大規模個展がドイツとスイス3か所を巡回。「Shigeko Kubota Video Sculptures」（daadgalerie、ベルリン、Museum Folkwang、エッセン、Kunsthaus Zürich）**
  ◎Chess/Staircase/Window/Door/River/Shigeko in Berlin ［daadgalerie］
- 「Video Classics」（The Bronx Museum、ニューヨーク）
  ◎Staircase

1982

- ［6月10日–6月13日］「National Video Festival」（Kennedy Center for the Performing Arts, Washington D.C.、ほか）
  ◎Staircase/Window

1983

- ［3月15日–5月29日］「Whitney Biennial 1983」（ホイットニー美術館、ニューヨーク）
  ◎River/Allan 'n' Allen's Complaint
- ［6月23日–30日］「"Eye to Eye" An event surveying recent Asian American artist works」（Asian Arts Institute、ニューヨーク）
  ◎［出品作不明］
- ［7月1日–9月4日］「第2回現代芸術祭―芸術と工学」（富山県立近代美術館）
  ◎Window/Staircase
- ［9月10日–25日］**［個展］（Japan American Cultural and Community Center、ロサンゼルス）**
  ◎［出品作不明］
- ［10月1日–31日］**「Shigeko Kubota/MATRIX 65」（The University of California, Berkeley Art Museum、カリフォルニア）**
  ◎River
- ［10月3日–1984年1月3日］「Video Art: A Hisotry」（ニューヨーク近代美術館）
  ◎My Father
- ［11月2日–11月26日］**「Shigeko Kubota Video Sculpture」（White Columns、ニューヨーク）**
  ◎Window (Snow/Flowers/Stars)/Video Haiku/Video Relief/Green Installations/Chess/Berlin Diary: Thanks to My Ancestors（以降Berlin Diary）/Duchampiana: Bicycle Wheel（以降Bicycle）
- ［12月6日–18日］**「Shigeko Kubota Video Sculptures」（Fondo del Sol, Visual Art and Media Center、ワシントンD.C.）**
  ◎Window (Snow/Flowers/Stars)/Video Haiku/Video Relief/Green Installations
- ［12月14日–12月23日］**「Ten-day Video Snow」（Grey Art Gallery、ニューヨーク）**
  ◎Window
- **［個展］（Japan House Gallery、ニューヨーク）**
  ◎Video Poem
- 「Transformations」（Focal Point Media Center、シアトル、ワシントン）
  ◎［出品作不明］
- ［展覧会名不明］（Palais de Beaux-Art、ブリュッセル）
  ◎［出品作不明］

1984

- ［2月］《河》が*Art in America*誌の表紙を飾る
- ［夏］東京都美術館で開催されたパイクの個展「ナムジュン・パイク展　ヴィデオ・アートを中心に」のあと、韓国へ旅行。
- ［9月14日–10月28日］「The Luminous Image」（Stedelijk Museum、アムステルダム）
  ◎Three Mountains
- ［11月23日–1985年1月1日］「A Survey: Artist's TV Lab, WNET/Thirteen」（ニューヨーク近代美術館）
  ◎［出品作不明］
- ［12月18日–12月29日］**「Shigeko Kubota: Marcel Duchamp's Grave (Revived)」（ザ・キッチン、ニューヨーク）**
  ◎Grave
- 「Societe des Expositions」（Palais des Beaux-Arts、ブリュッセル）
  ◎［出品作不明］
- ［展覧会名不明］（Milwaukee Art Museum、ウィスコンシン）
  ◎River
- ［展覧会名不明］（Sprengel Museum、ハノーヴァー）
  ◎Nude Descending a Staircase
- 「TiJD show」（Louisiana Museum、コペンハーゲン）
  ◎Staircase

1985

- New York Foundation for the Artsのフェローシップを得る。
- ［3月9日–3月30日］**「Shigeko Kubota Video Installation: Niagara Falls」（ザ・キッチン、ニューヨーク）**
  ◎Niagara Falls（以降Niagara）
- ［7月18日–9月8日］「The Box Show」（Tamayo Museum、メキシコシティ）
  ◎Window (Snow/Flowers/Stars)
- ［11月6日–1986年1月6日］［不明］（Kulturhuset, The Stockholm Culture House、スウェーデン）
  ◎Staircase
- ［11月14日–12月22日］「TV Sculpture」（Hofstra Emily Lowe Gallery, Hofstra University、ニューヨーク）
  ◎Green Installation/Window (Snow/Flowers/Stars)
- ［展覧会名不明］（Kunsthalle Mannheim、西ドイツ）
  ◎［出品作不明］

1986

- [1月31日-3月30日]**「Broken Diary: SoHo Soap/Rain Damage, Story of a SoHo Artists' Co-op」(The New Museum、ニューヨーク)**
  ◎Broken Diary: SoHo Soap/Rain Damage(以降SoHo Soap)
- [9月18日-10月12日]「**Shigeko Kubota Video Sculpture and Drawings」(Piezo Electric Gallery、ロサンゼルス)**
  ◎Window (Star?)/Chess/Rock Video Cherry blossoms(以降Rock Video)
- [9月21日-1987年1月18日]「The Window in Twentieth Century Art (Neuberger Museum of Art, Purchase、ニューヨーク、ほか)
  ◎Window
- [9月27日-11月2日]「The Other Television: Video by Artists」(Fort Wayne Museum of Art、インディアナ)
  ◎River
- [11月19日]トークイベント「Cycles: Revolutions in the Electronic Art」(The Center for New Television、シカゴ)
  ◎Trip to Korea(SC)
- **[個展](New Langston Arts Gallery、サンフランシスコ)**
  ◎Rock Video
- [展覧会名不明](Fort Wayne Museum of Art、インディアナ)
  ◎[出品作不明]
- [展覧会名不明](Villa Stuck、ミュンヘン)
  ◎[出品作不明]

1987

- グッゲンハイムのフェローシップを得る。
- [6月12日-9月20日]「documenta 8」(カッセル、ドイツ)
  ◎Niagara/Broken Diary: Chapter 12/SoHo Soap
- [7月29日-8月11日]「JAPAN 87 ビデオ・テレビ・フェスティバル」(青山スパイラル、東京)
  ◎Niagara
- [10月1日-1988年1月3日]「A Centennial Tribute apropos of Marcel Duchamp」(フィラデルフィア美術館)
  ◎Chess

1988

- NEA/Visual Artsの助成金を獲得。
- [1月15日-2月6日]「Uebrigens Sterben Immer Die Anderen. Marcel Duchamp und die Avantgarge seit 1950」(Museum Ludwig、ケルン)
  ◎[出品作不明]
- [2月8日]アシスタントであり共同製作者のアル・ロビンスが亡くなる。
- [2月18日-3月30日]「Video Art: Expanded Forms」(ホイットニー美術館、ニューヨーク)
  ◎Window
- [5月22日-9月5日]「Interaction: Light, Sound, Motion」(Aldrich Museum of Contermporary Art、リッジフィールド)
  ◎Dry Mountain, Dry Water
- [8月24日-9月25日]「The 3rd Australian Video Festival」(Art Space、シドニー)
  ◎[出品作不明]
- [9月11日-9月16日]「Shigeko Kubota und Keigo Yamamoto」(Japanisches Kulturinstitut、ケルン)
  ◎Video-Byobu
- 「3rd Videonale」(Japanisches Kulturinstitut、ボン)
  ◎[出品作不明]

1989

- [3月16日-4月23日]「Video-Skulptur retrospektiv und aktuell: 1963-1989」(Kölnischer Kunstverein、ケルン、ほか)
  ◎Three Mountains
- [4月20日-5月30日]「The Arts for Television」(ニューヨーク近代美術館)
  ◎Merce by Merce by Paik
- [7月22日-8月27日]「第4回現代芸術祭—映像の今日」(富山県立近代美術館)
  ◎Window/Staircase

1990

- [4月11日-6月3日]「Sydney Biennale: The Readymade boomerang, Certain relations in 20th century Art」
  ◎Window/River/Bicycle wheel 1
- [5月26日-8月30日]「Venice Biennale Ubi Fluxus ibi motus 1990-1962」
  ◎Stairs/Adam and Eve/Window Snow/Bicycle
- [夏]「Taormina Arte」(Villa Comunale Park, Taormina、シチリア)
  ◎The Gate for Culture

1991

- [4月26日-9月15日]**アメリカ初の回顧展「Shigeko Kubota Video Sculpture」がAmerican Museum of Moving Image(MMI)で開催され、ヨーロッパ、日本などに巡回。**
  ◎Chess/Video Poem/Grave/Staircase/Door/Meta-Marcel (Snow)/Three Mountains/River/Berlin Diary/Video Haiku/Bicycle/Green Installation/Window (Flowers)/Window (Stars)/Niagara Falls/Rock Video/Adam and Eve/Auto-Tire Wheel/Bycycle 1, 2, 3/Video Byobu III (Birds)/Window (Snow with Computer Writing)/[21点]
- [9月5日-11月10日]「Consumer Tools: Personal Visions」(ニューヨーク近代美術館)
  ◎Navajo Sky
- [9月14日、15日]シンポジウム「Video '92 & Beyond」(American Musuem of the Moving Image、ニューヨーク)
- [10月10日-11月10日]「ARTEC '91 第2回名古屋国際ビエンナーレ」(名古屋市美術館、ほか)
  ◎Auto-Tire Wheel

1992

- [1月18日-3月20日]**「クボタ シゲコ ビデオ インスタレーション」(原美術館、東京)、MMIより巡回。**
  ◎Chess/Grave/Staircase/Meta-Marcel (Snow)/Three Mountains/River/Bicycle/Window (Flowers)/Window (Stars)/Rock Video/Adam and Eve/Bycycle 1, 2, 3/[21点]
- [10月10日-11月29日]**「Shigeko Kubota 1975-1992」(Stedelijk Museum、アムステルダム)、MMIより巡回。**
  ◎[出品作不明]
- [4月9日-7月16日]「New Acquisitions, Video: Joan Jonas, Nam June Paik, William Wegman」(ニューヨーク近代美術館)
  ◎Merce and Marcel

- [10月10日–11月29日]「彫刻の遠心力–この十年の展開」(国立国際美術館、大阪)
  ◎Staircase/Window/Bicycle 1, 2, 3

1993

- **「Shigeko Kubota, Video Sculpture」(Ford Astistico, Eisfabrik, Hannover/Wiesser Raum, Hamburg/Kusthalle in Kiel, Kiel)MMIより巡回。**
  ◎[出品作不明]
- [6月14日–10月10日]「第43回ヴェネチア・ビエンナーレ Passagio a Oriente」
  ◎Garden of Eden. Video Dreamscape[Korean Grave, Jogging Lady, Bicycle Wheel, etc.]
- [9月3日–10月13日]「第2回リヨン・ビエンナーレ Et tous ils changent le monde」
  ◎Video feedback: Windmill, windflower
- 「VIDEOFORMES, 8e Festival International d'Art Vidéo」(クレモン=フェラン)
  ◎[出品作不明]
- 「Feuer, Erde, Wasser, Luft」(Mediale、ハンブルグ)
  ◎[出品作不明]
- [8月27日–9月5日]「Electronic Art/Philips 1993」(ベルリン)
  ◎[出品作不明]
- 「Matthew Barney, Shigeko Kubota, Bruce Nauman, Marcel Odenbach, Sierrick Sorin」(Barbara Gladstone Gallery、ニューヨーク)
  ◎[出品作不明]
- [11月13日–1月16日]「In the Spirit of Fluxus」(ウォーカー・アート・センター、ミネアポリス、ほか)
  ◎[出品作不明]

1994

- [2月5日–3月30日]「戦後日本の前衛美術」展(横浜美術館)
  ◎Window/Bicycle 1, 2, 3
- [5月11日–?]**「Shigeko Kubota Video as a Form of Spiritual Collision with the World」(ムディマ財団、ミラノ)**
  ◎[出品作不明]
- [6月5日–8月21日]「The First Generation: Women and Video, 1970–1975」(ロングビーチ美術館、ほか)
  ◎[出品作不明]
- [9月14日–1995年1月8日]「戦後日本の前衛美術」展(グッゲンハイム美術館ソーホー分館、ニューヨーク、ほか)
  ◎Window/Bicycle 1, 2, 3/Staircase
- [11月4日–1995年3月26日]「Duchamp's Leg」(ウォーカー・アート・センター、ミネアポリス)
  ◎[出品作不明]
- 「Set in Motion」(Frieda and Roy Furman Gallery, Walter Reade Theater, Lincoln Center、ニューヨーク)
  ◎Allan and Allen/Skater

1995

- [2月2日]The American Film Institute Award for Independent Film and Video Artists(マヤ・デレン賞)を受賞。
- [3月11日–6月18日]「記憶への視線」(ハラミュージアムアーク、群馬)
  ◎Bicycle 1, 2, 3
- [5月27日–9月5日]「Adding it up: Print Acquisitions 1970–1995」(ニューヨーク近代美術館)
  ◎Fluxkit
- [6月8日–8月31日]「ASIANA, Contemporary Art From the Far East」(Palazzo Vendramin Calergi、ヴェネチア)
  ◎[出品作不明]
- [7月7日–9月10日]「Collection in Context - Gazing Back: Shigeko Kubota and Mary Lucier」(ホイットニー美術館、ニューヨーク)
  ◎Staircase/Window
- [9月19日–11月20日]「光州ビエンナーレ '95 INFO-ART」
  ◎Niagara/Skater/Video flowers, etc.
- [11月10日–12月10日]「第4回イスタンブール・ビエンナーレ」
  ◎Niagara

1996

- [2月9日–3月16日]**「Shigeko Kubota: Video Sculptures Duchampiana」(Galerie de Paris)**
  ◎[カタログに記載なし]
- [2月]**[個展](Eric Fabre Galerie、パリ)**
  ◎[出品作不明]
- [3月5日–4月28日]「Les cases conjuguées en hommage à Teeny Duchamp」(ジュ・ド・ポーム美術館、パリ)
  ◎[出品作不明]
- [4月2日–5月6日]「美術の内がわ・外がわ—何故、眼差しは交わったのか—(シリーズART IN TOKYO No.8)」(板橋区立美術館)
  ◎Window
- [4月4日]パイクが脳梗塞で倒れる。
- [5月2日–8月2日]**「Shigeko Kubota: Video is a Ghost of Yourself」(Lance Fung Gallery、ニューヨーク)**
  ◎Video Rock Garden/Video Clouds/Small Windmill/Medium Windmill/Large Wnidmill/Video Tree/Video Flower/Video Snake/Video Coyote/Video Rock Garden (small)
- [6月19日–8月25日]**「Shigeko Kubota」(ホイットニー美術館、ニューヨーク)**
  ◎Bird II/Jogging Lady/Korean grave/Pissing Boy/Videoflower/Videotree/Windflower (Nail)/Windflower (Purple)/Windflower (Red Tape)/Windmill II/Windmill III/Videoflower I/Videoflower II/Videotree/Windmill/Running Coyote/Sitting Coyote/Snake

1998

- [1月19日–2月28日]**「久保田成子展」(鎌倉画廊、東京)**
  ◎Staircase/Adam and Eve/Sexual Healing

2000

- [2月11日–4月26日]パイクの大規模な回顧展「The Worlds of Nam June Paik」がグッゲンハイム美術館(ニューヨーク)で開催。実現のために公私に渡り尽力。
- [3月2日–4月1日]**「Shigeko Kubota: Sexual Healing」(Lance Fung Gallery、ニューヨーク)**
  ◎Video Flowers/Sexual Healing(SC)ほか、132頁参照
- [5月19日]アメリカ国籍を取得。
- [6月17日–8月16日]「現代美術百貨展」(山梨県立美術館)
  ◎Flux Medicine

2004

- [11月3日–12月19日]「マルセル・デュシャンと20世紀美術」(国立国際美術館、大阪、ほか)
  ◎Staircase/Window/Bicycle 1, 2, 3
- [11月20日–2005年2月20日]「フルクサス展—芸術から日常へ」(うらわ美術館)
  ◎Flux Medicine

2005

- [7月24日–9月11日]「前衛の女性 1950–1975」(栃木県立美術館)
  ◎ハイレッド・センター・イヴェント集/Fluxus Medicine/Flux Napkins/Video Poem/Marcel Duchamp and John Cage/Staircase

2006

- [1月29日]パイク、マイアミで死去。
- [6月25日–9月25日]「Into Me/Out of Me」(MoMA PS1、ニューヨーク)
  ◎Vagina Painting [photo]

2007

- [1月21日–3月19日]「国立新美術館開館記念展20世紀美術探検 アーティストたちの三つの冒険物語」(国立新美術館、東京)
  ◎Flux Medecine
- [3月6日–6月3日]「Art, Anti-Art, Non-Art: Experimentations in the Public Sphere in Postwar Japan」(Getty Research Institute、ロサンゼルス)
  ◎Flux Medecine
- [9月6日–10月20日]「Shigeko Kubota: My Life with Nam June Paik」(Maya Stendhal Gallery、ニューヨーク)
  ◎Nam June Paik I/Nam June Paik II/Pissing Boy/Jogging Lady/Tree (with green trunk)/Tree (on bucket)/Korean Grave/Bird I/Bird II

2008

- [9月10日–2009年3月23日]「Here is Every. Four Decades of Contemporary Art」(ニューヨーク近代美術館)
  ◎Staircase
- [9月30日–12月25日]「不協和音–日本のアーティスト6人」(豊田市美術館)
  ◎Staircase/Bicycle 1, 2, 3

2010

- [9月15–2011年5月2日]「Counter Space: Design and the Modern Kitchen」(ニューヨーク近代美術館)
  ◎[出品作不明]

2011

- [9月21日–2012年1月16日]「Thing/Thought: Fluxus Editions, 1962–1978」(ニューヨーク近代美術館)
  ◎Fluxkit (Napkin and Medicine?)

2012

- [11月18日–2013年2月25日]「Tokyo 1955–1970: A New Avant-Garde」(ニューヨーク近代美術館)
  ◎内科画廊での個展案内状/G.マチューナスへの手紙

2013

- [2月11日–3月23日]「ハイレッド・センター:『直接行動』の軌跡」展(名古屋市美術館、ほか)
  ◎ハイレッド・センター・イヴェント集
- [11月9日–12月23日]「女性アーティスト展　私たちは越えていく」(高岡市美術館、富山)
  ◎Staircase/Window

2014

- [7月23日]「Shigeko Kubota Rock Video: Cherry Blossom」(ハイライン、ニューヨーク)
  ◎Rock Video

2015

- [7月23日]ニューヨークにて乳がんのため死去。
- [9月11日]「久保田成子ヴィデオ・アート財団設立。
- [9月25日–11月21日]「The Experimental Television Center: A History, Etc . . .」(205 Hudson Street Gallery、ニューヨーク市立大学ハンターカレッジ)
  ◎[出品作不明]

2016

- [4月9日–7月24日]「シリーズ・映像のクリエイティビティ　ナム・ジュン・パイクとシゲコ・クボタ—折元立身が70年代ニューヨークで出会ったアーティストたち」(川崎市民ミュージアム)
  ◎Marcel Duchamp and John Cage(SC)

2018

- [2月8日–4月15日]「Before Projection: Video Sculpture 1974–1995」(MIT List Visual Atrs and Center、ケンブリッジ、ほか)
  ◎River
- [3月6日–4月14日]「Colossal World: Japanese Artists and New York, 1959s to Present」(White Box、ニューヨーク)
  ◎Bicycle/Photo portraits by Tom Haar

2019

- [9月6日–2020年2月23日]「Body Electric」(イエルバブエナ芸術センター、サンフランシスコ、ほか)
  ◎Video Poem
- [10月30日–2020年1月18日]「Japan is America」(Fergus McCaffrey、ニューヨーク)
  ◎Merce by Merce by Paik
- [11月1日–2020年2月2日]「窓展:窓をめぐるアートと建築の旅」(東京国立近代美術館、ほか)
  ◎Window (Three tapes)
- [11月18日–2020年1月30日]Shigeko Kubota: a woman artist, her life(Boa: basedonart、デュッセルドルフ)

◎（シングル・チャンネル作品、ドローイング、エフェメラ）

- ［11月1日−12月15日］「Shigeko Kubota: Restored in Beacon」（Mother Gallery、ビーコン、ニューヨーク）
  ◎Staircase/Grave/Bicycle 1, 2, 3/Chess/Window/Marcel Duchamp and John Cage(SC)/Rock Video(SC)

2020

- ［2月6日−6月6日］「Mercer Street」（McCaffrey、ニューヨーク）
  ◎Bicycle 1, 2, 3/Video Haiku
- ［2月20日−3月29日］「Techne Triennial: Topologies of the Real」（CAFA Art Museum、北京）
  ◎Photographs of Marcel Duchamp and John Cage's Reunion Chess Match
- ［12月27日−2021年3月21日］「Refocusing on the Medium: the Rise of East Asia Video Art」（OCAT上海館、上海）
  ◎Bicycle 1

2021

- ［3月20日−6月6日］「Viva Video!: The Art and life of Shigeko Kubota」没後初、1992年以来日本初の大規模な個展「Viva Video! 久保田成子」展開催（新潟県立近代美術館）。国立国際美術館、東京都現代美術館へ巡回。

Shigeko Kubota Chronology

Notes

[Notes on the Chronology]

- The chronology is made up of solo shows, group exhibitions, and other events that have been deemed important in the artist's career arranged in chronological order. It was assembled by referring to catalogs, pamphlets, magazines, and other publications related to the artist's work as well as the artist's diary entries and other writings, and the following interview:

  Oral History Interview with Shigeko Kubota, conducted by Miwako Tezuka, October 11, 2009, Oral History Archives of Japanese Art (URL: www.oralarthistory.org/archives/kubota_shigeko/interview_01.php).

[Notes on Exhibitions]

- Although the survey focuses primarily on exhibitions that were held in Japan and the U.S., some information on the artist's activities in Europe and Asia has also been provided. However, the information on areas outside Japan and the U.S. may not be comprehensive.
- Information on the exhibitions is given in the following order: [Exhibition period] (omitted when unknown), *title of exhibition* ([exhibition title unknown]when unknown), name of venue (as of the time of the event), name of Japanese prefecture (or name of city for foreign events—omitted when the name of the prefecture or city appears in the name of the venue). However, the name of the venue and city have been omitted for recurring international exhibitions such as the Venice Biennale. For group exhibitions that traveled or were held at multiple venues, only the name of the main venue has been given followed by the name of the city or country, and the word "et.al." In the case of solo exhibitions, however, the name of every venue has been given.
- For reference purposes, exhibitions that appear in the artist's CV or the chronologies included in the catalogs listed below have been included even when it proved impossible to locate a primary document related to the event. In these cases, the title is listed as "exhibition title unknown."

  Shigeko Kubota: Video Sculpture (New York: American Museum of Moving Image, 1991).

  Shigeko Kubota (New York: Whitney Museum of American Art, 1996).

[Notes on the Exhibited Works]

- In light of the fact that the artist basically gave her works English titles, exhibited works are provided in English after ◎. When it is unknown, this has been indicated with the word "unknown" or the phrase "not listed in the catalog." The list of works is not in any particular order. Titles are connected with a slash. The year of production has been omitted. Except for video sculptures and single-channel works, the number of pieces has been given in brackets for drawings and other works. When several works bear a same title, single-channel videos are indicated with (SC).

1937

- [Aug. 2]Born as the second of four daughters Ryuen and Fumie Kubota in Maki-machi, Nishikan-ku, Niigata-city.

1944

- [Apr.]Entered Primary School of Niigata University.

1945

- Temporarily moved to her father's family home in Takada-city during the war.

1947

- [Apr.]Transferred to Primary School in Maki-machi

1950

- [Mar.]Graduated from Primary School in Maki-machi

1953

- [Apr.]Graduated from Naoetsu Municipal Middle School
- [Apr.]Entered Niigata Prefectural Naoetsu High School. Her father was the principle there and invited Tatsuji Terashima as an art teacher from Tokyo.
- [Summer]Ran away from home and lodged at a relative's place, Jozenji Temple (Joetsu City), for a few months.

1954

- [Oct. 9–Oct. 26]*Sunflower* entered *the 8th Niki-ten exhbition* (Tokyo Metropolitan Art Museum).

1956

- [Mar.]Graduated from Naoetsu High School.
- [Apr.]Entered Tokyo University of Education and majored in sculpture. Joined the student movement.

1958

- [Sept. 22–Oct. 10]Sculpture *Kubi* A entered *the 22nd Shinseisaku Exhibition* (Tokyo Metropolitan Art Museum).

1959

- [May 26–June 7]Received an encouragement award for *Shiseki* at *the 14th Niigata Prefectural Art Exhibition* (Kobayashi Department Store, Niigata).

1960

- [Mar.]Graduated from Tokyo University of Education.

1960

- [Apr.]Started teaching at 2nd Ebara Middle School in Shinagawa-Ward, Tokyo.
- [After April]Stayed with her aunt and dancer Chiya Kuni and befriended members of Group Ongaku and other artists through Chiya Kuni Dance Institute.

1961

- [Sept. 22–Oct. 10]*Shiseki 5* [Death Stone 5] and *Shiseki 34* [Death Stone 34] were selected for *the 25th Shinseisaku Exhibition* (Tokyo Metropolitan Art Museum).

1962

- [Sept. 22–Oct. 10]Her sculpture, *Shiseki T* [Death Stone T] was selected for *the 26th Shinseisaku Exhibition* (Tokyo Metropolitan Art Museum).

1963

- [Mar. 2–Mar. 16]Showed two metal sculpture *we can make it, Suddenly* at *the 15th Yomiuri Independent Exhibition* (Tokyo Metropolitan Art Museum).
- [Dec. 1–7]**First solo exhibition, *1st. Love, 2nd. Love . . . Shigeko Kubota Sculpture Solo Exhibition* (Naiqua Gallery).**
  ◎1st. love / 2nd. love / 3rd. love
- [Dec. 3–5]Performed *a drop of water* in *Sweet 16* (Sogetsu Kaikan Hall, Tokyo).

1964

- [Jan. 26–27]Participated in Hi-Red Center's *Shelter Plan* at the Iimperial Hotel, Tokyo.
- [Mar. ?]Retired from 2nd Ebara Middle School.
- [May 24 or 31]Participated in Yoko Ono's *Morning Piece.*
- [May 29]Attended *Works of Nam June Paik* at Sogetsu Art Center. Nam June Paik praised her Naiqua Gallery show.
- [June 17–22]Participated in *OFF MUSEUM* (Tsubakikindai-Gallery, Tokyo), organized by Ushio Shinohara.
  ◎Miss Universe
- [July 4]Flew to New York with Mieko (Chieko) Shiomi. Lived in an apartment prepared by George Maciunas and began participating in Fluxus activities.
- [Oct. 12–17]Submitted a work to *Yasunao Tone's solo show* (Investigation Event) at Naiqua Gallery. [title unknown, black underwear on the wall]
- [Nov. 4]Took publicity photos of *Vagina Painting* at Peter Moore's studio. The event was postponed.

1965

- [Around June 27 or around July 4]Performed *Vagina Painting* as part of *the Perpetual Flux Fest at Cinemateque.*
- [–1966]Enrolled at New York University to obtain a student's visa.
- [Sept. 6–14]Included her work in *Flux Week* exhibition at Gallery Crystal in Tokyo.
  ◎[title unknown] (same work at Tone's solo show 1964)
- [Sept. 8]Participated in Dick Higgins' *Long Constellation No. 10 Graphis No.131* as a performer, as part of the 3rd Annual New York Avant Garde Festival, at Judson Hall, New York.
- [Sept. 25]Participated in the Flux Concert *THE 83RD FLUXUS CONCERT: FLUXORCHESTRA*, at Carnegie Recital Hall, playing the violin.

1966

- [–1967]Enrolled at New School of Social Research to extend her student visa.
- [Sept. 9]Participated in *the 4th Annual New York Avant Garde Festival* in Central Park.
  ◎peeping into the balla

1967

- [Jan. 21, 22, 27–29, Feb. 3–5]Participated as a Vietnamese in Carolee Schneemann's anti-Vietnam performance, *Snows* at Martinique Theater, New York.
- [–1968]Enrolled in the Brooklyn Museum Art School to extend her student visa.
- She occasionally participated in concerts of the Sonic Arts Union of which David Behrman was a founding member. Accompanied SAU concert tour in Italy and Belgium in April. After marrying composer Behrman, she moved to Stony Point, about sixty km from New York City.

1968

- [Mar. 5]Photographed *Reunion* chess event between John Cage and Marcel Duchamp in Ryerson Theatre, Tronto.
- [Mar. 9]Met Mr. and Mrs. Duchamp on the airplane to Buffallo to go see Merce Cunningham's *Walk Around the Time.*
- Taught Japanese to make her ends meet.

1969

- [Apr.–May]Sonic Arts Union Europe Tour (Stockholm, Sweden; Aquilla, Italy; and Brussells, Belgium)
- [May]Occassionally wrote a report on the New York art scene for Japanese art magazine *Bijutsu Techo.*

1970

- Self-published a book, *Marcel Duchamp and John Cage.*
- [Nov.]Moved to Los Angeles, following Paik, after separating from Behrman.

1971

- Audited lectures of Allan Kaprow and others at California Institute of Art. First exposure to the video camera and made *Self Portrait.*

- [June 1]Returned to New York.
- [Nov. 19]*8th Annual New York Avant Garde Festival* (69th Regiment Armory, New York).
  ◎[unknown]

1972

- [Mar.]Acquired a SONY Portapak through Mrs. Abe.
- [May 1–]Traveled throughout Europe and took video (Frankfrut, Bremen, Amsterdam, Paris, Rouen, Nice, Venice, et al.).
- Moved into an artists' building, Westbeth in New York City.
- [June 30]**The first live presentation of her video, *Live and Videotape Concert*, The Kitchen, New York.**
  ◎Cage-Tudor-Duchamp / Europe on half inch a Day
- [Sept. 5]***Video Birthday Party (60th) of John Cage by Shigeko Kubota*, The Kitchen, New York.**
  ◎John Cage in Bremen, New York, San Francisco and Toronto
- [Sept. 16, 23, 30]Participated in the *Women's Video Festival*, The Kitchen, New York.
  ◎Joa: Impasse of the Infidelity
- [Sept. 30]***Daily Performance: Shigeko Kubota Video Tapes*, Experimental Television Center Binghamton at Everson Museum, Syracuse, New York.**
  ◎Three Channels Video Performance (Marcel Duchamp-John Cage Chess match / Europe on a Tape a Day with slight time variations) (sic.)
- [Oct. 3–29]*Videotapes*, de Saisset Art Gallery, University of Santa Clara, California.
  ◎[unknown]
- [Oct. 28–30]*9th Annual New York Avant Garde Festival*, South Street Seaport, Alexander Hamilton Boat.
  ◎Video Birthday Party for John Cage II
- [Nov. 21]Participated in the *An Evening of Video Exhibition*, Wesleyan University, Middletown, Connecticut.
  ◎Video Birthday Party for John Cage, No.3 / Europe on 1/2 inch a day / Impasse of Infidelity / Marcel Duchamp and John Cage
- [Dec. 16]The first live concert of women's group, White Black Red & Yellow at The Kitchen, New York.
  ◎Riverrun—Video Water Poem
- *First Annual New York Video Festival*, The Kitchen, New York.
  ◎[unknown]

1973

- Video Artist in Residence, School of the Art Institute Chicago, Illinois (1981, 1982, 1984)
  ◎[unknown]
- **[solo show] Wabash Transit Gallery, School of the Art Institute of Chicago.**
  ◎[unknown]
- [Apr. 17–May 18]*Circuit: A Video International*, Everson Museum of Art, Syracuse, New York, et al.
  ◎[Europe on 1/2 inch a Day]
- [Apr. 20, 21]The second (and last) live concert of women's group, White Black Red & Yellow at The Kitchen, New York.
  ◎Video Fortunetelling
- [May 4–14]*About 405 East 13th Street (#1)*, 405 East 13 Street, New York.
  ◎Water Event
- [May 28]*Second Annual Video Arts Festival: Shigeko Kubot*a, The Kitchen, New York.
  ◎A36-24-36
- [June]Visited Chinle, Arizona and stayed in a Navajo Indian reservation. Took video for *Video Girls and Video Songs for Navajo Sky* (Hereafter Navajo Sky).
- [Sept. 28, Oct. 12, 14]*Second Annual Women's Video Festival*, The Kitchen, New York.
  ◎Navajo Sky
- [Dec. 9]Participated in the *10th Annual New York Avant Garde Festival*, Grand Central Station,New York.
  ◎[unknown]
- [Dec. 31]Returned home in Japan and videorecorded her father in sickbed.

1974

- [Jan. 7–9]Organized *Tokyo-New York: Video Express* with Video Hiroba and Underground Center, Tenjo Sajiki, Tokyo.
  ◎[unknown]
- [Jan. 23–25]Participated as a guest speaker at the symposium "Open Circuits: The Future of Television," Museum of Modern Art, New York.
- [Feb. 13]*Video Celebration for John Cage*, Harvard University, Cambridge.
  ◎[unknown]
- [Feb. 18]*Women in Film and Video*, State University of New York, Buffalo.
  ◎Navajo Sky
- [Apr. 18, 19, 20, 21]*About 405 East 13th Street (#2)*, 405 East 13 Street, New York.
  ◎[unknown]
- [May 30–June 16]*ART NOW 74: A Celebration of the American Arts*, John F. Kennedy Center for the Performing Arts, Washington, D.C.
  ◎Navajo Sky
- [June 15–30]*Tokyo Biennale 1974*, Kyoto City Museum of Art.
  ◎作品(work)
- Purchased a loft on Mercer St. throlugh George Maciunas and moved there with Paik.
- [July 7]Father died. Made *My Father*.
- [July–Aug.]*Project 1974*, Kölnischer Kunsteverein, Cologne.
  ◎[unknown]
- [Nov.]Started video curator job at the Anthology Film Archives (till 1982).
- [Nov. 16]*11th Annual Avant Garde Festival of New York*, Shea Stadium, New York.
  ◎Video Wind, Video Stripe
- [Nov. 30]*Soup and Tart*, The Kitchen, New York.
  ◎[unknown]

1975

- Had a miscarriage. Recorded *Hospital Diary*.
- Received a Creative Artists Public Service Program Grant.
- Received a National Endowment for the Arts Fellowship (also in 1978 and 1980).
- [Apr. 10–26]*Women's Video Festival*, Women's Interart

Center, New York.
◎Marcel Duchamp and John Cage
- [May 30–June 7]The first video sculpture exhibition, *Video Poem by Shigeko Kubota*, The Kitchen, New York.
  ◎Duchamp's Grave (Hereafter Grave) / Self-portrait (Later Video Poem)
- [June]*Projected Video*, Whitney Museum of American Art, New York.
  ◎Chess (tape)
- [Sept. 17–Nov. 2]*Video Art*, Institute of Contemporary Art, University of Pennsylvania, Philadelphia.
  ◎Europe on 1/2 inch a day
- [Sept. 27]*12th Annual Avant Garde Festival of New York*, Gateway National Recreation Area, New York.
  ◎[unknown]
- [Nov. 1–Jan. 31, 1976]*Projects: Video VI*, Museum of Modern Art, New York.
  ◎Video Girls and Video Songs for Navajo Sky
- [Nov. 25–Dec. 19]*Shigeko Kubota: Two Pieces*, Everson Museum of Art, Syracuse, New York.
  ◎[unknown]
- *Two Installations*, and/or Gallery, Seattle, Washington.
  ◎Grave / Video Poem
- *Southland Video Anthology*, Long Beach Museum of Art, California.
  ◎A Day at the California Institute of the Arts (with Shuya Abe)

1976

- [Jan. 24–Feb. 17]*Shigeko Kubota: 3 Video Installations. Duchampiana*, René Block Gallery, New York. First showing *Duchampiana* series.
  ◎Nude Descending A Staircase (Hereafter Staircase) / Video Chess (Hereafter Chess) / Grave
- [Apr. 1–3]*Living Video Environment Video Installations by Shigeko Kubota at her studio* (Part of The Moving Image New York City organized by Anthology Film Archives)
  ◎Staircase / Grave
- [Apr. 19–June 20]*Projects: Video III*, Museum of Modern Art, New York.
  ◎My Father
- [June 9–26]*Rooms*, MoMA PS1, New York.
  ◎[unknown]
- [June 10–27]*Women's Video Festival NYC*, Women's Interart Center, New York.
  ◎My Father / Grave
- *New York-Downtown Manhattan: SoHo-Berlin Festival*, Academie der Kunste, Berlin.
  ◎Grave
- [July 23–Aug. 1][solo show], and/or Gallery, Seattle, Washington.
  ◎Staircase
- [Aug.]Traveled throughout the West with Robert (Bob) Harris. Video taken then became the base for Three Mountains.

1977

- "Indie" Award, Association of Independent Video and Filmmakers, New York.
- [Jan. 22–Feb. 26]*Meta-Marcel by Shigeko Kubota 3 Video Sculptures: Window, Door, Mountain*, René Block Gallery, New York.
  ◎Window / Door / Mountain
- [Mar. 21]Married Nam June Paik. Hospitalized for masterectomy in the same year.
- [June 19]*13th Annual Avant Garde Festival of New York* , The World Trade Center, New York.
  ◎[unknown]
- [June 24–Oct. 2]*documenta 6*, Kassel.
  ◎Staircase
- [Sept. 18–Oct. 16]*Duchampiana: 3 Video Sculptures Shigeko Kubota*, Long Beach Museum of Art, California.
  ◎Staircase / Grave / Meta Marcel: Window (Hereafter Window)
- [unknown]*Duchampiana*, Museo de Arte Carrillo Gil, Mexico City.
  ◎Staircase

1978

- Taught Video Art, School of Visual Arts, NY and Kunst Akademie in Dusseldorf.
- [Jan. 21–Feb. 3]*Shigeo Kubota 4 Video Sculptures: Duchampiana*, Japan House Gallery, New York.
  ◎Grave / Window / Chess / Video Poem
- [Feb. 6–19]*PAN-CONCEPTUALS '78*, Gallery Tamura, Tokyo."
  ◎[unknown]
- [Mar. 16–May 2]*Projects: Shigeko Kubota*, Museum of Modern Art, New York.
  ◎Staircase
- [May 20]*14th Annual Avant Garde Festival of New York and the 2nd Annual Cambridge River Festival*, Cambridge, Massachusetts.
  ◎[unknown]
- [July 14–18]*Shigeko Kubota: Video Poem*, Galerie René Block, West Berlin.
  ◎Video Poem
- [Oct. 5–29][solo show] Art Gallery of Ontario, Toronto.
  ◎Video Poem / Staircase / My Father
- [Nov. 10–Dec. 31]*Shigeko Kubota: Nude Descending a Staircase*, Everson Museum of Art, Syracuse, New York.
  ◎Staircase
- [Dec. 3–Jan. 21, 1979]*Couples*, Institute for Art & Urban Resources, P.S.1, Long Island City, New York.
  ◎Window (Snow)

1979

- Received Rockefeller Fellowship.
- Received D.A.A.D. (Deutscher Akademischer Austauschdienst) Fellowship, and stayed in Berlin.
- [May 22–June 3]*Shigeko Kubota, Taka Iimura, New Video*, Whitney Museum of American Art, New York.
  ◎Three Mountains
- [Sept. 28–Oct. 21]*Three Mountains & Snow*, Aspen Center for the Visual Arts, Colorado.
  ◎Three Mountains / Window (Snow)
- [Oct. 28–Dec. 16]*Videoweeks Essen '79*, Museum Folkwang, Essen.

◎[unknown]

1980

- Received a New York State Council on the Arts Fellowship (also in 1982 and 1984).
- [Jan. 20–Mar. 2]*Fur Augen und Ohren: von der Spieluhr zum akustischen Environment*, Akademie der Kunste, Berlin.
  ◎Three Mountains
- [May 9–11]*Video-Informative Series 2*, Institut Alemany de Barcelona.
  ◎Staircase
- [June 18–Aug. 24]*Encounter par les yeux: objets et environments sonores*, Musée d'Art Moderne de la Ville de Paris.
  ◎Video Chess / Window
- [Sept. 23]Talk and Show "Video Sculpture: Mental Landscape into Physical Landscape," *Video Viewpoints*, Museum of Modern Art, New York.

1981

- Video Artist in Residence, Brown University, Providence, Rhode Island.
- The Museum of Modern Art purchased Duchampiana: Nude Descending a Staircase as the first video installation for its collection.
- [June 26–Aug. 23]*Options 9*, Museum of Contemporary Art, Chicago.
  ◎Grave / Staircase / Video Chess / Window / Video Haiku - Hanging Piece (Hereafter Video Haiku)
- [Aug. 1–Sept. 6, 11–28]*The Exhibition of Marcel Duchamp*, The Museum of Modern Art, Seibu Takanawa, Nagano, The Seibu Museum of Art, Tokyo.
  ◎Window / Staircase
- [Sept. 30–Oct. 17]**[solo show] Atholl McBean Gallery, San Francisco Art institute Annual Exhibition.**
  ◎Staircase / Window
- [Dec. 12–Jan. 24, 1982]**Shigeko Kubota: Video Sculptures, toured from daadgalerie, Berlin, Museum Folkwang, Essen, Kunsthaus Zürich**
  ◎Chess / Staircase / Window / Door / River / Shigeko in Berlin [daadgalerie. Other venues unknown]
- *Video Classics*, The Bronx Museum, New York.
  ◎Staircase

1982

- [June 10–13]*National Video Festival*, Kennedy Center for the Performing Arts, Washington D.C. et al.
  ◎Staircase / Window

1983

- [Mar. 15–29]*Whitney Biennial 1983*, Whitney Museum of American Art, New York.
  ◎River / Allan 'n' Allen's Complaint
- [June 23–30]*"Eye to Eye" An event surveying recent Asian American artist works*, Asian Arts Institute, New York
  ◎[unknown]
- [July 1–Sept. 4]*Art and Technology*, The Museum of Modern Art, Toyama.
  ◎Window / Staircase
- [Sept. 10–25]**[solo show] Japan American Cultural and Community Center, Los Angeles.**
  ◎[unknown]
- [Oct. 1–31]***Shigeko Kubota / MATRIX 65*, The University of California, Berkeley Art Museum.**
  ◎River
- [Oct. 3–Jan. 3, 1984]*Video Art: A Hisotry*, Museum of Modern Art, New York.
  ◎My Father
- [Nov. 2–Nov. 26]***Shigeko Kubota Video Sculpture*, White Columns, New York.**
  ◎Window (Snow / Flowers / Stars) / Video Haiku / Video Relief / Green Installations / Chess / Berlin Diary: Thanks to my Ancestors (Hereafter Berlin Diary) / Duchampiana: Bicycle Wheel (Hereafter Bicycle)
- [Dec. 6–18]***Shigeko Kubota Video Sculptures*, Fondo del Sol, Visual Art and Media Center, Washington D.C.**
  ◎Meta Marcel: Window (Snow / Flowers / Stars) / Video Haiku / Video Relief / Green Installations
- [Dec. 14–23]***Ten-day Video "Snow"*, Grey Art Gallery, New York.**
  ◎Meta-Marcel: Window
- **[solo show] Japan House Gallery, New York.**
  ◎Video Poem
- *Transformations*, Focal Point Media Center, Seattle, Washington.
  ◎[unknown]
- [exhibition title unknown] Palais de Beaux-Art, Bruxelles
  ◎[unknown]

1984

- [February]River was featured on the cover of *Art in America* magazine.
- [Summer]Trip to Korea with Paik after his show in Tokyo (*Nam June Paik: mostly video*, Tokyo Metropolitan Museum).
- [Sept. 14–Oct. 28]*The Luminous Image*, Stedelijk Museum, Amsterdam.
  ◎Three Mountains
- [Nov. 23–Jan. 1, 1985]*A Survey: Artist's TV Lab, WNET/Thirteen*, Museum of Modern Art, New York.
  ◎[unknown]
- [Dec. 18–29]***Shigeko Kubota: Marcel Duchamp's Grave (Revived)*,The Kitchen, New York.**
  ◎Grave
- *Societe des Expositions*, Palais des Beaux-Arts, Bruxelles.
  ◎[unknown]
- [exhibition title unknown] Milwaukee Art Museum, Wisconsin.
  ◎River
- [exhibition title unknown] Sprengel Museum, Hanover.
  ◎Staircase
- *TiJD* show, Louisiana Museum, Copenhagen.
  ◎Staircase

1985

- Received a New York Foundation for the Arts Fellowship.
- [Mar. 9–30]***Shigeko Kubota Video Installation: Niagara Falls*, The Kitchen, New York.**
  ◎Niagara Falls (Hereafter Niagara)
- [July 18–Sept. 8]*The Box Show*, Tamayo Museum, Mexico City.
  ◎Window (Snow / Flowers / Stars)
- [Nov. 6–Jan. 6, 1986][title unknown] Kulturhuset, The Stockholm Culture House, Sweden
  ◎Staircase
- [Nov. 14–Dec. 22]*TV Sculpture*, Hofstra Emily Lowe Gallery, Hofstra University, New York.
  ◎Green Installation / Window (Snow / Flowers / Stars)
- [*exhibition title unknown*] Kunsthalle Mannheim, West Germany.
  ◎[unknown]

1986

- [Jan. 31–Mar. 30]***Broken Diary: SoHo Soap/Rain Damage, Story of a SoHo Artists' Co-op*, The New Museum, New York.**
  ◎Broken Diary: SoHo Soap/Rain Damage (Hereafter SoHo Soap)
- [Sept. 18–Oct. 12]***Shigeko Kubota Video Sculpture and Drawings*, Piezo Electric Gallery, Los Angeles.**
  ◎Window (Star?) / Chess / Rock Video Cherry Blossoms (Hereafter Rock Video)
- [Sept. 21–Jan. 18, 1987]*The Window in Twentieth Century Art*, Neuberger Museum of Art, Purchase, New York, et al.
  ◎Window
- [Sept. 27–Nov. 2]Talk event, *The Other Television: Video by Artists*, Fort Wayne Museum of Art, Indiana.
  ◎River
- [Nov. 19]Talk Event "Cycles: Revolutions in the Electronic Arts" presented by The Center for New Television, Chicago.
  ◎Single Channel Video (Trip to Korea)
- **[solo show] New Langston Arts Gallery, San Francisco.**
  ◎Rock Video
- *[exhibition title unknown]*, Fort Wayne Museum of Art, Indiana.
  ◎[unknown]
- *[exhibition title unknown]*, Villa Stuck, Munich.
  ◎[unknown]

1987

- Received a Guggenheim Fellowship.
- [June 12–Sept. 20]*documenta 8*, Kassel.
  ◎Niagara / Broken Diary / Chapter 12 / SoHo Soap
- [July 29–Aug. 11]*Japan 87 Video Television Festival*, Spiral, Tokyo.
  ◎Niagara
- [Oct. 1–Jan. 3, 1988]*A Centennial Tribute apropos of Marcel Duchamp*, Philadelphia Museum of Art.
  ◎Chess

1988

- Received an NEA grant in Visual Arts.
- [Jan. 15–Feb. 6]*Uebrigens Sterben Immer Die Anderen. Marcel Duchamp und die Avantgarge seit 1950*, Museum Ludwig, Cologne.
  ◎[unknown]
- [Feb. 8]Al Robbins, assistant / collaborator of Kubota passed away.
- [Feb. 18–Mar. 30]*Video Art: Expanded Form*, Whitney Museum of American Art, New York.
  ◎Meta-Marcel: Window
- [May 22–Sept. 5]*Interaction: Light, Sound, Motion*, Aldrich Museum of Contermporary Art, Ridgefield.
  ◎Dry Mountain, Dry Water
- [Aug. 24–Sept. 25]*The 3rd Australian Video Festival*, Art Space, Sydney.
  ◎[unknown]
- [Sept. 11–16]*Shigeko Kubota und Keigo Yamamoto*, Japanisches Kulturinstitut, Cologne.
  ◎Video-Byobu
- *3rd Videonale*, Japanisches Kulturinstitut, Bonn.
  ◎[unknown]

1989

- [Mar. 16–Apr. 23]*Video-Skulptur retrospektiv und aktuell: 1963–1989*, Kölnischer Kunstverein, Cologne, et al.
  ◎Three Mountains
- [Apr. 20–May 30]*The Arts for Television*, Museum of Modern Art, New York.
  ◎Merce by Merce by Paik
- [July 22–Aug. 27]*4th Contemporary Art Festival: Image of Today*, The Museum of Modern Art, Toyama.
  ◎Window / Staircase

1990

- [Apr. 11–June 3]*Sydney Biennale: The Readymade boomerang, Certain relations in 20th century Art*
  ◎Window / River / Bicycle 1
- [May 26–Aug. 30]*Venice Biennale Ubi Fluxus ibi motus 1990–1962*
  ◎Stairs / Adam and Eve / Window Snow / Bicycle
- [Summer]*Taormina Arte*, Villa Comunale Park, Taormina, Sicilia.
  ◎The Gate for Culture

1991

- [Apr. 26–Sept. 15]***Shigeko Kubota Video Sculpture*, American Museum of Moving Image, New York. Traveled to multiple venues including Europe, Japan.**
  ◎Chess / Video Poem / Grave / Staircase / Door / Window (Snow) / Three Mountains / River / Berlin Diary / Video Haiku / Bicycle / Green Installation / Window (Flowers) / Window (Stars) / Niagara / Rock Video / Adam and Eve / Auto-Tire Wheel / Bycycle 1, 2, 3 / Video Byobu III (Birds) / Window (Snow with Computer Writing) / [21 pieces]

- [Sept. 5–Nov. 10]*Consumer Tools: Personal Visions*, Museum of Modern Art, New York.
  ◎Navajo Sky
- [Sept. 14, 15]**Symposium "Video '92 & Beyond," American Musuem of the Moving Image, New York.**
- [Oct. 10–Nov. 10]*Artec 91, International Biennale*, Nagoya, et al.
  ◎Auto-Tire Wheel

1992

- [Jan. 18–Mar. 20]***Kubota Shigeko Video Installation*, Hara Museum, Tokyo. MMI exhibition travels to Japan.**
  ◎Chess / Grave / Staircase / Window (Snow) / Three Mountains / River / Bicycle / Window (Flowers) / Window (Stars) / Rock Video / Adam and Eve / Bycycle 1, 2, 3 / [21 pieces]
- [Oct. 10–Nov. 29]***Shigeko Kubota Video Sculptuur*, Stedelijk Museum, Amsterdam. MMI exhibition travels to Amsterdam.**
  ◎[unknown]
- [Apr. 9–July 16]*New Acquisitions, Video: Joan Jonas, Nam June Paik, William Wegman*, Museum of Modern Art, New York.
  ◎Merce and Marcel
- [Oct. 10–Nov. 29]*Centrifugal Sculpture: An Aspect of Japanese Sculpture in the Late Decade*, The National Museum of Art, Osaka.
  ◎Staircase / Window / Bicycle 1, 2, 3

1993

- ***Shigeko Kubota, Video Sculpture*, Ford Astistico, Eisfabrik, Hannover / Wiesser Raum, Hamburg / Kusthalle in Kiel, Kiel. MMI exhibition travels to Amsterdam.**
  ◎[unknown]
- [June 14–Oct. 10]"Passagio a Oriente," *La Biennale di Venezia XLV Esposizione Internazionale d'Arte 1993*, Venice.
  ◎Garden of Eden. Video Dreamscape [Korean Grave, Jogging Lady, Bicycle, etc.]
- [Aug. 27–Sept. 5]*Electronic Art/Philips 1993*, Berlin.
  ◎[unknown]
- [Sept. 3–Oct. 13]"Et tous ils changent le monde," *2ème Biennale d'art contemporain*, Lyon.
  ◎Video feedback / Windmill, windflower
- [Nov. 13–Jan. 16, 1994]*In the Spirit of Fluxus*, Walker Art Center, Minneapolis, et al.
  ◎[unknown]
- *VIDEOFORMES, 8e Festival International d'Art Vidéo*, Clermont Ferrand.
  ◎[unknown]
- *Feuer, Erde, Wasser, Luft*, Mediale, Hamburg, Germany.
  ◎[unknown]
- *Matthew Barney, Shigeko Kubota, Bruce Nauman, Marcel Odenbach, Sierrick Sorin*, Barbara Gladstone Gallery, New York.
  ◎[unknown]

1994

- [Feb. 5–Mar. 30]*Japanese Art After 1945: Scream Against the Sky*, Yokohama Museum of Art, Kanagawa.
  ◎Window / Duchampiana: Bicycle 1, 2, 3
- ***Shigeko Kubota Video as a Form of Spiritual Collision with the World*, Fondazione Mudima, Milano.**
  ◎[unknown]
- [June 5–Aug. 21]*The First Generation: Women and Video, 1970–1975*, Long Beach Museum of Art, LA, et al.
  ◎[unknown]
- [Sept. 14–Jan. 8, 1995]"
Japanese Art After 1945: Scream Against the Sky, Guggenheim Museum SoHo, New York."
  ◎Window / Bicycle 1, 2, 3 / Staircase
- [Nov. 4–Mar. 26, 1995]*Duchamp's Leg*, Walker Art Center, Minneapolis, Minnesota.
  ◎[unknown]
- *Set in Motion*, Frieda and Roy Furman Gallery, Walter Reade Theater, Lincoln Center, New York.
  ◎Allan and Allen / Skater

1995

- [Feb. 2]Received Maya Deren Award from the American Film Institute Award for Independent Film and Video Artists.
- [Mar. 11–June 18]*Visions from Memory*, Hara Museum ARC
  ◎Bicycle 1, 2, 3
- [May 27–Sept. 5]*Adding it up: Print Acquisitions 1970–1995*, Museum of Modern Art, New York.
  ◎Fluxkit
- [June 8–Aug. 31]*ASIANA, Contemporary Art From the Far East*, Palazzo Vendramin Calergi, Venice.
  ◎[unknown]
- [July 7–Sept. 10]*Collection in Context - Gazing Back: Shigeko Kubota and Mary Lucier*, Whitney Museum of American Art, New York.
  ◎Staircase / Window
- [Sept. 19–Nov. 20]"INFO-ART", *Kwangju Biennale '95*, Korea.
  ◎Niagara / Skater / Video flowers
- [Nov. 10–Dec. 10]"New Orient/Ation," *4. Uluslararasi Istanbul Bienali (4th International Istanbul Biennial)*
  ◎Niagara

1996

- [Feb. 9–Mar. 16]***Shigeko Kubota: Video Sculptures Duchampiana*, Galerie de Paris.**
  ◎[Not listed in the catalog]
- [Feb.]**[solo show] Eric Fabre Galerie, Paris.**
  ◎[unknown]
- [Mar. 5–Apr. 28]*"Les cases conjuguées" en hommage à Teeny Duchamp*, Jeu de Paume, Paris.
  ◎[unknown]
- [Apr. 2–May 6]*Inside of Works, Outside of Works*, Itabashi Art Museum
  ◎Window
- [Apr. 4]Paik had a stroke.
- [May 2–Aug. 2]***Shigeko Kubota: Video is a Ghost of Yourself*, Lance Fung Gallery, New York.**
  ◎Video Rock Garden / Video Clouds / Small Windmill / Medium Windmill / Large Wnidmill / Video Tree / Video Flower / Video

Snake / Video Coyote / Video Rock Garden (small)

- [June 19–Aug. 25]***Shigeko Kubota*, Whitney Museum of American Art, New York.**
  ◎Bird II / Jogging Lady / Korean grave / Pissing Boy / Videoflower / Videotree / Windflower (Nail) / Windflower (Purple) / Windflower (Red Tape) / Windmill II / Windmill III / Videoflower I / Videoflower II / Videotree / Windmill / Running Coyote / Sitting Coyote / Snake

1998

- [Jan. 19–Feb. 28]***Kubota Shigeko*Kamakura Gallery, Tokyo.**
  ◎Staircase / Adam and Eve / Sexual Healing

2000

- [Feb. 11–Apr. 26]A major retrospective of Paik, *The Worlds of Nam June Paik*, was held at the Guggenheim Museum, New York. Worked both privately and publicly to make this happen.
- [Mar. 2–Apr. 1]***Shigeko Kubota: Sexual Healing*, Lance Fung Gallery, New York.**
  ◎Video Flowers / Sexual Healing (SC) et. al. See p. 132
- [May 19]Received an American citizenship.
- [June 17–Aug. 16]*Department Start of Contemporary Art*, Yamanashi Prefectural Museum of Art.
  ◎Flux Medicine

2004

- [Nov. 3–Dec. 19]*Marcel Duchamp and 20th Century Art*, National Museum of Art, Osaka.
  ◎Staircase / Window / Bicycle 1, 2, 3
- [Nov. 20–Feb. 20, 2005]*Fluxus - Art into Life*, Urawa Art Museum, Saitama.
  ◎Flux Medicine

2005

- [July 24–Sept. 11]*Japanese Women Artists in Avant-garde Movements, 1950–1975*, Tochigi Prefectural Museum of Art.
  ◎Hi-Red Center Events / Fluxus Medicine / Flux Napkins / Video Poem / Marcel Duchamp and John Cage / Staircase

2006

- [Jan. 29]Paik passed away in Miami.
- [June 25–Sept. 25]*Into Me / Out of Me*, MoMA PS1, New York.
  ◎Vagina Painting [photo]

2007

- [Jan. 21–Mar. 19]*Living in the material world "things" in art of the 20th century and beyond*, The National Art Center, Tokyo.
  ◎Flux Medecine
- [Mar. 6–June 3]*Art, Anti-Art, Non-Art: Experimentations in the Public Sphere in Postwar Japan*, Getty Research Institute, Los Angeles.
  ◎Flux Medecine
- [Sept. 6–Oct. 20]***Shigeko Kubota: My Life with Nam June Paik*, Maya Stendhal Gallery, New York.**
  ◎Nam June Paik I / Nam June Paik II / Pissing Boy / Jogging Lady / Tree (with green trunk) / Tree (on bucket) / Korean Grave / Bird I / Bird II

2008

- [Sept. 10–Mar. 23, 2009]*Here is Every. Four Decades of Contemporary Art*, Museum of Modern Art, New York.
  ◎Staircase
- [Sept. 30–Dec. 25]*Dissonances*, Toyota Municipal Museum of Art, Aichi.
  ◎Staircase / Bicycle 1, 2, 3

2010

- [Sept. 15–May 2, 2011]*Counter Space: Design and the Modern Kitchen*, Museum of Modern Art, New York.
  ◎[unknown]

2011

- [Sept. 21–Jan. 16, 2012]*Thing / Thought: Fluxus Editions, 1962–1978*, Museum of Modern Art, New York.
  ◎Fluxkit (Napkin and Medicine?)

2012

- [Nov. 18–Feb. 25, 2013]*Tokyo 1955–1970: A New Avant-Garde*, Museum of Modern Art, New York.
  ◎Invitation to her Naiqua Gallery exhibition / Letter to G. Maciunas

2013

- [Feb. 11–Mar. 23]*Hi-Red Center: The Documents of "Direct Action"*, Nagoya City Art Museum, Aichi, et al.
  ◎Hi-Red Center Events edited by Kubota
- [Nov. 9–Dec. 23]*Women Artists*, Takaoka Art Museum, Toyama.
  ◎Staircase / Window

2014

- [July 23]***Shigeko Kubota Rock Video: Cherry Blossom*, High Line, New York.**
  ◎Rock Video

2015

- [July 23]Died from breast cancer in New York.
- [Sept. 11]Shigeko Kubota Video Art Foundation was established.
- [Sept. 25–Nov. 21]*The Experimental Television Center: A History, Etc . . .*, 205 Hudson Street Gallery, Hunter College.
  ◎[unknown]

2016

- [Apr. 9–July 24]*[no English title given: Series: Creativity in Video Nam June Paik and Shigeko Kubota–Artists whom Tatsumi Orimoto met in New York in the 1970s]*, Kawasaki City Museum.
  ◎Marcel Duchamp and John Cage (SC)

2018

- [Feb. 8–Apr. 15]*Before Projection: Video Sculpture 1974–1995*, MIT List Visual Atrs and Center, Cambridge, et al.
  ◎River
- [Mar. 6–Apr. 14]*Colossal World: Japanese Artists and New York, 1959s to Present*, White Box, New York.
  ◎Bicycle Wheel, photo portraits by Tom Haar

2019

- [Sept. 6–Feb. 23, 2020]*Body Electric*, Yerba Buena Center for Arts, San Francisco, et al.
  ◎Video Poem
- [Oct. 30–Jan. 18, 2020]*Japan is America*, Fergus McCaffrey, New York.
  ◎Merce by Merce by Paik
- [Nov. 1–Dec. 15]*Shigeko Kubota: Restored in Beacon*, Mother Gallery, Beacon, New York.
  ◎Staircase / Grave / Bicycle 1, 2, 3 / Chess / Window / Marcel Duchamp and John Cage (single-channel) / Rock Video (SC)
- [Nov. 1–Feb. 2, 2020]*The Window: A Journey of Art and Architecture through Window*, The National Museum of Modern Art, Tokyo.
  ◎Window (Three tapes)
- [Nov. 18–Jan. 30, 2020]*Shigeko Kubota: a woman artist, her life*, Boa: basedonart, Dusseldorf.
  ◎Single-channel video, drawings and ephemera.

2020

- [Feb. 6–June 6]*Mercer Street*, McCaffrey, New York.
  ◎Bicycle 1, 2, 3 / Video Haiku
- [Feb. 20–Mar. 29]*Techne Triennial: Topologies of the Real*, CAFA Art Museum, Beijing.
  ◎Photographs of Marcel Duchamp and John Cage's Reunion Chess Match
- [Dec. 27–Mar. 21, 2021]*Refocusing on the Medium: the Rise of East Asia Video Art*, OCAT Shanghai.
  ◎Bicycle 1

2021

- [Mar. 20–June 6]A major solo exhibition (the first posthumous and first in Japan since 1992), *Viva Video!: The Art and life of Shigeko Kubota*, exhibition opens at the Niigata Prefectural Museum of Modern Art, and travels to The National Museum of Art, Osaka (June 29–Sept. 13) and Museum of Contemporary Art Tokyo. (Nov. 16–Feb. 23, 2022).

文献目録

Bibliography

凡例

- 本目録は、2021年2月までに日本国内・国外で発表された、久保田成子の自筆文献、および久保田について言及された文献およびインターネット上の記事をまとめたものである。
- 日本国内で発表されたものについては可能なかぎり網羅した。
- 日本国外については、英語で発表されたものを中心に調査し、記した。
- 文献は「自筆・インタビュー」「展覧会図録（個展）」「展覧会図録（グループ展）」「その他」のカテゴリーごとに、和書・洋書の順に日付順に記載した。
- 和書（展覧会図録含む）は、著者名「記事／論文名」『書名』発行所、発行年、掲載頁の順に記した。
- 洋書（展覧会図録含む）は、Author, "Title." *Book title* (Place of publication: Publisher, Year), pageの順に記した。
- インターネット上の記事は、和文は、著者名「記事名」掲載日、URL、アクセス日の順に記し、欧文は、Author, "Title." Date of upload, URL, Date of accessの順で記した。
- 本目録の作成にあたっては、以下の図録の文献目録を特に参考にした。
  - *Shigeko Kubota: Video Sculpture* (New York: American Museum of Moving Image, 1991).
  - *Shigeko Kubota: My Life With Nam June Paik* (New York: Maya Stendhal Gallery, 2007).
- 書誌にアクセスできず複写資料の確認となり、頁数不明の場合がある。
- 著者名・記事タイトルの記載がない文献は［著者名なし］［タイトルなし］と記した。
- フルクサスに関連する文献については、久保田に直接言及があるもののみ取り上げた。
- 展覧会に関連するエフェメラはここに含まない。

Notes

- This bibliography comprises printed materials, including web articles, that were written by and about Shigeko Kubota, and published in Japan and abroad prior to February 2021.
- Every effort has been made to include all of the texts published in Japan.
- The survey and documentation of non-Japanese sources focuses primarily on English-language materials.
- The bibliography is divided into four categories, "Publications by and interviews with the artist," "Exhibition catalogs (solo)," "Exhibition catalogs (group show)," and "Publications about the artsit." The entries are arranged in a chronological order, from Japanese to non-Japanese publications..
- Information on both Japanese and non-Japanese publications (including exhibition catalogs) is provided in the following order: author, "title of article or paper." *title of book* (place of publication: date), page number.
- Information on both Japanese and non-Japanese web articles is provided in the following order: author, "title of article." date of upload, URL, and last date accessed.
- In compiling this bibliography, the following exhibition catalogs served as primary references:
  - *Shigeko Kubota: Video Sculpture* (New York: American Museum of Moving Image, 1991).
  - *Shigeko Kubota: My Life With Nam June Paik* (New York: Maya Stendhal Gallery, 2007).
- In some cases, page numbers in the bibliography remain unclear as the information is based on reproductions of otherwise unattainable documents.
- The absence of an author's name or title in a source is indicated with the phrase "unknown" or "untitled."
- Fluxus-related references are limited to those that directly mention Kubota.
- Exhibition-related ephemera are not included.

自筆・インタビュー　Publications by and interviews with the artist

- 久保田成子「海外の新刊書紹介　アンディー・ウォーホールの小説《a》」『美術手帖』第312号1969年5月、130–133頁。
- ジャッド・ヤルカット（著）、久保田成子（訳）「性と音楽とコンピューター・アート　白南準の芸術」『美術手帖』第312号、1969年5月、172–181頁。
- ジャッド・ヤルカット（著）、久保田成子（訳）「特集《新しい自然》エア・アート　磯辺行久－空に浮く城」『美術手帖』第314号、1969年6月、106–121頁。
- 久保田成子「特集《新しい自然》エア・アート　芸術は芸術の灰である　ウィロビー・シャープ　インタビュー」『美術手帖』第314号、1969年6月、122–127頁。
- 久保田成子「ニューヨーク通信　創造的媒体としてのTV」『美術手帖』第317号、1969年9月、168–175頁。
- 久保田成子「晩年のデュシャンとチェス・ゲーム」『美術手帖』第319号、1969年11月、80–89頁。
- 久保田成子「爆発する“セックス革命”」『美術手帖』第322号、1970年1月、84–93頁。
- 久保田成子「ドラッグ・カルチュア明と暗」『美術手帖』第332号、1970年9月、54–64頁。
- 久保田成子「芸術家とエコロジーとコミューンと」『美術手帖』第341号、1971年4月号、94–107頁。
- 久保田成子「ヴィデオ——開かれた回路」『芸術倶楽部』第9号、1974年6月30日発行、173–181頁。
- 久保田成子「父、「生と死」」『久保田隆円先生記念誌』、「久保田隆円記念誌」刊行委員会、1980年、225–226頁。
- 久保田成子「ルート2　デュシャンピアナの連作から」『美術手帖』第487号、1981年10月、10–11頁。
- ［著者名なし］「総特集　映像の現在　久保田成子インタビュー　ビデオ／アート／人生／を語る」『月刊イメージフォーラム』第50号、1984年11月、46–57頁。
- 白南準、久保田成子「フルクサスの思い出から」『美術手帖』第600号、1988年10月、275、290–294頁。
- 久保田成子「オート・タイヤズ　久保田成子」『ARTEC '91　第2回名古屋国際ビエンナーレ』名古屋国際ビエンナーレ開催協議会編、1991年、38–41頁。
- 富山加津江（インタビュー）「一つのオデッセイが終わった　NYで大規模なビデオ・スカルプチャー個展を開く」、久保田成子「ビデオ・スカルプチャー久保田成子　作品コメンタリー」『月刊イメージフォーラム』第139号、1991年10月号、15–29頁、114–119頁。
- 久保田成子「ビデオ作品解説」『クボタ シゲコ ビデオ インスタレーション』原美術館、1992年、10–11頁。
- 「特集　HOW TO MAKE A VIDEO インタビュー久保田成子」『VIDEO CULTURE』松下電器産業株式会社ビデオ事業部、ビデオムービー事業部、No.19、1992年、2–3頁。
- 久保田成子「無題（鎌倉画廊での個展に寄せて）」、『久保田成子展』鎌倉画廊、1998年、頁数なし。（web　https://www.kamakura.gallery/kubotashigeko/1998.html　accessed May 22, 2021.）
- ［著者名なし］「しごとのデッサン　久保田成子　フルクサス・カップル」『京都新聞』1999年5月29日。
- 久保田成子「千谷さんへ」「邦千谷様　叔母様」「邦千谷先生」『凛として、花として』（編集：邦千谷舞踏研究所編集委員会）、アトリエサード、2008年、75–77頁。
- 手塚美和子（インタビュー）、金岡直子（書き起こし）「久保田成子オーラル・ヒストリー」日本美術オーラル・ヒストリー・アーカイヴ、2009年10月11日付、ニューヨーク市マンハッタン、久保田成子自宅にて。http://www.oralarthistory.org/archives/kubota_shigeko/interview_01.php accessed May 22, 2021.
- 久保田成子「直江津高校の思い出一創立百周年を祝して一」『新潟県立直江津高等学校創立100周年記念誌』新潟県立直江津高等学校創立100周年記念事業実行委員会、2012年、100–102頁。
- 久保田成子「Hi-Red Centerの思い出」『ハイレッド・センター：『直接行動』の軌跡』、「ハイレッド・センター」展実行委員会、2013年、22–23頁。
- 久保田成子・南禎鎬（著）、高晟埈（訳）『私の愛、ナムジュン・パイク』平凡社、2013年。
- 貝瀬拓弥「人ものがたり　がらっぱちアーティスト　ビデオ彫刻家久保田成子さん（77）①階段」新潟日報、2015年6月18日、夕刊1面。
- 貝瀬拓弥「人ものがたり　がらっぱちアーティスト　ビデオ彫刻家久保田成子さん（77）②少女時代」新潟日報、2015年6月19日、夕刊1面。
- 貝瀬拓弥「人ものがたり　がらっぱちアーティスト　ビデオ彫刻家久保田成子さん（77）③失望」新潟日報、2015年6月23日、夕刊1面。
- 貝瀬拓弥「人ものがたり　がらっぱちアーティスト　ビデオ彫刻家久保田成子さん（77）④出会い」新潟日報、2015年6月24日、夕刊1面。
- 貝瀬拓弥「人ものがたり　がらっぱちアーティスト　ビデオ彫刻家久保田成子さん（77）⑤再会」新潟日報、2015年6月25日、夕刊1面。
- 貝瀬拓弥「人ものがたり　がらっぱちアーティスト　ビデオ彫刻家久保田成子さん（77）⑥巨匠」新潟日報、2015年6月26日、夕刊1面。
- 貝瀬拓弥「人ものがたり　がらっぱちアーティスト　ビデオ彫刻家久保田成子さん（77）⑦ヒット」新潟日報、2015年6月29日、夕刊1面。
- 貝瀬拓弥「人ものがたり　がらっぱちアーティスト　ビデオ彫刻家久保田成子さん（77）⑧結婚」新潟日報、2015年6月30日、夕刊1面。
- 貝瀬拓弥「人ものがたり　がらっぱちアーティスト　ビデオ彫刻家久保田成子さん（77）⑨暗転」新潟日報、2015年7月1日、夕刊1面。
- 貝瀬拓弥「人ものがたり　がらっぱちアーティスト　ビデオ彫刻家久保田成子さん（77）⑩原風景」新潟日報、2015年7月2日、夕刊1面。

- Shigeko Kubota, ed. *Hi Red Center* (New York: Fluxus, c. 1965).
- Shigeko Kubota, *Marcel Duchamp and John Cage*(Tokyo: Takeyoshi Miyazawa, 1970).
- Shigeko Kubota, [Answer to the Question], *Art-Rite* 7 (Autumn 1974), p. 12.
- Shigeko Kubota, “Video Poems.” *Arts Magazine*, vol.49, no.4 (Dec. 1974), cover (photo), p. 48.
- Shigeko Kubota, “Video Poem.” “Anthology Film Archives Video Program: From Film to Video.” In Ira Schneider and Beryl Korot, eds. *Video Art: an Anthology* (New York and London: Harcourt Brace Jovanovich, 1976), pp. 82–83, 150–155.
- Shigeko Kubota, “Duchampiana.” *Tracks: A journal of artists' writings*, 3, 3 (Fall 1977), p. 63.
- Shigeko Kubota, “Women's Video in the U.S. and Japan.” In Douglas Davis and Allison Simmons, eds. *The New Television: A Public/Private Art* (Cambridge, Mass.: The MIT Press, 1977), pp. 96–101.
- Shigeko Kubota, “Video Sculpture: Two Phases.” “Mountain Series.” “Twenty Questions About my Work.” *Shigeko Kubota Video Sculptures* (Berlin: daadgalerie; Essen: Museum Folkwang; Kunsthaus Zurich, 1981) pp. 13, 19, 23, 27, 31, 35, 37, 42, 53, 59.
- Sharon Grace (interview), “Television, Electronic Kids, and Duchamp: An Interview Through the Wires with Shigeko Kubota.” *Art Com* (Fall 1981), p. 21.
- Barbara Schnierle (interview), “Es lebe Video???” *Tip* magazine (West Berlin: Dec. 18–31, 1981), pp. 54, 55.
- Shigeko Kubota, “Video Sculpture: Two Phases.” *Video*, 80, 4 (Spring/Summer 1982), pp. 34–35.
- Jeanine Mellinger and D.L. Bean, “Shigeko Kubota.” Interview in *Profile* (Video Data Bank) 3, 6 (Nov. 1983), entire volume.
- Shigeko Kubota, “Duchampiana.” translated from English to German by Caroline Nathusius-Priebe, Alfred M. Fischer and Dieter Daniels, eds. *Ubrigens sterben immer die anderen: Marcel Duchamp und die Avantgarde seit 1950* (Cologne: Museum Ludwig, 1988), pp. 64, 292–94, 327.
- Shigeko Kubota, “Passaggio a Oriente e Passaggio dall'Oriente.”*XLV Esposizione Internazionale d'Arte*, vol.2 (Venezia: Marsilio, 1993), pp. 556–

557.
- Shigeko Kubota, "Wind-video" *Et tous ils changent le monde: 2ème Biennale d'art contemporain, Lyon* (Paris: Réunion des musées nationaux, 1993), pp. 179–180, 277, 285.
- Shigeko Kubota, "Artsit's Statement: Niagara Falls." Kim Hong-hee and Cynthia Goodman, eds. *Kwangju Biennale 1995: InfoArt* (Kwangju Biennale Foundation, Korea/Sam Shin Gak, 1995), p. 177–181.
- Shigeko Kubota, "Shigeko Kubota." *4th International Istanbul Biennial* (Istanbul Foundation for Culture and Arts, 1995), pp. 184–185, 312.
- Shigeko Kubota, "Sexual Healing." *NY Arts* (date unknown, 2000), pp. 43–45.
- Phong Bui, "Shigeko Kubota with Phong Bui." *The Brooklyn Rail* (Sept. 2007). https://brooklynrail.org/2007/09/art/kubota accessed Sept. 10, 2020

展覧会図録（個展） Exhibition catalogs (solo)

- メアリ・ジェーン・ジェイコブ「序文」、ブルックス・アダムス「久保田成子のビデオ彫刻─伝記的考察」『クボタ シゲコ ビデオ インスタレーション』原美術館、1992年、4–9頁。
- 『久保田成子展』鎌倉画廊、1998年、頁数なし。

- Cindy Neal, "5 Video Sculptures." *Option 9: Shigeko Kubota* (Chicago: Museum of Contemporary Art, Chicago, 1981).
- Zdenek Felix, "Video, Tod und Wiedergeburt."; Barbara London, "For Shigeko."; John G. Hanhardt, "Video Transformations." *Shigeko Kubota Video Sculptures* (Berlin: daadgalerie; Essen: Museum Folkwang; Kunsthaus Zurich, 1981), pp. 5–7, 10–11, 39.
- Constance Lewallen, [No title.] *Shigeko Kubota/MATRIX 65* (Berkeley, CA: University Art Museum, Oct. 1983), n.p.
- Mary Jane Jacob, "Introduction."; Brooks Adams, "Kubota's Video Sculpture: A Biographical Perspective."; Moira Roth, "The Voice of Shigeko Kubota: 'A Fusion of Art and Life, Asia and America...'"; JoAnn Hanley, "Reflections in a Video Mirror." *Shigeko Kubota: Video Sculpture* (New York: American Museum of Moving Image, 1991).
- Achille Bonito Oliva, *Shigeko Kubota: Video as a Form of Spiritual Collision with the World* (Milan: Fundazione Mudima, 1994).
- *Shigeko Kubota Video Sculptures DUCHAMPIANA* (Paris: Galerie de Paris, 1996).
- John G. Hanhardt, *Shigeko Kubota* (New York: Whitney Museum of American Art, 1996).
- *Shigeko Kubota: My Life With Nam June Paik* (New York: Maya Stendhal Gallery, 2007).

展覧会図録（グループ展） Exhibition catalogs (group show)

- 『第11回日本国際美術展』（主催：毎日新聞社・日本国際美術振興会）、東京都美術館、京都市美術館、1974年、頁数なし。
- 『第2回現代芸術祭─芸術と工学』富山県立近代美術館、1983年、76–77頁。
- 『電視 ELECTROVISIONS JAPAN 87 VIDEO TELEVISION FESTIVAL Catalogue』（企画：Video Gallery SCAN）、スパイラル、1987年、95–96頁。
- 『第4回現代芸術祭─映像の今日』富山県立近代美術館、1989年、62頁。
- 『彫刻の遠心力：この10年の展開』国立国際美術館、1992年、18、50–55、100–102頁。
- 『戦後日本の前衛美術』横浜美術館、1994年、104、120–121、211頁。
- 『記憶への視線』ハラミュージアムアーク、1995年、7頁。
- 『美術の内がわ・外がわ─何故、眼差しは交わったのか─（シリーズ ART IN TOKYO No.8）』板橋区立美術館、1996年、5–8、40–41、86頁。
- 『内科画廊─'60年代の前衛』京都造形大学・京都芸術短期大学芸術館 GALLERY RAKU、2000年、頁数なし。
- 『現代美術百貨展』山梨県立美術館、2000年、74、95頁。
- 『マルセル・デュシャンと20世紀美術』国立国際美術館、横浜美術館、2004年、138–139頁。
- 『フルクサス展─芸術から日常へ』うらわ美術館、2004年、13、17、201頁。
- 由本みどり「フルクサスと日本人女性芸術家たち」『前衛の女性 1950–1975』栃木県立美術館、2005年、20–29、120–123、151–152頁。
- 『国立新美術館開館記念展20世紀美術探検──アーティストたちの三つの冒険物語──』国立新美術館、2007年、212、286頁。
- ジーノ・ディマッジオ「不協和音」、アキレ・ボニト・オリヴァ「精神状態を征服した6人の日本人アーティスト」、ジァン・カルロ・カルツァ「日本美術における女性的価値の過去と現在」、由本みどり「前衛を超えて：日本人女性芸術家たちの位置」、マニュエラ・ガンディーニとの対話「久保田成子の若き日々」『不協和音─日本のアーティスト6人』豊田市美術館、2008年、7、14、18、21、25、31–43、105、108、140、147–152、192、198、200、202、204、210頁。
- 『女性アーティスト展　私たちは越えていく』高岡市美術館、2013年、13–14、42–43、61–62頁。
- 『窓展：窓をめぐるアートと建築の旅』平凡社、2019年、16、178頁。

- Kynaston McShine, *Information* (New York: The Museum of Modern Art, 1970), p. 179.
- Wulf Herzogenrath, *Projekt '74: Kunst bleibt Kunst, Aspecte internationaler Kunst am Anfang der 70erjahre* (Cologne: Kolnischer Kunstverein, 1974), p. 427.
- *Art Now 74: A Celebration of the American Arts* (Washington, D.C.: John F. Kennedy Center for the Performing Art, 1974), pp. 55, 93.
- Suzanne Delehanty, *Video Art* (Philadelphia: Institute of Contemporary Art, 1975), p. 29.
- Essays on video by Wulf Herzogenrath and David A. Ross, *Documenta 6*, Vol. 2. (Kassel: Druck Verlag GMbh, 1977), pp. 312–313.
- John G. Hanhardt, *Shigeko Kubota/Taka Iimura: New Video* (New York: Whitney Museum of American Art, 1979), n.p.
- Feliz Zdenek, *Videoweeks Essen '79* (Essen: Museum Folkwang, 1979), pp. 10–12.
- *Video: entre I'art i Ia comunicacio*, Series Informatives 2 (Barcelona: Collegi D'Arquitectes/Institut Aleman, 1980).
- *Video Classics* (New York: The Bronx Museum, 1981).
- W. Herzogenrath, et al., M. Baudson, ed., *TIJD de Vierde Dimensie in de Kunst* (Brussels: Palais des Beaux-Arts, TIJD, 1983), p. 252.
- *National Video Festival* (Washington, D.C.: The American Film Institute, The John F. Kennedy Center for the Performing Arts, 1983), pp. 89–90.
- John G. Hanhardt, et al. *1983 Biennial Exhibition* (New York: Whitney Museum of American Art, 1983), p. 34.
- John G. Hanhardt, "Video Art: Expanded forms, notes toward a history," Dorine Mignot, ed. *Het Lumineuze beeld = The Luminous image* (Amsterdam: Stedelijk Museum, 1984), pp. 61, 126–129, 183–184.
- John Berger, Renate Berger, Christel Burmeir, Heidrum Ludwig, Annelie Pholen, and Heinz Thiel. Joachim Buchner, ed., *Nackt in der Kunst* (Hanover: Sprengel Museum, 1984), pp. 97–98.
- Robert Littman, *Imagenes en Cajas* (Mexico City: Museo Rufino Tamayo, 1985).
- John Minkowsky, *The Other Television: Video by Artists* (Fort Wayne, Indiana: Fort Wayne Museum of Art. 1986), pp. 6–8.
- Shirley Nielson Blum and Suzanne Delehanty, *The Window in Twentieth Century Art* (New York: Neuberger Museum, 1986), pp. 54, 102.
- Brooks Adams, "Shigeko Kubota." *documenta 8*, vol.2 (Kassel: Weber and Weidemeyer, 1987), n.p. (images), pp. 136–137, 320.
- "Shigeko Kubota Video Installation: Niagara Falls" (images) *documenta 8*,

vol.3 (Kassel: Weber and Weidemeyer, 1987), n.p.
- Clive Phillpot and Jon Hendricks, *Fluxus: selections from the Gilbert and Lila Silverman collection* (New York: The Museum of Modern Art, 1988), p. 54.
- John G. Hanhardt, *Video Art Expanded Forms* (New York: Whitney Museum of American Art at the Equitable Center, 1988), cover, p. 3.
- Vittorio Fagone, John G. Hanhardt, Wulf Herzogenrath, and Friedemann Malsch, Edith Decker, et al., *Video Skulptur retrospektiv und aktuell 1963–1989* (Cologne: DuMont, 1989), pp. 52, 184–87.
- Achille Bonito Oliva, *Ubi Fluxus 1990 Ibi Motus 1962* (Venice: Venice Biennale, Milan: Nuovi Edizioni Gabriele Mazzota, 1990), pp. 193–96.
- Marco Meneguzzo, "Shigeko Kubota."*XLV Esposizione Internazionale d'Arte*, vol.2 (Venice: Marsilio, 1993), pp. 554–555.
- Kristine Stiles, "Between Water and Stone: Fluxus Performance, A Metaphysics of Acts." Elizabeth Armstrong and Joan Ruthfuss, eds. *In the Spirit of Fluxus* (Minneapolis: Walker Art Center, 1993), pp. 19, 56, 77, 82, 98.
- Ann-Sargent Wooster, "The Way We Were." In JoAnn Hanley, *The first generation: women and video, 1970–75* (New York: Independent Curators Inc., 1993), pp. 29–30, 72–73.
- Alexandra Munroe, *Japanese Art After 1945: scream against the sky* (New York: Harry N. Abrams, 1994), pp. 71, 77, 81, 218, 219, 220, 239–241, 292, 300, 372, 377, 406.
- *Set in Motion* (New York: New York State Council on the Art, 1994), pp. 17–18, 40, 52.
- Eugenie Tsai, "Reflections."; Kerri Sakamoto, "Through Veils of Light." *Gazing Back: Shigeko Kubota and Mary Lucier* (New York: Whitney Museum of American Art, 1995), n.p.
- Kristine Stiles, "Uncorrupted Joy: International Art Actions." In Paul Schimmel, *Out of Action: Between Performance and the Object, 1949–79* (Los Angeles: Museum of Contemporary Art/Thames and Hudson, 1998), p. 279.
- John G. Hanhardt, *The Worlds of Nam June Paik* (New York: Guggenheim Museum, 2000), p. 25.
- Cornelia Butler, *WACK! Art and the Feminist Revolution* (Cambridge, MA: MIT Press. 2007), pp. 38, 255–256.
- Charles Marewether, *Art Anti-Art Non-Art: Experiments in the Public Sphere in Postwar Japan 1950–70* (Los Angeles: Getty Research Institute, 2007), pp. 20–21, 32, 80–83, 85, 124.
- Doryun Chong, *Tokyo 1955–1970: A New Avant-Garde* (New York: The Museum of Modern Art, 2012), p. 207.
- Henriette Huldisch, *Before Projection: Video Sculpture 1974–1995* (Cambridge, MA: MIT List Visual Arts and Center, 2018), pp. 16, 22, 25, 69–72, 107–109, 125.

その他 Publications and articles about the artist

- 「十七歳少女、みごと栄冠　久保田さん二紀会展に入選」『毎日新聞』新潟版、1954年10月8日、8面。
- 篠原有司男「OFF MUSEUM展」『美術ジャーナル』第49号、美術ジャーナル社、1964年、10–13頁。
- 篠原有司男『前衛の道』美術出版社、1968年、132頁。
- 針生一郎『現代の美術　art now 第11巻　行為に賭ける』講談社、1972年、33頁。
- ［著者名なし］「ART & TECHNOLOGY 第2回現代芸術祭　芸術と工学 7月1日–9月4日」『どおむ　富山県立近代美術館ニュース9』富山県立近代美術館、1983年7月、頁数なし。
- ［著者名なし］「特集＝フルクサス」『アールヴィヴァン』11号、西武美術館、1983年、7、27、57、63、65、67、120頁。
- ［著者名なし］「科学万博のナムジュン・パイク夫妻」『美術手帖』第550号、1985年9月、10–11頁。
- 島敦彦「久保田成子の『メタ・マルセル：窓』をめぐって」『収蔵作品についての報告』富山県立近代美術館、1986年、42–45頁。
- 飯村隆彦『80年代芸術フィールド・ノート　ニューヨークの映像、美術、パフォーマンス』1988年、朝日出版社、107頁。
- ジョナス・メカス（編)、木下哲夫（訳)『メカスの友人日記——レノン／ヨーコ／マチューナス』1989年、160–163頁。
- ジョアン・ハンリー「ビデオ・スカルプチャー久保田成子　ビデオ・ミラーのリフレクション」『月刊イメージフォーラム』第139号、1991年10月、121–123頁。
- ［著者名なし］「『クボタ　シゲコ　ビデオ　インスタレーション』フルクサス運動やデュシャンの生き方から多大な影響を受けたビデオアート」『Hanako』1992年1月30日、57頁。
- ［著者名なし］「斬新なビデオアートが刺激的『クボタ　シゲコ　ビデオ　インスタレーション』」『月刊実業の日本』No.2、1992年2月。
- ［著者名なし］「ART：世界的な女性アーティストの回顧展　ついに開催　「クボタ　シゲコ　ビデオ　インスタレーション」」『an・an』No.811、1992年2月。
- ［著者名なし］「沿線ガイド　ビデオの芸術そろえ　久保田成子さんの個展」『産経新聞』1992年2月2日。
- 吉原悠博「クボタ　シゲコ　ビデオインスタレーション　脳細胞の過剰な欲求が生んだ眼球とモニターの関係を実現する」『ぴあ』1992年2月6日。
- （俊）「県人アート　久保田成子ビデオインスタレーション ビデオの可能性を追求　人間存在の根源に迫る」『新潟日報』1992年2月7日、11面。
- ［著者名なし］「芸術的試み次々　クボタシゲコ　ビデオインスタレーション　日本的な感覚漂う」『朝日新聞』1992年2月8日、夕刊、23面。
- ［著者名なし］「key persons：「作品は日記のようなもの」 里帰りした在米アーティスト　久保田成子」『アポ』1992年2月20日、13、128頁。
- かわなかのぶひろ「アート　新しい映像に挑む気合」『読売新聞』1992年2月22日夕刊、9面。
- ［著者名なし］「よくわかるビデオ・インスタ展　クボタ　シゲコ　ビデオ　インスタレーション」『ピーチ　missアソビジョン』、no.47、1992年3月。
- ［著者名なし］「クボタシゲコ　ビデオインスタレーション」『ハラミュージアム　リヴュー』No.19、1992年4月、頁数なし。
- 花井カオル「『クボタ　シゲコ　ビデオ　インスタレーション』展　ぼくたちの多彩な欲望を孕みながら宇宙を透視しようと脈動する空間」『太陽』1992年5月、101頁。
- 「XLV Biennale di Venezia［東洋への道］展：久保田成子（展示写真)」『美術手帖』1993年9月、73頁。
- トーマス・ケライン（著)、ジョン・ヘンドリックス（編)、コリーヌ・バイヤー（監修)、『フルクサス』クレオ、1994年、72、73、126頁。
- イメージフォーラム（編)、『日本実験映像40年史』キリンプラザ大阪、1994年、28頁。
- ［著者名なし］「Scream Against The Sky　戦後日本美術展開催」『OCS News』Vol. 20、No. 487、1994年9月30日（表紙に《デュシャンピアナ：階段を降りるヌード》写真掲載)。
- ［著者名なし］「特集　フルクサス発　インターメディア・アートの出発点から」『STUDIO VOICE』vol. 232、インファス、1995年4月、16、24頁。
- ［著者名なし］「ぴーぷる　ビデオと彫刻を結んで」『OCS News』No. 496、1995年2月17日、4頁。
- バーバラ・ロンドン「久保田成子　驚くべき自在さで創作を続けるアーティスト」『月刊イメージフォーラム』1995年6月号、56–57頁。
- 和多利浩一「アート・トラスト：東洋と西洋の支点でアート見直し」『朝日新聞』1996年2月17日、夕刊、9面。
- 草原真知子「「民主の地」での国際美術展：光州ビエンナーレ」『季刊インターコミュニケーション』No. 16、1996年4月、27–28頁。
- 富山加津江「NYの久保田成子ビデオアート展　独自性と公共性に高い評価」『朝日新聞』1996年8月7日、夕刊、3面。

- (菅)「美術：久保田成子展　デュシャンを下敷き　日本に自然な郷愁も」『読売新聞』1998年1月22日、夕刊、21面。
- 田中三蔵「久保田成子／丸山常生展　ビデオで生む内省とユーモア」『朝日新聞』1998年2月5日、夕刊、5面。
- 高島直之「ニューヨーク在住3作家が問い詰める『近代のすきま』 # 25-04 久保田成子展、河原温展、荒川修作／マドリン・ギンズ展」『季刊インターコミュニケーション』No. 25、1998年7月、88-89頁。
- 宮田有香「『内科だった　画廊だった——』ふたたび〈内科画廊——'60年代の前衛展〉開催まで⑪」『あいだ』80号、2002年8月2日、31-32頁。
- ヘレナ・レキット（編）、ペギー・フェラン（著）『アート＆フェミニズム』ファイドン、2005年、65、191頁。
- 塩見允枝子『フルクサスとは何か——日常とアートを結びつけた人々』フィルムアート社、2005年、78、81頁。
- 飯村昭子「ニューヨーク人間模様　其の12 ビデオ彫刻家・久保田成子」『よみタイム』2007年10月19日、16頁。
- 由本みどり「久保田成子展　ヴィデオで綴る人生の喜怒哀楽　My life with Nam June Paik at Stendhal Gallery, New York, U.S.A. Sept. 6-Oct. 20. 2007」『イメージ＆ジェンダー』vol. 8、2008年3月、139-141頁。
- 西岡一正「6様の前衛鮮やか　豊田市美術館で「不協和音」展　ビデオ彫刻・電気服…半世紀の軌跡たどる」『朝日新聞』2008年11月25日、16面
- 田中三蔵「ニッポン人・脈・記　前衛バカ伝説③　ニューヨーク 貧しき日々」『朝日新聞』2009年3月19日、夕刊、1面
- 黒ダライ児『肉体のアナーキズム　1960年代・日本美術におけるパフォーマンスの地下水脈』グラムブックス、2010年9月16日、182、205、408頁。
- 濱田真由美「ヴィデオ・アーティスト久保田成子についての調査ノート」『新潟県立近代美術館研究紀要』第11号、2012年3月、17-23頁。
- クリス・メイ＝アンドリュース、伊奈新祐：訳、『ヴィデオ・アートの歴史　その形式と機能の変遷』三元社、2013年、22、303頁。
- シンポジウム記録集『戦後日本美術の新たな語り口を探る　ニューヨークと東京、二つの近代美術館展覧会を通して見えてくるもの』国際交流基金、2014年3月、79頁。
- 濱田真由美「ヴィデオ・アーティスト　久保田成子の初期制作について—フルクサスおよびナムジュン・パイクとの関係を中心に—」『鹿島美術研究』年報31号、公益財団法人鹿島美術財団、2014年11月、555-564頁。
- ［著者名なし］［見出しなし／訃報］『朝日新聞』2015年7月27日、38頁。
- 濱田真由美「文化：光る先駆性　久保田成子の芸術（上）「ビデオ彫刻」を創出　前衛的な表現に強い関心」『新潟日報』2015年10月2日。
- 濱田真由美「文化：光る先駆性　久保田成子の芸術（下）夫の制作支えて開眼　NY近代美術館にも収蔵」『新潟日報』2015年10月3日。
- 『霧の抵抗　中谷芙二子展』水戸芸術館現代美術ギャラリー、2018年、352-353頁。
- 濱田真由美「久保田成子ヴィデオ・アート財団における作品調査」『新潟県立近代美術館紀要』第17号、2019年3月、52-58頁。
- ハル・フォスター、ロザリンド・E・クラウス、イヴ‐アラン・ボワ、ベンジャミン・H・D・ブークロー、デイヴィッド・ジョーズリット（著）、尾崎信一郎、金井直、小西信之、近藤学（編）『Art since 1900：図鑑1900年以後の芸術』東京書籍、2019年、528、650頁。
- 山本浩貴「フルクサスのアーティストたち」『現代美術史　欧米、日本、トランスナショナル』中公新書、2019年、66-67頁。
- 富井玲子「現代美術の『試験管』——内科画廊と1960年代日本の貸画廊制度」『美術運動史研究会ニュース』177号、美術運動史研究会、2020年2月、1-7頁。

- Jiirgen Becker and Wolf Vostell, *Happenings: Fluxus, Pop Art, Nouveau Réalisme* (Hamburg: Rowohlt Verlag, 1965), p. 202.
- Micheel Smith, "Theatre Journal: Snows." *The Village Voice* (January 26, 1967), p. 27.
- Maryse Holder, "Women's Video Art Festiva." *Off Our Backs*, 3, 2 (October, 1972), p. 18.
- *Artscanada*, the issue of video art (October 1973), p. 38
- Ingrid Wiegand, "Video Poems." *The SoHo Weekly News* (June 12, 1975), pp. 32, 38.
- Text by Nam June Paik, John Hanhardt, Ira Schneider and Beryl Korot, eds. *Video Art: an Anthology* (New York and London: Harcourt Brace Jovanovich, 1976), pp. 98, 220, 223-24.
- Mona Da Vinci, "On Art: Neo-Futurism is on the Move." *The SoHo Weekly News* (Feb. 12, 1976), p. 20.
- Ingrid Wiegand, "On Video: Video Installations." *The SoHo Weekly News* (Feb. 12, 1976), p. 40.
- David Bourdon, "Women Paint Portraits on Canvas and Off." *The Village Voice* (Feb. 16, 1976), pp. 127-28.
- Peten Frank, "Shigeko Kubota at René Block." *ART news*, 75, 4, (Apr. 1976), pp. 121-22.
- Nancy Grove, "Shigeko Kubota." *Arts Magazine*, 50, 8 (Apr. 1976), p. 18.
- David Bourdon, "Shigeko Kubota at René Block." *Art in America*, 64, 4 (July-Aug. 1976), pp. 105-106.
- Jonathan Price, "Shigeko Kubota and the Video of Wipe, Flash, Crash." *Women Artists Newsletter*, 2, 6 (Dec. 1976), pp. 1, 4.
- Jonathan Price, *Video Visions: A Medium Discovers Itself* (New York: New American Library, 1977).
- Davidson Gigliotti, "On Video: Duchamp Through Another Monitor." *The SoHo Weekly News* (Feb. 10, 1977), pp. 28-29.
- Deborah Perlberg, "Shigeko Kubota, René Block." *Artforum*, 15, 8 (Apr. 1977), pp. 60-61.
- Ann-Sargent Wooster, "New York Reviews: Shigeko Kubota (RenéBlock)." *Art News*, 76, 4 (Apr. 1977), pp. 127-28.
- Valentin Tatransky, "Shigeko Kubota: René Block." *Arts Magazine*, 51, 9 (May 1977), p. 29.
- Jiirgen Hohmeyer, "Unruhe an neuen Fronten." *Der Speigel* (June 27, 1977), p. 170.
- Peter Sager, "Im Dschungel der Median: Photographie und Video auf der Documenta 6." *Die Zeit* (July 8, 1977).
- David Bourdon, "A Critic's Diary: The New York Art Year." *Art in America*, 65, 4 (July-Aug. 1977), p. 74.
- [unknown] "The Young Generation: A Cross Section." *Art in America*, (Sept.-Oct. 1977), p. 90. Ruth Askey, "Shigeko Kubota's Duchampiana." *Artweek* 8, 33 (Oct. 8, 1977), p. 7.
- Gregory Battcock, ed., *New Artists Video* (New York: Dutton, 1978), pp. 97, 181-82, 187-88.
- Richard Cork, "What Does Documenta Document?" *Studio International*, 194, 988 (Jan. 1978), pp. 44-45.
- Robert Sklar, "Good Morning, Lanesville." *American Film Institute*, 3, 4 (Feb. 1978), pp. 30-32.
- John Trayna, "How to Produce a Cable TV Telethon." *Videography*, 3, 10 (Oct. 1978), pp. 40-42.
- Charles Dreyfus, "From History of Fluxus." *Flash Art*, 84-85 (Milan: Oct.-Nov. 1978), p. 29.
- Ken Friedman, "On Fluxus." *Flash Art*, 84-85 (Milan: Oct.-Nov. 1978), p. 30.
- Harry Ruhé, *FLUXUS, The most radical and experimental art movement of the sixties* (Amsterdam: A, 1979), n.p.
- Jean Dupuy, ed. *Collective Consciousness: Art Performances in the Seventies* (New York: Performing Arts Journal Publications, 1980), pp. 109, 121, 189-90.
- Pat Wadsley and Jill Kirschenbaum, "Golden Age of Video Art." *Cue Magazine*, 49, 1 (Jan. 18, 1980), p. 21.Henry Scott Stokes, "Art Museum a Symbol of Turnabout in Japan." *The New York Times* (Oct. 11, 1981), pp. 78-79.
- TS, "Graphisches Kabinett: Shigeko Kubota Video Sculptures." *Kunsthaus Zurich*, 4. 82 (Zurich: 1982), pp. 16-19.
- Bettina Gruber and Maria Vedder, eds.*Kunst und Video: Internationale*

Entwicklung und Kunstler (Cologne: DuMont, 1983), p. 160.
- Grace Glueck, "Gallery View: Video Comes into Its Own at Whitney Biennial." *The New York Times* (April 24, 1983), A33.
- Victor Ancona, "Video Fuses with Traditional Media at Whitney Biennial." *Videography*, 8, S (May 1983), pp. 78–79.
- Bonnie Davidson, "Tube-Ular Sculptures." *TV-Cable Week* (New York: July, I983), pp. 22–23.
- Constance Lewallen, "Gallery Programs/Exhibitions: Video and the River." *University Art Museum* (Berkley: University of California, Oct. 1983), p. 2.
- Ann-Sargent Wooster, "Shigeko Kubota." *The Village Voice* (Nov. 9–15, 1983), p. 71.
- Joan Shepard, "The Arts Community: Shigeko Kubota shows video sculpture." *Daily News* (Nov. 13, 1983), p. MB9.
- Grace Glueck, "Shigeko Kubota (White Columns)." *The New York Times* (Nov. 18, 1983), p. M88.
- Michael Shore, "Videosyncracy." *New York Beat* (Dec. 1983), p. 28.
- Jane Addams Allen, "Galleries: Japanese tradition woven into video installations." *The Washington Times* (Dec. 8, 1983), p. 3B.
- Ann-Sargent Wooster, "Slow Scan: Shigeko Kubota's White Columns. November 2–26." *East Village Eye*, 5, 39 (Dec. 1983–Jan. 1984), p. 35.
- Brooks Adams, "Zen and the Art of Video." *Art in America*, 72, 2 (Feb. 1984), pp. 122–26.
- Nancy Princenthal, "Shigeko Kubota—White Columns." *ART news*, 83, 2 (Feb. 1984), pp. 159–60.
- Lisa Liebmann, "Shigeko Kubota, White Columns." *Artforum*, 22, 7 (March 1984), p. 95.
- Shelley Rice, "The Luminous Image: Video Installations at the Stedelijk Museum." *Afterimage*, 12, 5 (Dec. 1984), pp. 13–15.
- Dorine Mignot, "The Luminous Image: 22 Video-Installationen im Stedelijk Museum, Amsterdam." *Kunstforum International*, 77–78 (Jan.–Feb. 1985), p. 71.
- Ann-Sargent Wooster, "Slow Scan: Marcel Duchamp's Grave (revived) at the Kitchen." *East Village Eye*, 6, 51 (Feb. 1985), p. 48.
- Ann-Sargent Wooster, "Slow Scan: Techno Nature." *East Village Eye*, 6, 54 (May 1985), p. 50.
- Barbara London, "Video: A Selected Chronology, 1963–1983." *Art Journal*, 45, 3 (Autumn, 1985), pp. 249–262.
- Robert Graham and René Payant, eds. *Video* (Montreal: Artexte, 1986), p. 28.
- John G. Hanhardt, ed. *Video Culture: A Critical Investigation*, (Rochester, New York: Visual Studies Workshop Press, 1986), pp. 21–22.
- Nancy Buchanan, "Shigeko Kubota: 'Reunion'." *High Performance*, 9, 4 (1986), p. 86.Suzanne Pach, "Museums-Reife." *Videoaktiv*, 2 (Munich: Mar.–Apr.1986), pp. 90–93.
- Molly Barnes, "Shigeko Kubota." *Artscene* 6, 2 (Oct. 1986), pp. 90–93.
- Katy Tanney, "Delicate Video Structures." *Artweek*, 17, 10 (Oct. 1986), p. 6.
- David Prescott, "A Video Artist To See, An Electronic Composer to Hear." *Chicago Tribune* (Nov. 14, 1986), p. 86.
- Stephan Schmidt-Wulffen, "Documenta 8: Kunst auf dem Prufstand." *Kunstforum International*, 90 (July–Sept. 1987), p. 216.
- Jack Flam, "Major German Exhibition Shows Off the Art of Today." *The Wall Street Journal* (Aug. 13, 1987), p. 18.
- Nancy Marmer, "Documenta 8: The Social Dimension." *Art in America*, 75, 9 (Sept, 1987), p. 197.
- Jon Hendricks, ed. *Fluxus Codex* (New York: Harry N. Abrams, 1988), pp. 52–53, 66, 69, 75, 98, 109–110, 114, 116, 122–25, 128, 266–67, 283, 306–307, 370, 499, 510.
- Roberta Smith, "Sly, Sardonic Feminism from a West German Exhibition." *New York Times* (March 11, 1988) C.31.
- Catherine Francblin, "Marcel Duchamp et l'Avant-garde 1950–1970." *Art Press*, 124 (Apr. 1988), pp. 36–37.
- Ken Friedman, *Rethinking Fluxus* (New York: Henie Onstad Foundations, 1989), p. 15.
- Margot Lovejoy, *Postmodern Currents* (Ann Arbor, Michigan: UMI Research Press, 1989), p. 198.
- Dieter Daniels, "Shigeko Kubota und Keigo Yamamoto." *Kunstforum*, 18 (Jan.–Feb. I989), p. 165.
- Alfred Nemeczek, "Video-Aus Einer Marotte Wird Kunst." *Art Das Kunstmagazin*, 3 (Mainz, West Germany: March 1989), p. 64.
- John G. Hanhardt, "Video Art: Expanded Forms." *Leonardo*, 23, 4 (1990), pp. 437–439.
- Jack Hobbs and Richard Salome, *The Visual Experience* (Worcester, Massachusetts: Davis Publications, Inc., 1990), pp. 128–29, 151.
- Lucy Lippard, *Mixed Blessing* (New York: Pantheon Books, 1990), p. 188.
- Davidson Gigliotti, "The Allure of the Electronic." *Afterimage* (March 1990), pp. 12–17.
- Michael Shapiro, "The Japanese in New York: Shigeko Kubota Video Artist." *Manhattan Catalog*, 5, 1 (Spring–Summer 1990), p. 42.Gabriele Coassin, "Video Magazine." *Nastro d'Artista* (Dec. 1990), pp. 132–138.
- Frances DeVuono, "Fluxus-Closing In, Salvatore Ala." *Art News*, 90, 1 (Jan. 1991), p. 157.
- [unkown] "ART: Shigeko Kubota." *The New Yorker* (May 13, 1991), p. 14.
- Roberta Smith, "Sleek Video Sculptures by Shigeko Kubota." *The New York Times* (May 24, 1991), p. C26.
- Ann-Sargent Wooster, "Shigeko Kubota." *Arts Magazine* 66 (Dec. 1991), p. 69.
- Ann-Sargent Wooster, "Shigeko Kubota: I Travel Alone." *High Performance*, 14, 4 (Winter 1991), pp. 26–29.
- A transcript of a panel discussion, *Video '92 and Beyond* (New York: American Museum of Moving Image, 1992).
- Leza Lowitz, "Fine Arts: Talent, Luck and Videotape." *Asahi Evening News* (Feb. 1, 1992), p. 9.
- Lorna Ryan, "Arts: Expatriate video sculptor Kubota pays hommage to Duchamp." *The Japan Times* (Feb. 2, 1992), p. 10.
- Tatsumi Shinoda, "Today's Art Scene: Kubota Shigeko: Beyond Duchamp." *Mainichi Daily News* (Feb. 6, 1992), p. 9.
- [unkown], "Shigeko Kubota: video sculptuur." *Stedelijk Museum Bulletin* (Amsterdam: October 1992), pp. 65–67.
- [unkown], "Shigeko Kubota: Video Sculpture by Mary Jane Jacob." *Woman's Art Journal*, 15, 1 (Spring/Summer, 1994), p. 55.
- Anne Barday Morgan, "Video Installations: Shigeko Kubota, Michael Odenbach, Matthew Barney, Patrick Sorin, Bruce Nauman." *Art Papers*, 18 (June/July, 1994), p. 61.
- Rosalind Krauss, Benjamin Buchloh, Hal Foster, et al. "The Reception of the Sixties." *October*, 69 (Summer, 1994), pp. 3–21.
- Pepe Karmel, "Art in Review: 'Gazing Back' Shigeko Kubota and Mary Lucier." *The New York Times* (August 25, 1995), p. C15.
- Pierre Restany, "Biee 1995: interview," *D'ARS*, 146 (Autumn/Winter 1995), pp. 45–47.
- Mason Klein, "Shigeko Kubota and Mary Lucier at The Whitney Museum of American Art." *Frieze* (Nov./Dec. 1995), pp. 62–63.
- John G. Hanhardt, "Video/Media Culture of the Twentieth Century." *Art Journal*, 54, 4 (Winter 1995), p. 20.
- Grace Glueck, "Art Review: Sculpture with Video and a Lot of Activity." *The New York Times*, (July 19, 1996), p. C28.
- Claire Machaver, "Video Images Enhance Her Sculpture." *New York Law Journal* (July 26, 1996).
- Larry Qualls, "Five Video Artists." *Performing Arts Journal*, Vol. 18, No. 3 (Sept., 1996), p. 1, 3–4.
- Susan Hapgood. "Shigeko Kubota at the Whitney and Lance Fung." *Art in America*, 84, 9 (Oct. 1996), p. 113.
- Robert C. Morgan, "Shigeko Kubota, Meret Oppenheim." *Art Press*, 217, 10 (1996), p. 70.
- Rebecca Schneider, *The Explicit Body in Performance* (New York: Routledge, 1997), p. 38.

- Kathy O'Dell, "Fluxus Feminus." *TDR*, 41, 1 (Spring, 1997), pp. 43–60.
- Mary Ann Milford, "Asian/American Art: A/Part of/From the Postmodern Dialectic." *India International Centre Quarterly*, 24, 4 (Winter 1997), pp. 96–98, 113, 122.
- Roselee Goldberg, *Performance: live art since 1960* (New York: Harry N. Abrams Publishers. 1998), pp. 15, 38–39, 128–129.
- Amelia Jones, *Body Art/Performing the Subject* (Minneapolis: University of Minnesota Press, 1998), p. 99.
- Lowell Cross, "'Reunion': John Cage, Marcel Duchamp, Electronic Music and Chess." in "Power and Responsibility: Politics, Identity and Technology in Music." *Leonardo Music Journal*, 9, (1999), pp. 35–42.
- Michael Rush, *New Media in Art* (London: Thames & Hudson, 1999), pp. 126, 128.
- Michael Rush, "Shigeko Kubota; Sexual Healing." *Art in America*, 88, 6 (June 2000) p. 77.
- Kim Levin, "Shigeko Kubota." *The Village Voice*, 45, 11 (March 21, 2000).
- Susan Valdes-Dapena, "Shigeko Kubota: Lance Fung Gallery." *Sculpture*, 19, 7 (2000), p. 65–66.
- Tracey Warr and Amelia Jones, *The Artist's Body* (London: Phaidon, 2000).
- Karl Ruhrberg, Klaus Honnef, Klaus, Christiane Fricke, Manfred Schneckenburger, Ingo F. Walther, *Art of the 20th century* (Taschen, 2000), p. 596.
- Melinda Barlow, "Red, White, Yellow, and Black: Women, Multiculturalism, and Video History." *Quarterly Review of Film and Video*, 17, 4 (2000), p. 297–312.
- Ann Landi, "Screen Idyll: Nam June Paik Creates a Blinking Flashing Light Show at the Guggenheim." *Art News*, 99, 1 (Jan. 2000), pp. 146–148.
- Lydia Haustein, *Videokunst* (Munich: Verlag C. H. Beck, 2003), p. 81.
- Michael Rush, *video art* (London: Thames & Hudson, 2003), p. 59–61.
- Margot Lovejoy, *Digital Currents: Art in the Electronic Age* (London: Routledge, 2004), pp. 98, 138.
- Midori Yoshimoto, *Into Performance: Japanese Women Artists in New York* (New Brunswick, N.J.: Rutgers University Press, 2005), pp. 1–10, 169–200.
- Chris Meigh-Andrews, *A History of Video Art. The Development of Form and Function* (Oxford and New York: Berg, 2006), p. 8.
- Janet Koplos, "Shigeko Kubota at Maya Stendhal." *Art in America*, 96: 5 (June 2007), p. 187.
- Kara Kelley Hallmark, *Encyclopedia of Asian American Artists* (Westport C.T.: Greenwood Publishing Group, 2007), pp. 98–101.
- Janet Koplos, "Shigeko Kubota at Maya Stendhal." *Art in America*, 96, 5 (May 2008), p. 189.
- Lois Fichner-Rathus, *Understanding Art* (Independence, KY, 2009), pp. 200–201.
- Midori Yoshimoto, "Fluxus International: New York, Tokyo, and Beyond." Doryun Chong, Michio Hayashi, Kenji Kajiya, Fumihiko Sumitomo, eds. *From Postwar to Postmodern: Art in Japan 1945–1989* (New York: The Museum of Modern Art, 2012), p. 197.
- Chris Wahl, "Between Art History and Media History: A Brief Introduction to Media Art." Julia Noordegraaf, Sabacosetta G., Barbara Le Maître, and Vinzenz Hediger, eds. *Preserving and Exhibiting Media Art: Challenges and Perspectives*, (Amsterdam: Amsterdam University Press, 2013), pp. 27, 45, 58.
- *Symposium Report, In Search of a New Narrative of Postwar Japanese Art: What Becomes Visible through the Exhibitions at the Two Modern Art Museums in New York and Tokyo* (Tokyo: The Japan Foundation, 2014), p. 79.
- William Grimes, "Shigeko Kubota, a Creator of Video Sculptures, Dies at 77." *The New York Times* (July 27, 2015), B10
- Caroline Jones, "Shigeko Kubota." *Artforum* (June 2015), web.
- Alex Greenberger, "Shigeko Kubota, a Fluxus artist, and a Pioneer of Video Art, Dies at 77." *Artnews* (July 28, 2015), web.
- Jordan Carter, "Shigeko Kubota and International Pop." *Sightlines*, Walker Art Center magazine (Aug. 20, 2015). https://walkerart.org/magazine/pop-virus-shigeko-kubota-and-international-pop. accessed Nov. 25, 2020.
- Barbara London, "Shigeko Kubota: Media Maverick." *Millennium Film Journal*, 63 (Spring 2016), pp. 85–86.
- Karen Kedmey, "How Shigeko Kubota Pioneered Video as a Personal Medium." *ARTSY* (Feb. 6, 2018) https://www.artsy.net/article/artsy-editorial-shigeko-kubota-pioneered-video-personal-medium. accessed Nov. 18, 2020.
- Klaus Biesenbach and Bettina Funcke, eds. *MoMA PS1: A history* (New York: The Museum of Modern Art, 2019), pp. 62–63.
- Reiko Tomii, "'A Test Tube' of New Art: Naiqua and the Rental Gallery System in 1960s Japan." *Afterall: A Journal of Art, Context and Enquiry* (Spring/Summer 2019), (London: Central Saint Martins University of Arts London), pp. 146–161.
- Luciana Galliano, *Japan Fluxus* (London: Lexinton Books, 2019), pp. 45–46, 48–50, 63, 66, 67, 79–80, 82, 106, 117, 124, 126.
- Barbara London, *Video Art: The First Fifty Years* (New York: Phaidon, 2020), pp. 32, 35, 48–49, 58, 69, 83–84.
- Katie McCabe, *More Than A Muse: Creative Partnerships That Sold Talented Women Short* (London: Quadrille, 2020), pp. 189–197, 242–43.

出品リスト

List of Exhibited Works

凡例

- 本リストは、「Viva Video! 久保田成子展」出品作品・資料について、新潟県立近代美術館での展示および本カタログ図版ページの構成に沿って概ね年代順に記載している。ただし、巡回会場では出品内容が異なる場合がある。
- 久保田成子の作品について、[本カタログ掲載ページ]、作品名または資料名、制作年、メディウム、サイズ（縦×横×奥行）、所蔵先（敬称略）の順に和文と英文で記している。それ以外の関連作品や資料は、必要に応じて当該作者名を付しているが、資料についてはメディウムやサイズを記載しない場合がある。ただし、制作年は和英共通とする。（例：「1964年頃」は、「c.1964」）また、先頭にページ数の記載がないもの（「-」）は、本カタログに画像掲載がない。画像が本展出品作と異なる場合は、図版ページのキャプションに記した。
- 各データは、MMI個展カタログを中心とした既存の図録、関連資料、所蔵館提供資料および久保田成子ヴィデオ・アート財団提供資料を参考にした。

［作品タイトルについて］
発表後にタイトルおよびシリーズ名の付加や変更等が行われている場合、概ね変更後のデータを採用している。渡米後に発表された作品の原題は、基本的に英語である。本展における日本語の作品タイトルは、作家による過去の記述等を参照し、原題から和訳した。
［制作年について］
作品の構想または制作開始年と完成の年をダッシュ (-) でつないでいる（例：1968-1975）。また、本展出品にあたり、主要部分の修復作業が行われている作品については、作業年をスラッシュ (/) の後に加えている（例：1976/2021）。
［素材について］
本リストでは、本展出品作品の素材について表記しており、制作当時と異なる場合がある（ブラウン管モニターから液晶モニターへの変更など）。本展における映像は、所蔵先提供のデジタルデータを用いており、再生機については表記しない。

Notes

- The list of works, consisting of the works and documents in *Viva Video! The Art and Life of Shigeko Kubota*, has in principle been arranged chronologically based on the exhibition at the Niigata Prefectural Museum of Modern Art and the order of the plates contained in this catalogue. However, the content of the exhibition may differ at subsequent exhibition venues.
- Information on Shigeko Kubota's works are provided in the following order in Japanese and English: page number on which the work appears in this catalogue, title of work or document, year of production, medium, size (H × W × D), and collection (honorifics omitted). Some documents may lack medium or dimensions. When necessary, the artist's name has also been provided for related works and documents. Only one production year has been given for both Japanese and English (for example, "c.1964"). For entries without page numbers, a hyphen is used to indicate that no image has been included in the catalogue. When the image featured in this catalog differs from what is shown in the exhibition, it is noted in the caption of the image.
- Information on the works is based on the MMI solo exhibition catalogue and other exhibition catalogues, related documents, and materials provided by the collectors as well as those provided by the Shigeko Kubota Video Art Foundation.

[a. Titles of Works]
In cases in which the title of a work or series was appended or changed after it was first shown, the later version of the title has in principle been used. The titles of the works that the artist made after moving to the U.S. were primarily given in English. The Japanese titles of works in this exhibition were translated from the English based on descriptions and other information provided by the artist.
[Year of Production]
A dash has been used between the year in which a work was conceived or initially produced and the year in which it was completed (for ex., 1968-1975). When a significant part of a work in the exhibition has been restored, the year in which the restoration occurred appears after the year of production and a slash (for ex., 1976/2021).
[Materials]
In this list, the materials used to make the works have been indicated; in some cases, however, they differ from the materials used at the time of production (for ex., cathode-ray tube displays have been replaced with liquid-crystal displays, etc.). The video works in the exhibition make use of digital data provided by the collectors. Information on the playback equipment has been omitted.

---

p. 9
- 《向日葵》
Sunflower
1954
油彩／キャンバス
Oil on canvas
72.5 × 60.5 cm
個人蔵
Private Collection
＊新潟会場のみ出品 (only exhibited in Niigata)

\-
- 1954年のスケッチブック
Sketchbook in 1954
個人蔵
Private Collection
＊新潟会場のみ出品 (only exhibited in Niigata)

\-
- ［題不詳］
[Unknown]
c. 1956
石膏
Plaster
37 × 30 × 30 cm
個人蔵
Private Collection
＊新潟会場のみ出品 (only exhibited in Niigata)

---

p. 10
- ［複製写真］1956年、1957年のアルバムより（教育大学山岳部、邦千谷、高橋清アトリエ等）
[Reproduction photo] Photo album in 1956 and 1957 (Tokyo University of Education, Chiya Kuni, Kiyoshi Takahashi's studio)
提供：久保田成子ヴィデオ・アート財団
Courtesy Shigeko Kubota Video Art Foundation
＊画像は一部（The image is detail)

\-
- ［複製写真］《首A》
[Reproduction photo] *Kubi (Head) A*
1958
写真提供：久保田成子ヴィデオ・アート財団
Photo courtesy Shigeko Kubota Video Art Foundation

\-
- ［写真］《死石5》
[Photo] *Shiseki (Death Stone) 5*
1961
個人蔵
Private Collection

\-
- ［複製写真］《死石T》
[Reproduction photo] *Shiseki (Death Stone) T*
1962
写真提供：久保田成子ヴィデオ・アート財団
Photo courtesy Shigeko Kubota Video Art Foundation

---

p. 11 左 (left)
- ［複製写真］《死石T》を制作する久保田成子
[Reproduction photo] Kubota with *Shiseki (Death Stone) T*
c.1962
写真提供：久保田成子ヴィデオ・アート財団
Photo courtesy Shigeko Kubota Video Art Foundation

---

p. 11 右下 (bottom right)
- ［写真］第15回日本アンデパンダン展（読売アンデパンダン展）出品作品《We can make it》《Suddenly》、展示風景

[Photo]*We can make it* and *Suddenly* shown at the *15th Yomiuri Independent Exhibition*
1963
個人蔵
Private Collection

p. 12
- ［写真］「1st. LOVE, 2nd. LOVE... 久保田成子彫刻個展」会場風景
[Photo] Installation view of the *1st. LOVE, 2nd. LOVE..., Shigeko Kubota Sculpture Exhibition*
1963
個人蔵
Private Collection

p. 11 右上 (top right)、p. 13
- 久保田成子から瀧口修造宛て封書（内科画廊での個展案内状、写真、略歴、自筆手紙）
A letter from Shigeko Kubota to Shuzo Takiguchi with an invitation of Kubota's solo exhibition, photograph, and CV
1963
慶應義塾大学アート・センター蔵
Collection of Keio University Art Center

p. 14
- 「Sweet 16」プログラム
Program of *Sweet 16*
1963
刀根康尚蔵
Collection of Yasunao Tone

-
- ［写真］久保田の叔母、邦千谷（邦千谷舞踊研究所）
[Photo] Chiya Kuni, Kubota's aunt at Kuni Chiya Dance Institute
撮影年不詳（year unknown)
個人蔵
Private Collection

-
- 「白南準作品発表会」プログラム
Program of *N. J. PAIK: COMPOSITION*
1964
西山輝夫蔵
Collection of Teruo Nishiyama

-
- 「白南準作品発表会」チケット
Ticket of *N. J. PAIK: COMPOSITION*
1964
西山輝夫蔵
Collection of Teruo Nishiyama

-
- 平田実《ナムジュン・パイク「白南準作品発表会」》
Minoru Hirata, *Nam June Paik's "N. J. PAIK: COMPOSITION"*
1964/2011
写真
Photograph
東京都現代美術館蔵
Collection of Museum of Contemporary Art Tokyo

-
- 城之内元晴《シェルタープラン》
Motoharu Jonouchi, *Shelter Plan*
1964
16mmフィルムからデジタル変換（モノクロ、サイレント）
Digitalized from 16mm film, (b&w, silent)
19"00'
東京都現代美術館蔵　協力：城之内美稲子
Collection of Museum of Contemporary Art Tokyo, Courtesy Mineko Jonouchi

-
- ハイレッド・センター《「シェルター計画」カルテ（久保田成子）》
Hi-Red Center, *Carte (Shigeko Kubota) for "Shelter Plan"*
1964
インク／紙（活版印刷）
Ink on paper (letterpress printing)
19.4 × 27.1 cm
個人蔵
Private Collection

-
- ハイレッド・センター《「シェルター計画」より「シェルター模型（川仁宏）」》
Hi-Red Center, *Shelter Model (Hiroshi Kawani) from "Shelter Plan"*
1964
写真、木
Photograph and wood
20.6 × 5.6 × 3.5 cm
東京国立近代美術館蔵
Collection of The National Museum of Modern Art, Tokyo
＊新潟会場のみ出品 (only exhibited in Niigata)

-
- ［複製写真］ハイレッド・センター《「シェルター計画」より「人体展開図写真（風倉匠）」》
[Reproduction photo] Hi-Red Center, *Photographic Plans for Shelter Model (Sho Kazakura) from "Shelter Plan"*
1964
26.7 × 28.4 cm
写真提供：東京国立近代美術館
Photo courtesy The National Museum of Modern Art, Tokyo
＊新潟会場のみ出品 (only exhibited in Niigata)

-
- ハイレッド・センター《「シェルター計画」より「人体展開図写真(横尾忠則)」》
Hi-Red Center, *Photographic Plans for Shelter Model (Tadanori Yokoo) from "Shelter Plan"*
1964
ゼラチン・シルバー・プリント
Gelatin silver print
26.0 × 32.0 cm
東京国立近代美術館蔵
Collection of The National Museum of Modern Art, Tokyo
＊大阪会場のみ出品 (only exhibited in Osaka)

-
- ハイレッド・センター《「シェルター計画」より「人体展開図写真（風倉匠）」》
Hi-Red Center, *Photographic Plans for Shelter Model (Sho Kazakura) from "Shelter Plan"*
1964
湿式印刷
Wet printing
26.7 × 28.4 cm
東京国立近代美術館蔵
Collection of The National Museum of Modern Art, Tokyo
＊東京会場のみ出品 (only exhibited in Tokyo)

-
- 「OFF MUSEUM」ポスター
Poster of *OFF MUSEUM*
1964
シルクスクリーン
Silkscreen
27.0 × 78.7 cm
東京都現代美術館蔵
Collection of Museum of Contemporary Art Tokyo

-
- ［雑誌］『美術ジャーナル』第49号、1964年6月
[Magazine] *Bijutsu Journal*, No. 49, June 1964
東京都現代美術館図書室蔵
Collection of Museum of Contemporary Art Tokyo Art Library

p. 17 右上 (top right)
- 平田実《刀根康尚「インヴェスティゲイション・イヴェント」》
Minoru Hirata, *Yasunao Tone, "The Investigation Event"*
1964/2011
写真
Photograph
34 × 26 cm
東京都現代美術館蔵
Collection of Museum of Contemporary Art Tokyo

p. 17 左上 (top left)
- 《ハイレッド・センター「イヴェント集」》
編集：久保田成子、デザイン・製作：ジョージ・マチューナス
Hi-Red Center "Bundle of Events", edited by Shigeko Kubota, designed and produced by George Maciunas
1965
印刷／紙（両面）
Offset printing on paper, double-sided
55.9 × 43.3 cm
西山輝夫蔵
Collection of Teruo Nishiyama

p. 18-19
- 《フルクサス・スーツケース》
Fluxus Suitcase
1964
アルミニウム製スーツケース
Aluminum suitcase
22.86 × 66.04 × 40.64 cm
久保田成子ヴィデオ・アート財団蔵
Collection of Shigeko Kubota Video Art Foundation

p. 20
- 久保田成子からジョージ・マチューナスへの手紙
Letter to George Maciunas from Shigeko Kubota
1964
複製（原資料：インク、コラージュ／紙）
Reproduction (Original document: ink on paper with collage addition)
98.5 × 28.1 cm
写真提供：ニューヨーク近代美術館
Photo courtsy: The Museum of Modern Art, New York

p. 21 上 (top)
- フルクサス《フルクサス I》
Fluxus, *Fluxus I*
after 1964
フルクサス・メンバーによるマルチプル、木
Collection of multiples by Fluxus artists, wood
22.4 × 24.0 × 5.4 cm
国立国際美術館蔵
Collection of The National Museum of Art, Osaka
＊画像は一部（The image is detail)

p. 21 中央 (middle)

- 《フルックス・ナプキン》(「フルクサスⅠ」に所収)
Flux Napkin in Fluxus I
1965
紙ナプキン、コラージュ
Paper napkin with collage
国立国際美術館蔵
Collection of The National Museum of Art, Osaka
写真提供：ニューヨーク近代美術館
Photo courtesy The Museum of Modern Art, New York

-

- フルクサス《フルックスキット》
Fluxus, *Fluxkit*
after 1964
フルクサス・メンバーによるマルチプルや印刷物、アタッシェケース
Collection of multiples and printed items by Fluxus artists, attaché case
30 × 44 × 9.5 cm
東京都現代美術館蔵
Collection of Museum of Contemporary Art Tokyo

p. 21 下 (bottom)
- 《フルックス・メディシン》(「フルックスキット」に所収)
Flux Medicine in *Fluxkit*
1966
薬用カプセル、薬瓶、スポイト、絆創膏、薬説明書、ラベル付プラスチックケース
Medicine capsule, bottle, dropper, bandage, instructions of medicine in plastic case with label
10 × 12 × 2.5 cm
東京都現代美術館蔵
Collection of Museum of Contemporary Art Tokyo

-

- オノ・ヨーコ《グレープフルーツ》
Yoko Ono, *Grapefruit*
1964
本
Book
14 × 14 × 3.3 cm
東京都現代美術館蔵
Collection of Museum of Contemporary Art Tokyo

-

- ［複製写真］小野洋子から久保田成子への献辞(《グレープフルーツ》1964年に記載)
[Reproduction photo] Dedication to Kubota from Yoko Ono on her book *Grapefruit*, 1964
写真提供：久保田成子ヴィデオ・アート財団
Photo courtesy Shigeko Kubota Video Art Foundation

-

- 塩見允枝子《スペイシャル・ポエム No. 5「開くイヴェント」》招待状
Mieko Shiomi, Invitation Letter of *Spatial Poem No. 5 "open event"*
1972
印刷／紙
Printing on paper
27.8 × 21.4 cm
国立国際美術館蔵
Collection of The National Museum of Art, Osaka

-

- 塩見允枝子《スペイシャル・ポエム　No.5「開くイヴェント」》久保田成子によるオリジナル・レポート
Original report by Shigeko Kubota on *Spatial Poem No.5 "open event"* by Mieko Shiomi
1972
印刷／紙
Printing on paper
国立国際美術館蔵
Collection of The National Museum of Art, Osaka

-

- 塩見允枝子『スペイシャル・ポエム』
Mieko Shiomi, *Spatial Poem*
1976
本
Book
21 × 27.3 cm
新潟県立近代美術館蔵
Collection of The Niigata Prefectural Museum of Modern Art

-

- 《ふたつ目のジョージ・マチューナス 1972年、ひとつ目のジョージ・マチューナス 1976年》
George Maciunas With Two Eyes 1972, George Maciunas With One Eye 1976
1994
シングルチャンネル・ヴィデオ（モノクロ、サウンド）
Single-channel video (b&w, sound)
7'00"
映像提供：エレクトロニック・アーツ・インターミックス（EAI）
Courtesy Electronic Arts Intermix (EAI), New York

-

- ［写真］ジョージ・マチューナス、フランチェスコ・コンツと久保田成子（ロフトにて）撮影：ベアテ・ニッチュ
[Photo] Kubota with George Maciunas and Francesco Conz in her loft, photo by Beate Nitsch
1974
個人蔵
Private Collection

-

- グッゲンハイム美術館のベン・ヴォーティエ展オープニングにて（1972年）　撮影：久保田成子
Opening at Ben Vautier's show at Guggenheim Museum in 1972, photo by Shigeko Kubota
1995
パステル、水彩、鉛筆／写真
Hand writing with pastel, watercolor, pencil on photo
21.5 × 30.3 cm
個人蔵
Private Collection

p. 22
- ［複製写真］エリック・アンダーセン《Opus45》に参加する久保田成子　撮影：ピーター・ムーア
[Reproduction photo] Kubota performing in Eric Andersen's *Opus 45*, photo by Peter Moore
1965
協力：エリック・アンダーセン
Courtesy Eric Andersen

-

- 「フルックス・オーケストラ」ポスター
Poster of *Fluxorchestra*
1965
印刷／紙
Offset printing on paper
43.1 × 29.9 cm
国立国際美術館蔵
Collection of The National Museum of Art, Osaka

p. 24
- 《ヴァギナ・ペインティング》　撮影：ジョージ・マチューナス
Vagina Painting, photo by George Maciunas
1965/1996
ゼラチン・シルバー・プリント（オリジナルネガよりプリント）
Gelatin silver print, printed from the original negative
25.3 × 20.2 cm
ハリー・ルーエ／ギャラリー A、アムステルダム蔵
Collection of Harry Ruhé/Galerie A, Amsterdam
写真提供：ニューヨーク近代美術館
Photo courtesy The Museum of Modern Art, New York

p. 25 下 (bottom)
- ［複製写真］《ヴァギナ・ペインティング》スタジオ写真　撮影：ピーター・ムーア
[Reproduction photo] Contactsheet of the photos of *Vagina Painting* taken at Peter Moore's studio
1964
提供：久保田成子ヴィデオ・アート財団
Courtesy Shigeko Kubota Video Art Foundation

p. 25 上 (top)
- 「永続的なフルックスフェスト」『Fluxus Vacuum TRapEzoid』(フルクサス新聞No. 5)
"Perpetual Fluxfest" from *Fluxus Vacuum TRapEzoid* (Fluxus Newspaper No. 5)
1965
印刷／紙
Offset printing on paper
55.6 × 43 cm（二つ折　fold in half）
東京都現代美術館蔵
Collection of Museum of Contemporary Art Tokyo

-

- 「永続的なフルックスフェスト」『Fluxus Vaudeville TouRnamEnt』(フルクサス新聞No. 6)
"Perpetual Fluxfest" from *Fluxus Vaudeville TouRnamEnt* (Fluxus Newspaper No. 6)
1965
印刷／紙
Offset printing on paper
86.3 × 56 cm
東京都現代美術館蔵
Collection of Museum of Contemporary Art Tokyo

-

- 「1965年夏のフルックスフェストより 1. 久保田成子：ヴァギナ・ペインティング」『Fluxus 3 newspaper eVenTs for the pRicE of $1』(フルクサス新聞No. 7)
"From 1965 Summer Fluxfest 1: Shigeko Kubota: Vagina Painting," from *Fluxus 3 newspaper eVenTs for the pRicE of $1* (Fluxus Newspaper No. 7)
1966
印刷／紙
Offset printing on paper
56 × 43.2 cm（二つ折　fold in half）
東京都現代美術館蔵
Collection of Museum of Contemporary Art Tokyo

p. 26

・［スライドショー］ソニック・アーツ・ユニオン関連写真資料
[Slide show] Digital photo of Sonic Arts Union
1967-69
写真提供：メアリー・ルシエ
Photo courtesy Mary Lucier
＊画像は一部（The image is detail）

p. 26 下（bottom）
・メアリー・ルシエ《ポラロイド・イメージ・シリーズ：シゲコ》（アルヴィン・ルシエによる《私は部屋に座っている》を伴う）
Mary Lucier, *Polaroid Image Series: Shigeko*, with Alvin Lucier, *I am sitting in a room*
1970/2006
モノクロポラロイド写真からのスライドをデジタル変換
Digitalized from original slides from Polaroid b&w photographs
23'00"
メアリー・ルシエ蔵
Collection of Mary Lucier

-
・キャロリー・シュニーマン《スノーズ》
Carolee Schneemann, *Snows*
1967
16mmフィルムからヴィデオ変換（カラーとモノクロ、サウンド）
16 mm film on video (color and b&w, sound)
20'24"
映像提供：エレクトロニック・アーツ・インターミックス（EAI）
Courtesy Electronic Arts Intermix (EAI), New York

p. 27
・［写真］キャロリー・シュニーマン《スノーズ》より　撮影：シャーロット・ヴィクトリア、バッジャーニ、アレック・ソボルースキ、ハーバート・ミグドル
[Photos] Carolee Schneemann, *Snows*, photo by Charlotte Victoria, Baggiani, Alec Sobolewski and Herbert Migdoll
1967
個人蔵
Private Collection

-
・キャロリー・シュニーマン《スノーズ》ポスター
Poster of Carolee Schneemann's *Snows*
1967
複製
Reproduction
写真提供：キャロリー・シュニーマン財団
Photo courtesy Carolee Schneemann Foundation

p. 28
・『マルセル・デュシャンとジョン・ケージ』
Marcel Duchamp and John Cage
1970
本、ソノシート
Book with a 33 1/3 rpm record
15.5 × 21.5 × 1.7 cm
新潟県立近代美術館・万代島美術館蔵
Collection of The Niigata Prefectural Museum of Modern Art/The Niigata Bandaijima Art Museum

p. 29
・［写真］マルセル・デュシャンによるサインのある『美術手帖』第295号、1968年
[Photo] Page in *Bijutsu Techo*, No. 295, March 1968 with Marcel Duchamp's autograph
1968/1990
個人蔵
Private Collection

-
・『マルセル・デュシャンとジョン・ケージ』のための写真原版
Photographic plate of *Marcel Duchamp and John Cage*
1970
15.4 × 21.3 cm
宮澤依子蔵
Collection of Yoriko Miyazawa

-
・ティニー・デュシャンから宮澤壯佳（『マルセル・デュシャンとジョン・ケージ』発行者）への書簡
Letter to Takeyoshi Miyazawa, publisher of *Marcel Duchamp and John Cage* from Teeny Duchamp
1970
宮澤依子蔵
Collection of Yoriko Miyazawa

-
・［雑誌］久保田成子「晩年のデュシャンとチェス・ゲーム」『美術手帖』第319号、1969年11月
[Magazine] Shigeko Kubota, "Duchamp in his late years and Chess Game," *Bijutsu Techo*, No. 319, Nov. 1969
新潟県立近代美術館蔵
Collection of The Niigata Prefectural Museum of Modern Art

-
・携帯用ヴィデオカメラ「ビデオ・デンスケ SONY DVC-2400」（ポータパック）
Portable Video Camera, SONY DVC-2400 (Portapak)
1967
ソニー株式会社蔵
Collection of Sony Corporation

-
・［写真］「エレクトロニック／アートIII：シャーロット・モーマンとパイク-アベ・ヴィデオ・シンセサイザー」展での久保田とパイク　撮影：トム・ハール
[Photo] Kubota and Paik at the opening of *Electronic Art III : Paik-Abe Video Synthesizer with Charlotte Moorman*, photo by Tom Haar
1971
個人蔵
Private Collection

p. 30 下（bottom）
・［写真］久保田成子ポートレート　撮影：トム・ハール
[Photo] Shigeko Kubota Portrait, photo by Tom Haar
1972
個人蔵
Private Collection

-
・［写真］ヴェネツィアでの久保田成子
[Photo] Kubota in Venice
c. 1972
個人蔵
Private Collection

-
・久保田成子から宮澤壯佳へのポストカード（ブレーメンから、1972年5月5日消印）
Postcard from Kubota to Takeyoshi Miyazawa from Bremen, postmarked on May 5, 1972
宮澤依子蔵
Collection of Yoriko Miyazawa

-
・久保田成子から阿部修也へのポストカード（ニースから、1972年6月2日消印）
Postcard from Kubota to Shuya Abe from Niece, postmarked on June 2, 1972
東京都現代美術館蔵
Collection of Museum of Contemporary Art Tokyo

-
・［写真］「久保田成子：ライヴとヴィデオテープによるコンサート」での久保田とパイク　撮影：ピーター・ムーア
[Photo] Kubota and Paik at *Shigeko Kubota: Live and Videotape Concert*, photo by Peter Moore
1972
個人蔵
Private Collection

p. 31
・「久保田成子：ライヴとヴィデオテープによるコンサート」ポスター
Poster of *Shigeko Kubota: Live and Videotape Concert*
1972
複製
Reproduction
提供：久保田成子ヴィデオ・アート財団蔵
Courtesy Shigeko Kubota Video Art Foundation

p. 30
・《ブロークン・ダイアリー：ヨーロッパを一日ハーフインチで》
Broken Diary: Europe on 1/2 Inch a Day
1972
シングルチャンネル・ヴィデオ（モノクロとカラー、サウンド）
Single-channel video (b&w and color, sound)
30'48"
映像提供：エレクトロニック・アーツ・インターミックス（EAI）
Courtesy Electronic Arts Intermix (EAI), New York

-
・「久保田成子によるジョン・ケージの（60歳の）ヴィデオ・バースデー・パーティー」ポスター
Poster of *Video Birthday Party (60th) of John Cage by Shigeko Kubota*
1972
個人蔵
Private Collection

-
・「デイリー・パフォーマンス：久保田成子　ヴィデオテープ」ポスター
Poster of *Dail Performance: Shigeko Kubota Video Tapes*
1972
個人蔵
Private Collection

-
・［複製写真］第9回ニューヨーク・アヴァンギャルド・フェスティヴァルにおける久保田成子と作品
[Reproduction photo] Kubota and her work at *9th Annual New York Avant Garde Festival*
1972
写真提供：メアリー・ルシエ
Photo courtesy Mary Lucier

p. 32 下（bottom）
- 「ホワイト ブラック レッド イエロー」ポスター
デザイン：久保田成子
Poster of *White Black Red & Yellow*, designed by Shigeko Kubota
1972
複製
Reproduction
写真提供：メアリー・ルシエ
Photo courtesy Mary Lucier

-
- 「ホワイト ブラック レッド イエロー」ポスター
デザイン：メアリー・ルシエ
Poster of *White Black Red & Yellow*, designed by Mary Lucier
1973
複製
Reproduction
写真提供：メアリー・ルシエ
Photo courtesy Mary Lucier

---

p. 35
- 「第2回ヴィデオ・アーツ・フェスティヴァル：久保田成子」ポスター
Poster of *Second Annual Video Arts Festival: Shigeko Kubota*
1973
複製
Reproduction
写真提供：メアリー・ルシエ
Photo courtesy Mary Lucier

-
- メアリー・ルシエ《シゲコのヴィデオ・マリリン》
Mary Lucier, *Shigeko's Video Marilyn*
1973/2021
印刷／紙（久保田成子《A 36 - 24 - 36》を撮影したモノクロ写真を組み合わせ、カラー紙に印刷したオリジナルより、本展のために色加工、印刷）
Print on archival paper (Originally printed on colored paper from b&w negatives of Kubota's *A 36 - 24 - 36*. Colorized and re-printed for this exhibition)
62.54 × 78.89 cm
メアリー・ルシエ蔵
Collection of Mary Lucier

---

p. 34
- 《ブロークン・ダイアリー：ヴィデオ・ガールズとナヴァホの空のためのヴィデオ・ソング》
Broken Diary: Video Girls and Video Songs for Navajo Sky
1973
シングルチャンネル・ヴィデオ（モノクロとカラー、サウンド）
Single-channel video (b&w and color, sound)
31'56"
映像提供：エレクトロニック・アーツ・インターミックス（EAI）
Courtesy Electronic Arts Intermix (EAI), New York

---

p. 36
- 《ブロークン・ダイアリー：私のお父さん》
Broken Diary: My Father
1973-75
シングルチャンネル・ヴィデオ（モノクロ、サウンド）
Single-channel video (b&w, sound)
映像提供：エレクトロニック・アーツ・インターミックス（EAI）
Courtesy Electronic Arts Intermix (EAI), New York

---

p. 37 下（bottom）
- 「トーキョー・ニューヨーク・ビデオ・エキスプレス」チラシ（複写）
Flyer of *Tokyo-New York: Video Express* (photocopy)
1974
協力：プロセスアート、イメージフォーラム
Courtesy Processart and Image Forum

-
- ［雑誌］久保田成子「ヴィデオ――開かれた回路」『芸術倶楽部』第9号、1974年6月
[Magazine] Shigeko Kubota, "Video: Open Circuits," *Geijutsu Kurabu*, No. 9, June 1974
国立国際美術館蔵
Collection of The National Museum of Art, Osaka

---

p. 86
- ［写真］アンソロジー・フィルム・アーカイヴズでの久保田成子　撮影：ホリス・メルトン
[Photo] Kubota at Anthology Film Archives, photo by Hollis Melton
1974
個人蔵
Private Collection

-
- アンソロジー・フィルム・アーカイヴズ関連資料
Documents related to Anthology Film Archives
1974
個人蔵
Private Collection

-
- ［カタログ］『The New Television』（1977年）より "Open Circuits: The Future of Television"（1974年）について
[Catalog] "Open Circuits: The Future of Television" (1974) on *The New Television*, 1977
国立国際美術館蔵
Collection of The National Museum of Art, Osaka

---

p. 38-39
- 《ヴィデオ・ポエム》
Video Poem
1970-75/2018
ジッパー付ナイロン袋、小型扇風機、ブラウン管モニター、テキスト、シングルチャンネル・ヴィデオ
Nylon sleeping bag with zippers, small electric fan, CRT monitor, wall text and single-channel video
サイズ可変 Dimensions variable
久保田成子ヴィデオ・アート財団蔵
Collection of Shigeko Kubota Video Art Foundation

---

p. 54-55
- 《デュシャンピアナ：マルセル・デュシャンの墓》
Duchampiana: Marcel Duchamp's Grave
1972-75/2019
合板、モニター（枠付）11台、鏡、プロジェクション、シングルチャンネル・ヴィデオ、サウンド
Plywood, eleven monitors with bezel, mirrors, projector, single-channel video and sound
サイズ可変 Dimensions variable
久保田成子ヴィデオ・アート財団蔵
Collection of Shigeko Kubota Video Art Foundation

---

p. 56-59
- 《デュシャンピアナ：ヴィデオ・チェス》
Duchampiana: Video Chess
1968-75
合板、ガラス板、プラスチック製駒、モニター、テキスト、写真、シングルチャンネル・ヴィデオ、サウンド
Plywood, glass sheets, plastic chess pieces, monitor, wall text, photographs, single-channel video and sound
73.8 × 62.6 × 62.6 cm
久保田成子ヴィデオ・アート財団蔵
Collection of Shigeko Kubota Video Art Foundation

-
p. 60-62
- 《デュシャンピアナ：階段を降りる裸体》
Duchampiana: Nude Descending a Staircase
1975-76/83
合板、ブラウン管モニター4台、テキスト、シングルチャンネル・ヴィデオ
Plywood, four CRT monitors, wall text and single-channel video
180 × 90 × 170 cm
富山県美術館蔵
Collection of Toyama Prefectural Museum of Art and Design

-
- 「久保田成子 3ヴィデオ・スカルプチャー：デュシャンピアナ」案内ハガキ
Flyer of *Shigeko Kubota 3 Video Sculptures: Duchampiana*
1976
個人蔵
Private Collection

-
- ［雑誌］「若い世代の一断面」『Art in America』1977年、9・10月
[Magazine] "The Younger Generation: A Cross Section" *Art in America*, Sept.& Oct., 1977
個人蔵
Private Collection

-
- 「久保田成子 4ヴィデオ・スカルプチャー：デュシャンピアナ」チラシ
Flyer of *Shigeo Kubota 4 Video Sculptures: Duchampiana*
1978
個人蔵
Private Collection

---

p. 63-65
- 《デュシャンピアナ：ドア》
Duchampiana: Door
1976-77/2021
合板、ドア、モニタ　2台、テキスト、シングルチャンネル・ヴィデオ、サウンド
Plywood, doors, two monitors, wall texts, single-channel video and sound
サイズ可変 Dimensions variable
久保田成子ヴィデオ・アート財団蔵
Collection of Shigeko Kubota Video Art Foundation

---

p. 66-67
- 《メタ・マルセル：窓（雪）》
Meta-Marcel: Window (Snow)
1976-77/2019
合板、ガラス窓、ブラウン管モニター
Plywood, glass windows and CRT monitor
76 × 58.5 × 55 cm
久保田成子ヴィデオ・アート財団蔵
Collection of Shigeko Kubota Video Art

Foundation

p. 68-69
- 《メタ・マルセル：窓（三つのテープ）》
Meta-Marcel: Window (Three tapes)
1976-83/2019
合板、ガラス窓、モニター、テキスト、シングルチャンネル・ヴィデオ
Plywood, glass windows, monitor, wall text and single-channel video
76 × 58.5 × 55 cm
富山県美術館蔵
Collection of Toyama Prefectural Museum of Art and Design

p. 72-73, 74-75
- ［スライドショー］構想スケッチ
[Slide show] Conceptual sketches
1977, 1979
写真提供：久保田成子ヴィデオ・アート財団
Photo courtesy Shigeko Kubota Video Arts Foundation

p. 76-77
- ドローイング［Berlin Video Diary］
Drawing [Berlin Video Diary]
1979
水彩、ペン／紙（セルフポートレートが印刷された便箋）［7点］
Watercolor and pen on paper (letter paper with self-portrait) [seven pieces]
27.94 × 21.59 cm
久保田成子ヴィデオ・アート財団蔵
Collection of Shigeko Kubota Video Art Foundation

p. 78-81
- 《三つの山》
Three Mountains
1976-79/2020
合板、モニター5台、プラスチック製鏡、4チャンネルヴィデオ、サウンド
Plywood, five monitors, plastic mirrors, four channel video and sound
96.5 × 151 × 151 cm, 170 × 254 × 152 cm, 170 × 254 × 152 cm
久保田成子ヴィデオ・アート財団蔵
Collection of Shigeko Kubota Video Art Foundation

p. 189
- ドローイング［Autobiographical Landscape］
Drawing [Autobiographical Landscape]
制作年不詳（year unknown）
色鉛筆／紙
Color pencil on paper
30.8 × 46 cm
久保田成子ヴィデオ・アート財団蔵
Collection of Shigeko Kubota Video Art Foundation

-
- ドローイング［My Father's Country］
Drawing [My Father's Country]
1978
パステル／紙
Pastel on paper
45.7 × 61.6 cm
久保田成子ヴィデオ・アート財団蔵
Collection of Shigeko Kubota Video Art Foundation

p. 79
- ドローイング［Three Mountains for Whitney］
Drawing [Three Mountains for Whitney]
1978
パステル、鉛筆／紙
Pastel and pencil on paper
45.7 × 61.6 cm
久保田成子ヴィデオ・アート財団蔵
Collection of Shigeko Kubota Video Art Foundation

p. 94-95
- 《河》
River
1979-81/2020
ステンレス、プラスチック製鏡、波再生機、水、ブラウン管3台、シングルチャンネル・ヴィデオ
Stainless steel, plastic mirror, wave machine, water, three CRT monitors, single-channel video
サイズ可変 Dimensions variable
（ステンレス構造　Stainless steel structure：82 × 300 × 90 cm）
久保田成子ヴィデオ・アート財団蔵
Collection of Shigeko Kubota Video Art Foundation

-
- ドローイング［Study of River］
Drawing [Study of River]
1979
パステル、鉛筆／紙
Pastel and pencil on paper
55.9 × 74.9 cm
久保田成子ヴィデオ・アート財団蔵
Collection of Shigeko Kubota Video Art Foundation

-
- ドローイング［River of Blood］
Drawing [River of Blood]
1980
アクリル、パステル、水彩／紙
Acrylic pastel and watercolor on paper
55.9 × 74.9 cm
久保田成子ヴィデオ・アート財団蔵
Collection of Shigeko Kubota Video Art Foundation

-
- ドローイング［River of Blood］
Drawing [River of Blood]
1980
パステル、鉛筆／紙
Pastel and pen on paper
55.2 × 74.9 cm
久保田成子ヴィデオ・アート財団蔵
Collection of Shigeko Kubota Video Art Foundation

-
- ナムジュン・パイク、久保田成子《パイクによるマースによるマース　パート2：マースとマルセル》
Nam June Paik and Shigeko Kubota, *Merce by Merce by Paik Part Two: Merce and Marcel*
1978
シングルチャンネル・ヴィデオ（カラー、サウンド）
Single-channel video (color, sound)
13'05"
映像提供：エレクトロニック・アーツ・インターミックス（EAI）
Courtesy Electronic Arts Intermix (EAI), New York

p. 96-97
- 《ヴィデオ俳句—ぶら下がり作品》
Video Haiku - Hanging Piece
1981
吊り構造、モーター、球体モニター、ヴィデオカメラ、プラスチック製鏡
Hanging structure, motor, Videosphere, video camera and plastic mirror
サイズ可変 Dimensions variable（鏡寸法　mirror size: 30 × 107 × 107 cm）
久保田成子ヴィデオ・アート財団蔵
Collection of Shigeko Kubota Video Art Foundation

p. 98-100
- 《デュシャンピアナ：自転車の車輪1, 2, 3》
Duchampiana: Bicycle Wheel One, Two, Three
1983-90
自転車の車輪、木の椅子、モーター、モニター（各1台、2台、3台）、シングルチャンネル・ヴィデオ
Bicycle wheels, wooden stools, motors, monitors (one, two and three for each), and Single-channel video
148 × 64 × 39.5 cm each
公益財団法人アルカンシエール美術財団／原美術館コレクション
Foundation Arc-en-Ciel/Hara Museum Collection

p. 100 右（right）
- ドローイング［3 Speed Bicycle］
Drawing [3 Speed Bicycle]
1977
パステル／紙
Pastel on paper
30.8 × 46 cm
久保田成子ヴィデオ・アート財団蔵
Collection of Shigeko Kubota Video Art Foundation

-
- ［雑誌］『Art in America』（1984年2月）表紙（《河》掲載）
[Magazine] Cover of *Art in America*, Feb, 1984, with *River*
新潟県立近代美術館蔵
Collection of The Niigata Prefectural Museum of Modern Art

-
- 「ヴィデオ・アート」展（ホイットニー美術館、1988年）カタログ
Exhibition catalog of *Video Art: Expanded Forms* (Whitney Museum of American Art, 1988)
個人蔵
Private Collection

-
- 「久保田成子：ヴィデオ・インスタレーション」（原美術館、1992年）案内状
Invitation of *Kubota Shigeko: Video Installation* (Hara Museum, 1992)
個人蔵
Private Collection

-
- 安齊重男《久保田家　1981年8月1日　高輪美術館　軽井沢》
Shigeo Anzai, *Kubota Family, August 1, 1981, Takanawa Museum, Karuizawa*
1981/2020
ゼラチン・シルバー・プリント
Gelatin silver print
22.6 × 15.4 cm
国立国際美術館蔵
Collection of The National Museum of Art, Osaka

-
・安齊重男《久保田成子　1990年5月23日　ジュ－デッカ　ヴェネチア》
Shigeo Anzai, *Shigeko Kubota, May 23, 1990, Giudecca, Venezia*
1990/2020
ゼラチン・シルバー・プリント
Gelatin silver print
22.6 × 15.4 cm
国立国際美術館蔵
Collection of The National Museum of Art, Osaka

-
・安齊重男《久保田成子　1990年5月23日　ジュ－デッカ　ヴェネチア》
Shigeo Anzai, *Shigeko Kubota, May 23, 1990, Giudecca, Venezia*
1990/2020
ゼラチン・シルバー・プリント
Gelatin silver
22.6 × 15.4 cm
国立国際美術館蔵
Collection of The National Museum of Art, Osaka

---

p. 102
・《ブロークン・ダイアリー：韓国への旅》
Broken Diary: Trip to Korea
1984
シングルチャンネル・ヴィデオ（カラー、サウンド）
Single-channel video (color, sound)
9'05"
映像提供：エレクトロニック・アーツ・インターミックス（EAI）
Courtesy Electronic Arts Intermix (EAI), New York

---

p. 103
・《ブロークン・ダイアリー：ソーホー・ソープ／雨の被害》
Broken Diary: SoHo Soap/Rain Damage
1985
シングルチャンネル・ヴィデオ（カラー、サウンド）
Single-channel video (color, sound)
8'25"
映像提供：エレクトロニック・アーツ・インターミックス（EAI）
Courtesy Electronic Arts Intermix (EAI), New York

-
・「ブロークン・ダイアリー：ソーホー・ソープ／雨の被害、ソーホー・アーティストの共同住宅」案内ハガキ
Flyer of *Broken Diary: SoHo Soap/Rain Damage, Story of a SoHo Artists' Co-op*
1986
個人蔵
Private Collection

---

p. 104-107
・《ナイアガラの滝》
Niagara Falls
1985/2021
プラスチック製鏡、合板、モニター 10台、スプリンクラー、プール、水、プロジェクション、4チャンネルヴィデオ、サウンド
Plastic mirrors, plywood, ten monitors, sprinkler system, basin, water, projectors, four-channel video and sound
247.2 × 331 × 306 cm
久保田成子ヴィデオ・アート財団蔵
Collection of Shigeko Kubota Video Art Foundation

---

p. 104 左下（bottom left）
・《ナイアガラの滝》ドローイング
Drawing of *Niagara Falls*
1985
複製（原資料：水彩スティック、鉛筆／紙）
Reproduction (Original drawing: Watercolor-stick and pencil on paper)
27.94 × 21.59 cm
提供：久保田成子ヴィデオ・アート財団
Courtesy Shigeko Kubota Video Art Foundation

-
・「ヴィデオ・インスタレーション：ナイアガラの滝」案内ハガキ
Flyer of *Video Installation: Niagara Falls*
1985
個人蔵
Private Collection

---

p. 120-121
・《スケート選手》
Skater
1991-92
木、プラスチック製鏡、モニター 7台、回転機材、プロジェクション、シングルチャンネル・ヴィデオ
Wood, plastic mirrors, seven monitors, turntable, projectors and single-channel video
195 × 199 × 177 cm
久保田成子ヴィデオ・アート財団蔵
Collection of Shigeko Kubota Video Art Foundation

---

p. 126-127
・《韓国の墓》
Korean Grave
1993
木、プラスチック製鏡、モニター 12台、プロジェクション、2チャンネルヴィデオ
Wood, plastic mirrors, twelve monitors, projectors and two-channel video
130 × 281 × 246 cm
久保田成子ヴィデオ・アート財団蔵
Collection of Shigeko Kubota Video Art Foundation

---

p. 132-133
・《セクシュアル・ヒーリング》
Sexual Healing
1998
シングルチャンネル・ヴィデオ（カラー、サウンド）
Single-channel video (color, sound)
4'10"
映像提供：エレクトロニック・アーツ・インターミックス（EAI）
Courtesy Electronic Arts Intermix (EAI), New York

-
・「久保田成子：セクシュアル・ヒーリング」案内ハガキ
Invitation of *Shigeko Kubota: Sexual Healing*
2000
個人蔵
Private Collection

-
・「久保田成子：ナムジュン・パイクとの私の人生」案内状
Invitation of *Shigeko Kubota: My Life with Nam June Paik*
2007
個人蔵
Private Collection

-
・パイクから成子への手紙（複写）
Letter with drawing from Paik to Shigeko (photocopy)
2001
個人蔵
Private Collection

-
・「Videoは時間のARTである」スケッチブックより
'Video is Art of Time' from sketchbook
1995
水彩、ペン／紙
Watercolor and pen on paper
個人蔵
Private Collection

-
・吉原悠博《River：ある前衛芸術家の形見》
Yukihiro Yoshihara, *River; A memento of an avant-garde artist*
2021
シングルチャンネル・ヴィデオ（カラー、サウンド）
Single-channel video (color, sound)
23'10"

図版クレジット　Photo Credits

数字は掲載頁番号を示す。
The following numbers indicate page numbers in which images are reproduced.

- Courtesy Shigeko Kubota Video Art Foundation: 10, 11 left, 29 left, 31, 34, 39 bottom, 54 bottom, 69 right, 72-75, 78, 94, 100 left, 101 bottom, 102, 103, 104 bottom, 109, 115, 116, 119, 128, 131, 132 top, 183-184, 185 left, 204, 215 top and right, 216, jacket
- Courtesy Yuuka Miyata 宮田有香: 13 top
- Courtesy Tokyo National Research Institute for Cultural Properties 東京文化財研究所: 13 bottom
- Photo by Minoru Hirata 平田実 © HM Archive: 17 top right
- Courtesy Keio University Art Center 慶應義塾大学アート・センター: 17 bottom
- Photo by Yukihiro Yoshihara 吉原悠博: 18-19, 38, 56, 58-61, 63-64, 68, 70-71, 80-81, 84/93 spread, 97, 99, 105-106, 120-121, 126-127, 138-139
- Courtesy The Museum of Modern Art, New York / © 2021 Digital image, The Museum of Modern Art, New York / Scala, Florence: 20, 21 middle
- Photo by Ichiro Otani 大谷一郎: 21 bottom
- Photo by Peter Moore © 2021 Barbara Moore / Licensed by VAGA at Artists Rights Society (ARS), NY, Courtesy Paula Cooper Gallery / Courtesy Eric Andersen: 22
- Courtesy Alison Knowles and The Museum of Modern Art, New York / © 2021 Digital image, The Museum of Modern Art, New York / Scala, Florence: 23 top
- Photo by Larry Miller © Copyright Larry Miller / Courtesy Larry Miller & Sara Seagull: 23 bottom, 117
- Photo by George Maciunas / Courtesy The Lila and Gilbert Silverman Collection, The Museum of Modern Art, New York / Licensed by Scala, Florence: 24
- Photo by Peter Moore © 2021 Barbara Moore / Licensed by VAGA at Artists Rights Society (ARS), NY, Courtesy Paula Cooper Gallery, New York / Courtesy Shigeko Kubota Video Art Foundation: 25 bottom, 78 bottom, 88
- Photo by Mary Lucier © Mary Lucier / Courtesy Mary Lucier: 26, 32, 35, 39 top, 45, 49, 52, 202
- Photo by Alec Sobolewski, 27 top middle; Charlotte Victoria, 27 top left; Herbert Migdoll, 27 bottom / Courtesy Carolee Schneemann Foundation
- Courtesy Electronic Arts Intermix (EAI): 27 top right, 30 top, 36, 103 top left, 132 bottom
- Photo by Shigeko Kubota 久保田成子: 29 left
- Photo by Tom Haar © Tom Haar / Courtesy Tom Haar: 30 bottom
- Photo by Peter Moore / Courtesy Shigeko Kubota Video Art Foundation: 29 right, 40/53 spread, 54 top, 55, 62, 65, 66, 78 top, 82, 83, 95 top, 98 left, 101 top, 110, 114
- Photo by Ingeborg Lommatzsch / Courtesy DAAD: 57, 95 bottom
- Photo by Ron Amstutz / Courtesy Whitney Museum of American Art: 67
- Photo by Hollis Melton © Hollis Melton: 85
- Photo by Robert Haller / Courtesy Anthology Film Archives: 96 left, 142
- Photo by Midori Yoshimoto: 96 right
- Photo by Nam Sang: 104 top
- Photo by Yoshitaka Uchida 内田芳孝: 108
- Courtesy Kamakura Gallery 鎌倉画廊: 112
- Photo by Ian Roberts / Courtesy Ian Roberts: 122-125, 134-137
- Photo by Shigeo Anzai 安齊重男 © Estate of Shigeo Anzai / courtesy of Zeit-foto. 画像提供：国立新美術館ANZAÏフォトアーカイブ Courtesy ANZAÏ Photo Archive, The National Art Center, Tokyo
- Photo by Adam Reich / Courtesy Shigeko Kubota Video Art Foundation: 131 bottom
- Photo by Atsuhiko Shima 島敦彦: 145
- Courtesy Toyota Municipal Museum of Art 豊田市美術館: 215 middle
- Reproduced from *Mainichi Shimbun*, Niigata edition, October 8, 1954, p. 8.『毎日新聞』新潟版、1954年10月8日、8面より転載: 8
- Partially reproduced with permission from *Shigeko Kubota: Video Sculptures* (the Museum Folkwang Essen, the Berliner Künstlerprogramm des Deutschen Akademischen Austauschdienstes (DAAD, Berlin, the Kunsthaus Zürich, 1981, pp. 46-47): 33
- Reproduced from *40 Years of Japanese Experimental Film and Video* (Kirin Plaza Osaka, 1994).『日本実験映像40年史』（キリンプラザ大阪、1994年28頁）: 37 top
- Reproduced from *Et tous ils changent le monde/2éme Biennale d'art contemporain, Lyon* (Paris: Réunion des musées nationaux, 1993, p. 179): 129
- Reproduced from *La Biennale di Venezia: XLV Esposizione Internazionale d' Artte* (Venice: Marsilio, 1993, p. 556): 130 bottom

・本書は、下記の展覧会にあわせて刊行されました。

Viva Video! 久保田成子展

・新潟県立近代美術館
会期：2021年3月20日（土・祝）-6月6日（日）
主催：新潟県立近代美術館／読売新聞社／美術館連絡協議会／ TeNYテレビ新潟
協賛：ライオン／ DNP大日本印刷／損保ジャパン
協力：新潟県立美術館友の会／長岡市立中央図書館
助成：テラ・アメリカ美術基金／文化庁・令和２年度文化庁優れた現代美術の国際発信促進事業／公益財団法人ポーラ美術振興財団／公益財団法人三菱UFJ信託地域文化財団／公益財団法人野村財団

・国立国際美術館
2021年6月29日（火）-9月23日（木・祝）
主催：国立国際美術館／読売新聞社／美術館連絡協議会
協賛：ライオン／ DNP大日本印刷／損保ジャパン／公益財団法人ダイキン工業現代美術振興財団
助成：テラ・アメリカ美術基金／文化庁・令和２年度文化庁優れた現代美術の国際発信促進事業／公益財団法人ポーラ美術振興財団

・東京都現代美術館
2021年11月13日（土）-2022年2月23日（水・祝）
主催：公益財団法人東京都歴史文化財団 東京都現代美術館／読売新聞社／美術館連絡協議会
協賛：ライオン／ DNP大日本印刷／損保ジャパン／日本テレビ放送網
助成：テラ・アメリカ美術基金／文化庁・令和２年度文化庁優れた現代美術の国際発信促進事業／公益財団法人ポーラ美術振興財団

・展覧会企画
濱田真由美（新潟県立近代美術館）
橋本梓（国立国際美術館）
西川美穂子（東京都現代美術館）
由本みどり（ニュージャージー・シティー大学准教授／ギャラリーディレクター）

テラ・アメリカ美術基金は、アメリカ合衆国の美術を国内外の観客に更に慣れ親しみ、よりよく理解し、楽しんでもらう目的のためにあります。オリジナルの芸術作品を体験することの重要性に気付いたことから、シカゴにある基金のコレクションを増やし、作品を展示するだけではなく、触れあいと研究のための機会を設けています。アメリカ芸術についての異文化間の会話を進めるため、基金は革新的な展覧会、研究、そして教育プログラムを支援し、協力しています。そういった活動の根底には、芸術には異なる文化を見分けながらも、それらを結びつける力があるという信念があります。

・This book is published as the following exhibition's catalog.

Viva Video!: The Art and Life of Shigeko Kubota

・The Niigata Prefectural Museum of Modern Art
March 20-June 6, 2021
Organized by The Niigata Prefectural Museum of Modern Art, The Yomiuri Shimbun, The Japan Association of Art Museums, Television Niigata Network Co., Ltd.
Sponsored by Lion Corporation, Dai Nippon Printing Co., Ltd. (DNP), Sompo Japan Insurance Inc.
Cooperated by The Niigata Prefectural Art Museum Friendship Society, Nagaoka City Central Library
Supported by Terra Foundation for American Art, The Agency for Cultural Affairs Government of Japan in the fiscal 2020, The Pola Art Foundation, The Mitsubishi UFJ Trust Cultural Foundation, Nomura Foundation

・The National Museum of Art, Osaka
June 29-September 23, 2021
Organized by The National Museum of Art, Osaka, The Yomiuri Shimbun, The Japan Association of Art Museums
Sponsored by Lion Corporation, Dai Nippon Printing Co., Ltd. (DNP), Sompo Japan Insurance Inc., Daikin Foundation for Contemporary Arts
Supported by Terra Foundation for American Art, The Agency for Cultural Affairs Government of Japan in the fiscal 2020, The Pola Art Foundation

・Museum of Contemporary Art Tokyo
November 13, 2021-February 23, 2022
Organized by Museum of Contemporary Art Tokyo operated by Tokyo Metropolitan Foundation for History and Culture, The Yomiuri Shimbun, The Japan Association of Art Museums
Sponsored by Lion Corporation, Dai Nippon Printing Co., Ltd. (DNP), Sompo Japan Insurance Inc., Nippon Television Network Corporation
Supported by Terra Foundation for American Art, The Agency for Cultural Affairs Government of Japan in the fiscal 2020, The Pola Art Foundation.

・Curated by;
Mayumi Hamada, Curator of The Niigata Prefectural Museum of Modern Art
Azusa Hashimoto, Curator of The National Museum of Art, Osaka
Mihoko Nishikawa, Curator of Museum of Contemporary Art Tokyo
Midori Yoshimoto, Associate Professor of Art History and Gallery Director at New Jersey City University

"The Terra Foundation for American Art is dedicated to fostering exploration, understanding, and enjoyment of the visual arts of the United States for national and international audiences. Recognizing the importance of experiencing original works of art, the foundation provides opportunities for interaction and study, beginning with the presentation and growth of its own art collection in Chicago. To further cross-cultural dialogue on American art, the foundation supports and collaborates on innovative exhibitions, research, and educational programs.
Implicit in such activities is the belief that art has the potential both to distinguish cultures and to unite them."

THE NIIGATA PREFECTURAL MUSEUM OF MODERN ART
新潟県立近代美術館

Viva Video!　久保田成子

2021年6月20日　初版印刷
2021年6月30日　初版発行

・編集
濱田真由美（新潟県立近代美術館）
橋本梓（国立国際美術館）
西川美穂子（東京都現代美術館）
由本みどり（ニュージャージー・シティ大学准教授／ギャラリーディレクター）
吉住唯（河出書房新社）

・編集協力
久保田成子ヴィデオ・アート財団

・翻訳
由本みどり
近藤学
桜本有三
クリストファー・スティヴンズ
橋本梓

・デザイン
佐々木暁

・編者
新潟県立近代美術館
国立国際美術館
東京都現代美術館

・発行者
小野寺優

・発行所
株式会社河出書房新社
〒151-0051
東京都渋谷区千駄ヶ谷2-32-2
電話　03-3404-1201（営業）
　　　03-3404-8611（編集）
https://www.kawade.co.jp/

・印刷・製本
凸版印刷株式会社

・プリンティングディレクター
十文字義美（凸版印刷株式会社）

Printed in Japan
ISBN978-4-309-29141-3

Viva Video! The Art and Life of Shigeko Kubota

Published on June 30, 2021
First Edition

• Editors:
Mayumi Hamada (The Niigata Prefectural Museum of Modern Art)
Azusa Hashimoto (The National Museum of Art, Osaka)
Mihoko Nishikawa (Museum of Contemporary Art Tokyo)
Midori Yoshimoto (Associate Professor/Gallery Director, New Jersey City University)
Yui Yoshizumi (Kawade Shobo Shinsha)

• Editorial support:
Shigeko Kubota Video Art Foundation

• Translators:
Midori Yoshimoto
Gaku Kondo
Yuzo Sakuramoto
Christopher Stephens
Azusa Hashimoto

• Design:
Akira Sasaki

• Edited by
The Niigata Prefectural Museum of Modern Art
The National Museum of Art, Osaka
Museum of Contemporary Art Tokyo

• Publisher:
Masaru Onodera

• Published by
Kawade Shobo Shinsha Ltd. Publishers
2-32-2, Sendagaya, Shibuya-ku, Tokyo
151-0051 Japan
+81-(0)3-3404-1201 (Sales Department)
+81-(0)3-3404-8611 (Editorial Department)
https://www.kawade.co.jp/

• Printing and binding:
Toppan Printing Co., LTD.

• Printing director:
Yoshimi Jumonji (Toppan Printing Co., LTD.)